ORGANISATIONAL
BEHAVIOUR
CORE CONCEPTS AND APPLICATIONS
FOURTH AUSTRALASIAN EDITION

T0319687

ORGANISATIONAL BEHAVIOUR
CORE CONCEPTS AND APPLICATIONS
FOURTH AUSTRALASIAN EDITION

Jack **WOOD**

Rachid **ZEFFANE**

Michele **FROMHOLTZ**

Retha **WIESNER**

Rachel **MORRISON**

Aharon **FACTOR**

Tui **MCKEOWN**

John **SCHERMERHORN**

James **HUNT**

Richard **OSBORN**

WILEY

Fourth edition published 2016 by
John Wiley & Sons Australia, Ltd
42 McDougall Street, Milton Qld 4064

First edition published 2006
Second edition published 2010
Third edition published 2013

Typeset in 10/12 ITC New Baskerville LT Roman

National Library of Australia
Cataloguing-in-Publication entry

Creator:	Wood, J.M. (Jack Maxwell), 1945– author.
Title:	Organisational behaviour: core concepts and applications/Jack Wood, Rachid Zeffane, Michele Fromholtz, Retha Wiesner, Rachel Morrison, Aharon Factor, Tui McKeown, John Schermerhorn, James Hunt, Richard Osborn.
Edition:	4th Australasian edition.
ISBN:	9780730314714 (pbk.)
Notes:	Includes index.
Subjects:	Organizational behavior.
Other Authors/Contributors:	Zeffane, Rachid, author.
	Fromholtz, Michele, author.
	Wiesner, Retha, author.
	Morrison, Rachel, author.
	Factor, Aharon, author.
	McKeown, Tui, author.
	Schermerhorn, John R., Jr., author.
	Hunt, James G., 1932– author.
	Osborn, Richard, author.
Dewey Number:	302.35

Cover and internal design images: © Shutterstock.com/Nicemonkey

Typeset in India by diacriTech

Printed in Singapore by
C.O.S. Printers Pte Ltd

10 9 8 7 6 5 4 3 2

BRIEF CONTENTS

CONTENTS

PART ONE   INTRODUCTION   1

CHAPTER 1   WHAT IS ORGANISATIONAL BEHAVIOUR?   3

PART TWO   MANAGING INDIVIDUAL BEHAVIOUR AND PERFORMANCE   39

CHAPTER 2   INDIVIDUAL ATTRIBUTES AND THEIR EFFECTS ON JOB PERFORMANCE   41

CHAPTER 4 LEARNING, REINFORCEMENT AND SELF-MANAGEMENT 123

CHAPTER 7   TEAMWORK AND TEAM BUILDING   247

PART FOUR   MANAGING ORGANISATIONAL PROCESSES AND PERFORMANCE   283

CHAPTER 8   ORGANISATIONAL STRUCTURE AND DESIGN   285

CHAPTER 9 ORGANISATIONAL CULTURE 331

What would you do? 341

Counterpoint 347

International spotlight 350

The effective manager 9.1 351
Using organisational culture to help the organisation compete

Ethical perspective 352

CHAPTER 10 POWER, POLITICS AND INFLUENCE IN ORGANISATIONS 363

CHAPTER 11 LEADERSHIP 401

CHAPTER 12   DECISION MAKING   453

PART FIVE   CASE STUDIES   561

TUTORIAL ACTIVITIES AT A GLANCE

CHAPTER	Individual activity	Group activity
1 What is organisational behaviour?	Global awareness	Management foundations
2 Individual attributes and their effects on job performance	Your personality type	Building a more positive self-concept
3 Motivation and empowerment	Are you motivated to work hard at your studies?	What do you want from a job — motivators or hygienes?
4 Learning, reinforcement and self-management	Learning awareness questionnaire	Getting creative with remuneration
5 Job design, goal setting and flexible work arrangements	The case of the casual workforce	Motivation by job enrichment
6 Groups and group dynamics	Analysing a group	Analysing your groups
7 Teamwork and team building	Identifying norms that influence teams	Brainstorming
8 Organisational structure and design	Vertical and horizontal specialisation: organising XYZ Paper Company	Assessing organisational structure and design
9 Organisational culture	Which culture fits you?	Your university culture
10 Power, politics and influence in organisations	Influence tactics	Machiavellianism
11 Leadership	Survey of leadership	Leadership in action
12 Decision making	Decision-making biases	The fishing trip
13 Communication, conflict and negotiation in organisations	Conflict management strategies	Conflict resolution
14 Organisational change and innovation	Innovative attitude scale	Force field analysis

CASES AND REAL-WORLD EXAMPLES AT A GLANCE

CHAPTER	Opening vignette	OB in action
1 What is organisational behaviour?	Complexity and today's organisations	Fast food specialisation, BreadTalk (Singapore), Baby boomers at work (Australia/New Zealand), Transforming training for apprentices in Australia, Outsourcing to India (Australia/India), Workplaces of the future
2 Individual attributes and their effects on job performance	Staff engagement and retaining workers (Australia/New Zealand)	Chorus of inspired staff (New Zealand), Women in management (Australia/New Zealand), What are Australians dreaming of?, Challenges faced by mature-aged employees
3 Motivation and empowerment	The puzzle of motivation	Workforce ageing — an issue for employers (New Zealand), Frustrated by 'red tape', Workplace motivation and culture (China), Why are people leaving their jobs? (New Zealand), What will employees find rewarding?, Empowerment — What nurses want
4 Learning, reinforcement and self-management	The unintended consequences of rewards — when incentives backfire	Learning from failure, Pay for performance (incentive pay), Punishment and shame in organisations, Extinction in action — if you don't hear from me, you know you're doing fine, Self-management versus empowerment, The trouble with learning, Pixar: the ultimate learning organisation, A knowledge management officer for every organisation?
5 Job design, goal setting and flexible work arrangements	The third metric	Kiwis want flexibility and opportunity for growth (New Zealand), Clear goals means increased job satisfaction, Flexibility and autonomy beat all!, Subjective wellbeing — meaningful work and family focus creates lasting happiness, All, nothing or both? Flexibility allows mothers to make good career choices
6 Groups and group dynamics	Working in groups is not for everyone — the new 'groupthink'	New Zealand and Australian military task force foils drug smugglers, The importance of workplace friends, Group problem solving
7 Teamwork and team building	Teamwork in the defence forces — is it a matter of life or death?	Sushi team bonding (New Zealand), Team IQ (Australia/Asia), Trust drives empowerment in Chinese hotels (Asia), The Pirates Dilemma, Brainstorming is brilliant (New Zealand), Virtual team intelligence
8 Organisational structure and design	Structure, design and partnerships	The global financial crisis and organisational design, Australian wool exporter conquers Chinese market (Australia/Asia), The Chinese perception of quality, Breaking the silos at Sony and the New Zealand public sector

Ethical perspective	Counterpoint	What would you do?	International spotlight	Sustainability	Case study
Paid parental leave — whose responsibility is it?	Globalisation for good or evil?	IQ testing in recruitment	The dimensions of culture	Corporate social responsibility in South-East Asia	Resene Paints Ltd (New Zealand)
An ethical predicament	Gen Ys are not all the same	Sickies — staff absenteeism	Global managerial competencies		Perceptions, attitudes and job dissatisfaction: a tricky issue
Bridging the gender pay gap (Australia/New Zealand)	Satisfying generational needs — reality or myth?	Knowledge of pay process	Supply and demand of labour — a global phenomenon	Sustainability motivates (New Zealand)	Employee empowerment at the Bank of New Zealand
Paying for performance	Incentives modify behaviour … but not always in the way we hope!	Australia's maths crisis. Is poor self-efficacy to blame?	What is more rewarding than money? The case of Korea	Piece rates and 'the China price'	Experiential learning in organisations … just do it! (New Zealand)
The quest for work–life balance	Putting a price tag on friends, Is a bad job better than no job at all?	Having to do boring work … even the simplest of jobs can offer fulfilment, Feeling stressed and disengaged at work?	From bags to tickets to customer service (Singapore)		Brolly Sheets and 'mumpreneur' Diane Hurford (Australia/New Zealand)
Managing emotions and moods at work — how far can managers go?	Too much group work?	Improving health care — the impact of effective groups	Groups and cultural difference (China)	Vigilantes of the sea	Workgroup behaviour in a New Zealand factory
Fair treatment of team members and perceptions of justice	When 'teams' do not work!	When the senior executive team is to blame	Bain Southeast Asia: a great place to work (Asia)		Understanding the self (New Zealand)
Health check (Australia)	Social media and workplace productivity	Coordination in temporary organisations, The pros and cons of growth and acquisition	Fonterra: from local prominence to global reach (New Zealand)	Organisational structures for sustainability	Why do bosses need to go 'undercover'?

CHAPTER	Opening vignette	OB in action
9 Organisational culture	Organisational culture and values	Maintaining creativity in times of organisational growth, Corporate clothing gives a sense of unity, Organisational culture and customer service at GASP clothing, Ethical dilemmas and the workplace, Coworking around the world (New Zealand)
10 Power, politics and influence in organisations	Organisational politics, power and corruption	Empowering employees, Empowering women, The nasty side of office politics (New Zealand), Boys' clubs alive and well (Australia)
11 Leadership	Paving the way for innovation	Leadership across the generations, Leadership at The Physio Co (Australia), Exerting influence without authority, Preparing for a crisis, Regional leadership development in the Pacific (Australia/New Zealand), The cost of absenteeism
12 Decision making	How top CEOs make decisions	BP risks safety and environment in Gulf of Mexico, New Zealander creates Unified Inbox (New Zealand), Dealing with a flood of decisions (Australia), Groupthink involved in space shuttle tragedy, Bendigo and Adelaide Bank consider stakeholder interests in decision making (Australia)
13 Communication, conflict and negotiation in organisations	The changing social media face of organisations	Eliminating noise in communication, The etiquette of email communication, Skills for dealing with disgruntled employees
14 Organisational change and innovation	Leading change when going public	Planting seeds of success, Driving change that is environmentally friendly, Google: the trick to grow exponentially and still stay innovative

Includes New Zealand content

Includes Asian content

Ethical perspective	Counterpoint	What would you do?	International spotlight	Sustainability	Case study
Ethical cultural change at Siemens	The role of culture in adopting sustainability in business	Dress to express	Dover Park Hospice: embracing volunteers into its culture (Singapore)		The need for cultural change at ADFA and the ADF
Power and bullying	Managing up: exercising personal power	Working in the Woomera detention centre	The challenge of managing across cultures (Asia)		When leadership brawls become ugly
Companies with few females in governing positions may be short-changing their investors	Reality check: the perils of leadership	The trust predicament	The challenges of leading cross-cultural virtual project teams	Views from a sustainability leader	Sustainability leadership is alive and well at the Good Guys (Australia)
Discrimination evident in employers' recruitment decisions	Asian leaders value creativity and intuition more than New Zealand leaders (New Zealand/Asia)	Escalation of commitment by bank loan officers and university students	The precautionary principle		Decision making in the Victorian bushfires
Organisational control and social media	The virtue and vice of workplace conflict	Underlying conflict	Email and conflict escalation	Communication and sustainability	The perils of social media
Utilising tools to keep stress in check	Dealing with resistance through clear communication and anchoring (Asia)	Creating an innovation culture	Stimulating social innovation through crowdfunding		LEGO — when innovation is not the Holy Grail

HOW TO USE THIS BOOK

Organisational Behaviour: Core Concepts and Applications, 4th Australasian edition, has been designed with you, the student, in mind. We aim to provide you with a tool that best communicates the subject matter and facilitates learning. The following elements have been developed to assist you.

LEARNING OBJECTIVE Learning objectives listed at the start of each chapter help you identify the essential elements of that chapter. For ease of study, these learning objectives are revisited in the chapter summary.

 WHAT WOULD YOU DO? Regularly throughout the text, you will be asked to put yourself in the shoes of a decision maker and to propose a solution to an organisational issue.

 **OB IN ACTION** These boxed features throughout the text show how people can make a difference in the way organisations operate by highlighting progressive or innovative practices from the real world.

 **SUSTAINABILITY** Sustainability features explore issues of human and ecological wellbeing in the context of organisational and management practices.

 **ETHICAL PERSPECTIVE** Ethical perspective features highlight situations and dilemmas that may affect investor, consumer and staff attitudes, the long- and short-term economic viability of the organisation, and management practices.

 **INTERNATIONAL SPOTLIGHT** International spotlight features elaborate on the management practices of organisations around the world, particularly focusing on those operating in the Asia–Pacific region.

 COUNTERPOINT Counterpoint features provide an opposing view to stimulate discussion, analysis and the development of critical thinking skills.

 **THE EFFECTIVE MANAGER** Practical tips and checklists provide advice on how to achieve high performance in dynamic and demanding work environments.

STUDY GUIDE

Each chapter concludes with an integrated study guide. Designed for self-study, it includes:

- a list of key terms
- review, application and research questions
- a running project
- individual and group activities
- a case study.

CHAPTER 4 study guide

Key terms

behaviourists, *p. 125*
classical conditioning, *p. 126*
cognitive evaluation theory, *p. 141*
cognitive learning, *p. 128*
continuous reinforcement, *p. 133*
extinction, *p. 138*
extrinsic rewards, *p. 131*
intermittent reinforcement, *p. 133*
intrapersonal conflict, *p. 143*
law of contingent reinforcement, *p. 132*

law of effect, *p. 131*
law of immediate reinforcement, *p. 132*
learning, *p. 125*
merit pay, *p. 144*
negative reinforcement, *p. 136*
non-contingent reward, *p. 138*
operant conditioning, *p. 127*
organisational behaviour modification, *p. 131*
organisational learning, *p. 148*

piece rate, *p. 133*
positive reinforcement, *p. 132*
punishment, *p. 136*
reverse-incentive effect, *p. 141*
self-determination theory, *p. 141*
shaping, *p. 132*
social learning, *p. 128*
stimulus, *p. 126*
successive approximation, *p. 132*
teaching organisation, *p. 151*

Review questions

1. Explain the law of effect.
2. What are extrinsic rewards and how are these related to learning and reinforcement?

3. Distinguish between negative reinforcement and punishment.
4. Summarise the main features of a learning organisation.

Application questions

1. Describe the classical conditioning process and provide examples of its impact on behaviours and emotions.
2. Mentoring, based on social learning theory, is often used to teach less experienced managers new skills. Discuss the operation and efficacy of mentoring programs in the contemporary workplace.
3. Punishment strategies should be used sparingly by managers. Explain why.
4. What are some of the ethical issues to consider when linking pay to performance?
5. Turn back to the International Spotlight. What are some cultural issues to consider when using incentives for the purpose of achieving greater performance?
6. Critically analyse the difference between a learning organisation and organisational learning.
7. McDonalds, Nike, Levis, The Gap and many other companies have been widely criticised for using

cheap labour in developing countries (refer back to the Sustainability boxed feature on 'Piece rates and "the China price").
   (a) Do you buy products from these companies? Does having information about human rights abuses make you want to avoid their products? Why? Why not?
   (b) Why is it that China is able to continue to pay parts of its labour force at such a low rate? Think about demand and supply (of both products and labour).
   (c) Think about the lack of intrinsic reward that jobs in Chinese factories provide. Few people would choose to work in one if given a choice. What other types of incentive schemes might possibly work in this environment?

END-OF-BOOK CASE STUDIES

Additional situational and real-life cases enable you to apply what you have learnt to key concepts from multiple chapters.

CASE STUDY 2

MANAGEMENT STYLE AND EMPLOYEE–MANAGEMENT RELATIONS[1]

Background

Fiji Ships and Heavy Industries Limited (FSHIL), once known as Government Shipyard and Public Slipways (GSPS), was initially a wholly Fijian government-owned entity. Fiji, one of the most developed of the Pacific Island economies, is an island nation located in the heart of the Pacific Ocean, southwest of Honolulu, midway to the equator and New Zealand. GSPS was later corporatised as Shipbuilding (Fiji) Limited (SFL) to pave the way for its privatisation process. When SFL underwent receivership in 1999, the Fijian government made a successful $6.25 m bid to acquire the assets from the receivers. It was in 2002 (effective 1 January 2003) that the Board decided to change the company name to FSHIL to better reflect the extensive range of heavy engineering work carried out by the company. In the same year, an international search was done for the appointment of a CEO.

November 2002 saw the appointment of a CEO who came to FSHIL from Papua New Guinea. The new CEO had thirty years of experience in shipbuilding and ship repairs and had been a ships engineer in the ten years prior. His role became effective in 2003. In the period prior to the appointment of this full-time CEO, FSHIL had an acting CEO — one that had to work to gain the acceptance of his employees. The way the acting CEO carried himself and how he not only consulted the union/workers, but was also receptive to their suggestions and requests encouraged the employees to accept the acting CEO. With the introduction of the new CEO, problems began to surface between management and the 'managed'.

The situation breakdown

The CEO was unhappy with what he witnessed after joining FSHIL, contending that he had been brought into a politically sensitive shipyard that was not doing well, had old machinery and an overly tarnished reputation. He asserted that the biggest and the most difficult of all challenges was Fiji's laidback culture towards commercial operations. He had positive plans to further upgrade the shipyard, but was held back by finances and investor confidence. The members of the FSHIL in-house union decided that they would prefer to be a part of the Transport Workers Union (TWU) and to resign from the in-house union.

Following is a breakdown of the events in 2003 following the introduction of the new CEO and the in-house union's decision to change unions.

August	25	The secretary of the in-house union writes to the general secretary of TWU to join with them.
September	1	TWU writes to the CEO seeking voluntary recognition. The CEO advises that he will respond after the Board meeting on 4 September 2003.
	4	The first termination under the new CEO is made at FSHIL. The technical services manager (with 30 years' shipbuilding experience) receives a termination letter (effective immediately) from the CEO, with payment for only the one-month's pay that was stipulated in the manager's contract and no reason given for the termination. The technical services manager requests a written explanation for the reason of his termination from the CEO, but receives no response — he had only served eighteen months of his three-year contract.

ABOUT THE AUTHORS

Professor Jack Wood (PhD, Alberta, Canada) has held numerous senior management positions in higher education, including Deputy Vice-Chancellor International and Corporate at Central Queensland University; Professor of Management, Associate Dean International and Director of International Programs within the Faculty of Business and Economics at Monash University; MBA Director at both the University of Sydney and Monash University; and he was the Foundation Professor in Management at Monash–Mt Eliza Business School. He has published over ninety articles on management education, and is the author of and a contributor to a number of books in this field. His major research interests are knowledge management, the virtual workplace, work time options and improvements to the performance of Australian expatriate management, with special reference to Asia. He has been an Australian delegate to Asia–Pacific Economic Cooperation (APEC) meetings in Osaka, Japan, and has also worked as a consultant for the Organisation for Economic Co-operation and Development (OECD) in Paris and for the New Ways to Work organisation in San Francisco. Jack Wood has served as an executive member of the Australia and New Zealand Academy of Management (ANZAM) for a number of years.

Dr Rachid Zeffane BSc Economics (Algiers), MSc (Management) and PhD (Management and Organisational Behaviour) (Wales) is Associate Professor in Management (and formerly Chairman) of the Department of Management, Marketing and Public Administration in the College of Business Administration, University of Sharjah, United Arab Emirates. He was formerly Associate Professor in Management at the Bowater School of Management and Marketing, Deakin University, and has also held academic positions at Griffith University (Qld) and the University of Newcastle (NSW). He has extensive national and international experience in teaching and research in the areas of organisational behaviour and management at both undergraduate and postgraduate levels, and has also led several executive programs. He has over fifty publications in international journals, including two papers selected for the prestigious *Classic Research in Management*, edited by Professor Derek Pugh (1998). His research work appears in leading international journals such as the *International Journal of Human Resource Management, Journal of Management Studies, Social Science Research, Organization Studies, Human Systems Management* and the *International Journal of Employment Relations*. He has also consulted to major Australian organisations on a variety of management-related issues and projects.

Michele Fromholtz is an Adjunct Lecturer in Management at Charles Sturt University, New South Wales. She holds a BBA, a BA, a MPA and a GradCertUnivLearn&Teach. She has been employed in public sector organisations and involved in several community organisations. She has also served on boards of directors for a local Business Enterprise Centre, a Chamber of Commerce and Industry, and a Writers Centre. Most of her consultancy and research work has been in the areas of human behaviour in regional and community development. She also has a strong interest in organisational culture and workplace folklore, and the decision-making behaviour of public policy implementers.

Dr Retha Wiesner is Deputy Director of the Australian Centre for Sustainable Business and Development (ACSBD), and Associate Professor in the School of Management and Enterprise at the University of Southern Queensland. Retha's research and scholarly focus is on how business leaders can propel their businesses and maximise performance outcomes for their firms through entrepreneurial strategies and high performance management and organisational behaviour strategies. She has led large research and development projects of over $5 million in the last five years. She has published extensively in Australia and overseas, and is actively involved as a research consultant in Australian organisations. She has co-authored nine books in the areas of organisational behaviour, management and human resource management.

Dr Rachel Morrison was awarded her PhD in organisational psychology from Massey University (NZ) after completing postgraduate and professional qualifications in applied psychology at Auckland University (NZ). She currently teaches undergraduate and postgraduate organisational behaviour within the Faculty of Business and Law, AUT University (NZ). She has published articles in a variety of academic management and psychology journals, and has co-edited two books: *Friends and Enemies in Organizations: A Work Psychology Perspective* and *Relationships in Organizations: A Work Psychology Perspective,* authoring several chapters within these volumes. Her research interests include relationships in the workplace, gender and equity issues, virtual social networks, work–life balance, and social capital and liabilities.

Aharon Factor (BSc, MSc, PhD) began his academic career studying at Kings College, University of London, and holds a PhD from the Aarhus Business School, University of Aarhus, in Denmark. He has a diverse working background with experience as a sustainability consultant and subsequent engagement with academic teaching and research. He currently works as a lecturer in business sustainability at Swinburne University of Technology, and previously at Curtin University of Technology and the University of New England. His field of research is focused upon the sustainability behaviours of Australian small- and medium-sized businesses. He has worked in this area with the Australian Government in Canberra and the Australian Academy of Sciences.

Tui McKeown (BA (Hons), MA, PhD) is a Senior Lecturer in the Department of Management, Monash University. She has been working in education for over twenty years. Her research agenda is aimed at an active examination of the changing nature of work — with a specific focus on the independent contractor as a way of working which offers a practically grounded understanding of the nature, dimensions and relations of work. Tui's work on independent contracting offers an applied crossing point between small business, self-employment and entrepreneurship. She has published both domestically and internationally in academic and practitioner journals and books. Tui is a board member of Independent Contractors Australia, the Small Enterprise Association of Australia and New Zealand, and of the South Oakleigh Wildlife Shelter.

John Wiley and Sons, Australia: Terry Burkitt (Publishing Manager), Kylie Challenor (Managing Content Editor), Beth Klan (Project Editor), Tara Seeto (Senior Publising Assistant) Tony Dwyer (Production Controller), Jess Carr (Copyright and Image Researcher), Delia Sala (Graphic Designer), Rebecca Cam (Digital Content Editor).

ACKNOWLEDGEMENTS

The authors and publisher would like to thank the following copyright holders, organisations and individuals for their permission to reproduce copyright material in this book.

Images

• 123RF: **4, 147** © Paulus NR; **7** © Lisa Young; **35** © Oleksiy Mark; **46** © Andres Rodriguez; **47** © Erik Reis; **48** © blueskyimage; **63** © Dinis Tolipov; **82** © auremar; **87** © ginasanders; **108** © Syda Productions; **133** © Bartlomiej Magierowski; **135** © Angela Waye; **143** © Ed Sweetman; **332** © rido; **337 (top)** © Ivan Mikhaylov; **340** © Cathy Yeulet; **417** © Alexander Raths. • Breadtalk: **9** Breadtalk. • Shutterstock: **18, 26, 341** © bikeriderlondon; **24, 168, 192, 194, 219, 224, 234, 342, 344, 454, 499, 528** © Monkey Business Images; **28** © stockphoto mania; **42** © ValeStock; **44, 227, 374** © Konstantin Chagin; **49, 164, 184, 338, 433** © Pressmaster; **54** © BlueSkyImage; **66** © hartphotography; **69** © Marcin Balcerzak; **107, 293** © ChameleonsEye; **124** © Rafael Franceschini; **128** © PEPPERSMINT; **130** © Matej Kastelic; **140** © tmcphotos; **158** © Glynnis Jones; **166** © Blend Images; **169** © Fedor Selivanov; **173, 252** © Africa Studio; **177, 369** © wavebreakmedia; **183, 547** © Minerva Studio; **188, 337 (bottom), 532** © michaeljung; **210** © Max Somma; **213** © Margo Harrison; **215** © racorn; **233** © StockLite; **244, 439** © Sergey Nivens; **249** © Ruta Production; **255, 263, 511** © Rido; **259** © Filip Fuxa; **265** © Paul Vasarhelyi; **286** © Alexey Lysenko; **291, 570** © TK Kurikawa; **297** © Kzenon; **303, 438, 478** © Andrey_Popov; **334** © turtix; **350** © Barabasa; **353** © Robert Fruehauf; **366** © JuliusKielaitis; **368** © Creativa Images; **384** © iofoto; **388** © Roger Jegg - Fotodesign-Jegg.de; **388** © ventdusud; **389** © LuckyImages; **398** © ausnewsde; **406** © OPOLJA; **411** © EDHAR; **418** © Rawpixel; **426** © HitManSnr; **436** © NotarYES; **437** © Khakimullin Aleksandr; **461** © Dragon Images; **463** © Feng Yu; **465** © Brisbane; **474** © Goodluz; **479** © Nils Versemann; **492** © Quka; **498** © scyther5; **501** © Stuart Jenner; **514** © Photosebia; **534** © gualtiero boffi; **548** © Twin Design; **552** © lev radin; **557** © Stefano Tinti; **562** © gpointstudio; **564** © vichie81; **567** © StacieStauffSmith Photos. • Copyright Clearance Center: **44 (top)** Republished with permission of the *Academy of Management Review* from Blumberg & Pringle, 'The missing opportunity in organizational research…', vol. 7 (1982), p. 565; **129** Adapted from Kreitner & Luthans, 'A Social Learning Approach to Behavioral Management', *Organizational Dynamics* (Autumn 1984), p. 55, © 1984, with permission from Elsevier; **392** Reprinted from *Organizational Dynamics* from Velasquez, Moberg & Cavanagh, 'Organizational statesmanship and dirty politics' (August 1983), p. 73, © 1983, with permission from Elsevier. • Getty Images: **80** © Larry Busacca. • Harvard Business School Publishing: **94** Adapted & reprinted by permission of *Harvard Business Review*, Frederick Herzberg 'One more time: how do you motivate employees?', *Harvard Business Review* (September–October 1987), Exhibit 1, © 2002 Harvard Business School Publishing Corporation, all rights reserved. • iStockphoto: **117** Juanmonino. • Emerald Group Publishing Ltd: **187** Figure 3, M Le Favre, J Matheny & GS Kolt, 'Eustress, distress, and interpretation in occupational stress', *Journal of Managerial Psychology*, vol. 18 (2003), pp. 726–44, published by Emerald Group Publishing Ltd. • *The New Zealand Herald*: **200** © Paul Estcourt. • AAP Newswire: **222** © Eliza Muirhead/AAP Image; **326** BBS Public Relations/AAP Image; **456** © AFP photo/US Coast Guard; **485** © Dan Himbrechts/AAP Image. • Australian Defence Image Library: **248** © CPL David Gibbs/Commonwealth of Australia, Department of Defence. • McGraw Hill USA: **311** © Hodgetts & Luthans, *International Management* (1997). Reproduced with the permission of The McGraw-Hill Companies, Inc. • Alamy Australia Pty Ltd: **358** © Ray Warren Creative. • Newspix: **364** © Renee Nowytarger; **371** © Campbell Brodie; **460** © Ray Strange/News Ltd. • Loren Murray: **402** © Loren Murray. • Elsevier: **423** Reprinted from Kimberly B Boal & Robert Hooijberg, 'Strategic leadership research: moving on', *Leadership Quarterly*, vol. 11.4 (2000), © 2000, with permission from Elsevier; **429** Reprinted from Michael E Brown & Linda K Trevino, 'Ethical leadership: a review and future directions', *Leadership Quarterly*, vol. 17.6 (2006), p. 598, © 2006, with permission from Elsevier; **431** Reprinted from Lewis W Fry, Steve Vitucci & Marie Cedillo, 'Spiritual leadership and army transformation: theory, measurement and establishing a baseline', *Leadership Quarterly*, vol. 16.5 (2005), p. 838, © 2005, with permission from Elsevier. • Mohan Munasinghe: **432** Mohan Munasinghe, *Making development more sustainable: sustainomics framework and practical applications*, 1st ed. (Colombo, Sri Lanka: MIND Press, 2007), p. 34. • NASA: **470** © NASA. • Our Social Times: **524** © Our Social Times. • John Wiley & Sons Inc.: **531** From Robert H Miles, *Corporate comeback*, Jossey Bass, © 1997. Reprinted with permission of John Wiley & Sons, Inc.; **537** Adapted from N Tichy, *Managing strategic change: technical, political and cultural dynamics*, © 1983. Reprinted with permission of John Wiley & Sons, Inc.

Text

• CIPD: **53–4** from 'How would you deal with an ethical dilemma at work?', *People Management*, 19 April (2013), with the permission of Chartered Institute of Personnel and Development, London. • Sunsuper: **61** Sunsuper Dreams Index, based on a survey of 500 Australians and reproduced with the permission of Sunsuper Pty Ltd. • US Department of Health & Human Services: **73–4** from *Job demands and worker health* (HEW Publication no. [NIOSH] 75–160) (Washington DC: US Department of Health, Education and Welfare, 1975), pp. **253–4**. • Medical Observer: **87** Extract from A Bracey, 'Red tape, bureaucracy "strangling" general practice', *Medical Observer* (December 2013), © 2014 Cirrus Media Pty Limited, all rights reserved. • New Zealand Herald: **107** Extract from A Kenworthy & A Gifford, 'NZI Sustainable Business Awards: breaking the business-as-usual mould', *The New Zealand Herald*, 24 November (2013), © The New Zealand Herald; **200–1** Interview quotes from Diane Hurford in C Sykes, 'Small Business: Parenthood inspires entrepreneurs', *The New Zealand Herald*, 27 January (2014), www.nzherald.co.nz, © *The New Zealand Herald*. • Ralph Surette: **108–9** From R Surette, 'Fixing what ails nurses in the health-care system', *rabble.ca*, 7 April (2014). • McGraw Hill USA: **116** © Robert N Lussier, *Human relations in organizations: a skill building approach*, 2nd ed. (Homewood, IL: Richard D Irwin, 1993). Reproduced with the permission of The McGraw-Hill Companies, Inc. • Claire Snowdon-Darling: **164** Extract from 'Are women able to achieve the third metric', *The Huffington Post*, 2 August (2013), © Claire Snowdon-Darling. • Copyright Clearance Center: **243–4** Adapted from R McLennan & T Liew, 'Work group behaviour in a New Zealand factory', *Journal of Sociology*, vol. 16, no. 84 (1980), pp. 84–5. • Australian Army: **248** Excerpts from Address by the Chief of Army, Lieutenant General David Morrison, AO, at the launch of the fourth value of the Australian Army, 'Respect', at Lavarack Barracks Townsville, on Thursday 4 July 2013, © Australian Army. • John Wiley & Sons, Inc.: **357** Developed from C Hymowitz, 'Which corporate culture fits you?', *Wall Street Journal* (17 July 1989), p. B1, from *Organizational behavior*, 11th US ed. Published by John Wiley & Sons 2010; **473–4, 478, 522–3** J Schermerhorn Jr, J Hunt, R Osborn & M Uhl-Bien, *Organizational behavior*, 11th US ed. Published by John Wiley & Sons 2010; **483–4** Adapted from Max H Bazerman, *Judgement in managerial decision making*, 3rd ed., Wiley, NY, © 1994. Reprinted with permission of John Wiley & Sons, Inc. • ABC: **370–2** 'Woomera detention centre doctor speaks out' is reproduced by permission of the Australian Broadcasting Corporation and ABC Online, © 2004 ABC. All rights reserved. • Duane Dale: **468–9** Excerpt from: 'Decisionmaking methods: advantages and disadvantages', © Lois Frey, Duane Dale and Bob Biagi.

Every effort has been made to trace the ownership of copyright material. Information that will enable the publisher to rectify any error or omission in subsequent editions will be welcome. In such cases, please contact the Permissions Section of John Wiley & Sons Australia, Ltd.

INTRODUCTION

CHAPTER 1

WHAT IS ORGANISATIONAL BEHAVIOUR?

LEARNING OBJECTIVES

After studying this chapter, you should be able to:

1. define organisational behaviour and explain why organisations exist

2. discuss the role of managers in organisations

3. discuss some of the key issues affecting organisations today

4. explain why managers, and organisational members generally, need a thorough understanding of organisational behaviour principles.

COMPLEXITY AND TODAY'S ORGANISATIONS

The twenty-first century is marked by significant change in global politics, turbulent economic conditions, scientific and technological dynamism, as well as fundamental social change and global population expansion. Together, these different aspects form the macro-environment and impinge dramatically upon the behaviour of modern organisations. Organisational survival depends fundamentally on the ability of organisational members to recognise and understand the implications that fluctuations, change and emerging influences represent for the organisation. From an external perspective, therefore, modern organisations are in increasing need of constant monitoring and responsiveness to a whole host of stakeholders. The complex issues presented by these stakeholders may represent economic, environmental and societal considerations for an organisation. John Elkington, in his book *Cannibals with forks: The triple bottom line of 21st Century business*,[1] referred to these three organisational considerations, or 'pillars', as the 'triple bottom line.' This conception of the triple bottom line in the twenty-first century recognises the integral relationship between the sustainability of the organisations and the sustainable development of humankind. Sustaining both the enterprise, humankind and the planet is the focus of the Natural Step approach: people, profit and planet. The way people function and behave in an organisation is, therefore, of importance both to organisations and society at large.

Just as the relationship between the macro environment and today's organisations are complex, so too are the internal environments of organisations. The role of people and complexity within organisations is increasingly being recognised by twenty-first century businesses. Many organisations now feature policies and programs that integrate the needs of a diverse range of employees. This diversity includes biographical characteristics such as age and gender, race and ethnicity, disability, religion, sexual orientation and gender identity, and disabilities. Increasingly, organisations are recognising the importance of cognitive and emotional stability and the need to promote positive attitudes and job satisfaction. In essence, the drive to understand the individual in the organisation is of utmost importance to modern organisations. This has significant ramifications for managing the workforce in a complex and dynamic world. If organisations are to survive in the twenty-first century, decision-making, group and team dynamics must be aligned with the complexities and ever-changing demands of the macro-environment.

Complexity in twenty-first century organisations is, therefore, both a feature of integrally related external and internal forces. Understanding the dynamics of organisational behaviour in the twenty-first century thus necessitates a holistic approach that identifies the systemic nature of the modern organisation. In accordance with this broader remit, the triple bottom line approach has instigated a response by organisations to manage not only their costs, but to measure their environmental and social impacts as well. This has resulted in companies, such as Tesco in the United Kingdom and Nike, scrutinising ethical practices in their supply chain across the globe and has promoted the Fairtrade movement. Problems, though, abound with aligning the values of people and planet and the attainment of money.[2]

Many organisations have an emphasis on trust and supporting their employees. For some organisations, depending upon the types of people and leaders they attract, this would not work. But when it does work, it reflects many of the fundamental ingredients of a successful organisation: its members are engaged; ideas are shared; its workers are supported; the organisation is delivering a product that mostly satisfies its customers; and the customers make the company profitable.

Throughout this book you will learn about the complex field of organisational behaviour — what people and groups do in organisations, and why. We will place a particular emphasis on learning the skills you will need to be an effective manager within the organisations of today and tomorrow. Organisations of all kinds depend on managers to help ensure the work experiences of others are both productive and satisfying. Managers must act and think in the right ways, and they must do so even as great changes take place in the environment. Some significant influences on organisations today are: globalisation, information and communications technology, the emergence of a knowledge-based economy, an increasingly diverse workforce, and some significant changes in how employers and employees view each other. Climate change too is increasingly becoming a prominent issue for business. Managers need to understand the climate change debate and its consequences for their strategies and operations. These types of changes require the presence of input from both managers and other organisational members who are committed to learning and practising effective organisational behaviour. We hope this book will help you along that path.

What is organisational behaviour?

Formally defined, **organisational behaviour** is the study of individuals and groups in organisations. It emerged as an academic discipline during the late 1940s and has been prominent as an academic subject in business schools since then.

Organisational behaviour has strong ties to the behavioural sciences such as psychology, sociology and anthropology, as well as to allied social sciences such as economics and political science. It draws on this variety of scholarly vantage points to build concepts, theories and understandings about human behaviour in organisations. Organisational behaviour is unique in its focus on applying these diverse insights to create better understanding and management of human behaviour in organisations.

Among the special characteristics of organisational behaviour are the following.

- *Applied focus.* The ultimate goals of the field are to help people and organisations achieve high performance levels, and to help ensure all organisation members achieve satisfaction from their task contributions and work experiences.[3]
- *Contingency orientation.* Rather than assume that there is a universal way in which to manage people and organisations, organisational behaviour scholars adopt a **contingency approach**.[4] That is, they recognise that behaviour may vary systematically depending on the circumstances and the people involved. For example, organisational behaviour scholars recognise that 'cultural differences' among people may affect the way theories and concepts of management apply in different countries.[5] Management practices cannot simply be transferred from one part of the world to another without considering the cultural implications of the different settings in which they are to be applied.
- *Emphasis on scientific inquiry.* Organisational behaviour uses scientific methods to develop and empirically test generalisations about behaviour in organisations.[6] The three key characteristics of scientific thinking that underpin organisational behaviour research and studies are: the controlled and systematic process of data collection; the careful testing of proposed explanations; and only acceptance of explanations that can be scientifically verified.

Organisational behaviour is the study of individuals and groups in organisations.

A **contingency approach** is the attempt by organisational behaviour scholars to identify how situations can be understood and managed in ways that appropriately respond to their unique characteristics.

Organisational behaviour is not a static discipline. Managers are constantly seeking new insights and ideas to improve their effectiveness. Maybe you have already heard of some of these concepts: best practice, benchmarking, the learning organisation, the virtual workplace and knowledge management, to name a few. The study of organisational behaviour is improving our understanding of old and new concepts alike; such issues as stress, emotional intelligence and instinctive drive, all of which you will learn about as you progress through this book.

The field of organisational behaviour helps managers both deal with and learn from their workplace experiences. Managers who understand organisational behaviour are better prepared to know what to look for in work situations, to understand what they find, and to take (or help others to take) the required action.

Effective managers need to understand the people that they rely on for the performance of their unit. While each person, team/group and organisation is complex and unique, an individual's, team's/group's or organisation's performance depends on their *capacity* to work, *willingness* to work and *opportunity* to work. This concept can be summarised by the performance equation (figure 1.1). The **performance equation** views performance as the result of the personal and/or group attributes, the work effort they make and the organisational support they receive.

Performance equation Job performance = attributes × work effort × organisational support.

FIGURE 1.1 The performance equation

Job performance	=	attributes	×	work effort	×	organisational support

This equation can be applied to the three different units of analysis that form the structure of this book: individual, group/team, and organisation. The multiplication signs indicate that all three factors must be present for high performance to be achieved. This means that each factor should be maximised for each unit of analysis (individual, group/team and organisation) in a work setting if the maximum level of accomplishment is to be realised. Every manager must understand how these three factors, acting either alone or in combination, can affect performance. We will use this equation as the theoretical guide for much of the material presented in this book. Part 2 looks at individual behaviour and performance. In chapter 2 we will address individual attributes required to generate performance capacity; chapters 3 and 4 deal with motivation and volition to generate a *willingness* to perform; and chapter 5 points at how organisations can provide individuals with the best *opportunity* to perform. Part 3 of the book looks at organisational performance from a group/team level and organisational level and Part 4 combines individual performance, group performance and organisational processes in the context of organisational behaviour. Even though these concepts are presented in different parts and chapters of this book, they are highly related. Remember the multiplication sign in the performance equation indicates that all three factors (attributes, work effort and organisational support) must be present to gain a high level of performance.

For practitioners, the performance equation raises the question of whether performance is predictable. It is suggested that cognitive ability, or intelligence (as measured by IQ), is a reasonable predictor of job performance.[7] However, many human resource managers would argue that additional testing is required to ensure a good fit between capability and expected performance. Over recent decades the concept of 'emotional intelligence' (EI or EQ) has surfaced, sparking hopes for creating another way to predict performance. **Emotional intelligence** is defined as a form of social intelligence that allows us to monitor and shape our emotions and those of others.

Emotional intelligence is a form of social intelligence that allows us to monitor and shape our emotions and those of others.

Daniel Goleman suggests that emotional competence is a learned capability, based on emotional intelligence, that results in outstanding work performance.[8] In these domains EI is considered to be a competency for performance. For example, a person with a level of emotional intelligence is competent in recognising their own strengths and weaknesses.

Reuven Bar-On developed a self-assessment instrument (emotional quotient inventory, or EQi)[9] measuring traits and abilities related to social knowledge. The EQi is a measure of psychological wellbeing and adaptation, and can be a measure related to performance. Jack Meyer and Peter Salovey profess that EI is composed of mental abilities and skills.[10] They see EI as a form of intelligence that processes and benefits from emotions. They believe that other measures of intelligence fail to take into account individual differences in the ability to perceive, process and manage emotions. Chapter 2 expands on the notion of emotional intelligence as one of the individual attributes as a predictor for the capacity to perform.

Why do organisations exist?

Simply stated, organisations exist because individuals are limited in their physical and mental capabilities. Organisations are mechanisms through which many people combine their efforts and work together to accomplish more than any one person could alone.

The purpose of any organisation is to produce a product or service. Large and small businesses produce a diverse array of consumer products and services such as motor vehicles, appliances, telecommunications and accommodation. Not-for-profit organisations produce services with public benefits, such as health care and rehabilitation, public education and park maintenance.

A clear statement of purpose, or 'goal statement', is important to guide the activities of an organisation and its members. To illustrate, the following are goals of some prominent organisations:

- 'to help people and businesses throughout the world to realise their full potential' (Microsoft Corporation)[11]
- 'to be the world's mobile communications leader — enriching customers' lives, helping individuals, businesses and communities be more connected in a mobile world' (Vodafone Group)[12]
- 'to be Asia Pacific's best multimedia solutions group' (SingTel)[13]
- 'to maximise income and provide long-term sustainable returns to unit holders through the strategic acquisition, professional management and ongoing development of office, retail and industrial assets' (KIWI Income and Property Trust)[14]
- 'to create long-term value through the discovery, development and conversion of natural resources, and the provision of innovative customer and market-focused solutions' (BHP Billiton)[15]
- 'to make a difference to people's lives by making the desirable affordable and supporting New Zealand's communities and the environment. By putting the customer first, we will succeed. Everything we do flows from this principle' (The Warehouse).[16]

Fast food specialisation

The division of labour and task specialisation will be quite clear in your favourite fast-food restaurant — McDonald's, Eagle Boys, Hungry Jacks, KFC or Subway. Certain people take your order and your money, others cook the food, and still others clean after everyone else has gone home for the night. By dividing the labour and training employees to perform highly specialised tasks, these companies strive for excellence in task accomplishment. Whilst this division of labour may have benefits for consumers — as a result of task specialisation, consumers are usually served promptly in such establishments.

OBinAction

To achieve its purpose, any organisation depends on human effort. The **division of labour** is the process of breaking the work to be done into specialised tasks that individuals or groups can perform: it is a way of organising the efforts of many people to their best advantage. A good division of labour helps an organisation mobilise the work of many people to achieve its purpose.

A well-functioning organisation with a clear purpose and appropriate division of labour, like those of fast-food restaurants, achieves **synergy**, which is the creation of a whole that is greater than the sum of its parts. Synergy in organisations occurs when people work well together while using available resources to pursue a common purpose. In psychology this is called a 'gestalt'.[17]

Within an effective organisation, this 'gestalt' is created by the organisation's division of labour, task specialisation and hierarchy of authority, as well as by effective managerial behaviour. However, in recent times, this approach — which focuses on rationality, speed and efficiency — has been criticised. Some say that it has replaced the flair of creativity and design that were once essential elements in cooking, as well as diminished the importance of relationships in serving customers.[18] According to George Ritzer, the so-called 'McDonaldization', whereby the principles behind the management of fast food franchises in North America are dominating more and more segments of society globally, has led to a homogenisation of commercial life that is increasingly making it impersonal and even dehumanising.

The 'McDonaldization' effect

Simon Crowe, the founder of the Australian hamburger chain Grill'd, refers to the focus on 'the friendliest staff' and the general focus on effective management practice, not just efficient food production.[19] A more holistic manner of managing fast food outlets is also evident in the Australian outlet Spudbar, which sells baked potatoes, salads and soups. The Melbourne-based Spudbar was founded in 2000 by Clay and Laura Thompson. In 2008, there were eight Spudbars in Melbourne and a master franchisee had been signed in both Western Australia and New Zealand. The group is expanding and has three business models — a kiosk, a compact strip shop and a larger strip shop. The group's goal is to have 20 stores up and running by the end of 2008.[20]

Organisations as open systems

Organisations ultimately depend for their success on the activities and collective efforts of many people. People are the essential **human resources** of an organisation — the individuals and groups whose performance contributions enable the organisation to serve a particular purpose. But organisations need more than people if they are to survive and prosper. They also need **material resources**, which are the technology, information, physical equipment and facilities, raw materials and money necessary for an organisation to produce some useful product or service.

Many organisational behaviour scholars believe that organisations can be best understood as **open systems** that transform human and material resource 'inputs' received from their environment into product 'outputs' in the form of finished goods and/or services. The outputs are then offered to the environment for consumption. If everything works, measured via feedback, the environment accepts these outputs and allows the organisation to obtain the resource inputs it needs to continue operating in the future (figure 1.2).

Of course, things can go wrong; an organisation's survival depends on satisfying environmental demands. When the organisation's goods and/or services are not well received by the environment, it will sooner or later have difficulty obtaining the resource inputs it needs to operate.

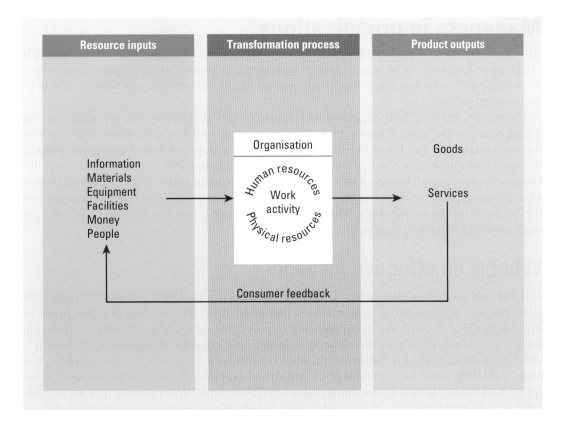

| Resource inputs | Transformation process | Product outputs |

Information
Materials
Equipment
Facilities
Money
People

Organisation

Human resources
Work activity
Physical resources

Goods

Services

Consumer feedback

FIGURE 1.2 How an organisation operates as an open system

BreadTalk

One company that is responding to its environment is BreadTalk. Founded in 2000, BreadTalk has grown to become one of the most recognisable local brands in the food and beverage industry in Singapore.[21] The BreadTalk group now includes 800 outlets and a team of 7000 employees in 15 territories, including Singapore, Hong Kong, China and the Middle East. BreadTalk today also owns ten Michelin Star restaurants, and operates 50 food courts in countries including Singapore, China, Hong Kong, Malaysia, Taiwan and Thailand.[22]

In addition, other companies have expanded the BreadTalk concept to Australia and New Zealand. Think about how BreadTalk's experience reflects the system in figure 1.2. By 2012, BreadTalk had launched its latest concept, Generation 4 which, according to the Chairman of BreadTalk Group Ltd, will allow the company to set up its franchises across China. The concept seeks to connect with customers' lifestyles through the promotion of healthy eating options supported by innovative research.

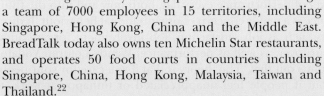

OBinAction

Managers in organisations

Now that we share a basic understanding of organisations, we can speak more precisely about what it means to be a manager. A **manager** is a person in an organisation who is responsible for work that is accomplished through the performance contributions of one or more other people.

Today, the focus of both management research and practice is not so much on the manager as on the work team or unit. A **work team** or **unit** is a task-oriented group that includes a manager and his or her direct reports. Such groups are found in organisations of all types, and they can be small or large. Examples include departments in a retail store, divisions of a corporation, branches of a bank, wards in a hospital and teams in a manufacturing plant. Even a university class can be considered a work team; the lecturer is its manager and the students are team members. The study of such work teams has become a key area of organisational behaviour research.

What is an effective manager?

It is not easy to define what makes a manager an effective manager within a business context. The list of managerial competencies identified over the past few decades helps us understand more clearly the competencies required for effective management. However, such research also illustrates the difficulties in defining effective management because it is still hard to achieve expert consensus on what constitutes a basic core of competencies. It is even more difficult to find agreement on prioritised rankings of such competencies.[23] Many of the best known writers in the management literature typically emphasise one managerial competence at the expense of all others. Tom Peters, for example, stresses that good managers are *doers*. (Wall Street says they 'do deals'.) Michael Porter emphasises that they are *thinkers*. Zalesnick and Bennis believe good managers are really *leaders*, whereas, historically, Fayol and Urwick have portrayed good managers as *controllers*.[24]

Fundamentally, any manager should seek two key results for a work unit or work team: **task performance**, which is the quality and quantity of the work produced or the services provided by the work unit; and **human resource maintenance**, which is the attraction and continuation of a capable workforce over time. This latter notion, while too often neglected, is extremely important. It is not enough for a work unit to achieve high performance on any given day; it must be able to achieve this level of performance every day, both now and into the future. Good human resource maintenance is a major concern of organisational behaviour. It directs a manager's attention to matters such as job satisfaction, job involvement, organisational commitment, absenteeism and turnover, as well as performance. Wendy Lenton, Vodafone Director of People and Brand, points out that 'The theory is that if you care for your people, your people will care for you, but if people feel unappreciated or unhappy at work, the anxiety manifests into ill health, low motivation, low productivity and absenteeism.'[25]

This book treats high performance and good human resource maintenance as results that any manager should seek. Indeed, the two results can be seen as the criteria for an **effective manager** — that is, a manager whose work unit achieves high levels of task accomplishment and maintains itself as a capable workforce over time. This concept of the 'effective manager' offers an important framework for understanding organisational behaviour and developing personal managerial skills. A special text feature, 'The effective manager', is used in this and later chapters to help remind us of these applications.

Managing task performance

Recall that task performance is the quality and quantity of the work produced or the services provided. An effective manager must be concerned with the 'productivity' of work units and their members. Formally defined, **productivity** is a summary measure of the quantity and

---

A **manager** is responsible for work that is accomplished through the performance contributions of others.

Work teams or **units** are task-oriented groups that include a manager and his or her direct reports.

Task performance is the quality and quantity of work produced.

Human resource maintenance is the attraction and continuation of a viable workforce.

An **effective manager** is a manager whose work unit achieves high levels of task accomplishment and maintains itself as a capable workforce over time.

Productivity is a summary measure of the quantity and quality of work performance that also accounts for resource use.

quality of work performance achieved (task performance) that also accounts for resource use. It is not acceptable simply to 'get a job done'; any job must be done with the best use of available resources — human and material. Productivity is a benchmark of managerial and organisational success.

The best organisations want **value-added managers**, whose efforts clearly enable their work units to achieve high productivity and improve 'bottom-line' performance. Value-added managers create high-performance systems in which individuals and groups work well together, to the benefit of the entire organisation and its clients or customers. Value-added managers are also the most likely to reap the rewards of satisfying careers. In an age of organisational restructuring and downsizing, often designed to reduce the number of management levels, value-added managers have little trouble justifying their jobs. The advice of consultant Tom Peters is worth considering: 'Middle Managers: Act like a consultant. Make friends with the line, create projects ... Your job, salary, and esteem are all in mortal danger ... are you ready?'[26] In many ways, this book is about you becoming a value-added manager.

Today's managers are confronted with a considerable dilemma. They are seeking ever-increasing added value from their stock of human capital. For example, NetApp Australia pursues this through a very open organisational system that allows employees accessibility to the managers, and enabling them to give feedback readily and responsively. On the other hand, while such approaches may improve worker productivity, they also have the potential to increase worker stress, burnout and absenteeism, and ultimately to result in a decline in worker productivity. To maximise the potential benefits of new initiatives, we must balance them against a careful consideration of quality of work life issues. One hallmark of a socially responsible organisation is its success not only in achieving high performance outcomes, but also in helping its members experience high levels of job satisfaction. The next section provides more detail on the broader issue of human resource maintenance.

> **Value-added managers** are managers whose efforts clearly enable their work units to achieve high productivity and improve 'bottom-line' performance.

Human resource maintenance

The need to ensure long-term and sustainable high performance helps to focus a manager's attention on the need to 'maintain' all of a work unit's resources (human and material resources alike). Just as managers should not allow a valuable machine to break down for lack of proper maintenance, they should never allow a valuable human contribution to be lost for lack of proper care.

Through their daily actions, the best managers in the new workplace will be able to create conditions in which people achieve their highest performance potential while experiencing a high quality of work life. The concept of **quality of work life** (QWL) gained deserved prominence in organisational behaviour study as an indicator of the overall quality of human experience in the workplace. It expresses a special way of thinking about people, their work and the organisations in which their careers are fulfilled. It establishes a clear objective that high productivity should be achieved along with job satisfaction for the people who do the required work. In particular, the following benchmarks of managerial excellence highlight true commitments to quality of work life:[27]

> **Quality of work life** refers to the overall quality of human experience in the workplace. QWL activities represent special applications of the many organisational behaviour concepts and theories discussed throughout this book.

* *participation* — involving people from all levels of responsibility in decision making
* *trust* — redesigning jobs, systems and structures to give people more freedom at work
* *reinforcement* — creating reward systems that are fair, relevant and contingent on work performance
* *responsiveness* — making the work setting more pleasant and able to serve individual needs.

It is important to remember that a broader social value associated with work makes any manager's responsibilities more complex. QWL is an important component in the quality of life: negative work experiences can affect a person's non-working life. Some of the most worrisome social ills — for example, alcoholism and drug abuse — may be linked with the adjustment problems of people who are unable to find meaning and self-respect in their work.[28] The social importance of managers as major influences on the quality of work life experienced by other people is well established. The study of organisational behaviour recognises that poor management can decrease overall quality of life, not just the quality of work life. It also recognises that good management can increase both.

Emotional intelligence

Emotional perception is a key human characteristic that enables individuals to cope with their social environment.[29] This characteristic provides humans with an emotional intelligence by providing critical information for understanding internal experiences and negotiating social environments. Subsequently, those individuals who are open to emotional signals become more engaged with advanced information processing regarding both themselves and other people's emotional experiences. These more emotionally in-tune individuals are also more likely to demonstrate the ability to adapt to both internal and external personal environments. This behaviour has been well researched, with studies showing that emotional intelligence is strongly associated with issues such as human wellbeing, academic accomplishment and the ability of students to manage university life positively.[30]

Emotional intelligence is comprised of four key skill sets that shape how the individual perceives, integrates, understands and manages their emotions. The first determinant of emotional intelligence is the precision by which a person will identify and show emotions. These emotions can then help an individual to differentiate between safe and unsafe environments, and integrate emotions with a person's cognition. This second skill set, integration, then shifts cognitive processes to open up to new perspectives, creativity and problem-solving capabilities. The third skill set, emotional understanding, concerns the understanding of emotional information and the combination of emotional information. The fourth skill set builds upon the first three skill sets to open up feelings and develop growth.[31]

Emotional intelligence can, therefore, be defined as the 'ability to identify, assess and manage both one's own emotions, and emotions of others, in order to successfully achieve one's goals'.[32] Emotions provide vital information so that the individual is able to understand their social setting accurately and to manage it successfully.

The term 'emotional intelligence' was first established by David Goleman in his *Harvard Business Review* paper. This work detailed his findings from research across almost 200 global companies. He found that traditional notions of leadership success such as intelligence, determination, vision and toughness were not as important in determining business performance as the five key areas of emotional intelligence: self-awareness, self-regulation, motivation, empathy and social skills.[33] While many people may not weigh the importance of these personal characteristics as relevant to business, David Goleman found a direct correlation between emotional intelligence and business performance.

WhatWould
You**Do?**

IQ testing in recruitment

Classic concepts of 'intelligence' have traditionally been measured by the IQ test. This test assumes that personal capabilities in critical thinking, learning and environmental adaptation can be formally delineated and examined, and that these results will provide a true indication of a personal success.[34]

Indeed, research by David Goleman shows that 75 per cent of professional success cannot be accounted for by the IQ test. He correlated test scores with individual performances and found that the maximum weight that could be attached to an IQ test was 25 per cent.[35] Goleman's findings suggest that the IQ test cannot be indicative of who will fail and who will succeed.

Imagine that you are a recruitment manager. Your company is now experiencing a significant number of senior managers and executive staff who are being placed on personal leave due to stress and mental health problems associated with increasing levels of change and diversity in the workplace. Many of these staff members were hired through decades of IQ testing of applicants. Although these staff members have been able to cope in periods where change occurred relatively slowly and the diversity of the workforce was less, it is now becoming increasingly difficult for these staff members to make effective decisions.

Questions

1. How would the increase in personal leave by senior managers and executives inform future hiring arrangements?
2. What aspects of the five key elements of emotional intelligence could the recruitment team use to ensure an effective business performance by future leaders of the organisation?

The management process

Managers use the **management process** of planning, organising, leading and controlling the use of organisational resources to achieve high performance results in both task performance and human resource maintenance. These four functions of management are planning, organising, leading and controlling (see also figure 1.3).

The **management process** involves planning, organising, leading and controlling the use of organisational resources.

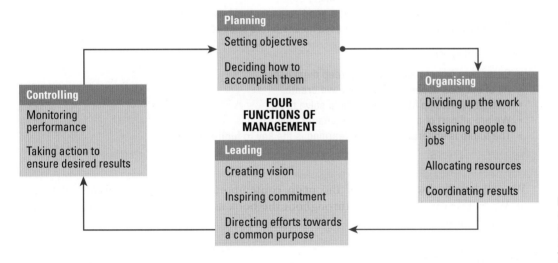

FIGURE 1.3 Planning, organising, leading and controlling — four functions of management

1. **Planning** is the process of setting performance objectives and identifying the actions needed to accomplish these objectives.
2. **Organising** is the process of dividing up the work to be done and coordinating the results to achieve a desired purpose.
3. **Leading** is the process of directing the work efforts of other people to help them to accomplish their assigned tasks.
4. **Controlling** is the process of monitoring performance, comparing the results with the objectives and taking corrective action as necessary.

There is no doubt that the task of managing both efficiently and effectively is becoming more complex. So far we have briefly discussed foundational organisational behavioural themes. In addition to these well-established organisational behaviour principles, today's business environment requires managers to deal with emerging and fast evolving challenges. The next part of this chapter will place the key concepts of organisational behaviour into the real world environment in which the managers of today and tomorrow will work.

Planning is the process of setting performance objectives and identifying the actions needed to accomplish them.

Organising is the process of dividing the work to be done and coordinating the results to achieve a desired purpose.

Leading is the process of directing and coordinating the work efforts of other people to help them to accomplish important tasks.

Controlling is the process of monitoring performance, comparing results with objectives and taking corrective action as necessary.

Contemporary themes in organisational behaviour

Among the biggest challenges that managers must deal with are: globalisation, the changing nature of the economy, the changing nature of work, the changing nature of the workforce, and the changing nature of the relationships between employers and employees. These in turn create another challenge: that of managing change itself. One approach is **process re-engineering** — formally defined as 'the fundamental rethinking and radical redesign of business processes to achieve dramatic improvements in critical contemporary measures of performance such as cost, quality, service and speed'.[36] The result involves a substantial shift in values, as shown in The effective manager 1.1.

THE EffectiveManager 1.1

Moving from traditional to re-engineered values

Traditional work values

- The boss pays our salaries; keep the boss happy.
- To keep your job, stay quiet and don't make waves.
- When things go wrong, pass problems to others.
- The more direct reports the better; a good manager builds an empire.
- The future is predictable; past success means future success.

Re-engineered work values

- Customers pay our salaries; help keep them happy.
- All of our jobs depend on the value we create.
- Accept ownership for problems; help solve them.
- We are all part of a team; a good manager builds teams.
- The future is uncertain; constant learning is the key to future success.

We will briefly discuss some of the main contemporary issues in organisational behaviour. We will revisit these themes throughout the book as your knowledge of organisational behaviour builds.

Globalisation

Globalisation is not a new concept. The pros and cons — indeed the definition — of globalisation have been the topic of much debate for decades. We look at this debate in the Counterpoint later in this chapter. For our purposes we will define globalisation as the process of becoming more international in scope, influence or application. In a business context, **globalisation** is characterised by networks that bind countries, institutions and people in an interdependent global economy.[37]

Success in the increasingly global business environment will depend on a new breed of 'global manager' with global management skills and competencies. **Global management skills and competencies** include a strong and detailed understanding of international business strategy, cross-cultural management, international marketing, international finance, managing e-business and the internet, risk management, managing sustainable organisations, re-engineering organisations, managing the virtual workplace, knowledge management, international economics and trade, and Asian languages. The effective manager 1.2 suggests ten important attributes of the successful global manager.

IT company NetApp has several global initiatives in place geared at fostering a stronger international presence. The company has initiated a NetApp Innovation Award that recognises innovators from three major regions — the Americas, the Asia–Pacific and Europe/the Middle East/Africa — who are able to make IT dramatically more proactive, productive, and essential to creating business value. They have also a Global Corporate Citizenship initiative that aims to support strategic partnerships to help make our global communities better, stronger and more vibrant places in which to live, work and do business.[38] It is important for managers to study and learn about the management and organisational practices of their counterparts in other nations. What is being done well in other settings may be of great value at home, whether that 'home' is Australia, Singapore or anywhere else in the world. Whereas the world at large once looked to the North Americans and Europeans for management insights, today we recognise that no one culture possesses all the 'right' answers to our management and organisational problems.

Ten attributes of the global manager

The global manager is able to:
1. negotiate effectively in different business environments
2. solve problems quickly and under different circumstances
3. motivate and communicate well with people from different cultures
4. understand different government and political systems
5. manage and create a sustainable environment
6. convey a positive attitude and enthusiasm when dealing with others
7. manage business in both traditional and virtual environments
8. view different economies as belonging to a single global market
9. be culturally sensitive and adaptable
10. manage the 'triple bottom line' — society, economy and the environment.

COUNTER**POINT**

Globalisation for good or evil?

Nearly twenty years ago, in referring to the technological revolution in the field of mass communication, Marshall McLuhan recognised the logical progression of humankind towards a 'global village' under the auspices of electronic media. For Marshall McLuhan, contemporary global socioeconomic and political developments may be characterised by redefining all existing structures that form the 'world village'. This means that humankind will dramatically advance 'from the nation-state to the global structures', thus reaching a transformation so profound that the future will belong entirely to this 'global village'.[39]

In the twenty years since Marshall McLuhan's insights into globalisation, the impact of multinational corporations (MNCs) on their host countries almost always causes controversy. This is most noticeable in developing nations that find they are overpowered by sizeable MNCs. On many occasions, MNCs are offered lower tax rates, cheap labour and substandard working conditions in comparison to the developed nations' standards, and local workers are generally used only for the lower-scale positions. MNCs can subsequently face a public relations nightmare when stories of child labour, physical abuse of workers and slave wages come to the surface. On the other hand, for workers who are socially and economically impoverished, the arrival of these MNCs can improve the existence and survival of their families. The issues are complex and there are no easy solutions. Globalisation is expected to continue, particularly as

(continued)

more developing countries and formerly communist countries become further open to international trade and investment. But is this a positive or a negative development? Consider the debate surrounding what are colloquially known as sweatshops.

The BBC television program *Panorama* aired a story about a factory in Cambodia that manufactured products for companies such as The Gap and Nike. Reportedly, in this factory children under the age of 15 were working more than 12 hours a day in terrible conditions on what Westerners would consider extremely low wages.[40] As a result of negative press, Nike and The Gap removed the production of their goods from Cambodia, costing hundreds of locals their jobs and the country millions of dollars in contracts. Similar pressures forced a German garment maker to lay off 50 000 child workers in Bangladesh. Oxfam later discovered that many of the children then became destitute and turned to prostitution and crime to sustain themselves, and some ultimately starved to death. Similarly, in Nepal, after a crackdown in the carpet industry, UNICEF reported that thousands of young girls turned to prostitution to survive. In Pakistan, after a controversy regarding sweatshop soccer balls, manufacturers including Nike and Reebok shut down their plants, costing tens of thousands of workers their jobs. This resulted in the mean family income in Pakistan falling by more than 20 per cent.[41]

Of course MNCs have ethical duties in terms of their own actions and those of their subcontractors and suppliers. There are labour laws and standards for pay, safety and the use of coercion.[42] However, it is difficult to determine exactly what these standards are and who sets them. The question is: Should these be 'Western' standards or the standards of the country in which the factory operates?

International trade has increased 3000 per cent since the 1960s[43] and this has been accompanied by an increase in civil and political freedom worldwide.[44] Many developing nations are increasing their overall prosperity at a higher rate than the developed nations have been capable of doing. For example, China, in the period before the global credit crunch, doubled its income per capita every 10 years, partly aided by a high prevalence of sweatshops. Compare this to Great Britain, where it took 58 years to do the same thing during the industrial revolution.[45]

Alongside the rise of China's global influence, Brazil, Russia and India are emerging as a critically important block of global players known as BRIC. Globalisation in these economies, as China demonstrates, not only manifests economic change, but exerts cultural tensions that will require multi-stakeholder engagement to create common norms across Asia in order to mitigate the vast magnitude of cultural conflicts.[46]

Questions

1. Summarise the issues surrounding globalisation and the growing rise of the BRIC block.
2. From these summaries, prepare a case *for* globalisation and prepare a case *against* globalisation, integrating both BRIC and 'Western' perspectives.

The changing nature of work

Work itself is changing rapidly due to globalisation, advances in technology, the growth in the services sector, and especially an increasing reliance on knowledge to generate new products and services. These changes require workers with different skills to the workers of the past, including the ability to continuously learn new skills and adapt to changing needs. Managing such workers presents a number of new challenges for managers. We will look at some of the biggest changes in the following sections.

Technology

Technology has emerged as an ever-present, dominant force in our lives. Just as 100 years ago people could not have accurately predicted the technology that is commonplace now, we can not foresee all the technological advances ahead of us. What is certain is that continuing change in information and communications technology will have massive implications for workers, managers and organisations alike.

High technology allows machines to do many routine chores more cheaply and accurately than people can; it makes available more information for planning and control to more people at all levels of organisational responsibility; and it is causing both people and organisational structures to change old habits and adopt new ways of doing things. For example, the use of email has revolutionised office communication. It is a convenient medium among billions of email users worldwide.[47] However, email has potentially negative consequences in the workplace. The main problems are that written forms are more official, less easy to withdraw and suffer from the absence of other additional communication modes — such as body language and intonation of voice. In addition, there is a growing body of research that suggests email reduces a person's ability to build rapport and impairs the establishment of trust. These problems are exacerbated by cultural issues when email users are in different countries.[48] Nevertheless, email has proven to be a convenient communication medium that has changed work practices significantly.

Knowledge management

Another major driver of organisational change is the growth of the knowledge-based economy in which prosperity is built on 'intellectual capital' — the use of information in people's minds — rather than on physical resources. The OECD defines a **knowledge-based economy** as 'an economy in which the production, distribution and use of knowledge is the main driver of growth, wealth creation and employment across all industries — not only those industries classified as high tech or knowledge intensive'.[49]

Recognition of knowledge and the contribution that knowledge creation, distribution and use can make towards improved levels of performance and productivity is not new; economies have always relied on knowledge expansion and application through research and development to create new products and improvements in productivity. What is new is the speed at which knowledge is being created and the pace at which it is being transformed into new goods and services.

In a knowledge-based economy, the central questions for high-performing organisations are:
- What do we know and what knowledge do we have?
- How do we organise to make best use of this knowledge?
- Who can add value to what we know?
- How quickly can we learn something new?
- How quickly can we deliver this new knowledge into the global marketplace?

Much knowledge resides within employees, including their skills, creativity and experience. It also exists in other areas such as the organisation's systems, processes and structures, and in the relationships that organisations have with their customers, suppliers and other stakeholders. **Knowledge management (KM)** focuses on processes designed to improve an organisation's ability to capture, share and diffuse knowledge in a manner that will improve business performance.

An important aspect of knowledge management is retaining people who possess the knowledge the organisation or the country needs. Workers are increasingly mobile and are taking their knowledge with them to their new workplaces across the globe. Such movement across national boundaries is commonly referred to as **brain drain**.

A **knowledge-based economy** is an economy in which the production, distribution and use of knowledge is the main driver of growth, wealth creation and employment across all industries — not only those classified as high-tech or knowledge intensive.

Knowledge management (KM) focuses on processes designed to improve an organisation's ability to capture, share and diffuse knowledge in a manner that will improve business performance.

Brain drain refers to a characteristic of today's skilled workforce whose members are now more mobile and prepared to take their knowledge with them to their new workplaces as they pursue opportunities across the globe.

Baby boomers at work

Demographic changes in Australia and New Zealand are transforming the employment landscape. In 2011, the first of the baby boomer generation, those born between 1946 and 1964, reached the age of 65. In fact, according to the Australian Bureau of Statistics the baby boomers comprise 25 per cent of the Australian population and will have a significant impact on the Australian economy and society for many decades to come. From 2010 onwards, there will be fewer people of employable age to support the current high-level debt structure.[50] With fewer new workers available than there are jobs, one obvious strategy to fill the skills gaps will be to actively recruit from older segments. This challenges recruiters to consider that the factors that attract younger workers are not always the same as for older workers. Can you think of some likely differences?

The changing nature of the workforce

The composition of the workforce is changing. Managers must be aware of, and able to successfully manage in the context of, the following trends.

* The size of the workforce is growing more slowly than in the past, especially as a result of the global economic slowdown.
* The average age of the workforce is rising.
* More women are entering the workforce.
* The proportion of ethnic minorities in the workforce is increasing.
* The proportion of immigrants in the workforce is increasing.
* Workforce mobility is increasing.
* 'Labour packaging' is growing through short-term migrant labour importation in many Asian and Middle Eastern countries.
* International careers and mobile managers are becoming commonplace.
* International experience is becoming a prerequisite for career progression to many top-level management positions.[51]

Perhaps the most notable change in the workforce is that it is more diverse than at any time in history. The term workforce diversity refers to the presence of demographic differences among members of a given workforce.[52] These differences include gender, race and ethnicity, culture, age and able-bodiedness.

In the next sections, we will look at the changing nature of the workforce in terms of culture, age and gender.

Culture

The workforce is becoming more multicultural as a result of migration, and as workforces increasingly span more than one country. Australia and New Zealand are among the most multicultural countries in the world. Almost one in three members of the workforce in major Australian cities such as Sydney and Melbourne was born outside Australia. About one in three people in the Auckland region of New Zealand was born overseas. Managers — whether or not they are directly involved in international business — must be able to effectively manage people from different cultures and make the most of the advantages that a diverse workforce can bring. For example, diversifying the workforce can be used as a

Workforce diversity means a workforce consisting of a broad mix of workers from different racial and ethnic backgrounds, of different ages and genders, and of different domestic and national cultures.

market strategy. A diverse workforce can provide business with a competitive advantage by capitalising on language skills, cultural knowledge, business networks and knowledge of business practices in overseas markets, and intelligence about overseas markets, including intimate knowledge of consumer tastes and preferences. Businesses can use the skills to improve productivity and innovation in the workplace, developing domestic niche markets and entering new, or increasing market share in, overseas markets.[53]

Styles of leadership, motivation and decision making, and other management roles vary among different countries, as outlined in the following examples.[54]

- *Leadership.* A study of international airlines found substantial differences in leadership styles despite the fact that the technology, types of jobs, skills required and basic operations are very similar from one company to another.[55]
- *Motivation.* Managers must avoid being parochial or ethnocentric. They cannot assume all people will be motivated by the same things and in the same ways as they are. Most of the popular theories of work motivation have been developed in the United States. These theories may help explain the behaviour of North Americans, but serious questions must be raised about how applicable they are to other cultures.[56] While North Americans, for example, value individual rewards, Japanese people prefer group rewards.
- *Decision making.* Latin American employees may feel uncomfortable with a boss who delegates too much authority to them. In France, decisions tend to be made at the top of companies and passed down the hierarchy for implementation. In other cultures, such as the Scandinavian, employees want their managers to emphasise a participative, problem-solving approach. In Japan, many companies use the ringi system for making decisions. Ringi is a group decision approach whereby all affected company members affix their sign of approval to widely circulated written proposals. Culture may even play a role in determining whether a decision is necessary at all — that is, whether the situation should be changed. Australians and New Zealanders tend to perceive situations as problems to be solved; other cultures, such as the Thai and Indonesian, tend to accept situations as they are. Thus, an Australian is more likely to decide that a workplace problem exists and that something should be done about it.[57]

Geert Hofstede, a Dutch scholar and consultant, has identified five dimensions of national culture — power-distance, uncertainty avoidance, individualism–collectivism, masculinity–femininity and long-term–short-term orientation — which provide one way of understanding differences across national cultures (see the International spotlight).[58]

The dimensions of culture

Hofstede's five dimensions of national culture can be described as follows:

1. *Power–distance* — the degree to which people in a country accept a hierarchical or unequal distribution of power in organisations. Indonesia, for example, is considered a high power–distance culture, whereas the Netherlands is considered a relatively low power–distance culture.
2. *Uncertainty avoidance* — the degree to which people in a country prefer structured rather than unstructured situations. France, for example, is considered a high uncertainty avoidance culture, whereas Hong Kong is considered a low uncertainty avoidance culture.
3. *Individualism–collectivism* — the degree to which people in a country focus on working as individuals more than on working together in groups. Germany, for example, is considered a relatively individualistic culture, whereas Sweden is considered a more collectivist culture.
4. *Masculinity–femininity* — the degree to which people in a country emphasise so-called masculine traits, such as assertiveness, independence and insensitivity to feelings,

(continued)

International
SPOTLIGHT

as dominant values. Japan, for example, is considered a highly masculine culture, whereas the Netherlands is considered a more feminine culture.

5. *Long-term–short-term orientation* — the degree to which people in a country emphasise values associated with the future, such as thrift and persistence, over values that focus on the past or present, such as social obligations and tradition. China, for example, is high on long-term orientation, while the United States is more orientated towards the short term.[59]

Continuing research on these cultural dimensions examines how countries can be grouped into clusters sharing generally similar cultures. Scholars are interested in such cluster maps as they try to determine how management practices can and do transfer across cultures.

One such grouping is shown in figure 1.4. 'Anglo' countries tend to score relatively low on the long-term–short-term dimension, whereas the Asian 'Dragons' — Hong Kong, Singapore, Japan, South Korea and Taiwan — score relatively high on this dimension. Hofstede and Bond argue that the long-term value and influence of Confucian dynamism may, at least in part, account for the surge of economic successes by these Asian nations.[60]

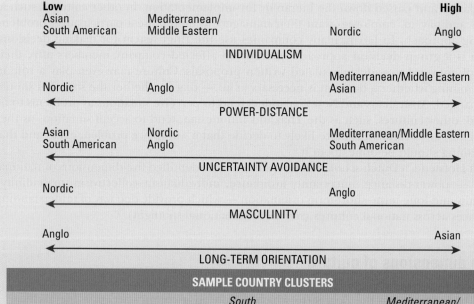

FIGURE 1.4 A sample of 'country clusters' based on Hofstede's five dimensions of national cultures

Sources: Based on Geert Hofstede, 'Cultural constraints in management theories', *Academy of Management Executive*, vol. 7 (February 1993), pp. 81–94; and Betty Jane Punnett, *Experiencing international management* (Boston: PWS-Kent, 1989), p. 19.

Age

In Australia, almost 25 per cent of the population will be 65 years or older by 2051; almost 20 per cent may be 85 years or older.[61] New Zealand also has an ageing population. By 2051 half the New Zealand population will be older than 45 years, compared with a median age of 35 years in 2001.[62] Japan will have the most rapidly ageing population of any major power, and will experience an increasing shortage of labour. The ageing of the workforce has a number of important implications for organisations. These include:

- the possibility of a labour shortage — not enough workers with the right skills for the work that needs to be done
- a loss of 'organisational memory' as the baby boomer generation (born between 1946 and 1964) reaches retirement (from 2006) and leaves the workforce
- an increasing representation of generations X (born after 1964) and Y (born after 1978) at senior levels within organisations as the baby boomer generation retires
- the need for new types of employment relationships to meet the needs of generations X and Y. For example, workers from generations X and Y are looking for different types of rewards for their work — they are less focused on just pay and job security. Google, for example, is one of the fastest growing companies in history and has a powerful reputation among high-performing IT workers of generation Y. Non-pay worker benefits at Google include free movie days, gourmet lunches, shuttles with built in Wi-Fi to get staff to work, and purchase grants for hybrid cars. This comes in addition to a flexible 70:20:10 workload and time formula, where 70 per cent is core company work, 20 per cent is for personal development and training that will benefit the company, and 10 per cent is for innovation and creativity time. The flexibility and lifestyle benefits of Google's employment package have strong appeal for generation Y[63]
- greater workforce mobility and less loyalty to the organisation due to the different attitudes of members of generations X and Y. They expect to have a series of jobs and multiple careers over their working lives. This is in stark contrast to older generations who tended to work for one company, perhaps rising through the ranks over the years
- the much higher levels of technical competence brought to the workplace by generation X and Y employees compared with their predecessors.

Gender

The past 40 years has been characterised by an increasing number of women entering the workforce, a breaking down of the traditional idea that some jobs are gender-specific (for example, nurses are women, mechanics are men), and increasing numbers of women in senior positions within organisations. For example, women now comprise 30 per cent of the three most senior levels of management. However, the top tier is still predominantly male orientated, and 54 per cent of the top 200 Australian publicly listed companies do not have a female in an executive management role.[64] As you can see in table 1.1, the Australian labour force status (2011) shows significant gender differences for both full-time and part-time workers.

	Participation in the workforce (%)	Full-time ('000s)	Full-time (%)	Part-time ('000s)	Part-time (%)
Male	72.9	5224.6	83.4	1037.7	16.6
Female	59.2	2815.5	54.3	2365.1	45.7
Total	66	8040.1	70.3	3402.7	29.7

TABLE 1.1 Australian labour force status

Source: Extracted from Australian Bureau of Statistics, *Labour Force Australia*, (January 2011) Canberra: ABS, 2011.

The rate of participation of women in the labour force continues to increase over time. More women are participating in the workforce during their peak child-bearing years (age 25–34). Back in 1980, only 59 per cent of women who were of child-bearing age were involved in the workforce. This participation rate has jumped more than 12 per cent since then, showing a substantial shift in the composition of the Australian labour force.[65]

One of the greatest implications of increased female participation in the workforce is for organisations to learn how to manage work–family relations such as maternity leave; this will be discussed later. The increased female presence in the workforce has also influenced organisational behaviour in terms of employer–employee relations.

A 2012 Australian census of woman in leadership shows that the situation did not change dramatically between 2010 and 2012, with only one more chair established in the ASX200. Helen Conway, the Director of Equal Opportunity for Women in the Workplace, claims significant systemic inequity continues to prevent talented and capable women from contributing at the highest level.[66]

The changing nature of employer–employee relations

The relationship between employers and employees is changing in how the organisation views its members and how people view employers. In the new workplace, employment is cut and streamlined for operational efficiency, businesses have flatter and more flexible structures, and the workforce is more diverse and dispersed.

Globalisation has significantly altered the employment relationship, creating challenges for organisations, managers and employees. Wage earners find themselves working at home for foreign employers. More senior executives are arriving at their positions with the benefit of 'overseas experience'. And more junior executives are being asked and encouraged to take on such assignments. Consequently, today's managers must be able to both 'think globally' and 'act locally' in pursuing their opportunities.

Human rights and social justice are increasingly pursued in the new workplace, just as they are in the world at large. All managers must deal with growing pressures for self-determination from people at work. Workers want input into major decisions that have a direct effect on their working lives.[67] Workers want more freedom to determine how and when to do their jobs. They want the benefits of increased participation accrued through workplace initiatives such as industrial democracy, job enrichment, autonomous work groups, flexible working hours and family-friendly workplaces. All of these initiatives are changing the nature of day-to-day human resource management.

To create value-adding human capital, the twenty-first-century manager must be well prepared to deal with not only the pressures outlined but also pressures for the following.

- *Employee rights.* People expect their rights to be respected on the job as well as outside their work environment, including the rights of individual privacy, due process, free speech, free consent, freedom of conscience and freedom from sexual harassment.
- *Job security.* People expect their security to be protected, including security of their physical wellbeing (in terms of occupational safety and health matters, as well as economic livelihood), guaranteed protection against layoffs and provisions for cost-of-living wage increases.
- *Employment opportunity.* People expect — and increasingly demand — the right to employment without discrimination on the basis of age, sex, ethnic background or disabilities. Among these demands are concerns to further the modest but important gains made in recent years by women and other groups that have been marginalised in the workplace. The concept of the 'glass ceiling' has been introduced into management vocabulary to describe the discriminatory barriers that women may face as they seek to advance their careers in organisations. Progress will be applauded, but it will not be accepted as a substitute for true equality of opportunity.
- *Equity of earnings.* People expect to be compensated for the 'comparable worth' of their work contributions. The fact that certain occupations (such as nursing) have been traditionally dominated by women, whereas others (such as carpentry) have been traditionally dominated by men is no longer accepted as justifying pay inequity. Equal pay for equal work, equity of rewards involving a comparison of inputs to output, and other related issues such as money and motivation continue to be widely discussed topics.

We will now briefly examine a few of the major issues in the changing employment relationship.

Work–life balance

Increasingly, workers are seeking balance between their work and the other aspects of their lives. The Australian Work and Life Index (AWALI) measures how work affects the rest of life for employed Australians. It measures how often work interferes with responsibilities or activities outside work, how often it restricts time with family or friends, how often it affects connections and friendships in the local community, overall satisfaction with work–life 'balance', and how often people feel rushed and pressed for time. A recent AWALI report found that although the global financial crisis has resulted in an economic downturn in Australia, this has not improved the problems of work–life balance, with work–life interference staying fairly steady. The researchers conclude that, unfortunately, negative work–life interference appears to be recession-proof.[68]

In highly competitive labour markets it is important for organisations to both be attractive to new employees and be retentive of them. This promotes increased organisational awareness and actions for the implementation and management of work–life balance (WLB) strategies.[69] The OECD report 'How's life in Australia?' investigated the quality of work–life balance in Australia, and reveals that it is the only aspect of life in Australia that is not highly ranked compared to other OECD countries (OECD Better Life Initiative). The 2014 Australian Government budget, however, brings funding cuts and cessations to key employment initiatives such as the 'Award Modernisation Process', Building Australia's Future Workforce Evaluation, Career Advice for Parents, Connection and Job Seeker Workshops amongst many other employment initiatives.[70] Key amongst these is the cessation of the government assistance to workers at Ford Australia. This is part of action by the government to cease funding of Ford Australia and in consequence the imminent ending of manufacturing of Ford cars in Australia. Although the government is, therefore, cutting investment in human capital this is being absorbed by industry. Randstad World of Work Report 2011–2012 surveyed some 3226 employees and employers across Australia, and found that 92 per cent of employers set to maintain or increase investment in human capital. Nevertheless, the report found that with the baby boomers moving into retirement, increasingly skill shortages will plague the Australian workplace. The report, therefore, reveals that the retention of employees will be an escalating issue and that work–life balance will be critical to retaining highly skilled employees.[71]

ETHICAL
Perspective

Paid parental leave — whose responsibility is it?

An International Labour Organization study has identified that over 120 nations provide paid maternity leave. The research highlighted that countries including Ethiopia, Morocco, South Africa, India, Thailand and Haiti offered superior maternity leave provisions for women than those in Australia. Recently, New Zealand started offering paid maternity leave support for women and from January 2011, Australia also started doing so; leaving the United States as the only OECD country that does not provide paid maternity leave. The issue of paid maternity leave is important because it is expected that about 80 per cent of all women in industrialised countries will work outside the home throughout their child-rearing years.[72] A recent Australian report explained that 'shortages of skilled labour are expected. Women's participation in the labour force will be relied upon more heavily in the future.'[73] What happens to family income when women fall pregnant? There is now a growing body of evidence from around the world that the pay gap between mothers and childless women is greater than it is between men and women generally.

(continued)

One of the more vital and controversial questions in many countries is: 'Whose responsibility is it to pay for maternity leave?' There are three main options: the employee, the employer or the government. The most talked about option is to force employers to pay for maternity leave, like other types of leave. However, there are only two industrialised nations (Switzerland and Singapore) that require employers to bear the full costs of paid maternity leave.[74] In other countries this cost is shared between employer, employee and government.

Australia's birth rate has declined to 1.7 per woman.[75] The government acknowledges some responsibility for child rearing in the form of maternity payments, immunisation payments, child-care payments, stay-at-home parental allowances and family tax benefits.[76] Until recently, these payments did not meet the minimum standards under the United Nations' Convention on the Elimination of All Forms of Discrimination against Women (CEDAW), which Australia ratified in 1983. At the time of ratification, the Australian Government advised that, due to differing state and federal industrial awards, it was not in a position to implement maternity leave with pay throughout Australia, though these measures were already in place in States like New South Wales and Victoria.[77] However, the change back to a federal Labor government in 2007 precipitated a new focus on maternity leave in Australia.

In January 2008, the then Deputy Prime Minister Julia Gillard announced the Productivity Commission Inquiry to examine the effectiveness of different models of support for parents with newborn children, their likely impact on work and family preferences and workforce participation generally.[78] The Australian federal parliament passed into law its first universal paid parental leave scheme in January 2011 and, since then, eligible parents have received 18 weeks' leave, paid at the federal minimum wage (at $570 a week in 2011). To qualify for the scheme, the nominated parent must work at least 330 hours in 10 of the 13 months before the child's birth or adoption, with a maximum two-month break, and their income cannot exceed $150 000 a year. Women who need to take time off work because of difficulties during their pregnancy are eligible, if they would have otherwise met the work test. The scheme also requires employers to top it up with any program they already have in place. Despite this, there are those who feel the scheme is still insufficient.

In contrast to Julia Gillard's scheme, Tony Abbott in his first prime ministership proposed a change in the parental leave scheme that was to allow parents to receive 100 per cent of their former salary for six months, with a ceiling of $50 000. This scheme had been scaled back from its original proposal over concerns of payments to wealthier parents. Nevertheless, women earning over $100 000 a year were to receive the payment at its upper limit. The proposed scheme was scrapped in early 2015, with Abbott announcing it would be replaced by a new, childcare-focused policy.[79] With the end of the baby boomers and the effect of increasing skill shortages in the workplace, further development of subsidised childcare schemes across the political spectrum is likely to continue.

Transforming training for apprentices in Australia

OBinAction

The twenty-first century is challenging organisations to develop employee competencies that will transform their organisations and ensure that they remain competitive in turbulent and changing business environments. The Australian Printing Association, for example, is implementing a project to assist Australian printing companies to keep up with the latest developments in digital technology. Key amongst the aims of the project is the enhancement flexibility, innovation and effectiveness of training methods. Amongst the project approaches is an apprenticeship model that is relevant to the needs of the industries' apprentices, employers and training providers. The association is collaborating with the Australian Manufacturing Workers Union and state printing industry associations throughout Australia in rolling out a training model that will be implemented across Australia in the coming 32 months.[80]

Woolworths are also following this competency-progression approach. The 'Accelerated Skill Development Program' is a project that is changing Woolworths's approach to training across its Australian business network. The project involves Service Skills Australia — the Industry Skills Council that represents Australian service industries such as wholesale, retail and personal services, tourism and hospitality. The program uses a personalised training platform, reforming pre-apprenticeships and apprenticeships for butchers and bakers and provides mentoring for apprentice's managers. This program will improve completion and retention rates in Woolworths's trainee and apprenticeship programs and develop consistency across the Woolworths chain nationally.[81]

Outsourcing

As we have already seen, countries, cultures and peoples around the world are increasingly interconnected. One result is that it is increasingly possible to transfer jobs from one country to another. Job migration (the transfer of jobs from one country to another) and global outsourcing (the replacement of domestic jobs with contract workers in another country) are popular to countries such as India, the Philippines and Russia, especially in IT-related jobs. With increasing use of virtual workspaces enabled by communications and information technology, it is easy to contract for many types of work anywhere in the world, at the lowest price. To remain competitive, organisations and workers themselves must continually change to achieve high performance.

Outsourcing to India

OBinAction

India places a high value on education and many workers have one or two degrees. Through successful global marketing of its knowledge-based workforce, many companies in a variety of industries (IT, aerospace, finance, telecommunications) are now outsourcing their work to India. Often the workers are shown video footage from the country they service; they watch local television shows via cable and partake in accent reduction courses, all in an effort to 'fit' with the culture they are servicing. One of the largest growth areas is finance. AXA Asia Pacific has its back office functions and data entry work done in India, and part of the ANZ Bank's IT operations are also undertaken there. Organisations like GE Capital (which runs credit card operations for Coles Myer, Shell and Buyers Edge), HSBC Bank and American Express have relocated credit card fraud departments to India. Interestingly, whenever you call these organisations, irrespective of where you are

(continued)

in the world, your call will be answered by someone in either Delhi or Mumbai, the emerging call-centre capitals of the world. Many companies outsource labour to developing countries where skills are often high and labour costs are significantly cheaper. However, companies must carefully consider both internal (cost) and external (customer experience) factors when outsourcing services, as many customers struggle to accept call centres that are not locally based, and it could, in turn, affect a customer's trust in and loyalty to a certain brand, company or organisation. In addition, despite mainly doing outsourced jobs in the past, companies in emerging economies like those in India have been learning and innovating so much so that they are redesigning business processes to do things better and faster than the companies that originally outsourced business to them from the developed world. Some observers have said that emerging economy firms, through 'frugal innovation', will unleash a wave of low-cost, disruptive innovations that will challenge the dominance of established players.[82]

This human capital has proved a successful commodity for India. In 1995, the Indian outsourcing sector turned over about US$100 million.[83] By 2008, it undertook 65 per cent of all IT outsourcing and 43 per cent of offshored business-process work. In 2011, Brazil, Russia and China were important players with 125 offshore locations offering both IT and BPO services, but none match India's enormous supply of IT and engineering graduates. Although 2002 to 2016 has witnessed some 2.1 million business services being transferred from Europe and America to Brazil, Russia, China and India, we will see a slowdown of offshoring from Europe and America to these countries with an eventual halt to the practice by 2022.[84] Various reasons underpin this changing dynamic, including the soaring costs of Indian labour and a lack of good analysts and developers in India and China. In addition, American and European companies have been disappointed by the relationship with outsourcing companies and their closeness to their operations. Such dynamics have influenced the labour turnover in outsourcing firms.

Casualisation of the workforce

One of the key themes from the chapter so far has been that organisations and the environments in which they operate are rapidly changing. Organisations are seeking greater flexibility and adaptability to respond to these changes. Increasingly, organisations are seeking people who can adapt to changing needs. Another method has been to change the composition of their workforce to consist of core workers and contingent workers. The contingent workers are usually employed on a casual basis. **Casual work** is work where the number and schedule of work hours vary and there is little or no security of ongoing employment. The number of casual workers and casual jobs has increased greatly in Australia in recent years: in 1984, 15.8 per cent of the Australian workforce was employed casually, and in 2013 this number had increased to 19 per cent. At its peak in 2007, the percentage was as high as 25 per cent.[85] While employing casual staff gives managers the ability to quickly increase or decrease the number of workers to meet demand, there are significant downsides for both employer and employees. For example, employees suffer a loss of job security and predictability of income; they may have less loyalty to their employer; and they may be less likely to invest in new skills or knowledge that could benefit the employer.[86]

Casual work is work where the number and schedule of work hours vary and there is little or no security of ongoing employment.

Telecommuting

The complexities of the twenty-first century also conspire to shape the trend of remote working, most commonly practised as 'telecommuting'. Telecommuting has been promoted over the past twenty years as an alternative form of working. Benefits include reducing traffic congestion and reducing energy and pollution. Telecommuting can also reduce costly overheads, improve employee productivity, reduce office space area and ultimately improve organisational competitiveness (Myers and Hearn).[87] While there are benefits to employees in terms of work–life balance (for example, saved travelling time and being able to work in their home environment), employees can become socially isolated and may miss out on opportunities for promotion and so on. An investigation by the New South Wales State Chamber of Commerce found that 23 per cent of survey respondents had employees who regularly worked from home or who worked via remote links. A further 24 per cent of respondents had employees who teleworked occasionally.[88]

Workplaces of the future

Complexity in society will increasingly place pressure on future workplaces to be collaborative, adaptable and dynamic. Central to driving change in this new working environment will be the entrepreneurial culture of the younger generation. According to Dr Marie Puybaraud, Director of the Global WorkPlace Innovation (GWI) program at Johnson Controls, gaining business advantage will also require a strong grasp of collaboration and collectivism in order to manage expected future disruptions that the new complex world will bring to the workplace. Furthermore, she describes how the Johnson Controls Global Workplace Innovation Roadmap has planned for changes such as the use of big data to inform decision-making processes; the prioritising of a people-focused workplace; the fluid movement of employees; and the evolution of offices into entrepreneurial incubators. Dr Puybaraud also describes how, in a time when technology potentially may increase productivity by 20 to 25 per cent, the need for face-to-face engagement by managers will increasingly be the most valuable communication mode.

The impact on the workplace will mean a more spatially dynamic and mobile engagement with technologies, and a break away from the office desk. A more entrepreneurial approach to responding to market needs and human resource management will also be required, especially considering the findings of McKinsey, as cited by Dr Puybaraud, that in Western countries there will be a lack of 38 to 40 million highly skilled workers by 2030. Finally, she also asserts that in the future workplace there will be a need for networks that can 'crowdsource' products, generate new markets and sustain existing strong markets. Furthermore, there will become a stronger focus on building an organisational culture across a collaborative and mobile workplace and greater attention to the wellbeing of employees both in the workplace and at home. Overall, Dr Puybaraud points to a world where the physicality of the office workplace will become important in developing performance through innovation, social networking and collaboration.[89]

Ethics and values

With an increasingly interconnected world, the growing representation of generation X and Y employees and employers, and a greater appreciation of the fragility of the natural environment, organisations, their members and the communities they exist within are placing more emphasis on ethical behaviour. The concepts of corporate social responsibility (that organisations have a responsibility to the societies that sustain them) and triple bottom line reporting (that organisations need to consider society and the environment, as well as their economics) are among the most prominent organisational responses to the increased emphasis placed on ethics and values.

Formally defined, **ethical behaviour** is behaviour that is morally accepted as good and right, as opposed to bad or wrong, in a particular setting. Business scandals resulting in the collapse of high-profile companies such as stockbroking and asset management firm Opes Prime and telecommunications company One.Tel have highlighted the importance of ethics in managerial behaviour. Today a trend is clear: the public is demanding that government officials, managers, workers in general and the organisations they represent all act in accordance with high ethical and moral standards.

Ethical managerial behaviour is behaviour that conforms not only to the dictates of law but also to a broader moral code that is common to society as a whole. But exactly what moral code governs a person's choices is a subject of debate.

Corporate social responsibility (CSR) refers to the notion that corporations have a responsibility to the society that sustains them. This responsibility includes such things as providing employment, caring for the environment, contributing to charities and operating in a way that meets the society's needs. CSR is not necessarily a concept that should be regulated. The Business Council of Australia (BCA) represents the top 100 companies in Australia who contribute 219 000 staff hours annually to community groups. The BCA is strongly opposed to new regulations aimed at mandating CSR, as it is their belief that it will encourage organisations to simply comply with legislation rather than encouraging them to be truly socially responsible.[90]

Ethical behaviour is behaviour that is morally accepted as 'good' and 'right' as opposed to 'bad' and 'wrong' in a particular social context.

Corporate social responsibility (CSR) is the obligation of organisations to behave in ethical and moral ways. It generally refers to the notion that corporations have a responsibility to the society that sustains them.

Sustainability

Corporate social responsibility in South-East Asia

Until recently, promotion of corporate social responsibility (CSR) has been local in nature. For example, in 2009, the CSR Club was launched by the 27 members of Thai Listed Companies Association, with the key objective to build networking among CSR practitioners in Thailand.[91] Similarly, in 2010, seven Singapore companies were awarded for the first time for their special contributions to CSR at the International Singapore Compact Summit.[92] The growing recognition of the importance of CSR among organisations in the various ASEAN countries combined with the

identification that there were synergies to be gained by cooperation and also that many of the organisations had regional operations led to the formation of the new Network.

In 2011, the Association of South-East Asian Nations (ASEAN) Corporate Social Responsibility (CSR) Network was established to encourage firms and organisations in the region to increase their CSR efforts. The ASEAN CSR Network has five founding members, under the umbrella of the ASEAN Foundation: (1) Indonesia Business Links; (2) Malaysia International Chamber of Commerce; (3) Philippines League of Corporate Foundations; (4) Singapore Compact for CSR; and (5) The CSR Club of the Thai Listed Companies Association.[93]

In 2013, CSR Asia conducted a survey of leading stockmarket companies in Hong Kong, Malaysia, Singapore and Indonesia. The findings reveal that of 80 leading companies CSR was associated with children, health and education, and investment in non-profit organisations. Little rationale or concern for environmental impact was shown throughout these South-East Asian countries.[94]

An **ethical dilemma** occurs when a person must make a decision that requires a choice among competing sets of principles. Such a situation may arise when a member of an organisation decides whether to do something that could be considered unethical, but that benefits the person or the organisation or both. Is it ethical, for example, to pay to obtain a business contract in a foreign country? Is it ethical to allow your company to dispose of hazardous waste in an unsafe fashion? Is it ethical to withhold information in order to discourage a good worker from taking another job? Is it ethical to conduct personal business on company time? Ethical dilemmas are common in life and at work. Research suggests that managers encounter such dilemmas in their working relationships not only with superiors and employees but also with customers, competitors, suppliers and regulators. Common issues underlying the dilemmas involve honesty in communications and contracts, gifts and entertainment, kickbacks, pricing practices and employee terminations.[95]

An **ethical dilemma** occurs when a person must make a decision that requires a choice among competing sets of principles.

Why study organisational behaviour?

By now you should understand why it is important for managers — and every other member of an organisation — to have a good understanding of organisational behaviour.

The success of companies like Google and NetApp, who have adopted cutting edge behavioural and attitudinal practices as a means of fostering productivity in the workplace, sends a clear message to other employers. Twenty-first-century managers will need to make appropriate behavioural changes if they want to succeed in today's competitive marketplace.

Your learning about organisational behaviour may begin with this book and a course as part of your formal education. But it can and should continue in the future as you benefit from actual work experiences. Your most significant learning about organisational behaviour may come with time as your career progresses. But it will do so only if you prepare well and if you are diligent in taking maximum advantage of each learning opportunity that arises.

The learning and education of the future is perhaps best conceptualised by the terms 'lifelong learning' and 'recurrent learning'. The essence of these propositions is that education and learning should continue over the lifespan of the individual from the full variety of actual work and life experiences. It is both a personal responsibility and a prerequisite to long-term career success. Day-to-day work experiences, conversations with colleagues and friends, counselling and advice from mentors, training seminars and workshops, professional reading and videotapes, and the information available in the popular press and mass media all provide frequent opportunities for continual learning about organisational behaviour. In progressive organisations, supportive policies and a commitment to extensive training and development are among the criteria for organisational excellence. The opportunities for lifelong learning and recurrent education are there; you must make the commitment to take full advantage of them at all times.

Summary

Organisational behaviour defined

Organisational behaviour is the study of individuals and groups in work organisations. This body of knowledge assists managers to interact effectively with their employees and improve organisational performance. Effective managers need to understand the people that they rely on for the performance of their unit. An individual's, team's/group's or organisation's performance depends on their capacity to work, willingness to work and opportunity to work. This concept can be summarised by the performance equation, which views performance as the result of the personal and/or group attributes, the work effort they make and the organisational support they receive.

Why organisations exist

Organisations are collections of individuals working together to achieve a common purpose or goal. Organisations exist because individuals are limited in their physical and mental capabilities. By working together in organisations, collections of individuals are able to achieve more than any individual could by working alone. The purpose of an organisation is to produce a product or to provide a service. To produce such outputs, organisations divide work into required tasks to organise the efforts of people to their best advantage. This process is termed 'division of labour'. Organisations can be portrayed as 'open systems' in that they obtain human and material inputs from their external environment, then transform these inputs into product outputs in the form of finished goods or services, which they then offer back to the external environment for consumption. If the environment values these outputs, then the organisation will continue to survive; if not, then it may fail to obtain subsequent inputs for future production and it may cease to operate.

The role of managers

A manager is responsible for work that is accomplished through the performance contributions of one or more other people. The management process involves planning, organising, leading and controlling. Managers should seek two key results for a work unit or work team: task performance, which is the quality and quantity of the work produced or the services provided by the work unit; and human resource maintenance, which is the attraction and continuation of a capable workforce over time. An effective manager's work unit achieves high levels of productivity and maintains itself as a capable workforce over time by keeping the psychological contract in balance. The psychological contract is individuals' expectations regarding what they and the organisation expect to give and receive from each other as an exchange of values. In a 'healthy' psychological contract, the contributions made to the organisation are believed to be in balance with the inducements received in return. The insights provided through the study of organisational behaviour can help managers help others maintain healthy psychological contracts with their employers. They can also help managers build and maintain work environments that offer their members a high quality of work life, which is marked by participation, independence, equity and responsiveness.

Key issues affecting organisations

Globalisation is the process of becoming increasingly international in character. A managerial career in today's work environment will sooner or later bring contact with international issues and considerations. Managing to perform effectively in a globalised marketplace requires many new skills and competencies.

Changes to the nature of work are largely due to globalisation, advances in technology, the growth in the services sector and, especially, an increasing reliance on knowledge to generate new products and services. Increasingly, the environmental impacts associated with the production and use of these products and services are coming under greater scrutiny by consumers. These changes to the nature of work require workers and managers with new skills and abilities.

The workforce is becoming diverse: more multicultural, older, and there are more women working than ever before. There are, however, remaining challenges for women and equity in the workplace and these issues demand change in organisational behaviour and practice. Managing such a workforce requires new approaches.

Workers are seeking greater work–life balance. They are also seeking a greater variety of incentives for their work contribution. More workers expect to have a series of jobs or careers over their lifetime. Employers should not expect the same degree of loyalty as in the past. Employers are seeking a more flexible, adaptable workforce that can keep pace with the ever-increasing speed of change in the marketplace. Outsourcing and the use of casual workers are among the ways organisations are responding to this need.

Organisations are under increasing pressure to conduct themselves in an ethical manner and to acknowledge that they have a responsibility to the society that sustains them.

The need to understand organisational behaviour

Learning about organisational behaviour is both a personal responsibility and a prerequisite to long-term career success. The field of organisational behaviour helps managers both deal with and learn from their workplace experiences. Managers who understand organisational behaviour are better prepared to know what to look for in work situations, to understand what they find and to take (or help others to take) the required action.

CHAPTER 1 study guide

Key terms

brain drain, *p. 17*

casual work, *p. 26*

contingency approach, *p. 5*

controlling, *p. 13*

corporate social responsibility (CSR), *p. 28*

division of labour, *p. 8*

effective manager, *p. 10*

emotional intelligence, *p. 6*

ethical behaviour, *p. 28*

ethical dilemma, *p. 29*

global management skills and competencies, *p. 14*

globalisation, *p. 14*

human resource maintenance, *p. 10*

human resources, *p. 8*

knowledge-based economy, *p. 17*

knowledge management (KM), *p. 17*

leading, *p. 13*

management process, *p. 13*

manager, *p. 10*

material resources, *p. 8*

open systems, *p. 8*

organisational behaviour, *p. 5*

organising, *p. 13*

performance equation, *p. 6*

planning, *p. 13*

process re-engineering, *p. 14*

productivity, *p. 10*

quality of work life, *p. 11*

synergy, *p. 8*

task performance, *p. 10*

value-added managers, *p. 11*

work team or unit, *p. 10*

workforce diversity, *p. 18*

Review questions

1. What is organisational behaviour and why do managers need to understand it?
2. What are the factors that accelerate organisational change today?
3. What is an effective manager? What are the competencies an effective global manager requires?
4. Why is it important for managers to have a *global* view of learning in organisations?

Application questions

1. Why is human resource maintenance important to effective management? What negative effects on business performance may result from managers' neglect of people issues? Can managerial performance be measured using a single criterion? Explain your answer.
2. What is meant by the term 'global management'? What distinguishes it from other types of management?
3. How have developments in information technology changed the nature of the workplace and the practice of management? How do virtual organisations differ from other organisations?
4. What is the psychological contract? Why is it important to understanding employment? What major challenges to the quality of work life are presented by the conditions and environment of today's organisations?
5. Why is an understanding of cultural differences important to business? What are some steps that managers can take to develop greater cross-cultural awareness? How would you describe the Australian culture if you were attempting to attract foreign investment?
6. What is corporate social responsibility and how is this influencing organisational behaviour?

Research questions

1. Write a report to answer the following question:

    In this time of dramatic changes in the business environment, how will organisations be managed in ten years' time? Give examples and suggestions.

    Your research on this question can pursue a wide variety of alternatives. At a minimum, you must support your report by readings from at least two business publications (for example, *Asian Business Review, Business Review Weekly, Bulletin Magazine, World Executive Digest, Asia Inc.* or *Asia Week*) approved by your lecturer and at least one journal (for example, *Australian Journal of Management, Management (NZ), Asia Pacific Journal of Human Resources* or *Asian Journal of Management*) approved by your lecturer.

2. Training managers and employees to make the most of a diverse workforce can be extremely useful. Visit Diversity@work (www.diversityatwork.com.au) and find out how diversity can be good for business. Use the resources available at the site to test your knowledge of diversity awareness in the workplace.

Running project

The running project appears at the end of each chapter in this book. By completing the exercises in the running project you will gain important insights into organisational behaviour and management in the new workplace. Each exercise requires you to collect and analyse information relating to the material discussed in that chapter.

The first step is to choose an organisation to study. Remember that we will be asking you for information about a broad range of management approaches and processes at your chosen organisation, so you must choose an organisation for which this information is readily available. We suggest using one of the following approaches.

1. Choose a well-known company. This option means you are likely to have access to information through newspapers, magazines, the company's corporate website and your library's resources.
2. Better still, choose a smaller company that you can access directly. This approach has much to offer if management will agree to talk to you at length (remember that you'll need to talk to them regularly throughout your study of this book). For example, you might choose the company you work for. For this approach, make sure you can secure substantial cooperation and information from your chosen company. Your instructor may have some guidance for you before you make a decision.
3. Your instructor may provide suggestions on which company to study.

Your task for chapter 1 is to choose the organisation you will study and to obtain enough information about that company to carry out the following instructions and answer the questions asked.

1. Identify the purpose or goals of the organisation.
2. Draw the organisation as an 'open system'. List the inputs, transformations and outputs.
3. What knowledge management processes does the organisation have in place to provide feedback?
4. Describe the business environment, both in terms of specific environment and general environment.

Individual activity

Global awareness

As we note in this chapter, the environment of business is becoming more global. The following assessment is designed to help you understand your readiness to respond to managing in a global context.

You will agree with some of the following statements and disagree with others. In some cases, you may find it difficult to make a decision, but you should force a choice.

Record your answers next to each statement according to the scale on the following page.

Strongly agree = 4	Somewhat disagree = 2
Somewhat agree = 3	Strongly disagree = 1

_____ 1. Some areas of Malaysia are very much like Indonesia.

_____ 2. Although aspects of behaviour such as motivation and attitudes within organisational settings remain diverse across cultures, organisations themselves appear to be increasingly similar in terms of design and technology.

_____ 3. Spain, France, Japan, Singapore, Mexico, Brazil and Indonesia have cultures with a strong orientation towards authority.

_____ 4. Japan and Austria define male–female roles more rigidly and value qualities like forcefulness and achievement more than Norway, Sweden, Denmark and Finland.

_____ 5. Some areas of Malaysia are very much like Brunei.

_____ 6. Australia, the United Kingdom, the Netherlands, Canada and New Zealand have cultures that view people first as individuals and place a priority on their own interests and values, whereas Colombia, Pakistan, Taiwan, Peru, Singapore, Mexico, Greece and Hong Kong have cultures in which the good of the group or society is considered the priority.

_____ 7. The United States, Israel, Austria, Denmark, Ireland, Norway, Germany and New Zealand have cultures with a low orientation towards authority.

_____ 8. The same manager may behave differently in different cultural settings.

_____ 9. Denmark, Canada, Norway, Singapore, Hong Kong and Australia have cultures in which employees tolerate a high degree of uncertainty, but such levels of uncertainty are not well tolerated in Israel, Austria, Japan, Italy, Argentina, Peru, France and Belgium.

_____ 10. Some areas of Malaysia are very much like the Philippines.

For interpretation, see page 36.

Group activity

Management foundations

Objectives

1. To understand the management foundations recommended by the Association to Advance Collegiate Schools of Business (AACSB). (These are the skills and personal characteristics that should be nurtured in university students of business for success in the new workplace of the twenty-first century.)
2. To assess your abilities in the ten management foundations
3. To select areas for development through planning
4. To examine diversity within the class members' responses

Total time: 10–20 minutes

Step 1: Self-assessment

Rate yourself by placing a number from 1–7 on the line before each of the ten management foundations to best describe how frequently you exhibit this behaviour. Be honest; you will not be asked to share your score in class.

Usually = 7   Infrequently = 3
Frequently = 6   Seldom = 2
Often = 5   Rarely = 1
Sometimes = 4

_____ 1. *Resistance to stress*. I get the job done under stressful conditions.

_____ 2. *Tolerance for uncertainty*. I get the job done under ambiguous and uncertain conditions.

_____ 3. *Social objectivity*. I act free of racial, ethnic, gender and other prejudices or biases.

_____ 4. *Inner work standards*. I personally set and work to high performance standards on my own.

_____ 5. *Stamina*. I work long, hard hours.

_____ 6. *Adaptability*. I am flexible and adapt to change.

_____ 7. *Self-confidence*. I am consistently decisive and display my personal presence.

_____ 8. *Self-objectivity*. I evaluate my personal strengths and weaknesses, and understand my motives and skills relative to tasks I need to do.

_____ 9. *Introspection*. I learn from experience, awareness and self-study. (I do not make the same mistake twice.)

_____ 10. *Entrepreneurism*. I address problems and take advantage of opportunities for constructive change.

Finally, consider this question: 'If I asked my friends and coworkers to answer these questions for me, would they select the same frequencies that I did?' You may want to ask them to select scores for comparison.

Step 2: Best practice manager

Repeat the process of rating against the ten management foundations, but this time assess how frequently you consider a 'best practice' manager should exhibit these behaviours.

Step 3: Gap analysis

Compare your self-assessment ratings with those for the best practice manager. Identify any significant differences (greater than one point) in the two sets of ratings. Select the three management foundations in which the greatest gaps were evident when you compared the ratings.

Step 4: Self-development

Review the three management foundations with the greatest gaps (identified in step 3). Develop some suggestions for self-improvement in each of these three areas.

Procedure for group discussion

1. The lecturer should determine the number of students who are most in need of improvement for each of the ten management foundations.
2. Discuss whether there is diversity, or whether all students elected the same foundations.
3. Beginning with those identified by the largest number of students, discuss how to improve performance against the management foundations.
4. Continue to discuss the foundations in priority order (from highest to lowest numbers identifies) until all ten are discussed, or the time runs out for the exercise.

Case study: Resene Paints Ltd[96]

'Cast a glance down any New Zealand street. Chances are, every building will have been touched by Resene.' The manufacture of paints is a chemical-intensive process, and it is unlikely that firms in this industry are seen as pathbreakers in terms of sustainability. However, innovation in paint-making has been the key to Resene Paints, a New Zealand family-run paint company. Its efforts in promoting sustainable innovation in the paint industry have seen it recently recognised as the Sustainable Business of the Year at the NZI National Sustainable Business Network Awards.

In 1946, Eastbourne builder Ted Nightingale was looking for an alkali-resistant paint to cover his concrete buildings. However, as there was nothing available at that time, he applied his own blend of Kiwi innovativeness and developed his own paint — in a cement mixer in his garage. The innovations continued with the development of the first waterborne paint in New Zealand under the brand Resene (a name derived from the main ingredient of paint — resin). Initially, the market responded slowly to the new paint technology, as there was disbelief that waterborne paint would not wash off walls with water, but Resene won them over with demonstrations run in shop windows. A series of innovations followed that saw Resene leading the way in colour paints development and the production of coatings for residential, commercial and industrial needs.

Resene has a long-established focus on sustainability,[97] and has been an early adopter and innovator. In the late 1960s, it removed lead from decorative paints well ahead of other manufacturers. In 1996, Resene joined the Environmental Choice program, an independent eco-label scheme which makes it easier for consumers to select paints that are more environmentally friendly. Other sustainable initiatives include the development of New Zealand's first volatile organic compound (VOC)-free interior wall paint, as well as paints that have a high renewable content and formulations that reflect more of the sun's energy. The company has also started a paint recovery and recycling program, Resene PaintWise. Resene has also been awarded $1 million of research and development services as winner of the What's Your Problem New Zealand? competition, set up by the Crown Research Institute Industrial Research to create a world-first water-borne paint based on sustainable ingredients. This innovation will provide a true alternative to the paint industry's history of reliance on the oil and gas sector for high-performance paints. Today, the company has three main considerations:

- to manufacture paints in a manner that has the least impact on the environment

- to market and promote paints and paint systems that are environmentally friendly
- to maintain a strong focus on recycling and reuse.

This sees a strong commitment to the local environment, where environmentally conscious products are produced and supported by a long-term vision of waste reduction.

The company has grown — with three generations of the Nightingale family now involved in the business — to over 50 company-owned ColorShops and 20 franchisee outlets with around 500 staff in New Zealand with another 150 employees in sites and outlets in Australia and Fiji. Its paint and colour technology is exported to many countries around the world, and its chemists are internationally respected for their development of high-quality products. The company is not only focused on itself and its customers, but also on its other stakeholders, including its employees, the professional painters who use its products and the community. New employees at its New Zealand ColorShops are given full training, including the nationally recognised NZQA Certificate in Retail from the Retail Institute. The judges of the Sustainable Business of the Year Awards have been especially impressed by Resene's EcoDecorator program, which, despite its challenging audience of professional painters, has made significant inroads in encouraging the adoption of sustainable practices across the painting industry.

As Nick Nightingale, Resene's Managing Director, notes, 'Resene's major competitors are big players with plenty of resources behind them. But the edge we have is our flexible, innovative approach. It's something we will always be able to rely on'.

Questions

1. Identify the three main categories that ought to be covered in a triple bottom line report, and outline the main issues under each that Resene Paints has highlighted.
2. Using the information in this chapter, what comments can you make about the nature of the employee–employer relationship at Resene?
3. Predict the overall organisational performance using the performance equation in figure 1.1.

Interpretation of individual activity

All of the statements are true. Thus, your score should be close to 40. The closer your score is to 40, the more you understand the global context of organisational environments. The closer your score is to 10, the less you understand the global context. For developmental purposes, you should note any particular items for which you had a low score and concentrate on improving your knowledge of those areas.

End notes

1. J Elkington, *Cannibals with forks: The triple bottom line of 21st Century business* (Oxford: Capstone Publishing, 1997).
2. *The Economist*, 'Idea: Triple bottom line' (17 November 2009).
3. See PR Lawrence and JW Lorsch, *Organisations and environment: managing differentiation and integration* (Homewood, IL: Richard D Irwin, 1967).
4. ibid.
5. G Hofstede, 'Cultural constraints in management theories', *Academy of Management Executive*, vol. 7 (1993), pp. 81–94. See also G Hofstede, *Culture's consequences* (Beverly Hills, CA: Sage, 1980).
6. See U Sekaran, *Research methods for managers*, 2nd ed. (New York: John Wiley & Sons, 1992).
7. J Arnold, *Work psychology. understanding human behaviour in the workplace*, 4th ed. (Edinburgh Gate, Harlow: Pearson Education Limited, 2005).
8. D Goleman, *Working with emotional intelligence* (New York: Bantam, 2000).
9. R Bar-On, *The emotional intelligence inventory (EQi): technical manual* (Toronto: Multi Health System, 1997).
10. JD Mayer and P Salovey, 'What is emotional intelligence?' in P Salovey and DJ Sluyter (eds), *Emotional development and emotional intelligence* (New York: Basic Books, 1997).
11. Microsoft Corporation, 'Our mission', www.microsoft.com.
12. Vodafone Group, 'Vision & values', www.vodafone.com.
13. Singtel, 'Company profile', http://info.singtel.com/about-us/vision-mission.
14. KIWI Income and Property Trust, 'Investment philosophy', www.kipt.co.nz.
15. BHP Billiton, 'Charter', www.bhpbilliton.com.
16. The Warehouse, 'Core purpose and values', www.thewarehouse.co.nz.
17. M Wertheimer [an address before the Kant Society, Berlin, 7 December 1924], reprinted in WD Ellis, *Source book of Gestalt psychology* (New York: Harcourt, Brace And Co, 1938).
18. G Ritzer, *McDonaldization: the reader*, 3rd ed. (Thousand Oaks, CA: Pine Forge Press, 2009).
19. Grill'd, 'Our Story', www.grilld.com.au.
20. L White, 'Spudbar signs on master franchises', *Australasian Business Intelligence* (22 May 2008).

21. BreadTalk, 'Our company', www.breadtalk.com.
22. ibid.
23. A Fish and J Wood, 'Cross-cultural management competence in Australian business enterprises', *Asia Pacific Journal of Human Resources*, vol. 35, no. 1 (1996), pp. 274–301.
24. H Mintzberg, 'Rounding out the manager's job', *Sloan Management Review* (Fall 1994), pp. 11–26.
25. L Hoffman, 'Mutual benefits', *Human Resources* (24 August 2005), www.humanresourcesmagazine.com.au.
26. T Peters, *Thriving on chaos* (New York: Knopf, 1991).
27. R Champion-Hughes, 'Totally integrated employee benefits', *Public Personnel Management*, vol. 30, iss. 3 (Washington, 2001); MJ Sirgy, D Efraty, P Siegel, D Lee, 'A new measure of quality of work life (QWL) based on need satisfaction and spill-over theories', *Social Indicators Research*, vol. 55, iss. 3 (Dordrecht, September 2001).
28. M Joseph Sirgy, D Efraty, P Siegel, D Lee, 'A new measure of quality of work life (QWL) based on need satisfaction and spill-over theories', *Social Indicators Research*, vol. 55, iss. 3 (Dordrecht, September 2001).
29. KPA Debusk and E J Austin, 'Emotional intelligence and social perception', *Personality and Individual Differences*, vol. 51, no. 6 (2011), pp. 764–8.
30. JAA Abe, 'Positive emotions, emotional intelligence, and successful experiential learning', *Personality and Individual Differences*, vol. 51, no. 7 (2011), pp. 817–22.
31. TR Schneider, JB Lyons and S Khazon, 'Emotional intelligence and resilience', *Personality and Individual Differences*, vol. 55, no. 8 (2013), pp. 909–14.
32. S Suciu, D Petcu and V Gherhes, 'Emotional intelligence and leadership', *Annals. Economics Science Series Timisoara*, issue no. 16 (2010), pp. 549–55.
33. D Goleman, 'What makes a leader?', *Harvard Business Review*, vol. 76, no. 6 (1998), pp. 93–102.
34. S Suciu, D Petcu and V Gherhes, 'Emotional intelligence and leadership', *Annals. Economics Science Series Timisoara*, issue no. 16 (2010), pp. 549–55.
35. D Goleman, 'What makes a leader?', *Harvard Business Review*, vol. 76, no. 6 (1998), pp. 93–102.
36. M Hammer and J Champy, *Re-engineering the corporation*, (New York: HarperCollins, 1993); M Hammer and J Champy, 'The promise of re-engineering', *Fortune* (3 May 1993), pp. 94–7.
37. Deresky, *International management: managing across borders and cultures*, 4th ed. (Prentice Hall, 2003).
38. http://www.netapp.com.
39. MR Beschloss and S Talbott, *La cele mai înalte nivele* (Bucureşti: Ed. Elit. 1993).
40. BBC News, http://news.bbc.co.uk.
41. R Balko, 'Sweatshops and globalisation', http://aworldconnected.org, also cited in M Street, *Taking sides: clashing views on controversial issues in management* (Iowa: McGraw-Hill, 2005), pp. 336–42.
42. D Arnold and N Bowie, 'Sweatshops and respect for persons', *Business Ethics Quarterly*, vol. 13, no. 2 (2003), pp. 221–42.
43. M Street, *Taking sides: clashing views on controversial issues in management* (Iowa: McGraw-Hill, 2005), p. 306.
44. ibid.
45. R Balko, 'Sweatshops and globalisation', http://aworldconnected.org/article.php/525.html, also cited in M Street, *Taking sides: clashing views on controversial issues in management* (Iowa: McGraw-Hill, 2005), pp. 336–42.
46. JE Mittleman, *Contesting Global Order, Development, Global Governance and Globalisation* (Oxon: Routledge, 2011), pp. 16–17.
47. J Gottschalk, 'The risks associated with the business use of email', *Intellectual Property & Technology Law Journal*, vol. 17, no. 7 (July 2005), pp. 16–18.
48. N Eason, 'Don't send the wrong message, when email crosses borders, a faux pas could be just a click away', *Business 2.0*, vol. 6, no. 7 (August 2005), p. 102; S Harris, 'Uh oh', *Government Executive*, vol. 37, no. 1, (January 2005), pp. 66–71.
49. OECD, *The knowledge based economy* (Paris: OECD, 1996).
50. L van Onselen, 'Babyboomers unprepared for retirement', *Macrobusiness* (23 January 2013), www.macrobusiness.com.au.
51. See also *Workforce 2000: Competing in a seller's market. Is corporate America prepared?* (Indianapolis: Tower Perrin/ Hudson Institute, 1990).
52. See JP Fernandez, *Managing a diverse workforce* (Lexington, MA: D. C. Heath, 1991); J O'Mara, *Managing workplace 2000* (San Francisco: Jossey-Bass, 1991).
53. Department of Immigration and Multicultural and Indigenous Affairs, 'Productive diversity: Australia's competitive advantage', www.immi.gov.au.
54. See G Hofstede and MH Bond, 'The Confucius connection: from culture roots to economic growth', *Organizational Dynamics*, vol. 16 (1988), pp. 4–21; G Hofstede, 'Cultural constraints in management theories', *Academy of Management Executive*, vol. 7 (February 1993), pp. 81–94; and Adler, op. cit.
55. Fritz Rieger and Durhane Wong-Rieger, 'Strategies of international airlines as influenced by industry, societal and corporate culture', *Proceedings of the Administrative Sciences Association of Canada*, vol. 6, part 8 (1985), pp. 129–41.
56. See G Hofstede, 'Motivation, leadership, and organization: do American theories apply abroad?', *Organizational Dynamics*, vol. 9 (Summer 1980), pp. 42–63; N Adler (1991), op. cit., pp. 123–48.
57. N Adler (1991), op. cit.
58. G Hofstede, *Culture's consequences: international differences in work-related values*, abridged ed. (Beverly Hills, CA: Sage, 1984); G Hofstede and MH Bond, 'The Confucius connection: from culture roots to economic growth', *Organizational Dynamics*, vol. 16 (1988), pp. 4–21.
59. G Hofstede, 'Cultural constraints in management theories', *Academy of Management Executive*, vol. 7 (February 1993), pp. 81–94.
60. Developed from G Hofstede, 'Motivation, leadership, and organization: do American theories apply abroad?', *Organizational Dynamics*, vol. 9 (Summer 1980), pp. 42–63; G Hofstede and MH Bond, op. cit.; G Hofstede (1993), op. cit.
61. H van Leeuwen, 'Population could rise by 56 per cent', *Australian Financial Review* (23 July 1996), p. 5. See D Jackson, 'Australia's impending demographic revolution',

Australian Bulletin of Labour, vol. 22, no. 3, (September 1996), pp. 194–211.

62. Information from Statistics NZ, 'National population projections (2001 (base) — 2051)', media release (24 October 2002), www.stats.gov.nz.

63. J Sullivan, 'The Last Word', *Workforce Management*, vol. 86 (2007), p. 42.

64. A Horin and C Munroe, 'Looking down on the glass ceiling', *The Age* (Melbourne, 3 April 2004), p. 3.

65. Australian Bureau of Statistics (2005) 'Labour Force, Australia Detailed', Electronic Delivery, Monthly, cat. No. 6291.0.55.001, ABS, Canberra, cited in Australian Bureau of Statistics 2007, Australian Social Trends, 'Maternity Leave Arrangements', cat. No. 4102.0, ABS, Canberra.

66. Equal Opportunity for Women in the Workplace Agency, *2012 Australian census of woman in leadership* (Sydney, 2012), p. 4.

67. E Davis and R Lansbury, *Managing together* (Sydney: Longman, 1996).

68. B Pocock, N Skinner, and S Pisaniello, 'How much should we work: working hours, holidays and working life: the participation challenge', *The Australian Work and Life Index 201* (Adelaide: Centre for Work + Life, University of South Australia, 2010).

69. HD Cieri, B, Holmes, J Abbott and T Pettit, 'Achievements and challenges for work/life balance strategies in Australian organisations', *International Journal of Resource Management*, vol. 16, no. 1 (January 2005), pp. 90–103.

70. Budget Papers No.2: Budget Measures, Part 2 Expenses Measures, Employment, 2014–2015, www.budget.gov.au.

71. Randstad World of Work Report, 2011–2012, www.randstad.com.au.

72. International Labor Organisation, 'More than 120 nations provide paid maternity leave', ILO press release 98/7.

73. S Linacre (2007), *Australian Social Trends 2007: Maternity leave arrangements*, Australian Bureau of Statistics, cat. No. 4102.0.

74. International Labor Organization, '*More than 120 nations provide paid maternity leave*', ILO press release 98/7, (16 February 1998).

75. F Farouque, 'So will you do it for your country?', *The Age* (Melbourne, 15 May 2004).

76. Australian Government, 'Family Assistance Office', www.familyassist.gov.au.

77. Human Rights and Equal Opportunity Commission, '*Commissioner calls on Government to remove Australia's reservation to CEDAW*', press release (30 June 2004), www.hreoc.gov.au; Attorney-General's Department, Right to maternity leave, fact sheet, accessed 18 May 2012, www.ag.gov.au.

78. S Peatling, 'Maternity leave back on ALP's to-do list', *Sydney Morning Herald* (30 January 2008), www.smh.com.au.

79. A Robinson, 'Tony Abbott amends paid parental leave scheme', *Essential Baby* (30 April 2014), www.essentialbaby.

com.au; 'Business presses Abbott on PPL levy', *Business Spectator* (3 February 2015).

80. Australian Government Skills Connect, *Printing industry in the 21st Century* (22 July 2013), http://skillsconnect.gov.au.

81. Australian Government Skills Connect, *Woolworths transforming training for apprentices* (20 July 2013), http://skillsconnect.gov.au.

82. 'A special report on innovation in emerging markets', *The Economist* (17 April 2010).

83. M Lawson, 'Making the switch from Dubbo to Delhi', *Australian Financial Review* (20 March 2003), http://afr.com; AFP, 'India set to emerge as a major outsourcing hub for global aerospace industry' (13 February 2005), www.independent-bangladesh.com.

84. 'India's outsourcing business, On the turn', *The Economist* (19 January 2013).

85. Australian Bureau of Statistics, 'One in five Australian workers are casual employees', media release (18 April 2013), www.abs.gov.au; Human Rights and Equal Opportunity Commission, *Report of the national pregnancy and work inquiry*, ch. 10 at p. 147, www.hreoc.gov.au; Australian Bureau of Statistics, Australian Social Trends, June 2009.

86. P Robinson, 'Exploding the myth of the happy casual worker', *The Age* (Melbourne, 28 July 2004), p. 2.

87. N Myers and G Hearn, 'Australian Communication and Control: Case Studies in Australian Telecommunication', *Journal of Communication*, vol. 27, no. 2 (2000), pp. 39–64.

88. New South Wales State Chamber of Commerce, *Getting a grip on IT* (May 2005), www.thechamber.com.au.

89. M Puybaraud, 'Workplaces of the future', *Tomorrow's World, New Statesman*, 31 January–6 February 2014 issue, p. 6.

90. M Zonneveldt, 'Business lobby fights new rules', *Herald Sun* (Melbourne, 17 October 2005), p. 30.

91. http://thailca.com/csrclub.

92. www.csrsingapore.org.

93. www.aseanfoundation.org.

94. CSR Asia, *Corporate community investment impact measurement in Hong Kong, Indonesia, Malaysia and Singapore* (June 2013), www.csr-asia.com.

95. See SN Brenner and EA Mollander, 'Is the ethics of business changing?', *Harvard Business Review*, vol. 55 (January–February 1977), pp. 50–7; SW Gellerman, 'Why 'good' managers make bad ethical choices', *Harvard Business Review*, vol. 64 (July–August 1986), pp. 85–90; BL Toffler, *Tough choices: managers talk ethics*, (New York: John Wiley & Sons, 1986); JG Longnecker, JA McKinney and CW Moore, 'The generation gap in business ethics', *Business Horizons*, vol. 32 (September/October 1989), pp. 9–14; JB Cullen, V Victor and C Stephens, 'An ethical weather report: assessing the organization's ethical climate', *Organizational Dynamics* (Winter 1990), pp. 50–62.

96. www.resene.co.nz.

97. 'Just good business case study: top coat for paint company', *New Zealand Management* (1 April 2009), p. 20.

MANAGING INDIVIDUAL BEHAVIOUR AND PERFORMANCE

CHAPTER 2

INDIVIDUAL ATTRIBUTES AND THEIR EFFECTS ON JOB PERFORMANCE

LEARNING OBJECTIVES

After studying this chapter, you should be able to:

1. explain the individual performance equation

2. discuss the demographic characteristics that distinguish individuals

3. discuss competency characteristics that distinguish individuals

4. discuss personality characteristics that distinguish individuals

5. list some strategies that managers can adopt to capitalise on workforce diversity in their organisations

6. define and describe possible values of workers

7. define and describe possible attitudes of workers

8. explain the importance of job satisfaction as a specific organisational attitude, and determine how this variable can affect job performance

9. describe the perceptual process and common perceptual distortion of stereotyping.

STAFF ENGAGEMENT AND RETAINING WORKERS

Marriott Hotels and Resorts were voted Best Employer in Australia and New Zealand in the 2013 Hewitt Associates' survey. The study provides insights on a set of actions and benchmark

comparisons that an organisation needs to develop to sustain a high performance workforce, using data from 125 organisations and over 100 000 employees within Australia and New Zealand. The hotel management firm, with more than 3700 properties across multiple brands spanning the globe, originated from a root beer concession stand in 1927. The founder J. Willard Marriott's first motto was, 'Take care of your associates and they'll take care of the customer, the customer will come back and the business will take care of itself'. This sentiment emphasises a 'people first' culture which is still at the core of Marriott's operations. According to Vice president Neeraj Chadha, an engaged workforce is only possible through strong quality leadership. She believes leaders need to live, breathe and believe in the company's culture and philosophy and have the ability to recognise effort and give people opportunities. Despite the company's strong global employment culture, it appreciates local sensitivities.

It is clear that Marriott has strong human resource policies which facilitate employee engagement. Brisbane Marriott human resources director Nayna Panjanani says the group's commitment to training and development is illustrated through the provision of 40 hours of further training for each associate within the company. She argues that acquisition, development and retention are core to the group's recruitment strategy. 'We believe we hire the best and we treat them the best,' Panjanani says. 'We don't look for a specific skill set in new employees — we look for an attitude. We promise to give our people the necessary skills and we want to prepare our people for a global career.' Internationalisation of staff, as part of a broader succession planning strategy, is emphasised in Marriott with many local associates earmarked for international roles in the fast-growing Asian markets. 'What we do is sit down as a management team and discuss global opportunities for our associates. Our best-performing associates and graduate associates from the hospitality education providers (who we work closely with) are picked up and fast-tracked.'

Several lessons from Aon Hewitt Best Employers are evident. There should be a connection between engagement improvement programs and the organisation's business strategy to increase relevancy and alignment to business priorities; leaders and managers should have the ability to keep staff motivated and focused on critical priorities; staff need to be engaged with the organisation's vision and strategy to facilitate a strong link between their behaviour and strategy outcomes; the most important workforce segments should be identified to implement business strategy and targeted engagement strategies; create a strong link between performance and reward practices; and talent attraction should be a priority in building a differentiated and compelling employment brand.

Such benefits have recently been used by employers to retain workers during the upcoming skills shortage. As unemployment drops, workers have become more confident in seeking new opportunities, and business owners are willing to pay more to get talented staff.

The 2013 Best Employer study found that Best Employers have more than twice as many 'highly engaged' employees than other organisations, which is a major driver for increased discretionary effort. Employees who are highly engaged tend to say positive things about their organisation, and intend to stay with the company for longer and strive to excel. Accountability for engagement improvement and effective execution are two crucial factors making a difference to staff in these companies.[1]

Introduction

People are different! Contemporary organisations are dealing with some key issues that a manager must address when attempting to influence individual performance. Accordingly, as managers, it is important that we stop and ask what makes them different. In this chapter we first examine in detail three broad categories important in our study of organisational behaviour: demographic or biographical characteristics; competency characteristics; and personality characteristics.

We then briefly address individual differences in planning strategies you can use to deal with the increasing diversity in the workforce. Next, as students or as managers of people, it is extremely important to understand your own values and how they differ from those held by others. This is especially the case in pluralist societies such as Australia and the United States. In a pluralist society we particularly need to understand differences in perceptions across cultures.

Consequently, in this chapter we examine values, attitudes and perceptions as they relate to the workplace. This includes a comprehensive discussion on job satisfaction and workplace behaviour. We also discuss perception as an attribute for work performance and reflect on the perceptual process and cognitive frameworks affecting perceptions. These concepts, together with demography, competency and personality, are critical to your understanding of the importance of responding to individuality in the workplace.

Individual performance factors

In chapter 1 we presented the organisational behaviour model that should help us explain and predict human behaviour in the workplace. As discussed, the performance equation (see figure 2.1) views performance as the result of the personal attributes of individuals, the work effort they make and the organisational support they receive. The multiplication signs indicate the three factors that must be present for high performance to be achieved. Every manager must understand how these three factors can affect performance results.

Job performance	=	individual attributes	×	work effort	×	organisational support

FIGURE 2.1 The basic performance equation

We will use this equation as the theoretical guide for the material presented in this chapter. Notice that:
- individual attributes relate to a *capacity* to perform
- work effort relates to a *willingness* to perform
- organisational support relates to the *opportunity* to perform.[2]

Individual attributes

Several broad categories of attributes create individual differences that are important in the study of organisational behaviour. These include demographic or biographic characteristics (for example, gender, age or ethnic background); competency characteristics (aptitude/ability, or what a person can do); personality characteristics (a number of natural and learned traits reflecting what a person is like, including individual innate or instinctive drives); values, attitudes and perceptions that influence how we interpret the world. The importance of these various attributes depends on the nature of the job and its task requirements. Managerially speaking, individual attributes must match task requirements to facilitate job performance (figure 2.2).

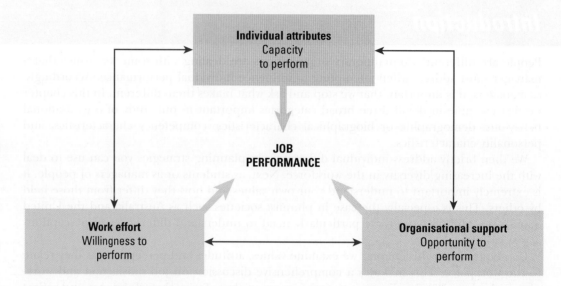

FIGURE 2.2 Dimensions of individual performance factors

Source: Suggested by Melvin Blumberg and Charles D Pringle, 'The missing opportunity in organizational research: some implications for a theory of work performance', *Academy of Management Review*, vol. 7 (1982), p. 565.

Chorus of inspired staff

Few companies can say their underlying goal is for individuals when they are sitting at home at the age of 75 and reflecting on their past career to think it was the best place at which they worked. Sara Broadhurst, general manager of human resources at New Zealand's largest telecommunications infrastructure firm, believes her company Chorus is heading in that direction. She says communicating the company's strategy clearly is done through its annual Line of Sight workshops in which everyone takes part. 'We start with the big global picture and then we hone that down to the New Zealand picture. People are engaged from the outset with the global outlook and then from the New Zealand picture we look at our company goals, then individual group goals, and these cascade through the business. 'We then ask people what their goals are for the year. Everyone talks about the business and their goals and there's a lot of interrelation between departments as they discover where there is crossover.' These workshops provide staff with a means through which they can connect with the company and gain an understanding of the linkages between their personal and organisational objectives. They also provide departments with a way to gauge where there's potential crossover and staff gain an understanding. This creates a real sense of where the company is heading and a sense of engagement throughout the company.

Another initiative which drives engagement is a group of Chorus guides with whom employees can discuss any issues they may have. In Broadhurst's view they act as a great temperature check for the company. Chorus takes great pride in the fact it sees people as individuals, which was evident from an initiative involving the use of psychometric tests to gauge employees own personal values. This fed into a results collation to gain a better understanding of how the teams work within the company.[3]

Work effort

To achieve high levels of performance, even people with the right individual attributes must have the willingness to perform; that is, they must display adequate work effort. For many reasons different individuals display different levels of willingness to perform. **Motivation to work** describes the forces within an individual that account for the level, direction and persistence of effort expended at work. A highly motivated person works hard. *Level* of effort refers to the amount of energy that is put forth by the individual (for example, high or low level of effort to complete a task). *Direction* refers to an individual's choice when presented with a number of alternatives (for example, quality versus quantity) and *persistence* refers to the length of time a person is willing to persevere with a given action (trying to achieve a goal or abandon it when it is found difficult to attain the goal).

Motivation to work refers to the forces within an individual that account for the level, direction and persistence of effort expended at work.

Organisational support

The third component of the individual performance equation is organisational support.[4] Even people whose individual characteristics satisfy job requirements and who are highly motivated to exert work effort may not be good performers because they do not receive adequate support in the workplace. Organisational behaviour researchers refer to such inadequacies as **situational constraints** and these may include: a lack of time; inadequate budgets; inadequate tools, equipment and supplies; unclear instructions; unfair levels of expected performance; and inflexibility of procedures.

Let us now turn to the first set of variables in our model — individual attributes — and examine three in particular: demography, competency and personality. The relevant part of the individual performance equation is shown in figure 2.3.

Situational constraints are organisational inadequacies which do not allow workers to perform adequately.

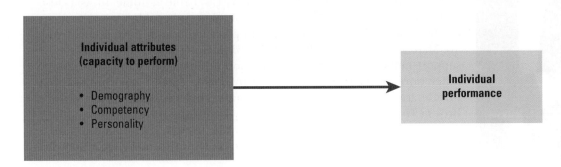

FIGURE 2.3 Part of the individual performance equation

Demographic differences among individuals

Demographic characteristics are background variables (for example, age and gender) that help shape what a person becomes over time.

Demographic characteristics, sometimes called *biographical characteristics*, are the background variables that help shape what a person has become. Key demographic characteristics are gender, age and racial background. Usually, demographic characteristics are easy to determine by appearance or from a person's personnel file. It is useful to think of these characteristics both in current terms (for example, a worker's current income) and in historical terms (for example, where and in how many places a person has lived, and family socio-economic status).

In terms of gender differences and work performance, research suggests that men and women show no consistent differences in their analytical skills and problem-solving abilities. However, women tend to treat their staff in a less autocratic way than men, engage more in transformational behaviour and deliver more rewards for good performance.[5] Hence, there is a difference in leadership behaviour between men and women that may affect overall work performance.

In terms of age differences and work performance, older workers are often stereotyped to be set in their ways. On the other hand, there is a positive relationship between seniority and performance because older persons have greater experience, resulting in higher skills and knowledge. In addition, more experienced workers tend to have lower turnover and less absenteeism.[6]

In terms of ethnicity and work performance, there is no evidence ethnicity is related to individual work performance providing ethnic groups are managed appropriately. This means that managers should be culturally aware and sensitive, be clear in their communication with workers from a non–English speaking background (NESB) and recognise the potential for stereotyping and discrimination.[7]

OBin**Action**

Women in management

Australia and New Zealand still have a lot of work to do to match their Asian counterparts when it comes to women in management positions; however, the New Zealand picture is certainly improving. Research from the Grant Thornton International Business Report (IBR) showed that the proportion of women who currently hold senior management positions globally has dropped from 24 to 20 per cent in the last two years; whereas in New Zealand it has risen from 27 to 32 per cent. New Zealand is comfortably ahead of its Australian neighbours (27 per cent), as well as the United Kingdom (23 per cent) and the United States (15 per cent). Nevertheless, across the world, Thailand boasts the greatest percentage of women in senior management (45 per cent), followed by Georgia (40 per cent), Russia (36 per cent), Hong Kong and the Philippines (both 35 per cent). The countries with the lowest percentages are India, the United Arab Emirates and Japan, where fewer than 10 per cent of senior management positions are held by women.[8]

With women still taking on the primary carer role at home, in Asia close and extended families are particularly of value and enable women to focus on their careers and take advantage of placements away from home. Jenny To, Managing Director of Pernod Ricard in Hong Kong, argues that family support helped her when she took a job in Shanghai, stating that 'Many other working mothers find it hard to pursue career opportunities that involve travel'. Theresa Chan, Corporate Finance Director for Warner Bros in Hong Kong, states that mobility is an issue for women executives. 'Travelling is a barrier for women especially in Asia; it's difficult to find a job with good career prospects that doesn't involve travelling.' Boonsiri

Somchit-Ong, Corporate Vice President Finance of Advanced Micro Devices Global Services in Malaysia, also views lack of mobility as limiting. 'A lot of good jobs are international and you have to make the decision about whether or not to go for them. Often I think, "If I was single I'd do this".'[9] A recent report from McKinsey highlights the importance of corporate culture as a key ingredient in women's confidence in their chances of success. It concludes that any gender-diversity programs such as development programs for women ought to be implemented in congruence with changes in the environment — for example, an inclusive corporate culture embracing diversity.[10]

Competency differences among individuals

The second category of individual attributes relates to competency. Competency is a broad concept relating to the aptitudes and abilities of people at work. **Aptitude** represents a person's capability to learn something. **Ability** reflects a person's existing capacity to perform the various tasks needed for a given job. Aptitudes are potential abilities, while abilities are the knowledge and skills that an individual already possesses.[11] In addition, emotional competence plays a role in the ability to handle the work pressures.

In terms of our individual performance model, competency is an important consideration for a manager when selecting candidates for a job. Once people with the appropriate aptitudes or abilities have been selected, on-the-job and continuing education/training or professional development activities can be used to enhance their required job skills.

Many different aptitudes and abilities are recognised as relevant to work performance and some have been extensively researched in the workplace. As a result, various tests are currently available to measure individual capacity. We can categorise abilities as cognitive abilities, physical abilities and emotional intelligence.

Aptitude is the capability to learn something.

Ability is the capacity to perform the various tasks needed for a given job.

Cognitive abilities refer to our mental capacity to process information and solve problems.

Physical abilities refer to our natural and developed motor capacities for speed, strength, flexibility and so on, as well as our use of the five senses.

Cognitive abilities

As a college or university student, you have probably taken some tests of **cognitive abilities** while at school or when you are applying for a job. Some provide a measure of general intelligence or the 'G Factor' (such as the Stanford-Binet IQ test); others represent capacity in more specific areas such as verbal comprehension, spatial ability, numerical ability and memory.[12] Researchers still disagree over the extent to which our intelligence is determined at birth. The consensus view is that genetics and life experience together shape our capacity, although we are all born with some limits to development in specific areas.

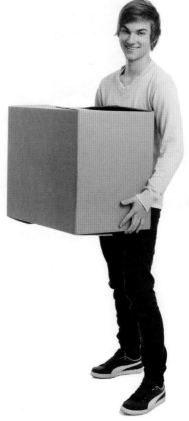

Physical abilities

Tune in to the Olympics, the World Cup or the Asia–Pacific Games and it is soon apparent that we all differ in terms of our **physical abilities**. Different sports require different levels of speed, strength, flexibility and stamina. The same is true of many different jobs. Fire-fighters need strength and stamina to withstand extreme physical conditions. Electricians need colour-perfect vision to work with electrical circuitry (about 10 per cent of the male population is red–green colour blind, while only a small proportion of females are). Manual dexterity has long been recognised as a crucial skill for people engaged in detail work, such as microsurgery and jewellery making.

If a particular job has a certain physical requirement, it is important that it is measured objectively, rather than through the inappropriate use of stereotypes. For example, in the past, a person had to weigh a minimum of 45 kilograms to become a mail officer at Australia Post. This requirement was based on the assumption that small people are incapable of lifting heavy objects. This has prevented many Asian women, who often weigh less than 45 kilograms, from seeking work as mail officers. The validity of this stereotypical criterion was successfully challenged in court.[13] These days, the criterion for assessing potential mail officers is that they must be able to lift up to 16 kilograms in weight.

Emotional competence

Until fairly recently, emotions were given little attention by researchers in organisational behaviour. Generally speaking, emotions were seen as impediments to sound decision making and an ordered approach to workplace relations. This kind of thinking is quickly being replaced by a view that sees emotions as a normal part of our workplace experiences. In fact, recent research has revealed the centrality of emotions to all areas of human functioning.[14] For example, to make decisions we are guided by our values, which are in turn based on our emotions. Reasoning and emotion are intertwined.

Emotional intelligence is one aspect of our emotional functioning that complements the cognitive form of intelligence already discussed. So what is emotional intelligence? It is a form of social intelligence that allows us to monitor and shape our emotional responses and those of others. For many people, it is even more important than cognitive intelligence for success in life. The concept of emotional intelligence was popularised by Daniel Goleman in 1995 with the publication of his book on the topic, although others had been researching the area for some time.[15]

We now turn to the specific dimensions that make up emotional intelligence. A sound place to start is with the research instruments that are under development to assess it. There are several of these, and each has a slightly different way of constructing and defining the dimensions or components of emotional intelligence. The oldest and most researched was developed by Reuven Bar-On as a self-report instrument of emotional wellbeing.[16] It includes various measures of self-awareness and regard, interpersonal competence, adaptability, stress management and general mood state. An instrument that focuses more closely on awareness and management of emotions is the Multifactor Emotional Intelligence Scale.[17] The four dimensions on the MEIS are as follows:

- identifying emotions — awareness of, and the ability to identify, the emotions you and others are feeling
- using emotions — the capacity to weigh up the emotional aspects of values and attitudes when confronting problems and making decisions
- understanding emotions — the ability to understand complex emotions and to recognise how emotions pass through stages over time
- managing emotions — the ability to exercise self-control and self-regulation, and to empathise with and influence others.

Emotion management is well and truly placed on the organisational agenda. Emotion is a valuable resource to be harnessed in order to gain employee commitment (willingness) and

Emotional intelligence is a form of social intelligence that allows us to monitor and shape our emotions and those of others.

Emotion management is exercising emotional self-control and self-regulation influenced by the context in which individuals find themselves.

a competitive advantage. Some researchers have the pessimistic view that emotion can be commodified via a 'commercialisation of intimate life'.[18] Others celebrate the recognition of emotion as a vital part of organisational life, and harness these energies in a positive way to improve customer service and counteract employees' emotional exhaustion.[19] For example, on a recent Virgin Blue flight, the air crew were obviously having a good time. The customer service manager's commentary during the usually boring demonstration of air safety equipment was very humorous and set the scene for interpersonal relations between crew members, as well as between crew members and passengers. There were smiles all around.

Emotion is a lived interactional experience with an organisational dark side. For example, emotional burnout in front-line service work, the everyday stresses and strains of organisational life, and the difficulty of working with bullies or harassers are a reality that managers face. However, not all emotion is controlled by the organisation. Employees are social beings who enter the organisation with life histories and experiences. They may take up organisationally prescribed roles, experience frustrations and often have to present themselves differently to customers or clients. There is no clear divide between public and private worlds of emotion.[20]

If you are good at knowing and managing your own emotions and are good at reading the emotions of others, you are likely to perform better in your interactions with others. There are four essential emotional intelligence competencies that should be developed for leadership success, as well as success in other interpersonal situations:

- *self-awareness:* the ability to understand our emotions and their impact on us and others
- *social awareness:* the ability to empathise and understand the emotions of others
- *self-management:* the ability to think before acting and control disruptive impulses
- *relationship management:* the ability to establish rapport with others to build good relationships.[21]

Emotional adjustment traits measure how much an individual experiences emotional distress or displays unacceptable acts, such as impatience, irritability or aggression. Individuals with Type A orientation are characterised by impatience, desire for achievement and perfectionism. In contrast, those with a Type B orientation are characterised as more easygoing and less competitive in relation to daily events. Type A people tend to work fast and to be abrupt, uncomfortable, irritable and aggressive. Such tendencies indicate 'obsessive' behaviour — a fairly widespread (but not always helpful) trait among managers. On the other hand, Type B managers tend to be much more laid-back and patient in their dealings with others.

Emotional labour

The concept of emotional labour relates to the need to show certain emotions in order to do a job well — it is a form of self-regulation to display organisationally desired emotions in one's job. Good examples come from service settings such as airline check-in personnel or flight attendants. They are supposed to appear approachable, respective and friendly while taking care of the things you require as a customer. Emotional labour isn't always easy; it can be hard to be constantly 'on', projecting the desired emotions associated with one's work. If you're having a bad mood day or just experienced an emotional run-in with someone, being 'happy' and 'helpful' with a customer might seem too much to ask. This can cause emotional dissonance; that is, we are expected to act with one emotion while we are feeling another.[22]

Perhaps one of the most emotionally exhausting professions is nursing. Often nurses cannot publicly show their private emotions. For example, when a nurse cares for a particular patient during the process of dying, and especially when he or she has cared for this person for a long period of time, the nurse will experience a strong emotional response to the patient's death. At the same time, the nurse is likely to care for several other patients in the ward. In consideration of his or her other patients, the nurse cannot share the privately felt emotions publicly. Thus, to be effective, nurses need to be highly competent social actors and emotion managers.

Emotion constantly crosses boundaries between self and society, private and public, formal and informal. Employees continually juggle their mixed emotions in order to both enjoy and endure the rigours of organisational life.[23] Managing employee emotions in the workplace includes recognising the potential transformative power of human action, while managers also need to recognise the emotive forces that inhibit organisationally desirable behaviours. For this, managers themselves need to be emotionally competent.[24]

Emotions across cultures

Issues of emotional intelligence, emotion and mood contagion, and emotional labour become even more complicated in cross-cultural situations. The frequency and intensity of emotions has been shown to vary among cultures. In mainland China, for example, research suggests that people report fewer positive and negative emotions as well as less intense emotions than appear in other cultures. Yet, people's interpretations of emotions and moods appear similar across cultures, with the major emotions of happiness, joy and love all valued positively.

Norms for emotional expression can vary across cultures. In collectivist cultures that emphasise group relationships, individual emotional displays are less likely to occur and less likely to be accepted than in individualistic cultures. Informal standards called display rules govern the degree to which it is appropriate to display emotions. For example, British culture tends to encourage downplaying emotion, while Mexican culture is much more demonstrative in public. Germans are much more 'serious', so shoppers would be unlikely to respond positively to friendly greetings from staff when they enter a store. In Israel, cashiers are encouraged to look sombre, as a smiling cashier is equated with inexperience.

Personality differences among individuals

Personality is the overall profile or combination of traits that characterise the unique nature of a person.

The third basic attribute of individuals is personality. We use the term personality to represent the overall profile or combination of characteristics that captures the unique nature of a person as that person reacts and interacts with others. Personality combines a set of physical and mental characteristics that reflect how a person looks, thinks, acts and feels. Understanding personality contributes to an understanding of organisational behaviour by helping us to see what shapes individuals, what they can do (competency) and what they will do (motivation). We expect there to be a predictable interplay between an individual's personality and the tendency to behave in certain ways. A common expectation, for example, is that introverts (people who are more interested in their private thoughts and feelings than in their external environment) tend to be less sociable than extroverts. Personality is a vital individual attribute for managers to understand.

Personality determinants

The nature/nurture controversy is the argument over whether personality is determined by heredity, or genetic endowment, or by one's environment.

An important question in looking at personality is what determines it. Is personality inherited or genetically determined? Or are personality attributes determined by experience? You may have heard someone say something like, 'She acts like her mother'. Or someone may argue that: 'Michael is the way he is because of how he was raised' or indeed: 'She is a born leader'. These arguments illustrate the nature/nurture controversy — that is, is personality determined by heredity (or genetic endowment) or one's environment? Figure 2.4 shows that these two forces actually operate in combination. Heredity consists of those factors that are determined at conception, and includes physical characteristics and gender in addition to personality factors. Environment consists of cultural, social and situational factors.

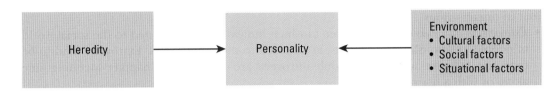

FIGURE 2.4 Heredity and environmental links with personality

Heredity

Psychologists acknowledge that the mind is made up of three domains: the cognitive domain (such as skills and learned behaviour); the affective domain (emotions); and the conative domain (instinctive approaches). Conative actions are those derived from striving instincts. Previous studies of components of the mind often ignored the notion of conation or instinct. **Instinct** is described as inherited patterns of unreasoned and unchangeable responses to particular actions and behaviours. At the beginning of modern psychology both emotion and conation were considered central to its study. However, interest in these topics declined as measuring overt behaviour and cognition received more attention. The notion of instinct as the primary source of motivation was abandoned for several reasons, the common one being that this may place human beings on the same level as other animals.[25] Striving instincts are subconscious and immeasurable. However, conative *actions* can be quantified.[26]

Personality measurement tools are heavily criticised for lacking statistical reliability and validity. However, *quantitative* validity and reliability may very well be irrelevant. The perceived outcomes of participating in a program that improves understanding of interpersonal relations at work (or the qualitative results of such participation) are clearly valued by many organisations, as can be seen by the success of the management consultancies running them.

> **Instinct** is made up of inherited patterns of unreasoned and unchangeable responses to particular actions and behaviours.

Environment

Cultural values and norms play a substantial role in the development of an individual's personality and behaviours. For example, contrast the individualism of Australian culture with the collectivism of Mexican culture.[27] Social factors reflect such things as family life, religion and the many formal and informal groups in which people participate throughout their lives. Finally, situational factors can influence personality; for example, the opportunity to assume increasingly challenging goals or to come back from failure can help build a person's feeling of self-worth.

There is considerable debate concerning the impact of heredity on personality. The most general conclusion is that heredity sets the limits on just how much personality characteristics can be developed, whereas the environment determines development within these limits. The limits appear to vary from one characteristic to the next.

Personality traits

Organisational behaviour literature describes numerous personality traits and characteristics. In this section we will consider some of the personality traits that have been linked with behaviour in organisations. Firstly, we will outline the 'big five personality dimensions', and we will follow this with a discussion of other key characteristics that have attracted considerable research interest.

Five key dimensions of personality

In a fascinating study of how we describe people's personalities, researchers identified 17 953 English-language terms that had been used over the years. They sorted the terms into groups with similar meanings, and finally distilled them into five key dimensions of personality.[28] Research has generally confirmed the relevance of each dimension to behaviour in organisations.

The **five key dimensions of personality** are extroversion–introversion; conscientiousness; agreeableness; emotional stability; and openness to experience.

- *Extroversion–introversion* is the degree to which individuals are oriented to the social world of people, relationships and events, as opposed to the inner world. Extroverts tend to be outgoing, talkative and sociable, while introverts are quiet and are happier spending time alone or with a few close friends.
- *Conscientiousness* is the extent to which individuals are organised, dependable and detail focused, versus disorganised, less reliable and lacking in perseverance.
- *Agreeableness* is the extent to which individuals are compliant, friendly, reliable and helpful, versus disagreeable, argumentative and uncooperative. One measure of this dimension is the Employee Reliability Scale.[29] Low-reliability individuals tend to be hostile towards rules, have feelings of detachment from others, and are thrill-seeking, impulsive and socially insensitive. Those with high scores have favourable attitudes to teamwork, helping others and punctuality, and are more adaptable.
- *Emotional stability* is the degree to which individuals are secure, resilient and calm, versus anxious, reactive and tending to mood swings.
- *Openness to experience* is the extent to which individuals are curious, open, adaptable and interested in a wide range of things, versus resistant to change and new experiences, less open to new ideas and preferring routine.

Research shows relationships between these dimensions and overall job performance. Conscientiousness is the most prevalent predictor of job performance across a wide range of occupations.[30] Extroversion is a predictor of job performance in sales and managerial roles. Openness to experience is important for the performance of students and those involved in training and professional development. Emotional stability is one dimension that does not necessarily predict job performance. Theories as to why this is so refer to the risk management aspect of job performance. Emotionally stable people may be generally more relaxed and less nervous about risk. In jobs where employees have to be careful about physical, financial or psychological dangers, a degree of nervousness and insecurity may actually be helpful.

Locus of control

Locus of control is the internal–external orientation — that is, the extent to which people feel able to affect their lives.

Internals are persons with an internal locus of control, who believe they control their own fate or destiny.

Externals are persons with an external locus of control, who believe what happens to them is beyond their control.

One widely used instrument is Rotter's locus of control, which measures the internal–external orientation of a person — that is, the extent to which a person feels able to affect his or her life.[31] People have general conceptions about whether events are controlled by themselves primarily, which indicates an internal orientation, or by outside forces or their social and physical environment, which indicates an external orientation. Internals, or persons with an internal locus of control, believe they control their own fate or destiny. In contrast, externals, or persons with an external locus of control, believe much of what happens to them is beyond their control and is determined by environmental forces.

For example, *internals* would agree with statements like 'people's misfortunes result from the mistakes they make' and 'by taking an active part in political and social affairs, people can control world events'.

On the other hand, *externals* would agree with statements such as 'many of the unhappy things in people's lives are partly due to bad luck' and 'as far as world affairs are concerned, most of us are the victims of forces we can neither understand nor control'.

In the work context and generally speaking, internals seek more information, experience stronger job satisfaction, perform better on learning and problem-solving tasks, have greater self-control and are more independent than externals.

Authoritarianism/dogmatism

Both 'authoritarianism' and 'dogmatism' deal with the rigidity of a person's beliefs. A person high in authoritarianism tends to adhere rigidly to conventional values and to obey recognised authority. This person is concerned with toughness and power. People high in dogmatism see the world as a threatening place. They often regard legitimate authority as absolute, and accept or reject others according to how much they agree with accepted authority. Superiors possessing these latter traits tend to be rigid and closed.[32]

We may expect highly authoritarian individuals to present a special problem because they are so susceptible to obey authority that they may behave unethically in their eagerness to comply.[33] Authoritarianism has been directly linked with 'crimes of obedience' and unethical behaviour.[34] For example, authoritarianism is a required trait in military organisations throughout the world. One recent example of a crime of obedience was the abuse of Iraqi prisoners by US soldiers at Abu Ghraib, and there have been many historical examples including Jewish genocide during World War II and the 1968 My Lai massacre in Vietnam.[35] However, authoritarianism is not confined to the military; for example, under instruction, Arthur Andersen employees shredded documents to cover up the impending corporate scandal that allegedly led to the demise of one of the US's largest accountancy organisations and sparked the Enron scandal.[36]

Authoritarianism is a personality trait that focuses on the rigidity of a person's beliefs.

Dogmatism is a personality trait that regards legitimate authority as absolute.

Machiavellianism

Another interesting personality dimension is Machiavellianism, which owes its origins to Niccolo Machiavelli. The name of this sixteenth-century author evokes visions of a master of guile, deceit and opportunism in interpersonal relations. Machiavelli earned his place in history by writing *The prince*, a nobleman's guide to the acquisition and use of power.[37] From its pages emerges the personality profile of a **Machiavellian** — that is, someone who views and manipulates others purely for personal gain.

Manipulation is a basic drive for some people in social settings. And although some people view manipulation of others as being deceitful and sinful, others see manipulation as an important attribute for succeeding in an organisation. Thus, it is easy to see why Machiavelli's ideas have been both so avidly read and so heavily criticised over the years.[38]

Machiavellians are people who view and manipulate others purely for personal gain.

ETHICAL
Perspective

An ethical predicament

What would you do if there was a conflict between your own ethics and those of the company you work for?

(a) Live with the conflict because you believe there is always going to be a gap between personal and professional ethics.

(b) Discuss the conflict with work colleagues, promoting the idea that more be done in the areas of concern to you.

(c) Discuss your reservations externally in an attempt to build up external pressure and scrutiny.

(d) Hand in your notice on the basis you should not work professionally for an organisation that has any obvious conflict with your personal standards of ethics.

(e) Take your case to senior management, volunteering to do additional work on the policies of concern.

Claire Warren, deputy editor at People Management, argues that deciding what to do when you think your company is acting unethically is neither easy nor straightforward. She says her choice would be (e); however, she works within a small team and she is able to quite freely voice any issues she may have. What if one works in a much larger team, or was more junior, or less confident?

(continued)

It was evident from research conducted by the Chartered Institute of Management Accountants that 80 per cent of businesses worldwide have committed to ethical performance, but this still leaves a 20 per cent gap. Chief executive Peter Cheese of CIPD, a professional body for human resources and people development, argues that the solution may lie in organisations espousing a values-based leadership. Organisations need to very strongly define their corporate purpose and values, and leaders need to define what they mean and then ensure their message is understood by all the levels throughout the organisation.[39]

Even though sometimes there is a conflict between the values of some executives and what's happening in the organisation, they sometimes may stay quiet in the boardroom on issues they should actually speak up about, often for fear of losing face or because they are trying to manipulate a situation. This tendency is often part of the game playing going on in executive boardrooms, but it may have significant undesirable consequences for the organisation.

These types of games seem to be more prevalent in the behaviour of individuals who rate high on Machiavellianism. Some strategies individuals can follow to minimise these types of games are to:

- make their thinking more visible (for example, 'Here's what I think and here's how I got there', 'I noticed that … and it led me to conclude …')
- publicly test conclusions and assumptions (for example, 'What do you think about what I have just said?', 'Do you see any flaws in my reasoning?', 'Do you see this differently?')
- use language to skilfully inquire about another's point of view through asking others to make their thinking processes visible (for example, 'What leads you to conclude that?', 'Can you help me understand your thinking better?')
- compare their assumptions to others (for example, 'Am I correct in saying that your assumption is …?' and 'My assumptions is that … and while I can't be sure, it would seem that your assumption is that …'[40]

Individual differences and workplace diversity

Increasing diversity is creating unparalleled workplace challenges. Significant variations are occurring in skill levels, education, physical abilities, cultural backgrounds, lifestyles, personal values, individual needs, ethnicity and social values. This increasing diversity is changing the mix of skills required to effectively manage the workforce.

Organisations that can incorporate the opportunities created by diversity into their business strategies and management practices can gain a significant competitive advantage.

Essentially, managers need to ensure everyone in the organisation is sensitive to individual differences and to seek innovative ways to match increasingly diverse workers with job requirements. This may mean developing innovative recruiting strategies to attract new sources of labour and creating flexible employment conditions to better use the increasingly diverse range of workers.

Working with workplace diversity

Implementing a diversity management program

- Examine current structures and processes — do they harbour any systemic biases to disadvantage some groups? Whose priorities do they reflect? Who is excluded (for example, from decisions made in corridors or on the golf course)?
- Take a long-term view — attitudes may need to change and this will not happen overnight.
- Get support for change from the top (commitment, resources, money, time), as nothing will change without it.
- Get the involvement of all those who will be affected by change.

Benefits of a workplace that is open to diversity

- With shortages of skilled labour in some occupational areas, recruitment of staff is easier for organisations that welcome diversity.
- Diverse workplaces have contacts with customers and business partners from a wider range of cultures and groups.
- Diverse perspectives bring creativity and innovation.
- Problems are solved using a wider range of ideas and perspectives.

The organisation also needs to utilise various aspects of education and training in working with diverse employees, using a broad range of programs — from basic skills to workshops designed to encourage managers and employees to value those with different demographic backgrounds. Note that training should be ongoing. Some organisations involve managers in conducting the training, to help provide a feeling of responsibility for making workplace diversity successful.

Turn back to figure 2.3 on page 45. Notice that in figure 2.5 we now add the other three important individual attribute variables:

1. values
2. attitudes
3. perception.

We will now discuss these variables.

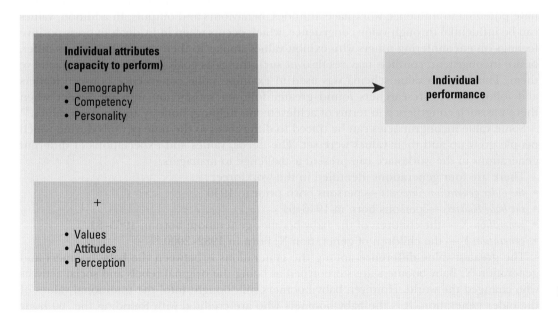

FIGURE 2.5 The individual performance equation

Values

Values can be defined as broad preferences concerning appropriate courses of action or outcomes. As such, they reflect a person's sense of right and wrong, or what 'ought' to be.[41] 'Equal rights for all' and 'people should be treated with respect and dignity' are examples of values held by people. Values tend to influence attitudes and behaviour. If, for example, you value equal rights for all and you work for an organisation that treats its managers much better than it does its workers, you may form the attitude that your organisation is an unfair place to work, and you may seek employment elsewhere.

Sources and types of values

People's values develop as a product of the learning and experiences they encounter in the cultural setting in which they live. Because learning and experiences differ from one person to another, value differences result. Such differences are likely to be deep-seated and difficult (although not impossible) to change; many have their roots in early childhood and the way in which a person was raised.[42]

Psychologist Gordon Allport and his associates developed a classification of human values in the early 1930s.[43] However, although that classification had a major impact on the literature, it was not specifically designed for people in a work setting. More recently Meglino and associates have developed a values schema aimed at people in the workplace.[44] There are four values in this classification:

1. *achievement* — getting things done and working hard to accomplish difficult things in life
2. *helping, and concern for others* — being concerned with other people and helping others
3. *honesty* — telling the truth and doing what you feel is right
4. *fairness* — being impartial and doing what is fair for all concerned.

The Meglino framework was developed from information obtained in the workplace, where these four values were shown to be especially important. Thus, the framework should be particularly relevant for studying organisational behaviour.

Patterns and trends in values

Values are important to managers and to the field of organisational behaviour because they have potential to influence workplace attitudes, behaviours and outputs. In addition, values can be influential through **value congruence**, which occurs when individuals express positive feelings on encountering others who exhibit values similar to their own. When values differ, or are incongruent, conflicts may result over such things as goals and the means to achieve them. The Meglino value schema was used to examine value congruence between leaders and followers. The researchers found greater follower satisfaction with the leader when there was such congruence in terms of achievement, helping, honesty and fairness values.[45]

Some value incongruencies can be traced to differences in the time periods during which people grew up and their values were set. The needs, values and expectations of different generations in the workplace can present a challenge to managers.

There are four generations identified in the workforce:

- *the older generation/veterans* — persons born prior to 1946
- *the baby boomers* — persons born in 1946–64
- *generation X* — the children of the baby boomer generation; born in 1965–81
- *generation Y* — the children of generation X; born in 1982–2000.[46]

The greatest value difference among the generations is between the baby boomers and generation X. Baby boomers are stereotyped as being the original rebels and social activists who changed the world. However, baby boomers still 'bought into' the traditional values of the older generation. It is the baby boomers who are credited with founding the '60 hour working week'; they are supposedly driven, hardworking, loyal, and respectful to seniority and traditional workplace values. Baby boomers still see a distinction between managers and workers; they are union members and are often naturally authoritarian in their leadership styles.[47]

In contrast, generation X are stereotyped as being self-reliant, they value autonomy, they dislike supervision and demand better balance of work life and home life. They are savvy and information driven and tend to be more cynical than other generations. This explains their aversion to political activism; they prefer to focus on what's real and achievable in a practical way. There is no organisational loyalty as their careers have been dominated by downsizing and layoffs, so if they are not learning or growing they will simply move on. This generation have not bought into the 'manager versus worker' polarised view; they see organisations as a partnership and so prefer teamwork and conciliation rather than dictatorship and militancy.[48]

Interestingly, generation Y have been described as generation X on steroids! This generation's expectations, performance, self-esteem and maintenance are all high. Generation Y demand flexibility from day one; they are results driven and have no respect for past accomplishments; their only interest is today and the future. Generation Y, in particular, are empowered and have grown up in an era where rights were entrenched in the workplace, hence they generally see no place for unions.[49]

Of course, these characterisations are just that! Managers need to be aware of value incongruence when working with different generations. However, they also need to be careful not to create stereotypes. We will discuss stereotyping in more detail later in this chapter.

Table 2.1 summarises the workplace characteristics of the various generations. Understanding the characteristics about individuals makes it easier to look at workplace characteristics and how they manifest themselves in business.[50] The characteristics listed in table 2.1 represent only a few of those that have been studied by various authors, and not every person in a generation will share all of them. Nevertheless, they do provide an indication of general patterns found in the workplace. Keep in mind that there may also be an overlap between the characteristics of individuals born at different times.

Research suggests that individual rewards systems are the key to managing the different generational values and this may require a much more hands-on approach to management, with monitoring of work performance and expectations spelled out.[51]

TABLE 2.1 Workplace characteristics of different generations

Source: G Hammill, 'Mixing and managing four generations of employees, *FDU Magazine* (Winter/Spring 2005).

	Veterans (1922–1945)	Baby boomers (1946–64)	Generation X (1965–81)	Generation Y (1982–2000)
Work ethic and values	Hard work, respect authority, sacrifice, duty before fun, adhere to rules	Workaholics, work efficiently, crusading causes, personal fulfilment, desire quality, question authority	Eliminate the task, self reliance, sceptical	What's next?, multitasking, tenacity, entrepreneurial, goal oriented
Work is …	An obligation	An exciting adventure	A difficult challenge, a contract	A means to an end, fulfilment
Leadership style	Directive, command and control	Consensual, collegial	Everyone is the same, challenge others, ask why	Research still to determine
Interactive style	Individual	Team player, enjoys having meetings	Entrepreneur	Participative
Communications	Formal, memo	In person	Direct, immediate	Email, voicemail

(*continued*)

TABLE 2.1 (*continued*)

	Veterans (1922–1945)	Baby boomers (1946–64)	Generation X (1965–81)	Generation Y (1982–2000)
Feedback and rewards	No news is good news, satisfaction in a job well done	Don't appreciate it, money, title recognition	'Sorry to interrupt but how am I doing?', freedom is the best reward	Whenever I want it, at a push of a button, meaningful work
Messages that motivate	Your experience is respected	You are valued, you are needed	Do it your way, forget the rules, balance	You will work with other bright, creative people
Work and family life	Ne'er the twain shall meet	No balance, work to live	Balance	Balance

Now look at table 2.2. The values reported here are based on responses from a sample of US managers and human resource professionals.[52] The responding organisational specialists were asked to identify the work-related values they believe to be most important to individuals in the workforce, both now and in the near future. The nine most popular values are listed in the table. Even though individual workers place their own importance on these values, and many countries have diverse workforces, this overall characterisation is a good place for managers to start when dealing with employees in the new workplace.

TABLE 2.2 The top nine work-related values

Source: D Jamieson and J O'Mara, *Managing workforce 2000* (San Francisco: Jossey-Bass, 1991), pp. 28–9.

1. Recognition for competence and accomplishments	People want to be seen and recognised, both as individuals and teams, for their value, skills and accomplishments. They want to know that their contribution is appreciated.
2. Respect and dignity	This value focuses on how people are treated — through the jobs they hold, in response to their ideas, or by virtue of their background. The strong support for this value indicates that most people want to be respected for who they are; they want to be valued.
3. Personal choice and freedom	People want more opportunity to be free from constraints and decisions made for and about them by authorities. They want to be more autonomous and able to rely more on their own judgement. They wish to have more personal choice in what affects their lives.
4. Involvement at work	Large portions of the workforce want to be kept informed, included and involved in important decisions at work, particularly where these decisions affect their work and quality of life at work.
5. Pride in one's work	People want to do a good job and feel a sense of accomplishment. Fulfilment and pride come through quality workmanship.
6. Lifestyle quality	People pursue many different lifestyles and each person wants theirs to be of high quality. Work policies and practices have a great impact on lifestyle pursuits. The desire for time with family and time for leisure were strongly emphasised.
7. Financial security	People want to know that they can succeed. They want some security from economic cycles, rampant inflation or devastating financial situations. This appears to be a new variation on the desire for money — not continual pursuit of money, but enough to feel secure in today's world, enjoy a comfortable lifestyle and ride out bad times.

8. Self-development	The focus here is on the desire to improve continually, to do more with one's life, to reach one's potential, to learn and to grow. There is a strong desire by individuals to take initiative and to use opportunities to further themselves.
9. Health and wellness	This value reflects the ageing workforce and increased information on wellness. People want to organise life and work in ways that are healthy and contribute to long-term wellness.

However, we should be aware of applied research on value trends over time. Values change as the world is changing. For example, the 9/11 tragedies will have changed value ranking. When employees talk about security, this is no longer assumed to be financial security but also personal security at work.

Attitudes

Like values, attitudes are an important component of organisational behaviour. Attitudes are influenced by values, but they focus on specific people or objects, while values have a more general focus. 'Employees should be allowed to participate' is a value; your positive or negative feeling about your job as a result of the participation it allows is an attitude. Formally defined, an **attitude** is a predisposition to respond in a positive or negative way to someone or something in our environment. When you say that you 'like' or 'dislike' someone or something, you are expressing an attitude. One important work-related attitude is job satisfaction. This attitude expresses a person's positive or negative feelings about various aspects of their job and/or work environment.

Regardless of the specific attitude considered, it is important to remember that an attitude, like a value, is a concept or construct; that is, one never sees, touches or actually isolates an attitude. Rather, attitudes are *inferred* from the things people say (informally or formally) or do (their behaviour).

An **attitude** is a predisposition to respond in a positive or negative way to someone or something in your environment.

Components of attitudes

Study figure 2.6 (overleaf) carefully. This shows attitudes as accompanied by antecedents and results. The 'beliefs and values' antecedents in the figure are the **cognitive components** of an attitude: the beliefs, opinions, knowledge or information a person possesses. **Beliefs** represent ideas about someone or something, and the conclusions people draw about them; they convey a sense of 'what is' to an individual. 'My job lacks responsibility' is a belief shown in figure 2.6. Note that the beliefs may or may not be accurate. 'Responsibility is important' is a corresponding aspect of the cognitive component that reflects an underlying value.

The **affective component** of an attitude is a specific feeling regarding the personal impact of the antecedents. This is the actual attitude, such as 'I do not like my job'. The **behavioural component** is an intention to behave in a certain way based on specific feelings or attitudes. This intended behaviour is a predisposition to act in a specific way, such as 'I am going to quit my job'.

In summary, the components of attitudes systematically relate to one another as follows:[53]

$$\text{Beliefs and values} \xrightarrow[\text{predispose}]{\text{create}} \text{attitudes} \xrightarrow{\text{that}} \text{behaviour.}$$

Look again at figure 2.6 (overleaf). It is essential to recognise that the link between attitudes and behaviour is tentative. An attitude results in intended behaviour. This intention may or may not be carried out in a given circumstance. For example, a person with a favourable attitude towards unions would have an attitude predicting such intentions as saying positive things about unions. However, other practical factors in a given situation may override

The **cognitive components** of an attitude are the beliefs, opinions, knowledge or information a person possesses.

Beliefs represent ideas about someone or something and the conclusions people draw about them.

The **affective components** of an attitude are the specific feelings regarding the personal impact of the antecedents.

The **behavioural components** of an attitude are the intentions to behave in a certain way based on a person's specific feelings or attitudes.

these intentions. For example, hearing a good friend say negative things about unions may lead to the suppression of the tendency to say something positive in the same conversation. The person has not changed his favourable attitude in this case, nor has he carried out the associated intention to behave.

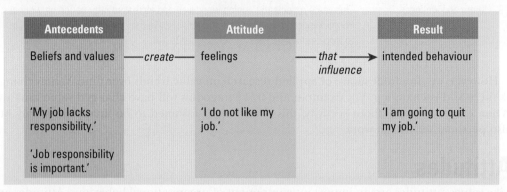

FIGURE 2.6 A work-related example of the three components of attitudes

Even though attitudes do not always predict behaviour, the link between attitudes and potential or intended behaviour is important for managers to understand. Think about your work experiences or conversations with other people about their work. It is not uncommon to hear concerns expressed about someone's 'bad attitude'. These concerns typically reflect displeasure with the behavioural consequences with which the poor attitude is associated. As we will show, unfavourable attitudes in the form of low job satisfaction can result in costly labour turnover. Unfavourable attitudes may also result in absenteeism, tardiness and even impaired physical or mental health. One of the manager's responsibilities is to recognise attitudes and to understand both their antecedents and their potential implications.

Attitudes and cognitive consistency

One additional avenue of research on attitudes involves cognitive consistency; that is, the consistency between a person's expressed attitudes and actual behaviour. Let us go back to the example depicted in figure 2.6. A person in this illustration has an unfavourable attitude towards a job. She knows and recognises this fact. Now assume that her intentions to leave are not fulfilled and that she continues to work at the same job each day. The result is an inconsistency between the attitude (job dissatisfaction) and the behaviour (continuing to work at the job).

Festinger, a noted social psychologist, uses the term cognitive dissonance to describe a state of inconsistency between an individual's attitudes and his or her behaviour.[54] Let us assume that you have the attitude that recycling is good for the economy but you do not recycle. Festinger predicts that such an inconsistency results in discomfort and a desire to reduce or eliminate it. There are three ways of achieving this reduction or elimination.

- *Changing the underlying attitude.* You decide that recycling really is not very good after all.
- *Changing future behaviour.* You start recycling.
- *Developing new ways of explaining or rationalising the inconsistency.* Recycling is good for the economy, but you do not recycle because the plastic recycling bags and procedures require more resources than are saved through recycling.

Job satisfaction as an attitude

Formally defined, job satisfaction is the degree to which an individual feels positively or negatively about work. It is an emotional response to one's tasks as well as to the physical and social conditions of the workplace. As a concept, job satisfaction also indicates the degree to which the expectations in someone's psychological contract are fulfilled.

Cognitive dissonance is a state of perceived inconsistency between a person's expressed attitudes and actual behaviour.

Job satisfaction is the degree to which individuals feel positively or negatively about their jobs.

What are Australians dreaming of?

Sunsuper surveyed more than 500 people across all age groups and genders, and found that the reasons behind the respondents' dreams portray quite a bleak picture. The research was commissioned to understand what underpinned the dreams and achievements of Australians throughout their lives, including retirement. Sunsuper's General Manager, Customer Engagement, Teifi Whatley, says: 'Australians are dreaming and setting goals in their droves, but it is more often than not driven by the negative reality of what could happen if those dreams aren't realised'. The reasons Australians dream have to do with two main factors: having freedom, and being recognised for their achievements in life. Whatley further adds: 'The actions the majority of Australians are taking to help make their dreams come true include saving money, setting deadlines and looking to others for inspiration'.[55]

OBinAction

Age	Top three dreams	Positive drivers	Negative drivers
20s	1. Travel 2. Career 3. Study for improvement	1. Have fun, relax and enjoy life 2. Being successful and recognised for achievements 3. Success, accomplishment and recognition	1. No independence 2. Being left behind and not having finances to enjoy life 3. Dissatisfied with work, being stuck in a rut
30s	1. Study for improvement 2. Buying a car 3. Travel	1. Success, accomplishment and recognition 2. Independence and going wherever you like 3. Have fun, relax and enjoy life	1. Dissatisfied with work, being stuck in a rut 2. Reliant on public transport — loss of independence 3. No time nor the resources to enjoy life
40s	1. Partner/togetherness 2. Travel 3. Asset ownership	1. Close bond with someone special 2. Have fun, relax and enjoy life 3. To be debt free and independent	1. No security of a life partner and not missing out on family 2. No time nor the resources to enjoy life 3. Not having financial means to provide, enjoy life and retire
50s	1. Partner/togetherness 2. Asset ownership 3. Family time	1. Close bond with someone special 2. To be debt free and independent 3. Feel close and bonded with family	1. No security of a life partner and not missing out on family 2. Not having financial means to provide, enjoy life and retire 3. Missing out on special family moments
60s	1. Partner/togetherness 2. Family time 3. Health	1. Close bond with someone special 2. Feel close and bonded with family 3. The ability to relax and enjoy life	1. No security of a life partner — being alone 2. Missing out on special family moments 3. Poor health and its impact on the ability to enjoy life

TABLE 2.3 Australians' top three dreams by age group

Source: C Hughes, 'Australian dreams driven by nightmares — study finds', 16 March 2011, *Sunsuper*.

Dr Rebecca Huntley, Director of the Ipsos Mackay Report, says that the results of this survey are indicative of minds and moods of Australians. The findings echo the results of

(continued)

a survey by Careerone.com.au, which found that job dissatisfaction had hit a record high, with 82 per cent of Australian workers open to changing jobs and 37 per cent actively pursuing new roles.[56]

The negative drivers behind the dreams of Australians are obviously a source of stress in the lives of working adults. Within the context of job satisfaction, research indicates that stress plays a role in job and life satisfaction, and the spillover effects of stressful lives could have a significant negative effect on employees' work.[57]

Organisational commitment is the degree to which a person strongly identifies with, and feels a part of, the organisation.

Job involvement is the degree to which a person is willing to work hard and apply effort beyond normal job expectations.

Two attitudes closely related to job satisfaction are 'organisational commitment' and 'job involvement'. Organisational commitment refers to the degree to which a person strongly identifies with, and feels a part of, the organisation. Job involvement refers to the degree to which a person is willing to work hard and apply effort beyond normal job expectations.

Job satisfaction is among the important attitudes that influence human behaviour in the workplace. Thus, organisational behaviour researchers are interested in accurately measuring job satisfaction and understanding its consequences for people at work. On a daily basis, managers must be able to infer the job satisfaction of others by careful observation and interpretation of what they say and do while going about their jobs. Among the many available job satisfaction questionnaires, two popular ones are the Minnesota Satisfaction Questionnaire (MSQ) and the Job Descriptive Index (JDI).[58] The MSQ measures satisfaction with working conditions, opportunities for advancement, freedom to use one's own judgement, praise for doing a good job and feelings of accomplishment, among others.

The effective manager 2.2 shows five important facets of job satisfaction from the JDI that summarise the factors that can influence whether people develop positive feelings about their work.

THE **EffectiveManager** 2.2

Facets of job satisfaction (from the Job Descriptive Index)

1. *The work* — responsibility, interest and growth
2. *Quality of supervision* — technical help and social support
3. *Relationships with coworkers* — social harmony and respect
4. *Promotion opportunities* — chances for further advancement
5. *Pay* — adequacy of pay and perceived equity compared with the pay that others receive.

Job satisfaction and workplace behaviour

It is helpful to view job satisfaction in the context of two decisions people make about their work. The first is the decision to belong — that is, to join the organisation, attend work regularly and remain with the organisation. The second is the decision to perform — that is, to work hard in pursuit of high levels of task performance.

Job satisfaction, absenteeism and turnover

Absenteeism is the failure of people to attend work on a given day.

Turnover is the decision by people to terminate their employment.

Job satisfaction influences absenteeism, or the failure of people to attend work. In general, satisfied workers are more regular in attendance and are less likely to be absent for unexplained reasons. Job satisfaction can also affect turnover, or decisions by people to terminate their employment: satisfied workers are less likely to leave, while dissatisfied workers are more likely to leave when they can.[59]

Gen Ys are not all the same

The top four things Gen Ys all over the world are looking for in an employer are:

* the chance to learn and develop
* the opportunity to do work that excites them
* a job aligned to their talents
* a mentor at work.

However, in a generation Y study comparing Asia with the rest of the world, it was found that Asian-based Gen Ys' key influencers are in fact different to their counterparts in the rest of the world. In the western world Gen Ys tend to look first to parents and then peers and mentors. Although peers and parents are viewed as equally important in Asia, there are differences when looking a bit closer at specific countries. For example, in China after parents, members of the older generation are the next most influential. Peers, mentors and the media come next. In India after parents, academics are the most influential. In their decision to work for an organisation company brand features higher on the list of Gen Ys in Asia than Gen Ys elsewhere.

Asian-based Gen Ys view themselves as different to their older coworkers. This emphasises the importance of enabling an understanding of generational diversity. Understanding what makes people act differently in different generations can significantly lessen potential inter-generational conflict and team work.

The opportunity to work overseas is rated much higher among Gen Ys in Asia than the rest of the world.

In view of these findings, strengths-based recruitment and development is important. In other words it is about selecting candidates that are made for the job rather than those that are just capable of doing it. In development terms, it means focusing on what an employee likes doing and does well and assisting them in developing those strengths further.[60]

It's very often the kudos that goes with [working for a reputable company]. We have seen that with some professions, especially law firms: people only want to work with the top-tier firms. And if it's Virgin, that has a brand pull with the younger professionals.

Furthermore, young professionals find extravagant reward schemes — such as European holidays for high-achieving employees and in-house free vending and coffee machines — very attractive.[61]

Questions

1. Brainstorm some strategies that managers can employ to keep young professional staff.
2. It is clear from this discussion (and table 2.3 on p. 61) that young professionals have very high expectations of employers. What are some non-monetary things managers can do to keep young high-quality professional staff?

In addition to job satisfaction, both absenteeism and turnover are of major concern to managers as a part of their human resource maintenance responsibility. The costs of turnover, especially, are high. They include the expenses of recruiting, selecting and training replacements, as well as productivity losses caused by any operational disruptions and low morale.

Clearly, the intention to remain or belong (the notion of organisational commitment, which we referred to earlier) is closely related to job satisfaction. However, how these two are related is not totally clear as yet. Does job satisfaction produce commitment? Or, if we are committed to the organisation, will that lead to satisfaction with our work? Look at figure 2.7 closely — which way do you think it is?

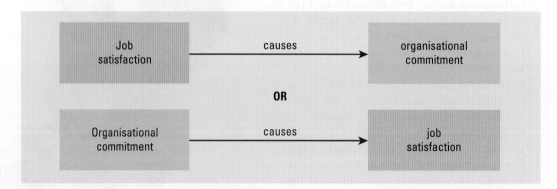

FIGURE 2.7 Hypothesised links between job satisfaction and organisational commitment

The link between job satisfaction and overall job performance

Performance is a summary measure of the quantity and quality of task contributions made by an individual or group to the work unit and organisation.

Recall the performance equation (figure 2.1, p. 43). **Performance** is defined as the quantity and quality of individual, group or organisational accomplishments. What is the relationship between job satisfaction and performance? This question assumes that satisfaction and performance may be related but does not say how. There is considerable debate on this issue — sometimes called the job satisfaction–performance controversy — which involves three alternative points of view,[62] and is by no means solved.[63]

(a) Satisfaction causes performance (S→P).
(b) Performance causes satisfaction (P→S).
(c) Rewards cause both performance and satisfaction (R→P, S).

Argument A: satisfaction causes performance

If job satisfaction causes high levels of performance, the message to managers is quite simple: to increase people's work performance, make them happy. However, research indicates that there is no simple and direct link between individual job satisfaction at one point in time and work performance at a later point in time. This conclusion is widely recognised among organisational behaviour scholars, even though some continue to argue that the S→P relationship may exist to various degrees, depending on the exact situation; for example, some evidence suggests an S→P relationship is more likely for professional or higher-level employees than for non-professionals or those at lower job levels.[64] These alternative views continue to be debated.

Argument B: performance causes satisfaction

If high levels of performance cause job satisfaction, the message to managers is quite different. Rather than focusing first on people's job satisfaction, attention should be given to helping people experience high performance accomplishments. From this outcome, job satisfaction would be expected to follow. Research indicates that an empirical relationship exists between individual performance measured at a certain time and later job satisfaction. A model of this relationship, based on the work of Edward E Lawler and Lyman Porter,[65] is presented in figure 2.8.[66]

In the figure, performance accomplishment leads to rewards that, in turn, lead to satisfaction. Rewards in this model are *intervening variables* — that is, they 'link' performance with later satisfaction. In addition, a *moderator variable* — perceived equity of rewards — further affects the relationship. The moderator indicates that performance will lead to satisfaction only if rewards are perceived as equitable. If individuals feel their performances are unfairly rewarded, the P→S effect will not hold.

This viewpoint is important for managers to understand, not because it resolves the job satisfaction–performance controversy, but because it highlights the importance of rewards in the management process.

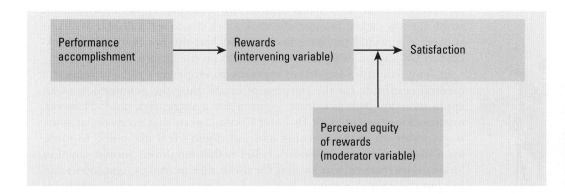

FIGURE 2.8 Simplified version of the Porter–Lawler model of the performance–satisfaction relationship

Argument C: rewards cause both satisfaction and performance

This final argument in the job satisfaction–performance controversy is the most compelling. It suggests that a *proper* allocation of rewards can positively influence both performance and satisfaction. Research indicates that people who receive high rewards report higher job satisfaction. But research also indicates that performance-contingent rewards influence a person's work performance.[67] Large rewards are given for high performance; small or no rewards are given for low performance. Additionally, while giving a low performer only small rewards may lead to initial dissatisfaction, the expectation is that the individual will make efforts to improve performance to obtain greater rewards in the future.

The point is that managers should consider satisfaction and performance as two separate but interrelated work results that are affected by the allocation of rewards. Whereas job satisfaction alone is not a good predictor of work performance, well-managed rewards can have a positive influence on both satisfaction and performance. The What would you do? discusses staff absenteeism, and the International spotlight outlines some global managerial competencies.

Thus far, we have discussed individual differences in terms of demography, competency, personality, values and attitudes. This last section focused on job satisfaction as an attitude and we have expanded on that by linking job satisfaction and workplace behaviour, arguing the links between satisfaction and performance. Now turn back to the individual performance equation earlier in this chapter. Employees' capacity to perform is dependent on individual attributes (demography, personality and competency) that are influenced by values, attitudes and perceptions. The next section outlines the perceptual process and includes stereotyping as a way for individuals to select, organise, interpret, retrieve and respond to information from the world around them.

Sickies — staff absenteeism

A 'sickie' occurs when an employee fails to turn up for work without a legitimate reason. Worker absenteeism can have a significant impact on a business's bottom line. Surveys show almost half of all Australian workers take the odd sickie.[68] Unscheduled absences that are not due to illness are estimated to cost Australian employers more

than $7 billion a year in lost productivity and disruption. However, sickies are not only an Australian phenomenon; unauthorised absenteeism occurs internationally. Asia and Africa have the lowest rates of absenteeism, whereas the United States and Western European countries such as Germany and France have the highest rates, with Australia and New Zealand falling in the middle.[69]

Caring for (sick) family members and worker job dissatisfaction are cited by most workers as the main causes of absenteeism. Some reasons for taking a sickie are far less obvious; for example, an Air New Zealand employee was sacked because she took a sick day to see a Robbie Williams concert. She would not have been caught had she not flown from Auckland to Wellington using her staff discount on the airfare.[70]

In some countries legislation supports an employer's right to request a medical certificate for the purpose of establishing the genuineness of an application for paid sick leave — even for a single sick day.[71] However, organisational psychologist Dr Peter Cotton asserts that everyone, at some stage, wakes up in the morning and just doesn't feel like going to work, for a variety of reasons. Cotton's belief is that employers should sanction 'doona days' twice a year so that for those rare mornings, employees can just put the doona back over their head and not go into work. The belief is that this will help to reduce stress, particularly in an era where up to 20 per cent of workers in Australia and New Zealand work more than 50 hours per week.[72]

Questions

1. In a small group, brainstorm some 'real' reasons for single-day absenteeism.
2. What are some strategies that managers can employ to reduce the financial impact of 'sickies'?

International
SPOTLIGHT

Global managerial competencies

Global managers must understand and respond to customers, governments and competitors across the world. To be successful, global managers must develop key global and cultural competencies: high energy levels, work composure, listening skills, cultural self-awareness, cultural consciousness, ability to lead multicultural teams, ability to negotiate across cultures and a global mindset.[73]

- High energy levels. This is required for handling increased work activity, longer hours and often extensive global travelling.
- Work composure. Managers must have the flexibility to handle the pressures involved, maintaining a calm and professional manner even when under duress.
- Listening skills. Good listening skills are essential for interpreting the nuances of communications with the ability to recognise what is not said as well as what is directly spoken.[74]

- Cultural self-awareness. The starting pointing for cultural sensitivity is an understanding of the influence of one's own culture. A clear appreciation of one's own cultural values, assumptions and beliefs is a prerequisite for developing an appreciation of other cultures.[75]
- Cultural consciousness. A critical requirement for global managers is the ability to adapt to cultural requirements and manage cultural diversity.[76]
- The ability to lead multicultural teams. This requires working collaboratively with people with different cultural perspectives and developing cultural sensitivity.[77]
- The ability to negotiate across cultures. Global managers are required to negotiate with people from different countries and cultures. Negotiating styles and approaches vary substantially with each culture.[78]
- A global mindset. An essential global management competency has been described as 'global thinking', a 'global mindset' or a 'global perspective'. Managers need to appreciate the strategic implication of global business and develop a long-term orientation. A global mindset allows a manager to scan the global environment from a very broad perspective.[79]

In Australia and New Zealand, providers of diplomas, undergraduate bachelor degrees, majors and masters programs are actively preparing students for global business and global management.

Perception and the perceptual process

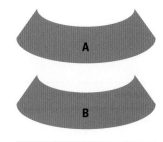

Look at the two shapes on the left and compare them. Objectively, A and B are the same length, but they do not look that way to most people. Now think back to the last soccer, football or netball game you watched. How similarly did you and a friend supporting the other team see the game? What about the referee's calls in close situations? Did you agree with them?

This example illustrates the notion of **perception**, or how we select, organise, interpret and retrieve information from the environment.[80] As the example shows, perception is not necessarily the same as reality; nor are the perceptions of two people necessarily the same when describing the same event. The process is outlined in figure 2.9.

Through perception, people process information inputs into decisions and actions. Perception is a way of forming impressions about oneself, other people and daily life experiences. It is also a screen or filter through which information passes before having an effect on people.

Perception is the process through which people receive, organise and interpret information from their environment.

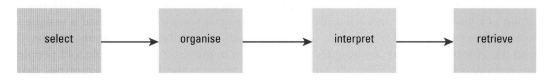

FIGURE 2.9 The perceptual process

Factors influencing the perceptual process

A number of factors contribute to perceptual differences and the perceptual process among people at work. These include the characteristics of the perceiver, the setting and the perceived.

- *The perceiver.* A person's needs or motives, past experiences, values, attitudes and personality may all influence the perceptual process. A person with a negative attitude towards unions, for example, may look for antagonism even during routine visits by local union officials to the organisation.
- *The setting.* The physical, social and organisational context of the perceptual setting can also influence the perceptual process. Hearing a subordinate call the boss by his or her first name may be acceptable in Australia and New Zealand, but not in Germany or Malaysia.
- *The perceived.* Characteristics of the perceived, such as contrast, intensity, size, motion and repetition or novelty, are also important in the perceptual process. A bright red sports car will tend to stand out from a group of grey sedans; whispering or shouting will stand out from ordinary conversation; very small or very large people will tend to be perceived differently from and more readily than average-sized people; and moving objects will stand out from those not moving.

Perceptions are influenced by values and attitudes and, in turn, influence behaviour. For example, a manager may feel that employees are not performing well and perceive the reason to be lack of effort (an internal factor). This manager would likely respond with attempts to 'motivate' the employees to work harder. Exploring the possibility of changing external, situational factors to remove job constraints and providing better organisational support might be ignored. This oversight could sacrifice major performance gains.

Perceptual distortions can make the perceptual process inaccurate and affect the response. A halo effect occurs when one attribute of a person is used to develop an overall impression, for example, that a smiling person is nice. This usually occurs at the organisation stage of perceptual process. Another example of perceptual distortion is projection — where one's personal attributes are assigned to other individuals. This usually occurs at the interpretation stage of perception. A common perceptual distortion is stereotyping.

Stereotyping occurs when information is being organised and sorted in different categories or stereotypes. This process is heavily influenced by schemas or cognitive frameworks that represent organised knowledge about a given concept developed through experience. Stereotypes obscure individual differences. They can prevent managers from accurately assessing people's needs, preferences and abilities.

Schemas are cognitive frameworks developed through experience.

Stereotyping

As stated earlier, demographic differences between individuals can influence work performance; for example, length of service may indicate greater knowledge and skill. Different demographic characteristics, such as gender, age and ethnicity, are particularly important to managers in light of equal employment opportunity and workforce diversity management.

Demographic variables, in particular, are often the source of inappropriate generalisations, misconceptions and perceptions — for example, 'young people today are lazy and lack motivation', or 'men are cold and insensitive'. *Stereotyping* occurs when an individual is assigned to a group or category (for example, old people) and the attributes commonly associated with the group or category are assigned to the person in question (for example, old people are not creative). Demographic characteristics may serve as the basis for stereotypes that obscure individual differences, preventing people from getting to know others as individuals and from accurately assessing their potential performance. Someone who believes that older people are not creative, for example, may mistakenly decide not to appoint an inventive 60-year-old person to an important job.

Perceptions about age and performance

There is a common stereotype or misconception concerning age, in relation to learning and flexibility. Many people associate older people with a sense of inertia. However, the truth is that this depends on the individual. Many older people have shown themselves to be flexible. Further, age and performance have been found to be unrelated; that is, older people are no more likely than younger people to be unproductive.[81] In addition, older workers are less likely than younger workers to leave a job, so there is a managerial advantage if they are performing well. Overall, contrary to common opinion, the data suggests that most older workers are likely to be good workers.[82]

The research findings on age are particularly important, given that the workforce is ageing. The figures on the changing age demographic in Australia show that important shifts are occurring. There are currently 170 000 new entrants into the workforce every year; however, it is estimated that by 2030 this figure will drop to 125 000 new entrants. Currently, for every person over 65 there are 5.3 people of working age (usually considered to be from ages 15 to 64). By 2022 the figure is expected to drop to 3.5, and in 2042 it will be even lower at 2.5.[83]

However, ageism remains prevalent in the workplace in many Western countries. In Australia and the United States, research shows that older managers are more at risk of being retrenched and, if retrenchment occurs, that the older worker will have more difficulty in finding new employment that matches his or her old job in terms of income or security.[84] In Japan, once workers reach 50 they are increasingly being pushed into early retirement.[85] However, in rural China, agricultural workers continue their employment until well in their seventies.[86] This reflects the more traditional views in Asia that older workers are to be respected and not disparaged.[87]

Challenges faced by mature-aged employees

OBinAction

Stereotypes about older workers are rife including employers' attitude that older workers are disinterested or lack the ability to undertake training and development; they are unable to change; and older workers lack competence because of ageing processes.[88] This stereotyping of older workers is especially problematic in places such as Australia where there is a debate about raising the retirement age of workers from 65 to 67 or 70. Furthermore, older workers may have very few opportunities to refute negative stereotypes as workplace training programs often discriminate against older workers by focusing on abilities that are typically superior in younger workers such as information communication technologies and mental processing or motor speed.

Older workers with limited schooling may especially suffer from lack of motivation and confidence with regard to acquiring new skills, owing to weak literacy and numeracy skills. In a survey of older workers employed in regional areas in Australia female workers generally took greater advantage of training opportunities than males. This greater preference by women for computer-based learning could be a reflection of the higher proportion of (computer literate) female office workers in the study, whereas desire for early retirement amongst men may be related to their manual occupational status, which tends to become more physically demanding as they get older.[89]

Perceptions about gender and performance

Perceptions about gender and performance have been difficult to combat, particularly for women. As mentioned earlier, there are few gender-related differences affecting performance; nevertheless there are still inequalities.

The fight for equal pay between men and women continues. Since 1972, Australian women have received equal pay for equal work — that is, if they perform the same work as a man. According to the National Women's Consultative Council report, this is estimated to have benefited 18 per cent of adult female employees. However, despite equal pay and anti-discrimination legislation, women still earn less than men in all categories of earnings, all components of earnings, all major occupational groupings and all industries. It is important to note that while the average weekly earnings data in table 2.4 can be used to compare, at the very broad level, average earnings between males and females, such comparisons do not take into account a range of compositional differences, such as differences in occupation or hours worked, which contribute significantly to the differences observed between male and female earnings. However, regardless of the figure used, or the comparisons made, women's average earnings are consistently and demonstrably lower than those of their male counterparts.

TABLE 2.4 Average weekly total earnings of male and female adult employees (all employees)

Source: Australian Bureau of Statistics, *Average Weekly Earnings, Australia*, May 2013, cat. no. 6302.0 (Canberra: ABS, 2013).

	Males ($)	Females ($)
Adult employees		
— full-time ordinary weekly earnings	1 603.10	11267.40

What seems to be consistently ignored is the difference in earnings between women with children and women without children, where the gap is significant and increasing.[90] There is evidence that the family responsibilities of women is having a significant effect on their earning ability, because their work choices are based on working flexibility rather than high income.[91]

Perceptions about ethnicity and performance

A growing proportion of the new workforce is composed of an increasingly broad spectrum of employees from differing ethnic backgrounds.[92] This is particularly true of the Asia — Pacific region, where many organisations have multicultural workforces. Dealing with diverse ethnicities in the workplace is a contemporary management issue that strongly rejects the notion of ethnic stereotyping. Stereotyping can easily result in discrimination, which is against the law.

Good managers try to make decisions and take action with a true understanding of the work situation. A manager who is skilled in influencing the perceptual process will try to have a high level of self-awareness, seek information from various sources to confirm or contradict personal impressions of a decision situation, and be empathetic — that is, be able to see a situation as it is perceived by other people and avoid common perceptual distortions that may bias his or her views of people and situations. In addition, good managers are aware of various kinds of interpretive schemas of their employees and their possible impact, avoid inappropriate actions and actively influence the perceptions of other people.

Summary

The individual performance equation

The individual performance equation views performance as the result of the personal attributes of individuals, the work efforts they put forth and the organisational support they receive. Individual performance factors are highlighted in the equation: performance = individual attributes × work effort × organisational support. Individual attributes consist of demographic, competency and personality characteristics. Work effort is reflected in the motivation to work. Organisational support consists of a wide range of organisational support mechanisms, such as tools, resources, instructions and other educational strategies, which provide the opportunity for an individual to perform if they have the capacity and willingness.

Demographic characteristics of individuals

Demographic characteristics of individuals are background variables that help shape what a person has become. Some demographic characteristics are current (for example, a worker's current health status); others are historical (for example, length of service).

Competency characteristics of individuals

Competency characteristics among individuals consist of aptitude (the capability to learn something) and ability (the existing capacity to do something). Aptitudes are potential abilities. Abilities can be classified as cognitive abilities, physical abilities and emotional intelligence.

Personality characteristics of individuals

Personality captures the overall profile or combination of characteristics that represent the unique nature of a person as that person reacts and interacts with others. We expect there to be a predictable interplay between an individual's personality and a tendency to behave in certain ways. Personality traits important in organisational behaviour are locus of control, authoritarianism/dogmatism, Machiavellianism, and the 'big five' personality dimensions.

Capitalising on workplace diversity

Increasing diversity is creating workplace challenges. Significant variations are occurring in skill levels, education, physical abilities, cultural backgrounds, lifestyles, personal values, individual needs, and ethnic and social differences. Workplaces that are open to diversity create a diversity management plan.

Values and attitudes

Values are global concepts that guide actions and judgements across a variety of situations. Values are especially important in organisational behaviour because they can directly influence outcomes such as performance or human resource maintenance; they can also have an indirect influence on behaviour by means of attitudes and perceptions. While treated as characteristics of individuals in this chapter, values can also reflect differences among various societal and organisational cultures. Attitudes are influenced by values but focus on specific people or objects; in contrast, values have a more global focus. Attitudes are predispositions to respond in a positive or negative way to someone or something in one's environment. They operate through intended behaviour to influence actual behaviour or other variables.

Job satisfaction

Job satisfaction is a specific attitude that indicates the degree to which individuals feel positively or negatively about their jobs. It is an emotional response to one's tasks as well as to the physical and social conditions of the workplace. Often, job satisfaction is measured in terms of feelings about various job facets, including the work, pay, promotion, coworkers and supervision. Job satisfaction is related to employee absenteeism and turnover, but the relationship to performance is controversial. Current organisational behaviour thinking rejects the notion that satisfaction causes performance, and instead argues that rewards influence both satisfaction and performance.

The perceptual process

Individuals use the perceptual process to select, organise, interpret and retrieve information from their environment. Perceptions are influenced by a variety of factors, including social and physical aspects of the situation as well as personal factors such as needs, experience, values, attitudes and personality. A manager who is skilled in influencing the perceptual process will be able to see a situation as it is perceived by other people and avoid common perceptual distortions that may bias his or her views of people and situations. In addition, managers must avoid stereotyping as this can have social and legal implications.

CHAPTER 2 study guide

Key terms

ability, *p. 47*
absenteeism, *p. 62*
affective components, *p. 59*
aptitude, *p. 47*
attitude, *p. 59*
authoritarianism, *p. 53*
behavioural components, *p. 59*
beliefs, *p. 59*
cognitive abilities, *p. 47*
cognitive components, *p. 59*
cognitive dissonance, *p. 60*
demographic characteristics, *p. 46*

dogmatism, *p. 53*
emotion management, *p. 48*
emotional intelligence, *p. 48*
externals, *p. 52*
five key dimensions of
personality, *p. 52*
instinct, *p. 51*
internals, *p. 52*
job involvement, *p. 62*
job satisfaction, *p. 60*
locus of control, *p. 52*
Machiavellians, *p. 53*

motivation to work, *p. 45*
nature/nurture controversy, *p. 50*
organisational commitment, *p. 62*
perception, *p. 67*
performance, *p. 64*
personality, *p. 50*
physical abilities, *p. 47*
schemas, *p. 68*
situational constraints, *p. 45*
turnover, *p. 62*
value congruence, *p. 56*
values, *p. 56*

Review questions

1. Describe and explain the individual performance equation used in this chapter.
2. Name the factors influencing an individual's capacity to perform.
3. List and briefly explain the five key dimensions of personality.
4. Name the factors that influence the perceptual process and explain each of them.

Application questions

1. Personality testing is widely used as a recruitment and selection strategy. What are the advantages and disadvantages of such a strategy and why? In your answer please use examples.
2. The year is 2018 and you are employed by the 'Commission of Inquiry into the Ageing Workforce'. Your role is to prepare a report on current employment trends in relation to age, their broader implications for the economy and society, and creative strategies to address problem issues. What would you write?
3. Colleges and universities are 'workplaces' for generating, acquiring and sharing new knowledge. There is great diversity within the student population, but this may not be used in the classroom teaching strategies that you experience. Develop a 'diversity management program' suitable for use by teachers

and lecturers in the classroom that would reflect the diversity of the student group, and capitalise on its potential within this group to enhance learning. Explain the ideas behind your diversity management program.
4. Explain the relevance of emotional intelligence and emotional management to the workplace. Illustrate your answer with examples.
5. Read the 'International spotlight' in this chapter. What values and attitudes do individuals need to develop to become successful *global* managers? How do these values and attitudes differ from what a *local* manager must develop?
6. 'Workplace values and attitudes typically undergo significant change from one generation of workers to the next.' Do you agree? Explain and give examples.

Review the discussion of diversity in terms of the basic attributes of individuals in organisations. Write a report that answers the following questions.

(a) Research and describe the current diversity of the Australian workforce.

(b) Select at least five items for comparison and compare data on Australian workforce diversity with data from at least three other developed countries. Present your findings in a table. What were facilitators and barriers to the comprehensiveness of your analysis? Can you draw a conclusion on how well 'diversity' is understood in other developed countries?

(c) When comparing different developed countries, can you conclude if Australia's workforce is more or less diverse than those of other countries? Why or why not?

(d) What is the implication of workforce diversity in terms of *global* business management?

(e) Search the internet for an organisation in the transport, health, hospitality, banking or retail industry and notice the values that it espouses in its mission or goal statement and related materials. Do you think that these values are the most appropriate for this organisation? Can you find any evidence that this organisation is putting its values into practice? How does the organisation monitor the values and attitudes of its staff through surveys or other measures?

Running project

1. Using the information you have available about your organisation, perform the following activities.
2. What does management look for in potential employees to ensure a good fit between the employee and the job requirements?
3. Identify the types of organisational support provided to employees.
4. How diverse is the workforce of your organisation? Assess the strategies your organisation has in place to encourage and benefit from workforce diversity.
5. Determine what management and employees do to ensure job satisfaction.

Individual activity

Your personality type

How true is each statement for you?

	Not true at all		Not true or untrue		Very true	
I hate giving up before I'm absolutely sure that I'm beaten.	1		2	3	4	5
Sometimes I feel that I should not be working so hard, but something drives me on.	1		2	3	4	5
I thrive on challenging situations. The more challenges I have, the better.	1		2	3	4	5
In comparison to most people I know, I'm very involved in my work.	1		2	3	4	5

(continued)

	Not true at all	Not true or untrue		Very true	
It seems as if I need 30 hours a day to finish all the things I'm faced with.	1	2	3	4	5
In general, I approach my work more seriously than most people I know.	1	2	3	4	5
I guess there are some people who can be nonchalant about their work, but I'm not one of them.	1	2	3	4	5
My achievements are considered to be significantly higher than those of most people I know.	1	2	3	4	5
I've often been asked to be an officer of some group or groups.	1	2	3	4	5

Source: From Job Demands and Worker Health (HEW Publication No. [NIOSH] 75–160) (Washington, DC: US Department of Health, Education and Welfare, 1975), pp. 253–254.

Scoring

Add all your scores to create a total score = _____.

Interpretation

Type A personalities (hurried and competitive) tend to score 36 and above. Type B personalities (relaxed) tend to score 22 and below. Scores of 23–35 indicate a balance or mix of Type A and Type B.

Group activity

Building a more positive self-concept

Objective

To develop a more positive self-concept

Total time: 5–15 minutes

Preparation

The objective of this activity is to develop a more positive self-concept. According to humanistic theory, the self-concept is important in the development of personality. This may not be an easy exercise for you, but it could result in improving your self-concept, which has a major impact on your success in life. Complete the following three-step plan for building a positive self-concept.

You may be asked to share your plan with a person of your choice in class. (Your lecturer should tell you if you will be asked to do so.) If so, do not include anything you do not wish to share; write a second set of plans that you are willing to share.

Step 1: Identify your strengths and areas for improvement

What do you like about yourself? What can you do well (reflect on some of your accomplishments)? What skills and abilities do you have to offer people and organisations? What are the things about yourself or your behaviour that you could improve to help build a more positive self-concept?

Step 2: Set goals and visualise them

Based on your areas of improvement, write down some goals in a positive, affirmative format; three to five is recommended as a start. Once you achieve these goals, go on to others — for example, 'I am positive and successful' (not 'I need to stop thinking/worrying about failure') or 'I enjoy listening to others' (not 'I need to stop dominating the conversation'). Visualise yourself achieving your goals; for example, imagine yourself succeeding without worrying, or visualise having a conversation you know you will have, without dominating it.

Step 3: Develop a plan and implement it

For each of your goals, state what you will do to achieve it. What specific action will you take to improve your self-concept by changing your thoughts or behaviour? Number your plans to correspond with your goals.

Procedure for group discussion

Break into teams of two or three members. Try to work with someone with whom you feel comfortable sharing your plan.

Using your prepared plan, share your questions and responses one at a time. It is recommended that you each share one question/answer before proceeding to the next. The choice is yours, but be sure you get equal 'air time': for example, one person states 'what I like about myself' and the other person follows with their response. After you both share, go on to cover 'what I do well', and so on. During your sharing you may offer each other helpful suggestions, but do so in a positive way; remember, you are helping one another build a more positive self-concept. Avoid saying anything that could be considered confronting or critical.[93]

Case study: Perceptions, attitudes and job dissatisfaction: a tricky issue

Stephen To was entrusted to manage the training department for a NASDAQ-listed information technology company in the Asia-Pacific region. The company's presence spans across the globe. His task was simple and unambiguous: to lead a group of highly skilled IT professionals in providing high quality technical training to internal and external customers.

His team was made up of four technical trainers and a training administrator, Sandra. All the team members were in the department before his appointment as the department's head. The fourth trainer, however, was recruited by Stephen and subsequently caused a lot of controversy within the department.

His name is Michael, a 24-year-old graduate from a reputable university in Malaysia. Although he was young, he was recruited owing to his outstanding presentation and technical skills during an interview. The other trainers, however, thought he was too young and hence would not have enough experience to handle a class. Michael proved them wrong and turned out to be a star performer in the team. He was lavished with compliments from training attendees and as a result became quite arrogant in his behaviour. Michael was aware of the praise received and approached Stephen, suggesting that he be promoted to Senior Technical Trainer and given a pay rise. Knowing the promotion would not be welcomed by other team members, Stephen tactfully declined his request. Michael took the rejection badly and threatened to leave the company. From that point onwards, he started turning up late for work and even failed to turn up for work occasionally. His performance consequently started deteriorating.

To make things worse, Sandra, the training administrator, was starting to mirror Michael's unacceptable behaviour. She too started turning up late for work and sporadically failed to turn up at work. Whenever Stephen asked her why she was late, she would explain that she had put in additional hours on the previous day.

On one occasion, both Michael and Sandra failed to turn up for work on the same day. Customers turned up at the training venue and knowing that Michael was absent, Stephen instructed Peter, the other trainer in the department, to stand in for Michael. Peter felt he was treated unfairly and was very reluctant to accept the job assigned. After much persuasion from Stephen, Peter obliged unwillingly.

Unsurprisingly, the training turned out to be a total disaster. The already agitated participants showed little patience with Peter's dispassionate training.

Complaints were filed to upper management and consequently, Michael was asked to resign and Stephen was demoted for his inability to manage the team.

Questions

1. Refer to the individual performance equation in the early part of this chapter. Use this equation to identify and discuss the problems in the case.
2. The case is a good illustration of a work-related example of the three components of attitudes. Discuss these three components as they relate to the case. In doing so state any assumptions you make.
3. Recommend some strategies Stephen could have taken to effectively deal with the perceptions, attitudes and behaviour of employees.
4. You are at the beginning of your studies in organisational behaviour. What additional knowledge about human behaviour would help you to better understand the problems which occurred in the case and pose suitable solutions?

1. M Eggleton, Hotel's five-star values pay off AON Hewit Best Employers Awards, *Weekend Professional, Weekend Australian*, 1–2 (2013), p. 44; Aon Hewit, *2013 Best employers Australia and New Zealand insights presentation*, (2013), pp. 3–8.

2. Melvin Blumberg and Charles D Pringle, 'The missing opportunity in organizational research: some implications for a theory of work performance', *Academy of Management Review*, vol. 7 (1982), pp. 560–9.

3. M Eggleton, 'Chorus of the contented as employees meet their aspirations', *Weekend Professional, Weekend Australian*, 1–2 (June 2013), p. 44.

4. See Thomas N Martin, John R Schermerhorn Jr and Lars L Larson, 'Motivational consequences of a supportive work environment', in *Advances in motivation and achievement: motivation enhancing environment*, vol. 6 (Greenwich, CT: JAI Press, 1989), pp. 179–214.

5. R Schermerhorn, J Hunt, R Osborn and M Uhl-Bien, *Organizational behavior*, 11th ed. (Hoboken: John Wiley & Sons, 2010).

6. ibid.

7. ibid.

8. 'NZ bucks trend as proportion of women in senior management falls globally', *Grant Thornton* (2011), www.grantthornton.co.nz.

9. Chartered Institute of Management Accountants, *Reflections from Asia Pacific leaders — Strategies for career progression* (London, United Kingdom, 2010), www.cimaglobal.com.

10. S Sankier, C Werner, I Mailer and C Kossoff, *Gender diversity in top management: moving corporate culture, moving boundaries* (McKinsey & Company, 2013), www.mckinsey.com.

11. C Jaffee, 'Measurement of human potential', *Employment Relations Today*, vol. 27, issue 2 (Summer 2000), p. 15; E Smith, 'Communities of competencies: new resources in the workplace', *Journal of Workplace Learning*, vol. 17, issue 1/2 (2005), p. 7.

12. C Spearman, *The abilities of man* (New York: Macmillan, 1927).

13. *Dao v Australian Postal Commission* (1987) 162 CLR 317.

14. E Smith, 'Communities of competencies: new resources in the workplace', *Journal of Workplace Learning*, vol. 17, issue 1/2 (2005), p. 7; S Perkel, 'Primal leadership: realizing the power of emotional intelligence', *Journal of Management Consultancy*, vol. 15, issue 3 (September 2004), p. 56; K Petrides, A Furnham and Martin G Neil, 'Estimates of emotional and psychometric intelligence: evidence for gender-based stereotypes', *The Journal of Social Psychology*, vol. 144, issue 2 (April 2004), p. 149; L Herkenhoff, 'Culturally tuned emotional intelligence: an effective change management tool?', *Strategic Change*, vol. 13, issue 2 (March/April 2004), p. 73.

15. D Goleman, *Emotional intelligence* (New York: Bantam, 1995); D Goleman, *Working with emotional intelligence* (New York: Bantam, 2000).

16. R Bar-On, 'Emotional intelligence and self-actualization' in J Ciarrochi, J Forgas and JD Mayer (eds), *Emotional intelligence in everyday life: a scientific inquiry* (New York: Psychology Press, 2001).

17. JD Mayer and P Salovey, 'What is emotional intelligence?' in P Salovey and DJ Sluyter (eds), *Emotional development and emotional intelligence* (New York: Basic Books, 1997).

18. A Hochschild, *The commercialization of intimate life* (Berkley, Los Angeles: University of California Press, 2003).

19. N Kinnie, S Hutchinson and J Purcell, 'Fun and surveillance: the paradox of high commitment management in call centres', *International Journal of Human Resource Management*, vol. 11, no. 5 (2000), pp. 967–85.

20. S Bolton, *Emotion management in the workplace* (Basingstoke: Palgrave McMillan, 2005).

21. Schermerhorn et al., p. 63.

22. ibid, pp. 66–67.

23. Bolton, 2005.

24. R Stock, 'Watch those emotions — they're the new IQ', *Sunday Star Times* (Wellington, New Zealand, 21 December 2003), p. D8.

25. K Kolbe and D Kolbe, 'Management by instinct leads the way to change', *Kolbe Corp* (1999), www.kolbe.com.

26. P Burgess, *The ID Impact Survey. A measure of actual improvement in leadership, capability and team effectiveness* (Link-up International, 2003); P Burgess (ed.), *The development of the ID system including reliability and validity* (version 2.1) (Link-Up International, 2003).

27. See Geert Hofstede, *Culture's consequences: international differences in work-related values*, abridged ed. (Beverly Hills, CA: Sage, 1984).

28. G Allport and H Odbert, 'Trait names: a psycholexical study', *Psychological Monographs*, vol. 47 (1936), pp. 211–14.

29. See J Hogan and R Hogan, 'How to measure employee reliability', *Journal of Applied Psychology*, vol. 74 (1988), pp. 273–9.

30. S Judge Robbins, B T Millett and T Waters-Marsh, *Organisational Behaviour*, 5th edition (French's Forest: Pearson, 2008).

31. JB Rotter, 'Generalized expectancies for internal versus external control of reinforcement', *Psychological Monographs*, vol. 80 (1966), pp. 1–28.

32. Don Hellriegel, John W Slocum, Jr and Richard W Woodman, *Organizational behavior*, 5th ed. (St Paul: West, 1989), p. 46.

33. See John A Wagner III and John R Hollenbeck, *Management of organizational behavior* (Englewood Cliffs, NJ: Prentice Hall, 1995), ch. 4.

34. V Lee Hamilton and Herbert C Kelman, *Crimes of obedience: towards a social psychology of authority and responsibility* (London: Yale University Press, 1990).

35. Herbert C Kelman, 'The policy context of torture: a social-psychological analysis', *International Review of the Red Cross*, vol. 87, no. 857 (March 2005).

36. P Waldmeir, 'Anderson conviction overturned', *Financial Times* (London, 1 June 2005), p. 15.

37. Niccolo Machiavelli, *The prince*, trans. George Bull (Middlesex: Penguin, 1961).

38. K Cyriac and R Dharmaraj, 'Machiavellianism in Indian management', *Journal of Business Ethics*, vol. 13, no. 4 (April 1994), pp. 281–6; Myron Gable and Martin T Topol, 'Machiavellian managers: do they perform better?', *Journal of Business and Psychology*, vol. 5, no. 3 (Spring 1991), pp. 355–65.

39. C Warren, 'How would you deal with an ethical dilemma at work?', *CIPD* (19 April 2013), www.cpid.co.uk.

40. P Donovan, 'Executive games', *Human Resources Leader* (14 April 2009), pp. 30–31.

41. See PE Jacob, JJ Flink and HL Schuchman, 'Values and their function in decisionmaking', *American Behavioral Scientist*, vol. 5 (supplement 9, 1962), pp. 6–38.

42. See M Rokeach and SJ Ball Rokeach, 'Stability and change in American value priorities, 1968–1981', *American Psychologist* (May 1989), pp. 775–84.

43. Gordon Allport, Philip E Vernon and Gardner Lindzey, *Study of values* (Boston: Houghton Mifflin, 1931).

44. Bruce M Meglino, Elizabeth C Ravlin and Cheryl L Adkins, 'Value congruence and satisfaction with a leader: an examination of the role of interaction', unpublished manuscript (University of South Carolina, 1990), pp. 8–9; Bruce M Meglino, Elizabeth C Ravlin and Cheryl L Adkins, 'The measurement of work value congruence: a field study comparison', *Journal of Management*, vol. 1, no. 1 (1992), pp. 33–43.

45. ibid.

46. 'Generation X and Y: who they are and what they want', *Board Matters Newsletter*, vol. 8, no. 3 (November 2008), www.governance.com.au.

47. P Kitchen, 'HR staffers learn about generational difference at Woodbury NY conference', *Knight Ridder Tribune Business News* (Washington, 14 May 2005), p. 1; Jason Rawlins, 'Work values change with new generations of workers; revolution in the workplace', transcript of Australian Broadcasting Corporation radio program AM (23 October 2004), p. 1; AR Earls, 'Clash of generations in workplace genxers, boomers seen as having different life goals, values, career expectations,' *Boston Globe* (Boston, Mass, 10 August 2003), p. G1.

48. ibid.

49. ibid.

50. G Hammill, 'Mixing and matching four generations of employees', *FDU Magazine* (Winter/Spring 2005), www.fdu.edu/newspubs/magazine.

51. ibid.

52. See D Jamieson and J O'Mara, *Managing workforce 2000* (San Francisco: Jossey-Bass, 1991), pp. 28–9.

53. See Martin Fishbein and Icek Ajzen, *Belief, attitude, intention and behavior: an introduction to theory and research* (Reading, MA: Addison-Wesley, 1975).

54. Leon Festinger, *A theory of cognitive dissonance* (Palo Alto, CA: Stanford University Press, 1957).

55. C Hughes, 'Australian dreams driven by nightmares — study finds', *Sunsuper* (16 March 2011), www.sunsuper.com.au.

56. P McLeod, 'Top pay no longer key lure for young', *The Australian* (14 May 2011), www.theaustralian.com.au.

57. R Ilies, KM Schwind, DT Wagner, MD Johnson, DS DeRue and DR Ilgen, 'When can employees have a family life? The effects of daily workload and affect on work–family conflict and social behaviors at home', *Journal of Applied Psychology*, vol. 92, no. 5 (2007).

58. The Job Descriptive Index (JDI) is available from Dr Patricia C Smith, Department of Psychology, Bowling Green State University; the Minnesota Satisfaction Questionnaire (MSQ) is available from the Industrial Relations Center and Vocational Psychology Research Center, University of Minnesota.

59. For job satisfaction trends, see *Work in America: report of a special task force to the Secretary of Health, Education, and Welfare* (Cambridge, MA: MIT Press, 1973); George H Gallup, *The Gallup Poll*, 1972–1977, vol. 1 (Wilmington, DE: Scholarly Resources, 1978); Charles N Weaver, 'Job satisfaction in the United States in the 1970s', *Journal of Applied Psychology*, vol. 65 (1980), pp. 364–7; 'Employee satisfaction', Inc. (August 1989), p. 112; Alan Farnham, 'The trust gap', *Fortune* (4 December 1989), pp. 56–78.

60. J James, S Bibb, & S Walker, 'Generation Y: Comparison between Asia and the rest of the World', *'Global Tell is how it is' Summary Research Report, Asia* (November 2008), www.talentsmoothie.com.

61. McLeod, 2011.

62. Charles N Greene, 'The satisfaction–performance controversy', *Business Horizons*, vol. 15 (1972), p. 31; Michelle T Iaffaldano and Paul M Muchinsky, 'Job satisfaction and job performance: a meta-analysis', *Psychological Bulletin*, vol. 97 (1985), pp. 251–73; Greene, op. cit., pp. 31–41; Dennis Organ, 'A reappraisal and reinterpretation of the satisfaction-causes-performance hypothesis', *Academy of Management Review*, vol. 2 (1977), pp. 46–53; Peter Lorenzi, 'A comment on Organ's reappraisal of the satisfaction-causes-performance hypothesis', *Academy of Management Review*, vol. 3 (1978), pp. 380–2.

63. B El-Bedayneh and S Sonnad, 'An analysis of the self-rated job performance and job satisfaction relationships in Jordanian hospitals' (1990), www.mutah.edu.jo.

64. See Stephen P Robbins, *Organizational behavior*, 6th ed. (Englewood Cliffs, NJ: Prentice Hall, 1993), p. 188.

65. E Lawler and L Porter, 'The effects of performance on job satisfaction' *Industrial Relations*, vol. 7 (1967), pp. 20–8.

66. Lyman W Porter and Edward E Lawler III, *Managerial attitudes and performance* (Homewood, IL: Richard D Irwin, 1968).

67. P Podsakoff, W Todor and R Skov, 'Effect of leader contingent and non-contingent reward and punishment behaviours on subordinate performance and satisfaction' *Academy of Management Journal*, vol. 4 (1982), pp. 810–21.

68. The Hallis Turnover and Absenteeism Survey was released in early 2004.

69. See www.cch.com.au.

70. 'Sick worker went to concert', *Dominion Post* (Wellington, New Zealand, 9 November 2002), p. A20.

71. For example *Workplace Relations Act 1996* (Cth), Schedule 1A, 1C (1) in Australia.

72. C Larmer, 'Doona days', *Sunday Telegraph* (Sydney, 8 May 2005), p. 2.

73. AG Cant, 'Internationalizing the business curriculum: developing intercultural competence', *Journal of American Academy of Business*, vol. 5, issue 1/2 (2004), pp. 177–82.

74. 'Management Competencies for the global marketplace', *PSP Metrics* (Fall 2005), http://psp-hrd.com/newsletters.asp.

75. NJ Adler, *International dimensions of organizational behavior*, 4th ed. (Canada: South-West, 2002); RT Moran and JR Ricsenburger, *The global challenge: building the new worldwide enterprise* (London: McGraw-Hill, 1994); S Sokuvitz and AM George, 'Teaching culture: the challenges and opportunities of international public relations', *Business Communications Quarterly*, vol. 66 (June 2003), pp. 97–106.

76. MW McCall and GP Hollenbeck, *Developing global executives: the lessons of international experience* (Boston: Harvard Business School, 2002); RT Moran and JR Ricsenburger, *The global challenge: building the new worldwide enterprise* (London: McGraw-Hill, 1994).

77. NJ Adler and S Bartholomew, 'Managing globally competent people', *The Academy of Management Executive*, vol. 6, no. 3 (1992), pp. 52–65; RT Moran and JR Ricsenburger, *The global challenge: building the new worldwide enterprise* (London: McGraw-Hill, 1994); ME Mendenhall, TM Kuhlman and OK Stahl (eds), *Developing global business leaders: policies, processes and innovations* (Westport, CT: Quorum, 2001).

78. NJ Adler, *International dimensions of organizational behavior*, 4th ed. (Canada: South-West, 2002); NJ Adler and S Bartholomew, 'Managing globally competent people', *The Academy of Management Executive*, vol. 6, no. 3 (1992), pp. 52–65; RT Moran and JR Ricsenburger, *The global challenge: building the new worldwide enterprise* (London: McGraw-Hill, 1994).

79. NJ Adler and S Bartholomew, 'Managing globally competent people', *The Academy of Management Executive*, vol. 6, no. 3 (1992), pp. 52–65; RM Kanter, 'Afterward: what thinking globally really means' in RS Barnwik and RM Kanter (eds), *Global strategies* (Boston: Harvard Business Press, 1994), pp. 227–32; RT Moran and JR Ricsenburger, *The global challenge: building the new worldwide enterprise* (London: McGraw-Hill, 1994).

80. HR Schiffmann, *Sensation and perception: an integrated approach*, 3rd ed. (New York: John Wiley & Sons, 1990).

81. M Aadomt, *Applied industrial/organizational psychology*, 4th ed. (Southbank Vic.: Thomson, 2004).

82. S Saunders, 'A certain age — job market discrimination', *Weekend Australian* (18 October 2003), p. C12.

83. 'Looming labour crisis puts the focus on grey force', *Sydney Morning Herald* (2 October 2002), p. 4.

84. Human Rights and Equal Opportunity Commission, *Age matters: a report on age discrimination* (Sydney: Commonwealth of Australia, May 2000).

85. William Holstein, 'Japan rises again', *Chief Executive*, issue 182 (October 2002), pp. 50–2.

86. L Pang, A de Brauw, S Rozelle, 'Working until you drop: the elderly of rural China', *The China Journal*, issue 52 (July 2004), pp. 73–94.

87. R Hoar, 'Seven over 70', *Management Today* (October 2003), p. 60.

88. E Gringart, E Helmes, & CP Speelman, 'Exploring attitudes towards older workers among Australian employers: an empirical study', *Journal of Ageing and Social Policy*, vol. 17, no. 3 (2005), pp. 85–103.

89. HK Pillay, K Kelly & MJ Tones, Career aspirations of older workers: An Australian study', *International Journal of Training and Development*, vol. 10, no. 4 (2006), pp. 298–305.

90. J Woldfogel, 'Understanding the family gap in pay for women with children', *Journal of Economic Perspectives*, vol. 12, no. 1 (Winter 1998), pp. 137–56.

91. A Berstein, 'Women's pay: why the gap remains a chasm; a new study spells out the costly impact of family obligations', *Business Week* (New York, 14 June 2004), p. 58; J Humphries, 'Towards a family-friendly economics', *New Political Economy*, vol. 3, issue 2 (July 1998), p. 223.

92. See Taylor H Cox and Stacy Blake, 'Managing cultural diversity: implications for organizational competitiveness', *Academy of Management Executive*, vol. 5, no. 3 (1991), p. 45; P Burns, A Myers and A Kakabadse, 'Are natural stereotypes discriminating?', *European Journal of Management*, vol. 13, no. 2 (1995), pp. 212–17.

93. ibid.

CHAPTER 3

MOTIVATION AND EMPOWERMENT

LEARNING OBJECTIVES

After studying this chapter you should be able to:

1. discuss the complexities of motivating and empowering today's workforce

2. explain the difference between the two main types of motivation theories — content and process

3. outline the major theoretical contributions from the content theories of motivation of Maslow, Alderfer, McClelland and Herzberg

4. explain the process theories of motivation, including equity theory and expectancy theory

5. explain how managers can use an integrated model of content and process motivation theories to enhance productivity and human resource maintenance

6. explain how other perspectives move beyond traditional theories of motivation to include ideas like self-concept, self-efficacy, temperament and congruency

7. discuss empowerment and explain how the empowerment process works.

THE PUZZLE OF MOTIVATION

Before starting this chapter it is worth considering some ideas that have been put forward by well-known author Daniel Pink in his book *Drive*,[1] which investigates what motivates people at work. In the book, Pink discusses what he calls 'the puzzle of motivation'.

Although there is a great deal of research that indicates reward and punishment (carrots and sticks) will indeed change behaviour, the specific work-related behaviours on which this will work are really quite limited, especially in today's complex work environments. Daniel Pink calls into question the whole notion that if you reward someone for something you will get more of the desired behaviour. Performance-based rewards do work well for simple, straightforward, mechanical or manual tasks; carrots and sticks are outstanding in this context. It is also no doubt true that, for simple tasks involving mechanical skill, larger rewards lead to better performance.

On the other hand, rewards have been found to have the *opposite* effect on tasks involving conceptual thinking or problem solving. Pink's main idea is that financial incentives actually limit creativity and undermine performance by interfering with our natural tendencies to direct our own lives (have autonomy), to learn, and to create new things (these relate both to Aldefer's ERG needs and the 'motivators' in Herzberg's two-factor theory in this chapter) — these activities are intrinsically rewarding; people *want* to engage in them, so do not need to be incentivised.

Pink does not suggest people should not be paid, but rather that financial incentives work best for people in routine jobs; that is, those jobs which do not offer adequate intrinsic rewards. He believes people should be paid above market rates and according to their contribution so that they are not dissatisfied with their pay; thereby taking the issue of money 'off the table' (see the notion of dissatisfaction in Herzberg's two-factor theory).

One of Australia's biggest home grown tech successes, award-winning enterprise software company Atlassian, is a great example of a company that has harnessed the talents of its staff in this manner. Once every quarter they have a 'FedEx Day' (recently renamed 'ShipIt Day' due to the unauthorised use of the FedEx brand) where staff are given 24 hours to work on whatever they want as long as it isn't part of their regular jobs (and they have to 'deliver overnight' just like FedEx couriers).[2] That one day of autonomy has created a huge array of new products, software and computer fixes. Atlassian is saying to its employees, 'You probably *want* to do something interesting … here you go!'

Pink's basic claim is that employees doing complex and creative work will be motivated if their intrinsic needs as well as their financial ones are met. The take home message? Don't offer an 'innovation bonus'; just give innovative people the chance to innovate!

Introduction

One of the keys to effective management lies in harnessing the motivation of employees in order to achieve the organisation's goals and objectives. Motivation is therefore a key topic in the study of organisational behaviour. This chapter discusses several motivation theories and the concept of empowerment in terms of how they may contribute towards increasing both productivity and the quality of working life. The theories in this chapter are an important foundation for the ideas to be developed throughout the rest of this book. Before looking at the separate theories, two key points should be made. First, **motivation to work**

Motivation to work refers to the forces within an individual that account for the level, direction and persistence of effort expended at work.

refers to forces within an individual that account for the level, direction and persistence of effort expended at work:

- *level:* the amount of effort a person puts forth (for example, a lot or a little)
- *direction:* what the person chooses when presented with a number of possible alternatives (for example, to exert effort on achieving product quality or product quantity)
- *persistence:* how long a person sticks with a given action (for example, to try for product quantity or quality, and to give up when it is difficult to attain).

Second, it is important to emphasise that motivation to work (or willingness to perform) is one of three components of the individual performance equation, which was presented in chapter 2 (the other two are the capacity to perform and organisational support). High performance in the workplace depends on the combination of these three individual performance equation factors (as will be emphasised later in the chapter when motivation theories are integrated).

Motivating and empowering the workforce

Each employee is different, each organisation's workforce may have different characteristics, and at different times or in different locations there may be different circumstances that affect motivation and empowerment strategies in different ways. In order to meet the challenge of motivating employees, managers must be concerned with the context in which this is being done. Managers also need to understand the challenges of the work effort–motivation cycle.

Contemporary issues affecting motivation and empowerment

When considering motivation, contemporary organisations are not just dealing with existing employees — they must also consider how they might attract future employees. They are concerned about attracting and retaining employees, especially in a competitive labour market. The business media carries much discussion relating to competition for talented workers as well as on attracting and retaining staff, engaging employees, providing employee benefits, rewards and remuneration programs and helping employees to balance work and life demands. These and many other contextual factors for motivation illustrate how difficult and complex it can be for employers to motivate employees and to enhance their performance. Organisations that fail to recognise these contextual factors and their implications for workplace motivation risk losing their best people to other organisations with more exciting, satisfying or rewarding opportunities. Some particular contemporary issues that underpin these concerns are labour skills shortages, an ageing population and workforce mobility. These are briefly summarised below. Motivation is applied in workplaces through the use of various strategies such as the provision of workplace rewards, job designing and flexible work places. These are taken up in chapters 4 and 5 respectively.

Labour skills shortages

Leading up to and during 2008, the business media carried a lot of advice about labour and skills shortages and competition for talent. Shortages among employees such as accountants, chefs, metal tradespersons and construction workers were very evident. Regionally uneven, the shortages in the Northern Territory, South Australia and Queensland were increasing while a survey of more than 500 businesses in Australia found that 73 per cent of Victorian companies nominated the inability to employ skilled staff as a barrier to their success.[3] Skills shortages in New Zealand were the main constraint on expansion for just under one-third of organisations in the services sector and 44 per cent of building firms were experiencing problems finding skilled staff. There were also high vacancy levels for agriculture and fishery workers, and for machine operators and assemblers, with shortages perceived to be worse on the South Island.[4]

With the global financial downturn that began in late 2008 and continued through 2009 and 2010, a sudden change in the labour market was seen. The large-scale retrenchments of the 1990s returned, with unemployment rising, overshadowing the focus on skills shortages and talent wars. However, skills shortages can and do coexist with high unemployment[5] and despite a sudden shift in the labour demand, some skills shortages will remain and in the future new shortages may develop. Both Australia and New Zealand had modified their immigration policies to attract more skilled immigrants.[6] Interestingly, the Australian Institute of Management 2014 National Salary Survey suggests a weakening in demand for labour, and has forecast little in the way of pay increases for Australian employees in the near future.[7] Companies reported finding it somewhat less difficult to recruit skilled staff in 2014 compared to 2013 (with the exception of construction and engineering), which suggests that the power may once again be with employers in hiring negotiations.

Employers are more likely to consider applicants from underutilised groups, such as people with disabilities, in times of labour shortages, which can result in a more balanced and diverse workforce.

High levels of competition for 'talented' workers may continue in some areas despite economic downturn and many employers will need to maintain their efforts for attracting and retaining talent. One of many explanations about why skills shortages emerged was that some professions had a poor public image in terms of compensation, career path and development opportunities and young people chose to seek out other careers.[8] Salary is still a key driver for skilled employees to change roles, so organisations do need to offer competitive financial incentives to attract and retain good staff.[9] Whenever labour shortages occur (such as when there are particular skills shortages or as the population ages) there will be a growing need for organisations to carefully consider employee needs and expectations as well as how they can attract and retain trained and skilled workers and older employees. A method they might use is looking at groups that have previously been underutilised — such as people with disabilities, indigenous people, older people, women who wish to work part-time and international workers.[10] Profiles of employees over time may necessitate adjustments so employee benefits and rewards suit the different personalities in a workplace.

The ageing population

In conjunction with skills shortages, the ageing population is contributing to a potential 'experience deficit' as older workers retire.[11] In Australia, the median age will rise from 35 years to between 43–46 years by 2051[12] and the rate of effective growth in labour supply will be slower than population growth.[13] There will still be services that need to be provided to the community but organisations may have trouble finding enough employees to work to provide those services. There are numerous advantages to hiring older workers: they bring varied skills to the workplace, and they are often the staff members with the most experience. It is to the advantage of businesses to continue to benefit from their skills and knowledge for as long as possible.[14] In New Zealand, those aged over 65 will increase from 600 000 in 2012 to 1.2 million in 2036, and will exceed the number of children aged 0–14 years. More than one in five New Zealanders (22 per cent) will be aged over 65 by 2031, compared with 13 per cent in 2012.[15]

Responses by organisations to these looming problems vary. Studies reveal 80 per cent of Australian businesses are struggling to compete for talent and 59 per cent of businesses are aware the ageing population is affecting their work environment. However, only about 46 per cent of businesses are doing any workforce planning and about 17 per cent have strategies for recruiting and retaining older workers.[16] Some organisations still focus on hiring only younger employees[17] and consider older workers who are looking for employment to be too old.[18] Considering the particular needs of older employees is important for staff retention levels and for attracting new employees from older age groups. For example, health and wellbeing programs may be more attractive to older employers. Such programs have been shown to provide a 3:1 return on investment by PricewaterhouseCoopers[19] and, along with employment itself, to have value in preventing illness in older age.[20] It is also evident that many older people emphasise the importance of job satisfaction and self-worth in their work, and some report that they would not work unless they could have work that was satisfying and worthwhile.[21] More men than women are interested in working in their retirement.[22] As the research that follows shows, older workers are still discriminated against; however, they are going to become increasingly valued in the near future, especially in the context of competitive labour markets.

Workforce ageing — an issue for employers

OBin**Action**

The Australian population is ageing. From 1996 to 2006, those aged from 50 to 59 years grew from 10 per cent to 13 per cent of the total population, or from around 1.8 million to 2.6 million people.[23] By 2021, the number of people aged 65 and over is likely to total 4 million, and the number of people retiring will exceed those entering the Australian labour force. While an ageing workforce means declining labour participation, Australia's declining fertility rates also mean it faces markedly slower population growth. Over the entire decade of 2010 to 2020, the working population in Australia is projected to increase by just 125 000 compared with an annual increase of 170 000 prior to that.[24]

Perhaps unsurprisingly, the Retirement Intentions Survey conducted by the NSW Department of Premier and Cabinet found that 57 per cent of the 2005 workforce was planning to retire by 2015. This issue is particularly important for Australia because of its reliance on the mining and agricultural sectors for export earnings. Although technology has improved labour efficiencies and enables ageing workers to remain in these sectors, these industries continue to require a largely youthful skilled workforce which will be increasingly hard to secure.

New Zealand is also experiencing a significant change in the structure of its population. The number of people aged 65 and over (65+) has doubled since 1980, and is likely to double again by 2036. The largest growth will occur between 2011 and 2036, as the baby boomers (those born from 1946 to 1965) move into the 65+ age group. By 2036, there will be between 21 and 24 per cent of New Zealanders aged over 65 (compared with 14 per cent in 2012). By 2061, approximately 26 per cent of the population will be aged over 65.[25] Another study of workforce ageing investigated what actions and adjustments New Zealand organisations are making to meet the challenges the ageing population presents.[26] What they found, in essence, is that a majority of employers are not taking workforce ageing seriously enough. Many employers also still actively discriminate against older workers, even though it's illegal.

The report's author, Judith Davey, director of the Institute for Research on Ageing, states, 'Employers must surely be aware of emerging labour shortages, and, by discriminating, they are making the situation worse — creating their own shortages'.

So, why not retain older workers beyond the time they would normally leave the workforce or actively recruit older workers? It seems employers generally prefer the work attitudes of 'mature' workers, but it is not always easy to recruit them. Older workers are described as 'stable, diligent, hardworking, mature in dealing with clients, respectful of privacy, reliable and loyal'. They also reportedly 'bring experience and life skills to the workplace and are more likely to stay in their jobs than younger workers'.

(continued)

To get older workers to stay on the payroll, more enlightened employers are adopting more flexible work practices, such as part-time work and job sharing; flexible working hours (outside rush hours) and less demanding hours of work. They are using them in relieving or casual positions; providing better health support and monitoring; providing assistance for more physical tasks; allowing older workers to work from home and using them as mentors. But part-time workers can cost more, particularly if employers have to supply extra office equipment and facilities; and the administrative costs associated with managing them can be higher. Providing additional workplace and time flexibility can be tricky to organise.[27]

As well as encouraging older workers to remain in organisations, some have argued that immigration levels can be increased to address population aging.[28] Because migrants are predominantly of workforce age, migration will assist with maintaining workforce growth. In addition, if they are skilled they will raise general skill levels and productivity. This is currently happening in Australia and New Zealand. Governments recognise that the greatest gains come from young skilled migrants. The Australian Government has shifted the balance of Australia's Migration Program from less than 30 per cent skilled in 1995–96 to close to 70 per cent (128 550) in 2013–14.[29] It is worth noting, however, that increased migration cannot entirely prevent our population from ageing. This is because migrants who come to Australia will age along with the rest of the population.

Workforce mobility

Another feature of many workplaces is the mobility of the workforce. This relates to the willingness of workers to move from job to job and from organisation to organisation. Many young people opt to travel and work overseas for extended periods. As a result of the Australian resources boom, many people are being tempted to accept jobs that require them to work in hot and isolated locations — sometimes thousands of kilometres from their homes — for high financial rewards. For some it is a case of flying in and flying out for work and missing time with family or being subjected to excessive tiredness from travelling long distances.[30] Mobility also relates to the trend for organisations to seek whole workforces from other locations (such as from different states, provinces or countries). Many organisations are already familiar with multicultural workforces, either domestically or in various global locations. Motivation of different cohorts within the workforce may require local or cross-cultural knowledge and an understanding of the psychological bond an employee has with the organisation. The following International spotlight discusses the importance and prevalence of sourcing workforces from other locations.

International **SPOTLIGHT**

Supply and demand of labour — a global phenomenon

Labour shortages have significantly contributed to the need to increase the mobility of workers around the globe. Organisations in some countries have had problems attracting and retaining good workers, but the workplace issues of an ageing population and widespread skills shortages described above in the previous 'OB in Action' have not been prevalent worldwide. While the population statistics for Australia and New Zealand are similar to those for other developed countries such as Northern America and much of Europe, many countries have older or younger populations. For example, Japan, Latvia, Slovenia, Italy and Estonia are expected to have the oldest populations midway through this century — with a median age of around 52 years. Much younger populations are anticipated in future years in Africa, Asia (broadly), Latin America and the Caribbean.[31] As populations age and when labour markets become strained in Australia and New Zealand, it is predicted that skilled people in 'younger' nations will be attracted to more rewarding job opportunities available to workers who are prepared to migrate elsewhere. This trend towards migrating for better work conditions and pay might result in a 'brain drain' from 'younger' countries, but it will also likely help meet rising organisational demands in associated nations. In Australia, where labour shortages and an ageing population have caused considerable concern, the federal government has a Migration Occupations in Demand List (MODL) that explicitly states the occupations that will be favoured for immigration purposes. These range from the general to the specific, for example, civil engineers and computing professionals specialising in PeopleSoft.[32] A range of options for employers to help cope with 'importing' workers is also available.[33] For instance, a program assisting electricians with migrating to Australia from India, Sri Lanka, the United Kingdom, South Africa and the Philippines began in September 2007. The workers are given assistance in gaining provisional licences and getting work under supervision as well as help with gap training until full licences can be obtained. Immigration New Zealand also has lists for immediate skills shortages and long-term shortages.[34]

The implications for focusing on motivating workers are significant. It is likely workforces will be more diverse in the future. In some organisations, the majority of the workforce may be from diverse cultural backgrounds. Our current approaches to understanding needs and the cognitive processes of motivation may need to broaden if we are to move beyond Western cultural biases. For example, individualistic Western cultures (such as Australia and the United States) may have different ways of perceiving what people need from their work than what Islamic cultures do. In Islamic cultures, work is valued for sustaining confidence and self-reliance and it has moral, psychological and social (relational) dimensions.[35] Such differences require more research and societal understanding.

Immigrant workers might have new needs that develop as their circumstances change. For example, the challenge of working in a new country without the security of family and community ties they had at 'home' may affect their motivational experience. Importing workforces can appear to be straightforward, but there are inherent problems. Managers of migrant workers need to be alert to cultural differences in motivation if they want to attract and retain these workers and also encourage productivity in the workplace.

The Human Rights Commission in New Zealand recently published a report with a focus on migrant workers.[36] The report states that work is arguably the single most important element in the integration of immigrants to New Zealand. 'Work is about income, about individual fulfilment, about identity and about social inclusion and cohesion. Amazingly, though, many migrants find it hard to access decent employment despite years of experience and qualifications recognised elsewhere.'[37] This issue of 'underemployment' is an important one. Migrants often face prejudice and discrimination and often find themselves in a frustrating double bind of employers wanting 'New Zealand work experience' which they can't provide due to not having been able to get a job without New Zealand work experience! This situation is changing, however, and more and more organisations in New Zealand actively recruit migrants and refugees.[38]

The work motivation challenge

Managers in organisations affected by such changes and pressures must build or rebuild loyalty and commitment, and create a positive organisational climate in which employees are motivated to achieve at high levels of work performance.

This challenge is examined in more detail in figure 3.1 (overleaf). The figure shows how an individual's willingness to perform is directly related to the needs, expectations and values of the individual, and their link to the incentives or aspirations presented by the organisational reward system. Rewards fulfil individual goals such as financial remuneration and career advancement.

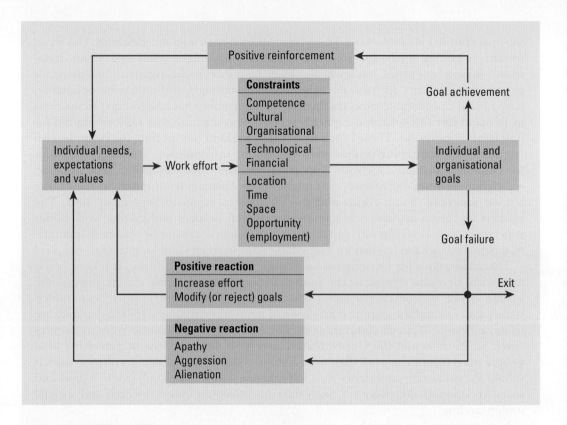

FIGURE 3.1 Understanding the work effort–motivation cycle

The degree of effort expended to achieve these outcomes will depend on:
- the individual's willingness to perform, and his or her commitment to these outcomes in terms of the value attached to a particular outcome
- the individual's competency or capacity to perform the tasks
- the individual's personal assessment of the probability of attaining a specific outcome
- the opportunity to perform (which is central to empowerment, discussed later in the chapter).

A number of organisational constraints or barriers, if not minimised, may restrict high levels of individual performance.

Figure 3.1 shows that if the outcome or goal is attained, then the individual experiences a reduction in pressure or tension, and goal attainment positively reinforces the expended effort to achieve the outcome. As a result of this positive experience, the individual may repeat the cycle. On the other hand, if the outcome is frustrated after a reasonable passage of time then the individual experiences goal frustration and arrives at a decision point. The individual is presented with three alternatives:

1. exit from the organisation
2. renew attempts at goal achievement, or modify or abandon the goals
3. adopt a negative response to the frustration experience, and perform at below-optimum levels.

The challenge for managers is to create organisations in which the opportunities to perform through competency building and empowerment are maximised and the impediments to performance are kept to a minimum to avoid the negative consequences of goal frustration. The next OB in action describes an example of a common performance impediment; that of 'red tape' in organisational processes. Figure 3.1 shows the complexity of the work motivational process and emphasises the importance of individual needs, expectations and values as key elements of this process. Some of these issues are addressed in the rest of this chapter.

Frustrated by 'red tape'

The term 'red tape' refers to excessive regulation or rigid conformity to formal rules in an organisation's bureaucracy. Excessive red tape is a great example of an organisational constraint to employee effectiveness.

Exemplifying this, Australian GPs spend at least nine hours every week dealing with red tape they feel 'strangles' general practice.[39] Things such as issues with Medicare provider numbers and payments, registration requirements, and prescription permissions topped the red tape list. Australian Medical Association (AMA) president Dr Steve Hambleton states:

> AMA research shows that a large number of GPs spend up to nine hours or more each week meeting their red tape obligations. Every hour a GP spends doing paperwork equates to around four patients who are denied access to their doctor.

The AMA calculated that more than 25 000 patient consultations were lost each year as a result of red tape.[40]

The goal frustration experienced when motivated, engaged employees are prevented from doing their job should be a priority for organisations. The AMA makes several suggestions to combat the red tape; these include:

- a national simplified Medicare provider number system
- streamlining of the 'complex legal framework' for professional registration
- an overhaul of restrictions on chronic disease management.

Content and process motivation theories

Two main approaches to the study of motivation are known as the content and process theories. More recent approaches, based on personal values and self-concept, are also presented later in the chapter.

Content theories are primarily concerned with what it is within individuals or their environment that energises and sustains behaviour. In other words, what specific needs or motives energise people? We use the terms 'needs' and 'motives' interchangeably to mean the physiological or psychological deficiencies that one feels a compulsion to reduce or eliminate. If you feel very hungry (a physiological need), you will feel a compulsion to eliminate or satisfy that need by eating. If you have a need for recognition (a psychological need), you may try to satisfy that need by working hard to please your boss. Content theories are useful because they help managers understand what people will and will not value as work rewards or need satisfiers.

The **process theories** strive to provide an understanding of the cognitive processes that act to influence behaviour. Thus, a content theory may suggest that security is an important need. A process theory may go further by suggesting how and why a need for security could be linked to specific rewards and to the specific actions that the worker may need to perform to achieve these rewards. Process theories add a cognitive dimension by focusing on individuals' beliefs about how certain behaviours will lead to rewards such as money or promotion; that is, the assumed connection between work activities and the satisfaction of needs.[41]

Content theories offer ways to profile or analyse individuals to identify the needs that motivate their behaviours.

Process theories seek to understand the thought processes that take place in the minds of people and that act to motivate their behaviour.

Content theories

Maslow, Alderfer, McClelland and Herzberg proposed four of the better-known content theories. Each of these content theories has made a major contribution to our understanding of work motivation. Some have provided a basis for more complex theorising in later years.

Maslow's hierarchy of needs theory

Abraham Maslow's hierarchy of needs theory (figure 3.2) identifies higher-order needs (self-actualisation and esteem) and lower-order needs (social, safety and physiological requirements). Maslow's formulation suggests a prepotency of these needs; that is, some needs are assumed to be more important (potent) than others, and must be satisfied before the other needs can serve as motivators. Thus, the physiological needs must be satisfied before the safety needs are activated, and the safety needs must be satisfied before the social needs are activated, and so on.

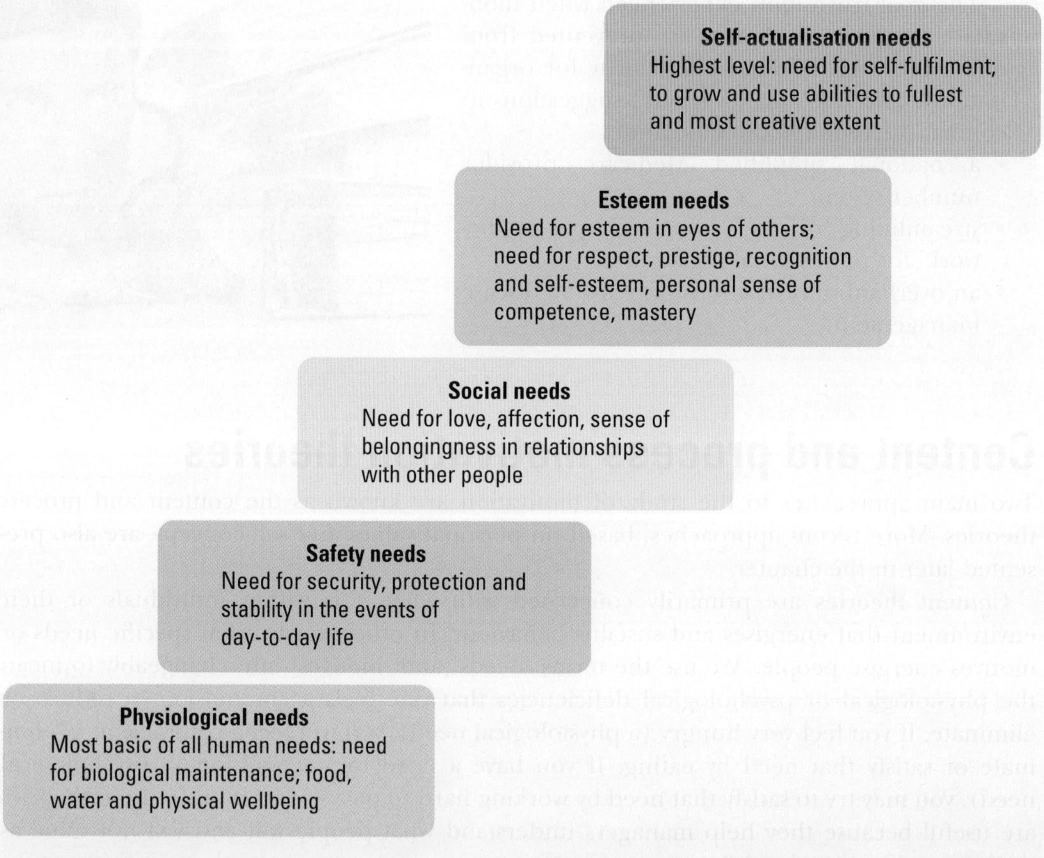

Self-actualisation needs
Highest level: need for self-fulfilment; to grow and use abilities to fullest and most creative extent

Esteem needs
Need for esteem in eyes of others; need for respect, prestige, recognition and self-esteem, personal sense of competence, mastery

Social needs
Need for love, affection, sense of belongingness in relationships with other people

Safety needs
Need for security, protection and stability in the events of day-to-day life

Physiological needs
Most basic of all human needs: need for biological maintenance; food, water and physical wellbeing

FIGURE 3.2 Maslow's hierarchy of needs

The physiological needs are considered the most basic; they consist of needs for such things as food, water and the like. Individuals try to satisfy these needs before turning to needs at the safety level, which involve security, protection, stability and so on. When these needs are active, people will look at their jobs in terms of how well they satisfy these needs.

The social needs of a sense of belonging and a need for affiliation are activated once the physiological and safety needs are satisfied. The higher-order needs depicted in figure 3.2 consist of the esteem and self-actualisation needs — that is, being all that one can be. Here, challenging work and recognition for good performance assume centre stage.

Maslow: the research

Some research suggests that there is a tendency for higher-order needs to increase in importance over lower-order needs as individuals move up the managerial hierarchy.[42] Other studies report that needs vary according to a person's career stage,[43] the size of the organisation[44] and even geographic location.[45] However, there is no consistent evidence that the satisfaction of a need at one level will decrease its importance and increase the importance of the next higher need.[46] It is interesting to note that, despite being widely adopted and referred to, Maslow retained concerns and criticisms about his own theory. For example, in his later writing he appears to have questioned the position of self-actualisation at the peak of the hierarchy. He moved beyond this precept to a belief in self-transcendence as the highest level need (where the individual transcends his or her identity and ego to higher level aesthetic, mystical and emotional experiences).[47] As the Counterpoint shows, there may be many limitations to our knowledge of needs in terms of how they apply to different people.

COUNTERPOINT

Satisfying generational needs — reality or myth?

Content motivation theories present us with a range of ways of understanding the needs of employees in the workplace but these may be insufficient. It seems that the ways in which we talk about employee motivation are growing. We are embracing a wider set of needs and making distinctions between different cohorts of employees. Perhaps the most predominant discussions relate to differences between what different generations need or want. For example, it has been argued generation Y will need a lot of mentoring, constant feedback and teamwork while baby boomers might need more help embracing new technology.[48]

While there is a flurry of interest in generational needs, there are those who don't like measuring personnel needs by generational differences. Jim Bright, who is a Professor of Career Education and Development at the Australian Catholic University (ACU National) as well as a partner at international career development consultancy Bright & Associates, argues differences in life stages can be used to help measure the characteristics of different cohorts of people. Consider the idea young people may have always wanted to have new experiences, to have challenging and interesting work and to be well rewarded for their work. Bright says this desire would have been experienced by young people one hundred years ago just as it would have been felt by young people today. This theory follows that there is always going to be a 'younger generation' with certain needs in any society. Bright says the needs of generation Y will change at other life stages, such as when they start their families, when their social lives stabilise and when they have more domestic and financial responsibilities. Rather than needs being determined by the generation people are born into, the stage of life they are experiencing at any particular time may dictate their needs. Bright says that most importantly, organisations should see people as individuals and respond to individual needs as best as they can — often by being as flexible as they can.[49]

Consider the quote below:

> Our youth now love luxury. They have bad manners, contempt for authority; they show disrespect for their elders and love chatter in place of exercise; they no longer rise when elders enter the room; they contradict their parents, chatter before company; gobble up their food and tyrannize their teachers.

It is much like what the baby boomers say about the younger generation X and Ys with whom they work but, in fact, is often attributed to the Greek philosopher Socrates (469–299BC) who lived over two thousand years ago! Even if he didn't actually say it, it was certainly written around that time in ancient history.

(continued)

One theory on why the generational debate is so prevalent in Australia is that with increasing globalisation and, until recently, low unemployment, there is more competition for talented employees. This competition has meant employers have had to become more sensitive to the needs of employees or potential employees in order to attract or retain the best employees they can.[50]

Questions

1. The 'life stage' explanation of needs suggests that people's needs change over time. How might this statement differ if you adopted an approach based on different needs for different generations (such as baby boomers, Gen X and Gen Y)?
2. In what ways can employers respond effectively and flexibly to all the individual needs their workers may have?

To what extent does Maslow's theory apply only to Western culture? In many developing nations the satisfaction of lower-order needs, such as basic subsistence and survival needs, consumes the entire lifetimes of many millions of individuals, with little opportunity to progress to higher-level need satisfaction. But in societies where regular employment is available, basic cultural values appear to play an important role in motivating workplace behaviour. In those countries high in Hofstede's uncertainty avoidance, such as Japan or Greece, security tends to motivate most employees more strongly than does self-actualisation. Workers in collectivist-oriented countries such as Pakistan or China tend to emphasise social needs (see, for example, the next boxed feature).[51]

OBinAction

Workplace motivation and culture

An issue that has received an increasing amount of research attention lately is that of Guanxi. Guanxi (pronounced *guan-shee*) refers to networks of relationships and favours that influence business activity throughout China. It is an ancient system and is based on informal relationships; as opposed to Western management practice, which is based largely on formal agreements and written contracts. With the increasing economic power of China, Western businesspeople are faced with an increasing need to be able to not only operate in non-Western systems, but also understand the perspectives and values of the millions of Chinese currently working outside of China.[52] Guanxi systems depend on reputations and trust between individuals and mean that social interactions and social needs become much more important than in Western (individualist) contexts.

An interesting implication of China's existing social networks is that online alternatives such as LinkedIn (www.linkedin.com) have had trouble breaking in to the Chinese market (China has the world's biggest online population at 564 million).

Wei Wuhui, a professor at Jiaotong University in Shanghai, claims online alternatives will have a hard time supplanting its deeply embedded role. He states:

> I don't think the Chinese middle class has the same needs in terms of professional networks as people in the West, because of the concept of guanxi … In China people do not want to meet with people they don't know. The Chinese have a culture based on relationships among family members and close friends.[53]

Perhaps unsurprisingly, just one per cent of LinkedIn's 200 million worldwide users come from China.

In general, a person's frame of reference will determine the order of importance of their needs, and societal culture influences that frame of reference.[54] We must also be careful to consider ethnic or other cultural groups within countries. For example, in New Zealand the Maori, non-Maori and other ethnic groups could present different cultural contexts for motivation. We will now discuss Alderfer's, McClelland's and Herzberg's theories in contrast to Maslow's hierarchy of needs theory. A comparison of these theories is provided in figure 3.3 below.

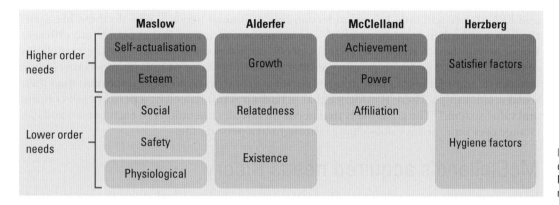

FIGURE 3.3 Comparison of Maslow's, Alderfer's, McClelland's and Herzberg's motivation theories

Alderfer's ERG theory

Clayton Alderfer has developed a modification of Maslow's hierarchy with the ERG theory. **ERG theory** is more flexible than Maslow's theory in three basic respects.[55] Firstly, the theory collapses Maslow's five need categories into three: **existence needs** relate to a person's desire for physiological and material wellbeing; **relatedness needs** represent the desire for satisfying interpersonal relationships; and **growth needs** are about the desire for continued personal growth and development. Secondly, while Maslow's theory argues that individuals progress up the hierarchy as a result of the satisfaction of lower-order needs (a satisfaction–progression process), ERG theory includes a 'frustration–regression' principle, whereby an already satisfied lower-level need can become activated when a higher-level need cannot be satisfied. Thus, if a person is continually frustrated in their attempts to satisfy growth needs, relatedness needs will again surface as key motivators. Thirdly, according to Maslow, a person focuses on one need at a time. In contrast, ERG theory contends that more than one need may be activated at the same time.

ERG: the research

Research on ERG theory is relatively limited and includes disclaimers.[56] One of the earlier articles on this topic suggested interesting findings such as that growth needs are higher for respondents with more highly educated parents and women have lower strength of existence needs and higher strength of relatedness needs than men.[57] Another study from China argues that gender makes some difference to motivational preferences using Alderfer's approach in a Chinese context.[58] In regards to gender, males are more likely to be driven by growth and existence needs. The same study also inferred complex links between personality types and motivation using Alderfer's and Maslow's theories.

Additional research is needed to shed more light on its validity, but the supporting evidence on ERG theory is stronger than that for Maslow's theory. For now, the combined satisfaction–progression and frustration–regression principles provide the manager with a more flexible approach to understanding human needs than does Maslow's strict hierarchy. Importantly, Alderfer's theory emphasises that performance constraints outside the control of the individual (see figure 3.1 on p. 86), or innate disposition (such as lack of competence or

ERG theory categorises needs into existence, relatedness and growth needs.

Existence needs are about the desire for physiological and material wellbeing.

Relatedness needs are about the desire for satisfying interpersonal relationships.

Growth needs are about the desire for continued personal growth and development.

low intrinsic work motivation), may cause a decline in effort or negative behaviour. Managers need to examine the workplace environment continually to remove or reduce any organisational constraint that will restrict opportunities for personal growth and development.

The problem with needs hierarchy models

ERG theory adds to Maslow's theory by describing how people can regress down the hierarchy when they fail to fulfil higher needs, and seems to explain human motivation somewhat better than Maslow's hierarchy. In spite of this, studies have shown that both Maslow's theory and ERG theory add little to our understanding of human needs.[59] Why do these hierarchy theories not explain employee needs? The most obvious answer is that people are different from one another! A single hierarchy of needs cannot possibly account for the complexity of human motivation. Some people consider social status to be of utmost importance, while others may consider higher education or personal growth to be far more important than their social relationships. There is evidence that behaviour is influenced by a person's self-concept and value system.[60] Thus, it is likely that needs hierarchies are unique to each person and can change over time, just as values change throughout a person's life.

McClelland's acquired needs theory

In the late 1940s the psychologist David McClelland distinguished three themes or needs that he feels are important for understanding individual behaviour. These needs are:

- the **need for achievement (nAch)** — that is, the desire to undertake something better or more efficiently, to solve problems or to master complex tasks
- the **need for affiliation (nAff)** — that is, the desire to establish and maintain friendly and warm relations with others
- the **need for power (nPower)** — that is, the desire to control others, to influence their behaviour or to be responsible for others.

McClelland's basic theory is that these three needs are acquired over time, as a result of life experiences. People are motivated by these needs, which can be associated with different work roles and preferences. The theory encourages managers to learn how to identify the presence of nAch, nAff and nPower in themselves and in others, and how to create work environments that are responsive to the respective need profiles of different employees. One study indicates that motivation has links to emotional intelligence (see chapter 2). For example, those with a higher perceived ability to regulate their emotions are more likely to be motivated by achievement needs, while those who score highly in terms of being able to appraise the emotions of others are more likely to be motivated by affiliation needs.[61]

McClelland and his colleagues began experimenting with the Thematic Apperception Test (TAT) as a way of measuring human needs.[62] The TAT is a projective technique that asks people to view pictures and write stories about what they see. In one case, using projective techniques, McClelland tested three executives on what they saw in a photograph of a man sitting down and looking at family photos arranged on his work desk. In terms of nAch, McClelland scored the stories given by the three executives as follows:[63]

- person dreaming about family outing — nAch = + 1
- person pondering new idea for gadget — nAch = + 2
- person working on bridge-stress problem — nAch = + 4.

To provide a more complete profile, each picture would also be scored in terms of nAff and nPower. Each executive's profile would then be evaluated for its motivational implications based on the three needs in combination.

One of the most important aspects of McClelland's theorising is that he challenges and rejects many other psychological theories that suggest the need to achieve is a behaviour that is only acquired and developed during early childhood. Alternatively, psychologists such as Erickson have supported a view that the learning of achievement-motivated behaviour can only occur during critical stages of a child's development; if it is not obtained then it

The **need for achievement (nAch)** is the desire to do something better, solve problems or master complex tasks.

The **need for affiliation (nAff)** is the desire to establish and maintain friendly and warm relations with others.

The **need for power (nPower)** is the desire to control others, influence their behaviour and be responsible for others.

cannot be easily learned or achieved during adult life.[64] McClelland's research contradicts this viewpoint; he maintains that the need to achieve is a behaviour that an individual can acquire through appropriate training in adulthood.

McClelland: the research

Research lends considerable insight into nAch in particular and includes some interesting applications in developing nations. McClelland trained business people in Kakinada, India, for example, to think, talk and act like high achievers by having them write stories about achievement and participate in a business game that encouraged achievement. The business people also met with successful entrepreneurs and learned how to set challenging goals for their own businesses.

Over a two-year period following these activities, the people from the Kakinada study engaged in activities that created twice as many new jobs as those who did not receive training.[65] Research on Chinese entrepreneurship confirms McClelland's view that the stronger a person's nAch, the greater likelihood that the person would be likely to start a business.[66]

Other research also suggests that societal culture can make a difference in the emphasis on nAch. Anglo-American countries such as Australia, the United States, Canada and the United Kingdom (countries weak in uncertainty avoidance and high in masculinity) tend to follow the high nAch pattern. In contrast, strong uncertainty, high femininity countries, such as Portugal and Chile, tend to follow a low nAch pattern. There are two especially relevant managerial applications of McClelland's theory. Firstly, the theory is particularly useful when each need is linked with a set of work preferences (table 3.1). Secondly, if these needs can truly be acquired, it may be possible to acquaint people with the need profiles required to succeed in various types of jobs. For example, McClelland found that the combination of a moderate to high need for power and a lower need for affiliation enables people to be effective managers at higher levels in organisations. Lower nAff allows the manager to make difficult decisions without undue worry of being disliked.[67] High nPower creates the willingness to have influence or impact on others, though misuse of that power may result in sabotage by those mistreated or prevented from rising to the top of the organisation.[68]

Individual needs	Work preference	Example
High need for achievement	Individual responsibility; challenging but achievable goals; feedback on performance	Field salesperson with a challenging quota and the opportunity to earn individual bonus; entrepreneur
High need for affiliation	Interpersonal relationships; opportunities to communicate	Customer service representative; member of a work unit that is subject to a group wage bonus plan
High need for power	Influence over other persons; attention; recognition	Formal position of supervisory responsibility; appointment as head of special task force or committee

TABLE 3.1 Work preferences of persons high in need for achievement, affiliation and power

Herzberg's two-factor theory

Frederick Herzberg's research was based on in-depth interview techniques learned during his training as a clinical psychologist. This interview approach — called a 'critical incident technique' — has been the subject of considerable debate among academics over many decades, but the findings of his theory have been valuable. Herzberg began his research on motivation by asking workers to comment on two statements:
1. 'Tell me about a time when you felt exceptionally good about your job.'
2. 'Tell me about a time when you felt exceptionally bad about your job.'[69]

The **motivator–hygiene theory** distinguishes between sources of work dissatisfaction (hygiene factors) and satisfaction (motivators); it is also known as the two-factor theory.

After analysing nearly 4000 responses to these statements (figure 3.4), Herzberg and his associates developed the two-factor theory, also known as the **motivator–hygiene theory**. They noticed that the factors identified as sources of work dissatisfaction (subsequently called 'dissatisfiers' or 'hygiene factors') were different from those identified as sources of satisfaction (subsequently called 'satisfiers' or 'motivator factors').

According to Herzberg's two-factor theory, an individual employee could be simultaneously both satisfied and dissatisfied because each of these two factors has a different set of drivers and is recorded on a separate scale. According to Herzberg's measurement the two scales are:

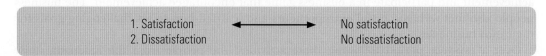

1. Satisfaction   ⟷   No satisfaction
2. Dissatisfaction   No dissatisfaction

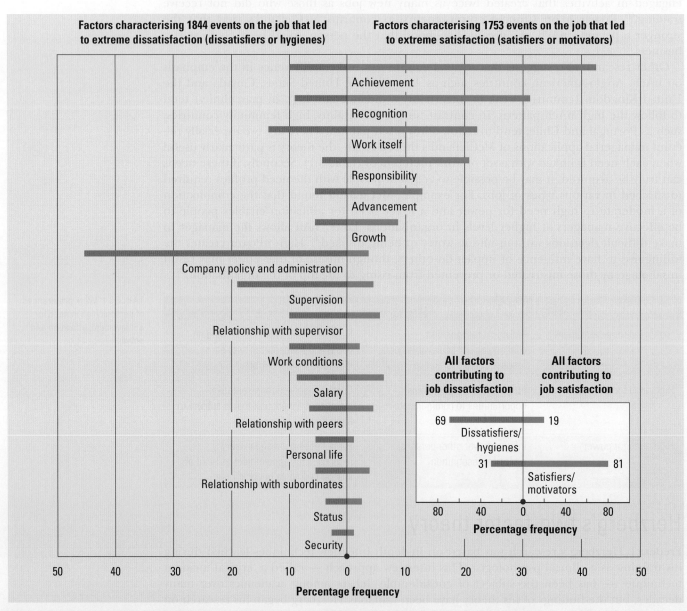

FIGURE 3.4 Herzberg's two-factor theory: sources of satisfaction and dissatisfaction as reported in 12 investigations

Source: Adapted & reprinted by permission of Harvard Business Review, Exhibit 1 from 'One More time: How Do You Motivate Employees?' by Frederick Herzberg, Sept–Oct 87. © 2002 Harvard Business School Publishing Corporation; all rights reserved.

Effective managers have to achieve two distinct outcomes as now discussed: (1) to maximise job satisfaction and (2) to simultaneously minimise job dissatisfaction.

Satisfiers or motivator factors

To improve satisfaction, a manager must use motivator factors as shown on the right side of figure 3.4. These factors are related to job content — that is, what people do in their work. Adding these satisfiers or motivators to people's jobs is Herzberg's link to performance. These cover such things as sense of achievement, recognition and responsibility. According to Herzberg, when these opportunities are absent, workers will not be satisfied and will not perform well. Building such factors into a job is an important topic (see the following research relating to why people leave their jobs) and it is discussed at length in chapter 5.

Motivators (motivator factors) are satisfiers that are associated with what people do in their work.

Job content refers to what people do in their work.

Why are people leaving their jobs?

OBinAction

In 2004, Mercer Human Resource Consulting conducted a survey called 'What's working' — the Mercer survey of Australia at work.[70] They found that nearly 25 per cent of Australian employees reported planning to look for a new job in the next 12 months. This survey has now been repeated and, startlingly, now 40 per cent are seriously considering leaving their jobs![71] The figure is even higher for younger workers (52 per cent of those aged 25–34 are considering leaving). Even if only half of those people saying they're contemplating leaving actually leave, Australian businesses face a potentially huge cost — ranging somewhere between $50 billion and $180 billion.

On a more micro level, reviewing the cost of staff turnover for individual companies is perhaps even more disturbing. Mercer estimates that staff turnover costs range from 50 per cent to 150 per cent of annual salary depending on the role and level of seniority. So, in a company with 250 employees earning $49000 each and, using Mercer's forecast 2011 staff attrition rate of 40 per cent, the cost of turnover for that company would be more than $5.5 million per year.

So, why are people most likely to leave their jobs? Although base salary ranked as very important in the latest Mercer survey, base pay alone is not enough to keep employees engaged (just as Herzberg proposed). It was incentive pay (or pay for performance) that drew some of the biggest scores. This type of pay is more closely linked to Hertzberg's 'recognition' (a motivator). In 2004, the Mercer Survey of Australia at Work found that the most important aspects of work for Australian employees were: first, the existence of opportunities for advancement; second, training; and, third, a clear career path.

Interestingly, another study also found that it is seldom money that makes people leave. An unpublished Saratoga Institute study of 19500 former employees of 18 organisations, conducted from 1996 to 2003, revealed that 89 per cent of managers believe that employees mainly stay or leave because of money. But, in fact, 88 per cent of employees say they leave for reasons other than money. The full Saratoga study is summarised in Leigh Branham's book *The 7 hidden reasons employees leave*.[72]

Another survey of close to 3000 people conducted in 2010 by New Zealand's largest job hunting site Seek (www.seek.co.nz) ascertained the most common reasons Kiwis gave for leaving their last jobs.[73] The most common reason people gave for leaving their last job was not that they sought a better salary, but rather that they were seeking a new challenge. The search for challenging work clearly links with Herzberg's motivator factors of 'the work itself' and 'achievement' (job content). The third and fourth most common reasons people left their jobs were feeling unappreciated and having bad management. Again, this supports Herzberg's notion that negative relationships with one's supervisor (job context) create dissatisfaction.

(continued)

When asked to identify what they loved about their current jobs, only a tiny three per cent of respondents stated that it was their salary that made them happy. On the other hand, for those *unhappy* in their work, poor salary was the third most frequent response in terms of contributing to people hating their job.

The examples above link in nicely with Herzberg's theory, which predicts that (so long as you are being paid a fair wage) *more* money has little impact on your experience of work or your happiness in your job. Intrinsic aspects of work, or the recognition received, will motivate and satisfy, while the feeling of not being paid *enough* will create dissatisfaction and the desire to leave.

Dissatisfiers or hygiene factors

Hygiene (hygiene factors) are dissatisfiers that are associated with aspects of a person's work setting

Job context refers to a person's work setting.

Hygiene factors are associated with the **job context**; that is, they are factors related to a person's work setting. Improving working conditions (e.g. special offices and air conditioning) involves improving a hygiene, or job context, factor. It will prevent people from being dissatisfied with their work but will not make them satisfied. This can be an important distinction from the motivator factors. Lambert[74] argues that dissatisfiers are issues that employees are unhappy about in their work but that are not necessarily the causes of them leaving an organisation. Many organisations do put in effort to address job context factors as the following example shows.

OBinAction

What will employees find rewarding?

A recent *New York Times* article[75] documented a Silicon Valley trend where the focus on benefits is shifting from traditional things everyone offers to practical ideas very few do. For example Evernote's 250 employees (every full-time worker, from receptionist to top executive) have their houses cleaned twice a month for free. It is the latest innovation from Silicon Valley: the employee perk is moving from the office to the home. Facebook gives new parents $4000 in spending money (Google offers $400). Stanford School of Medicine is piloting a project to provide doctors with housecleaning and in-home dinner delivery. Genentech offers take-home dinners and helps employees find last-minute baby sitters when a child is too sick to go to school. Because technology such as smartphones has allowed work to easily 'bleed into' home life, some companies are trying to address the impact of home life on work. It is worth noting, however, that there is a very real possibility that relieving people of chores at home will simply free them up to work more!

Similarly, the *Huffington Post* published an article titled 'Best job perks: Companies provide employees with everything from catered meals to free alcohol'[76]. And indeed the 'perks' being offered by tech companies are truly astounding. They include things such as $3000 for child care expenses (Facebook), $5000 in adoption assistance (Facebook), a running tab at the coffee shop (Jetsetter), take-home dinners (Genentech), free skate park, snowboard park, and ski slope (Burton), performance-based paid tropical vacations (ZocDoc), metal, wood, welding, and electronics workshop rooms (Google), free beer, vodka, tequila, whiskey (Thrillist), personal trainers and nutritionists (Deloitte) and on-site lap pools (Google).

The Guild Group is one company that attends to job context factors. The company caters to the insurance, financial, legal and accounting needs of healthcare and childcare professionals. It won the Australian Human Resources Institute (AHRI) 2007 award for Excellence in People Management. The Guild Group has a new head office in Melbourne, with great care having been taken in relation to the design, construction and ergonomics of the space, as well as in considering the environment. The Guild Group has a carbon offset program, a greenhouse audit, corporate university programs and leave provisions including paternity leave and 12 weeks of maternity leave.[77]

Table 3.2 shows other examples of hygiene factors in work settings.

TABLE 3.2 Sample hygiene factors found in work settings

Hygiene factors	Examples
Organisational policies, procedures	Attendance rules Holiday schedules Grievance procedures Performance appraisal methods
Working conditions	Noise levels Safety Personal comfort Size of work area
Interpersonal relationships	Coworker relations Customer relations Relationship with boss
Quality of supervision	Technical competence of boss
Base salary	Hourly wage rate or salary

As table 3.2 shows, salary or money is included as a hygiene factor. This is perhaps surprising and is discussed further in the next section.

Money: motivator or hygiene factor

Herzberg found that low salary makes people dissatisfied, but that paying people more does not satisfy or motivate them. It is important to bear in mind that this conclusion derives from data that found salary had considerable cross-loading across both motivators and hygiene factors (see the bars that cross the central vertical line at zero percentage frequency in figure 3.4). Because most of the variance could be explained within the hygiene or job context group of factors, Herzberg concluded that money was not a motivator.

New ideas are constantly being explored to link money and motivation. Direct employee involvement in the financial future of the organisation is being widely encouraged through Employee Share Ownership Programs (ESOPs).[78] The extent to which these ESOPs are provided varies around the world[79] and may depend on factors such as favourable taxation. In Australia, approximately 6 per cent of all employees have employee shares.[80] Earlier statistics suggested that differences in share ownership exist based on criteria such as state, industry and occupation, working arrangements, and gender. For example, managers and administrators have a higher proportion of employee shares than the total (11.9 per cent) and full-time employees have more shares than part-time employees (7.0 per cent compared to 3.4 per cent).[81] Schemes exist in organisations such as Wesfarmers, Foster's and Eyecare Partners.[82]

It is difficult to explain the impact of such schemes on work motivation within Herzberg's framework, because these schemes have an impact on Herzberg's job content factors (such as responsibility and accountability) but also have a direct impact on money and its link to work motivation and performance. The link between money, ESOPs and work motivation remains complex and inconclusive to date.

Some Australian studies have found that the link between money and motivation also depends on other key factors such as the work status of the employee. One study found that casual workers employed on a part-time basis placed a higher value on job security than on monetary reward. The implications of this finding are far reaching because the growth in the part-time workforce in Australia and New Zealand is far greater than the growth of the full-time workforce.

Herzberg: the research and practical implications

Organisational behaviour scholars debate the merits of the two-factor theory.[83] While Herzberg's continuing research and that of his followers support the theory, some researchers have used different methods and are unable to confirm the theory. It is therefore criticised as being method-bound — that is, supportable only by applying Herzberg's original method. This is a serious criticism because the scientific approach requires that theories be verifiable when different research methods are used. The critical incident method used by Herzberg may have resulted in respondents generally associating good times in their jobs with things under their personal control, or for which they could give themselves credit. Bad times, on the other hand, were more often associated with factors in the environment under the control of management.

Herzberg's theory has also met with other criticisms.

1. The original sample of scientists and engineers probably is not representative of the working population.
2. The theory does not account for individual differences (for example, the similar impact of pay regardless of gender, age and other important differences).
3. The theory does not clearly define the relationship between satisfaction and motivation.[84]

Such criticisms may contribute to the mixed findings from research conducted outside the United States. In New Zealand, for example, supervision and interpersonal relationships have been found to contribute significantly to satisfaction and not merely towards reducing dissatisfaction. And certain hygiene factors have been cited more frequently as satisfiers in Panama, Latin America and a number of countries other than the United States. In contrast, earlier evidence from countries such as Finland tends to confirm US results.[85] A study of a Norwegian company, Telenor, suggested the physical environment (incorporating the aspects of art, design and architecture) could be a motivator — since the pleasantness of the physical environment might impact on the mood, the wellbeing and the inspiration of workers.[86] This finding appears to work against the idea that 'working conditions' constitute hygiene factors. The same Norwegian study also indicated that respondents to their survey seemed to find it hard to distinguish between motivation and satisfaction, presumably accepting the two as related. In view of globalising workforces, these distinctions may have significant importance for managers endeavouring to motivate their employees.

However, Herzberg's theory does have value. For example, it may help to identify why a focus on job environment factors (such as special office fixtures, piped-in music, comfortable lounges for breaks and high base salaries) often do not motivate. It also highlights the value of job design and motivation as discussed in chapter 5.

Process theories

As useful as they are, content theories still emphasise the 'what' aspect of motivation — that is, 'If I have a security deficiency, I try to reduce or remove it'. They do not emphasise the thought processes concerning 'why' and 'how' people choose one action over another in the workplace. For this, we must turn to process motivation theories. Two well-known process theories are equity theory and expectancy theory.

Equity theory

Equity theory presents the idea that motivation is affected when people feel that work outcomes are unfair or inequitable, due to social comparison in the workplace.

Equity theory is based on the phenomenon of social comparison and is best known through the writing of J Stacy Adams.[87] Adams argues that when people gauge the fairness of their work outcomes compared with those of others, felt inequity is a motivating state of mind. That is, when people perceive inequity in their work, they experience a state of cognitive dissonance, and they will be aroused to remove the discomfort and to restore a sense of felt equity to the situation. Inequities exist whenever people feel that the rewards or inducements they receive for their work inputs or contributions are unequal to the rewards other people appear to have received for their inputs. For the individual, the equity comparison or thought process that determines such feeling is:

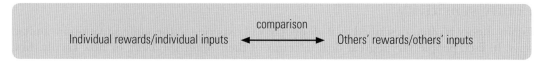

comparison

Individual rewards/individual inputs ⟷ Others' rewards/others' inputs

Resolving felt inequities

Felt negative inequity exists when an individual feels that they have received relatively less than others have in proportion to work inputs. **Felt positive inequity** exists when an individual feels that they have received relatively more than others have.

Both felt negative and felt positive inequity are motivating states. When either exists, the individual will likely engage in one or more of the following behaviours to restore a sense of equity:

1. change work inputs (for example, reduce performance efforts)
2. change the outcomes (rewards) received (for example, ask for a raise)
3. leave the situation (for example, quit)
4. change the comparison points (for example, compare self with a different coworker)
5. psychologically distort the comparisons (for example, rationalise that the inequity is only temporary and will be resolved in the future)
6. act to change the inputs or outputs of the comparison person (for example, get a coworker to accept more work).

Equity theory predicts that people who feel either under-rewarded or over-rewarded for their work will act to restore a sense of equity.

Adams's equity theory: the research

The research of Adams and others, accomplished largely in laboratory settings, lends tentative support to this prediction.[88] The research indicates that people who feel over-paid (felt positive inequity) increase the quantity or quality of their work, while those who feel underpaid (felt negative inequity) decrease the quantity or quality of their work. The research is most conclusive about felt negative inequity. It appears that people are less comfortable when they are under-rewarded than when they are over-rewarded.

Managing the equity dynamic

Figure 3.5 shows that the equity comparison intervenes between a manager's allocation of rewards and their impact on the work behaviour of staff. Feelings of inequity are determined solely by the individual's interpretation of the situation.

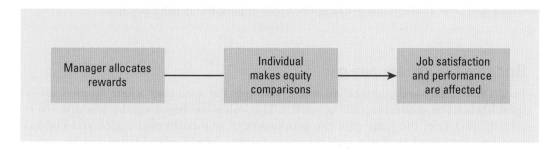

Manager allocates rewards → Individual makes equity comparisons → Job satisfaction and performance are affected

FIGURE 3.5 The equity comparison as an intervening variable in the rewards, satisfaction and performance relationship

Thus, it is incorrect to assume all employees in a work unit will view their annual pay rise as fair. It is not how a manager feels about the allocation of rewards that counts; it is how the recipients perceive the rewards that will determine the motivational outcomes of the equity dynamic. Managing the equity dynamic therefore becomes quite important to the

Felt negative inequity exists when individuals feel they have received relatively less than others have in proportion to work inputs.

Felt positive inequity exists when individuals feel they have received relatively more than others have.

manager, who strives to maintain healthy psychological contracts — that is, fairly balanced inducements and contributions — among staff.

Equity sensitivity

Equity theory is often described as if all people will experience the same situation in similar ways. In fact, people vary a great deal in terms of their *equity sensitivity*, or how keenly they experience unfairness in their work environment.[89] Instead of assuming that all individuals prefer to have equal outcome–input ratios, equity researchers have recognised that some individuals may be more sensitive than others to inequity. Huseman et al.[90] identified three categories to describe equity preferences: benevolents, entitleds, and sensitives. According to equity theorists, benevolents have the greatest tolerance for under-reward situations and prefer their ratio of outcomes to inputs to be less than that of a comparison other. Entitleds, on the other hand, tend to be very focused on outcomes. With less concern for inputs, they feel most comfortable in situations where they receive proportionally more than their work-mates. Sensitives act in accordance with Adam's equity theory and prefer their outcomes–input ratio to be equal to that of a comparison other. Rewards that are received with feelings of equity can foster job satisfaction and performance. In contrast, rewards that are received with feelings of negative inequity can damage these key work results. The burden lies with the manager to take control of the situation and make sure that any negative consequences of the equity comparisons are avoided, or at least minimised, when rewards are allocated. The effective manager shows how you can deal with these concerns.

THE
EffectiveManager 3.1

Steps for managing the equity process

- Recognise that an employee is likely to make an equity comparison whenever especially visible rewards, such as pay, promotions and so on, are being allocated.
- Anticipate felt negative inequities.
- Communicate to each individual your evaluation of the reward, an appraisal of the performance on which it is based, and the comparison points you consider to be appropriate.

Managing the equity dynamic across cultures can become very complex. Western expatriates working in multinational corporations typically adopt an individual frame of reference when making equity comparisons. For local employees in Eastern cultures, the value placed on rewards and the weighting attributed to a specific outcome may vary considerably from Western norms. The group, not the individual, is the major point of reference for such equity comparisons and if a multinational corporation tries to motivate by offering indi-vidualised rewards, employees may not respond as expected.[91]

The following Ethical perspective examines how both the public and private sectors in Australia and New Zealand are working towards bridging the gender pay gap.

ETHICAL
Perspective

Bridging the gender pay gap

In 2013, *The Economist* created an index showing the countries where women are most likely to be treated equally at work.[92] The index was based on the labour-force participation rate, the wage gap, the proportion of women in senior jobs and child care cost compared to wages, among other factors. New Zealand came out on top (with Australia ranking a respectable 5th). The process was repeated in 2014 and New Zealand had slipped in the rankings, being beaten only by the Nordic nations (well known for their gender equality policies).[93] By 2014, Australia had slipped to sixteenth place but still ranked above average for the OECD.

In spite of these encouraging results, equity in terms of pay is an ongoing issue in Australia and New Zealand. In New Zealand women in the public sector are paid on average 14 per cent less than their male counterparts, despite making up 60 per cent of the sector's workforce.[94] The New Zealand labour market average is only slightly better with a gender pay gap of 13 per cent.[95] Some industries fare worse than others, for example the New Zealand Institute of Chartered Accountants surveyed its own sector to discover that male chartered accountants with five years' experience earn $3605 more than their female counterparts, debunking the myth that pay gaps emerge when women start families (typically around 31 years old in New Zealand).

The private sector in New Zealand needs to lead the way in closing the pay gap, and this is happening to an extent. Many larger organisations understand that increasing diversity and bringing women through will actually improve their bottom line. There is a good business case for pay equality, and companies that understood the issue are more able to attract and retain the right talent.

In addition, New Zealand organisations can get recognition through a new award scheme aiming to raise awareness and promote change. The YWCA Equal Pay Awards will acknowledge businesses which have implemented equal pay policies or are beginning to take steps towards closing the gap. The awards will be backed by a range of resources, to be made available on the YWCA Auckland website, to help businesses work towards equal pay (www.akywca.org.nz).

In February 2014, the gap between what men and women earn in Australia was 17.1 per cent (a difference that equates to $262.60 per week).[96] Helen Conway (Director of the Workplace Gender Equality Agency, Australia) states, 'This persistent pay gap is both concerning and frustrating. And sadly, there is a pay gap in favour of men in every single industry'.

Australia's Workplace Gender Equality Agency (WGEA) offers free a payroll analysis tool to assist organisations in identifying two types of pay gap:

1. pay gaps between women and men doing the same or similar work
2. organisation-wide (or department-wide) gender pay gaps resulting from unequal gender representation at different levels of the organisation (or department).[97]

Expectancy theory

Victor Vroom's expectancy theory[98] seeks to predict or explain the task-related effort expended by a person. The theory's central question is: 'What determines the willingness of an individual to exert personal effort to work at tasks that contribute to the performance of the work unit and the organisation?'

Figure 3.6 (overleaf) illustrates the managerial foundations of expectancy theory. Individuals are viewed as making conscious decisions to allocate their behaviour towards work efforts and to serve self-interests. The three key terms in the theory are as follows.

1. **Expectancy:** the probability that the individual assigns to work effort being followed by a given level of achieved task performance. Expectancy would equal '0' if the person felt it was impossible to achieve the given performance level; it would equal '1' if a person was 100 per cent certain that the performance could be achieved.

2. **Instrumentality:** the probability that the individual assigns to a given level of achieved task performance leading to various work outcomes that are rewarding for them. Instrumentality also varies from '1' (meaning the reward outcome is 100 per cent certain to follow performance) to '0' (indicating that there is no chance that performance will lead to the reward outcome). (Strictly speaking, Vroom's treatment of instrumentality would allow it to vary from −1 to +1. We use the probability definition here and the 0 to 1 range for pedagogical purposes; it is consistent with the basic instrumentality notion.)

Expectancy is the probability that the individual assigns to work effort being followed by a given level of achieved task performance.

Instrumentality is the probability that the individual assigns to a level of achieved task performance leading to various work outcomes.

3. Valence: the value that the individual attaches to various work reward outcomes. Valences form a scale from –1 (very undesirable outcome) to +1 (very desirable outcome).

Expectancy theory argues that work motivation is determined by individual beliefs about effort–performance relationships and the desirability of various work outcomes from different performance levels. Simply, the theory is based on the logic that people will do what they can do when they want to.[99] If you want a promotion and see that high performance can lead to that promotion, and that if you work hard you can achieve high performance, you will be motivated to work hard. Estee Lauder, a leading skin care, fragrance and hair care company, is an example of a business where promotion within is well entrenched, thereby increasing employee belief that performance may lead to promotion.

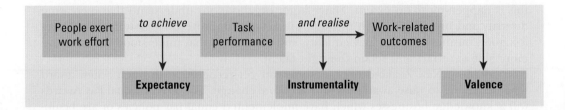

FIGURE 3.6 Expectancy theory terms in a managerial perspective

Multiplier effects and multiple outcomes

Vroom posits that motivation (M), expectancy (E), instrumentality (I) and valence (V) are related to one another by the equation: $M = E \times I \times V$.

This relationship means that the motivational appeal of a given work path is sharply reduced whenever any one or more of these factors approaches the value of zero. Conversely, for a given reward to have a high and positive motivational impact as a work outcome, the expectancy, instrumentality and valence associated with the reward must all be high and positive.

Suppose a manager is wondering whether the prospect of earning a merit pay rise will be motivational to a subordinate. Expectancy theory predicts that motivation to work hard to earn the merit pay will be low if the person:

1. feels they cannot achieve the necessary performance level (expectancy)
2. is not confident a high level of task performance will result in a high merit pay rise (instrumentality)
3. places little value (valence) on a merit pay increase
4. experiences any combination of these.

Expectancy theory is able to accommodate multiple work outcomes in predicting motivation. As shown in figure 3.7, the outcome of a merit pay increase may not be the only one affecting the individual's decision to work hard. Relationships with coworkers may also be important, and they may be undermined if the individual stands out from the group as a high performer.

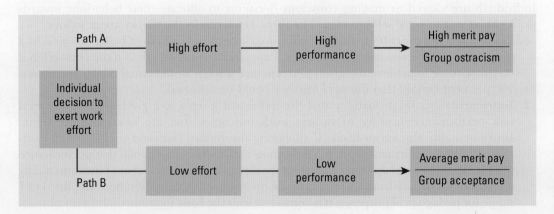

FIGURE 3.7 An example of individual thought processes, as viewed by expectancy theory

Although merit pay is both highly valued and considered accessible to the individual, its motivational power can be cancelled out by the negative effects of high performance on the individual's social relationships with coworkers. One of the advantages of expectancy theory is its ability to help managers account for such multiple outcomes when trying to determine the motivational value of various work rewards to individual employees.

Vroom: managerial implications

The managerial implications of Vroom's expectancy theory are summarised in table 3.3. Expectancy logic argues that a manager must try to understand individual thought processes, then actively intervene in the work situation to influence them. This includes trying to maximise work expectancies, instrumentalities and valences that support the organisation's production purposes. In other words, a manager should strive to create a work setting in which the individual will perceive that their own effort will lead to work outcomes that are valued by the organisation and rewarded fairly with things desired by the individual.

Expectancy term	The individual's question	Managerial implications
Expectancy	'Can I achieve the desired level of task performance?'	Select workers with ability; train workers to use ability; support individual ability with organisational resources; identify performance goals
Instrumentality	'What work outcomes will be received as a result of the performance?'	Clarify psychological contracts; communicate performance–reward possibilities; confirm performance–reward possibilities by making actual rewards contingent on performance
Valence	'How highly do I value the work outcomes?'	Identify individual needs or outcomes; adjust available rewards to match these.

TABLE 3.3 Managerial implications of expectancy theory

Expectancy theory might also be considered in the context of uncertainty in the workplace. It also suggests that managers need to understand the individual expectancy and instrumentality links for all workers. Although individuals will always be unique in their motivation, there may be new cohorts of workers in the organisation (such as those staying past retirement age and the Gen X and Gen Y employees) about whom generalisations may be made.

Knowledge of pay process

Instrumentality, at its core, is about whether an employee believes that their work or effort will be fairly and accurately rewarded, yet in a study of more than 6000 workers, less than half said that they knew how to increase their pay or bonuses and only a third reported understanding how their pay was determined.[100] This study found that although *performance management processes* are generally well understood by employees and managers, *pay processes* are not well understood. The research suggests that pay knowledge and performance management knowledge are positively associated with organisational effectiveness. In addition, improving pay and performance knowledge was found to have such a strong positive impact on pay satisfaction that organisations may be able to offset low base pay rates by simply being more transparent about how pay is determined!

(continued)

WhatWould
You**Do?**

Further, it was found that when people report having less base pay knowledge, they also report being less satisfied with their pay. Because pay satisfaction is related to several aspects of organisational effectiveness, such as commitment and engagement, lack of base pay knowledge can go some way towards explaining turnover and poor performance.

Questions
1. How might you go about increasing pay and performance knowledge for your workforce?
2. In addition to instrumentality, what could you do to improve levels of expectancy in a workforce?

In terms of outcome valence, the manager can identify individual needs or outcomes important to each individual, then try to adjust available rewards to match these. In this sense, the theory can be universally applied. Each individual may be different, though different cultural patterns of values will affect valence of rewards across cultures. It may also be possible to change the individual's perceptions of the valence of various outcomes, as shown in The effective manager 3.2.

THE **EffectiveManager** 3.2

Tips for influencing the perceived valence of work outcomes

- Find out the currently valued outcomes for each employee.
- Determine the outcomes that are currently available to them.
- Discuss how well the two sets match, and examine similarities between each individual's list and your list.
- Show how some available outcomes may be more desirable or less undesirable than the worker thinks (for example, promotion may be available, but the employee currently does not desire it because he or she feels uncomfortable with it).

Vroom: the research

There is a great deal of research on expectancy theory, and good review articles are available.[101] Although the theory has received substantial support, specific details (such as the operation of the multiplier effect) remain subject to question. Rather than charging that the underlying theory is inadequate, researchers indicate that problems of method and measurement may cause their inability to generate more confirming data. Thus, while awaiting the results of more sophisticated research, experts seem to agree that expectancy theory is a useful insight into work motivation.

One of the more popular modifications of Vroom's original version of the theory distinguishes between extrinsic and intrinsic rewards as two separate types of possible work outcomes.[102] **Extrinsic rewards** are positively valued work outcomes that the individual receives from some other person in the work setting. An example is pay. Workers typically do not pay themselves directly; some representative of the organisation administers the reward. In contrast, **intrinsic rewards** are positively valued work outcomes that the individual receives directly as a result of task performance; they do not require the participation of another person. A feeling of achievement after accomplishing a particularly challenging task is one example. The distinction between extrinsic and intrinsic rewards is important because each type demands separate attention from a manager seeking to use rewards to increase motivation. We discuss these differences more thoroughly in chapters 4 and 5.

Extrinsic rewards are positively valued work outcomes that the individual receives from some other person in the work setting.

Intrinsic rewards are positively valued work outcomes that the individual receives directly as a result of task performance.

Integrating content and process motivation theories

Each of the theories presented in this chapter is potentially useful for the manager. Although the equity and expectancy theories have special strengths, current thinking argues for a combined approach that points out where and when various motivation theories work best.[103] Thus, before leaving this discussion, we should pull the content and process theories together into one integrated model of individual performance and satisfaction.

First, the various content theories have a common theme, as shown in figure 3.8. Content theorists disagree somewhat as to the exact nature of human needs, but they do agree that:

$$\text{Individual needs} \xrightarrow{\text{activate}} \text{tensions} \xrightarrow{\text{that affect}} \text{attitudes and behaviour.}$$

The manager's job is to create a work environment that responds positively to individual needs. Poor performance, undesirable behaviours and/or decreased satisfaction can be partly explained in terms of 'blocked' needs, or needs that are not satisfied on the job. The motivational value of rewards (intrinsic and extrinsic) can also be analysed in terms of 'activated' needs to which a given reward either does or does not respond. Ultimately, managers must understand that individuals have different needs and place different importance on different needs. Managers must also know what to offer individuals to respond to their needs and to create work settings that give people the opportunity to satisfy their needs through their contributions to task, work unit and organisational performance.

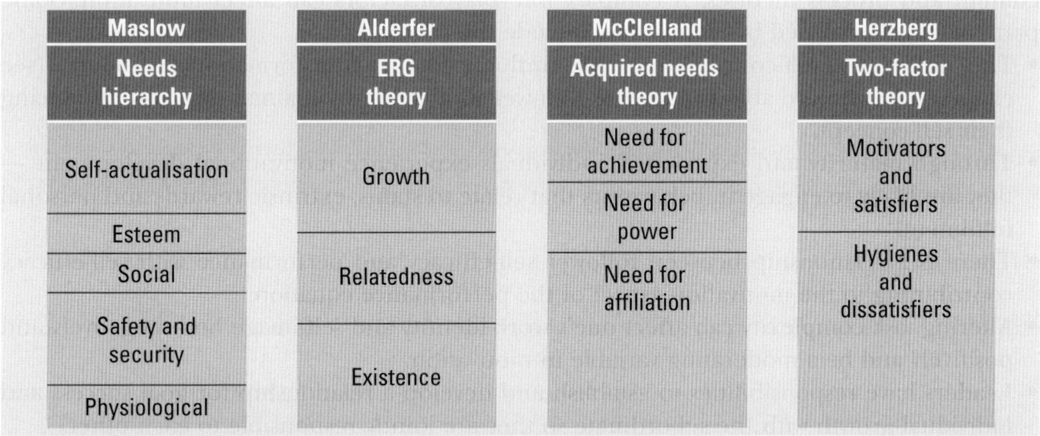

Maslow	Alderfer	McClelland	Herzberg
Needs hierarchy	**ERG theory**	**Acquired needs theory**	**Two-factor theory**
Self-actualisation	Growth	Need for achievement	Motivators and satisfiers
Esteem		Need for power	
Social	Relatedness	Need for affiliation	Hygienes and dissatisfiers
Safety and security			
Physiological	Existence		

FIGURE 3.8 Comparison of content motivation theories

Figure 3.9 (overleaf) is a model that goes further to integrate content and process theories. The model, as proposed by Lyman W Porter and Edward E Lawler, is an extension of Vroom's original expectancy theory.[104] The figure is based on the foundation of the individual performance equation (see chapter 2). Individual attributes and work effort, and the manager's ability to create a work setting that positively responds to individual needs and goals all affect performance. Whether a work setting can satisfy needs depends on the availability of rewards (extrinsic and intrinsic). The content theories enter the model as the manager's guide to understanding individual attributes and identifying the needs that give motivational value to the various work rewards allocated to employees. Research has linked individual attributes such as personality with motivation in terms of achievement factors and intrinsic and extrinsic motivation. For example, highly conscientiousness employees are likely to work well and achieve in environments high in intrinsic motivation opportunities.[105] Managers are also interested in promoting high levels of individual satisfaction as a part of their concern for human resource maintenance. You may recall that we concluded our chapter 2 review of the satisfaction–performance controversy by noting that when rewards are allocated on the basis of past performance (that is, when rewards are performance contingent), they can cause both future performance and satisfaction. Motivation can also occur when job satisfactions result from rewards that are felt to be equitably allocated. When felt negative inequity results, satisfaction will be low and motivation will be reduced. Thus, the integrated model includes a key role for equity theory and recognises job performance and satisfaction as separate, but potentially interdependent, work results.[106]

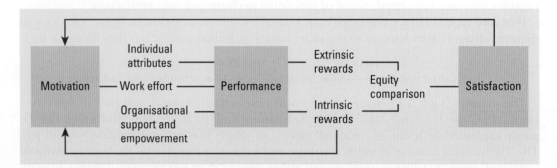

FIGURE 3.9 Predicting individual work performance and satisfaction: an integrated model

Other perspectives on motivation

In recent years more work has developed to explain other dimensions that contribute to our understanding of motivation. These extend beyond what is traditionally explained by content and process theories. A complex interplay of factors can affect motivation. Some particular ideas collated by Humphreys include the following.

- The follower's self-concept may be influenced by transformational leaders (see chapter 11) who are able to increase follower motivation by maintaining and enhancing their self-concept.
- Through maturity and experience, individuals experience motivational development — they are likely to engage in behaviours that relate to status, extrinsic rewards and personal fulfilment.
- There is a relationship between follower self-efficacy and performance with self-efficacy contributing to the motivation aspect of the performance equation.
- Altering task complexity can affect one's work identity and self-image both negatively and positively and be a moderating variable in motivation.
- Leaders have responsibilities to establish and develop a relationship for goal success and individual growth with the subordinate so they are jointly responsible to each other.
- There must be congruency between a leader's communication and a follower's values, and/or between the leader's focus and the follower's identity and values. Leader-follower congruency may affect leader's attempt to enhance a follower's self-concept.
- Some work indicates that different personalities can be explained as different temperaments. Temperament can impact upon how individuals are motivated, their likely satisfaction and goal-directed behaviour.[107]

Collectively, such factors can contribute to a congruent temperament model that suggests that motivation is enhanced when the leader can understand the employee, and respond appropriately with behaviours that are congruent with the follower's temperament and perspective.

There has also been quite a bit of work done researching why people often offer their services voluntarily or engage in altruistic deeds without having any anticipated rewards (intrinsic or extrinsic). Personal value systems and the idea of self-concept, as discussed in chapter 2, underlie this approach. **Self-concept** is the concept that individuals have of themselves as physical, social and spiritual or moral beings.

Self-concept is the concept that individuals have of themselves as physical, social and spiritual or moral beings.

Sustainability motivates

Auckland University of Technology (AUT) was a winner in the NZI Sustainable Business Awards for 2013. With a business and law faculty aimed at educating future businesspeople, it is perhaps not surprising that AUT is leading the way on sustainability in its own operations.

Recently the university has upgraded lighting throughout its facilities to increase efficiency, including the installation of solar-powered LED lighting to its North Shore campus car park. This saved approximately 1 000 000 kWh of power and about 140 tonnes of CO_2 emissions between 2011 and 2013, the equivalent of negating the effects of running 27 average-sized cars.

AUT also installed two high-efficiency boilers for heating and partially buried 'Molok' bins that compact their contents to reduce the need for recycling and waste collection.

Recycling has been increased by 40 per cent between 2009 and 2012; there are even eight worm farms installed at the School of Hospitality and Tourism to turn food scraps into compost, and cut waste to landfill by a fifth.

University staff are incentivised to make the switch to public transport, with a combination of the 'stick' (increased parking costs) and the 'carrot' (inter-campus shuttle service) that accounted for about 250 000 trips in 2012.

AUT now has a university-wide sustainability taskforce promoting these ideas across the organisation's entire culture.[108]

The self-concept approach comes from personality theory. It focuses on using the concept of the self as an underlying force that motivates behaviour, gives it direction and energy and sustains it. Self-concept is derived from many influences including family, social identity and reference groups, education and experience. Generally speaking, these aspects of personality are a guide to our behaviour and help us to decide what to do in specific situations. So, for example, a young person may choose to study medicine or dentistry at university, or to enter the family trade, because that is what was always expected of them and has therefore become an important part of their identity. Rewards such as money and status may be secondary considerations. Many acts are done out of a sense of responsibility, integrity or even humour, which relate to the self-concept aspect of personality.[109] This sort of approach would help to explain the nurse who waits with the relatives of a critically injured patient for hours after his shift is completed; or the person who works the shift of a friend who is studying for exams.

In contrast to a focus on needs or cognitive thought processes to explain motivation, the self-concept approach relies on other ways of understanding motivation to explain the full range of motivated behaviour. People may also draw on the values they hold, and the way that these values are a guide to behaviours that seem right or appropriate for them. For example, people internalise values that are espoused by the professional group (or the organisation) to which they belong. Behaviours consistent with such values might include saving lives and property at considerable personal risk, exposing unethical financial practices despite censure from management, or facing personal hardship.

A study by Camilleri found that there might be an altruistic motivation relationship between some public servants' commitment to serving the public interest and their sense of compassion. The relationship was evident for married public servants with children and bachelors but not for those married without children, or without children at home.[110] Having identified content and process theories and an integrated model of these two approaches, as well as considering the ideas of self-efficacy, self-concept, personal values and temperament in motivation, it is worth reflecting on how managers may be able to understand and implement these concepts in the workplace. Bearing in mind Richard Thompson's desire to do voluntary work and his change in career from auditing to a lower paying job in welfare work might help highlight aspects of the motivational elements discussed in this chapter.

Empowerment

Much of the motivational theory discussed in this chapter has addressed the question of what management can do to ensure employees positively contribute to the achievement of organisational goals. In the workplace in the twenty-first century, the worker is searching for recognition, involvement and a heightened sense of self-worth and the employer is often looking for a 'can do' mentality among employees that lessens the need for managerial control. Empowerment can do this. **Empowerment** is the process by which managers delegate power to employees to motivate greater responsibility in balancing the achievement of both personal and organisational goals. The key question for managers is how to facilitate employees' individual and joint contributions to the organisation and their own development. Empowerment focuses on liberating, not controlling, human energy, and on balancing the achievement of personal and organisational goals. Managers commonly attempt these processes by delegating more power to employees and encouraging them to take on leadership roles in the organisation.

Empowerment is the process by which managers delegate power to employees to motivate greater responsibility in balancing the achievement of both personal and organisational goals.

OBinAction

Empowerment — What nurses want

A study at Australia's Monash University called *What nurses want* found that nurses did not 'trust their employer to keep promises', had 'limited influence in important workplace decisions', had 'a poorer industrial relations climate than the general population' and viewed their management more poorly than other workers.[111]

So what can be done? The answer may be the Toyota Management System.[112] It has helped the Japanese car manufacturer be among the world's best, and recently it has been applied to hospitals. It is a bureaucracy-busting system in which any employee, upon discovering a problem, can 'stop the assembly line' instead of sweeping it under the rug for fear of being ignored or blamed. All available resources are then pulled in to not just solve the problem, but change the process that led to it, keeping it from recurring; eliminating or resolving the underlying bad practices. In hospitals, this means an internal hotline and the empowerment of nurses, resulting in improved morale and operational savings.

In the United States, where the practice is spreading, the Virginia Mason Health Centre in Seattle started in 2002 and is considered the leader. A recent medical journal article analysing the process concluded that the system had 'drastically increased the number of safety concerns that are resolved ... while drastically reducing the time it takes to resolve them. Transparent discussion and feedback have helped promote staff acceptance and participation'.[113]

In New Zealand efficiency improvements in hospitals due to the lean methodologies developed by Toyota (also called 'the productive ward') have been reported as being as much as 35 per cent. Other research has focused on the productivity of professional practice models (PPM). These models are characterised by increased responsibility and control by nurses over work processes, scheduling, professional development and quality. While the increased autonomy and empowerment inherent in PPM was not shown to achieve cost savings or improved nursing outputs, benefits including improved job satisfaction, retention, and less absenteeism were reported (all of which contribute to a hospital's bottom line).[114]

The concept of empowerment is founded on the belief that everyone has an internal need for self-determination and a need to cope with environmental demands directly. This suggests that appropriate empowerment strategies can raise the perception of low self-efficacy. **Self-efficacy** refers to a person's belief that they can perform adequately in a situation. It refers to a state of mind or mentality,[115] which is why its relationship with empowerment strategies is important (self-efficacy is discussed in more depth in chapter 4). Empowerment strategies are designed to improve self-efficacy by providing employees with greater autonomy and by increasing knowledge and control over factors directly related to job performance.

Some work on empowerment has identified the following stages (see figure 3.10, overleaf) in the empowerment process.[116]

- *Stage 1* Identify the conditions contributing to low self-efficacy. This could include organisational factors (such as poor communication systems and an impersonal bureaucratic climate); supervisory style factors (such as authoritarianism, an emphasis on failure or lack of communication of reasons for action or inaction); reward factors (such as rewards that are not performance-based, or the low incentive value of rewards); and job design factors (such as unclear roles, unrealistic goals, low levels of participation and low job enrichment).
- *Stage 2* Employ empowerment strategies and techniques that help to vest substantial responsibility in the hands of the individual who is closest to the problem requiring a solution.
  - *Cultivate a 'service wisdom'.* Trained and multiskilled employees should be able to handle non-routine situations, to understand the bigger picture and how their role affects other employees and the achievement of organisational goals.
  - *Encourage job mastery.* Provide coaching, training and appropriate experiences to ensure successful job performance.
  - *Create a freedom to act.* Treat employees as if they own their jobs, devolving power so employees can adequately resolve problems. Managers should set appropriate boundaries to the freedom to facilitate successful employee job performance without creating inappropriate licence.
  - *Provide emotional support.* Employees must feel that if they act within the designated boundaries, then managers will support their actions even if they make mistakes. Such support helps reduce stress and anxiety through clearer role definition, task support and concern for employee wellbeing.
  - *Provide appropriate feedback.* Employees need regular and detailed feedback so they know how they are performing against managerial expectations.
  - *Share the power.* Share as much power as possible, allowing for employee experience, education and task difficulty.
  - *Demonstrate active listening skills.* Learn to listen to feedback from experienced employees, because the person performing the task often has the best ideas on process improvement.
  - *Learn how to let go.* Treat employees as partners and equals rather than as subordinates and know when to let go when their work is successfully helping the business move in the right direction.

Self-efficacy refers to a person's belief that they can perform adequately in a situation.

- *Encourage diversity of approach.* Employees should have the discretion to use various job styles and methods provided they meet agreed organisational standards for the work.
- *Develop participative management skills.* Encourage employees to participate in major decisions that directly affect their daily working lives.
- *Encourage modelling.* Employees should be able to observe and model their work on examples of 'best practice' performance in particular skills and competency-based areas relevant to their own work assignments.
- *Create job enrichment.* Enrich jobs by making employees more accountable and responsible for key aspects of their work performance.
- *Stage 3* Provide self-efficacy information directly to the employee. This stage focuses on modifying employee behaviour and increasing the self-efficacy belief. Four approaches have been identified.
  - *Competency building.* Structure training and organisational learning so that employees acquire new skills through successive, moderate increments in task complexity and responsibility.
  - *Encouragement and persuasion.* Use verbal feedback and other persuasive techniques to encourage and reinforce successful job performance.
  - *Emotional support.* Provide emotional support for employees and minimise emotional arousal states such as anxiety, stress and the fear associated with making mistakes. Mistakes should be seen as part of the learning process.
  - *Modelling.* Allow employees to observe workers who perform successfully on the job.

  Both stages 2 and 3 are designed to remove and eradicate the conditions identified in stage 1, and to develop the positive feelings of self-efficacy within the individual employee.
- *Stage 4* Create a 'can do' mentality and an empowering experience for the employee.

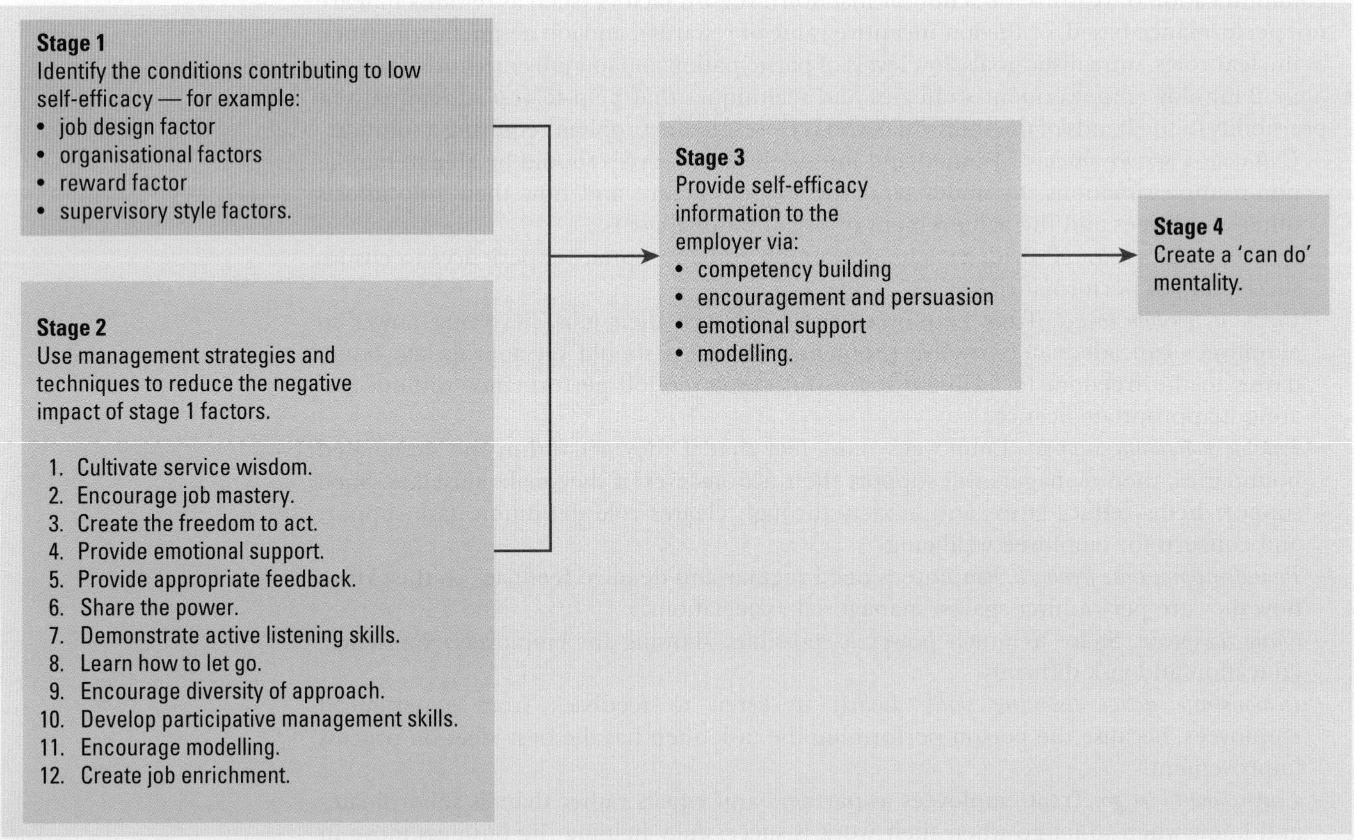

Stage 1
Identify the conditions contributing to low self-efficacy — for example:
- job design factor
- organisational factors
- reward factor
- supervisory style factors.

Stage 2
Use management strategies and techniques to reduce the negative impact of stage 1 factors.

1. Cultivate service wisdom.
2. Encourage job mastery.
3. Create the freedom to act.
4. Provide emotional support.
5. Provide appropriate feedback.
6. Share the power.
7. Demonstrate active listening skills.
8. Learn how to let go.
9. Encourage diversity of approach.
10. Develop participative management skills.
11. Encourage modelling.
12. Create job enrichment.

Stage 3
Provide self-efficacy information to the employer via:
- competency building
- encouragement and persuasion
- emotional support
- modelling.

Stage 4
Create a 'can do' mentality.

FIGURE 3.10 Modelling the empowerment process

If stages 2 and 3 are successful then they will increase the employee's effort–performance understanding. As we saw earlier in the chapter, expectancy theories of motivation are essential for high and sustained levels of performance. Here, performance is linked directly to the positive mentality of the individual.

Summary

Motivating and empowering today's workforce

In the contemporary world, a key challenge is to motivate and empower workers towards productive performance. With an ageing population, when there are labour shortages and with mobile workforces, organisations need to understand how to motivate and empower employees in order to attract and retain them and to enhance performance.

Difference between content and process motivation theories

There are two main types of motivational theories — content and process. Content theories examine the needs that individuals have. Their efforts to satisfy those needs are what drive their behaviour. Process theories examine the thought processes that people have in relation to motivating their behaviour.

Content theories of motivation

The content theories of Maslow, Alderfer, McClelland and Herzberg emphasise needs or motives. They are often criticised for being culturally biased, and caution should be exercised when applying these theories in non-Western cultures.

Maslow's hierarchy of needs theory arranges human needs into a five-step hierarchy: physiological, safety, social (the three lower-order needs), esteem and self-actualisation (the two higher-order needs). Satisfaction of any need activates the need at the next higher level, and people are presumed to move step by step up the hierarchy. Alderfer's ERG theory has modified this theory by collapsing the five needs into three: existence, relatedness and growth. Alderfer also allows for more than one need to be activated at a time and for a frustration–regression response. McClelland's acquired needs theory focuses on the needs for achievement (nAch), affiliation (nAff) and power (nPower). The theory argues that these needs can be developed through experience and training. Persons high in nAch prefer jobs with individual responsibility, performance feedback and moderately challenging goals. Successful executives typically have a high nPower that is greater than their nAff. Herzberg's two-factor theory treats job satisfaction and job dissatisfaction as two separate issues. Satisfiers, or motivator factors such as achievement, responsibility and recognition, are associated with job content. An improvement in job content is expected to increase satisfaction and motivation to perform well. In contrast, dissatisfiers, or hygiene factors such as working conditions, relations with coworkers and salary, are associated with the job context. Improving job context does not lead to more satisfaction but is expected to reduce dissatisfaction.

Process theories of motivation

Process theories emphasise the thought processes concerning how and why people choose one action over another in the workplace. Process theories focus on understanding the cognitive processes that act to influence behaviour. Although process theories can be very useful in explaining work motivation in cross-cultural settings, the values that drive such theories may vary substantially across cultures and the outcomes may differ considerably.

Equity theory points out that people compare their rewards (and inputs) with those of others. The individual is then motivated to engage in behaviour to correct any perceived inequity. At the extreme, feelings of inequity may lead to reduced performance or job turnover. Expectancy theory argues that work motivation is determined by an individual's beliefs concerning effort–performance relationships (expectancy), work–outcome relationships (instrumentality) and the desirability of various work outcomes (valence). Managers, therefore, must build positive expectancies, demonstrate performance-reward instrumentalities, and use rewards with high positive valences in their motivational strategies.

Integrating content and process motivation theories

The content theories can be compared, with some overlap identified. An integrated model of motivation builds from the individual performance equation developed in chapter 2 and combines the content and process theories to show how well-managed rewards can lead to high levels of both individual performance and satisfaction.

Other perspectives on motivation

Other theories go beyond content and process theories to draw links with personality theory, leadership, individual values, self-concept and self-efficacy. Such theories tend to place a lot of emphasis on leader responsibility for motivation and on the complexity of motivation. Theories that focus on self-concept and personal values seek to describe motivation as a desire that is derived from a person's self-concept. This self-concept guides individual behaviour.

Empowerment and the empowerment process

Empowerment is the process by which managers delegate power to employees to motivate greater responsibility in balancing the achievement of personal and organisational goals. For employees who experience low self-efficacy, managers can implement strategies to improve the employees' feelings of self-worth and their capacity to improve their performance.

CHAPTER 3 study guide

Key terms

content theories, *p. 87*
empowerment, *p. 108*
equity theory, *p. 98*
ERG theory, *p. 91*
existence needs, *p. 91*
expectancy, *p. 101*
expectancy theory, *p. 102*
extrinsic rewards, *p. 104*
felt negative inequity, *p. 99*
felt positive inequity, *p. 99*

growth needs, *p. 91*
higher-order needs, *p. 88*
hygiene (hygiene factors), *p. 96*
instrumentality, *p. 101*
intrinsic rewards, *p. 104*
job content, *p. 95*
job context, *p. 96*
lower-order needs, *p. 88*
motivation to work, *p. 80*
motivators (motivator factors), *p. 95*

motivator–hygiene theory, *p. 94*
need for achievement (nAch), *p. 92*
need for affiliation (nAff), *p. 92*
need for power (nPower), *p. 92*
process theories, *p. 87*
relatedness needs, *p. 91*
self-concept, *p. 106*
self-efficacy, *p. 109*
valence, *p. 102*

Review questions

1. Define 'work motivation' and identify the role of motivation in the individual performance equation.
2. Compare and evaluate the key differences between what each of the content theories offer in terms of explaining needs.
3. Explain the key differences between the expectancy and the equity theories of motivation.
4. Describe each of the four stages in the empowerment process.

Application questions

1. What challenges might there be in motivating (a) older workers who are nearing the time when they are able to retire and (b) highly talented younger workers? Consider strategies for attracting and retaining such workers in your answer.
2. Your organisation is very concerned about the low performance levels of some of its employees. What motivation strategies can the organisation adopt to improve performance levels?
3. 'It is impossible to know what employees want but if you give them good salaries or wages they can use the money to find ways to fulfil their own needs. Employers do not need to worry about anything else.' Discuss this statement.
4. Explain the application of the integrated model of motivation to each of the following occupational groups at an early career stage: police officers and marketing research professionals.
5. Discuss ways in which (a) a major retail store could empower its retail assistants in their jobs and (b) a bank could empower its tellers in their work.
6. Imagine that you are the manager of a small furniture design and manufacturing company. Several of the staff members have complained that the rewards and benefits provided by the company are inequitable. What practical steps can you take to evaluate current policies and practices, or to ensure that perceptions of inequity are rectified?

1. 'The need theories of motivation are culturally based.' Evaluate this statement, examining in detail one of the need theories of motivation. In answering this question, you are encouraged to read an original work of the theorist associated with the theory you chose, such as David McClelland's *The achieving society*, or the works of Douglas McGregor and Abraham Maslow.

2. Many companies in the service sector — large hotels and resorts, for example — are implementing empowerment strategies to improve the quality of service provided to residents and guests. Search the internet for an example of such a company, with particular emphasis on strategies used to empower front-line staff.

Running project

Using the information you have available about your organisation, answer the following questions.

1. How does management try to motivate employees?
2. Based on your answer to question 1, does this vary between permanent and casual employees? How and why?
3. To what extent does management use money, both wages/salary and performance-based pay, as a motivator? Are the self-concepts or personal values of individuals likely to have an impact on their efforts at work?
4. How does the organisation manage the equity process?
5. How does management empower the organisation's employees?

Individual activity

Are you motivated to work hard at your studies?

Complete the questions in this exercise, based on your work as a university student. This exercise should help to explain the level of effort you put into your studies at university, while also clarifying the way the expectancy theory of motivation is intended to work.

Connection 1: Expectancy (probability that your effort will result in a certain level of performance)

How often is it true for you personally that the first factor leads to the second factor in your studies?

	Never	Sometimes	Often	Always
Spending twice as many hours on an assignment results in a higher grade.				
Studying consistently throughout the semester leads to better results.				
Participating in class activities enhances my understanding of the subject or improves my grades.				
Being organised helps me handle the demands of being a student.				

Connection 2: Instrumentality (probability that your performance will result in various rewards and outcomes)

How likely are you to receive the following rewards if you work hard (put in the hours, study consistently, participate, try to be organised)?

	Never	Not very likely	Fairly likely	Very likely
A better academic record/transcript				
More/better employment options				
Peer acceptance				
Sense of accomplishment				
Building my knowledge/skills				
Feeling good about myself				
Avoidance of pressure and stress				
A 'pat on the back' from my parents/family				
Reward — holiday, dinner out, etc.				
Other (specify)				

Connection 3: Valence (value of the reward outcome to you)

How important are each of the following rewards to you?

	Not important	Moderately important	Fairly important	Very important
A better academic record/transcript				
More/better employment options				
Peer acceptance				
Sense of accomplishment				
Building my knowledge/skills				
Feeling good about myself				
Avoidance of pressure and stress				
A 'pat on the back' from my parents/family				
Reward — holiday, dinner out, etc.				
Other (specify)				

After you have completed the questions, review your answers in the light of what expectancy theory tells us about motivation:

- What do your answers in the 'expectancy' section tell you about your level of confidence in your abilities, or the things that have discouraged/encouraged you in the past?

- Refer to your responses in the 'instrumentality' section. What do they tell you about the rewards you experience from your studies? Are they predominantly extrinsic, intrinsic or a mix of both?
- Compare the rewards you experience (or expect to experience) from your studies with the rewards you value from the 'valence' section. How well do they match one

another? Are there any rewards that you value highly but do not expect to receive?

- Assess the 'multiplier effect' to explain the level of effort you put into your studies. Compare your results with those of others in the class. If your motivation to study is low, what can you do to improve it?

What do you want from a job — motivators or hygienes?

Objectives

1. To help you better understand how job factors affect motivation
2. To help you realise that people are motivated by different factors
3. To better understand Herzberg's motivation theory and determine if you agree with it.
   Total time: 10–30 minutes

Preparation

Complete the following 'Motivators or hygienes' assessment before coming to class.

Most workers want job satisfaction. The following 12 job factors may contribute to job satisfaction. Rate each according to how important it is to you. Place a number on a scale of 1 to 5 on the line before each factor.

Very important	Somewhat important		Not important
5	4	3	2	1

_____ 1. An interesting job
_____ 2. A good boss
_____ 3. Recognition and appreciation for the work I do
_____ 4. The opportunity for advancement
_____ 5. A satisfying personal life
_____ 6. A prestigious or status job
_____ 7. Job responsibility
_____ 8. Good working conditions (nice office)
_____ 9. Sensible company rules, regulations, procedures and policies
_____ 10. The opportunity to grow through learning new things
_____ 11. A job I can do well and at which I can succeed
_____ 12. Job security

To determine if hygienes or motivators are important to you, place your scores below.

Hygiene factors		Motivational factors	
	Score		Score
2.	_____	1.	_____
5.	_____	3.	_____
6.	_____	4.	_____
8.	_____	7.	_____
9.	_____	10.	_____
12.	_____	11.	_____
Total points	_____	Total points	_____

Add each column vertically. Did you select hygienes or motivators as being more important to you?

Procedure for class discussion

1. Break into groups of five or six members and discuss the job factors selected as important by group members. Come to a consensus on the three factors that are most important to the group. If the group has other factors not listed in the activity, you may add them.
2. Select a representative from your group to write the group's three most important job factors on the board.
3. The lecturer can then identify the most important job factors for the entire class.
4. Are the class selections motivators or hygienes? As a class, discuss whether you agree with Herzberg's two-factor theory.[117]

The Bank of New Zealand (BNZ) has introduced a new business model by empowering branch managers to think and act like business owners. Chris Bayliss visited a store in Christchurch in June 2007, soon after joining the bank as the director of retail banking. It was just past 9.00 am on a Tuesday, and the store was still closed. Most days, it opened at 9.00 am, but on Tuesdays and Wednesdays, it opened at 9:30 am to accommodate staff training. Corporate policy dictated the exact same schedule for all the stores. The problem was the growing line of impatient customers outside the store. Bayliss asked the store manager if this was a regular occurrence. She said it was, and that it was very frustrating. He asked if she would prefer to open earlier and reschedule the training. She enthusiastically said she would, and was given the go-ahead.

Within days, news of the policy change had spread across BNZ's retail network. Soon Chris was fielding requests from managers throughout New Zealand, all of whom, it seemed, were eager for the same prerogatives that had just been granted the Christchurch store.

Bayliss decided to give all the bank's branches the flexibility to set their own hours. In Takapuna, a North Auckland suburb, BNZ became the first bank to open on Sunday mornings. This allowed the store to serve the thousands of customers at the local farmers' market. In South Island ski towns, store managers chose to stay open until late in the evening, so skiers could use the bank after a day on the slopes. Within city centres, many store managers chose to align their schedules with nearby retailers rather than keep bankers' hours. Within six months, nearly 95 per cent of BNZ's 180 stores had altered their opening hours in some way.

This shift raised concerns at BNZ's headquarters, where a policy change would ordinarily occur only after a lengthy risk assessment and input from all the major functional heads. Some of the objections were political, but others were more practical, and resulted in new processes that were meant to help the new policy succeed. For example, to deal with a concern from marketing that hand-lettered signs being used to advertise branch hours looked tacky, a software template was developed that allowed store managers to print out a simple sign displaying local opening hours.

Bayliss kept encouraging store teams to take the initiative in coming up with ideas to better serve BNZ's customers. One of the more creative ideas was a 'trailer' bank that can be pulled behind a vehicle. A local store towed the trailer onto a beach on New Year's Day. BNZ staff clad in BNZ T-shirts blew up balloons, fired up a barbecue, and chatted with people in the gathering crowd about BNZ products. The HR team was concerned about possible perceptions that employees were being exploited by being made to work on New Year's Day, and that cooking sausages was breaching health and safety regulations. Bayliss wasn't really worried because the staff members felt empowered by the freedom to experiment. If they had been told to do it, it never would have happened. But it was their idea, and no one bothered to ask permission.

Store managers felt like they had received a promotion. The bank hadn't really given them a promotion, but had changed their roles. They were now expected to manage, inspire and lead people; to deliver great customer service; to understand how the business worked; and to run it like their own.

These are good example of changes and innovations initiated by employees — based on their knowledge and experience on the front line, supported by senior leadership, and backed up by policy and technology adjustments. Ultimately, it reflects well on the company's identity and reputation, and helps reinforce the fresh new branding the bank introduced in October 2008.

Chris sums up the spirit of the change by saying, 'What everyone learned is that when you treat people like adults, they act like adults'.

Background

BNZ was founded in 1861 and, on the verge of bankruptcy, was purchased by the National Australia Bank Group in 1992. Part of BNZ's strategy was an increased focus on the performance of local branches (known as stores), which typically had four to seven team members — the store manager, a few tellers and a few salespeople.

Chris Bayliss was appointed as the director of retail banking in April 2007, and decided that his first priority was to build competitive advantage by moving BNZ from a banking to a retail mindset. By doing this, he was aiming to better serve and impress customers. Chris strongly believes that front line staff know how to run their local branch, and he wanted them to feel and act like it was their own business.[118]

Questions

1. Evaluate whether the situation described at BNZ fits your textbook definition of empowerment.
2. Why are the changes to organisational culture at BNZ so important in ensuring that empowerment is genuinely embraced throughout the organisation?
3. What management strategies and techniques (see stage 2 of figure 3.10) are evident in the case study? How important is each to achieving empowerment in the organisation?
4. How would the changes be likely to impact on the self-efficacy of BNZ employees?

End notes

1. DH Pink, *Drive: The surprising truth about what motivates us* (New York, NY: Riverhead Books, 2009).
2. Atlassian, '*About us — Shipit days*', www.atlassian.com.
3. K Brown, 'Searching for talent', *Management Today* (October 2006), pp. 13–15. Referring to a study by the Australian Industry Group (AIG); Readers are encouraged to consult the following sources for updated figures: Department of Education, Employment and Workplace Relations, Australian labour Market Update (January 2008 and May 2008), www.workplace.gov.au; Department of Employment and Workplace Relations, '*Skills in demand*' www.workplace.gov.au, State lists of skills shortages, www.workplace.gov.au.
4. Department of Labour (New Zealand), '*Skills in the labour market — February 2008*' (28 February 2008), www.dol.govt.nz.
5. Chamber of Commerce & Industry Queensland — *Skills and Training Factsheet*, http://deta.qld.gov.au/resources/pdf/fs2-skills-shortages.pdf.
6. Workpermit.com, '*Changes to New Zealand Skilled Migrant Category*' (1 February 2008), www.workpermit.com; Department of Labour (New Zealand), '*Skills in the labour market — February 2008*' (28 February 2008), www.dol.govt.nz; ABC News, 'Immigration cut only temporary: Evans', *ABC News* (16 March 2009), www.abc.net.au/news.
7. Australian Institute of Management, '*National Salary Survey*' (2014).
8. Australian Centre for Retail Studies, Monash University, *Attracting and retaining a cross-generational workforce*, (Melbourne: ACRS, July 2007), www.buseco.monash.edu.au.
9. The Global Recruiter, '*AIM Survey Published*', www.theglobalrecruiter.com/news, (n.d.).
10. 'Skills shortages elevate HR to the boardroom', *Human Resources* (23 January 2007), pp. 1, 5.
11. D Parker, '[Skill shortage:] crisis ahead', *Management Today* (August 2004), pp. 26–9.
12. Australian Bureau of Statistics, '*Quick stats: New South Wales*' (2007), www.censusdata.abs.gov.au; and House of Representatives, Parliament of Australia, 'Navigating the ageing minefield', *About the House* (June 2007), pp. 19–25, www.aph.gov.au.
13. S Encel and R Ranzijn, 'Age and employment' in A Borowski, S Encel and E Ozanne (eds), *Longevity and social change in Australia* (Sydney: UNSW Press, 2007), p. 143.
14. '*Tips for hiring mature-age workers*', Fair Work Ombudsman (Australian Government) (21 March 2014).
15. Statistics New Zealand, '*National Population Projections: 2011 (base)–2061*', www.stats.govt.nz (19 July 2012).
16. C Donaldson, citing research by Aruspex in 'Workforce planning stumps HR', *Human Resources* (24 July 2007), pp. 1, 8; and citing research by Manpower in 'Human capital topics business risks' and 'Employers napping on ageing workforce', *Human Resources* (15 May 2007), pp. 5, 7.
17. 'HR must break the generational hoodoo', *Human Resources* (10 July 2007), pp. 1, 7.
18. K Shacklock and L Fulop, 'Managing older worker exit and re-entry practices: A "revolving door"', *Asia Pacific Journal of Human Resources*, vol. 45, no. 2 (August 2007), pp. 151–167.
19. 'CEOs concerned about workplace wellness', *Human Resources* (6 March 2007), p. 5.
20. T Myers, 'Our workforce is aging', *Management* (New Zealand, March 2007), pp. 60–62, 65, 67.
21. Shacklock and Fulop, op. cit.
22. ibid.
23. '*Responding to the challenge of Australia's ageing workforce: A NSW public sector perspective*', www.deloitte.com (Sydney: Deloitte Touche Tohmatsu, 2010).
24. NSW Business Chamber, '*The benefits of an ageing workforce*', www.nswbusinesschamber.com.au (2010).
25. Statistics New Zealand, '*National Population Projections: 2011 (base)–2061*', www.stats.govt.nz (19 July 2012).

26. J. Davey, '*Workforce ageing — an issue for employers*'. Working paper 08/04. (Wellington: Institute of Policy Studies and New Zealand Institute of Management, 2008). http://ips.ac.nz.

27. R. Birchfield, '*NZIM — Research: overaged are underrated — Implications of an Ageing Workforce*'. (Wellington: New Zealand Institute of Management, 2008).

28. The Treasury, '*Australia's demographic challenges*', demographics.treasury.gov.au.

29. Department of Immigration and Border Protection, '*Migration Programme statistics (2008–2014)*, www.immi.gov.au.

30. 'Roadworthy', *HRMonthly* (December 2007/January 2008), pp. 30–31.

31. Australian Bureau of Statistics, '*Scenarios for Australia's aging population*' (Australian Social Trends, 2004, 4102.0), www.abs.gov.au.

32. Department of Immigration and Citizenship, '*Is your occupation in demand?*', www.immi.gov.au (data for 30 July 2007).

33. ibid.

34. Department of Education, Employment and Workplace Relations, *Australian Labour Market Update* (January 2008), www.workplace.gov.au; Department of Labour (NZ), '*Skills in the labour market at a glance*' (28 February 2008), www.dol.govt.nz.

35. AJ Ali and A Al-Owaihan, 'Islamic work ethic: a critical review', *Cross-Cultural Management: An International Journal*, vol. 15, no. 1 (2008), pp. 5–19.

36. Human Rights Commission, *Brain gain: Migrant workers in New Zealand* (2009).

37. ibid.

38. ibid.

39. A Bracey, 'Red tape, bureaucracy 'strangling' general practice', *Medical Observer*, Cirrus Media Pty Limited (December 2013), www.medicalobserver.com.au.

40. ibid.

41. See JP Campbell, MD Dunnette, EE Lawler III and KE Weick, Jr, *Managerial behavior performance and effectiveness* (New York: McGraw-Hill, 1970), ch. 15.

42. LW Porter, 'Job attitudes in management: II. Perceived importance of needs as a function of job level', *Journal of Applied Psychology*, vol. 47 (April 1963), pp. 141–8.

43. DT Hall and KE Nougaim, 'An examination of Maslow's need hierarchy in an organizational setting', *Organizational Behavior and Human Performance*, vol. 3 (1968), pp. 12–35.

44. LW Porter, 'Job attitudes in management: IV. Perceived deficiencies in need fulfillment as a function of size of company', *Journal of Applied Psychology*, vol. 47 (December 1963), pp. 386–97.

45. JM Ivancevich, 'Perceived need satisfactions of domestic versus overseas managers', *Journal of Applied Psychology*, vol. 54 (August 1969), pp. 274–8.

46. MA Wahba and LG Bridwell, 'Maslow reconsidered: a review of research on the need hierarchy theory', *Academy of Management Proceedings* (1974), pp. 514–20; EE Lawler III and JL Shuttle, 'A causal correlation test of the need hierarchy concept', *Organizational Behavior and Human Performance*, vol. 7 (1973), pp. 265–87.

47. ME Koltko-Rivera, 'Rediscovering the later version of Maslow's hierarchy of needs: self-transcendence and opportunities for theory, research and unification', *Review of General Psychology*, vol. 10, no. 4 (2006), pp. 302–317.

48. 'Ageing population will demand more private/public cooperation', *Management* (New Zealand: August 2007), pp. 6–7.

49. P Stock, 'Generation Y is not a mutation', *Human Resources* (27 November, 2007), p. 3.

50. C Donaldson, 'Much ado about nothing: generational change', *Human Resources* (27 November 2007), p. 3.

51. See NJ Adler, *International dimensions of organizational behavior*, 2nd ed. (Boston: PWS-Kent, 1991), p. 153; RM Hodgetts and F Luthans, *International management* (New York: McGraw-Hill, 1991).

52. S Blanc, '*Business network giants face China "guanxi" battle*', Phys.org (24 February 2013), phys.org.

53. Adler, op. cit., ch. 11.

54. S Lovett, LC Simmons & R Kali, 'Guanxi versus the market: ethics and efficiency', *Journal of International Business Studies*, vol. 30, no. 2 (1999), pp. 231–47.

55. See CP Alderfer, 'An empirical test of a new theory of human needs', *Organizational behavior and human performance*, vol. 4 (1969), pp. 142–75; CP Alderfer, *Existence, relatedness, and growth* (New York: The Free Press, 1972); B Schneider and ClP Alderfer, 'Three studies of need satisfaction in organizations', *Administrative Science Quarterly*, vol. 18 (1973), pp. 489–505.

56. L Tracy, 'A dynamic living systems model of work motivation', *Systems Research*, vol. 1 (1984), pp. 191–203; J Rauschenberger, N Schmidt and JE Hunter, 'A test of the need hierarchy concept by a Markov model of change in need strength', *Administrative Science Quarterly*, vol. 25 (1980), pp. 654–70.

57. CP Alderfer and RA Guzzo, 'Life experiences and adults enduring strength of desires in organizations', *Administrative Science Quarterly*, vol. 24 (1979), pp. 347–61.

58. L Song, Y Wang and J Wei, 'Revisiting motivation preference within the Chinese context: an empirical study', *Chinese Management Studies*, vol. 1, no. 1 (2007), pp. 25–41.

59. J Rauschenberger, N Schmitt & JE Hunter, 'A test of the need hierarchy concept by a Markov model of change in need strength', *Administrative Science Quarterly* (1980), pp. 654–70.

60. B Verplanken and RW Holland, 'Motivated decision making: effects of activation and self-centrality of values on choices and behavior', *Journal of Personality and Social Psychology*, vol. 82, no. 3 (2002), p. 434.

61. A Christie, P Jordan, A Troth and S Lawrence, 'Testing the links between emotional intelligence and motivation', *Journal of Management and Organisation*, vol. 13, no. 3 (September 2007), pp. 212–226.

62. Sources pertinent to this discussion are DC McClelland, *The achieving society* (New York: Van Nostrand, 1961); DC McClelland, 'Business, drive and national achievement', *Harvard Business Review*, vol. 40 (July/August 1962), pp. 99–112; DC McClelland, 'That urge to achieve', *Think* (November/December 1966), pp. 19–32; GH Litwin and RA

Stringer, *Motivation and organizational climate* (Boston: Division of Research, Harvard Business School, 1966), pp. 18–25.

63. G Harris, 'To know why men do what they do: a conversation with David C. McClelland', *Psychology Today*, vol. 4 (January 1971), pp. 35–9.

64. EH Erikson, *Childhood and society*, 2nd ed. (New York: Vintage, 1963).

65. P Miron and DC McClelland, 'The impact of achievement motivation training in small businesses', *California Management Review* (Summer 1979), pp. 13–28.

66. RJ Taormina and S Kin-Mei Lao, 'Measuring Chinese entrepreneurial motivation', *International Journal of Entrepreneurial Behaviour & Research*, vol. 13, no. 4 (2007), pp. 200–21.

67. DC McClelland and DH Burnham, 'Power is the great motivator', *Harvard Business Review*, vol. 54 (March–April 1976), pp. 100–10; DC McClelland and RE. Boyatzis, 'Leadership motive pattern and long-term success in management', *Journal of Applied Psychology*, vol. 67 (1982), pp. 737–43.

68. CM Kelly, 'The interrelationship of ethics and power in today's organizations', *Organizational Dynamics*, vol. 5 (Summer 1987); C Farrell, 'Gutfreund gives Salmon's young lions more power', *Business Week*, vol. 32 (20 October 1986); J Solomon, 'Heirs apparent to chief executives often trip over prospect of power', *Wall Street Journal*, vol. 29 (24 March 1987).

69. The complete two-factor theory is well explained by Herzberg and his associates in F Herzberg, B Mausner and B Bloch Synderman, *The motivation to work*, 2nd ed. (New York: John Wiley & Sons, 1967); and F Herzberg, 'One more time: how do you motivate employees?', *Harvard Business Review*, vol. 46 (January/February 1968), pp. 53–62.

70. *'What's Working'* — the Mercer survey of Australia at work (Mercer Human Resource Consulting, 2004).

71. *'What's Working'* — the Mercer survey of Australia at work (Mercer Human Resource Consulting, 2011).

72. L Branham, *The 7 hidden reasons employees leave: how to recognize the subtle signs and act before it's too late* (New York: AMACOM, 2005).

73. Seek, *Satisfaction and motivation study 2010*, www.seek.co.nz.

74. L Lambert, 'Exit stage right', *HRMonthly* (February 2008), pp. 28–31.

75. M Richtel. 'House cleaning, the dinner? Silicon Valley perks come home,' *The New York Times* (October 2012).

76. B Ballenger. 'Best Job Perks: Companies Provide Employees With Everything From Catered Meals To Free Alcohol', *Huffington Post* (26 October 2012), www.huffingtonpost.com.

77. 'Maintaining momentum', *HRMonthly* (December 2007/ January 2008), pp. 24–25.

78. F Davis and R Lansbury (eds), *Managing together* (Melbourne: Longman, 1996).

79. Australian Employee Ownership Association (AEOA), *'News & Publications — 2008'* (including link to article 'Employee ownership around the globe'), www.aeoa.org.au.

80. ibid.

81. Australian Government (Department of Employment and Workplace Relations), 'Employee share ownership in Australia: Aligning interests' (*TNS Social Research*, 2012), www.employeeownership.com.au.

82. Wesfarmers, *'Letter to Australian Securities Exchange re Wesfarmers Employee Share Ownership Plan'*, (27 November 2007), www.wesfarmers.com.au (May 2008); Foster's, Careers *'Working with Foster's — The Benefits'*, http://careers.fosters.com.au (May 2008); and *Australian Employee Ownership Association (AEOA) News* (May 2008), www.aeoa.org.au.

83. See RJ House and LA Wigdor, 'Herzberg's dual-factor theory of job satisfaction and motivation: a review of the evidence and a criticism', *Personnel Psychology*, vol. 20 (Winter 1967), pp. 369–89; S Kerr, A Harlan and R Stogdill, 'Preference for motivator and hygiene factors in a hypothetical interview situation', *Personnel Psychology*, vol. 27 (Winter 1974), pp. 109–24.

84. See N King, 'A clarification and evaluation of the two-factor theory of job satisfaction', *Psychological Bulletin* (July 1970), pp. 18–31; M Dunnette, J Campbell and M Hakel, 'Factors contributing to job satisfaction and job dissatisfaction in six occupational groups', *Organizational Behavior and Human Performance* (May 1967), pp. 143–74; House and Wigdor, op. cit.

85. Adler, op. cit., ch. 6; NJ Adler and JT Graham, 'Cross cultural interaction: the international comparison fallacy', *Journal of International Business Studies* (Fall 1989), pp. 515–37; F Herzberg, 'Workers' needs: the same around the world', *Industry Week* (27 September 1987), pp. 29–32.

86. R Bjerke, N Ind and D De Paoli, 'The impact of aesthetics on employee satisfaction and motivation', *EuroMed Journal of Business*, vol. 2, no. 1 (2007), pp. 57–73.

87. See, for example, JS Adams, 'Toward an understanding of inequality', *Journal of Abnormal and Social Psychology*, vol. 67 (1963), pp. 422–36; JS Adams, 'Inequity in social exchange', in L Berkowitz (ed.), *Advances in experimental social psychology*, vol. 2 (New York: Academic Press, 1965), pp. 267–300.

88. See 'Toronto Sun Publishing Corporation', *Wall Street Journal* (9 March 1990), pp. B1–B2.

89. GL Blakely, MC Andrews and RH Moorman, 'The moderating effects of equity sensitivity on the relationship between organizational justice and organizational citizenship behaviors', *Journal of Business and Psychology*, vol. 20, no. 2 (2005), pp. 259–73.

90. RC Huseman, JD Hatfield and EW Miles, 'A new perspective on equity theory: the equity sensitivity construct', *The Academy of Management Review*, vol. 12, no. 2 (1987), pp. 222–34.

91. P Dowling, R Schuler and D Welch, *International dimensions of human resource management* (Melbourne: Wadsworth, 1994).

92. *The Economist*, 'The glass-ceiling index: Where is best to be a working woman in the rich world' (7 March 2013), www.economist.com/blogs.

93. *The Economist*, 'The glass-ceiling index: The best and worst places to be a working woman' (8 March 2014), www.economist.com/news.

94. P Dougan and M Backhouse, 'Bridging the gender pay gap: Pay-up time at public service', *NZ Herald* (2 April 2014).

95. Statistics New Zealand, *The New Zealand Income Survey* (June 2013 quarter), http://www.stats.govt.nz.

96. Australian Government Workplace Gender Equality Agency. '*National gender pay gap at 17.1%, employers tackle pay inequity*' (February 2014).

97. op. cit.

98. VH Vroom, *Work and motivation* (New York: John Wiley & Sons, 1964).

99. For an excellent review, see RT Mowday, 'Equity theory predictions of behavior in organizations' in RM Steers and LW Porter (eds), *Motivation and work behavior*, 4th ed. (New York: McGraw-Hill, 1987), pp. 89–110.

100. PW Mulvey, PV LeBlanc, RL Heneman and M McInerney, 'Study finds that knowledge of pay process can beat out amount of pay in employee retention, organizational effectiveness', *Journal of Organizational Excellence*, vol. 21, no. 4 (2002), pp. 29–42.

101. GR Salancik and J Pfeffer, 'A social information processing approach to job attitudes and task design', *Administrative Science Quarterly*, vol. 23 (June 1978), pp. 224–53.

102. See TR Mitchell, 'Expectancy models of job satisfaction, occupational preference and effort: a theoretical, methodological, and empirical appraisal', *Psychological Bulletin*, vol. 81 (1974), pp. 1053–77; MA Wahba and RJ House, 'Expectancy theory in work and motivation: some logical and methodological issues', *Human Relations*, vol. 27 (January 1974), pp. 121–47; T Connolly, 'Some conceptual and methodological issues in expectancy models of work performance motivation', *Academy of Management Review*, vol. 1 (October 1976), pp. 37–47; T Mitchell, 'Expectancy-value models in organizational psychology' in N Feather (ed.), *Expectancy, incentive and action*, (New York: Erlbaum, 1980).

103. Mitchell (1982), op. cit.

104. LW Porter and EE Lawler III, *Managerial attitudes and performance* (Homewood, IL: Richard D. Irwin, 1968).

105. JW Hart, MF Stasson, JM Mahoney and P Story, 'The big five and achievement motivation: Exploring the relationship between personality and a two-factor model of motivation', *Individual Differences Research*, vol. 5, no. 4 (2007), pp. 267–274.

106. This integrated model is not only based on the Porter and Lawler model but is consistent with the kind of comprehensive approach suggested by Evans in a recent review. See MG Evans, 'Organizational behavior: the central role of motivation' in JG Hunt and JD Blair (eds), *1986 yearly review of management of the Journal of Management*, vol. 12 (1986), pp. 203–22.

107. J Humphreys, 'Adapting the congruent temperament model with culturally specific work motivation elements', *Cross-Cultural Management: An International Journal*, vol. 14, no. 3 (2007), pp. 202–216.

108. A Kenworthy and A Gifford. 'NZI Sustainable Business Awards: Breaking the business-as-usual mould', *NZ Herald* (24 November 2013).

109. For further explanation of alternatives to process and content theories of motivation, see N Leonard, L Beauvais and R Scholl, 'Work motivation: the incorporation of self-concept-based processes', *Human Relations*, vol. 52, no. 8 (1999), pp. 969–98; R McKenna, 'Identity, not motivation: the key to employee–organisation relations' in R Wiesner and B Millett, *Management and organisational behaviour* (Brisbane: John Wiley & Sons, 2000), pp. 35–45.

110. E Camilleri, 'Antecedents affecting public service motivation', *Personnel Review*, vol. 36, no. 3 (2007), pp. 356–377.

111. P Holland, B Allen and B Cooper, '*What nurses want. Analysis of the first national survey on nurses' attitudes to work and work conditions in Australia*' (Clayton, Victoria: Department of Management, Monash University, 2012).

112. R Surette, '*Fixing what ails nurses in the health-care system*', Rabble.ca (7 April 2014).

113. N North and F Hughes, 'A systems perspective on nursing productivity', *Journal of Health Organization and Management*, vol. 26, iss. 2 (2012), pp. 192–214.

114. C Furman and R Caplan, 'Applying the Toyota production system: Using a patient safety alert system to reduce error', *The Joint Commission Journal on Quality and Patient Safety*, vol. 33, iss. 7 (2007), pp. 376–86.

115. ME Gist, 'Self-efficacy: implications in organizational behavior and human resource management', *Academy of Management Review*, vol. 12 (1987), pp. 472–85; A Bandura, 'Self-efficacy mechanism in human agency', *American Psychologist*, vol. 37 (1987), pp. 122–47.

116. JA Conger and RN Kanungo, 'The empowerment process: integrating theory and practice', *Academy of Management Review*, vol. 13, no. 3 (1988), pp. 471–82.

117. RN Lussier, *Human relations in organizations: a skill building approach*, 2nd ed. (Homewood, IL: Richard D. Irwin, 1993). Used with permission.

118. C Bayliss, 'Not just an ordinary day at the beach: organization innovation and employee empowerment at the Bank of New Zealand', *Management Innovation eXchange* (10 August 2010), www.managementexchange.com; '*BNZ: case study in decentralized, employee-led strategy*' (25 August 2009), www.elevatorview.com.

CHAPTER 4

LEARNING, REINFORCEMENT AND SELF-MANAGEMENT

LEARNING OBJECTIVES

After studying this chapter, you should be able to:

1. outline the four general approaches to learning

2. explain organisational behavioural modification and how reinforcement strategies are involved in it

3. discuss social learning theory and behavioural self-management

4. explain how to manage pay as an extrinsic reward

5. discuss the concepts of the learning organisation and the teaching organisation.

THE UNINTENDED CONSEQUENCES OF REWARDS — WHEN INCENTIVES BACKFIRE

'What gets rewarded gets repeated'
John E Jones (American lawyer and jurist from Pennsylvania)

A good example of how complex organisational incentives can be comes from the Chilean city Santiago; a city of six million people. The bus system in Santiago de Chile was voted the city's worst public service in 2003. The bus routes were very long and inefficient and the treatment of passengers was poor. On top of all this, the level of noise and environmental pollution was high due to poor maintenance of petrol engines as was the rate of accidents due to both careless driving and brake failure.[1]

Two systems of bus driver compensation exist in Santiago. Most drivers are paid per passenger transported, while a second system compensates drivers with a fixed wage. For the drivers whose wages depended on the number of fares sold, there was fierce competition for passengers. Although this incentive system did motivate drivers to begin their route on time, take shorter breaks, and drive efficiently, it also had serious unintended consequences.

Drivers being paid per passenger were incentivised to compete at street level with other buses, even those from the same company. This resulted in dangerous races to busy stops, or waiting for a red light in congested areas to prolong the stay at a busy junction (as buses could be boarded anywhere), or driving past stops with only a few passengers waiting and refusing schoolchildren altogether (they paid only one-third of the adult fare)![2]

Studies reported that Santiago's transit buses caused one fatal accident every three days and that drivers paid per passenger caused twice as many traffic accidents as drivers paid per hour. On the other hand, a typical bus passenger in Santiago waited roughly 10 per cent longer for a bus on a fixed-wage route relative to an incentive-contract route.[3]

Santiago now pays drivers partly by the distance travelled. Unfortunately, these drivers are no longer motivated to ensure that passengers pay the fare (about one-third are freeloaders), and drivers will pocket money paid by passengers who are willing to pay a lower fare in return for not having a ticket!

Introduction

The information age is the backdrop for global business.[4] New strategic information generates daily in vast quantities while current knowledge frequently becomes obsolete. This makes learning a critical factor for the survival of both the individual and the organisation.

In this chapter, we address three major questions.

1. *How do people acquire the knowledge, skills and competencies they need to be valuable participants in the workplace?* To answer this question, we need to understand the four different learning methods. These methods explain how we learn from our experiences of acting, thinking, observing and reflecting on our behaviour and interaction with others.
2. *How can a manager allocate extrinsic rewards, including pay, so desired work behaviours are encouraged and facilitated, rather than discouraged and inhibited?* To examine this question

we need to be especially familiar with learning and the management of various forms of reinforcement and rewards. It is possible to use extrinsic rewards effectively; they are an important part of any broad-based motivational strategy.

3. *What is organisational learning?* In this section we introduce and critically assess some of the elements necessary to combine individual learning and create a learning organisation. The notion of the teaching organisation reminds us the continual renewal of all organisational structures and processes is now essential for organisations to maintain competencies.

At the individual level, learning, reinforcement and self-management are important building blocks in organisational behaviour. In addition, rewards systems may help the modification of behaviours to a desired state. In this chapter, we discuss each of these topics and some ways in which managers can use them in the organisations of today and tomorrow.

At the organisational level, much is written about organisational learning and the learning and teaching organisation. We will briefly introduce these concepts at the end of this chapter after examining the importance of learning for the individual.

Learning as a modification of work behaviour

There is no doubt what people *do* is critical to organisational success and the scientific study of human behaviour has a central role in understanding and potentially influencing behaviours at work. So, it can be argued 'behaviour', rather than thought processes or feelings, is the unit of analysis in organisational behaviour research.[5] This is a philosophical stance adopted by **behaviourists**, who generally argue that in order to understand human behaviour scientists must focus on observational behaviour *deriving* from internal psychological processes.

Behaviourists argue that any construct that cannot be directly observed, such as internal psychological states, emotions and feelings, will fail to provide a systematic understanding of human behaviour. Rather, external exhibitions and the consequences of behaviour are given priority.

For example, BF Skinner and other learning theorists argue behaviour is environmentally controlled.[6] While work psychologists believe this represents a rather limited view of human psychology, behaviourist ideas have been successfully applied in organisations and many behavioural concepts are being incorporated into related theories, such as social cognitive theory. These areas of applied research help managers modify behaviours and influence the *willingness* of workers to improve overall performance.

Learning is defined as a relatively permanent change in behaviour resulting from experience. Learning is the process by which people acquire the competencies and beliefs which affect their behaviour in organisations. An understanding of basic learning principles will deepen your perspectives on the concepts and theories of motivation discussed in chapter 3. Managers with such awareness are well positioned to influence the willingness of their employees, necessary to achieve maximum positive outcomes from their work.

It is important to differentiate between learning and performance. Learning refers to the process of acquiring the capacity to perform through attaining the requisite skills or competencies. *Performance* implies the individual, in addition to acquiring these requisite skills or competencies, is motivated to engage in the appropriate behaviour to apply the learning.

Learning in organisations can occur in many ways and there are many different approaches attempting to maximise learning in the workplace. New employees often introduce new skills and competencies acquired in a former workplace or through formal education. In addition, many organisations invest considerable sums of money in improving the skills and competencies of their workforce through formal training programs. For example, management development training and education has attracted significant investment globally.

Behaviourists study observable behaviours and consequences of behaviour, and reject subjective human psychological states as topics for study.

Learning is a relatively permanent change in behaviour which occurs as a result of experience.

OBinAction

Learning from failure

Organisations are widely encouraged to learn from their failures, but it is advice most find easier to advocate than to truly embrace. Large and well-publicised organisational failures such as the Challenger shuttle tragedy (where the shuttle broke apart 73 seconds into the flight killing the whole crew in 1986),[7] the Colorado South Canyon firefighter deaths (which resulted in the deaths of 14 firefighters in 1994),[8] and the Enron accounting scandals (where the company lost billions of dollars in 2001 and company executives were indicted for a variety of charges and imprisoned) clearly exemplify the importance of learning from mistakes.

There are usually multiple causes of these types of large failures that are either ignored or that have become deeply embedded in organisational practice and are not viewed as mistakes. Research in organisational contexts ranging from the operating theatres to the boardrooms suggests that best practice in organisational learning requires proactively identifying and learning from small failures.[9] Small failures are often overlooked because, at the time they happen, they appear to be insignificant mistakes or one-off events, and so organisations fail to make good use of these important learning opportunities. Researchers in this area have found that when small failures are not widely identified, discussed and analysed, it is very difficult for larger failures to be prevented.[10]

It is important, however, to note that a great deal of learning in organisations also occurs informally in an unstructured and haphazard manner.

There are four general approaches to learning:

1. classical conditioning
2. operant conditioning
3. cognitive learning
4. social learning.

Each approach offers potentially valuable insights for managers, as well as the field of organisational behaviour.

Classical conditioning is a form of learning through association that involves the manipulation of stimuli to influence behaviour.

Stimulus is something that incites action.

Classical conditioning

Classical conditioning is a form of learning through association. This type of learning involves the manipulation of a **stimulus** (or stimuli) to influence behaviour (figure 4.1). We define a stimulus as something that incites action. Classical conditioning associates a previously neutral stimulus — that is, one that has no effect on behaviour — with another stimulus that does affect behaviour. The former thus becomes a conditioned stimulus, which, when it occurs, also draws forth the now conditioned response. This process is illustrated by the well-known experiments conducted by Ivan Pavlov, the Russian psychologist who 'taught' dogs to salivate (conditioned response) at the sound of a tone (conditioned stimulus) by ringing a bell just prior to feeding the dogs. The sight of the food caused the dogs to salivate. Eventually, the dogs 'learned', through the association of the bell with the presentation of meat, to salivate at the ringing of the bell alone. Classical conditioning is often termed *stimulus–response learning*.

Involuntary and reflexive human behaviours are also susceptible to classical conditioning. These are often associated with strong emotional reactions or vivid and painful experiences. For example, after witnessing a car crash at a certain intersection, passing this intersection again is likely to bring back this vivid memory, resulting in an emotional response.

The same principle of classical conditioning, in which two previously unrelated things (the stimulus and the response) are brought together in the mind of the person, applies in the work setting. However, both the manager and the employee may take a long time to figure out the stimulus and response connection shown in figure 4.1. In addition, classical conditioning at a higher order takes place where a second or third stimulus is introduced. Pavlov introduced a shape to the tone and, after several trials, dogs salivated to the shape alone. This is known as second-order conditioning. Humans may be conditioned to third or even higher orders. For example, consider the car crash already described. When the crash was seen, there was a certain piece of music playing. Hearing the music can cause a strong emotional response (fear and anxiety) that leads to altered driving behaviour. Now imagine it was raining at the time. The automated response of fear and anxiety is created when passing the place of the accident, when hearing the music and when it rains. The classical conditioning approach helps managers gain a better understanding of the emotional reactions of their staff. Further, the general stimulus–response notion sets the stage for operant conditioning.

Operant conditioning

Operant conditioning is learning achieved when the consequences of a behaviour lead to changes in the probability of its occurrence. You may think of operant conditioning as learning through reinforcement. Figure 4.1 clarifies how this operant, or behaviourist, approach contrasts with classical conditioning. The former approach views behaviour as 'operating' on its environment to produce consequences that affect its future occurrence. Operant conditioning is often termed stimulus–response learning that produces behaviour that will not appear spontaneously.

The noted psychologist BF Skinner popularised operant conditioning as a way of controlling behaviour by manipulating its consequences.[11] The method consists of a three-component framework: antecedents–behaviour–consequences, sometimes called ABC contingencies or 'if/then' relationships. Returning to figure 4.1, the antecedent (A) — the condition leading up to behaviour — may be an agreement between the boss and the employee to work overtime as needed. If the employee engages in the overtime behaviour (B), the consequence (C) — the result of the behaviour — is the boss's praise.

Whereas classical conditioning works only on involuntary behaviours, operant conditioning has a broader application to almost any human behaviour. So, according to some behaviourists, operant conditioning has substantial applications in the workplace, while others protest that people are much more self-controlled and thinking (a process also known as cognitive learning).

Operant conditioning is the process of controlling behaviour by manipulating its consequences.

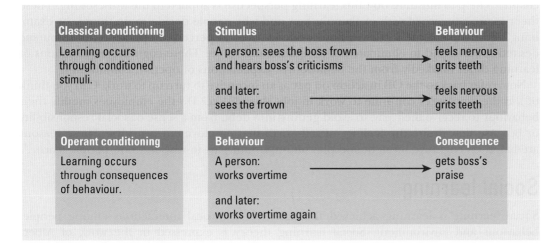

Classical conditioning	Stimulus	Behaviour
Learning occurs through conditioned stimuli.	A person: sees the boss frown and hears boss's criticisms	feels nervous grits teeth
	and later: sees the frown	feels nervous grits teeth

Operant conditioning	Behaviour	Consequence
Learning occurs through consequences of behaviour.	A person: works overtime	gets boss's praise
	and later: works overtime again	

FIGURE 4.1 Differences between the classical and operant conditioning approaches to learning

OBinAction

Pay for performance (incentive pay)

Although there is great deal of research indicating that money alone cannot motivate, engage or inspire employees (see, for example, the reinforcement perspectives section later in the chapter), the fact remains that, for many people, their pay is the reason they go to work and can work well in some contexts and when carefully administered. The following quote is from a farmer in Tennessee who implemented pay for performance in his plant nursery.

> My labour costs went down 50 per cent for the same amount of production … The hard-working person was making [twice, on a per hour average, than the slower ones]. I use incentive pay for other jobs as well … I wish I could use it for everything![12]

Researchers from Berkeley University (California) describe 'casual incentives' where workers never know when they will be given a reward (i.e. rewards are given on a variable interval schedule).[13] Casual rewards may include a few words of praise for a job well done, a thank-you, fifty dollars, or dinner at a local restaurant. The researchers suggest employers may want to allow workers to choose from a menu of several rewards.

When a reward is accompanied by specific praise such as, 'This is for packing twice as much fruit while reducing waste', the reward is more effective than simply, 'Thanks for all your hard work'.

To be of use, these casual incentives must be given at unexpected intervals; this is because a 'regular' bonus soon becomes part of the expected compensation package. Casual incentives communicate to employees that you have noticed their efforts.

Cognitive learning

Cognitive learning is learning achieved by thinking about the perceived relationship between events and individual goals and expectations.

Cognitive learning is learning achieved by thinking about the perceived relationship between events and individual goals and expectations. The process motivation theories reviewed in chapter 3 help to illustrate how this learning perspective is applied to the work setting. These theories are concerned with explaining how and why people decide to do things, by examining how people come to view various work activities as perceived opportunities to pursue desired rewards and to eliminate felt inequities and so on. These cognitive explanations of learning differ markedly from the behaviourist explanations of operant conditioning.

Now, refer back to the OB in action on pay as an incentive to turn up to work. Can you think of *why* the employees continue to work in jobs they dislike? Do the employees modify their behaviour to receive their pay, to avoid getting into debt, from a sense of social responsibility or because they desire the feelings of self-worth that employment provides? These reasons are based on cognitive thought and play an important part in why and how people learn.[14]

Social learning

Social learning is learning achieved through the reciprocal interaction between people and their environments.

Social learning is learning achieved through the reciprocal interactions among people, behaviour and environment. Social learning theory is expressed in the work of Albert Bandura[15] and uses such reciprocal interactions to integrate operant and cognitive learning approaches; that is, environmental determinism and self-determinism are combined. Behaviour is seen not simply as a function of external antecedents and consequences, or as only being caused by internal needs, satisfaction or expectations (see chapter 3), but as a combination of the two. Social learning theory stresses our capacity to learn from reinforcement and punishments experienced by other people and ourselves. Figure 4.2 illustrates and elaborates on this reciprocal interaction notion.

In figure 4.2, the individual uses modelling or vicarious learning to acquire behaviour by observing and imitating others. Then, the person attempts to acquire these behaviours by modelling them through practice. The 'models' could be the person's parents, friends or even well-known celebrities. In the work situation, the model may be a manager or coworker who demonstrates desired behaviours. Mentors or senior workers who befriend more inexperienced protégés can also be very important models. Interesting psychology-based work has investigated the link between television and real-life professional practice. The Resource Centre for Women in Science, Engineering and Technology (SET) in the United Kingdom recently hosted a conference presenting research into television plot lines about women with non-traditional occupations such as science, technology and engineering. SET has been eager to encourage higher participation rates of women in these occupations through modelling the occupations on television.[16] The latest research shows that in educational programs (including cartoons), the ratio of words spoken is 70:30 in favour of men.[17] In addition, a far narrower range of characters and a clearer set of stereotypes are portrayed for women than men. It is clear that gender misperceptions continue to filter through the social learning situations of popular culture.

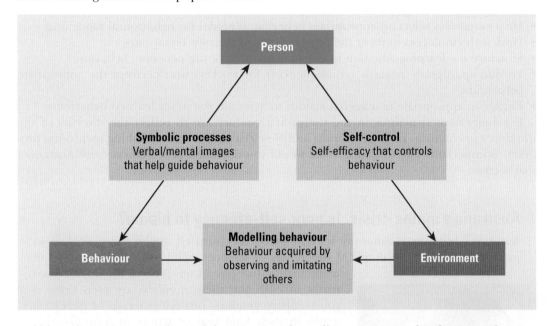

FIGURE 4.2 Social learning model

Source: Adapted from R Kreitner and F Luthans, 'A social learning approach to behavioral management: radical behaviorists "mellowing out"', *Organizational Dynamics* (Autumn 1984), p. 55.

Although mentors or role models may come from diverse sources, the shortage of appropriate mentors or role models is often a concern in the contemporary workplace. Indeed, some have argued a shortage of mentors for women in management is a major constraint on their progression up the career ladder. It is also a leading reason why many women are leaving the corporate world and moving into self-employment.[18]

If management structures are to reflect the diversity of the workforce in countries such as Australia, then establishing mentoring programs is important.

Self-efficacy and social learning

The symbolic processes depicted in figure 4.2 are also important in social learning. Words and symbols used by managers and others in the workplace can help communicate values, beliefs and goals and serve as guides to a person's behaviour. A 'thumbs up' or other symbol from the boss, for example, lets you know your behaviour is appropriate.

At the same time, an individual's self-control is important in influencing his or her behaviour. Self-efficacy is an important part of such self-control. People with high self-efficacy believe:

- they have the necessary ability for a given job
- they are capable of the effort required
- they are motivated to perform the required behaviour
- no outside events will hinder them from obtaining their desired performance level.[19]

In other words, high self-efficacy people believe they can manage their environmental cues and consequences and their cognitive processes to control their own behaviour. People with low self-efficacy believe, regardless of how hard they try, they cannot manage their environment well enough to be successful. For example, if you feel self-efficacious as a student, a low grade on one test will encourage you to study harder, talk to the lecturer or do other things to enable you to do well the next time. In contrast, a person low in self-efficacy might drop the course or give up studying.

Even people who are high in self-efficacy do not control their environment entirely. As a manager, you can have an impact on the environment and other factors shown in figure 4.2 (even though the impact is less than in the operant approach). This is especially the case in influencing another person's self-efficacy. A manager's expectations and peer support can go far in increasing a worker's self-efficacy and feelings of control.

Here are some key points for managers to consider in applying social learning theory.
- Identify appropriate job behaviours.
- Help employees select an appropriate behavioural model for behavioural modelling.
- Work with employees to meet the requirements of the new behaviours.
- Structure the learning situation to enhance learning of the necessary behaviours.
- Provide appropriate rewards (consequences) for workers who perform the appropriate behaviours.
- Engage in appropriate managerial actions to maintain the newly learned behaviours.[20]

If management structures in the twenty-first century are to reflect the diversity of the workforce in countries such as Australia and New Zealand, then establishing mentoring programs is important. The following What would you do? looks at self-efficacy and Australia's maths crisis.

WhatWould
You**Do?**

Australia's maths crisis. Is poor self-efficacy to blame?

Australia's business community is right to be very worried at the sharp decline in participation rates in the STEM disciplines of science, technology, engineering and mathematics. Just one in ten year 12 students studied maths in 2013 and these numbers are even worse if you compare genders. Just 6.6 per cent of girls took maths in their final year of school in Australia; that is half the rate for boys and represents a 23 per cent decline in the last decade. In New South Wales fewer than 2 girls in 100 take the trio of maths, physics and chemistry. A 'lack of confidence' is the most often cited reason for this steep decline.[21]

Self-efficacy, the confidence that you have the skills and abilities to successfully complete a task, assignment or job, is one of the key predictors of success. Some recent research with school children showed that self-efficacy beliefs at the age of 13 predicted better (junior school) grades; these relatively higher grades contributed to higher self-efficacy at the age of 16 which, in turn, contributed to better high school grades, even when prior academic achievement and socio-economic status were controlled for. This suggests that the *belief* that you are capable, skilled and smart has a greater influence on achievement that almost any other variable. Prior experience of success is a great way to improve the self-efficacy of both children and organisational employees.[22]

Questions

1. Can you think of some *industry-specific* reasons why women and girls are under-represented in STEM?
2. Can you think of some *social or environmental* reasons why women and girls are under-represented in STEM?
3. If you were a manager, how would you identify future leaders in STEM?
4. How would you motivate young women to choose STEM as a career?

Reinforcement as a strategy to modify work behaviour

Reinforcement plays a key role in the learning process. The foundation for this relationship is the law of effect, as stated by EL Thorndike: 'behaviour that results in a pleasant outcome is likely to be repeated, while behaviour that results in an unpleasant outcome is not likely to be repeated'.[23]

The implications of the law of effect are rather straightforward. Rewards are outcomes or environmental consequences that are considered by the reinforcement perspective to determine individual behaviour. In chapter 5 we discuss both intrinsic and extrinsic rewards. In terms of operant learning and reinforcement, our interest is in the latter.

Recall extrinsic rewards are positively valued work outcomes the individual receives from some other person. They are important external reinforcers or environmental consequences that can substantially influence people's work behaviours through the law of effect. Table 4.1 presents a sample of extrinsic rewards managers can allocate to their staff.[24] Some are contrived or planned rewards which have direct costs and budgetary implications, such as pay increases and cash bonuses. Various forms of pay are of such importance as planned extrinsic rewards a later section of this chapter is devoted to managing pay as an extrinsic reward. A second category includes natural rewards that have no cost other than the manager's personal time and efforts; examples are verbal praise and recognition in the workplace.

The **law of effect** refers to Thorndike's observation that behaviour that results in a pleasant outcome is likely to be repeated while behaviour that results in an unpleasant outcome is not likely to be repeated.

Extrinsic rewards are positively valued work outcomes the individual receives from some other person in the work setting.

TABLE 4.1 Sample of extrinsic rewards allocated by managers

Contrived rewards (some direct cost)		Natural rewards (no direct cost)
Refreshments	Promotion	Smiles
Piped-in music	Trips	Greetings
Nice offices	Company car	Compliments
Cash bonuses	Paid insurance	Special jobs
Merit pay increases	Stock options	Recognition
Profit sharing	Gifts	Feedback
Office parties	Sport tickets	Request for advice

Organisational behaviour modification brings together the application of the previously mentioned operant conditioning, reinforcement and extrinsic reward notions. It is the

Organisational behaviour modification is the systematic reinforcement of desirable work behaviour and the non-reinforcement or punishment of unwanted work behaviour.

systematic reinforcement of desirable work behaviour and the non-reinforcement or punishment of unwanted work behaviour. Organisational behaviour modification includes four basic reinforcement strategies:

1. positive reinforcement
2. negative reinforcement (or avoidance)
3. punishment
4. extinction.

Let us look at each of these strategies in some detail.

Positive reinforcement

BF Skinner and his followers advocate **positive reinforcement**: the administration of positive consequences that tend to increase the likelihood of the desirable target behaviour being repeated in similar settings. For example, a manager may nod to express approval to a staff member after they make a useful suggestion during a sales meeting.

An awareness of what has potential reward value (table 4.1) is necessary to use positive reinforcement well in the work setting. In using these rewards for reinforcement purposes, it is important to remember several points.

Positive reinforcers and rewards are not necessarily the same. Recognition is both a reward and a positive reinforcer if a person's performance later improves. However, some apparent rewards turn out not to be positive reinforcers; for example, a supervisor may praise a staff member in front of other group members for finding errors in a report, but the group members may then give the worker the silent treatment so the worker stops looking for errors. In this case, the supervisor's 'reward' does not serve as a positive reinforcer.

To have maximum reinforcement value, a reward must be delivered only if the desired behaviour is exhibited; that is, the reward must be contingent on the desired behaviour, as in the contingent ABC model. This principle is known as the **law of contingent reinforcement**. In the previous example, the supervisor's praise was contingent on the subordinate's finding errors in the report, even though this praise did not turn out to be a positive reinforcer.

Finally, the reward must be given as soon as possible after the desired behaviour. This is known as the **law of immediate reinforcement**.[25] If the supervisor praised the worker as soon as the errors were found, that praise would be consistent with this law.

A recent publication in the Journal of Population Economics[26] describes a study where were collected from over 800 Dutch organisations to investigate the productivity effects of performance related pay. Performance related pay can be either an individual scheme, such as a piece rate wage, or a collective scheme, such as profit sharing. The authors propose that performance related pay may stimulate productivity in two ways. First, a performance related pay scheme can be used to induce workers to exert the right amount of effort and second, when hiring new workers, piece rates can be used as a screening mechanism to encourage only the most able workers to apply. The overall finding was that that performance related pay increased productivity at the organisational level by 9 per cent compared to organisations without performance related pay.

Sometimes a desired organisational behaviour is quite specific and difficult to achieve. If this is the case a form of positive reinforcement, called shaping, may be used. **Shaping** is the creation of a new behaviour by the positive reinforcement of **successive approximations** to the desired behaviour. We attempt to mould individuals' behaviour by guiding their learning in a series of small graduated steps towards targeted behavioural outcomes.

If an employee constantly arrives at work 40 minutes late, but today arrives only 20 minutes late, under a shaping strategy to modify this behaviour we would reinforce this improvement. The frequency of the reinforcement would increase as the employee moves closer to the desired behavioural outcome.

Positive reinforcement is the administration of positive consequences which tend to increase the likelihood of repeating the behaviour in similar settings.

The law of contingent reinforcement is the view that for a reward to have maximum reinforcing value, it must be delivered only if the desired behaviour is exhibited.

The law of immediate reinforcement states the more immediate the delivery of a reward after the occurrence of a desirable behaviour, the greater the reinforcing effect on behaviour.

Shaping is the creation of a new behaviour by the positive reinforcement of successive approximations to the desired behaviour.

Successive approximation is when someone acts in a way that gets closer and closer to the desired behaviour in order to receive a reward.

Piece rates and 'the China price'

The China Price: The True Cost of Chinese Competitive Advantage[27] is a book that describes how China achieved its competitive edge by ruthlessly selling out both its workers and the environment. China is not solely to blame, however, as the Chinese factories are simply responding to intense pricing pressure from Western companies and this, combined with the endemic corruption and a lack of transparency, exacts an immense toll in human misery and environmental damage.

The 'China price' refers to the fact that Chinese manufacturers can undercut the prices offered by foreign competitors over a wide range of products and services by paying very low wages, often in the form of **piece rates**, to their workers. Today, as a result of the China price, China produces more than 70 per cent of the world's DVDs and toys; more than half of its bikes, cameras, shoes and telephones; and more than a third of its air conditioners, TVs, computer monitors and microwave ovens. The country has also established dominant market positions in everything from refrigerators to underwear.[28] Labour practices in China have led to many factories being labelled as 'unsustainable sweatshops'.

The actual incidence of piece rate wages in China is difficult to gauge, but it has been well established that the use of this compensation scheme is often detrimental to workers. Peter Navarro, writing in the *Financial Times*, states that 'the government wants to hide the fact that numerous companies illegally pay their workers far less than the stated minimum wage', particularly through the use of piece rates.[29] The purpose of paying workers in terms of their production is, of course, to provide an incentive for harder work and increased productivity. The practice is receiving increased academic attention,[30] and most of the data that is available about the industrial use of piece rates comes from factories in the Guangdong Province, which are notorious for their mistreatment of staff. Although many are paid by the hour, piece rates are employed especially where handcraft labour is used, and some workers receive a combination of both systems. An extensive report on the toy industry in China found a wide array of styles of compensation. The Kay Long factory's piece rate workers, for example, 'are paid only according to the number of pieces made', while workers at Wei Wang receive a base pay per month as well.[31]

In some cases, the idea of piece rates as a means of paying per amount produced has taken on another form. Some factories have been establishing quotas that workers must meet in order to earn their wage, with traditional piece rates being awarded for any amount in excess of the quota. Workers at City Toys and Wei De, two firms producing toys for McDonald's, have a fixed 'normal' rate for eight hours of work, which can only be collected if employees 'hit a fixed production quota everyday no matter how many hours it takes'.[32] Likewise, workers at the Kingmaker factory in Zhuhai, producing footwear for international consumption, are paid with piece rates and a base monthly wage, 'but only if they complete their monthly quota'.[33]

Source: The IHLO (Hong Kong Liaison Office of the international trade union movement). The IHLO has a mandate to monitor trade union and workers' rights and political and social developments in China.

Piece rate is a fixed ratio schedule where workers are paid for each unit or item at a fixed rate.

Continuous reinforcement is a reinforcement schedule that administers a reward each time a desired behaviour occurs.

Intermittent reinforcement is a reinforcement schedule that rewards behaviour only periodically.

Scheduling of positive reinforcement

Positive reinforcement can be given according to continuous or intermittent schedules. **Continuous reinforcement** administers a reward each time a desired behaviour occurs. **Intermittent reinforcement** rewards behaviour only periodically.

These alternatives are important because the two schedules may have very different impacts on behaviour.

1. Continuous reinforcement draws forth a desired behaviour more quickly than does intermittent reinforcement, but continuous reinforcement is more costly in the consumption of rewards and more easily extinguished when reinforcement is no longer present.

2. Behaviour acquired under intermittent reinforcement lasts longer when reinforcement is discontinued than does behaviour acquired under continuous reinforcement. In other words, it is more resistant to extinction.

As shown in table 4.2, intermittent reinforcement can be given according to fixed or variable schedules. The variable schedules are considered to result in more consistent patterns of desired behaviours than result from fixed reinforcement schedules. Fixed interval schedules provide rewards at the first appearance of a behaviour after a given time has elapsed; fixed ratio schedules result in a reward each time a certain number of the behaviours has occurred. A variable interval schedule rewards behaviour at random times, while a variable ratio schedule rewards behaviour after a random number of occurrences.

TABLE 4.2 Four ways to schedule intermittent positive reinforcement

Reinforcement schedule	Example
Fixed interval — give reinforcer after specific time passes	Weekly or monthly pay cheques
Fixed ratio — give reinforcer after specific number of responses	Piece rate pay or sales commissions
Variable interval — give reinforcer at random times	Occasional praise by boss on unscheduled 'walk arounds'
Variable ratio — give reinforcer after a random number of responses	Random quality checks with praise for zero defects

COUNTER**POINT**

Incentives modify behaviour … but not always in the way we hope!

In their now famous book *Freakonomics*,[34] Steven Levitt and Stephen Dubner write about how we all learn to respond to incentives and rewards, stating that an incentive is simply a means of urging people to do more of a good thing and less of a bad thing. A rather nice workplace application of the power (and sometimes unintended consequence) of incentives is described in the opening chapter of *Freakonomics*. The authors discuss real-estate agents, and, specifically, how these individuals behave in response to the incentive of receiving a commission for listing, showing and selling a house.

It would be nice to think that a real-estate agent is motivated to help the vendor (the person who hired them to sell the house) by getting the best possible price. But, in fact, on looking closely at the actual behaviour of real-estate agents, we can see that the incentives in place actually induce them to sell the house quickly and for a lower price.

Consider a $300 000 house; usually you would pay a 6 per cent commission ($18 000) to the agent. This is often split between the seller's agent and the buyer's, and each agent then kicks back roughly half to his or her agency. This means that only 1.5 per cent of the purchase price goes directly to the agent. So, of the $18 000 commission, an agent will take around $4500 — still not bad for placing a couple of ads and showing up to some open homes.

However, what if the house was actually worth $310 000 and with a little more effort, a few more weeks of open homes and increased advertising the agent could have sold it for that? After commission this will give you, the vendor an extra $9400. But the agent's share (1.5 per cent of the extra $10 000) is just $150. Agents will encourage you to take the first decent offer; they want to make deals and make them fast, and why not? Their share of a better offer is far too small an incentive to encourage them to do otherwise.

The problem is that the agent stands to personally gain only an additional $150 by selling your house for $10 000 more, which isn't much of a reward for quite a bit of extra work, so their job is to convince you that $300 000 is in fact a very good offer, and one you should certainly take!

With the rise in popularity of sites such as Trademe Property in New Zealand (www. trademe.co.nz/property) and No Agent Property in Australia (www.noagentproperty.com.au), where people can easily list and sell their houses privately, avoiding real-estate agent's fees altogether, one wonders whether the days of real-estate agents are numbered. Will more companies start charging a 'flat' rate on sales, rather than commission? Will agent's fees have to drop? What incentive is there for home owners to use agents at all?

In Australia, variable pay and non-financial benefits have also been gaining popularity for organisations wishing to experiment with changing reinforcement schedules. A recent remuneration report predicts base senior executive salaries will continue rising but variable benefits will rise equally if not more.[35] While absenteeism for senior executives may not be the big issue, attracting good senior talent is, and reinforcement schedules for ensuring this do tend to differ depending on the level of the organisational hierarchy observed.

Let us summarise this section on positive reinforcement by looking at The effective manager 4.1 guidelines.

Guidelines for allocating extrinsic rewards to ensure a positive reinforcement effect

THE **EffectiveManager** 4.1

1. Clearly identify the desired behaviours.
2. Maintain an inventory of rewards with the potential to serve as positive reinforcers for these people.
3. Recognise individual differences in the rewards that will have positive values for each person.
4. Let each person know exactly what must be done to receive a desirable reward. Set clear target antecedents and give performance feedback.
5. Allocate rewards contingently and immediately upon the appearance of the desired behaviours. Make sure the reward is given only if the desired behaviours occur.
6. Allocate rewards wisely in terms of scheduling the delivery of positive reinforcement.

The consequences associated with work behaviours are not always positive in nature. Often adverse consequences are put in place to influence employee motivation and behaviour. The following section deals with ways of manipulating adverse consequences.

Negative reinforcement (avoidance)

Negative reinforcement, or avoidance, is the withdrawal of negative consequences, which tends to increase the likelihood of the desirable behaviour being repeated in similar settings. There are two aspects here: first, the negative consequences, and second, the withdrawal of these consequences when desirable behaviour occurs. The term 'negative reinforcement' comes from this withdrawal of the negative consequences. This strategy is sometimes called avoidance because its intent is for the person to avoid the negative consequence by performing the desired behaviour; for instance, a worker who prefers the day shift is allowed to return to the day shift if they perform well on the night shift.

Both positive and negative reinforcement seek to encourage desirable behaviour. The first type of reinforcement provides pleasant consequences; the second provides unpleasant consequences, followed by their withdrawal when the desired behaviour occurs.

Punishment

Unlike positive reinforcement and negative reinforcement, punishment is not intended to encourage positive behaviour but to discourage negative behaviour. Formally defined, **punishment** is the administration of negative consequences or the withdrawal of positive consequences, which tends to reduce the likelihood of the behaviour being repeated in similar settings. For example, stimuli to weaken behaviours can include written and verbal reprimands, assignment of unpopular tasks, performance measurements and evaluation, transfer or dismissal.

There are major reservations about using punishment as a motivational tool. Research on punitive manipulation in the workplace is scarce. This may be because punishment is seen by the workers as arbitrary and capricious and leads to low satisfaction as well as low performance.[36]

Problems with the punishment strategy

Problems such as resentment and sabotage may accompany a manager's use of punishment. It also is wise to remember the following issues.

- Although a behaviour may be suppressed as a result of punishment, it may not be permanently abolished.
- The person who administers punishment may end up being viewed negatively by others.
- Punishment may be offset by positive reinforcement received from another source. Peers may reinforce a worker at the same time the manager administers the punishment. Sometimes, the positive value of such peer support may be strong enough to cause the individual to put up with the punishment. Therefore, the undesirable behaviour continues; for example, a student may be verbally reprimanded many times by a lecturer for being late to class, yet the grins offered by other students may justify the student's continuing tardiness.
- The behavioural response to punishment is typically less predictable and, therefore, may be less effective as a behavioural modification strategy.

In addition, the generational differences referred to in chapter 2 need to be taken into account when applying reinforcement strategies. Using the stereotypical classification of generations in organisations, punishment is considered to be increasingly ineffective for generation Y people. They are more likely to change their behaviour by simply moving on. Hence, positive reinforcement and extinction may be better strategies when managing staff from generation Y.[37]

When evaluating the merits of punishment, we need to consider organisational justice. Punishment viewed by employee observers to be unfair may affect others' attitudes and commitment. At the same time, punishment may be important for the maintenance of positive attitudes, by way of demonstrating organisational justice.[41] The notion of organisational justice is highly related to process theories for motivation (chapter 3) and, in particular, Adams's equity theory that stems from the principle of social comparisons and balance. Further, a range of procedural justice theories have influenced research into organisational justice.[42]

Punishment and shame in organisations

Punishment can take many forms. For example, people who do not show appropriate behaviours can be forced to work at an undesirable desk or checkout; an employee may be scheduled to work very early in the morning, or be expected to stay back on a Friday night. However, if managers are not aware of staff preferences, there is a risk the punishment may inadvertently be rewarding (some people may like to start work early or work on a Friday night). So, managers need to be aware of an individual's likes and dislikes. For example, being told to work alone or as part of a group may suit an introvert or an extrovert respectively.

Another important consideration when implementing punishment is the psychological consequence of receiving punishment for failing at a task or showing poor judgement. Most people will experience shame. Shame is *'one of the most powerful, painful, and potentially destructive experiences known to humans'*,[38] resulting in feelings of worthlessness inferiority and damaged self-esteem. Recent research has indicated that people will react in one of two ways when they experience shame; they will either be motivated to redo the task, make amends, and thereby affirm their capability (approach behaviour) or they will withdraw and remove themselves from situations where they could fail again (avoidance behaviour).[39] It is difficult to predict how employees will respond, however, and when considered in context with research that suggests harsh punishment within the workplace rarely sustains changes to long-term behaviour, this strategy should be used sparingly.[40]

Guidelines for using punishment to change behaviour

1. *Tell the individual what is being done wrong.* Clearly identify the undesirable behaviour being punished.
2. *Tell the individual what is right.* Clearly identify the desirable alternative to the behaviour being punished.
3. *Punish in private.* Avoid the public embarrassment associated with punishing someone in front of others.
4. *Punish in accord with the laws of contingent and immediate reinforcement.* Make sure the punishment is truly contingent on the undesirable behaviour and follows its occurrence as closely as possible.
5. *Make sure the punishment matches the behaviour.* Be fair in equating the magnitude of the punishment with the degree to which the behaviour is truly undesirable.

Extinction

Extinction is the withdrawal of the reinforcing consequences for a given behaviour.

Extinction is a reinforcement strategy that deals with the withdrawal of the reinforcing consequences for a given behaviour. For example, Jack is often late for work, and his coworkers cover for him (positive reinforcement). The manager instructs Jack's coworkers to stop covering for him, withdrawing the reinforcing consequences. The manager has deliberately used extinction as a means to stop an undesirable behaviour. This strategy decreases the frequency of, or weakens, the behaviour. The behaviour is not 'unlearned'; it simply is not exhibited. No longer reinforced, the behaviour will reappear if reinforced again. Whereas positive reinforcement seeks to establish and maintain desirable work behaviour, the goal of extinction is to weaken and eliminate undesirable behaviour. It is important to note here that almost any behaviour can be extinguished. Just as ignoring bad behaviours will cause them to occur less frequently, the occurrence of desirable behaviours will also lessen over time if there is no reward. For example, there is research evidence showing that performance tends to decline when managers withhold praise or stop congratulating employees for good work.[43] Consider the following OB in action box.

OBinAction

Extinction in action — if you don't hear from me, you know you're doing fine

The following quotes are from employees who were part of study conducted through Cornell University, looking at the effects of extinction on positive behaviour.[44]

> One of the major problems around here is that you don't know how you are doing until you make a mistake, then you get hammered. It really discourages risk taking and makes everyone nervous. We all want to do a good job, but it would just be nice to know that you are appreciated once in a while.

The same study presents the following vignette:

> XYZ Corporation is a food service company with several product groups. Keith Wilson works is one of nine product managers. Performance across product groups varies considerably. Over the past several months, Keith has worked hard to reduce his group's overall expenses by almost 20 per cent while increasing market share. On Monday, Keith is notified that the division manager will be visiting on Friday and wishes to meet with all product managers at lunch. Prior to the meal, the division manager shakes hands with and slaps several product managers on the back, thanking them all for their great contribution. Following lunch, he gives a brief speech on the importance of everyone to the organisation. He then disappears, not to be seen for the next two months. Keith leaves the luncheon wondering why he breaks his back when he receives no recognition for his efforts. In fact, he received the same praise as those managers whose operations were doing poorly. He is wondering if it might not be time to look for a new job.

The point here is to highlight the damage that can be done by failing to reinforce desired performance. Keith is upset because he feels that his efforts have been overlooked. In addition, by praising everyone no matter how good (or bad) their performance, the division manager is using a **non-contingent reward** (which has been shown to have no effect on employee satisfaction or performance). The division manager could have had much greater effect on motivation and performance if he had specifically recognised and thanked those who had done well. Over time, high performers whose achievements are not recognised will probably either reduce performance or leave the organisation. High performers with marketable skills have little difficulty finding alternative employment, while average performers remain and help to make an organisation average.

Non-contingent reward is a reward that is given arbitrarily; being unrelated to, or not requiring, a behavioural response.

Organisational behaviour modification strategies — a summary

Figure 4.3 summarises the use of each organisational behaviour modification strategy using the ABC framework. Each is designed to direct work behaviour towards practices desired by management. Both positive and negative reinforcement are used to strengthen the desirable behaviour of improving work quality when it occurs. Punishment is used to weaken the undesirable behaviour of high error rate, and consists of either administering negative consequences or withdrawing positive consequences. Likewise, extinction is used deliberately to weaken the undesirable, high-error-rate behaviour when it occurs. However, extinction is also used inadvertently to weaken the desirable, low-error-rate behaviour. Finally, do not forget these strategies may be used in combination, as well as independently.

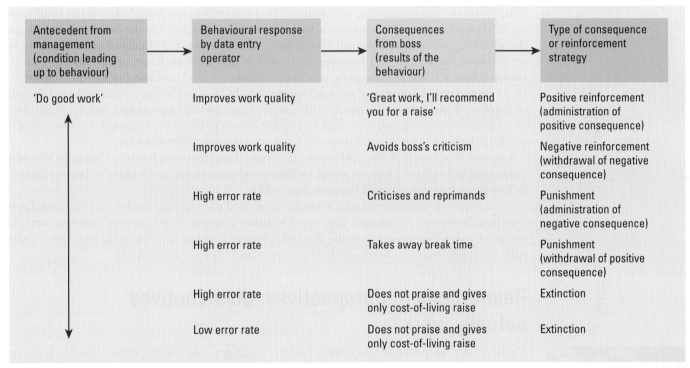

Antecedent from management (condition leading up to behaviour)	Behavioural response by data entry operator	Consequences from boss (results of the behaviour)	Type of consequence or reinforcement strategy
'Do good work'	Improves work quality	'Great work, I'll recommend you for a raise'	Positive reinforcement (administration of positive consequence)
	Improves work quality	Avoids boss's criticism	Negative reinforcement (withdrawal of negative consequence)
	High error rate	Criticises and reprimands	Punishment (administration of negative consequence)
	High error rate	Takes away break time	Punishment (withdrawal of positive consequence)
	High error rate	Does not praise and gives only cost-of-living raise	Extinction
	Low error rate	Does not praise and gives only cost-of-living raise	Extinction

FIGURE 4.3 Applying the ABC framework in a work setting

Certain aspects of behaviour modification theory need further research. Much of the research in this area is predicated on the use of positive reinforcement to modify behaviour. Less is known about the effects of punishment. The reactions to punishment would appear to be less predictable and less understood by researchers, and one only has to look at the penal systems in many countries to understand the need for further research in this area.

Reinforcement perspectives: using rewards carefully

The effective use of reinforcement strategies can assist in the management of human behaviour at work. Testimony to this effect is found in the application of these strategies in many large companies, including Westpac, Coles Group and government agencies such as Medicare Australia. Smaller companies can also use various reinforcement strategies to reward and retain good staff; for example, bonuses for high performing individuals, extra leave days and free lunches.[45] Reinforcement strategies are also supported by the growing number of consulting firms that specialise in reinforcement techniques. The point of agreement is that supportive and positive communication and reward strategies provided on several fronts seem to reinforce one another.[46]

However, we must recognise managerial use of these approaches is not without criticism. Some reports on the 'success' of specific programs are single cases analysed without the benefit of scientific research designs. Moreover, studies in this field often look at the short-term outcomes; rewards almost always buy temporary compliance, so it looks like the problems are solved. It's harder to spot the long-term outcomes which may not be as uniformly positive. In addition it is hard to conclude definitively whether reinforcement dynamics caused the observed results. One critic argues the improved performance may well have occurred only as a result of the goal setting involved; that is, because specific performance goals were clarified and workers were individually held accountable for their accomplishment.[47] Another concern is whether it is ethical to use behaviour modification strategies.[48]

It is possible that continuing research will primarily refine our knowledge of the reinforcement strategies rather than dramatically change existing insights. On the other hand, perhaps decades of psychological research establishing the undermining effects of extrinsic rewards on intrinsic motivation will become more widely accepted in large organisations. Future research may tell us, as managers, in what situations we can best use the various reinforcement strategies. Although the notion that we should be using them seems well established, perhaps we should temper such use with a strong managerial emphasis on employee involvement and genuine engagement, and by explicit efforts to avoid exploitation. In other words, we should always pursue reinforcement from strong ethical foundations.

It is also clear much of the work on reinforcement and learning has been based in Western cultures. As the global business world gathers pace, greater understanding of how to modify behaviour across cultures will become important.

More cross-cultural comparative research is needed to examine whether the research findings from Western cultures are supported in other cultures. If a Japanese manager were to use positive reinforcement to shape the behaviour of a Japanese worker, for example, would such a public display be accepted by the worker and/or their coworkers?

Reinforcement perspectives: do incentives actually work?

There is no doubt that employees' salary packages are an important factor both in determining the organisations that skilled people will choose to work for, and in terms of avoiding dissatisfaction and perceptions of inequity (refer to the section on equity theory in chapter 3). In addition, if there is little that is intrinsically rewarding about a given task, then people certainly require an extrinsic reward or incentive to induce them to do it (see the Sustainability box on Chinese factories earlier in this chapter). However, using incentive plans and performance-based rewards in contexts where employees find intrinsic enjoyment in their work, or to enhance motivation and engagement, is quite a different thing. While managers and consultants generally believe that people will do a better job if they are promised some sort of incentive, many studies in laboratories, workplaces, classrooms and other settings find that extrinsic rewards actually destroy intrinsic motivation![49]

But why should a reward reduce motivation? Research suggests that rewards do succeed at achieving temporary compliance but, when it comes to producing a lasting change in attitudes and behaviour, rewards are not particularly effective.[50] Once the rewards run out, people tend to revert to their old behaviours.

Studies show that offering incentives for losing weight, quitting smoking or using seatbelts often proves worse than doing nothing at all. One reason for this is that incentives (or extrinsic rewards) do not alter the attitudes that underlie our behaviours. Another reason is explained by **cognitive evaluation theory**, which holds that when people are offered a large payment for engaging in an activity, they infer that the activity must be tedious, risky or unpleasant (otherwise, why would someone offer them such a reward?). This inference produces the **reverse-incentive effect**.[51] Just as consumers perceive more expensive items, services or activities to be of higher quality than less expensive versions of the same thing, they will also be willing to offer more money for a more difficult, risky or unpleasant job. Therefore, when a greater incentive (in terms of money or anything else) is associated with an activity, people tend to infer that the activity is less enjoyable. The unavoidable outcome is decreased intrinsic satisfaction with the activity.

In addition, **self-determination theory** distinguishes between autonomous motivation and controlled motivation.[52] Autonomous motivation comprises both intrinsic motivation and the types of extrinsic motivation in which people have identified with an activity's value or worth. When people are autonomously motivated, they experience a sense of volition, choice or free will — that is, they want to engage in the activity.

Controlled motivation, on the other hand, relates to external regulation, where behaviour is dictated by contingencies of reward or punishment, as well as seeking approval from others and avoiding shame. An enormous amount of research has confirmed that autonomous motivation and controlled motivation lead to very different outcomes, with autonomous motivation resulting greater psychological health, better performance and greater long-term persistence and behaviour change.[53]

More than 20 studies over the last three decades have conclusively shown that people who expect to receive a reward for completing a task or for doing that task successfully simply do not perform as well as those who expect no reward at all.[54]

The *Harvard Business Review*[55] published an article outlining why many reward systems fail, and presents a six-point framework relating to the above ideas.

1. *Pay is not a motivator.*
2. *Rewards punish.*
3. *Rewards rupture relationships.*
4. *Rewards ignore reasons.*
5. *Rewards discourage risk-taking.*
6. *Rewards undermine interest.*

The recipient of a reward assumes, 'If they have to bribe me to do it, it must be something I wouldn't want to do'. Studies have found that the larger the incentive we are offered, the more negatively we will view the activity for which the bonus was received.[56] The activities themselves don't seem to matter; in this study, they ranged from participating in a medical experiment to eating unfamiliar food. Whatever the reason for the effect, however, any incentive or pay-for-performance system tends to make people less enthusiastic about their work, and therefore less likely to approach it with a commitment to excellence.

Social learning theory and behavioural self-management

Social learning theory is applied in the workplace to encourage employees to help manage or lead themselves. Table 4.3 (overleaf) shows some possible self-management strategies. Notice how these strategies build on social learning theory to emphasise both behavioural and cognitive focuses. Their use is designed to enhance self-efficacy and the worker's feeling of self-control. For example, 3M (the company which manufactures Post-It Notes) encourages employees to apply behavioural self-management actions (such as those listed in table 4.3) wherever possible. People are encouraged to 'work outside the box' to facilitate new product innovations.[57] Many high-profile sporting organisations throughout the world use sports psychologists to teach players the strategies listed in table 4.3 (overleaf).[58]

Cognitive evaluation theory explains the effects of extrinsic rewards on intrinsic motivation. When people are offered a large payment for engaging in an activity, they infer that the activity must be difficult, tedious, risky, or unpleasant in some way, so their enjoyment of the task is decreased.

Reverse-incentive effect is when people are offered a large incentive or reward for doing a task, they will judge that task to be more difficult, more boring, or more unpleasant than when a small (or no) reward is offered.

Self-determination theory is a theory of human motivation, development and wellness. The theory focuses on types, rather than just amount, of motivation, paying particular attention to autonomous (intrinsic) motivation, controlled (extrinsic) motivation, and amotivation (lack of motivation) as predictors of performance and wellbeing outcomes.

TABLE 4.3 Self-management strategies

Behaviour-focused strategies	
Behaviour	**Strategy**
Self-setting goals	Setting goals for your own work efforts
Managing cues	Arranging and altering cues in the work environment to facilitate your desired personal behaviours
Rehearsing	Physically or mentally practising work activities before you actually perform them
Self-observing	Observing and gathering information about specific behaviours that you have targeted for change
Self-rewarding	Providing yourself with personally valued rewards for completing desirable behaviours
Self-punishing	Administering punishments to yourself for behaving in undesirable ways (This strategy is generally not very effective.)
Cognitive-focused strategies	
Behaviour	**Strategy**
Building natural rewards into tasks	Redesigning where and how you do your work to increase the level of natural rewards in your job. Natural rewards that are part of, rather than separate from, the work (that is, the work, like a hobby, becomes the reward) result from activities that cause you to feel: • a sense of competence • a sense of self-control • a sense of purpose
Focusing thinking on natural rewards	Purposely focusing your thinking on the naturally rewarding features of your work
Establishing constructive thought patterns	Establishing constructive and effective habits or patterns in your thinking (for example, a tendency to search for opportunities rather than obstacles embedded in challenges) by managing your: • beliefs and assumptions • mental imagery • internal self-talk

OBinAction

Self-management versus empowerment

Frederic Laloux's recent book *Reinventing Organizations*[59] attempts to describe new ways to manage and to work in organisations in the context of current changes in social systems and culture. Laloux states that one of the key misperceptions about self-management is that 'it's about empowerment' (see chapter 3 for more on empowerment). The irony here is that, if employees need to be empowered, it is because the organisation is set up in such a way that power is concentrated at the top and (unless leaders are generous enough to share their power) those lower down are essentially powerless.

In true self-managing organisations, people are not empowered by the benevolence of others. Empowerment is a core part of the organisation itself; part of the structure, processes, and practices. Individuals do not have to ask, or fight, for power; they already have it. For people experiencing self-management for the first time, it can be difficult at first. With freedom comes responsibility: employees quickly learn they can no longer delegate problems or difficult decisions 'up the hierarchy' and let managers take care of them. Everybody needs to grow up and take full responsibility for their thoughts and actions — a steep learning curve for some people.[60]

Self-management is a social learning theory that can be applied by behaviour-focused strategies and cognitive-focused strategies. However, self-management for an organisational member includes managing inconsistencies between individual and organisational expectations and goals.

It is evident that self-management includes self-reflection or introspection, in which individuals contemplate their thoughts, feelings and actions. In the organisational context, self-reflection can lead to the discovery of incongruence between organisational goals and personal expectations. These **intrapersonal conflicts** often involve actual or perceived pressures from incompatible goals or expectations of the following types.

Approach conflict occurs when a person must choose between two positive and equally attractive alternatives. An example is a person having to choose between a valued promotion in the organisation or a desirable new job with another organisation. *Avoidance conflict* occurs when a person must choose between two negative and equally unattractive alternatives. An example is a person having to accept a job transfer to another town in an undesirable location or have their employment terminated. *Approach–avoidance conflict* occurs when a person must decide to do something that has both positive and negative consequences. An example is being offered a higher-paying job with responsibilities that will entail unwanted demands on personal time.

This chapter has emphasised workers as individuals. However, many of the self-management strategies can also be extended to self-managed teams, which are discussed later in the book. Managers are seeking strategies designed to increase the use of human potential in the workplace. Many Western organisations have experienced downsizing in recent decades, and now they are giving increased attention to new approaches designed to increase worker productivity. The success of this in Australia is evidenced by the productivity gains combined with the skills shortages that continue in some sectors despite challenging economic times.[61] Organisations are being designed to have flatter structures, provide increased worker empowerment and offer greater opportunities for self-management — all strategies designed to increase the use of personnel.

Intrapersonal conflict is conflict that occurs within the individual as a result of actual or perceived pressures from incompatible goals or expectations.

Managing pay as an extrinsic reward

The earlier part of this chapter focused on different kinds of reinforcement and extrinsic reward. Table 4.1 (p. 131) showed various forms of pay as one of these extrinsic rewards and reinforcers. Pay is an especially complex extrinsic reward. It can help organisations attract and retain highly capable workers, and it can help satisfy and motivate these workers to work hard to achieve high performance. But if workers are dissatisfied with the salary, pay can also lead to strikes, grievances, absenteeism, turnover and sometimes even poor physical and mental health. The various aspects of pay make it an especially important extrinsic reward.[62]

Multiple meanings of pay

To use pay effectively as a reward, a manager must understand why it is important to people. Various organisational behaviour theories recognise multiple meanings of pay and the potential of these meanings to vary from one person or situation to another. For example, when it comes to the relationship between pay and job satisfaction, each of the following theories (with which you should be familiar) offers a slightly different perspective.

According to Maslow's hierarchy of needs theory, pay is a unique reward that can satisfy many different needs. It is used directly to satisfy lower-order needs, such as the physiological need for food, and it is of symbolic value in satisfying higher-order needs, such as ego fulfilment.

According to McClelland's acquired needs theory, pay is an important source of performance feedback for high-need achievers. It can be attractive to persons with a high need for affiliation when offered as a group bonus, and it is valued by the high need-for-power person as a means of 'buying' prestige or control over others.

According to Herzberg's two-factor theory, pay in the form of base wage or salary can prevent dissatisfaction but cannot lead to motivation (although merit pay rises given as special rewards for jobs done well can cause increased satisfaction and motivation). However, Herzberg's research does show pay cross-loads across both his hygiene and motivating factors. This finding recognises many of the respondents in Herzberg's research perceived money as a motivating factor.

Expectancy and equity theories, as well as the various reinforcement strategies, give additional insight into the multiple meanings of pay and their potential relationships to job performance. These ideas (summarised in table 4.4) show how pay can serve as a motivator of work effort, when properly managed. This phrase is the real key; for pay to prove successful as a reward that is truly motivational to the recipient, it must be given:

1. contingent on the occurrence of specific and desirable work behaviours, and
2. equitably.

Merit pay and a variety of emerging creative pay practices are applications that need to be dealt with in more detail.

TABLE 4.4 The multiple meanings of pay as viewed from a performance perspective

Theory	The meaning of pay
Equity theory	Pay is an object of social comparison. People are likely to compare their pay and pay increases with those received by others. When felt inequity occurs as a result of such comparisons, work effort may be reduced in the case of negative inequity, or increased in the case of positive inequity.
Expectancy theory	Pay is only one of many work rewards individuals may value at work. When valence, instrumentality and expectancy are high, pay can be a source of motivation. However, the opportunity to work hard to obtain high pay will be viewed in the context of other effort–outcome expectancies and the equity dynamic.
Reinforcement theory	Pay is one of the extrinsic rewards a manager may use to influence the work behaviour of employees. Through the techniques of operant conditioning, pay can be used as a positive reinforcer when the laws of contingent and immediate reinforcement are followed.

Merit pay is a compensation system that bases an individual's salary or wage increase on a measure of the person's performance accomplishments during a specified time period.

Merit pay

Edward Lawler is a management expert whose work has contributed greatly to our understanding of pay as an extrinsic reward. His research generally concludes for pay to serve as a source of work motivation, high levels of job performance must be viewed as the path through which high pay can be achieved.[63] **Merit pay** is defined as a compensation system that bases an individual's salary or wage increase on a measure of the person's performance accomplishments during a specified time period. That is, merit pay is an attempt to make pay contingent on performance.

For some time, research has supported the logic and theoretical benefits of merit pay, but it also indicates the implementation of merit pay plans is not as universal or as easy as we may expect.[64]

To work well, a merit pay plan must:
- be based on realistic and accurate measures of individual work performance
- create a belief among employees the way to achieve high pay is to perform at high levels
- clearly discriminate between high and low performers in the amount of pay reward received
- avoid confusing 'merit' aspects of a pay increase with 'cost-of-living' adjustments.

These guidelines are consistent with the basic laws of reinforcement and the guidelines for positive reinforcement discussed earlier in the chapter.

However, total quality management guru W Edwards Deming has long been a critic of pay-for-performance schemes. Deming argues because performance is difficult to measure, all employees should receive a traditional salary or wage, and all future pay rises should be administered uniformly across the company to encourage cooperation and teamwork.

There are potential problems in linking pay to performance. However, many human resource experts and headhunters emphasise the importance of rewarding high performers for a private company's ability to attract top talent in a competitive global marketplace. As a result, a large number of Australian companies in the private sector (and a growing number of companies in New Zealand) maintain pay-for-performance schemes. A Morgan and Banks survey of 2100 businesses Australia-wide revealed 70.2 per cent of these companies had some form of performance-based pay system for senior executives and a further 60.5 per cent had a similar scheme for middle managers. Only 40.4 per cent of the same sample of companies had implemented any performance-based pay scheme for non-managerial employees.[65] Such schemes have many critics, because some Australian CEOs have received bonus payments of shares even when their performance has been less than meritorious.[66] Nevertheless, a more recent survey of pay rates in Australia and New Zealand reveals 'employers are now focusing more on variable pay and non-financial benefits that are meaningful to employees and support work/life balance'.[67]

By nature, performance-related pay is context- and time-related — so rewarding public servants is much more problematic than company CEOs. For example, in New Zealand, the situation for public service CEOs is complicated because of the lag between performance measured and outcomes reported. It can take years for new policies to take effect and to produce improved measurable achievements. In addition, government executives are often restricted from implementing radical changes by existing government policies, including policies related to funding. Further, apart from measurable financial efficiencies, quality of (governmental) services is difficult to measure. The New Zealand State Services Commission is dedicated to working on solutions for this complex problem.[68] The Ethical perspective looks at the issue of paying employees based on their performance.

Paying for performance

The concept of linking pay with performance is controversial. It can lead to inequities that are hard to reconcile. At one time, Macquarie Bank was in the news for the record performance pay amounts going to its senior executives. In the financial year prior to the global financial crisis, Macquarie Capital CEO Nicholas Moore earned $26.8 million. The following year, his pay was slashed to only $290 000. By 2010, the

(continued)

ETHICAL
Perspective

figure had increased to $9.5 million — almost 25 times the amount of Australia's Prime Minister, and more than 135 times the salary of the average Australian worker.[69] By 2014, his entry on the Mayne Report Rich List stated that he had earned 'over $30 million two years in a row'.[70] There have been inevitable comparisons of the performance of work in the financial sector with more 'caring' professions such as nursing or policing. The debate about the intrinsic value of senior executives was reignited; as were discussions about what levels of incentives are needed to attract and retain talented managers in various industries.

It is easy to criticise comparatively high performance payments. How can someone ever actually *earn* that amount of money (roughly $4000 per hour)? Do they really help managers continuously learn new and better ways of improving organisational performance? On the other hand, can corporate and individual social responsibility benefits manifest through a kind of 'trickle down' effect, whereby local charities and foundations benefit from the goodwill of highly paid executives?[71] For example, Mark Zuckerberg (founder of Facebook) and his wife, Priscilla Chan, gave over $922 million in 2013 alone.[72] Bill Gates, has been ranked number two (second only to Warren Buffet, CEO of Berkshire Hathaway) in a list compiled by *Bloomberg Business Week* of the world's 50 most generous philanthropists.[73] According to this list, his estimated lifetime giving is over $28 144 million (though his net worth has been estimated at $59 000 million!). In a 2008 documentary containing a rare interview with Microsoft co-founder Bill Gates, it was explained that based on Mr Gates' current personal net worth, he could have received $5 million in pay every day since Microsoft was founded in 1975.[74] Obviously, some years have been better than others for Microsoft, and for Bill Gates, but can you imagine suggesting an executive remuneration package of this magnitude into the business plan of any company when it first starts off?

Creative pay practices

Merit pay plans are an attempt to enhance the positive value of pay as a work reward and to use it as a positive reinforcer. Indeed, some argue merit pay plans are not consistent with the demands of today's organisations because they fail to recognise the high degree of task interdependence among employees, as illustrated particularly in total quality management programs. Still, others contend the nature of any incentive scheme should be tied to the overall organisational strategy and the nature of the desired behaviour; for example, the pay system of an organisation which needs highly skilled individuals in short supply should emphasise employee retention, rather than performance.[75]

Many organisations facing increased competition, in an attempt to become more competitive by getting more from their workers, use varying creative incentive schemes either singly or in combination. Such non-traditional practices are becoming more common in organisations with increasingly diverse workforces and a growing emphasis on total quality management or similar setups.[76] These creative schemes can include skill-based pay, gain-sharing plans, lump-sum pay increases, bonus share schemes and flexible benefit plans (see table 4.5).

TABLE 4.5 Creative pay practices

Pay practice	Description
Skill-based pay	A pay system that rewards people for acquiring and developing job-relevant skills that relate to organisational needs
Gain-sharing plans	A pay system that links pay and performance by giving workers the opportunity to share in productivity gains through increased earnings

Pay practice	Description
Lump-sum pay increases	A pay system in which people elect to receive their annual wage or salary increase in one or more lump-sum payments
Bonus share schemes	A share plan to reward high-performing executives
Flexible benefit plans	Pay systems that allow workers to select benefits according to their individual needs

There is a growing trend away from rewarding performance solely by financial outcomes. Many companies are now incorporating non-financial outcomes, such as a flexible benefit plan, into this performance-based pay equation. Additional criteria such as improved customer service, employee satisfaction with managerial style and increased market share are being added to the equation to obtain a clearer and more comprehensive profile of the measurement of effective managerial performance.[77]

The following International spotlight looks at how the effectiveness of incentives varies with different cultural and economic contexts.

What is more rewarding than money? The case of Korea

Organisational behaviour modification approaches have been researched and largely applied in Western contexts, such as the United States.[78] However, these programs cannot necessarily be assumed to work the same way in non-Western cultures. The way that employees value and respond to the various incentives (e.g. money, social recognition and feedback) used to change behaviour is likely to be quite different in different cultural contexts.

Organisational behaviour modification has been shown to be successful in United States firms.[79] However, there has been little research looking at the usefulness of various incentives when they are used in a different culture. Korea has very contrasting cultural values when compared with Western countries such as the United States, Australia and New Zealand. The two most relevant cultural dimensions when it comes to appropriately rewarding employees are *high vs low power distance* and *individualism vs collectivism*. According to Hofstede,[80] Korea has a high power distance culture. Therefore, Korean employees may be more inclined to try to impress their leaders. In addition, the incentive of social recognition by respected organisational leaders may be relatively more motivating to Korean employees. Objective financial incentives, on the other hand, may be more compatible with low power distance cultures such as the United States, Australia and New Zealand. This would suggest that Korean employees may be more influenced by

non-financial rewards such as social recognition. By contrast, employees in the United States, Australia or New Zealand may be more likely to respond to monetary incentives.

Another of Hofstede's dimensions is individualism vs collectivism. Since most organisational rewards are contingent on individual performance, it is likely that their impact would be greater in individualistic than in collectivistic cultures. This is because in collectivistic cultures, teamwork and group harmony are strongly emphasised over individual concerns. Employees with collectivist cultural values would be likely to respond better to incentives that benefit their whole work group (e.g. gain-sharing) or are less harmful for teamwork. In a strong collectivistic culture, such as Korea, there

(continued)

is a higher value placed on preserving group wellbeing. Social recognition is not as salient as monetary rewards in emphasising individual achievement, and is less detrimental to group harmony. Therefore, social recognition may have a more positive impact on collectively oriented Korean employees than monetary incentive, especially when compared to more individually oriented Western employees.

A recent study, conducted in a modern Korean internet service firm, examined the use of organisational behaviour modification strategies, comparing the relative impact of money, social recognition and feedback on employee performance.[81] This study found that that social recognition was consistently more effective than money in the Korean setting. This contradicts conventional wisdom in the United States, and the differences between the two countries may help explain this finding. As described above, Korean culture is characterised by both high power distance and collectivism. Therefore, these cultural values suggest Koreans may be more motivated by the incentives that provide a better chance to form a close relationship with their leaders and that preserve teamwork and group harmony. Thus, social recognition may be a relatively more effective incentive than money in Korea, as well as in other Asian countries with similar cultural values.

The learning organisation

The human race has experienced more rapid changes in the past 25 years than in the rest of humanity's existence. During the next 20 years or so, this pace of change is likely to accelerate. The challenge for organisations in this rapidly changing environment is to be flexible and adaptable enough to cope, because not only growth but, perhaps more importantly, organisational survival depends on these responses. This section introduces the concepts of the learning organisation and the teaching organisation.

The 'learning organisation' was popularised by Peter Senge in his book, *The fifth discipline.*[82] He argued a learning organisation is a medium to enhance the development and use of knowledge at an individual level and, consequently, at an organisational level. Such knowledge will lead to organisational change. Learning organisational models are attempting to harness this potential for change in order to achieve competitive advantage. Now refer back to the story on communities of competence that began this chapter. You can see in addition to achieving a competitive advantage for business, learning organisations can also enhance social services.

Organisational learning refers to the process of becoming a learning organisation and can be conceptualised as acquiring or developing new knowledge that modifies or changes behaviour and improves organisational performance. Underlying the concept of a learning organisation is a belief organisations can be transformed by improving communication processes and techniques so as to enrich relationships among members. The effective manager 4.3 looks at methods for creating a learning organisation.

Organisational learning is acquiring or developing new knowledge that modifies or changes behaviour and improves organisational performance.

THE
EffectiveManager 4.3

Creating a learning organisation

Managers can create a learning organisation by:
- building a powerful shared vision of future growth that will provide the focus for learning and a benchmark for future achievements
- developing strategies and action plans that will inspire the commitment of all personnel to achieve the future goals of the organisation
- making extensive use of a continuous process of consultation to achieve consensus and unity of thought

- encouraging continual renewal of all organisational structures and processes
- employing systems thinking to ensure the organisation focuses on both internal and external factors driving the change
- creating self-directed teams of employees that are supported to make decisions at appropriate levels.

  The degree to which an organisation can successfully create a learning environment can be measured by examining:
- the relationship between the employee and the organisation
- the value placed on the employee and their organisational contribution
- employee ownership and acceptance of responsibility
- employee empowerment.[83]

Certain preconditions are essential if a successful learning environment is to be created through these new communication processes.[84]

1. *Trust.* All organisational members must believe they can rely on an individual's word (spoken or written). Trust permeates all organisational relationships and strongly influences all aspects of coordination and control. Managerial actions such as encouraging supportive rather than defensive behaviour, aligning goals among and between organisational members, managing information flows and avoiding stereotyping assist in building a trusting environment.

2. *Commitment.* The company must develop an emotional and intellectual commitment to its actions and achievements.

3. *Perceived organisational support.* Organisational support reinforces a bond between the organisation and its employees, and creates a sense of involvement with organisational objectives. An emphasis on relationship building and organisational support also reinforces the growth of trust and commitment.

Organisational learning is about deliberately and continuously acquiring, processing and disseminating knowledge in order to transform the organisation to be more effective and/or competitive. However, more recent research is questioning the prescriptive nature and apparent ease of transformation into a learning organisation in much of the management literature.[85] This research indicates the process of learning in organisations is much more problematic than first understood and is presented in the OB in action that follows.

The trouble with learning

What do the terms 'learning' and 'learning organisation' mean? In common usage, people generally equate them with acquiring facts. However, acquired information needs to be interpreted and translated into usable knowledge and, most importantly, needs to be accompanied by changes in behaviour or attitudes. For organisations, knowledge acquisition is tied up with systems for disseminating (communicating) information. But the real meaning of learning is much broader than this. It encompasses the subtle changes that take place when people, individually or collectively, reinterpret or *reframe* their experiences, and, ideally, modify their behaviour accordingly. Learning from failure (see OB in action at the beginning of this chapter) is a good example of the learning organisation approach.

Learning organisations can only enable competitive advantage via learning if the knowledge is properly communicated to individual organisational members.[86] Knowledge sharing is vitally important to a learning organisation, as having a 'shared vision' underpins the collective nature of the organisational learning process. The problem is that when

OBin**Action**

(continued)

organisational members are all moving the same way, they may very well move in the wrong direction and 'actively damage the future direction of the company'.[87] This means despite all intentions of being 'open' to external feedback, and responsive to the organisational environments, organisational decision making is likely to be reactive. This reactivity is in direct contrast to an organisational learning process that is meant to be proactive.

Difficulties may also occur with learning and well-intentioned attempts to create a 'learning organisation' because existing mental models (beliefs and representations of reality) limit our ability to be adaptive.[88] Recent research in the United Kingdom, regarding the role of strongly held mental models in a team environment, asserts that these mental models may ultimately prevent desired creativity for innovation.[89] Strongly shared mental models are potentially 'closed' to new information; little new knowledge can emerge, and radically different and creative ideas are likely to be rejected. Hence, behaviour is unlikely to change.

Learning is a subjective process encompassing the absorption of new knowledge through emotional, intuitive and reflective filters and mental models. Real learning is a lifelong process and requires the skills of self-management, self-knowledge and self-evaluation.

Questions

1. What are the barriers and facilitators for organisational learning?
2. How can individual learning be transformed into organisational learning?
3. Think of an organisation where you have worked (or use your knowledge of your university or college). To what extent is the organisation a 'learning organisation'? Identify the facilitators and barriers to learning in these particular organisations.

Despite these concerns about learning in organisations, there are companies that are adaptive and foster a collective learning environment of trust, commitment and organisational support. Consider Pixar's focus on seeking out and proactively solving problems, described in the next OB in action.

OBinAction

Pixar: the ultimate learning organisation

A recent *Harvard Business Review* article 'Why leaders don't learn from success'[90] suggests that while most leaders recognise that they need to learn from failure, very few understand the need to understand and analyse their firm's success. Success can make us so overconfident that we believe we don't need to change anything. The authors use the Ducati motorbike racing team as an example. Success led the team to stop learning and only a failure caused it to start again. It was only after an unexpected third place finish that the team re-examined its approach to developing bikes. Pixar is one of the few organisations that retains a focus on continuous learning and improvement, even when faced with a string of successes!

Pixar is as close to a constant learning organisation as there is; they have a proven ability to reinvent and innovate, and genuine cultural humility. Pixar's founder Ed Catmull is known for his continued efforts to proactively seek out and solve new problems, recognising that he doesn't have all the answers on his own.[91]

Despite an unbroken string of 11 blockbuster films including *Toy story, Monsters inc.* and *Finding Nemo*, Catmull regularly says that 'success hides problems'. What Pixar has is a culture where the fear of complacency is a strong motivator — where new problems are identified, discussed and addressed openly and honestly.

As David Price describes in his book *The Pixar touch*,[92] Pixar began its life as a computer hardware company. Price writes that the late Steve Jobs (co-founder and chief executive officer of Apple Inc.) never expected Pixar to be a film company when he bought it from George Lucas in 1986. At that time, Pixar was the 45-person computer graphics department of Lucasfilms, and was headed by Catmull, whose dream since university had been to make a full-length digitally animated film. During the 1980s, Catmull was puzzled as to why so many successful companies ultimately failed. In a recent lecture at Stanford Business School he stated, 'I'm thinking, "If we're ever successful, how do I keep from falling into the traps these companies are falling into?"'

Today, Catmull sets the tone for a company culture that is unusually open and honest. He regularly solicits feedback from Pixar employees, who say that the mentality of constant improvement flows throughout the company. What interests Catmull the most, and appears to motivate his actions, is constantly identifying and solving new problems. When he gives a public speech or lecture, what's most noticeable is that he talks about the problems that Pixar has encountered and the mistakes that he has made. Pixar has, for example, nearly burned out its employees on numerous occasions.

Pixar director Brad Bird recounts being recruited to Pixar:[93]

> Steve Jobs, Ed Catmull, and John Lasseter said, in effect, 'The only thing we're afraid of is complacency, feeling like we have it all figured out. We want you to come shake things up. We will give you a good argument if we think what you're doing doesn't make sense, but if you can convince us, we'll do things a different way'. For a company that has had nothing but success to invite a guy who had just come off a failure and say, 'Go ahead, mess with our heads, shake it up'. When do you run into that?

The teaching organisation

The 1990s saw the rise to prominence of the learning organisation. Learning is a necessary competence, but it is insufficient to assure market leadership. The early decades of the twenty-first century are testing even the ideals of learning organisations. The companies that have outperformed competitors and increased shareholder returns have been those able to move beyond being a learning organisation to becoming teaching organisations.

The two types of organisation have many similarities. Fundamental to both is the common objective every person within the organisation continually acquires new knowledge and appropriate skills. However, the distinguishing aspect of a **teaching organisation** is its ability to be more agile and to build more continuity into its successes. This is a direct consequence of a teaching organisation's added focus on passing on learning experiences and knowledge.

A teaching organisation aims to pass on learning experiences to others and, in doing so, allow the organisation to achieve and maintain success.

A teaching organisation aims to convey learning experiences to others, and, in doing so, allow the organisation to achieve and maintain success. Leaders in teaching organisations feel responsible for sharing their knowledge with other staff as a means of helping the organisation to develop a knowledge base rapidly and accurately that is infused with hands-on experience.

The constant focus on developing its people to remain appropriately skilled and to become leaders allows a teaching organisation to become more agile and responsive to changes, because its members are always armed with the necessary knowledge and know-how to deal with new situations. An added benefit is the continuity of smooth leadership successions, preventing the potential disruption a leadership change can entail.

OBinAction

A knowledge management officer for every organisation?

Knowledge management is a broad concept that has been defined as 'a conscious strategy of getting the right knowledge to the right people at the right time'.[94] Knowledge has been described as one of the most 'strategically significant' resources of organisations;[95] both intellectual capital and employee talent have become areas of competitive advantage (and even of survival) for many organisations. As our working population ages by the year (refer to the earlier section on our aging population), the importance of not only transferring knowledge and continually up-skilling employees, but also of ensuring that critical organisational knowledge is not lost forever as the baby boomers retire, becomes increasingly important.

As the baby boomers transition out of the workforce, organisations will face risks and challenges in ensuring the transfer of knowledge of older (almost invariably, more experienced) workers.[96] While it is difficult to measure precisely how much it costs to lose critical knowledge, the costs certainly include lowered productivity, more errors, and decreased creativity. Another risk is simply that there will be a shortage of workers. The retirees are not being replaced quickly enough with young adults due to a relatively lower birth-rate in many developed countries.

A further challenge is how to retain and make the best of older workers who do remain in the workplace. The 'productivity risk' of having older workers on the payroll has been identified by some academics.[97] They claim that while age often brings valuable expertise and wisdom in some contexts it can also mean a lack of fully up-to-date skills, more health problems and absence, and lowered motivation.

The take home message here is that knowledge management professionals, now and into the future, will need to think about systems and processes such as job redesign and career planning to boost the work motivation and job performance of their older workers.[98]

Summary

Four general approaches to learning

Learning is a relatively permanent change in behaviour resulting from experience. It is an important part of rewards management. The four general approaches to learning are classical conditioning, operant conditioning, cognitive learning and social learning. Modern managers need to understand the principles of cognitive learning, which relate to the motivational theories discussed in chapter 5; operant conditioning, which is achieved when the consequences of behaviour lead to changes in the probability of its occurrence; and social learning.

Organisational behaviour modification and reinforcement strategies

Reinforcement is the means through which operant conditioning takes place. Its foundation is the law of effect, which states behaviour will be repeated or extinguished, depending on whether the consequences are positive or negative. Reinforcement is related to extrinsic rewards (valued outcomes that are given to the individual by some other person) because these rewards serve as environmental consequences that can influence people's work behaviours through the law of effect.

Organisational behaviour modification uses four reinforcement strategies to change behaviour: positive reinforcement, negative reinforcement (avoidance), punishment and extinction. Positive reinforcement is used to encourage desirable behaviour; the administration of positive consequences tends to increase the likelihood of a person repeating a behaviour in similar settings. Positive reinforcement should be contingent (administered

152   Part 2 • Managing individual behaviour and performance

only if the desired behaviour is exhibited) and immediate (as close in time to the desired behaviour as possible).

Negative reinforcement, or avoidance, is used to encourage desirable behaviour; the withdrawal of negative consequences tends to increase the likelihood a person will repeat a desirable behaviour in similar settings.

Punishment is the administration of negative consequences or the withdrawal of positive consequences, which tends to reduce the likelihood of a given behaviour being repeated in similar settings. Punishment is used to weaken or eliminate undesirable behaviour, but problems can occur. So, one must be especially careful to follow appropriate reinforcement guidelines (including the laws of contingent and immediate reinforcement) when using it. Punishment is likely to be more effective if combined with positive reinforcement.

Extinction is the withdrawal of the reinforcing consequences for a given behaviour. It is often used to withhold reinforcement for a behaviour that has previously been reinforced. This is done to weaken or eliminate the undesirable behaviour. It is an especially powerful strategy when combined with positive reinforcement.

Social learning theory and behavioural self-management

Social learning theory advocates learning through the reciprocal interactions among people, behaviour and environment. Therefore, it combines operant and cognitive learning approaches. Behavioural self-management builds on social learning theory to emphasise both behavioural and cognitive foci with a special emphasis on enhancing a worker's self-efficacy and feeling of self-control. Self-management is useful in treating workers both as individuals and as part of self-managed teams.

Managing pay as an extrinsic reward

Managing pay as an extrinsic reward is particularly important because pay has multiple meanings — some positive and some negative. As a major and highly visible extrinsic reward, pay plays a role in reinforcement and in the motivation theories discussed. Its reward implications are especially important in terms of merit pay. Other pay practices that are important and offer creative reward opportunities are skill-based pay, gain-sharing plans, lump-sum pay increases and flexible benefit plans.

Learning organisations and teaching organisations

A learning organisation is one in which members recognise the importance of communicating new knowledge for the benefit of the organisation. Such an environment can be encouraged if trust, commitment and a perception of organisational support exist. A teaching organisation is highly similar to a learning organisation; the difference lies in the focus on continuity in the passing on of necessary knowledge and 'know-how' from leaders to other members of the organisation. This ensures a teaching organisation is always agile and able to maintain its success.

CHAPTER 4 study guide

Key terms

behaviourists, *p. 125*
classical conditioning, *p. 126*
cognitive evaluation theory, *p. 141*
cognitive learning, *p. 128*
continuous reinforcement, *p. 133*
extinction, *p. 138*
extrinsic rewards, *p. 131*
intermittent reinforcement, *p. 133*
intrapersonal conflict, *p. 143*
law of contingent reinforcement, *p. 132*

law of effect, *p. 131*
law of immediate reinforcement, *p. 132*
learning, *p. 125*
merit pay, *p. 144*
negative reinforcement, *p. 136*
non-contingent reward, *p. 138*
operant conditioning, *p. 127*
organisational behaviour modification, *p. 131*
organisational learning, *p. 148*

piece rate, *p. 133*
positive reinforcement, *p. 132*
punishment, *p. 136*
reverse-incentive effect, *p. 141*
self-determination theory, *p. 141*
shaping, *p. 132*
social learning, *p. 128*
stimulus, *p. 126*
successive approximation, *p. 132*
teaching organisation, *p. 151*

Review questions

1. Explain the law of effect.
2. What are extrinsic rewards and how are these related to learning and reinforcement?
3. Distinguish between negative reinforcement and punishment.
4. Summarise the main features of a learning organisation.

Application questions

1. Describe the classical conditioning process and provide examples of its impact on behaviours and emotions.
2. Mentoring, based on social learning theory, is often used to teach less experienced managers new skills. Discuss the operation and efficacy of mentoring programs in the contemporary workplace.
3. Punishment strategies should be used sparingly by managers. Explain why.
4. What are some of the ethical issues to consider when linking pay to performance?
5. Turn back to the International Spotlight. What are some cultural issues to consider when using incentives for the purpose of achieving greater performance?
6. Critically analyse the difference between a learning organisation and organisational learning.
7. McDonalds, Nike, Levis, The Gap and many other companies have been widely criticised for using cheap labour in developing countries (refer back to the Sustainability boxed feature on 'Piece rates and "the China price"').

(a) Do you buy products from these companies? Does having information about human rights abuses make you want to avoid their products? Why? Why not?
(b) Why is it that China is able to continue to pay parts of its labour force at such a low rate? Think about demand and supply (of both products and labour).
(c) Think about the lack of intrinsic reward that jobs in Chinese factories provide. Few people would choose to work in one if given a choice. What other types of incentive schemes might possibly work in this environment?

Research questions

1. As you have read in this chapter, punishment is a management tool that continues to be used in the workplace despite increasing concerns about its effectiveness. Using the library, the internet and other resources you have access to, research the following questions. Share your responses in a 1000-word report, a 20-minute presentation or as part of an online blog.

    Thinking of your own workplace (or one you are familiar with):
    (a) How frequently is punishment used? Give examples.
    (b) Explain the behavioural and emotional response to punishment.
    (c) How does punishment prevent undesirable behaviour from reoccurring?
    (d) Do you think punishment has a place in modern workplaces? Why or why not?

2. Find an organisation online that publicises its employee rewards. How does the organisation motivate its employees? Would you like to work for this organisation? Why or why not? Compare your answer with those from others in your class and discuss why your answers may be the same or different.

Running project

Complete the following activities for your organisation.
1. Identify at least one example of each of the four approaches to learning.
2. Describe the formal and informal mentoring processes. If there are none in place, why are these considered unnecessary?
3. What extrinsic rewards does management use?
4. How does management deal with unwanted work behaviour exhibited by employees?
5. Identify whether your organisation exhibits elements of a learning or teaching organisation. Describe them. If the organisation is not a learning or teaching organisation, has this disadvantaged the organisation?

Individual activity

Learning awareness questionnaire

Introduction
This questionnaire contains statements about how you assess your own knowledge of your learning.

Instructions
Indicate the extent to which each of the following statements is true of either your actual behaviour or your intentions. Use the following scale for your responses. *Answer every statement*, even if you are not completely sure of your answer.

(Very true of me) = 5
(Often true) = 4
(Not applicable) = 3
(Seldom true) = 2
(Not true of me) = 1

_____ 1. I ask myself periodically if I am meeting my goals.

_____ 2. I try to use strategies that have worked in the past.

_____ 3. I understand my intellectual strengths and weaknesses.

_____ 4. I think about what I really need to learn before I begin a task.

_____ 5. I set specific goals before I begin a task.

_____ 6. I know what kind of information is most important to learn.

_____ 7. I consciously focus my attention on important information.

_____ 8. I learn best when I know something about the topic.

_____ 9. I periodically review to help me understand important relationships.

_____ 10. I ask myself questions about the material before I begin.

_____ 11. I think of several ways to solve a problem and choose the best one.

12. I can motivate myself to learn when I need to.
13. I use my intellectual strengths to compensate for my weaknesses.
14. I focus on the meaning and significance of new information.
15. I am a good judge of how well I understand something.
16. I ask myself how well I accomplished my goals once I'm finished.

17. I ask myself if I have considered all options after I solve a problem.
18. I learn more when I am interested in the topic.
19. I ask myself questions about how well I am doing while I am learning something new.
20. I ask myself if I learned as much as I could have once I finish a task.

To interpret your results, see page 158.

Group activity

Getting creative with remuneration

Objectives

1. To provide an experience of choices faced by managers when they make remuneration decisions.
2. To help you review some of the theoretical issues involved in attempts to motivate employees though learning, reinforcement and flexible benefit plans.
3. To apply these issues in a realistic and practical work setting.

Total time: 30 minutes

Instructions

In groups, you are to select a remuneration package that best fits each of the following employees' needs (they are listed under the employee profiles). When you have finished, one member of each group will report to the class their groups' remuneration selections for each employee. In the report the speaker must justify each selection made by using relevant theory and case knowledge.

Employee profiles

'The Nut House' is altering its pay structure to a more creative and flexible one to assist with employee motivation. However, each employee has at least 40 per cent of their package as a base salary. At the moment, all packages are paid as salary, and no performance bonuses are paid. Any additional hours worked by employees are not paid; instead, they receive time-in-lieu, which is to be taken one day at a time, on a Tuesday or Wednesday.

Fred

Fred is a middle manager who has been with the organisation for eight years. During that time he has never had a pay rise or a promotion. Fred is not skilled and obtained his position on the basis of bringing several very large customers to the organisation. Fred is unhappy at work. Fred has an aggressive manner when communicating with people. Fred has expressed no interest in learning new skills. Current salary package = $75 000.

Huong

Huong is an administrative officer who has been with the organisation for two years. She was looking for a slower-paced life where she could do her job and spend more time on her hobbies. Huong is well respected and an excellent worker who is keen to expand her knowledge at every opportunity. Current salary package = $35 000.

Carlos

Carlos is a middle manager who has been in the organisation for six years. Carlos is highly skilled and cannot be replaced easily; he is one of the hardest workers in the organisation and puts in long hours on the job. He is very well respected by everyone in the organisation and clients adore him. He never seems to take the time-in-lieu that he has accumulated. Carlos is looking for another job, where he can spend more time at home and to have an opportunity to undertake training and development. Current salary package = $90 000.

June

June is 63 years old and has been with the organisation for many years. She works two days per week. Although June is very good at her job, she has been taking more and more time off due to illness and other 'personal reasons', which is beginning to frustrate other members of staff. Current salary package = $18 000.

Kim

Kim is a 25-year-old marketing graduate who has worked in the sales department for three years. Kim intends working hard and being an executive by the time she is 30 years old. She has high aims that involve earning a lot of money, travel and driving a luxury car. Her current performance is average: she makes the sales margins, but there are also some complaints about her lack of customer service. Current salary package = $45 000.

Flexible options

Following are some of the more usual benefits available. This is not an exhaustive list and you may choose any other options that you think appropriate for the individual; be as creative as you can.

- Base salary
- Superannuation top-ups (no more than 20 per cent of total package)
- Gym membership $600
- Four-day working week $2000
- Part-time university education $2000
- Performance-linked salary
- Car allowance $10000 (tax free)
- Provision of lunch $3500
- 25 per cent pay cut per annum, for every fifth year off with full pay
- Holiday accommodation vouchers up to $2000
- Skill-based salary
- ASX 100 shares of the employee's choice $5000
- Medical benefits: single $2000, family $4000
- Mobile phone $1200
- Child-care/elder-care payments up to $4000 per annum per child/elder.

Case study: Experiential learning in organisations ... just do it!

The term 'experiential learning' differentiates the learning process from learning by rote, book learning or being 'taught'. As the Nike slogan says, 'Just do it' — and then learn through looking back and reflecting on what has been done, what worked and what didn't. In other words, experience it.

Henry Mintzberg is the author of a book simply entitled *Managing*.[99] Talking about his book to *Strategy + Business* magazine,[100] Mintzberg states that he and his colleagues were putting managers at round tables where they could 'reflect on their own work and others' experiences'. They did this to contrast with the traditional MBA approach of 'studying other (unknown) people's experiences'.

Experiential learning already underpins the way in which the New Zealand Institute of Management (NZIM) delivers its key learning programs. The approach, says NZIM Northern chief executive Kevin Gaunt:

enables participants to apply their theoretical learning on the programme and then have their understanding and application of the learning assessed ... Our key point of differentiation is that our learning programmes are delivered by experienced management practitioners. They then become the facilitators of the shared learning experiences.[101]

According to Gaunt, the approach is rooted in the organisation's history.

NZIM was established by managers after the Second World War to help returning servicemen to gain management experience for a new life on civvy street. Practicing managers were the teachers. This has continued to be our differentiator. But irrespective of the history, there is still a growing demand for this approach, and particularly among today's X and Y generations.

Experiential learning, according to the experts, doesn't really need a teacher, because it rests upon reflection and consideration of an individual's direct experience, but the process can be facilitated. For example, David A Kolb, the American educational theorist who made his name by describing the experiential learning process, believed that knowledge is continuously gained through both personal and environmental experiences. However, to gain genuine knowledge from an experience, certain abilities were required. The learner needed to:

- be actively involved in the experience
- reflect on the experience
- possess and use analytical skills to conceptualise the experience
- possess decision-making and problem-solving skills to use the new ideas gained from the experience.[102]

Mintzberg says the best way to learn is by reflecting and learning from your own experience.

When a competency issue comes up in a classroom of practicing managers, one of the most powerful things we can do is to stop everything and say, okay — there are 30 managers in this classroom. They have got an average of 15 years of managerial experience each and you ask the group: 'What have you done when you have encountered this issue?' Then you get people saying; 'Well, I had that exact issue. I dealt with it this way; it didn't work. But another time, I dealt with it that way, and it did work'. That kind of competency sharing can cut across all kinds of managerial issues that would never get discussed in a traditional classroom.[103]

However it is implemented, prevailing evidence suggests that experiential learning is a highly effective method. It works because the learner is engaged at a personal level, and the reflection and solution are tailored to address the individual's needs. According to Gaunt, NZIM also takes the experiential learning experience outside of the classroom.

We have partnered with the Sir Edmund Hillary Outdoor Pursuits Centre to provide its outdoor Executive Leadership courses. For example, a team of managers will go to Great Barrier Island for three or four days and work together to experience a range of physical and mental challenges. The Hillary Outdoor Pursuits Centre philosophy is based on experiential learning and their instructors are able to help the groups review their experiences to maximise their learning and then re-apply it in the workplace.

The relevance of experiential learning in today's world is obvious. Many of the situations managers and leaders now face are completely new, and the solutions to problems will, more often than not, be untried. New technologies, economic priorities, global externalities, trade relationships and environmental pressures are creating new challenges and opportunities. Old experiences may not provide relevant solutions in tomorrow's world so dated case studies will be less effective than ever. Shared, real-time experiences are the grist of tomorrow's learning mill.

Questions

1. Think about times when you have worked problems out for yourself, either in the classroom of in real life. Compare this learning to when you are simply told the answer or read it in a book.
2. When new employees join an organisation they are sometimes 'thrown in the deep end' (just expected to do their best and learn on the job). Other organisations choose instead to formally train and educate new recruits into their roles. Which would you prefer? Think about types of jobs/roles/organisations that would be well suited to each of the two strategies.

Interpretation of individual activity

Your ability to learn effectively may be enhanced by trying to improve your focus or abilities in the question areas where you rated yourself below '3'. Those questions on which you rated yourself greater than '3' are your perceived current learning strengths.

End notes

1. JC Muñoz, J Ortuzar and A Gschwender, 'Transantiago: the fall and rise of a radical public transport intervention', In W Saaleh and G Sammer (eds.), *Success and Failure of Travel Demand Management: Is Road User Pricing the Most Feasible Option?* (Ashgate, Aldershot, 2008).
2. ibid.
3. RM Johnson, DH Reiley and JC Muñoz, *The war of the fare: how driver compensation affects bus system performance*, working paper, (Washington, D.C.: National Bureau of Economic Research, 2006).
4. E Fisher, 'The "perfect storm" of reach: charting regulatory controversy in the age of information, sustainable development, and globalization,' *Journal of Risk Research*, vol. 11 (2008), pp. 541–63.
5. See TR Davis and F Luthans, 'A social learning approach to organisational behaviour,' *Academy of Management Review*, vol. 5 (1980), pp. 281–90.
6. For some of BF Skinner's works, see *Walden two* (New York: Macmillan, 1948); *Science and human behavior* (New York: Macmillan, 1953), *Contingencies of reinforcement* (New York: Appleton-Century-Crofts, 1969).
7. D Vaughan, *The Challenger Launch Decision: Risky Technology, Culture, and Deviance at NASA* (Chicago, IL: University of Chicago Press, 1996).
8. J Maclean, *Fire on the Mountain: The True Story of the South Canyon Fire* (New York: William Morrow, 1999).
9. MD Cannon and AC Edmondson, 'Failing to learn and learning to fail (intelligently): how great organizations put failure to work to innovate and improve', *Long Range Planning*, vol. 38 (2005), pp. 299–319.
10. AL Tucker and AC Edmondson, 'Why hospitals don't learn from failures: organizational and psychological dynamics that inhibit system change', *California Management Review*, vol. 45, no. 2 (2003), pp. 55–72.
11. BF Skinner's works, see Walden two (New York: Macmillan, 1948); Science and human behavior (New York: Macmillan, 1953), Contingencies of reinforcement (New York: Appleton-Century-Crofts, 1969).
12. GE Billikopf, 'APMP study on incentive pay. Quote from American Nurseryman magazine portion of study', (October 1995)

13. GE Billikopf, *Labor Management in Agriculture: Cultivating Personnel Productivity* (2014), www.cnr.berkeley.edu/ucce50/ag-labor/7labor.

14. ibid.

15. A Bandura, Social learning theory (Englewood Cliffs, NJ: Prentice Hall, 1977).

16. 'TV drama seen as key for women engineers,' Professional Engineering, vol. 17, issue 19 (10 November 2004), p. 9.

17. Y Cook. 'Prejudice under the Microscope.' The Independent, Tuesday 6 May 2008.

18. M Mattis, 'Women entrepreneurs: out from under the glass ceiling,' *Women in Management Review*, vol. 19, issue 3, (2004), p. 154.

19. T Peterson and R Amn, 'Self-efficacy: the foundation of human performance,' *Performance Improvement Quarterly*, vol. 18, no. 2, (2005), pp. 5–18.

20. See JD Zalesny and JK Ford, 'Extending the social information processing perspective: new links to attitudes, behaviors and perceptions,' *Organizational Behavior and Human Decision Processes*, vol. 47 (1990), pp. 205–46; ME Gist, C Schwoerer and B Rosen, 'Effects of alternative training methods of self-efficacy and performance in computer software training,' *Journal of Applied Psychology*, vol. 74 (1989), pp. 884–91; DD Sutton and RW Woodman, 'Pygmalion goes to work: the effects of supervisor expectations in a retail setting,' *Journal of Applied Psychology*, vol. 74 (1989), pp. 943–50; ME Gist, 'The influence of training method on self-efficacy and idea generation among managers,' *Personnel Psychology*, vol. 42 (1989), pp. 787–805.

21. J Mather, 'Australia's maths crisis', *The Australian Financial Review Magazine* (June 2014).

22. GV Caprara, M Vecchione, G Alessandri, M Gerbino and C Barbaranelli, 'The contribution of personality traits and self-efficacy beliefs to academic achievement: A longitudinal study', *British Journal of Educational Psychology*, vol. 81, no. 1 (2011), pp. 78–96.

23. EL Thorndike, *Animal intelligence* (New York: Macmillan, 1911), p. 244.

24. Based on Fred Luthans and Robert Kreitner, *Organizational behavior modification and beyond* (Glenview, IL: Scott, Foresman, 1985).

25. 'Paying employees not to go to the doctor,' *Business Week* (21 March 1983), p. 150; 'Giving goodies to the good,' *Time* (21 November 1985), p. 98; 'Incentive plans spur safe work habits, reducing accidents at some plants,' *Wall Street Journal* (27 January 1987), p. 1.

26. AC Gielen, MJM Kerkhofs and JC van Ours, 'How performance related pay affects productivity and employment', *Journal of Population Economics* (no. 23, 2010), pp. 291–301.

27. A Harney, *The China price: The true cost of Chinese competitive advantage* (New York: The Penguin Press, 2008).

28. Peter Navarro, 'The "China price" and weapons of mass production', *Financial Times* (2007).

29. ibid.

30. C Ichniowski and K Shaw, 'Beyond incentive pay: insiders' estimates of the value of complementary human resource management practices', *The Journal of Economic Perspectives* (2003), pp. 155–80.

31. China Labour Watch, *The toy industry in China: Undermining workers' rights and rule of law* (New York: China Labour Watch, 2005).

32. Hong Kong Christian Industrial Committee. 'McDonald's Toys: do they manufacture fun or more exploitation?' (2007).

33. China Labour Watch, *The kingmaker company's factory in Zhuhai, China: stolen wages, unfair labour practices* (New York: China Labour Watch, 2005).

34. SD Levitt and SJ Dubner, *Freakonomics. A rogue economist explores the hidden side of everything* (New York: Harper Collins, 2006).

35. J Ashworth, 'Pay Market Report — Australia & New Zealand 2008', CSi — The Remuneration Specialists Pty Limited, (2008), www.classalinfo.com.au.

36. AR Korukonda and James G Hunt, 'Pat on the back versus kick in the pants: an application of cognitive inference to the study of leader reward and punishment behavior,' *Group and Organization Studies*, vol. 14, no. 3 (1989), pp. 299–324.

37. P Kitchen, 'HR staffers learn about generational difference at Woodbury NY conference,' *Knight Ridder Tribune Business News* (Washington, 14 May 2005), p 1; Jason Rawlins, 'Work values change with new generations of workers: revolution in the workplace,' *transcript of the Australian Broadcasting Corporation radio program AM* (23 October 2004), p. 1; AR Earls, 'Clash of generations in workplace genxers, boomers seen as having different life goals, values, career expectations,' *Boston Globe* (10 August 2003), p. G1.

38. P Gilbert, 'The evolution of social attractiveness and its role in shame, humiliation, guilt, and therapy', *British Journal of Medical Psychology*, vol. 70 (1997), pp. 113–47.

39. IE de Hooge, M Zeelenberg and SM Breugelmans, 'A functionalist account of shame-induced behaviour', *Cognition and Emotion*, vol. 25, no. 5 (2011), pp. 939–46.

40. K Ntinas, 'Behavior modification and the principle of normalization: clash or synthesis?', *Behavioral Interventions*, vol. 22 (2007), pp. 165–77.

41. GA Ball, LK Trevino and HP Sims, 'Just and unjust punishment: influences on subordinate performance and citizenship,' *Academy of Management Journal*, vol. 37 (1994), pp. 299–322. Also see ch. 16 on organisational justice in M O'Driscoll, P Taylor and T Kalliath, Organisational psychology in Australia and New Zealand (Melbourne: Oxford University Press, 2003).

42. For an overview see M O'Driscoll, P Taylor and T Kalliath, Organisational psychology in Australia and New Zealand (Melbourne: Oxford University Press, 2003), ch. 16.

43. TR Hinkinand and CA Schriesheim, '"If you don't hear from me you know you are doing fine": the effects of management nonresponse to employee performance', *Cornell Hospitality Quarterly*, vol. 45, no. 4 (2004), pp. 362–72.

44. ibid.

45. Westpac Banking Corporation, www.westpac.com.au; BHP Billiton, www.bhpbilliton.com; National Australia Bank, 'NAB markets: Woolworths,' www.nabmarkets.com; The Health Insurance Commission, www.hic.gov.au; pers. com. with managing director of networking company on 10 May 2005.

46. N Nohria, B Groysberg and LE Lee, 'Employee Motivation: A Powerful New Model,' *Harvard Business Review* (July–August 2008), pp. 78–84.

47. Edwin A Locke, 'The myths of behavior mod in organizations,' *Academy of Management Review*, vol. 2 (October 1977), pp. 543–53. For a counterpoint see Jerry L Gray, 'The myths of the myths about behavior mod in organizations: a reply to Locke's criticisms of behavior modification,' *Academy of Management Review*, vol. 4 (January 1979), pp. 121–9.

48. The concern is raised in Robert Kreitner, 'Controversy in OBM: history, misconceptions, and ethics' in Lee Frederiksen (ed.), *Handbook of organizational behavior management* (New York: John Wiley & Sons, 1982), pp. 71–91.

49. M Gagne and EL Deci, 'Self-determination theory and work motivation', *Journal of Organizational Behavior*, no. 26 (2005), pp. 331–62; JL Freedman, JA Cunningham and K Krismer, 'Inferred values and the reverse-incentive effect in induced compliance', *Journal of Personality and Social Psychology*, vol. 62, no. 3 (1992), pp. 357–68

50. A Kohn, 'Why incentive plans cannot work', *Harvard Business Review*, vol. 71, no. 5 (1993), pp. 54–63; A Kohn, *Punished by rewards: the trouble with gold stars, incentive plans, A's, praise, and other bribes*, (Boston: Houghton Mifflin, 1993).

51. Gagne and Deci, op. cit.

52. EL Deci and RM Ryan, 'Self-determination theory: a macrotheory of human motivation, development, and wealth', *Canadian Psychology*, vol. 49, no. 3 (2008), pp. 182–5.

53. ibid.

54. A Kohn, 'Why incentive plans cannot work', op. cit.

55. ibid.

56. Freedman, Cunningham and Krismer, op. cit.

57. Charles C Manz and Henry P Sims, Jr, *Superleadership* (New York: Berkley, 1990).

58. T McLean, 'How to find the right frame of mind,' *Financial Times* (London, 22 April 2000), p. 22; A Johnson and J Gilbert, 'The psychological uniform: using mental skills in youth sport,' *Strategies*, vol. 18, no. 2 (2004), pp. 5–9; 'Improving the performance of expert workers,' *The Journal for Quality and Participation*, vol. 27, no. 1 (2004), pp. 9–11.

59. F Laloux, *Reinventing Organizations* (Belgium: Nelson Parker, 2014).

60. F Laloux, 'Misperceptions of self-management', Morning Star Self-Management Institute, (June, 2014), www.self-managementinstitute.org/misperceptions-of-self-management.

61. M LeFroy, 'Managing the Skills Shortage,' *My Small Business*, Fairfax, http://smallbusiness.smh.com.au.

62. MA Spinelli and GR Gray, 'How important is compensation for job satisfaction of retail trainers? Some evidence,' *Employee Benefit Plan Review*, vol. 58, no. 5 (November 2003), p. 29.

63. Edward E Lawler III, *Pay and organization development* (Reading, MA: Addison-Wesley, 1981).

64. For complete reviews of theory, research and practice, see Edward E Lawler III, *Pay and organizational effectiveness* (New York: McGraw-Hill, 1971); Lawler (1981), op. cit.; Edward E Lawler III, 'The design of effective reward systems' in Jay W Lorsch (ed.), *Handbook of organizational behavior* (Englewood Cliffs, NJ: Prentice Hall, 1987), pp. 255–71; K Bartol and A Srivastava, 'Encouraging knowledge sharing: the role of organisational reward systems,' *Journal of Leadership & Organisational Studies*, vol. 9, no. 1 (2002), pp. 64–76; S Appelbaum and B Shapiro, 'Pay for performance: implementation of individual and group,' *Management Decision*, vol. 30, no. 6 (1992), pp. 86–91.

65. M Lawson, 'Incentive schemes used mainly for chiefs,' *Australian Financial Review* (13 May 1996), p. 2.

66. Australian Council of Superannuation Investors Inc, 'CEO pay in the top 100 companies: 2002' (May 2003), www.acsi.org.au; J McConvill, 'Money can't buy you & performance,' *The Age* (10 June 2005).

67. J Ashworth, '*Pay Market Report* — Australia & New Zealand 2008', CSi — The Remuneration Specialists Pty Limited, www.classalinfo.com.au.

68. State Services Commission, www.ssc.govt.nz.

69. Australian Bureau of Statistics, *6302.0 — Average Weekly Earnings, Australia, Nov 2013* (20 February 2014), www.abs.gov.au/ausstats/abs@.nsf/mf/6302.0.

70. 'The Mayne Report rich list', *The Mayne Report* (7 February 2014), www.maynereport.com.

71. T Hardy, 'Philanthropy — a Fad That's Here to Stay,' *Money Management*, 2007, p. 24.

72. 'A look at the 50 most generous donors of 2013', The Chronicle of Philanthropy (9 February 2014), http://philanthropy.com/article/A-Look-at-the-50-Most-Generous.

73. 'The 50 most generous philanthropists', *Bloomberg Business week*, www.bloomberg.com.

74. C Trelford, D Miller, 'Bill Gates: How a Geek Changed the World,' BBC Productions and The Open University, 2008.

75. Jone L Pearce, 'Why merit pay doesn't work: implications from organization theory' in David B Balkin and Luis R Gomez-Mejia (eds), *New perspectives on compensation* (Englewood Cliffs, NJ: Prentice Hall, 1987), pp. 169–78; Jerry M Newman, 'Selecting incentive plans to complement organizational strategy' in David R Balkin and Luis R Gomez-Mejia (eds), *New perspectives on compensation* (Englewood Cliffs, NJ: Prentice Hall, 1987), pp. 214–24; Edward E Lawler III, 'Pay for performance: making it work,' *Compensation and Benefits Review*, vol. 21, no. 1 (1989), pp. 55–60.

76. See Daniel C Boyle, 'Employee motivation that works,' *HR Magazine*, vol. 37, no. 10 (October 1992), pp. 83–9. Kathleen A McNally, 'Compensation as a strategic tool,' *HR Magazine*, vol. 37, no. 7 (July 1992), pp. 59–66.

77. N Weinberg, 'Hidden treasure,' *Forbes* (New York, 28 October 2002), p. 58.

78. F Luthans and AD Stajkovic, 'Reinforce (not necessarily pay) for performance', *Academy of Management Executive* vol. 13 (1999), pp. 49–57; F Luthans, R Paul and D Baker, 'An experimental analysis of the impact of contingent reinforcement on salesperson's performance behavior', *Journal of Applied Psychology*, vol. 66 (1981), pp. 314–23; F Luthans, AD Stajkovic, BC Luthans and KW Luthans, K.W., 'Applying behavioral management Eastern Europe', *European Management Journal*, vol. 16 (1998), pp. 466–75.

79. AD Stajkovic and F Luthans, 'Behavioral management and task performance in organizations: conceptual background, meta-analysis, and test of alternative models', *Personnel Psychology*, vol. 56 (2003), pp. 155–94.

80. G Hofstede, *Culture's consequences: comparing values, behaviors, institutions, and organizations across nations* (Thousand Oaks, CA: Sage, 2001).

81. S Rhee, BC Luthans and JB Avey, 'Impact of behavioral performance management in a Korean application', *Leadership & Organization Development Journal*, vol. 29, no. 5 (2008), pp. 427–43.

82. P Senge, *The fifth discipline* (Sydney: Random House, 1992).

83. Randolph T Barker and Martin R Camarata, 'The role of communication in creating and maintaining a learning organisation: preconditions, indicators and disciplines,' *Journal of Business Communication*, vol. 35, no. 4 (1998), pp. 443–67.

84. D Blackman and S Henderson, 'Why learning organisations do not transform,' *The Learning Organization Journal*, vol. 12, no. 1 (2005), pp. 42–56; L Lee-Kelley and D Blackman, 'More than shared goals: the impact of mental models on team innovation and learning,' *Journal of Innovation and Learning*, vol. 2, no. 1 (2005), pp. 11–25; D Blackman, 'Is knowledge acquisition and transfer realisable?,' *Electronic Journal of Radical Organization Theory*, vol. 7, no. 1, (March 2001), www.mngt.waikato.ac.nz.

85. ibid.

86. Deborah Blackman and Steve Henderson, 'Why learning organisations do not transform,' *The Learning Organization Journal*, vol. 12, no. 1 (2005), pp. 42–56.

87. ibid.

88. L Lee-Kelley and D Blackman, 'More than shared goals: the impact of mental models on team innovation and learning,' *Journal of Innovation and Learning*, vol. 2, no. 1 (2005), pp. 11–25.

89. ibid.

90. F Gino and G Pisano, 'Why leaders don't learn from success', *Harvard Business Review* (April 2011) pp. 68–74.

91. P Sims, 'What Google could learn from Pixar', *Harvard Business Review: The Conversation* (August 2010), http://blogs.hbr.org.

92. DA Price, *The Pixar touch: the making of a company* (London: Vintage Books, 2009).

93. Sims, op. cit.

94. C O'Dell, C and CJ Grayson, *If only we knew what we know* (New York: Free Press, 1998).

95. RM Grant, 'Toward a knowledge-based theory of the firm', *Strategic Management Journal*, vol. 17 (1996), pp. 109–22.

96. TJ Calo, 'Talent management in the era of the aging workforce: the critical role of knowledge transfer', *Public Personnel Management*, vol. 37, no. 4 (2008), pp. 403–16.

97. R Strack, J Baier and A Fahlander, 'Managing demographic risk' *Harvard Business Review*, vol. 86, no. 2 (2008), pp. 119–28.

98. TJ Calo, op. cit.

99. H Mintzberg, *Managing* (San Fransisco: Berrett-Koehler Publishers, 2009).

100. A Kleiner, 'Management by reflection', *Strategy + Business* (March 2010).

101. R Birchfield, 'NZIM executive learning: experiential learning' *NZ Management Magazine* (May 2010).

102. ibid.

103. Kleiner, op. cit.

CHAPTER 5

JOB DESIGN, GOAL SETTING AND FLEXIBLE WORK ARRANGEMENTS

LEARNING OBJECTIVES

After studying this chapter, you should be able to:

1. explain the concepts of intrinsic motivation and intrinsic rewards

2. compare and contrast the alternative job design strategies and link them to intrinsic work rewards

3. discuss the job characteristics model and clarify how it employs job diagnosis techniques as a newer approach to job enrichment

4. explain how goal-setting theory is linked to job design, motivation and performance

5. discuss how flexible work arrangements contribute to workforce flexibility and individual satisfaction.

THE THIRD METRIC

Arianna Huffington is the chair, president, and editor-in-chief of the Huffington Post Media Group, a world famous syndicated columnist, and a celebrated author. She has recently coined the term 'The Third Metric'. The Third Metric is a way to redefine success beyond money and power (the traditional measures of success) and move towards a more holistic metric. Arianna Huffington believes that success should also be measured by our wellbeing, wisdom, and ability to make a difference in the world.[1]

In the context of these ideas numerous articles and blogs have been devoted to redesigning work in an effort to improve wellbeing and happiness. For example, Claire Snowdon-Darling (an alternative health expert) writes:

> The third metric is vital, I agree wholeheartedly and good goddess do I wanna be one of those 'up at dawn doing yoga followed by a green juice before skipping to my office' type of women but in reality I'm a 'drag my butt out of bed, put the clothes on I left on the floor last night, grab a protein shake, do the school run and roll into my office feeling stressed already' kind of women. So, how do we change this without putting more pressure on ourselves? … knowing how to say 'no' plays an important role. If we want to change the parameters of success and allow ourselves to have a life and wellbeing as well as money and power the seed of change has to start now.[2]

Similarly, Joanna Lyall (the Chief Planning Officer at Mindshare) discusses flexitime; stating that, traditionally, our way of working meant that work happened only in the office and only home life happened at home. Technology has changed all that. It is now possible to be online and electronically present at work no matter where you are. Many employees

almost entirely stop switching off. So, if we are not working 9–5, but are instead doing more in the evening or weekends to be freer during the traditional workday, when do we switch off from work and find balance? Joanna asks, is it really possible to 'do it all' and not let our health and happiness suffer?[3]

Innovative work arrangements such as flexitime require high trust between employers and employees and colleagues. It requires a collective commitment to delivering clear outputs. Being at your desk between certain hours is rapidly becoming irrelevant. If our days become less defined by the hours that we do and more so by our results, then the benefits both to organisations and individuals could be enormous.[4] This chapter explores these ideas and more by looking at job design and flexible work arrangements as a source of satisfaction and motivation in the work context.

Introduction

In chapter 3 we discussed motivation in relation to intrinsic and extrinsic rewards. We built on that treatment in chapter 4, emphasising various aspects of reinforcement and different kinds of pay plans as extrinsic rewards. In this chapter we give special emphasis to intrinsic rewards that work can offer and how to use job design, goal setting and flexible work arrangements to improve intrinsic job satisfaction.

Our society and the nature of workplaces are continuously changing, generating forces that impact upon how workers experience their work and their workplaces. Within the workplace, there is a deeper appreciation of how the job itself can affect an individual's motivation and job satisfaction. Organisations have moved well beyond simply trying to improve worker performance by offering limited extrinsic rewards such as higher wages or promotion.

There is more focus now on responding to the intrinsic rewards that workers get from doing their jobs, and on the goals that can help to guide and motivate them in their work. Designing the work to maximise employee outcomes is fundamental to this process. The theoretical aspects of job design are explained and job design theories or approaches (such as job characteristics, socio-technical, socio-information and multiskilling) are examined to demonstrate how the design of jobs can have an impact on workers. The alignment and achievement of organisational goals through a process of goal setting is also considered, since this impacts upon employees' jobs and their motivation, satisfaction and performance within them. Finally, a discussion of flexible work arrangements explores how the very arrangements in which workers are employed are being reconsidered and modified. These new arrangements take into account the demands that employees experience; they enhance the quality of their working lives and also enhance their capacity to work productively for their organisations.

Intrinsic motivation

Intrinsic work rewards were defined in chapter 3 as those rewards that an individual receives directly as a result of task performance. One example is the feeling of achievement that comes from completing a challenging project. Such feelings are individually determined and integral to the work. The individual is not dependent on an outsider, such as a manager, to provide these rewards or feelings. This concept is in direct contrast to extrinsic rewards, such as pay and conditions, which are externally controlled. The unique nature of intrinsic rewards can be seen when a social worker says: 'My working conditions are bad and my coworkers are boring, but I get a sense of satisfaction out of helping my clients'.[5]

Intrinsic work rewards are a very important part of motivating and satisfying employees in the workplace.[6] Herzberg's two-factor theory of motivation in chapter 3 particularly draws attention to the importance of intrinsic job content factors in improving satisfaction in the job (while extrinsic job context factors can lead to dissatisfaction). His ideas will be discussed further in this chapter when job enrichment is considered. Intrinsic work rewards play a key part in effective job design. The previous example illustrates that people can be motivated simply because they enjoy the experience of accomplishing tasks. This is described as intrinsic motivation, which is a desire to work hard solely for the pleasant experience of task accomplishment.

When we discussed extrinsic rewards in the last chapter, we saw the manager as responsible for allocating extrinsic rewards such as pay, promotion and verbal praise to employees, and for controlling general working conditions. To serve in this capacity, a manager must be good at evaluating performance, maintaining an inventory of valued work rewards and giving these rewards to employees contingent upon work performance.

Intrinsic motivation is a desire to work hard solely for the pleasant experience of task accomplishment.

Putting a price tag on friends

Some fascinating research published in the *Journal of Socio-Economics* explored the notion that it is social relationships that primarily promote happiness for individuals.[7] The author asks the question, 'Which is better for us: a large pay rise or more quality time spent with friends and relatives?' This seems like an almost impossible question to answer with any certainty and, historically, there has been no simple way to assess the size of different influences upon happiness and satisfaction with life in general.

Economists have, however, recently developed a way to do so. The process involves taking a random sample of individuals, recording their satisfaction levels at different

(continued)

COUNTER**POINT**

points in time, and then using statistical methods to work out the implied value of different life events. For example, economists have been able to show, using happiness surveys, that marriage (compared to being single) is worth around £70 000 (or A$125 000) a year for a person in Great Britain. Separation, on the other hand, is equivalent to around minus £170 000 (or A$301 000) a year.

Numerous empirical studies support the notion that people with strong social ties tend to report higher levels of happiness and satisfaction than those without social ties. This finding has been supported in school,[8] in the community,[9] and at work.[10] The author provides evidence that an increase in the level of social involvement is worth an extra £85 000 (A$151 000) a year in terms of life satisfaction (more than being married!). Actual changes in income, on the other hand, buy very little happiness.

A workplace implication of this research is that organisations that focus on fulfilling the social needs of employees (either by providing a friendly, social work environment, or by giving employees the flexibility to maintain their outside relationships) will have a happier, more satisfied workforce. Further, this impact is far greater than simply offering increased extrinsic rewards such as pay or bonuses.

Managing intrinsic work rewards presents an additional challenge for the manager. Still acting as an agent of the organisation, the manager must design jobs for individual employees so that intrinsic rewards become available to them as a direct result of feedback gained from working on assigned tasks. That is not to say that every manager should design every job to provide every employee with the maximum opportunity to experience intrinsic work rewards. This chapter will help you to understand:

- when people may desire intrinsic work rewards
- how to design jobs for people who desire greater intrinsic work rewards
- how to motivate those people who do not desire intrinsic work rewards.

Job design

Jobs are one or more tasks that an individual performs in direct support of an organisation's production purpose.

A **job** is one or more tasks that an individual performs in direct support of an organisation's production purpose. When a job is properly designed, it should facilitate both task performance and job satisfaction, partly through intrinsic motivation. Additional aspects of human resource maintenance (defined in chapter 5 as the attraction and continuation of a viable workforce) such as absenteeism, commitment and turnover, may also be influenced. These are costly outcomes — for example, it is estimated that the cost of staff turnover to Australian employers is $20 billion annually.[11] Lencioni argues that the three signs of a 'miserable job' are irrelevance, immeasurability and anonymity.[12] Clearly, there is a range of factors we can consider when examining the design of jobs and it is important that we understand whether jobs affect people positively or negatively.

Job design is the planning and specification of job tasks and the work setting in which they are to be accomplished.

Job design involves the planning and specification of job tasks and the work setting designated for their accomplishment. This definition includes both the specification of task attributes and the creation of a work setting for these attributes. It includes all the structural and social elements of the job, and their impacts on employee behaviour and performance. The objective of job design is to help make jobs meaningful, interesting and challenging. The manager's responsibility is to design jobs that will motivate the individual employee. Figuratively speaking, this is properly done when:

Individual needs + task attributes + work setting *lead to* performance and satisfaction.

Between 1900 and 1950 there were many developments in management theories that ranged from scientific studies of job efficiency to studies that were more concerned with the human response to the job. Four major approaches to job design were identified. Each approach was prescriptive in nature and assumed that all workers would respond to the strategies in the same manner. None of these approaches made allowance for variation in the motivational potential of the individual worker, though each still contributes to our understanding of job design today. The approaches were:

1. job simplification (job engineering)
2. job enlargement
3. job rotation
4. job enrichment.

Job simplification

Job simplification, often termed job engineering, involves standardising work procedures and employing people in clearly defined and specialised tasks. The machine-paced car assembly line is a classic example of this job design strategy.

This approach, deriving from the scientific managers such as Frederick Taylor, involves simplified jobs that are highly specialised and usually require an individual to perform a narrow set of tasks repetitively. The potential advantages include increased operating efficiency (which was the original intent of the job simplification approach), low-skill and low-cost labour, minimal training requirements and controlled production quantity. Some possible disadvantages of this 'de-skilling' include loss of efficiency due to low-quality work, high rates of absenteeism and turnover, and the need to pay high wages to get people to do unattractive jobs. For most people, simplified job designs tend to be low in intrinsic motivation. The jobs lack challenge and lead to boredom. In today's high-tech age, a natural extension of job simplification is complete automation — allowing a machine to do the work previously accomplished through human effort. Since simple work can be put into a routine, it tends to be easier to automate it.

> **Job simplification** is standardising work procedures and employing people in clearly defined and specialised tasks.

> **Automation** is a job design that allows machines to do work previously accomplished by human effort.

WhatWould YouDo?

Having to do boring work ... even the simplest of jobs can offer fulfilment

It is all very well recommending that people strive to do 'interesting' work, but the fact remains, for some people, at some point in their lives, there may be little choice. When they have no work experience, when they are very young and have yet to gain qualifications, and before their first 'real' job, many people take whatever work they can get. While gaining qualifications or still at high school, many students will engage in repetitive, simple and boring jobs where it is difficult to feel motivated. If nothing else, these jobs can provide both money and valuable work experience and may even motivate people to focus on their studies in order to avoid having to do this type of work indefinitely.

In addition, it is worth noting that a job you can 'leave behind' when you walk out the door is just what some people want — a job where you turn up, work hard and get paid, but doesn't take up headspace or interfere with other aspects of life.

Tom Morris, an academic at Notre Dame and the founder of the Morris Institute for Human Values, argues that the teachings of ancient philosophers can (and should) be applied to today's corporation, in his book *If Aristotle ran General Motors*.[13] Morris writes that even the most routine of jobs can be made interesting, fulfilling and challenging:

> A concern for truth should continually play an important role in how we think about our jobs and in the many ways we interact with others in our work. But a concern for beauty should guide us too.

(continued)

How, you might wonder, can a factory worker be an artist and experience this form of active beauty if he has to perform the same routine motions, over and over, all day long? This is part of the reason Jack Stack decided to teach everyone at the Springfield Remanufacturing Company what he began to call 'The Great Game of Business'.

Even the factory-floor worker engaged in repetitive acts of assembly can play the game of business, using his mind to devise more efficient processes and motions, connecting his specific job with the big picture of what's going on in the overall company life.

He may be able to see things no-one else can see and make suggestions for beautiful improvements no-one else could make. He alone may be in a position to create an elegant solution to a problem that no-one else can solve, or even notice.

We need to encourage the people who work around us to think of their jobs in this way, no matter what their jobs might be. Everyone can be a performance artist and an important player in the great game of business.

Questions

1. While completing your degree, do you think a simple, repetitive job that requires no mental effort, or a job (perhaps in your chosen field) that takes a great deal of energy is preferable?
2. What has been your own experience of 'boring' work, perhaps while studying, or early in your career? What were some of the positive things you got from this experience?

Job enlargement

Job enlargement involves increasing task variety by combining into one job tasks of similar skill levels that were previously assigned to separate workers.

Job enlargement emerged in the 1950s when many managers sought a job design strategy to reduce the boredom associated with the job engineering approach. The aim is to increase the breadth of a job by adding to the variety of tasks performed by a worker. Task variety is assumed to offset some of the disadvantages of job simplification, thereby increasing job performance and satisfaction for the individual. Job enlargement increases task variety by combining into one job two or more tasks previously assigned to separate workers. The only change in the original job design is that a worker now does a greater variety of tasks.

Often job enlargement has not lived up to its promise. For example, if a graphic designer who has been designing business brochures and posters is also given the task of preparing book cover layouts, the job has been enlarged even if the same basic technique of using computer design software is utilised. The designer's supervisor would still secure the business, conduct meetings with the client and oversee the tasks, so there is no more responsibility. Job enlargement may add variety and alleviate boredom with mundane tasks but there may be limits to how much it might stimulate and satisfy the designer.

Job rotation

Job rotation involves increasing task variety by periodically shifting workers among jobs involving different tasks at similar levels of skill.

Like job enlargement, **job rotation** increases task variety but generally it does so by periodically shifting workers among jobs involving different tasks at similar skill levels. Job rotation can be arranged around almost any time period, such as hourly, daily or weekly schedules. For example, a nurse may be rotated on a monthly basis, looking after geriatric patients one month, surgical patients the next and rehabilitation patients each third month. Job rotation is often used for younger employees who are 'learning the ropes' in an organisation, as the following example illustrates.

From bags to tickets to customer service

International
SPOTLIGHT

Job rotation is particularly appropriate if employees often do very routine work. At Singapore Airlines, for example, a ticket agent may take on the duties of a baggage handler. Extensive job rotation is one of the reasons Singapore Airlines is rated one of the best airlines in the world and has the reputation as being a highly desirable place to work.

On its website (www.singaporeair.com) Singapore Airlines makes a point of informing customers

about its job rotation schemes. It states that it is 'committed to developing employees into true airline professionals'. The diverse nature of the business provides varied scope for development. With Singapore Airlines' job rotation scheme, employees can look forward to job postings either within their own specialist field or across functional areas.[14]

Although Singapore Airlines has used job rotation to its advantage, the results — as with job enlargement — are not always so positive. If a rotation cycle takes employees through a series of similar jobs, they may experience many boring jobs instead of merely a single boring job. A nurse may be doing the same repetitive tasks, such as checking pulses and taking blood pressure and temperatures, in each ward. In different wards there may be different tasks like checking and changing wound dressings or feeding patients in geriatrics; however, the tasks may still seem routine.

While job rotation may decrease efficiency because people spend more time changing, it can add to workforce flexibility. Staff can be moved from one job to another. This is often the primary purpose of job rotation. Employers have a more adaptable workforce to accomplish work tasks when employees are on sick or recreation leave, or when they move from the organisation.

Perhaps the greatest weakness in the application of job rotation in the 1950s was that workers tended to be rotated horizontally (expanding the scope of the job) — that is, across tasks that demanded similar skill profiles. In other words, just as with enlargement, there was a horizontal loading of tasks, which means the breadth of the job is increased by the addition of a variety of tasks. Since the mid 1970s, job rotation has become an important part of work experience and corporate acculturation. New employees are often rotated around the company and across different divisions to gain a better understanding of the corporate structure and corporate work and communication networks. At Robert Bosch Australia, a producer of automotive parts, new apprentices are taken through a program of planned job rotation after their initial basic training.[15] Job rotation can often involve vertical loading, which enables increasing job depth by adding responsibilities, like planning and controlling, that were previously held by supervisors. Such experience often contributes to employee development and helps overcome many limitations of the earlier approaches to job rotation. China, for example, has used rotation schemes to send employees from central urban locations into rural areas to keep in touch with the needs of rural communities.[16] Global companies such as Pirelli, Kone and Standard Chartered Bank all offer job rotation as a feature of employment that encourages personal and career development and/or helps staff to diversify their experience.[17] Vertical loading is a key aspect of job enrichment.

Horizontal loading involves increasing the breadth of a job by adding to the variety of tasks that the worker performs.

Vertical loading involves increasing job depth by adding responsibilities, like planning and controlling, previously held by supervisors.

Job enrichment

Job enrichment is the practice of building motivating factors into job content.

Frederick Herzberg, whose two-factor theory is discussed in chapter 3, suggests that it is illogical to expect high levels of motivation from employees whose jobs are designed according to the rules of simplification, enlargement or rotation (with horizontal loading). Herzberg asks, '[Why] should a worker become motivated when one or more "meaningless" tasks are added to previously existing ones or when work assignments are rotated among equally "meaningless" tasks?'[18] Rather than pursuing one of these job design strategies, Herzberg recommends that managers practise job enrichment.

Job enrichment is the practice of building motivating factors into job content. This job design strategy differs from the previous ones in that it seeks to expand job content by adding planning and evaluating duties (normally performed by the manager) to the employee's job. The changes that increase the 'depth' of a job involve vertical loading of the tasks, as opposed to the horizontal loading involved in job enlargement and much job rotation.

The seven principles guiding Herzberg's approach to job enrichment are listed in table 5.1. Each principle is an action guideline designed to increase the presence of one or more motivating factors. Remember, in the job enlargement and rotation strategies, managers tend to retain all responsibility for work planning and evaluating; in contrast, the job enrichment strategy involves vertical loading, which allows employees to share in these planning and evaluating responsibilities, as well as do the actual work.

TABLE 5.1 Herzberg's principles of job enrichment

Principle	Motivators involved
1. Remove some controls while retaining accountability	Responsibility and achievement
2. Increase the accountability of individuals for their own work	Responsibility and recognition
3. Give a person a complete natural unit of work (module, division, area and so on)	Responsibility, achievement and recognition
4. Grant additional authority to employees in their activities; provide job freedom	Responsibility, achievement and recognition
5. Make periodic reports directly available to the worker rather than to the supervisor	Recognition
6. Introduce new and more difficult tasks that the individual has not previously handled	Growth and learning
7. Assign to individuals specific or specialised tasks; enable them to become experts	Responsibility, achievement, recognition and advancement

On the face of it, job enrichment seems appealing. However, it has some problems.
- Little, if any, diagnosis of the jobs is undertaken before they are redesigned.
- Cost–benefit data pertaining to job enrichment are not often reported and it may not always be worth it. Much of the time it is expensive to implement, especially if work flows need to be redesigned and facilities or equipment changed.
- Situational factors specifically supporting job enrichment have often not been systematically assessed.
- Many reports of the success of job enrichment have been evangelical in nature — that is, the authors overstate benefits and understate problems. There are few reported failures in the literature, possibly as a result of such bragging.
- Evaluations of job enrichment programs too often have not been conducted rigorously using the appropriate scientific method.

- Many trials of job enrichment have been undertaken with hand-picked employees, rather than a random sample of employees representing differing skill profiles and job environments.
- Job enrichment theory fails to recognise and emphasise that individuals may respond differently to job enrichment and that not all individuals will like it.
- Job enrichment falls into that category of workplace innovations that is much talked about but not widely practised. Despite the plethora of literature defining job enrichment, only a small number of case studies have actually been reported.[19]

The various strategies of job design are summarised on a continuum in figure 5.1. This figure shows how the strategies differ in their degree of task specialisation and as sources of intrinsic work rewards. The availability of intrinsic rewards is lowest for task attributes associated with simplified jobs, and highest for enriched jobs. Task specialisation is higher for simplified jobs and lower for enriched jobs.

The four basic approaches to job design (simplification, enlargement and rotation, and enrichment), as shown in figure 5.1, have provided vital insights into the complexity of effective job design. Collectively, they are an important platform for later theorists. However, the common factor underlying these approaches is that they are 'static'; that is, they assume that all individuals will respond in the same, positive manner to these approaches. They fail to recognise the 'dynamic' nature of individual behaviour — that workers can, and will, respond in a variety of ways to the implementation of any innovative job design approach. To be effective, a manager needs to be able to understand, identify and predict how an individual worker will respond to any job redesign approach.

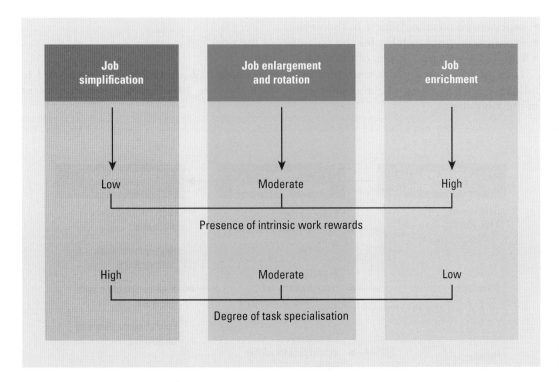

FIGURE 5.1 A continuum of job design strategies

The job characteristics model

Pioneering work by Turner and Lawrence (1965) and Hulin and Blood (1967, 1968) began to look at the role of individual differences in job design.[20] They were trying to understand how an individual would respond to job redesign. That work led to the diagnostic approach — a technique developed by Richard Hackman and Greg Oldham, which is the basis of their job characteristics model (sometimes abbreviated to JCM). This model addresses job design in a contingency fashion.[21] The diagnostic job design approach, which generated considerable research in the 1980s, recognises that there will be differences in the way any group of individuals responds to a change in the design of their jobs.

The current version of this newer approach to job enrichment, as depicted in Hackman and Oldham's **job characteristics model**, is shown in figure 5.2.[22] Five core job characteristics are identified as task attributes of special importance in the diagnosis of job designs. A job that is high in these core characteristics is said to be enriched. The core job characteristics are:

1. *skill variety* — the degree to which the job requires an employee to undertake a variety of different activities and use different skills and talents
2. *task identity* — the degree to which the job requires completion of a 'whole' and identifiable piece of work (that is, it involves doing a job from beginning to end with a visible outcome)
3. *task significance* — the degree to which the job is important and involves a meaningful contribution to the organisation or society in general
4. *autonomy* — the degree to which the job gives the employee substantial freedom, independence and discretion in scheduling the work and determining the procedures used in carrying it out
5. *job feedback* — the degree to which carrying out the work activities results in the employee obtaining direct and clear information on how well the job has been done.

Furthermore, Hackman and Oldham state critical psychological states which must be realised for people to develop intrinsic work motivation. These are:

* experienced meaningfulness in the work
* experienced responsibility for the outcomes of the work
* knowledge of actual results of the work activities.

These psychological states represent intrinsic rewards that are believed to occur and to influence later performance and satisfaction when the core job characteristics are present in the job design.

The **job characteristics model** identifies five core characteristics (skill variety, task identity, task significance, autonomy and job feedback) as having special importance to job designs.

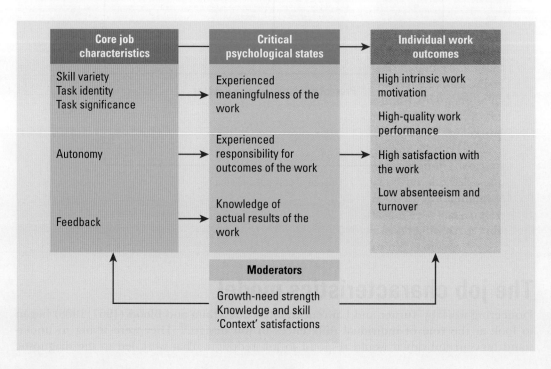

FIGURE 5.2 Core job characteristics and individual work outcomes

Kiwis want flexibility and opportunity for growth

OBinAction

According to the recent 'World of Work Report' commissioned by Randstad (a leading recruitment consultancy based in the Asia–Pacific region), almost half (49 per cent) of the Kiwi workforce will be seeking a new job in the coming year.[23] NZ employers who can't or don't offer what talented Kiwi workers are looking for will feel the bite of the talent shortage moving forward.

Paul Robinson, director of Randstad New Zealand was interviewed in the *NZ Herald* about the key findings of the report.[24] He is quoted as stating, 'With business conditions improving, workers in many industries are feeling more confident they will receive an increase in salary, growth or promotion'. Robinson says this is great for employees, but it also means that employers will need to address these expectations. Organisations will need to concentrate on how to retain a motivated and satisfied workforce while also attracting the best talent.

The report shows that most of those people looking to leave their jobs (63 per cent) will do so for career advancement, far more than those changing jobs to simply earn more money or benefits (45 per cent).

Robinson says this proves once again that New Zealanders are looking for more than money. 'For more than half of New Zealand employees, flexible working options are one of the top three most important benefits. Training and development opportunities, and being rewarded and recognised for strong performance are also important to Kiwi workers.'

Robinson makes the point that people are not always looking for a step up. 'Many are simply looking for an opportunity to be challenged, or to work on a project or area that will expand their skills, knowledge and experience.'

Individual differences: moderators of the job characteristics model

The job characteristics model recognises that the five core job characteristics do not affect all people in the same way. Unlike many earlier theories of job design, the job characteristics model recognises individual differences in response to changes in job design. A number of factors will influence the manner in which any individual employee responds to changes in the design of his or her job. These factors are called 'job design moderators'. Figure 5.2 shows three important individual difference moderators.

- *Growth-need strength.* This is the degree to which a person desires the opportunity for self-direction, learning and personal accomplishment at work. It is similar to Maslow's esteem and self-actualisation and Alderfer's growth needs. The theory predicts that people strong in growth-need will respond positively to enriched jobs, experiencing high internal motivation, high growth satisfaction, high-quality performance and low absenteeism and turnover. On the other hand, people low in growth-need strength will have negative reactions and will find enriched jobs a source of anxiety. They are likely to be at risk of being 'overstretched' in the job and possibly baulking at doing the job.[25]

- *Knowledge and skill.* Those with the knowledge and skill needed for performance in an enriched job are predicted to respond positively to the enrichment. Once again, we see how important a sense of competency or self-efficacy can be to people at work.
- *Context satisfaction.* This is the extent to which an employee is satisfied with the kind of contextual factors emphasised by Herzberg. For example, those satisfied with salary levels, supervision and working conditions are more likely than their dissatisfied colleagues to support job enrichment.

This list of moderators of the work outcome relationship of the job characteristics model is not intended to be exhaustive, because many other variables (such as high-order needs, workers' value systems, perceptions of social impact and social worth, conscientiousness and pro-social values) have also been examined as potential moderators of reactions to these job dimensions.[26] In general, people whose capabilities match the requirements of an enriched job are likely to experience positive feelings and to perform well; people who are inadequate or who feel inadequate in this regard are likely to have difficulties.

Testing and the motivating potential score

Hackman and Oldham developed the **job diagnostic survey** questionnaire to test each of the dimensions in their job characteristics model, as shown in figure 5.2. They also developed a **motivating potential score** (MPS) to summarise a job's overall potential for motivating those in the workplace. You can calculate this score using the following formula:

$$\text{MPS} = (\text{variety} + \text{identity} + \text{significance})/3 \times \text{autonomy} \times \text{feedback}$$

The scores for each of the dimensions come from the job diagnostic survey and show the great importance of autonomy and feedback in providing the results shown in figure 5.2. The MPS is especially useful for identifying low-scoring jobs that may benefit most from redesign.

The research

Considerable research has been done on the job characteristics approach. The approach has been examined in a variety of work settings, including banks, dentists' offices, corrective services departments, telephone companies, and such organisations as IBM and Texas Instruments. Job-design studies using this approach have also been reported in Australia.[27] A comprehensive review of the approach shows that:[28]

- on average, job characteristics affect performance, but not nearly as much as they affect satisfaction
- it is important to consider growth-need strength. Job characteristics influence performance more strongly for high growth-need employees than for low growth-need employees. The relationship to growth-need is about as strong as that to job satisfaction.
- employee perceptions of job characteristics are different from objective measures and from those of independent observers. Positive results are typically strongest when an overall performance measure is used, rather than a separate measure of quality or quantity.

Luthans also argues that employee perceptions are dynamic and change over time; sometimes even from day-to-day.[29] The degree of engagement or disengagement may be a critical factor.

The effective manager 5.1 summarises some guidelines for implementing a job enrichment program and for reviewing the process.

Experts generally agree that the job diagnostic approach that is the basis for Hackman and Oldham's job characteristics model is useful. A series of implementation concepts for the enrichment of core job characteristics is outlined in figure 5.3[30] and some impacts of enriching core job characteristics are listed in table 5.2 (overleaf). However, these experts urge caution in applying the technique, emphasising that it is not a universal panacea for job performance and satisfaction problems. It can fail when job requirements are increased beyond the level of individual capabilities and/or interest. It can also raise issues of changes in remuneration — if employees are taking on more responsibility, should they be paid more? In summary, jobs high in core characteristics (especially as perceived by employees) tend to increase both satisfaction and performance, particularly among high growth-need employees. It is clear that this approach is not always going to be successful or appropriate. For example, as the What would you do? (overleaf) shows, it can be difficult in the case of actively disengaged workers. The forthcoming Counterpoint illustrates that people are often looking for different things in their work and it highlights that sometimes, these unique factors may trigger career changes — regardless of how effectively an organisation designs its job positions.

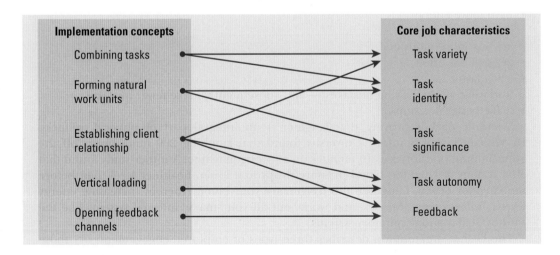

FIGURE 5.3 Implementation concepts and the core job characteristics

	Enriched	Unenriched
Skill variety	Decided own strategy for performing task and changed strategy at will	Were provided with explicit instructions for task to perform and strategy to use (e.g. 'first, open letters')
Task identity	Formed into groups of ten; performed all necessary operations on a certain proportion of customer requests	As an individual, performed just one of these operations on all requests
Task significance	Were briefed about importance of their jobs and how they fitted into the organisation as a whole	Received no formal instruction
Autonomy	Chose length and timing of breaks. Performed own inspections at intervals they determined	Except for breaks, stayed at workplace throughout the day. Had work periodically checked by inspectors
Feedback	Saw productivity posted on scoreboards at end of each day	Received no specific information about performance level

What Would You Do?

Feeling stressed and disengaged at work?

There has been increasing attention given to ways people can relieve stress in the workplace and, more and more, people have come to realise that laughter and humour are great remedies for stress.

Ross Smith has worked in the software industry for over twenty years, and is currently a Director of Test at Microsoft. He writes in the *Management Innovation eXchange* (www.managementexchange.com) about laughter at work and asks whether it is possible that laughter is a measure of success for a healthy, creative and innovative organisation.[31] If you are laughing, Ross says, it could be because you're succeeding ... it might also be *why* you're succeeding!

Salvatore Moccia (Professor of Strategic Management at Universidad CEU Cardenal Herrera) suggests that happy people:

- work better with others
- are more creative
- fix problems instead of complaining about them
- have more energy
- are more optimistic
- are way more motivated
- get sick less often
- learn faster
- worry less about making mistakes — and consequently make fewer mistakes
- make better decisions.[32]

Scientific data is proving that laughter is an integral part of physical wellness. Dr William Fry of Stanford University found that laughing 200 times burns off the same amount of calories as 10 minutes on a rowing machine. Another study found that after a bout of laughter, blood pressure drops to a lower, healthier level than before the laughter began. Laughter also oxygenates your blood (thereby increasing energy levels), relaxes your muscles, and works out all your major internal systems like the cardiovascular and respiratory systems.

The Gallup organisation describes three types of employee engagement: (1) those who are engaged (work with passion and help to drive their organisations forward);

(2) those who are not engaged (put in time but not much energy); and (3) those who are actively disengaged (actively unhappy and undermine other workers). Gallup's American economists estimate that close to 30 per cent of employees are not truly engaged at work and, in America, this failure-to-engage translates into US$300 billion yearly in lost productivity.[33] This does not include the cost of replacing the millions of disengaged employees who leave organisations annually because their emotional needs are not being met.

According to the Gallup 2009 Australian Engagement Study,[34] around 21 per cent of Australian workers (and 15 per cent of New Zealand workers) are actively disengaged employees — up from 18 per cent two years earlier.[35] Actively disengaged employees are more likely to have higher levels of absenteeism and safety incidents and are responsible for 80 per cent of engagement issues. In addition to this, they are less likely to provide excellent customer service, are less likely to be productive, are not as loyal, and can be disruptive. On the other hand, engaged employees (just 18 per cent in Australian workers, and 23 per cent of New Zealand ones) are responsible for around 80 per cent of the discretionary effort in organisations. In Australia, the Gallup statisticians found that a 4.1 per cent increase in output per worker would be the result of eliminating active disengagement from the workforce. This average output figure amounts to $4768 per person in the total workforce, or $42.1 billion overall.[36]

So, can laughter help with reducing disengagement? With terms like 'stress-related-illness' and 'burnout' becoming more commonplace, organisations are increasingly looking for ways to keep their workforce happy, healthy and productive. Until recently, most organisations tended to view laughter at work as a distraction from getting the 'real' job done. However, this belief may actually be counter-productive, and this is confirmed by scientific research. A recent study conducted at Canadian financial institutions found that managers who facilitated the highest level of employee performance used humour the most often.[37]

Questions

1. Using the guidelines in The effective manager 5.1, would you use job enrichment to redesign the jobs of your actively disengaged employees?
2. The job characteristics model has 'moderators' that impact how individuals respond to job redesign. Given the reasons for employees being actively disengaged, explain how these moderators might impact disengaged employees and engaged employees differently during job redesign.

Intrinsic motivation and job satisfaction are the result of a complex interplay of factors. The organisation cannot always understand and provide the particular balance of intrinsic and extrinsic job rewards that each individual would prefer. Being happy in life can mean being happy at work, or giving more to the job.[38] If a new job or situation (such as running a private business) helps a person achieve a harmony between work and life, or offers them greater fulfilment, that person is likely to switch to that job — even if their employer has endeavoured to retain employees by careful attempts at job enrichment.

Socio-technical job design

Technology can sometimes constrain the ability to enrich jobs. **Socio-technical job design** recognises this problem and seeks to optimise the relationship between the technology system and the social system. This is achieved by designing work roles that integrate with the technology system. Best known is the semi-autonomous work group approach, by which self-managed or autonomous work teams perform a job previously done on the assembly line (these teams are discussed in chapter 7).

Because it is difficult and costly to modify technology in an existing plant, and to change work practices and job design across the entire organisation, the socio-technical approach often works more effectively in a 'greenfield' site (that is, a new site with no established work practices).

Over the past decade some managers have begun to question the costs of maintaining and developing this socio-technical approach in some plants because of the rising costs associated with rapid knowledge obsolescence and multiskilling the workforce. However, this is not always a problem, or organisations can take action to minimise this effect. For example, while Boeing has different cockpits on its different aircraft, Airbus's strategy is to have the same cockpit on all the models in its fleet. This means that pilots require much less re-skilling when they move between different aircraft models. More research on the costs and benefits of the approach in contemporary environments, and of strategies to minimise problems, is needed to address such criticisms.

Social information and job design

Gerald Salancik and Jeffrey Pfeffer have reviewed the literature on the job diagnostic approach to job design.[39] They question whether jobs have stable and objective characteristics that individuals perceive and to which they respond predictably and consistently. As an alternative, their **social information-processing approach** argues that individual needs, task perceptions and reactions are a result of socially constructed realities. Thus, social information in the workplace influences workers' perceptions of the job and their responses to it. It is much like a student's perception of a class. Several of the student's friends may tell her that the lecturer is bad, the content is boring and the class requires too much work. The student may then think that the critical characteristics of the class are the lecturer, the content and the workload, and that they are all bad. All of this may take place before the student has even set foot in that class, and may substantially influence the student's class perception and response, regardless of the reality of the job characteristics approach.

Research on the social information-processing approach provides mixed results. Essentially, the results show that social information processing does influence task perceptions and attitudes, but the kinds of job characteristics described earlier remain important.

Multiskilling

Multiskilling programs help employees become members of a flexible workforce and acquire an array of skills needed to perform multiple tasks in a company's production or customer service process. The cross-training and multiskilling of employees allow them to assume broader responsibilities so they are better equipped to solve problems. Industry professionals are recognising this. For example, IBISWorld chairman Phil Ruthven says HR managers need to become more multiskilled, especially in finance and strategy, if they are going to be able to have an impact on business strategy and how it involves people in the organisation.[40] Multiskilling is also valuable in teams. In an environment that fosters multiskilling, there is always someone who can take over the role if a team member is absent. If suggestions for process improvements are required, members of the team have the requisite skills and expertise to make valuable contributions. Even in jobs where people work alone, their jobs may involve many skills.

Multiskilling is an innovative work practice that has helped improve organisational performance by 30 to 40 per cent in some cases. Strong links between a multiskilled workforce and improved productivity have been identified. More recently, the skills matrix has been used to measure employees' skill levels and compare them to the desired levels, which are often an upward moving target.

Overall, employees in a flexible workforce benefit from having a challenging and varied work experience, more control over their work environment, higher skill levels, higher pay opportunities and greater marketability in the job market.

Goal-setting theory

For any employee a reasonable question to ask the employer is: 'What is it you want me to do?' Without clear and appropriate goals, employees may suffer a direction problem and be unable to channel their work energies towards the right goal. A recent survey of European companies showed only one third of poor performers believed their supervisor or immediate manager was effective in establishing individual performance goals that were linked to business objectives or was effective in providing direct feedback on their individual performance.[41] Such problems are found in many work settings. Proper setting and clarification of task goals can eliminate, or at least reduce, these and other problems. Goal setting involves building challenging and specific goals into jobs and providing appropriate performance feedback.

Goal setting is the 'process of developing, negotiating and formalising the targets or objectives that an employee is responsible for accomplishing'. Expanding job design to include goal setting results in specific task goals for each individual. These task goals are important because they have a link with task performance. Over a number of years, Edwin Locke developed a set of arguments and predictions concerning this link. This set of predictions serves as the basis for goal-setting theory. Locke's research, and that of others, provides considerable support for the following predictions.[42]

> **Goal setting** is the process of developing, negotiating and formalising an employee's targets and objectives.

1. *Difficult goals are more likely to lead to higher performance than are less difficult ones.* They encourage effort that leads to greater outcomes. However, if the goals are seen as too difficult or as impossible, the relationship with performance no longer holds. An individual is likely to cease trying if the goal is unattainable.

2. *Specific goals are more likely to lead to higher performance than are no goals or vague or general ones.* Setting a specific goal of selling ten refrigerators a month should lead to better performance than a simple 'do your best' goal.

3. *Task feedback, or knowledge of results, is likely to motivate people towards higher performance by encouraging the setting of higher performance goals.* Feedback lets people know where they stand and if they are on or off course in their efforts; for example, think about how eager you are to find out how well you have done in an examination.

4. *Goals are most likely to lead to higher performance when people have the abilities and the feelings of self-efficacy required to accomplish them.* Individuals must believe that they are able to accomplish the goals and feel confident in their abilities.

5. *Goals are most likely to motivate people towards higher performance when they are accepted and there is commitment to them.* One way of achieving such acceptance or commitment is by participating in the goal-setting process. You then feel a sense of 'ownership' of the goals. However, Locke and Latham report that goals assigned by someone else can be equally effective. The assigners are likely to be influential authority figures. Also, the assignment implies that the employee can actually reach the goal. Third, assigned goals are often a challenge. Finally, assigned goals help define the standards people use to attain personal satisfaction with their performance.[43] According to Locke and Latham, assigned goals only lead to poor performance when they are curtly or inadequately explained.[44]

Goal setting: follow-up research

Research using and extending the five predictions discussed is now extensive. Indeed, there is more research for goal setting than for any other theory related to work motivation.[45] Several hundred studies have been conducted in countries including Australia, the United Kingdom, Germany, Japan and the United States.[46] Locke and Latham and their associates have been at the forefront of this work and they have recently integrated their predictions into a more comprehensive framework that links goals to performance. We show a simplified version of the Locke and Latham framework in figure 5.4.[47]

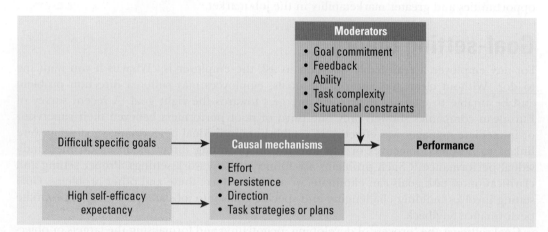

FIGURE 5.4 Simplified Locke and Latham goal-setting framework

Starting at the left, we see the difficult, specific goals mentioned earlier in predictions 1 and 2. These are joined by high self-efficacy (mentioned in prediction 4 and emphasised in chapters 3 and 4) and high expectancy (discussed as a part of expectancy motivation theory in chapter 3). The argument is that these factors operate through the linking mechanisms of effort, persistence, direction, and task strategies or plans to affect performance. At the same time, the moderators of goal commitment (prediction 5), feedback (prediction 3), ability (prediction 4), task complexity and situational constraints also operate to strengthen or weaken the relationship between goals and performance.

Locke's predictions concerning goal setting are still relevant. However, they have now been embedded in the simplified framework in figure 5.4. That framework includes some ideas discussed in the motivation chapter and relates to concepts from expectancy theory, as shown in our discussion in the previous paragraph of the role of expectancy and self-efficacy. Further, while our simplified framework does not show it, Locke and Latham argue that the instrumentality concept from expectancy theory (that is, that performance leads to rewards) operates through the link between challenging goals and valued rewards.[48] Again, the basic tenets of expectancy theory prove useful in explaining work behaviour. This relationship has sometimes led to the treatment of goal-setting theory as a process motivation theory, in addition to the equity and expectancy theories discussed in chapter 3. Further, the task-complexity notion discussed earlier suggests a link with job enrichment. As more enrichment is built into a job, the job becomes more complex and probably calls for new task strategies or plans. Finally, Locke's fourth prediction links goal-setting theory with ability as an individual attribute and with self-efficacy, which is so important in social learning theory.[49]

Goal setting and MBO

When we speak of goal setting and its potential to influence individual performance at work, the concept of management by objectives (MBO) immediately comes to mind. Over many years, this approach has been widely used in many large organisations in both the public and private sectors.[50] In Australia and New Zealand many senior executives employed within the public service (including some local government authorities) have performance-based contracts that identify clear goal-achievement milestones for each year. For example, the senior executives in the Australian Public Service must link their own specific agency goals with broader government goals and, at the same time, use these goals to motivate subordinates to achieve high performance.[51]

MBO involves managers working with their employees to establish performance goals and plans that are consistent with higher-level work unit and organisational objectives.[52]

Figure 5.5 shows a comprehensive view of MBO. The concept is consistent with the notion of goal setting and its associated principles (as already discussed). Notice how joint supervisor–employee discussions are designed to extend participation from the point of initial goal establishment to the point of evaluating results in terms of goal attainment. Key issues for mutual goal setting are summarised in The effective manager 5.2.[53]

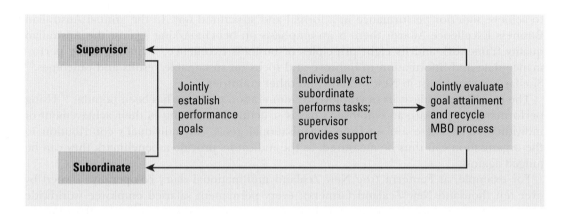

FIGURE 5.5 The management-by-objectives (MBO) process

In addition to the goal-setting steps previously discussed, a successful MBO system calls for careful implementation. This means that the previous steps are translated into the kinds of strategies or plans, mentioned earlier, that will lead to goal accomplishment. Employees must have freedom to carry out the required tasks; managers may have to do considerable coaching and counselling. As with other applied organisational behaviour programs, managers should be aware of MBO's potential costs as well as its benefits.

Despite substantial research based on case studies of MBO success, such research has not always been rigorously controlled and it reports mixed results.[54] In general, and as an application of goal-setting theory, MBO has much to offer. But it is not easy to start and keep going. MBO may also need to be implemented organisation-wide if it is to work well.[55]

Key issues for mutual goal setting in an MBO program

THE **EffectiveManager** 5.2

- What must be done? Start with higher-level goals, job descriptions stating tasks to be performed, outcomes expected, necessary supplies and equipment, and so on.
- How will performance be measured? Time, money or physical units may often be used to measure performance. If the job is more subjective, emphasise behaviours or actions believed to lead to success.
- What is the performance standard? Start with previous performance or the average performance of others doing this job. Where these measures do not exist, use mutual supervisor–subordinate judgement and discussion.

(continued)

- What are the deadlines for the goals? Discuss deadlines in terms of daily, weekly or longer terms.
- What is the relative importance of the goals? Not all goals are equally important. The manager and employee should decide the goal ranking together.
- How difficult are the goals? Watch especially for high task complexity and multiple goals. Come up with a clearly agreed decision.

Key performance indicators

Key performance indicators are standards against which individual and organisational performance can be measured.

The concept of individual goal setting has been further developed over the past few years to introduce the concept of **key performance indicators** (KPIs) — standards against which individual and organisational performance can be measured.

Such measurement is a step in the benchmarking process taken by companies wanting to achieve superior performance in a formal and structured way. In the annual Australian Business Excellence Awards there is an emphasis on benchmarking against the Australian quality framework and its eight principles of business excellence, including using performance data and information to improve and focus on sustainable results and outcomes.[56] Similar programs exist in New Zealand and other countries.

The use of such indicators in employee remuneration packages has been popular.[57] Using performance appraisals, an employee's pay is structured according to their achievement of individual KPIs. These are set from organisational goals. An individual's contribution to the organisation can thus be measured, as the indicators provide a benchmark they can be judged against.

For example, at Fonterra (the New Zealand multinational dairy co-operative owned by over ten thousand New Zealand farmers), every permanent salaried employee worldwide is invited to participate in an annual short-term incentive (STI) plan.[58] STI plans are an important communication device signalling to employees what is important to Fonterra and how success in the company is measured and rewarded. At the commencement of each year, a series of KPIs are identified and agreed. These KPIs include important financial measures from Fonterra's three-year strategic plan. Incentive programs drive Fonterra's performance by:

1. aligning the objectives of the company to ensure collaboration and a one team approach to achieve Fonterra's goals
2. establishing targets which are challenging yet achievable
3. linking specific levels of reward to individual, team and company performance
4. providing great opportunities when Fonterra's business and people are successful.

At the end of each operating year, performance against the KPIs is determined and independently reviewed and approved by the appointments, remuneration and development committee (AR&D).

The use of performance appraisals keeps employees accountable for their achievements. A KPI must be specific, measurable, achievable, realistic and time-framed (SMART).[59] It depends on the nature of the employee's job, the industry in which the employee works, the strategic direction and goals of the company, and the bottom line of the organisation.

Key performance indicators are often built around measurable or quantifiable targets, but they can extend to qualitative issues, such as staff initiative and communication skills. There can be a lot of debate about the suitability of KPIs. For example, Withers argues that KPIs are unsuitable for measuring improvement or contributions in software development.[60] Thus, the degree to which KPIs can be quantified and measurable can vary.

Clear goals means increased job satisfaction

It is essential that managers and leaders in organisations keep their followers motivated, both through clear goal setting and support for their followers' goal accomplishment.[61] There is increasing research being conducted about the influences of *goal ambiguity* (that is, not understanding the goal well, not being clear about the timeline and/or confusion about which aspects are most important). Goal ambiguity has been shown to reduce employee motivation,[62] to increase turnover,[63] and to decrease performance.[64]

Some recent research in the public sector in North America found that goal ambiguity dimensions are negatively associated with job satisfaction for employees.[65] The researcher provides some recommendations and strategies that leaders should consider in order to enhance the job satisfaction of their employees based on the notion that job satisfaction can be improved just by reducing levels of organisational goal ambiguity.

First, there should be increased and effective communication with employees about the organisation's goals and mission. This will result in increased levels of employee job satisfaction by helping them to understand the goals and mission and by reducing employee perceptions of organisational goal ambiguity. The job satisfaction of employees can be further influenced by the use of clear wording or a leader's effective goal support. The researcher suggests that satisfaction will be increased when managers set specific targets, establish a clear timeline for performance goals, and focus on only a few important performance goals.

Flexible work arrangements

Attempting to enhance worker satisfaction through job redesign involves mostly intrinsic factors relating to *doing the job*. Worker satisfaction (as well as avoidance of dissatisfaction) can also be achieved by changing job conditions, such as the timing or number of working hours and work location. For example, the employee may experience a more acceptable working environment (extrinsic change) if working hours are flexible enough to allow the achievement of other (personal) goals. This, in turn, may affect the employee's levels of work motivation and performance (intrinsic changes), because they are more satisfied with their job environment. The key drivers and practices of flexible work arrangements are now presented.

Major drivers of changing work arrangements

Organisations that utilise flexible strategies in the workforce have the potential to reap many benefits including:
- higher retention or less intention to leave
- lower absenteeism
- more capacity to meet peak demand and service outside hours
- improved job satisfaction

- increased commitment and motivation
- reduced work pressure
- more diversity in the workforce.[66]

The US Families and Work Institute reports flexible work practices provide a 'win–win' situation, with higher levels of employee engagement, retention, job satisfaction and wellbeing.[67] Not only do organisations and individuals gain benefits from flexible work practices — they also help to reduce the prevalence of work-related conditions such as employee burnout and stress (see chapter 14). Flexible work practices can assist individual workers deal with their work in the context of the following drivers.

Personal and family circumstances and work–life balance

The prevalence of households where both partners are working (dual-income families) and the rising number of one-parent families, along with increasing hours worked exacerbate the problems of balancing work and life pressures. Work can impact on family life and family life can impact on work.[68] In addition, some employees have other interests in their lives that they wish to or need to accommodate, such as caring for elderly parents, pursuing sports accomplishments or engaging in voluntary work. Substantial benefits can be gained for both employees and employers in considering the work–life balance for workers in very many different ways.

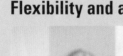

OBinAction

Flexibility and autonomy beat all!

Research reported by the University of Kent shows that self-employed people are happier about their work–life balance even though they work the longest hours.[69] This is because they have more control over their work day. Studies have supported the notion that autonomy is profoundly important for both subjective wellbeing[70] and psychosocial wellbeing[71] (far more so than income). Numerous studies have supported the notion that wealth does not make people happy, showing that the more people focus on materialistic goals, the lower their wellbeing. This result has been confirmed both in developed countries such as the United States[72] and Germany,[73] and in developing nations such as Russia and India.[74] People with high income but little autonomy are usually much less happy than people with a low income but control over what they do, so if you can find ways of controlling your life, you can be happy even on a low income (so long as you feel you have enough to meet your needs).

Work stress and burnout

Perhaps the most widely accepted model of work stress is the job demand-control-support (JDCS) model.[75] Negative consequences of work are believed to be related to both **job demands** and **job control**. Job demands are generally understood in terms of the amount of work that is required, such as workload, time pressure, and physical and emotional demands.[76] The second job characteristic, job control, refers to the extent to which a person is capable of controlling their tasks and the way they approach their work (such as when they do a task or the method they use). Combining the two dimensions of job demands and job control, Robert Karasek, the original theorist proposing the JDC model, stated that jobs high on demands and low on control (high-strain jobs) bear the highest risk of illness and reduced wellbeing. In jobs low on demands and high on control (low-strain jobs), the occurrence of adverse reactions is much less likely.[77] The JDC model was extended by integrating **job resources/support** as a third dimension.[78] The JDCS model predicts work situations characterised by high demands, low control and low support to be most harmful to workers' wellbeing.

Thus, resources and support are assumed to promote work-related wellbeing, while excessive demands and low control lead to impaired health and exhaustion. This dual process (the contrasting relationship between demands and impaired health, and between resources and motivation and engagement) is the basis of the job demand resource model and is well supported by empirical evidence across a range of occupations.[79]

Work stress and burnout are of increasing importance to both employers and employees. They are important to employees because stress can result in physical and psychological ill-health. They are important to employers because employee performance may be reduced — either directly by them becoming stressed, or indirectly by the long-term negative effects of stress and burnout. In addition, employers are coming under increasing pressure, through health and safety legislation, to take responsibility for and to manage their employees' work-related stress.[80]

It is important to differentiate between stress and burnout. Stress was originally defined as the body's response to any demand.[81] More recently, stress has come to mean distress — the negative physical and psychological consequences of a demand, whether that demand is physical, psychological or both.[82] In the work context, a demand could include issues such as workload, work patterns or almost any other aspect of the work environment.[83] Burnout, on the other hand, is a set of symptoms that usually occurs as a result of long-term exposure to stress, especially stress that has its origins in emotional labour.[84]

Emotional labour is the effort involved in maintaining an outwardly positive and/or caring attitude while inwardly feeling other emotions such as anger, frustration or even sadness. While stress can result in a wide range of physical symptoms (such as heart problems, high blood pressure, obesity and reduced immunity) and psychological outcomes (such as anxiety, depression, anger, irritability and difficulty in concentrating), burnout has a fairly specific set of symptoms. Burnout is characterised by overwhelming exhaustion, feelings of cynicism and detachment towards the job and a sense of ineffectiveness and failure.[85] Burnout mostly shows up in employees' interpersonal relationships, and can be very damaging to an organisation.

Both stress and burnout seem to be increasing in the workplace, probably due to increasing demands being placed on employees, often without any real compensation. Research shows that, although one-third of the Australian labour force still officially work standard hours, the majority of full-time employees work extended hours (often without extra pay).[86] The working conditions of so many employees, with increased pressure to work harder and longer, are associated with rising levels of work stress and burnout. This may, in part, be due to a mistaken belief that some stress is good for performance.[87] This idea is commonly held to be true, but is dangerously misleading. Stress has become synonymous with distress, and there is no evidence that any amount of distress enhances performance.[88] We all require some level of stimulation and motivation, but this is not the same as stress. Positive stress, sometimes termed eustress, is the opposite of distress. Eustress is an individual's response to stimulation, pressure or demands and can lead to challenge or excitement. It is not the amount of pressure or demand that results in either eustress or distress, but rather the nature of the demand and how that demand is interpreted by the individual.

Job resources/support are the aspects of the job that function to reduce job demands, enable achievement of work goals, and/or stimulate personal growth, learning and development.

COUNTERPOINT

Is a bad job better than no job at all?

It is generally believed that working is good for our mental health, and numerous studies have linked unemployment to poor psychological wellbeing.[89] A recent publication even linked unemployment to a significantly increased risk of *death* for those in their early and middle careers![90] In spite of this, some jobs are so bad that they are actually worse for employees' psychological wellbeing than not having a job at all.

A study in *Occupational and Environmental Medicine* describes research by the Australian National University.[91] In this study, data from over 7000 Australian adults were analysed over several years, evaluating links between the nature of their jobs and their mental health. The study found that 'the mental health of those who were unemployed was comparable or superior to those in jobs of the poorest quality'. Poor-quality jobs were defined as those with high demands, low pay and a lack of autonomy and security. Participants were asked, for example, whether a job was 'more stressful than I ever imagined', whether it was 'complex and difficult', or whether it caused them to 'worry about the future'. The worse the job, the poorer the worker's mental health.

To make sure the pattern wasn't simply caused by unhappy people tending to land in bad jobs because they were already unhappy, the researchers studied what happened when the unemployed subjects finally obtained work. They found that those who moved into high-quality jobs showed significant improvements in mental health. Those who took poor-quality jobs, however, showed clinically significant declines in mental wellbeing compared to their own previous state of mind and that of their jobless counterparts. Mental health measures included how often participants had recently felt nervous, depressed, calm or happy. Overall, the researchers concluded that work of poor psychosocial quality does not bestow the same mental health benefits as employment in jobs with high psychosocial quality.

Many of the ideas discussed previously in this chapter are relevant to workplace stress. The idea of person-environment fit (PE fit) is related to job design and the job characteristics model, and to methods of goal setting and performance monitoring, for example, MBO.[92] Theorists suggest that stress will be minimised when there is good 'fit' between a person's skills and abilities and the job situation they are in.[93] Stress increases as the fit between the person and their work environment becomes less. A job that demands too little of an employee (underload or too little stimulation) can be just as stressful as one that demands too much.[94]

However, employees' reactions to demands seem to be more complex than simple PE fit theory suggests. A job that is positively stimulating to one person may seem unbearably stressful to another, even though there appears to be a good PE fit in terms of skills and abilities and the demands of the job for both. Richard Lazarus's transactional theory of stress may help to explain this.[95] His theory suggests that not only is a stressful event 'one in which demands tax or exceed the person's resources', but that becoming stressed is also due to the individual's appraisal of that event. In other words, the way in which a person perceives and appraises a demand is central to the process that may result in stress. Lazarus proposes that people will evaluate a demand as being either potentially harmful and threatening, or as being stimulating and challenging, and their stress response will largely depend on this appraisal. Thus, high workloads and increasing pressure to perform can produce quite different responses in different individuals. For some, it is a positive source of challenge and stimulation. Increasingly, however, employees seem to find this pressure stressful, leading to stress-related diseases and burnout.

The perceptual interface model (figure 5.6) gives a simple guide to this process.[96] Some organisations are responding by offering extended breaks from the workplace, such as sabbatical leave, to help employees cope more effectively.[97] Even if normal working hours apply, some employees may suffer from stress and burnout due to the combined load and conflict of family and work commitments, or due to some disharmony between work and personal life. The following Ethical perspective discusses some concerns relating to these matters. Seeking balance between the demands and rewards of work and the demands and rewards of other aspects of one's life becomes increasingly important if workplace stress is to be reduced.

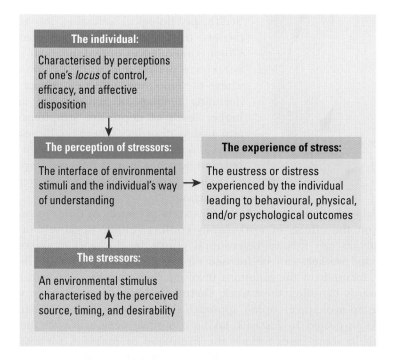

FIGURE 5.6 Perceptual interface model

Source: M Le Fevre, J Matheny and GS Kolt, 'Eustress, distress, and interpretation in occupational stress', *Journal of Managerial Psychology, 18*(7) (2003), pp. 726–44.

A longitudinal (three year) study using Australian university academics[98] examined the impact of selected job demands (academic workload and pressure) and job resources (such as funding, procedural fairness and job autonomy) on stress. During the time frame of this study changes to Australian government funding resulted in substantial increases in the student-to-staff ratios (an increased demand) and decreases in research funding (leading to decreased resources). The notion of academic workload captures some demands that are unique to academic work; for example the role conflict that many academics feel among the triple demands of research, teaching and administration. This study found that the more resources academic staff felt they had, the more committed they were to their university, and the less stress they experienced three years down the track.

The quest for work–life balance

More than ever before, workers, organisations, the business media and academic scholars are discussing work–life balance. Longer working hours, more demands in both the work and family domains and/or more workers who have family demands deciding to enter the workforce is creating higher levels of work pressure.

While concern for work–life balance is widespread, an understanding of the causes and effects of work–life imbalance and conflict are less well understood. Haar provides a rich picture of some contributing factors. For example, he argues it is not just a case of work affecting the family–home situation; the demands in the family home can also affect work. It can also be related to role conflict and ambiguity in the workplace

(continued)

ETHICAL
Perspective

as well as the fact that the conflict is ongoing. He says the impact on individuals can be important since work and family roles are both components of adult identity.[99] The consequences can include absenteeism and turnover, as well reduced levels of health, psychological wellbeing, job and life satisfaction, trust and organisational commitment.[100] Other consequences of dysfunctional relationships between a person and work are job burnout — where the employee suffers emotional exhaustion, declining feelings of achievement and possibly higher levels of depressive symptoms and mood and anxiety disorders. There might be a loss–spiral effect where the work–family conflict is followed by burnout, which is in turn followed by reductions in an ability to cope at work and even greater conflict and burnout.[101]

Haar explains that employees deal with excess pressures in different ways and this will impact on the effects of work–family conflict (either negatively or positively). Coping strategies can involve behavioural efforts by the worker and/or cognitive efforts. Affected workers can be focused on the problem of work–family conflict or alternatively, focused on the emotions involved. Some workers' focus can be action-oriented towards handling their work, thereby buffering against stress while others tend to have an avoidance coping approach that tends to have little benefit for the employee. As suggested by Lazarus, taking a positive perspective on the competing demands can in some cases reduce the likelihood of burnout, for example if the employee frames the additional workload as a chance to progress or impress. In other cases, increased focus on work can simply intensify the source of the conflict leading to burnout.[102] The degree of control an employee has is important, as is whether the employee perceives work and life pressures as being in harmony (or complementary) or not.[103] The results are that employees need to be more aware of the consequences of how they cope with their work–family and family–work conflicts as some approaches can heighten the burnout and stress levels. Employers can assist by helping employees recognise when they are not coping and by providing resources (including training and flexible work practice options).[104] It is important that employees can mobilise support from the organisation when necessary.[105]

Changing levels and modes of employment

Throughout the 1980s and the early 1990s, rising levels of unemployment dominated and impacted on work security and workload. More recently, unemployment figures have stabilised or decreased (though there is some dispute about the way in which figures are measured). For example, in New Zealand from 2003 to 2007 there was a decline in unemployment from around 4.5 to 3.4 per cent; this rose to 6.3 by the end of 2011,[106] but by mid-2014 had decreased somewhat to 5.6 per cent.[107] In Australia the unemployment rate has fluctuated, dropping from 5 per cent in April 2005 to 3.5 per cent during 2007. By early 2008, it had stabilised at 4 per cent,[108] but was rising again in response to the worldwide slowdown brought on by the global financial crisis. By mid-2014, the unemployment rate in Australia had continued to rise steadily to 6.2 per cent.[109] However, the shift from traditional full-time permanent to casual or part-time jobs has been substantial in some countries — as has an increase in the number of fixed-term contracted positions. Almost 30 per cent of the Australian labour force can be classified as working part-time.[110]

Skills shortages and the ageing population

The trends towards more competitive labour markets, with ageing populations and skills shortages, though recently reversing, have been mentioned in earlier chapters. These trends work in conjunction with the other drivers to encourage employers to provide more flexible work practices in order to attract and retain talented employees. By being more competitive, in terms of the flexibility of work arrangements, organisations may have a better chance of attracting the best candidates. Additionally, flexibility might enable them to be able to expand the pool of candidates from which they might draw their employees.

The population is ageing and this means increasing pressure on social services, so flexible work options are being explored to retain the productive skills of many older workers while simultaneously offering them a new balance between work and lifestyle.[111] Australia's population is expected to grow from 20 million to 33.4 million by 2051. It is expected the proportion of people aged 65 and over will increase from 13 per cent (in 2004) to around 19 per cent by 2021 and around 26–28 per cent by 2051.[112]

The responses to these trends are mixed. Some organisations are doing little to retain older employees and there is evidence that some are still pushing older employees out, despite age discrimination legislation.[113] However, many corporations are examining retirement phasing schemes through which admission to full retirement is staggered across a number of years, rather than occurring abruptly at a certain age.[114] When unemployment is low, it will be critical to retain as many older employees as possible in the workforce, as the pools of younger applicants will be proportionally decreasing. Offering them part-time work, phased retirement or contracted work will also help to retain older workers.[115]

In a study of the work exit and entry patterns of mature-aged workers, Shacklock and Fulop[116] report on previous studies that indicate that flexible working arrangements have been found to be successful in retaining older workers in the United States, Australia and New Zealand. The same study indicates most older people find flexible and reduced working hours the most attractive working arrangements; for example, working 2 or 3 days a week and on specific assignments that might last a few months. There is a desire to have less pressure and stress and more time to pursue other interests.[117]

The use of 'I-pros' (independent professionals) illustrates that many white-collar professional workers are being employed to fill short-term skills gaps in organisations.[118] The Adage Top 20 is a list of organisations displaying excellence in age management. It includes Insurance Australia Group (IAG).[119]

Positive organisational behaviour

Scholar Sunil Ramlall has discussed the notion that it is not only a person's job and work environment that can impact on someone's experience of work and wellbeing, but also the way that an employee thinks about (or frames) their work in relation to the rest of their life.[120]

Martin Seligman has described the manner in which scholars distinguish three kinds of work orientation: a job, a career and a calling.[121] A person performs a *job* for the pay cheque at the end of the week, and when the wage stops, the person quits. A *career* entails a deeper personal investment in work. Finally, a *calling* is a passionate commitment to work for its own sake.

Seligman also explains that part of what turns a job into a calling is the state known as flow.[122] Csikszentmihalyi defines flow as complete absorption in an activity, where the task is well matched to one's abilities.[123] He explains that flow is not the pleasure a person derives from a warm shower or any other positive experience, but the loss of self-consciousness that is experienced while totally engrossed in a task. People who experience flow are not only happier, but more productive.

Flow is complete absorption in an activity, where the task is well matched to one's abilities.

Changing technology and the capacity to work remotely

Information technology enables many changes to the way in which work is organised and located. Work can often be location independent, and there is often no need for the employee and the employer to meet regularly. Teleworking and working remotely from the office have been extensively discussed over several decades.[124] Despite a slow take-up, they have been increasing in popularity. One study suggests that countries are in one of four phases of progress with introducing such teleworking arrangements.[125] In the first phase, the environment for teleworking is *established*. In the second phase, greater *recognition and enlightenment* of the benefits of teleworking is achieved. The third phase involves a *building up of know-how* for operating teleworking in individual companies, while in the fourth phase, *diffusion* helps to spread teleworking widely.

Types of flexible work arrangements

Some of the important work options to emerge from the trends already outlined include a compressed work week, flexitime or flexi years, job-sharing, V-time and teleworking or working remotely. Nearly all these options are designed to influence employee satisfaction and to serve as both extrinsic and intrinsic motivating devices by helping employees to balance the demands of their working and non-working lives. In our fast-changing society, these arrangements are becoming more important as a way of dealing with our increasingly diverse workforce. It is important to remember there are other family friendly practices that assist workers and that may help alleviate their anxieties, such as corporate crèches[126] and home phone calls to check on children.[127]

The compressed work week

Compressed work week is any scheduling of work that allows a full-time job to be completed in fewer than the standard five days.

A **compressed work week** is any scheduling of work that allows a full-time job to be completed in fewer than the standard five days. The most common form of compressed work week is the 'four–forty'; that is, forty hours of work accomplished in four ten-hour days. Added time off is a major feature for the worker. The individual often benefits from increased leisure time, more three-day weekends, free weekdays to pursue personal business, and lower commuting costs. The organisation can benefit, too, through reduced energy consumption during three-day shutdowns, lower employee absenteeism, improved recruiting of new employees, and the extra time available for building and equipment maintenance, though results are inconsistent.[128]

The potential disadvantages of the compressed work week include increased fatigue from the extended workday and family adjustment problems for the individual; and, for the organisation, increased work scheduling problems and possible customer complaints due to breaks in work coverage. Possible constraints on the use of compressed work week schedules include union opposition and laws that require some organisations to pay overtime for work that exceeds eight hours of individual labour in any one day.

Proposed legislation to increase the accepted 'normal' hours of work may enhance employers' capacity to expand compressed working week strategies in Australia. One study found that reaction to the compressed work week was most favourable among employees who had participated in the decision to compress the work week, who had had their jobs enriched as a result of the new schedule, and who had strong higher-order needs. The enrichment occurred because fewer employees were on duty at any one time and job duties were changed and enriched to accommodate this reduction.[129] A further interesting finding is employees' reluctance to once more seek employment under the typical standard-hours model of five days/40 hours once they have experienced the lifestyle changes associated with a compressed work week.[130]

Flexible working hours or flexiyears

Flexible working hours (flexitime) is defined as 'any work schedule that gives employees daily choice in the timing of work and non-work activities'.[131] Flexitime is perhaps the most widely adopted work option in Western economies, such as Australia, though data on it is not always clear. Recent Australian Bureau of Statistics (ABS) data revealed the working arrangements of Australian workers (excluding owner managers in incorporated enterprises). It showed 39.9 per cent of workers had some say in their starting and finishing times. Of these workers, 26.2 per cent could determine their own times on a daily basis, 10.4 per cent had to negotiate with their employer and 3.3 per cent had other arrangements. Employees who were allowed to work extra hours to take time off comprised 38.2 per cent of the survey group, while 57.1 per cent did not have this option and 4.7 per cent did not know.[132] The potential advantages of flexitime are listed in figure 5.7.

Flexible working hours (flexitime) is any work schedule that gives employees daily choice in the timing of work and non-work activities.

Organisational benefits	Individual benefits
Lower absenteeism	More time for leisure and personal business, e.g. dentist, bank and better timing of commuting
Reduced tardiness	Less commuting time
Reduced turnover	Higher job satisfaction
Higher work commitment	Greater sense of responsibility
Higher performance	Easier personal scheduling

FIGURE 5.7 Organisational and individual benefits of flexible working hours

Proponents of this scheduling strategy argue that the discretion it allows workers in scheduling their own hours of work encourages them to develop positive attitudes and increased commitment to the organisation. Accenture is one company that benefits from offering flexitime to its employees.

In Australia since 1 January 2010, under the National Employment Standards (NES) eligible employees have a right to request flexible working arrangements. Now an employee who is a parent (or who has responsibility for the care of a child) may request a change in their working arrangements to assist them in caring for the child.[133] Examples of changes in working arrangements may include:

- changes in hours of work (e.g. reduction in hours worked, changes to start/finish times)
- changes in patterns of work (e.g. working 'split-shifts' or job-sharing arrangements)
- changes in location of work (e.g. working from home or another location).

Subjective wellbeing — meaningful work and family focus creates lasting happiness

OBinAction

In the study of wellbeing there is a theory called 'set-point theory' which basically holds that adult wellbeing set points (how happy or unhappy you are) do not change, except just temporarily, in the face of major life events. The theory holds that, with few exceptions (such as the death of one's child) our happiness will remain the same irrespective of things that happen to us.

More recent research, however, suggests that subjective wellbeing appears to depend partly on how we prioritise our life goals.[134] Pursuit of 'non-zero sum' goals (such as family and altruistic goals) leads to higher subjective wellbeing than the pursuit of zero

(continued)

sum goals (such as career advancement and material gains). This implies that simply striving to progress your career or become wealthy has little impact on happiness (in fact, research suggests it actually results in a lasting decline), whereas people who placed a higher priority on altruistic, helping activities (for example, engaging in meaningful work) and family goals had a long-term increase in life satisfaction.

It seems, then, that our set point *can* change. Research has shown that many people achieve long-lasting and permanent gains in subjective wellbeing as a result of getting married.[135] On the other hand, repeated spells of unemployment have been shown to have a 'scarring effect' from which most people do not fully recover; that is, they are permanently less happy.[136]

Thus, it is not just work itself that will make us happy, but doing work that has some 'greater good'; that is, the 'experienced meaningfulness of work' in the job characteristics model described earlier.

Job sharing

Job sharing is the assignment of one full-time job to two or more persons, who divide the work according to agreements made between themselves and the employer.

Another work-setting alternative is **job sharing**, whereby one full-time job is assigned to two or more people, who then divide the work according to agreements made between or among themselves and with the employer.[137] Under this scheme a job can be 'shared', which may require a high degree of coordination and communication between the job-sharing partners, or it may be 'split', which requires little cooperative interaction and coordination. Some jobs require a careful job-sharing approach, whereas in other cases a job split approach can work effectively. Work options such as job sharing and permanent part-time help facilitate better balance between work and family responsibilities. Job sharing often entails each person working half a day, although it may also be a weekly or monthly arrangement.

Job sharing has a lot to offer for the creation of a 'family-friendly workplace'. Organisations benefit from job sharing when they are able to attract talented people who would otherwise be unable to work. An example is the qualified teacher who also is a parent. Some teachers cannot be away from the home for a full day but are able to work half a day. Through job sharing, two staff members can be employed to teach one class. Many other opportunities for job sharing exist.

Some job sharers report less burnout and claim they feel recharged each time they report for work. Finding the right partnerships is very important, however, because the 'sharers' must work well with each other.[138] A recent Hays survey revealed 18 per cent of the 1700 employers surveyed were using job sharing as a work practice.[139] The following OB in action is about a company that has adopted a highly supportive approach to job sharing and other flexible work arrangements.

Reduced working hours and voluntary reduced work time (V-Time)

Voluntary reduced work time (V-Time or time–income trade-offs) is a scheme by which workers trade income for additional leisure time that is packaged to suit their needs.

Voluntary reduced work time, or **V-Time**, is also known as **time–income trade-offs**. Proposed by Fred Best[140] in 1979, it was considered that work sharing could be achieved through encouraging employees to trade either current or future work and income for leisure on a voluntary basis by packaging leisure in a way that best suited the needs of an individual.

In a bid to reduce unemployment, the French Government led this approach, but made the work–time reduction (10 per cent) *compulsory* rather than *voluntary*.[141] In Best's studies and in subsequent studies conducted in Australia by Mills and Wood and Bullock and Wood, the leisure packages available for trading were a reduced work day, a reduced work week, additional annual leave, sabbatical leave and earlier retirement.[142] For example, a 2 per cent reduction in 'current income' could be traded for any of the following:

- ten minutes off each working day
- 50 minutes' reduction in one work day each week
- five days' added paid vacation each year
- seven weeks' paid leave after six years of work
- earlier retirement at the rate of five working days for every year worked until retirement.

This trade-off could also be financed from 'future income', so that the employee takes a 2 per cent pay increase as an equivalent leisure package in one of the forms identified instead of as a salary increment.

V-Time has many potential advantages. From an employee's perspective, it provides major opportunities to improve the quality of work life and family life by establishing a new balance between work and leisure goals. From the employer's point of view, it provides opportunities for employees to self-fund periods away from the workplace, thereby reducing problems associated with depreciation of human capital (such as stress and burnout). However, if people are already working unpaid overtime, it is unlikely that such a scheme could work effectively. Given that a Senate inquiry in Australia was told that 'if all the nation's unpaid overtime was converted into paid work for new employees, unemployment would virtually disappear',[143] it seems difficult to imagine how V-Time would effectively benefit employees.

However, there can be many other ways of assisting employees (though not necessarily the unemployed) through the provision of reduced working hours. For example, many women are keen to resume work in a part-time capacity after maternity leave. Around 300 00 women have babies each year, and many of them are in the workforce.[144] Being able to do this is not always easy, with some organisations more supportive and some less supportive of female needs. To attract a wider pool of workers, such as working mothers, retiring baby boomers and others, some have suggested the principle of a 20-hour working week. Instead of seeing this is a problem, or as a convenient way to reduce labour costs, organisations need to view this as an opportunity to attract more talented workers. They will still need to be able to design the job so that it gives employees a sense of satisfaction — providing growth, recognition and so on.[145]

Remote working and the virtual office

It is now clear that the traditional office is no longer the sole focal point of employee activity.[146] Advances in communication and information technology, as well as changing attitudes towards trusting employees, are leading to more work being undertaken in 'virtual offices' *remote* from the central workplace. Workers can work from home, while on the road, while overseas and from any other location. Despite lack of physical proximity to each other, workers in different locations are able to interact extensively and cheaply with each other. For example, they might talk using technology such as voice over internet protocols (VoIP), and email using blackberries. Mobile workers using high-speed downlink packages can have rapid internet connection with online technical manuals, and enter work orders and reports while on the road that are instantly accessible to work colleagues.[147]

There are numerous options and forms of teleworking. The most common is working from home, but other options enable workers to work from well-equipped hotels, resorts, offices, telecentres and vehicles. All these options involve **telework principles** whereby a worker is enabled, for various reasons but especially information technology, to work remotely from the central organisation. Such technologies can also reduce the amount of travel workers might do in a large organisation. Instead of travelling to meet in person, they can utilise conferencing technology.

Telework principles relate to work conducted remotely from the central organisation using information technology.

All, nothing or both? Flexibility allows mothers to make good career choices

In 1989, Felice N Schwartz wrote a controversial *Harvard Business Review* article called 'Management women and the new facts of life'. Schwartz said that companies should recognise that women who may be willing to trade some career growth and earning power in order to have children are a 'precious resource'. Every effort should be made to retain them, and to do this they should be offered more flexibility and part-time work. Such arrangements would likely mean lower pay and a slower career trajectory, but 'most career-and-family women are entirely willing to make that trade-off'.[148]

A 2011 retrospective by Virginia Postrel in the *Wall Street Journal*[149] and a follow-up blog in *The Juggle*[150] discuss Schwartz's article, which, back in 1989, had ignited an outcry. Critics accused Schwartz of relegating women to dead-end jobs, or, as it quickly became dubbed, the 'mummy track' — according to Postrel, 'Lower pay for less work offended the reigning idea of a serious career'.

However, Schwartz ended up being right! By the 1990s, university-educated women began conceiving their career and family options in new ways, and the percentage of women who had both children and careers jumped significantly. Most of the gains came from new work patterns, such as part-time arrangements, that no longer forced women to make an all-or-nothing choice.

As it turned out, many women indeed have chosen to trade money for family. 'You just couldn't say so in public', Postrel writes. She doesn't delve into the changing roles and expectations of men, but it will be interesting to see whether more men eventually choose to make these same trade-offs. Will there be a 'flexi track' available to anyone — men and women (parent or not) — as opposed to a gendered 'mummy' or 'daddy' track? And will that track necessarily mean lower pay or promotions, especially if the work gets done efficiently and competently?

Flexiyear or **annual hours** is a system whereby total agreed annual hours are allocated by workers as they see fit.

In Austria and Germany several firms have considered the possibility of a **flexiyear** or **annual hours** model of employment. Workers decide on the number of hours they want to work in the coming year and then they can allocate them as they see fit. Their pay is equalised each month, but their hours can vary.[151] Such a system can reduce the need for overtime, match staff to fluctuating workloads such as those caused by seasonal demand, reduce absenteeism since options for taking time off are available, and remove the need for bringing in casual staff.[152]

Measures of who qualifies in any statistical count of remote workers requires further elaboration, and data collection must become more accurate. Trying to gain an accurate picture is difficult because many surveys are dated and also because working from home covers the self-employed such as farmers, dressmakers and masseurs. A survey conducted in Japan predicted the number of teleworkers in the country would double over a five-year period.[153] Data released by The Australian Telework Advisory Committee suggested around 2.4 million Australians worked from home recently; with around 1.4 million of these considered 'employees' (the others may be self-employed — such as farmers and those offering property, personal and communications services). A more narrow interpretation indicated around one million workers completed all or most of their hours of work at home, or had an arrangement with their employer to work at home. Most of the one million 'at home' workers were managers, administrators (male dominant) and advanced clerical and service workers (female dominant) and the most common age group represented was 35–44 years.[154]

A more up-to-date report by Sensis did not provide overall figures but suggested about 20 per cent of small to medium enterprises had at least one person who teleworked — with higher percentages of teleworkers noted in the communications, property and business services sector. In a state-by-state comparison, the ACT had the most teleworkers while NSW had the least. The report found metropolitan businesses were more likely to have teleworkers, as were businesses with 20–199 employees and businesses that were not family-based.[155] While many home workers operate home-based enterprises and/or are self-employed, employees also work at home, especially corporate managers and professionals. In many cases, the work is done in the evening or on weekends, suggesting these people take work home in addition to working at the office.[156]

Teleworkers work in virtual workplaces or offices. In virtual workplaces, productivity can rise substantially as a result of fewer interruptions and a quieter, more focused environment. The virtual office can offer more flexible work schedules, allowing employees to do work when and where they are most productive, whether early in the morning or late in the evening. It also fosters better customer service, because virtual workers may be constantly in the field in direct contact with their clients.

It is vital to match the right people to remote work. They must have disciplined work habits and the knowledge and technical skills to be able to work effectively without supervision. They might be better suited to remote work if they are self-starters and self-sufficient, rather than persons with high affiliation needs.[157] They must also be motivated to continually improve their work skills on their own, and to know when to call on outside support. Use of email, internet and software for work and work meetings is involved. The employee will benefit by saving in commuting time and expense and reducing personal expenditure on lunches, work clothes, laundry and so on. However, they may feel isolated from other employees and the workplace. They may be overlooked for training opportunities and promotions because they do not have a presence in the workplace.

Managers and coworkers often do not believe that employees can work effectively at home without being supervised. Employees may be expected to work harder to prove the effectiveness of the arrangement and/or because working at home blurred the hours of attending to home and work duties. There can also be an expectation that being at home means workers can work at any time.[158] It can be unclear who should bear the cost of infrastructure for telework in the home (computers, printers, wireless or internet broadband, airconditioning, heating, lighting). It does appear that workers are often not knowledgeable enough to provide adequate data security and that technology failure can be a strong cause for terminating telework arrangements (with inability to download large files being an example of the problems that arise).[159]

When an employee becomes a teleworker, advantages accrue to the community through the reduction of travel, traffic and pollution.[160] For the organisation, advantages include increased employee productivity and satisfaction, lower costs in providing office space and parking (providing ICT in the home or elsewhere can be much cheaper) and access to a larger pool of highly skilled workers, many of whom may not be willing to cope with the demands of the traditional office environment (for example, those in carer roles or with a physical disability). The potential business costs and problems may include insurance, security, local government zoning laws, office safety, remote support and supervision. Insurance issues involving the home office can be complex because responsibilities are not always clear. Others are data confidentiality and security, because employees often have confidential client information in their home office and must be responsible for security and backing up data to the main office's network.[161]

Summary

Intrinsic motivation and intrinsic rewards

Intrinsic motivation is the desire to work hard solely for the pleasant experience of task accomplishment. It builds upon intrinsic work rewards, or those rewards that an individual receives directly as a result of task performance. They are self-motivating and do not require external reinforcement. Together these can be important components of job design.

Job design strategies and intrinsic work rewards

In theory, job design involves the planning and specification of job tasks and the work setting in which they are to be accomplished. The manager's responsibility is to fit individual needs with task attributes and the work setting so both performance and human resource maintenance are facilitated. Job design strategies include four broad alternatives. Job simplification standardises work procedures and employs people in clearly defined and specialised tasks. Job enlargement increases task variety by combining two or more tasks previously assigned to separate workers. Job rotation increases task variety by periodically rotating employees among jobs involving different tasks. Job enrichment builds motivating factors into job content by adding planning and evaluating duties. The intrinsic work rewards made available by these strategies range on a continuum from low (job simplification) to high (job enrichment).

The job characteristics model and the diagnostic approach to job enrichment

The job characteristics model and the diagnostic approach to job enrichment recognise that not everyone wants an enriched job. Rather, they consider those with high and low growth needs and related concerns. They then look at the effect of five core job characteristics (ranging from skill variety to feedback from the job itself) on intervening critical psychological states that influence motivation, performance and satisfaction. The socio-technical approach to job design is also known as the semi-autonomous work group. The impact and role of technology is viewed as a factor in designing jobs, and steps are taken to optimise the relationship between technology and the social system to which employees belong. The social information-processing model argues that individual needs, tasks perceptions and reactions are a result of social constructions of reality. Multiskilling promotes the learning of a wide array of skills needed to perform multiple tasks within a company. Employees who are multiskilled are better equipped to shoulder greater responsibilities, and to take over when another employee is absent.

Goal-setting theory and job design, motivation and performance

Goal setting is the process of developing, negotiating and formalising the targets or objectives that an employee is responsible for accomplishing. It includes predictions that link it to job design and that serve as the basis for goal-setting theory. These predictions emphasise challenging and specific goals; knowledge of results; ability and a feeling of self-efficacy to accomplish the goals; and goal commitment or acceptance. A managerial technique that applies goal-setting theory is management by objectives (MBO). A manager and subordinate mutually agree on individual goals that are consistent with higher-level ones. A process is then implemented to monitor and assist the subordinate in task accomplishment, and the subordinate's performance is evaluated in terms of accomplished results. If implemented well, many positive aspects of goal-setting theory can be realised from MBO, but effective MBO systems are difficult to establish and maintain. Key performance indicators (KPIs) provide a benchmark against which employees' goals can be measured.

Flexible work arrangements and individual satisfaction

There are a number of flexible work arrangements that are increasingly important as a result of various drivers such as work–life balance, labour shortages and occupational stress. The compressed work week allows full-time work to be completed in less than five days.

Flexible working hours allow employees a daily choice in timing work and non-work activities. Job sharing occurs when two or more people divide one full-time job according to an agreement among themselves and the employer. Flexiyear, annual hours, job sharing and V-Time are all designed to enable workers to balance the competing demands on their time of work, leisure and education. These flexible work arrangements are becoming more important as a way of obtaining the services of an increasingly diverse workforce requiring a family-friendly workplace in our rapidly changing society. Information and communication technologies have had a significant impact on organisational design. The capabilities of this technology and lessening costs mean that the technology can often be taken with the worker, or to the worker. This enables workers to work remotely when they are travelling to and from their homes. Such teleworking allows work to be conducted remotely from the central organisation using information technology. These methods have several potential benefits, especially for those with child-care or other care duties, or for those with physical disabilities. For all employees it can involve reductions in employee expenditure on travel to work, lunches and work clothes, as well as saving on time. The potential costs are increased isolation of employees, and poorer communication and knowledge sharing, as well as costs like insurance and establishment of home offices. Data confidentiality and security and local government zoning laws can also present potential problems.

CHAPTER 5 study guide

Key terms

automation, *p. 167*

compressed work week, *p. 190*

flexible working hours (flexitime), *p. 191*

flexiyear or annual hours, *p. 194*

flow, *p. 189*

goal setting, *p. 179*

horizontal loading, *p. 169*

intrinsic motivation, *p. 165*

job, *p. 166*

job characteristics model, *p. 172*

job control, *p. 184*

job demands, *p. 184*

job design, *p. 166*

job diagnostic survey, *p. 174*

job enlargement, *p. 168*

job enrichment, *p. 170*

job resources/support, *p. 185*

job rotation, *p. 168*

job sharing, *p. 192*

job simplification, *p. 167*

key performance indicators, *p. 182*

motivating potential score, *p. 174*

multiskilling, *p. 178*

social information-processing approach, *p. 178*

socio-technical job design, *p. 178*

telework principles, *p. 193*

time–income trade-offs, *p. 192*

vertical loading, *p. 169*

voluntary reduced work time (V-Time or time–income trade-offs), *p. 192*

Review questions

1. What is the difference between intrinsic rewards and extrinsic rewards?
2. Explain the difference between horizontal and vertical job loading.
3. List and define the core job characteristics.
4. Explain the difference between job-sharing and the compressed work week.

Application questions

1. Consider a situation in which you performed a duty for someone — for example, doing an assignment, doing a job for your supervisor or even doing a favour for a friend. List the rewards you obtained from completing the duty. Distinguish between the intrinsic and extrinsic rewards.
2. Assume you are a university lecturer in this subject who is designing an assignment for students — consider the assignment design as being a job design. Use the job characteristics model to design an assignment that will maximise the intrinsic motivation for students doing the assignment. Explain the advantages of your assignment design.
3. Think about and explain how much your current 'job' (studying at college or university) involves social information processing. Provide two examples.
4. In view of the listed predictions on goal setting provided in the chapter, how would you set goals for yourself in completing a subject in your course? How would you think your instructor could be involved in this process of goal setting for you?
5. Consider the principles of working remotely or teleworking. How much of your study requires you to be located at your college or university and how much of it do you undertake remotely? Explain the role that information technology plays in enhancing this process. Discuss, based on your experience as a student, whether you think you would work effectively as a teleworker or telecommuter in the workforce.
6. Think about a job you have some familiarity with (for example, a bank teller, shop assistant, your teacher). Explain what advantages or disadvantages you would see for (a) that person, (b) the employer and (c) you as the customer if that person was working flexible hours.
7. Is it socially acceptable among your peers to say that you would be happy to sacrifice your career for family, and do you think it is the same or different for male versus female students? Why/why not?

Research questions

1. Many organisations have strongly developed conditions to support workplace flexibility for employees. Find two organisations in your community and investigate what flexible work arrangements they provide for their employees, and evaluate their apparent effectiveness.
2. Hewitt Associates, a global HR outsourcing company, announces each year the 'best employers' list for countries such as China, Hong Kong, India, the Philippines, Malaysia, Singapore, Thailand, Australia and New Zealand — and for Asia in general. For 2008 Bain & Company topped the Australian and New Zealand lists, with other winners including Federal Express, Inside Mobile, Medtronic Australia, NSW Teachers Credit Union, the GPT Group, Vedior Asia Pacific and Westaff (see http://was7.hewitt.com/bestemployers/anz/for the full list of the winners and the competition report). Analyse the characteristics of these 'best' employers in terms of their jobs and job-related practices. (Note that there are other relevant or similar awards, such as *Fortune* magazine's best employers and *Human Resources* HR awards for work–life balance and EEO Trust's awards).

Running project

Try to find the answers to the following questions about your organisation.

1. Has the nature of work, including technology utilised and/or the formal educational qualifications required for positions at the organisation increased over the past ten years? If so, has there been a corresponding change in job design and rewards? Explain. If not, why have the requirements increased? Do the requirements seem to match the job?
2. What intrinsic rewards do the employees at the organisation obtain from their work? If you have direct access to the organisation, it might be useful to speak directly with the employees.
3. Have any of the four approaches to job design been implemented? What was the outcome?
4. How does the organisation set goals for its employees? How does it communicate these goals and assess whether they are being met?
5. Describe any flexible work arrangements the organisation offers its employees. Assess the outcomes of these arrangements for both employees and the organisation.

Individual activity

The case of the casual workforce

Preparation

Casual work is a rising percentage of total employment in Australia and New Zealand. Go to the library and read about the current use of casual workers in business and industry. Alternatively, go to the internet, enter a government database (e.g. the Australian Bureau of Statistics), and locate some current statistics on the size of the casual labour force, the proportion that is self-employed and part time, and the proportion of casuals who are voluntary and involuntary.

Instructions

Collate the available information, taking into consideration the personal and social implications of a casual workforce. For each of the following scenarios, brainstorm five ways in which the current climate affects the state of mind and day-to-day business of each person, taking into account the current size and break-up of the casual labour force. For scenarios 1 and 2, consider how the employer would answer the question: 'What does the casual workforce mean to me?' For scenarios 3 and 4, from the employee's perspective, consider the question: 'What does being a casual worker mean to me?'

1. Human resources manager of a large discount retailer hiring casual workers
2. Owner of a local specialty music shop hiring casual workers
3. Recent college or university graduate working as a casual employee at the discount retailer in (1)
4. Single parent with two children in primary school, working as a casual employee of the music shop in (2).

Motivation by job enrichment

Procedure

1. Form groups of five to seven members. Each group is assigned one of the following categories:
   (a) Bank teller
   (b) Retail sales clerk
   (c) Managers, fast-food service (e.g. McDonald's)
   (d) Wait person
   (e) Receptionist
   (f) Restaurant manager
   (g) Clerical worker (or bookkeeper)
   (h) Janitor
2. As a group, develop a short description of job duties for the job your group has been assigned. The list should contain approximately four to six items.
3. Next, using job characteristics theory, enrich the job using the specific elements described in the theory. Develop a new list of job duties that incorporate any or all of the core job characteristics suggested by Richard Hackman and Greg Oldham, such as skill variety, task identity and so on. Indicate for each of the new job duties which job characteristic(s) was/were used.
4. One member of each group should act as the spokesperson and will present the group's ideas to the class. Specifically describe one or two of the old job tasks. Describe the modified job tasks. Finally, relate the new job tasks the group has developed to specific job core characteristics such as skill variety, skill identity, and so on.
5. The group should also be prepared to discuss these and other follow-up questions:
   (a) How would a manager go about enlarging but not enriching this job?
   (b) Why was this job easy or hard?
   (c) What are the possible constraints on actually accomplishing this enrichment in the workplace?
   (d) What possible reasons are there that a worker would *not* like to have this newly enriched job?

Source: 'Motivation by job enrichment' from Schermerhorn, Hunt and Osborn, *Organizational behavior*, 10th edn (USA: 2007), pp. W–79 to W–80, contributed by Diana Page, University of West Florida.

Case study: Brolly Sheets and 'mumpreneur' Diane Hurford

Mumpreneurs can be defined as mothers who move from traditional employment to owning and operating new ventures — either to better fit with their role as mothers, or motivated by opportunities identified by the experience of pregnancy or having children. Researchers propose that existing business practice in much of the commercial and corporate sectors in New Zealand and Australia operates to 'push' women who start families to explore other options and to redefine themselves as business women as well as mothers.[162]

For many women, self-employment fits around their family commitments. That is, the start-up decision is in some way motivated by the accommodation of family needs; family orientation drives the way in which the firm is managed, and mediates goals in relation to firm performance. Diane Hurford's Brolly Sheet business (www.brollysheets.co.nz and www.brollysheets.com.au) is a venture that is clearly the result of the lifestyle changes that stem from motherhood, as well as a case of 'necessity being the mother of invention'.

Diane grew up in Hamilton, New Zealand and designed Brolly Sheets in 2006 after finding she needed a fast and easy solution to changing her daughter's bed in the middle of the night while she was toilet training. A brolly sheet

is a waterproof, breathable, cotton slip, which goes over (rather than under) the bottom sheet. This meant she no longer had to strip the entire bed, and in solving her problem she saw the opportunity to solve it for others; and a business was born.

Mumpreneurs like Diane are profiled more and more often in the media and the *NZ Herald* recently interviewed

Diane[163] about her decision to start her own venture. On being asked what inspired her to set up Brolly Sheets she answers:

> I came up with the idea when my daughter Mia was nighttime toilet training and sleeping on the bottom bunk.
>
> Every night I'd always hit my head on the top bunk, because a normal mattress protector goes under the sheet, meaning I'd have to strip the whole bed.
>
> I thought if there was something that sat on top of the sheet it would be easy to get off, so I went to Spotlight and made one myself.

Because getting the product made in Australia or New Zealand was too expensive, Diane set up production in China, where they have 20 staff and the sheets can be made for a price people were prepared to pay (they sell for between $30 and $50). The business is a success, but it hasn't been without a great deal of hard work. When asked to give advice to other parents wanting to start their own baby-related venture, Diane states:

> I talk to quite a few mums who have an idea. A lot of women think, 'If I start a business I'll have the lifestyle I want because I can do it around the kids'. But the reality for me is it took three years of working harder and longer hours for less money than if I'd had a job. But it can be done. You can just take an idea and grow it into a successful business, but you've got to be prepared that it's going to take time.

Questions

1. Identify some 'push' factors within many corporate environments that discourage women with children from traditional employment.

2. Identify 'pull' factors encouraging women to start their own ventures after having children.

3. Do you think that starting your own business really does afford you more time with your children? Why/why not?

Interpretation for individual activity

People differ in their need for psychological growth at work. This instrument measures the degree to which you seek growth-need satisfaction. Score your responses as follows:

For items 1, 2, 7, 8, 11 and 12, give yourself the following points for each item:

1	2	3	4	5	6	7
Strongly prefer A			Neutral			Strongly prefer B

For items 3, 4, 5, 6, 9 and 10, give yourself the following points for each item:

7	6	5	4	3	2	1
Strongly prefer A			Neutral			Strongly prefer B

Add up all of your scores and divide by 12 to find the average. If you score above 4.0, your desire for growth-need satisfaction through work tends to be high and you are likely to prefer an enriched job. If you score below 4.0, your desire for growth-need satisfaction through work tends to be low and you are unlikely to be satisfied or motivated by an enriched job.

Source: JR Hackman & GR Oldham, *Work redesign* (Reading, MA: Addison-Wesley, 2008).

End notes

1. *The Huffington Post UK*, 'The third metric: all you need to know' (25 July 2013), www.huffingtonpost.co.uk.
2. C Snowdon-Darling, '*Are women able to achieve the third metric?*' (2nd August, 2013), www.huffingtonpost.co.uk.
3. J Lyall, '*Finding balance with flexi time*', (27 September 2013), www.huffingtonpost.com.
4. J Lyall, op. cit.
5. RJ Aldag and AP Brief, 'The intrinsic-extrinsic dichotomy: toward conceptual clarity', *Academy of Management Review*, vol. 2 (1977), pp. 497–8.
6. See HL Tosi, JR Rizzo and SJ Carroll, *Managing organizational behavior*, 2nd ed. (New York: Harper & Row, 1990).
7. N Powdthavee, 'Putting a price tag on friends, relatives, and neighbours: using surveys of life satisfaction to value social relationships', *The Journal of Socio-Economics*, vol. 37, (2008), pp. 1459–80.
8. K Ueno, 'The effects of friendship networks on adolescent depressive symptoms', *Social Science Research*, vol. 34, (2005), pp. 484–510.
9. RS Burt, 'Strangers, friends, and happiness', *Social Networks*, vol. 9 (1987), pp. 311–31.
10. R Morrison, 'Informal relationships in the workplace: Associations with job satisfaction, organisational commitment and turnover intentions', *New Zealand Journal of Psychology*, vol. 33, no. 3 (2004), pp. 114–28.
11. T Evans, 'Going concerns', *HRMonthly* (March 2008), pp. 18–21.
12. P Lencioni, *The three signs of a miserable job*, (Milton: John Wiley & Sons, 2007).

13. T Morris, 'If Aristotle ran General Motors', *The new soul of business* (New York: Henry Holt and Company, 1997).

14. Singapore Airlines, www.singaporeair.com.

15. Robert Bosch Australia, '*Your apprenticeships with us*', www.bosch.com.au.

16. *Hong Kong Standard* (August 1990), p. 6.

17. Pirelli, '*Career – job rotation*', www.pirelli.com; Kone, '*Company – Personnel*', www.kone.com; and Standard Chartered, '*Careers — Learning and development*', www.standardchartered.com.

18. Frederick Herzberg, 'One more time: how do you motivate employees?' *Harvard Business Review*, vol. 46 (January/February 1968), pp. 53–62.

19. See JR Hackman, 'On the coming demise of job enrichment' in EL Cass and FG Zimmer (eds), *Man and work in society* (New York: Van Nostrand, 1975).

20. See CL Hulin and MR Blood, 'Job enlargement individual differences, and worker responses', *Psychological Bulletin*, vol. 69 (1968), pp. 41–55; MR Blood and CL Hulin, 'Alienation, environmental characteristics and worker responses', *Journal of Applied Psychology*, vol. 51 (1967), pp. 284–90; AN Turner and PR Lawrence, *Industrial jobs and the worker: an investigation of responses to task attributes* (Boston: Harvard Graduate School of Business Administration, 1965).

21. For a complete description and review of the research, see JR Hackman and GR Oldham, *Work redesign* (Reading, MA: Addison-Wesley, 1980).

22. Adapted from JR Hackman and GR Oldham, 'Development of the job diagnostic survey', *Journal of Applied Psychology*, vol. 60 (1975), p. 161.

23. Ranstad, *The world of work report* (March, 2014), www.randstad.co.nz.

24. R Court, 'Flexibility high on worker's list', *The New Zealand Herald* (2nd April 2014), www.nzherald.co.nz.

25. See JR Hackman, G Oldham, R Janson and K Purdy, 'A new strategy for job enrichment', *California Management Review*, vol. 17, no. 4 (1975), p. 60.

26. See discussion on research into job design moderators in F Luthans, *Organizational behavior* (New York: McGraw-Hill, 1985); and A Grant, 'The significance of task significance: Job performance effects, relational mechanisms, and boundary conditions', *Journal of Applied (Psychology)* vol. 93, no. 1 (January 2008), pp. 108–24.

27. T Thomas, 'Every man is a manager at BHP's Queensland mill', *Business Review Weekly*, vol. 14, no. 3 (January 1992), pp. 56–7.

28. See JR Hackman and G Oldham, 'Development of the job diagnostic survey', *Journal of Applied Psychology*, vol. 60 (1975), pp. 159–70.

29. F Luthans, *Organizational Behavior*, 11th edn (Boston: Irwin, 2008), pp. 353–54.

30. Derived from Hackman, Oldham, Janson and Purdy (1975), op. cit., p. 62.

31. R Smith, 'Laugh harder, do better', *Management Innovation eXchange* (2011), www.managementexchange.com.

32. S Moccia, 'The good humor company', *Management Innovation eXchange* (2011), www.managementexchange.com.

33. Gallup Organization, www.gallup.com.

34. Gallup Organization, '*The Gallup Q12 Employee Engagement Poll 2008 results (Australia overview)* (2009), Gallup Consulting, www.destinationtalent.com.au.

35. J Stirling, 'Cultivate commitment', *The Weekend Australian* (22–23 March 2008), p. 1.

36. Gallup Organization (2009).

37. D Granirer, '*Laughing your way to organizational health: a lighter approach to workplace wellness*', About.com (2011), http://humanresources.about.com.

38. Jim Bright, 'Happy staff get a life', *The Sydney Morning Herald* (My Career Section) (9–10 February 2008), p. 7.

39. See G Salancik and J Pfeffer, 'An examination of need–satisfaction models of job attitudes', *Administrative Science Quarterly*, vol. 22 (1977), pp. 427–56; G Salancik and J Pfeffer, 'A social information processing approach to job attitude and task design', *Administrative Science Quarterly*, vol. 23 (1978), pp. 224–53.

40. P Ruthven talking to C Donaldson, 'Business outlook for 2008', *Human Resources* (22 January 2008), pp. 10–11.

41. C Donaldson, 'Managers underperform when managing underperformers', *Human Resources* (19 February 2008), p. 7.

42. See EA Locke, KN Shaw, LM Saari and GP Latham, 'Goal setting and task performance: 1969–1980', *Psychological Bulletin*, vol. 90 (July/November 1981), pp. 125–52. See also GP Latham and EA Locke, 'Goal setting — a motivational technique that works', *Organizational Dynamics*, vol. 8 (Autumn 1979), pp. 68–80; GP Latham and TP Steele, 'The motivational effects of participation versus goal-setting on performance', *Academy of Management Journal*, vol. 26 (1983), pp. 406–17; M Erez and FH Kanfer, 'The role of goal acceptance in goal setting and task performance', *Academy of Management Review*, vol. 8 (1983), pp. 454–63.

43. See EA Locke and GP Latham, 'Work motivation and satisfaction: light at the end of the tunnel', *Psychological Science*, vol. 1, no. 4 (July 1990), pp. 240–6.

44. ibid.

45. ibid.

46. For a complete review of goal-setting theory and research see EA Locke and GP Latham, *A theory of goal setting and task performance* (Englewood Cliffs, NJ: Prentice Hall, 1990).

47. Adapted from EA Locke and GP Latham, 'Work motivation and satisfaction: light at the end of the tunnel', *Psychological Science*, vol. 1, no. 4 (July 1990), p. 244. Reprinted by permission of Blackwell Publishers.

48. See EA Locke and GP Latham, 'Work motivation and satisfaction', *Psychological Science* (July 1990), p. 241.

49. ibid., pp. 240–6.

50. F Schuster and K Kendall, 'Where we stand — a survey of Fortune 500', *Human Resources Management* (Spring 1974), pp. 8–11.

51. Australian Public Service Commission, '*Senior executive leadership capability (SELC) framework*', www.apsc.gov.au.

52. For a good review of MBO, see Anthony P Raia, *Managing by objectives* (Glenview, IL: Scott, Foresman, 1974); Steven Kerr summarises the criticisms well in 'Overcoming the dysfunctions of MBO', *Management by Objectives*, vol. 5, no. 1 (1976).

53. F Luthans, *Organizational behavior*, 5th ed. (New York: McGraw-Hill, 1989), p. 282.

54. CC Pinder, *Work motivation theory, issues, and applications* (Dallas, TX: Scott, Foresman, 1984), p. 169.

55. Based on Cypress Semiconductor Corporation, *Harvard Business Review* (July/August 1990), pp. 88–9.

56. SAI Global, '*Awards*', '*Business Excellence Framework (2007)*' and '*Eight principles of business excellence*', www.sai-global.com.

57. P Roberts, 'Sharing the secrets of success', *Australian Financial Review* (3 July 1998), p. 42.

58. Fonterra, 'The natural source of dairy nutrition', *Fonterra Annual Report 2010*, Fonterra Co-operative Group Limited, www.fonterra.com.

59. A Moodie, 'Career surfing now the new wave', *Australian Financial Review* (22 May 1998), p. 58.

60. Stephen Withers, 'Are key performance indicators a true measure?', *Tech Management Tech Guides* (ZD Net Asia), www.zdnetasia.com (21 November 2007).

61. BM Bass, BJ Avolio, I Jung Dong and Y Berson, 'Predicting unit performance by assessing transformational and transactional leadership', *Journal of Applied Psychology*, vol. 88, no. 2 (2003), pp. 207–18. G Yukl, 'How leaders influence organizational effectiveness', *The Leadership Quarterly*, vol. 19, no. 6 (2008), pp. 708–22.

62. BE Wright, 'Public sector work motivation: A review of the current literature model and a revised conceptual model', *Journal of Public Administration Research and Theory*, vol. 11, no. 4 (2001), pp. 559–86.

63. CS Jung, 'Why are goals important in the public sector? Exploring the benefits of goal clarity for reducing turnover intention', *Journal of Public Administration Research and Theory*, doi:10.1093/jopart/mus1058, (2012).

64. YH Chun and HG Rainey, 'Goal ambiguity and organizational performance in US federal agencies', *Journal of Public Administration Research and Theory*, vol. 15, no. 4 (2005), pp. 529–57.

65. SY Chan, 'Organizational goal ambiguity and job satisfaction in the public sector', *Journal of Public Administration Research and Theory*, doi: 10.1093/jopart/mut020, (2013).

66. List developed from The Work and Age Trust, '*Flexible employment*', www.eeotrust.org.nz; and S Forsyth and A Polzer-Debruyne, 'The organisational pay-offs for perceived work–life balance support', *Asia Pacific Journal of Human Resources*, vol. 45, no. 1 (April 2007), pp. 113–23.

67. J Bourke and G Russell, 'Future perfect', *HRMonthly* (October 2007), pp. 32–36.

68. JM Haar, 'The downside of coping: Work–family conflict, employee burnout and the moderating effects of coping strategies', *Journal of Management & Organization*, vol. 12, no. 2 (September 2006), pp. 146–59.

69. University of Kent Careers and Employability Service. www.kent.ac.uk/careers/selfemployment.htm.

70. HT Reis, KM Sheldon, SL Gable, J Roscoe and RM Ryan, 'Daily well-being: the role of autonomy, competence, and relatedness', *Personality and Social Psychology Bulletin*, vol. 26, (2000), pp. 419–35.

71. CD Ryff and B Singer, 'The contours of positive human health', *Psychological Inquiry*, vol. 9 (1998), pp. 1–28.

72. T Kasser and RM Ryan, 'Further examining the American dream: differential correlates of intrinsic and extrinsic goals', *Personality and Social Psychology Bulletin*, vol. 22 (1996), pp. 280–7.

73. P Schmuck, T Kasser and RM Ryan, 'The relationship of well-being to intrinsic and extrinsic goals in Germany and the U.S.', *Social Indicators Research*, vol. 50 (2000), pp. 225–41.

74. RM Ryan, VI Chirkov, TD Little, KM Sheldon, E Timoshina and EL Deci, 'The American dream in Russia: extrinsic aspirations in two cultures', *Personality and Social Psychology Bulletin*, vol. 25 (1999), pp. 1509–24.

75. RA Karasek, 'Job demands, job decision latitude and mental strain: implications for job redesign', *Administrative Science Quarterly*, vol. 24 (1979), pp. 285–308; JA Häusser, A Mojzisch, M Niesel, and S Schulz-Hardt, 'Ten years on: a review of recent research on the Job Demand-Control (Support) model and psychological well-being', *Work & Stress*, vol. 24, no. 1 (2010), pp. 1–35.

76. M van der Doef, and S Maes, 'The job demand-control (support) model and physical health outcomes: a review of the strain and buffer hypotheses', *Psychology and Health*, vol. 13 (1998), pp. 909–936; M van der Doef, and S Maes, 'The job demand-control (support) model and psychological well-being: a review of 20 years of empirical research', *Work & Stress*, vol. 13 (1999), pp. 87–114.

77. RA Karasek (1979), op. cit.

78. E Demerouti, AB Bakker, F Nachreiner, and WB Schaufeli, The job demands-resources model of burnout', *Journal of Applied Psychology*, vol. 86 (2001), pp. 499–512; CM Boyd, AB Bakker, S Pignata, AH Winefield, N Gillespie, and C Stough, 'A longtitudinal test of the job demands-resources model among Australian academics', *Applied psychology: An international review*, vol. 60, no. 1 (2011), pp. 112–40.

79. Boyd et al. (2011), op. cit.

80. M Le Fevre, GS Kolt, and J Matheny, 'Eustress, distress and their interpretation in primary and secondary occupational stress management interventions: which way first?', *Journal of Managerial Psychology*, vol. 21 (2006), pp. 547–65.

81. H Selye, 'The stress concept: past, present, and future', in CL Cooper (ed.), *Stress research*, (New York: John Wiley & Sons, 1983), pp. 1–20.

82. M Le Fevre, GS Kolt, and J Matheny, 'Eustress, and distress: their interpretation in stress management interventions and implications for research, practice, and education', in *British Academy of Management Annual Conference 2004* (Scotland: St Andrews, 2004).

83. Health and Safety Executive, *Managing the causes of work-related stress: a step-by-step approach using the Management Standards* (Suffolk: HSE Books, 2007).

84. C Maslach, *Burnout: the cost of caring* (Englewood Cliffs, NJ: Prentice-Hall, 1982).

85. C Maslach, SE Jackson and MP Leiter, *Maslach Burnout Inventory Manual*, 3rd ed. (Palo Alto CA: Consulting Psychologists Press Inc., 1996).

86. R Callus and RD Lansbury (eds.), *Working futures: the changing nature of work and employment relations in Australia* (Sydney: The Federation Press, 2002), p. 245.

87. H Benson and RL Allen, 'How much stress is too much?', *Harvard Business Review*, 1980, p. 86–92.

88. Le Fevre, Kolt and Matheny (2006), op. cit.; Le Fevre, Kolt and Matheny (2004), op. cit.

89. U Janlert and A Hammarström, 'Which theory is best? Explanatory models of the relationship between unemployment and health', *BMC Public Health*, vol. 9 (2009).

90. DJ Roelfs, E Shor, KW Davidson and JE Schwartz, 'Losing life and livelihood: a systematic review and meta-analysis of unemployment and all-cause mortality', *Social Science and Medicine* (2011), pp. 1–15.

91. P Butterworth, LS Leach, L Strazdins, SC Olesen, B Rodgers and DH Broom, 'The psychosocial quality of work determines whether employment has benefits for mental health: results from a longitudinal national household panel survey', *Occupational and Environmental Medicine* (2011).

92. RD Caplan, 'Person-environment fit: past, present, and future', in Cooper (ed.) (1983), op. cit.

93. AL Kristof-Brown, RD Zimmerman and EC Johnson, 'Consequences of individuals' fit at work: a meta-analysis of person-job, person-organization, person-group, and person-supervisor fit', *Personnel Psychology*, vol. 58, no. 2 (2005), pp. 281–342.

94. D Feldman, C Leana and M Bolino, 'Underemployment and relative deprivation among re-employed executives', *Journal of Occupational and Organizational Psychology*, vol. 75 (2002), pp. 453–71.

95. RB Lazarus, JR Averill and EM Opton, 'The psychology of coping: issues of research and assessment', in DA Coehlo, D Hamburg and J Adams (eds), *Coping and adaptation* (New York: Basic Books, 1974), pp. 249–315.

96. Le Fevre, M., G.S. Kolt, and J. Matheny, 'Eustress, and distress: their interpretation in stress management interventions and implications for research, practice, and education', in *British Academy of Management Annual Conference*. 2004: St Andrews Scotland.

97. J Wood and J Duffie, 'Sabbatical: a strategy for creating jobs', *New Ways to Work Newsletter*, vol. 2, no. 1 (Winter 1982), pp. 5–6; J Wood and J Duffie, 'Sabbatical: a strategy for creating jobs' (part II), *New Ways to Work Newsletter*, vol. 2, nos 2–3 (Spring/Summer 1982), pp. 5–6.

98. Boyd et al. (2011), op. cit.

99. Haar, op. cit.

100. SA Lawrence, 'An integrative model of perceived available support, work–family conflict and support mobilisation', *Journal of Management & Organization*, vol. 12, no. 2 (September 2006), pp. 160–78; J Bourke and G Russell, 'Future perfect', *HRMonthly* (October 2007), pp. 32–36.

101. Haar, op. cit.

102. ibid.

103. Bourke and Russell, op. cit.

104. Haar, op. cit.

105. Lawrence, op. cit.

106. Statistics New Zealand, *Household Labour Force Survey: December 2007 quarter* (7 February 2008), www.stats.govt.nz;

Department of Labour, Employment and Unemployment: December 2011 Quarter, www.dd.govt.nz.

107. Statistics New Zealand, *Household Labour Force Survey*: June 2014 *quarter* (06 August 2014), www.stats.govt.nz.

108. Australian Bureau of Statistics, *Labour Force Australia, April 2008* (Canberra: ABS, 2008).

109. Australian Bureau of Statistics, *Labour Force Australia, August 2014* (Canberra: ABS, 2014).

110. ibid.

111. Australian Bureau of Statistics '*Population projections, Australia*', cat. no. 3222.0 (2 September 2003), www.abs.gov.au.

112. Australian Bureau of Statistics, *3222.0 — Population Projections* (for 2004 to 2101), www.ausstats.abs.gov.au (reissued 14 June 2006).

113. K Shacklock and L Fulop, 'Managing older worker exit and re-entry practices: A 'revolving door'?', *Asia Pacific Journal of Human Resources*, vol. 45, no. 2 (August 2007), pp. 151–67; C Donaldson, 'Employers napping on ageing workforce', *Human Resources* (15 May 2007), p. 7.

114. B O'Hara, *Put work in its place: how to redesign your job to fit your life,* (Victoria, BC: Work Well, 1988).

115. *Future of work*, 'Population ageing: where will it take us?', www.dol.govt.nz; 'Recognising phased retirement strategies', *HRMonthly* (July 2007), p. 12.

116. Shacklock and Fulop, op. cit.

117. ibid.

118. Cameron Cooper, 'Labour pains', *Management Today* (July 2007), pp. 22–5.

119. 'Grey-power blitzkrieg', *Management Today* (July 2007), p. 4; see also http://adage.com.au.

120. SJ Ramlall, 'enhancing employee performance through positive organizational behavior', *Journal of Applied Social Psychology*, vol. 38, no. 6 (2008), pp. 1580–600.

121. ME Seligman, 'How to see the glass half full', *Newsweek*, vol. 140 (16 September 2002), p. 48.

122. ME Seligman, *Authentic happiness: Using the new positive psychology to realize your potential for lasting fulfillment* (New York: Free Press, 2002).

123. M Csikszentmihalyi, 'Finding flow', *Psychology Today*, vol. 30, no. 4 (1997), p. 46.

124. J Nilles, *The telecommunications–transportation tradeoff: options for tomorrow* (New York: John Wiley & Sons, 1976).

125. Ministry of Posts and Telecommunications, '*Introducing teleworking in the Asia-Pacific Region – A reference guide*', www.soumu.go.jp.

126. S O'Carroll, 'Making work family friendly', *Human Resources* (5 February 2008), pp. 12–13.

127. C Rance, 'Port Kembla Coal Terminal: lightening the loads', case study in 'About time', *HRMonthly* (September 2005), pp. 22–9.

128. JC Latack and LW Foster, 'Implementation of compressed work schedules: participation and job redesign as critical factors for employee acceptance', *Personnel Psychology*, vol. 38 (1985), pp. 75–92.

129. AR Cohen and H Gadon, *Alternative work schedules: integrating individual and organizational needs* (Reading, MA: Addison-Wesley, 1978), pp. 38–46. See also JL Pearce

and JW Newstrom, 'Toward a conceptual clarification of employee responses to flexible working hours: a work adjustment approach', *Journal of Management,* vol. 6 (1980), pp. 117–34.

130. J Wood, *Altered work week study,* unpublished PhD thesis, Department of Educational Administration, University of Alberta, Canada (1977).

131. 'France aims to make job sharing work', *The Australian* (23 August 1996).

132. Australian Bureau of Statistics, *6342.0 – Working time arrangements,* (Canberra: ABS, November 2006, released 29 May 2007).

133. www.fairwork.gov.au.

134. B Headey, *The set-point theory of well-being needs replacing – on the brink of a scientific revolution?,* Melbourne Institute of Applied Economic & Social Research, University of Melbourne and DIW Berlin (2007).

135. RE Lucas, AE Clark, Y Georgellis and E Diener, 'Reexamining adaptation and the set point model of happiness: reactions to change in marital status', *Journal of Personality and Social Psychology,* vol. 84 (2003), pp. 527–39.

136. AE Clark, Y Georgellis, RE Lucas and E Diener, 'Unemployment alters the set point for life satisfaction', *Psychological Science,* vol. 15 (2004), pp. 8–13.

137. J Wood and G Wattus, 'The attitude of professionals towards job sharing', *Australian Journal of Management,* vol. 12, no. 2 (1987), pp. 103–21.

138. 'Job shares can mean two brains for the price of one', *Management Today* (August 1998), p. 10.

139. See Hays salary survey cited in 'More flexibility at work', *HRMonthly* (September 2007), p. 6.

140. F Best, 'Exchanging earnings for leisure: findings on an exploratory national survey on work time preferences', *R&D monograph* (Washington: US Department of Labor Employment and Training Administration, 1979); F Best, *Flexible life scheduling: breaking the education–work–retirement lockstep* (New York: Praeger, 1980).

141. 'France aims to make job sharing work', *The Australian* (23 August 1996), p. 29.

142. A Mills and J Wood, 'Attitudes of NSW employers towards voluntary reduced worktime', *Human Resources Management Australia,* vol. 24, no. 2 (May 1986), pp. 38–46; J Wood and F Bullock, 'Time–income tradeoffs: establishing a new equity between work, income and leisure' in R Castle, D Lewis and J Managan (eds), *Work, leisure and technology* (Melbourne: Longman Cheshire, 1986).

143. C Rance, 'Lost in transition', *HRMonthly* (March 2005), p. 22.

144. S O'Carroll, 'Making work family friendly', *Human Resources* (5 February 2008), pp. 12–13.

145. B Brown, 'Flexibility Inc', *Management Today* (November/December 2007), pp. 30–33.

146. M Gray, N Hodson and G Gordon, *Teleworking explained* (New York: John Wiley & Sons, 1993).

147. D Braue, 'Technology now?', *Management Today* (March 2007), pp. 28–30.

148. FN Schwartz, 'Management women and the new facts of life', *Harvard Business Review,* vol. 4, no. 5 (1989), pp. 5–14.

149. V Postrel, 'Mommy track without shame: a notorious article urging flexibility is proven right', *Wall Street Journal* (26 March 2011), p. C12.

150. RE Silverman, 'Is the "mommy track" still taboo?' *Wall Street Journal Blogs* (27 March 2011), http://blogs.wsj.com.

151. B Teriet, 'West German firms experiment with flexible working years', *Management Review* (April 1989), p. 29; 'Norsk Hydro's new approach takes root', *Personnel Management* (January 1988), pp. 37–40.

152. CMB South Yorkshire, '*Annual/annualised hours*', fact sheet, www.cmb.org.uk.

153. Ministry of Public Management, Home Affairs, Posts and Telecommunications, '*Communications News*' (Biweekly newsletter, 29 July 2002, vol. 13, no. 8), www.soumu.go.jp.

154. Australian Telework Advisory Committee (ATAC), *Telework in Australia,* paper II (March 2005), www.workplace.gov.au. These data draw from previous years and other studies such as the Household, Income and Labour Dynamics in Australia (HILDA) survey (2003) and Australian Bureau of Statistics (ABS) 'Location at work' survey. The paper is part of a taskforce activity by ATAC to identify trends and uptake of telework in Australia; See also www.teleworkaustralia.com.au.

155. Sensis, *The Sensis® Business Index: Teleworking* (Sensis: July 2007), www.teleworkaustralia.com.au.

156. P Callister, '*The future of work within households: understanding household-level changes in the distribution of hours of paid work*', (Department of Labour, New Zealand, 2001), www.dol.govt.nz.

157. Steve Hart, 'Remote working — It's about trust', *Management* (New Zealand, April 2008), pp. 48–51.

158. Australian Telework Advisory Committee (ATAC), op. cit., pp. 17–18.

159. ibid., pp. 19–20.

160. Telework New Zealand, '*Flexible work practices*', www.telework.co.nz.

161. 'Wired to the desk', *Fortune* (Summer 1999), pp. 164–75; RH Kepczyk, 'Evaluating the virtual office', *Ohio CPA Journal,* vol. 58, no. 2 (April/June 1999), pp. 16–17; KA Edelman, 'Open office? Try virtual office', *Across the Board,* vol. 34, no. 3 (March 1997), p. 34.

162. C Harris, RL Morrison, M Ho and K Lewis, 'Mumpreneurs: mothers in the business of babies', *paper presented at the Australia and New Zealand Academy of Management (ANZAM)* (3 December 2008), Auckland, New Zealand.

163. C Sykes, 'Small Business: Parenthood inspires entrepreneurs', *The New Zealand Herald* (27 January 2014), www.nzherald.co.nz.

Part 3

MANAGING GROUP DYNAMICS AND TEAM PERFORMANCE

CHAPTER 6

GROUPS AND GROUP DYNAMICS

LEARNING OBJECTIVES

After studying this chapter, you should be able to:

1. define a group and explain what types of groups exist in organisations

2. explain how groups meet individual and organisational needs

3. list and describe some of the key concepts that underpin managing effective groups

4. explain the inputs to groups that may contribute towards group effectiveness

5. define the dynamics and processes that occur within groups

6. describe the outputs of groups in terms of task and maintenance activities

7. explain the key features of intergroup dynamics and why it is important managers understand them.

WORKING IN GROUPS IS NOT FOR EVERYONE — THE NEW 'GROUPTHINK'

The advantages of working in a group and within teams are well known; most people report enjoying the experience of collectively solving problems and coming up with solutions. In fact, many of us actually expect our social needs to be met in friendly, collaborative workplaces. From primary school classrooms set up with shared tables and piles of beanbags (to foster group learning) through to university courses being assessed using group assignments, new employees are educated to expect, and hopefully enjoy, the experience of working in groups. But while teamwork can offer a stimulating, useful way to exchange ideas, manage information and build trust, not everyone likes or is suited to this way of working. Studies show that open-plan offices can make workers hostile, insecure and distracted. They are also more likely to suffer from high blood pressure, stress, the flu and exhaustion.[1] There is increasing evidence in the academic literature that interruptions increase the number of mistakes people make,[2] the length of time it takes to complete tasks, and even if the task is completed at all![3]

Susan Cain is the author of the book *Quiet: the power of introverts in a world that can't stop talking*.[4] She published an article in the *New York Times* critiquing the current trend towards working in groups and teams, having shared offices, and the emphasis on 'people skills' as being the most important thing for employees to possess.[5] Cain states, 'Our companies, our schools and our culture are in thrall to an idea I call the New Groupthink, which holds that creativity and achievement come from an oddly gregarious place'. She goes on to suggest people are in fact *more* creative when they have privacy and freedom from interruption. She states that the most creative people in a variety of fields are often very introverted (preferring solitude and disliking social interaction). The creative force behind Apple computers, Steve Wozniak, is a perfect example of the creative introvert. In his memoir Mr Wozniak offers the following advice to others:

> Most inventors and engineers I've met are like me … they live in their heads. They're almost like artists. In fact, the very best of them are artists. And artists work best alone … I'm going to give you some advice that might be hard to take. That advice is: Work alone … Not on a committee. Not on a team.

This chapter will outline both advantages and disadvantages of groups. As you read it, consider what type of work environment might work best for you.

Introduction

Group life is fundamental to the existence of the human species. We work in groups in our families, neighbourhoods, communities and political systems. Individuals seldom, if ever, behave without being influenced by the groups to which they belong. As we saw in the opening to this chapter, groups exist in organisations in many forms and are usually an important part of the organisation's operations and success. It is important to understand groups and the interactions between group members involved in the pursuit of organisational goals. All organisations involve interrelationships within and between groups, both within and outside the organisation.

The best organisations tap the full potential of groups as an important human resource. They understand what groups can contribute and the problems sometimes associated with groups, and they have managers who are comfortable leading and participating in groups of all types and sizes. The benefits of people working cooperatively apply to any organisation. However, groups have to be understood and managed skilfully if they are to produce quality results. Just putting people together does not guarantee success.

In the workplace, the use of small groups is increasingly viewed as a prescription for success. Therefore, an understanding of group processes is important in dealing with human behaviour in organisations. This chapter introduces you to the basic attributes of groups as they are found in organisations, and examines group and intergroup dynamics to provide you with the knowledge and skills to work in and manage groups better. The next chapter, on teams and teambuilding, is closely linked.

What is a group?

Formally defined in an organisation context, a **group** is a collection of two or more people who work with one another regularly to achieve one or more common goals. There is absolutely no restriction on the size of a group. In the right circumstances, 50 individuals in a theatre production unit may see themselves as a group. However, 20 is commonly considered the upper limit, because beyond this number interaction and/or unity become more difficult and the group tends to split into smaller subgroups. This does not necessarily mean a group of 20 people is always effective. Group effectiveness depends on a number of factors that will be discussed in the chapter.

In essence, a group is more than just a collection of people — say, passengers waiting to board a Qantas or Singapore Airlines flight, or a crowd watching a street procession. In a true group, members consider themselves mutually dependent to achieve common goals, and they interact with one another regularly to pursue those goals over a sustained period of time.

Groups are collections of two or more people who work with one another regularly to achieve one or more common goals.

Types of groups in organisations

Groups appear in various forms in organisations. All groups within organisations have purposes and we will consider some of these later. Regardless of these, it is useful to classify groups into different types. A common managerial distinction is between formal groups and informal groups.

Formal groups

A **formal group** is an 'official' group that is designated by formal authority to serve a specific purpose. Employees become members of formal groups because they are formally assigned to them. Within these groups, people are assigned positions, such as leading hand or supervisor. Another example is the work unit headed by a manager and consisting of one or more people reporting directly to the manager. Such a group has been created by the

Formal groups are 'official' groups that are designated by formal authority to serve a specific purpose.

organisation to perform a specific task. This 'task' may be described in general terms as the transformation of various resource inputs (such as ideas, materials and objects) into certain product outputs (such as a report, decision, service or commodity).

A manager is responsible for the group's performance while depending on the group's members to do the required work. Such challenges are found at all levels of managerial responsibility because any manager is responsible for the performance of at least one group. A popular view of organisations depicts them as interlocking networks of work groups. As shown in figure 6.1, this view identifies the important 'linking-pin' function of managers first described by Rensis Likert. Likert points out managers actually create the network structure by simultaneously serving as superiors in one work group and as subordinates in another at the next higher level. Whereas the manager of a branch bank is 'in charge' of the branch, they are also one of several branch managers who report to the person at the next higher level. So, all work groups are seen as interconnected, working together to create the 'total' organisation.

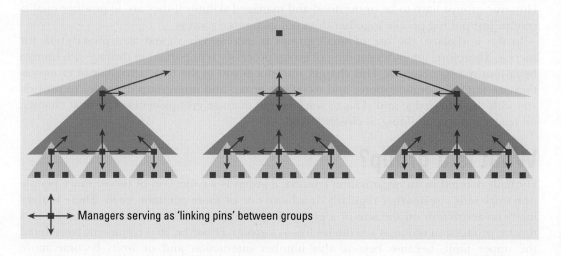

FIGURE 6.1 Likert's linking-pin model of an organisation as a complex network of interlocking groups

Source: Rensis Likert, *New patterns of management* (New York: McGraw-Hill, 1961). Reproduced with the permission of The McGraw-Hill Companies.

Managers serving as 'linking pins' between groups

There are different types of formal groups in organisations; some are relatively permanent and others are more temporary in nature.

Permanent formal work groups perform a specific function on an ongoing basis.

1. **Permanent formal work groups**, or command groups, often appear on organisation charts as departments (for instance, market research department) or divisions (for instance, consumer-products division), among other possibilities. Such groups can vary in size from small departments of just a few people to large divisions employing 100 or more people. However, in all cases, permanent formal work groups are officially created to perform a specific function on an ongoing basis. They continue in existence until a decision is made to change or reconfigure the organisation for some reason.

Temporary formal work groups are created for a specific purpose and typically disband once that purpose has been accomplished.

2. In contrast, **temporary formal work groups** (or task groups) are created for a specific purpose — to solve a specific problem or to perform a defined task — and typically disband once that purpose has been accomplished.[6] Good examples are the temporary committees and task forces that are important components of any organisation. Indeed, today's organisations tend to make considerable use of task forces for special problem-solving efforts. The managing director of a company, for example, may convene a task force to examine the possibility of implementing flexible work hours for non-managerial employees. Usually, such temporary groups appoint chairpersons or heads who are held accountable for results, much like the manager of a work unit. The head of a temporary group may be given a deadline or due date for submitting formal recommendations and/or for achieving a particular task. There are other ways of using groups in organisations too. For example, an organisation may use a 'focus group' to survey its employees, clients or customers about organisational products or processes.

New Zealand and Australian military task force foils drug smugglers

A task force is an example of a temporary formal group. Often, the combined expertise in a task force will create synergies and have successes impossible without the cooperation of several groups. In October 2014, the *New Zealand Herald* reported on a huge drug smuggling operation that was foiled by the Combined Task Force 150 (CTF-150), which is part of the Combined Maritime Forces.[7] New Zealand Defence Force commander Air Commodore Kevin McEvoy said:

OBinAction

> This was a great result for the combined New Zealand and Australian force and our Pakistan Navy colleagues at CTF-150, who led the operation. We often work with other nations on operations and it is good for our people to be involved in a large-scale operation that can make a real difference.

> The drug haul was its first successful counter-narcotics operation since the Pakistan Navy took command of the maritime security and counter-terrorism mission in August 2014. Task force head Commodore Sajid Mahmood, of the Pakistan Navy, said he was incredibly proud of the sailors and airmen involved in the complicated operation.

> CTF-150 has a long history of disrupting narcotics trafficking in the region, and Toowoomba, with the support of 5 Squadron of the RNZAF, have carried this on. Keep up the good work!

Informal groups

Social psychologists make an important distinction between the formal groups just discussed and informal groups. The latter emerge unofficially and are not formally designated as parts of the organisation. The key difference is formal groups are officially defined in the organisational structure, whereas informal groups begin spontaneously and without formal endorsement. Most formal groups include one or more informal groups that have emerged within them. Alternatively, informal groups can exist in organisations but overlap different formal groups. For example, members of different formal groups may belong to a single informal group, such as a Friday night social club. While they might not seem important to the organisation, these informal group links may affect members' behaviour in positive and negative ways. Sometimes wider sharing of information and support occurs through such informal group memberships.

Social networking websites represent another type of informal group. Those who are connected within a virtual social network are able to share information and problem-solve aspects of working life. *The Juggle* (blogs.wsj.com/juggle) is a blog set up by and for working mothers, with a focus on choices and tradeoffs people make as they juggle work and family. The virtual social networks that spring from sites such as this help people to feel that they are not alone in the problems that they face. *The Juggle* gives solutions to dilemmas and provides strategies to help people deal with difficult situations in organisations.

In other cases, informal groups can have political goals and their activities may destabilise the organisation or challenge its operations. Covertly, an informal group of executives engaging in nepotistic support for one another in promotion decisions, or coalitions to influence other key decisions, may undermine the organisation's capacity to achieve its goals effectively. Strikes by industrial unions are an overt example.

Two common types of informal groups are friendship groups and interest groups. Friendship groups consist of people with natural affinities for one another; they may tend to work together, sit together, take breaks together, and even do things together outside

Informal groups are groups that emerge unofficially and are not formally designated as parts of the organisation.

Friendship groups consist of people with natural affinities for one another who may do things together inside or outside the workplace.

the workplace. **Interest groups** consist of individuals who share common interests; they may be job-related interests, such as an intense desire to learn more about computers, or non-work interests, such as community service, sports or religion.

There are at least two reasons for the emergence of informal groups in organisations. First, they help people get their jobs done. Informal groups offer a network of interpersonal relationships with the potential to 'speed up' the work flow or 'gain favours' in ways that formal lines of authority fail to provide. Second, informal groups help people to satisfy individual needs (these are discussed more in the next section).

Figure 6.2 illustrates how informal groups add complexity to the linking-pin model of organisations shown earlier. These groups create a vast array of informal but very real networks that further relate people from various parts of the organisation to one another. Accordingly, managers must be skilled at understanding and working with groups in both their formal and informal forms.

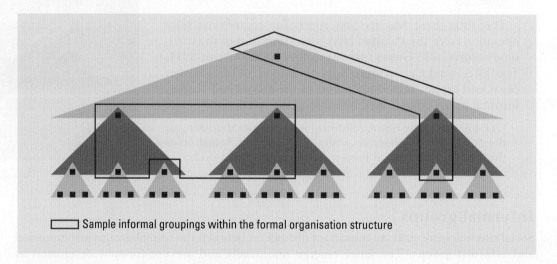

☐ Sample informal groupings within the formal organisation structure

FIGURE 6.2 How informal groups add complexity to Likert's linking-pin model of organisations

Purposes of groups in organisations

Groups can have a major impact on their members and on the organisation. In the workplace, a prime managerial concern is to help groups influence members' attitudes and behaviours in positive ways. Managers also aim to enhance collective member contributions to effective performance through groups and also through allowing group members to satisfy their individual needs. Thus, it is clear that groups have two key purposes in organisations.

1. *Groups can help to meet organisational needs.* The following examples give an indication of some of the many ways in which this may occur. Groups provide the context in which many people learn how to do their jobs. The job skills and knowledge of group members can be shared. This shared knowledge can be used to help solve difficult and unique problems, and it can be especially helpful to newcomers who require advice and assistance in their jobs. In an effective group, members are quick to offer support and performance feedback. This kind of support helps group members acquire job competencies and may even make up for deficiencies in the formal training and education practices of an organisation. How group members behave in the workplace serves as a 'model' for newcomers to follow. Group members communicate work performance expectations to one another, influencing one another's attitudes and beliefs about various aspects of the work setting. This influence may be positive or negative; that is, it may encourage or discourage high levels of work effort. A new employee soon learns from coworkers who are 'good' and 'bad' supervisors and who can be 'trusted'. These influences may even extend to how individuals feel about their job and the organisation; for example, a coworker may indicate 'this is a good job to have and a great place to work' or 'this is a

lousy job and you are better off looking for something else'. Naturally, managers would all like such influence within groups to be as positive and supportive of organisational goals as possible. The following example illustrates the importance of forming relationships with other employees in the workplace.

2. *Groups can satisfy the needs of their individual members.* Groups, both formal and informal, provide social interaction and interpersonal fulfilment. They can provide individual security in the form of direct work assistance and technical advice, or offer emotional support in times of special crisis or pressure. In informal groups, individuals may be able to find sympathy for their feelings and receive task assistance without having to reveal uncertainties to managers. By participating in group activities, members can acquire a sense of identification and offer opportunities for ego involvement. They can also achieve a sense of belonging from being with people who share similar values, attitudes and goals. In many ways, group involvement provides members with the full range of need satisfactions discussed in chapter 3.

The importance of workplace friends

OBinAction

The importance of informal groups and relationships in organisations should not be underestimated. As humans, we all need some form of social interaction; most people thrive on the simple act of connecting to others. For most of us, a large part of our social network is created in the workplace. We see these people every day and we have work in common. Our colleagues often get to know us in ways that our other friends and significant others simply don't.

Yet, despite the social opportunities that work can bring, what is the outcome when it doesn't happen for you? What do you do when you have no work friends — no-one to save you space at a meeting, or to look forward to catching up with on Monday? When this happens, there is often no lonelier place to be. Research looking into workplace friendships has found that, for some people, simply having no friends at work is enough to make them leave their jobs and seek employment elsewhere.[8]

Dorothy Tannahill-Moran is a career coach who states that being new to an organisation, or perhaps feeling that you are a bad fit with your colleagues, can be a lonely and unpleasant experience.[9] She maintains that work relationships can make or break a job — they can nourish you and help you excel in your career. When those bonds are not forming, there are things you can do to improve the situation. Perhaps existing friendship cliques seem too strong to penetrate? These people have probably worked together for a while and the bond is tight, and they may not realise how unfriendly they seem. Dorothy advises people in this situation to be patient and give a friendly smile. They need to make the effort to get to know each person at an individual level. It may even take some big work event, like a Christmas party, to be the final catalyst that forms the bond.

Effective managers will attempt to use groups in ways that benefit both the group members and organisations. Contemporary organisations use groups in many creative and productive ways. Examples of the efficacy of groups can be found in many settings, as managers increasingly recognise the usefulness of groups in organisations. The scholar Harold J Leavitt points out the following reasons in support of groups.[10]

- Groups can help foster innovation and creativity.
- Groups sometimes make better decisions than individuals do, and can help gain commitments needed to implement such decisions.
- Groups can guide members and exert control over them.
- Groups help offset the negative effects of increasing organisation size.
- Groups can help organisations accomplish important tasks.

While groups serve useful purposes in organisations, they can have various advantages and disadvantages as summarised in table 6.1 below. Some of the concepts in the table are discussed more fully on the following pages of this chapter.

TABLE 6.1 Potential advantages and disadvantages of groups

Advantages of groups	Disadvantages of groups
Groups bring together people for a specific purpose.	Some groups' specific purposes may conflict with the objectives of the organisation or with those of other groups.
Groups can achieve positive synergy.	Groups may result in negative synergy, especially when there are disruptive behaviours, ambiguous roles or interpersonal conflicts between group members.
Groups can become highly cohesive and high-performance entities.	Groups can become highly cohesive but work against organisational work goals.
Individuals can collaborate to achieve a joint goal.	Some people may be able to 'loaf' in groups while others do the work.
Groups of people with complementary skills, attitudes, experiences and viewpoints may enhance task accomplishment and decision making.	Groups of people with similar opinions and viewpoints may make uncreative or poor decisions while groups of people with extreme differences, or with strong subgroups, may experience dysfunctional levels of conflict in decision making.
People from collectivist societies are likely to work well in groups.	People from individualistic societies may not work well in groups.
Organising people into groups clarifies goals and activities and enables people to work together on large and complex tasks.	The more people are organised into specific task-related activities, the more they may become different from other groups working on different goals and activities, leading to problematic intergroup relations.
Groups can be an ideal collection of people to work on particular tasks.	Groups can be the wrong size or combination of people to accomplish what is necessary.
Informal groups can enable informal networks of individuals who support one another towards achieving organisational goals.	Informal groups can have members whose goals and behaviours conflict (intentionally or unintentionally) with organisational goals.

The success of organisations depends upon the success of its groups as well as the way networks of groups interlock and work with each other. Like individuals, groups must succeed for the organisation to prosper over the long run. At this point it is useful to highlight what makes an effective group.

Managing groups for effectiveness

Managers are concerned with productive workplace activity. Productive workplaces require efficient and effective performance activities at individual, group and organisational levels. In order to understand group effectiveness we need to consider what groups do and how they operate, and what might support or undermine group effectiveness.

Task performance and group maintenance

In order to function, and continue functioning, a group must achieve two things:
- *task performance* — achieving the group's task or tasks
- *group maintenance* — maintaining the social system of the group itself.

These two group activities are examined more fully when the outputs of group activity are described later in the chapter. However, it is appropriate to highlight at the outset why they are important. When properly managed, groups are conducive to achieving synergy — the creation of a whole that is greater than the sum of its parts. When synergy occurs, groups accomplish more than the total of their members' individual capabilities. Therefore, organisations and their managers have much to gain through the effective use of groups as human resources. Research shows groups often have three performance advantages over individuals acting alone.

1. When the presence of an 'expert' is uncertain, groups seem to make better judgements than those of the average individual operating alone.
2. When problem solving can be handled by a division of labour and the sharing of information, groups are typically more successful than individuals.
3. Given their tendencies to make more risky decisions, groups can be more creative and innovative than individuals in accomplishing their tasks.

Groups can also have problems. In essence, group problems can result in 'negative' synergy. A manager should endeavour to avoid these effects. The very word 'group', for example, produces both positive and negative reactions. It is said 'two heads are better than one', but we are also warned 'too many cooks spoil the broth'. The issue here is how well group members work together to accomplish a task. This includes a concern about social loafing, also called the 'Ringelmann effect'.[11] Ringelmann, a German psychologist, pinpointed this effect by asking people to pull as hard as they could on a rope, first alone and then in a group. He found average productivity dropped as more people joined the rope-pulling task. Thus, the Ringelmann effect acknowledges people may tend not to work as hard in groups as they would individually. There are two reasons: their contribution is less noticeable, and they prefer to see others carry the workload.

Social loafing is also another name for freeloading, which occurs when a person is placed in a group and removed from individual accountability. Because of differences in the degree of individualism or collectivism in different national cultures (see chapter 1), it is possible social loafing might occur more in individualist societies than in collectivist societies, in which people focus on working together in groups. Obviously, one of a manager's interests in studying organisational behaviour is to learn how to minimise social loafing and maximise the performance contributions of any group.

Other disruptive behaviours can affect group performance and functions and should be avoided. Disruptive behaviours are behaviours that harm the group process. A good group member avoids (and helps other group members avoid) the following behaviours:
- lack of direction or uncertainty of purpose
- being overly aggressive towards other members
- infighting
- lack of respect and/or trust for each other
- withdrawing and refusing to cooperate with others
- shirking of responsibilities for group tasks or processes
- playing around when there is work to be done
- using the group as a forum for self-confession
- talking too much about irrelevant matters
- trying to compete for attention and recognition.

Awareness of such dysfunctional group behaviours is vital for managers — being aware of potential problems can help a group take actions that will discourage or overcome such behaviours. Some of the ways in which behaviour within a group can affect group

Synergy is the creation of a whole that is greater than the sum of its parts.

Social loafing is the tendency of people not to work as hard in groups as they would individually.

Disruptive behaviour is any behaviour that harms the group process.

effectiveness will be discussed later in the chapter, especially in the section on group processes and group dynamics.

Group effectiveness

We can conclude an **effective group** is one that achieves high levels of both task performance and human resource maintenance over time. Practically speaking, an effective group gets its job done and takes good care of its members in the process. Being part of an effective group is motivating and rewarding for an individual. In terms of task performance, an effective group achieves its performance goals in the standard sense of timely and high-quality work results. For a permanent work group, such as a manufacturing section or division, this may mean meeting daily work targets. For a temporary group, such as a new policy task force, this may involve submitting a draft of a new organisational policy to the company managing director. In terms of human resource maintenance, an effective group is one whose members are sufficiently satisfied with their tasks, accomplishments and interpersonal relationships to work well together on an ongoing basis. For a permanent work group, this means that the members work well together day after day; for a temporary work group, it means the members work well together for the duration of the assignment. A classic listing of the characteristics of an effective group is found in The effective manager 6.1.

THE **EffectiveManager** 6.1

Ten characteristics of an effective group

1. A sense of urgency and direction; purpose and goals
2. A lot of work at the start, setting a tone, setting a 'contract' and/or specifying a clear set of rules
3. A broad sense of shared responsibility for the group outcomes and group process
4. Effective approaches to recognising problems and issues and making decisions
5. A high level of commitment and trust among members
6. A balance in satisfying individual and group needs
7. A climate that is cohesive yet does not stifle individuality
8. An ability to confront differences and deal with conflict
9. An ability to deal with minority opinions effectively
10. Communication patterns with a proven track record

For groups to be effective, managers need to be the key supports to help them get started and stay focused. The What would you do? describes an alternative to internal organisational groups and shows how group effectiveness and synergies can be harnessed to truly benefit both individuals and organisations.

WhatWould **You Do?**

Improving health care — the impact of effective groups

A small and highly effective group of Australasian medical specialists and entrepreneurs has won two prestigious British health services awards for a software package developed to save patients from hospital medical misadventure. Patientrack is a software response to a global health problem recognised by Dr Michael Buist, a New Zealand clinician and intensive care specialist now working in Australia.

Each year, up to 98 000 patients die from adverse events (i.e. something other than the illness for which they were hospitalised) in United States, 40 000 in the United Kingdom and 18 000 in Australia. Extrapolating those figures suggests around 3000 patients die in New Zealand hospitals from adverse events each year. The solution, Buist decided, lay with the use of information technology specifically designed to support the medical response processes. Patientrack is the outcome.

After 14 months of trialling by the Central Manchester University Hospitals National Health Service (NHS) Foundation Trust (CMFT), it was declared a success. The trials provided the developers with unprecedented insight into the ways in which hospitals respond to better management practices and procedures, and how IT can improve patient care outcomes. They showed, for example, that not only could they lower the number of patient deaths, they could also shorten hospital stays and make better use of resources.[12] In late 2014, the Patientrack system was adopted in Harrogate Hospital in the United Kingdom.[13] Patientrack will identify automatically patients who may be deteriorating, before sending alerts directly to the doctors and nurses who need to take action. Paper-based observation processes will be completely removed. Patientrack will allow nurses to capture observations in real-time at the patient bedside on handheld tablets, with clinicians also able to access that information from anywhere in the hospital.

Question

Refer to The effective manager 6.1. Which of the ten characteristics of effective groups may have been exemplified by the creators of Patientrack?

To begin with, it is normal for groups to address issues and problems they can manage most easily. Later, the problems become more difficult to solve and the groups may grow disinclined to change the perfect systems they have already worked out. This stage of group development can be difficult to endure. Mature groups may expand or change group membership and question established roles and processes as new problems arise. There is more about the stages of group development later in the chapter.

Groups as open systems

One way to gain a better understanding of what it takes to become effective as a group — and to remain so — is to view the group as an 'open system'. Consider the model presented in figure 6.3. This perspective depicts a group as an open system that interacts with its environment to transform group resource inputs into group outputs (a similar model is typically applied to organisations as open systems).

For present purposes, the environment of any given group consists of other individuals and groups with whom the group interacts within the organisation. The group depends on

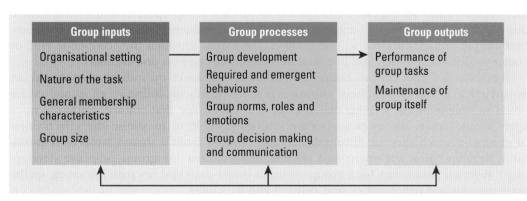

Group inputs	Group processes	Group outputs
Organisational setting	Group development	Performance of group tasks
Nature of the task	Required and emergent behaviours	Maintenance of group itself
General membership characteristics	Group norms, roles and emotions	
Group size	Group decision making and communication	

FIGURE 6.3 The work group viewed as an open system — transforming group inputs into group outputs

these elements to provide the resources, or inputs, it needs to operate. In return for these resources, the group is expected to give something back to the environment — group outputs, or work results, of real value. Once again, the interlocking nature of groups in organisations is clear. The many groups of an organisation are interdependent; they depend on one another to provide the support needed for their operating success.

To be truly effective, a group must achieve its goals in such a way other groups are helped in attaining theirs. Of course, this does not always happen. Sometimes, groups emphasise their own needs and neglect those of others. Sub-goal optimisation occurs when a group achieves its goals at the expense of the goals of others. The group identifies strongly with its own sub-goals and puts its efforts towards achieving those. In doing so, it loses an appreciation of the fact all the various groups should be working collectively for higher common goals, of which the group's sub-goal is a part. For example, a marketing department may increase sales by offering customers special product designs that are difficult for manufacturing to produce — marketing looks good because it achieves a high sales record, but manufacturing looks bad because it has cost overruns. This is a tendency that must be avoided. An effective group should serve the needs of the total organisation, not just its own. It should establish and maintain good input–output relations with other parts of the larger system, both individuals and groups. This 'give and take' helps the group gain the resource inputs it needs from the environment. It also helps the group perform in a manner that truly assists, rather than hinders, the performance efforts of other components of the organisation.[14]

> **Sub-goal optimisation** occurs when a group achieves its goals at the expense of the goals of others.

Inputs into the group process

The effectiveness of a group, as in all open systems, will depend in part upon the inputs to the system. The better the group inputs, the better the chance of group effectiveness. When considering inputs, we are considering both the inputs to the tasks the group performs and also the inputs to the maintenance of the group itself. We need to be concerned with the way in which a group operates if we wish to have the group continue as an effective entity in the organisation. Group inputs are the initial 'givens' in a group situation. They set the stage for all group action. If all the inputs are satisfactory, the group has a strong foundation for pursuing effectiveness. But if even some of the inputs are unsatisfactory, efforts to achieve effectiveness will suffer from the problems and shortcomings tracing back to the input insufficiencies. An informed manager can avoid many of these difficulties by remaining aware of how these major categories of group input factors — organisational setting, nature of the task, membership characteristics and group size — may influence group operations and outcomes. Look back at figure 6.3 to picture these group inputs as part of an 'open system'.

> **Group inputs** are the initial 'givens' in a group situation that set the stage for all group processes.

Organisational setting

The organisational setting can affect the way in which a group operates and what it accomplishes. Specifically, research suggests the setting can influence whether group members become psychologically close to one another, the extent to which they cooperate and/or compete with one another, and how well they communicate with one another.[15]

Organisational policies, procedures and cultures that focus on individualism could act as barriers to group effectiveness. Groups rely more heavily on collective effort and evolve better in organisational settings that nurture and encourage that culture. Naturally, managers should create the most supportive settings possible to maximise the effectiveness of groups in which they are involved. Managers should build a shared sense of responsibility, develop vision alignment and provide opportunities for group collective development. Relevant parameters for a group setting include: goals and rewards; resources, spatial arrangements and technologies; and cultures and structures.

Goals and rewards

Many of the insights we discussed in chapters 3, 4 and 5 — and, in particular, those about goals, needs and rewards — can be applied to the group as well as to the individual level of analysis. Appropriate goals and well-designed reward systems can help establish and maintain the 'motivation' for group members to work hard together in support of group-level accomplishments. On the other hand, groups can suffer if goals and rewards are focused too much on individual outcomes. As in the case of individuals, a group's performance can suffer when goals are:

• unclear
• insufficiently challenging
• arbitrarily imposed from the outside.

Sometimes, unclear goals and individualised rewards can have very negative consequences and this highlights the need to consider who is responsible for ensuring a group has clearly stated goals, is closely monitored in its activities and has appropriate reward practices.

Resources, spatial arrangements and technologies

The supporting resources, spatial arrangements and technologies of the group are important. Organisational resources important to the work group include adequate budgets, the right facilities, good work methods and procedures, and the best technologies.

These and related items provide groups with the background support needed to take optimum advantage of their performance opportunities. Any person, working alone or as part of a group, must be supported to achieve maximum success. A good manager, for example, 'supports' a work group by making sure the members have the resources they need to use their talents fully and achieve high performance results. This includes the right technologies to help them do their jobs effectively and the right spatial arrangements to enable communication and interaction to achieve work outcomes and maintain group social systems. In cases in which groups are physically dispersed, technological or other solutions must enable them to communicate and collaborate in their group activities; for example, teleworkers may feel ostracised from fellow group members unless efforts are made to include them.

When support is absent or minimal, the performance of a group is likely to suffer and additional side effects may occur. For example, when monetary resources are scarce, groups may engage in unhealthy competition to obtain them. Such intergroup competition can be dysfunctional in terms of the accomplishment of higher-level organisational goals.

Cultures and structures that value and support group activity and interaction

The 'cultures' of some organisations tend to be very individualistic; that is, they emphasise individual performance, individual advancement and individual rewards. This emphasis can make it more difficult to develop truly effective work groups. In contrast, groups can prosper in cultures that place a high value on individual contributions to group accomplishments. Because of the mounting intransigence of local organisational cultures, and the changing work environment that makes cultural learning more urgent, groups have become important resources in sensitising managers and their employees to the cultural dimensions of their work.

Structure counts too. Every group will develop an internal structure as it goes about its daily operations. In some groups, this structure may be 'tight' and 'rigid'; in others, it may be 'loose' and more 'flexible'. Neither one structure nor the other is essentially good or bad. Circumstances often dictate which form of group structure works best and this will also depend upon the organisational structure in which it must operate, including interaction with other groups. A rigid organisation structure, for example, can constrain a group that is trying to operate in a flexible manner; yet a group with a rigid structure may encounter difficulties working within organisational structures that are more flexible in nature.

Nature of the group task

Like organisational setting, the nature of the task to be performed is an important factor in group input. Different tasks place different demands on a group. A basic rule of thumb is that the difficulty of achieving group effectiveness increases with the degree of task complexity.[16] In other words, it is harder to accomplish complex tasks than to accomplish simple tasks. To master complex tasks, group members must apply and distribute their efforts more broadly than they do on simple tasks. They must also cooperate more to achieve desired results. When group members are successful in doing so, they usually experience high levels of satisfaction from knowing they are able to accomplish complex tasks. This often has a positive flow-on effect and works as a further reinforcer of group effectiveness.

Task complexity can be understood along technical and social lines. In terms of technical demands on a group, the key issues are: How unusual is the task that is to be accomplished? How difficult is the task? And how dispersed is the information needed to accomplish the task? Compared with simple tasks, complex tasks are technically more demanding. They require high performance on unique and difficult tasks, and they require more information processing to make this performance possible. In terms of social demands on a group, the key issues relate to ego involvement and agreements on issues of ends and means; that is, compared with simple tasks, complex ones are more socially demanding. They are very ego involving, but they also make it more difficult to reach agreement on either the ends or the means for accomplishing them.[17]

- *Ego involvement* refers to the degree to which members strongly and personally identify with the group tasks. Ego-involving tasks relate to deeply rooted personal values, affect personal lives and/or engage personal skills.
- *Ends agreement* refers to members' agreement about what they are trying to accomplish and the criteria for defining 'success'. Ends agreement is easier to achieve when the group task is clear and the outcomes are measurable.
- *Means agreement* refers to members' agreement about how the group should perform its task. Means agreement is easier for tasks in which one approach is clearly the best; it is much harder to attain when many alternatives exist.

Sustainability

Vigilantes of the sea

The Sea Shepherd Conservation Society (SSCS) is an international non-profit marine wildlife conservation organisation established in 1977. The aim of SSCS is to end the destruction of habitat and the slaughter of wildlife in the world's oceans.

In recent years, SSCS has received a great deal of attention for its direct-action tactics against Japanese whaling. The crew on the Sea Shepherd vessels work together, often putting their own safely on the line. They have high levels of ego involvement (strongly believing in the value of the mission), ends agreement (being in agreement about what they are trying to accomplish) and means agreement (the best way to achieve their goals). Sea Shepherd claims that the organisation's harassment of the Japanese whaling fleet in 2010 halved the number of whales killed. Several conservation groups have claimed that Japanese whaling has been reduced in the Southern Ocean, citing the Sea Shepherd's constant hounding of them — blocking supplies and blockading whaling ships — as the reason.[18]

The work of the SSCS has paid off. In late 2014, Australia joined New Zealand in a resolution that aims to put an end to Japan's whaling activities in the Southern Ocean. In an article published by *The Guardian* (UK) Oliver Milman outlines the Australian Government's opposition to whaling.[19] The resolution demands that strict new standards must be met for scientific whaling, with an emphasis on non-lethal methods for analysing whales. Permits would have to be issued by the full International Whaling Commission (IWC), rather than its scientific committee, meaning that Japan would not be able to get permission for whaling until 2016 because the IWC meets only every two years.

General membership characteristics

The attributes of individual group members are also important inputs that may affect both the way the group operates and what it accomplishes. The competency, demographic and psychological characteristics of the members are all important. Having the right competencies available within the membership can be a great asset to group performance. Although these talents alone cannot guarantee success, they establish an important baseline of potential performance accomplishments. And, if the input competencies are insufficient in any way, a group will operate with performance limits that are difficult to overcome. If group members suffer from too much personality conflict, for example, it is likely critical energies — energies that might otherwise be used to enhance task accomplishment — will be drained as members deal with these issues. In the case of a new task force, a good manager carefully chooses the membership to avoid such problems and the performance limitations that may accompany them.[20] To this end, the demographic and psychological make-up of a group becomes important. If members have difficulty getting along, talents may be wasted, as energies and attention are devoted to interpersonal problems. Whether this happens may depend in part on membership diversity and on how well this diversity is handled. Workforce diversity has already been examined in this book as an important issue in organisational behaviour. In the present context, it may be addressed from the perspective of diversity in the demographic and psychological characteristics of group membership. Important considerations include interpersonal compatibilities, membership heterogeneity and status.

The following International spotlight shows groups can operate differently in different countries.

Groups and cultural difference

Andrew 'Jock' McGregor is a former president of ANZ in China. He has lived in China since 1999 — mostly in Beijing and more recently in Shanghai. As a leader of his group, he spent a lot of time talking to members of his workplace, in the role of coach, mentor and trainer. It helped keep him informed of what was going on. He argued that running a business in China remains very different culturally, saying:

> If you want to get your point across, it's no good calling the whole group together and speaking to them all at once, nor is it any good raising your voice. You need to work with small groups of peers, otherwise you won't get dialogue; the juniors would be reluctant to speak up in front of their seniors as it's a sign of disrespect.[21]

Cultural dimensions, such as whether a country is predominantly individualistic or collectivist, also have an impact on how well people work together in a group or team. In Japan, collectivism is high and personal success hinges on the success of one's group and organisation. Teams tend to be more successful in Japan than in

International **SPOTLIGHT**

(continued)

individualistic countries such as the United States and Australia.[22]

Another relevant cultural dimension is related to communication styles. Individuals from high-context cultures (such as France, Korea and Brazil) use very indirect speech styles, whereas those from low-context cultures (such as Germany, America and Australia) tend to be much more direct. High-context communication requires much more attention to both the speaker and the setting because, in order to interpret the message, we need to be more aware of the context in which it takes place. When an individual from a high-context culture makes a statement (such as 'I have so much to do and I'm not sure I'll be finished in time to meet my deadline'), the request for help can easily be misunderstood by someone from a low-context culture (who would perhaps have asked 'Can you please help me to get this work done?').

There may also be cultural differences within countries. For example, people from the north of India are likely to consider being well mannered is highly important and they will avoid situations of public sparring and seek low-risk, conservative options in their behaviours. In contrast, southern Indian people value education so highly they are likely to pull rank to display their educational status.[23] Such distinctions may inhibit the ability of some group members (such as southern Indians) to contribute towards creative group activities or individuals may be overwhelmed by the status of other group members. Zeacom's New Zealand chief executive, Miles Valentine, says he had a steep learning curve when beginning to operate in the United States. He says people from the east coast are very direct while those from California never say 'no' — so, if you walk away thinking you have 'a deal', you might not.[24]

The implications of different cultures can have many impacts on how groups operate in organisations, especially in situations such as multicultural groups, in which it is hoped everyone will contribute to group decisions. Many organisations must deal with cultural issues in their groups; because they have cultural diversity in their workforce, groups in different global locations, or teams from different locations working remotely with each other.

Interpersonal compatibilities

The ability of diverse people to work well together in groups can be understood through the FIRO-B (fundamental interpersonal orientation) theory.[25] This theory helps explain how people orient themselves towards one another based on their needs to express and receive feelings of inclusion, control and affection. These needs can be measured by an instrument called the FIRO-B scale. They are defined as follows:

- the *need for inclusion*: the desire to be given prominence, recognition and prestige in the eyes of others
- the *need for control*: the tendency to exert control and to rebel or refuse control by others, or the tendency to be compliant and submissive
- the *need for affection*: the desire to be friendly and to seek close emotional ties with others.

FIRO-B theory points out that groups whose members are 'compatible' on these needs are more likely to be effective than groups whose members are more 'incompatible' on them. Symptoms of harmful incompatibilities include the presence of withdrawn members, open hostilities, struggles over control, and domination by a few members. William Schutz, the author of the FIRO-B theory, states the management implications this way: 'If, at the outset, we can choose a group of people who can work together harmoniously, we shall go far toward avoiding situations where a group's efforts are wasted in interpersonal conflicts'.[26]

Membership homogeneity–heterogeneity

Groups whose members have similar backgrounds, interests, values, attitudes and so on are called homogeneous groups. Groups whose membership is more diverse on these dimensions are called heterogeneous groups. The degree of homogeneity or heterogeneity within a group can affect its operations and results.

The effect of member diversity on group performance is inconclusive. One reason for this is heterogeneity or homogeneity can be considered on many different criteria. For example, a group may be homogeneous in age, but heterogeneous in terms of professional background of its members. It may be homogeneous in terms of ethnic background but heterogeneous in terms of member values. The value of group diversity may depend upon what the group is trying to achieve. For instance, a group with a heterogeneous membership often has a wide variety of skills and experiences that it can bring to bear on complex problems or tasks that require creativity or innovation.

A group may have some difficulty getting diverse members to work together to make success like this possible. The more heterogeneous the membership, the more that manager, group leader and/or group members may need to work to encourage interaction and communication.[27] In a more homogeneous group, the chances for harmonious working relationships among members may be higher, but the group may find that complex tasks are hard to accomplish if the skills and experiences of the members are limited or narrow in focus.

In other words, although management of interpersonal relations is easier in homogeneous groups, the group may suffer performance limitations as a result of a narrow range of talents. In most cases, strong group homogeneity tends to be more beneficial in situations in which group tasks are relatively simple and focused. In contrast, group diversity tends to provide better results in situations in which group tasks are complex and highly varied. So, it is important for managers to use good judgement when selecting members for work groups, committees and task forces to ensure the most productive mix of people is chosen.

> **Homogeneous groups** are groups whose members have similar backgrounds, interests, values, attitudes and so on.

> **Heterogeneous groups** are groups whose members have diverse backgrounds, interests, values, attitudes and so on.

Status

A person's status is an indicator of his or her relative rank, worth or standing in terms of prestige and esteem within a group. This standing can be based on any number of factors, including a person's age, work seniority, occupation, education, work accomplishments or status in other groups. A degree of status incongruence may occur when people operate in more than one group and there is a perceived difference in their status in one group compared to that in another. Status incongruence occurs when a person's expressed status within a group is inconsistent with his or her standing on these factors in another context. For example, in high power–distance cultures, such as Hong Kong and Malaysia, status incongruence is expected if the chair of a committee is not the highest-ranking or senior member of the group. In a low power–distance culture, this sort of status incongruence may be more acceptable, though there can still be problems; for example, if a young graduate is hired to supervise a group of experienced workers. This is important if members of the group are to be comfortable and harmonious when working together. When there is status incongruence, problems such as stress, dissatisfaction and frustration can occur. The way members deal with these issues can affect group performance.

> **Status** is the indication of a person's relative rank, worth or standing within a group.

> **Status incongruence** occurs when a person's expressed status within a group is inconsistent with their standing in another context.

Group size

The size of a group, defined as the number of its members, can make a difference to its effectiveness. One study looked at 80 work groups in a financial services firm and found group size was positively related to effectiveness.[28] As noted earlier, there is no hard and fast 'magic number' for group size. Some warning signs could indicate when groups, perhaps as a result of their numbers, have outgrown the cohesiveness among members. These warning signs become apparent when it is difficult to unite the group, either physically or verbally. Further, if group meetings are governed by a rigid agenda designed to make sure a maximum number of issues are communicated, and yet little is discussed, then the group may be too big.

Although it is difficult to pinpoint an ideal group size, a few general guidelines regarding the relationship between size and performance are recognised. Figure 6.4 depicts some of the possible trade-offs. As a group becomes larger, more potential human resources are available to divide up the work and accomplish necessary tasks. This relationship can boost performance, and member satisfaction also tends to increase — up to a point. As a group continues to grow larger, communication and coordination problems begin to set in among members. Satisfaction may dip and tendencies for more turnover and absenteeism increase, as do opportunities for more social loafing. Even logistical matters, such as finding time and locations for meetings, become more difficult with larger groups, causing performance problems.[29] Some networking groups are very conscious of these problems and put strict size limitations on their groups.

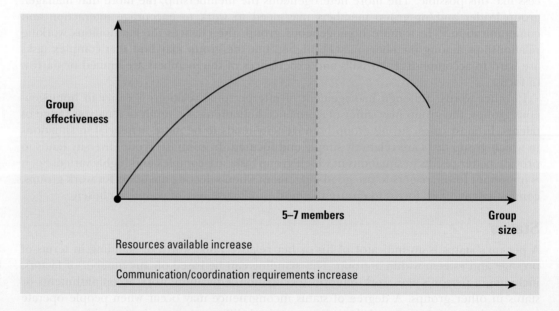

FIGURE 6.4 Trade-offs between group size and group effectiveness

In terms of general guidelines, the following patterns in group size can be noted. In problem-solving groups of fewer than five members, there are fewer people to share responsibilities. This typically results in more personal discussions and more participation by all members. In problem-solving groups of more than seven members, there tend to be fewer opportunities for participation, and members may be more inhibited in offering their contributions. There is also the possibility of domination by aggressive members and a tendency for the larger group to split into subgroups.[30] Thus, it appears that the best size for problem-solving groups is between five and seven members. In addition to the homogeneity–heterogeneity issue, this size guideline is useful for managers when they are forming committees and task forces to solve specific problems.

Another aspect of group size to consider is whether the number of members is odd or even. Groups with an even number of members seem more prone to sustained disagreement and conflict while working on tasks. One explanation is the even number makes it harder for a dominant coalition to form, or for one position to get a majority if a vote is taken. In contrast, it seems easier for members in odd-numbered groups to form coalitions and to take majority votes to resolve disagreements. Where speed is required, this form of conflict management behaviour is useful and odd-numbered groups may be preferred. In cases in which careful deliberations are required and the emphasis is more on consensus (such as in jury duty or complex problem solving), even-numbered groups may be more effective — that is, if the members do not deadlock.[31] Again, the choices made by the manager when initially forming the group may have an important impact on its eventual effectiveness.

Too much group work?

While group work is often considered to be a valuable and enjoyable aspect of working life, some university students hold the view that there is too much group work in undergraduate business and psychology courses (and perhaps you are among them). This is an important issue for all students, but particularly for potential new students considering university education.[32] Group skills are vital in all business forms, and successful start-up entrepreneurs are usually adept at working in groups. But should up to half the assessment in some courses be based on group work, where typically teams of three of four students work together on large projects? And is so much group work partly about universities passing underperforming students to get their fees, and academics having less end-of-semester marking? It's far easier to mark, say, eight group projects than 32 individual ones. In addition, it is far easier for students to pass courses with a heavy weighting on group projects.

Many students have had the experience of group members who ride the coat-tails of committed students. Proponents of group work will say that is the very point: the format helps you develop skills to deal with people who are not up to scratch (or, conversely, those who are more experienced) — useful skills for business life.

Questions

1. Is there too much group work in university business courses, and what has been your experience with it?
2. Have you been frustrated by having to work with underperforming students who coasted along and got a good mark?

Group processes and group dynamics

According to the 'open systems' group model described earlier, **group dynamics** are the forces operating in groups that affect task performance and human resource maintenance. If the group is an open system that transforms group inputs into group outputs, then group dynamics are the 'processes' through which this transformation is accomplished.

Group dynamics are the forces operating in groups that affect group performance and member satisfaction.

In organisational behaviour and in management practice, it is common to use the term 'group processes' interchangeably with 'group dynamics'; both refer to the internal operations of a group. In this section we will consider the stages of group development, emergent and required behaviours, norms and roles, and emotions, and finally, we will briefly acknowledge group communication and decision making.

Stages of group development

One way to improve the internal operations of groups and to facilitate group effectiveness is to recognise different stages of group development. Groups typically pass through different stages in their life cycles. Any given group, be it a work group, committee or task force, may be in a different stage of development at any one point in time. Depending on the stage, the group may have different challenges and management needs and it is important to understand these to either manage or function within the group. Members of new groups, or groups with significant changes of membership, often behave differently from members of groups that have been together for longer periods of time. In both cases, group effectiveness may be influenced by how well group members and leaders deal with the problems typical of each stage of development.

Models of group development tend to describe it as a sequential process (in which the development goes through a number of steps) or as a recurring process (in which groups tend to return to or move between different group concerns such as task orientation and emotional expression).[33] The five sequential stages of Tuckman's model will now be discussed,[34] followed by an explanation of Gersick's 'punctuated equilibrium' model.

Forming stage

In the forming stage of group development, a primary concern is the initial entry of members to a group. At this point, individuals ask a number of questions as they begin to identify with other group members and with the group itself: What can the group offer me? What will I be asked to contribute? And can my needs be met at the same time as I contribute to the group? People are interested in discovering what is considered acceptable behaviour, determining the real task of the group and defining group rules. All this is likely to be more complicated in the workplace than in other settings. Members of a new task force, for example, may have been in the organisation for a substantial period of time. Such factors as multiple group memberships and identifications, prior experience with group members in other contexts, and impressions of organisation philosophies, goals and policies may affect how these members initially behave in the newly formed task force.

Storming stage

The storming stage of group development is a period of high emotion and tension among the group members. Hostility and infighting may occur during this stage. Typically, the group experiences many changes. Membership expectations (the required activities) tend to be clarified and elaborated. Attention begins to shift towards obstacles standing in the way of group goals. Individuals begin to understand one another's interpersonal styles and make efforts to find ways in which to accomplish group goals while also satisfying individual needs. Outside demands, including premature expectations for performance results, may create pressures at this time. Depending on the group's size and membership composition, coalitions or cliques may appear in the form of emergent and informal subgroups. Conflict may develop over leadership and authority, as individuals compete to impose their preferences on the group and to achieve their desired status position. At this stage, discussions about the task, alternatives and possible actions occur. Group members may acknowledge their emotional responses to the task and attempt to justify their legitimacy.

Initial integration stage

The **initial integration stage** of group development (sometimes referred to as the norming stage) is the point at which the group begins to come together as a coordinated unit. At this point, the interpersonal probes and jockeying behaviours of the storming phase give way to a precarious balancing of forces. In their pleasure at the new sense of harmony, group members will most likely strive to maintain this balance. The group as a whole will try to regulate individual behaviour towards this end; minority viewpoints and tendencies to deviate from or question group directions will be discouraged. Initial integration provides group members with a preliminary sense of closeness; consequently, members will want to protect the group from disintegration. Indeed, holding the group together may become more important than successfully working on the group's tasks. Therefore, some group members may wrongly perceive this stage as a stage of ultimate maturity. In fact, the sense of premature accomplishment needs to be carefully managed as a stepping stone to a higher level of group development and not an end in itself.

> The **initial integration stage** is the third stage of group development, at which the group begins to come together as a coordinated unit; it is sometimes called the norming stage.

Total integration stage

The **total integration stage** of group development (sometimes referred to as the performing stage) sees the emergence of a mature, organised and well-functioning group. The integration begun in the previous stage is completed during this period. The group is now able to deal with complex tasks and to handle membership disagreements in creative ways. Group structure is stable, and members are motivated by group goals and are generally satisfied. The primary challenges of this stage relate largely to continuing work on human resource maintenance and task performance, but with a strong commitment to continuing improvement and self-renewal. An effective group at this stage of development is made up of members who:

> The **total integration stage** is the fourth stage of group development, which sees the emergence of a mature, organised and well-functioning group; it is also referred to as the performing stage.

- continue to work well together
- understand their individual and collective responsibilities to other groups and to the larger organisation
- are able to adapt successfully as opportunities and demands change over time.

A group that has achieved the level of total integration typically scores high on the criteria of group maturity shown in figure 6.5 (overleaf).

Adjourning stage

A well-integrated group is able to disband, if required, when its work is accomplished. Thus, it is sometimes appropriate to address a fifth stage, the **adjourning stage**, of group development.[35] This is an especially important stage for the many temporary groups that are increasingly common in the new workplace, including task forces, committees and the like. Members of these groups must be able to convene quickly, do their jobs on a tight schedule and then adjourn, often to work together again in the future. The willingness of members to disband when the job is done and to work well together in future responsibilities, group or otherwise, is an important long-run test of group success.

> The **adjourning stage** is the fifth stage of group development, in which members of the group disband when the job is done.

Gersick's[36] idea of punctuated group development or 'equilibrium' suggests groups tend to undergo two long phases of inertia 'punctuated' by a concentrated period of change that is more revolutionary or transitional. This occurs about midway through the life cycle of a group with a fixed task, usually when complacency and a sense of having time is lost to the panic which is accompanied by an approaching deadline. Depending on the urgency and nature of the task(s), and the life cycle of the group, such groups will experience different patterns of development and change.

There are links between Gersick's and Tuckman's models. It can be argued the midpoint transition of Gersick's model occurs after the forming, storming and initial integration stages of Tuckman's model. At this point, the group receives a 'wake-up alarm' and has to rapidly reassess its goals and direction, perhaps because this was not sufficiently undertaken in the storming stage. Once the new direction is established, the group is likely to move into the total integration stage.[37]

Figure 6.5 provides some measures for examining a group and considering what level of maturity it has reached.

Required and emergent behaviours

George Homans believes it is useful to distinguish among the activities, sentiments and interactions of group members. He also believes it is useful to examine the required and emergent forms of each.[38] **Required behaviours** are those contributions the organisation formally requests from group members as a basis for continued affiliation and support. They may include work-related behaviours such as being punctual, treating customers with respect and helping coworkers.

Emergent behaviours are tasks group members do in addition to, or in place of, what is formally asked of them by the organisation. Whereas required behaviours are formally designed with the group's purpose in mind, emergent behaviours exist purely as matters of individual or group choice. They are what people do that extends beyond formal job requirements but helps get the job done, such as telephoning an absent member to make sure they are informed about what happened during a group meeting. As figure 6.6 (overleaf) illustrates, emergent behaviours exist as a 'shadow' standing beside the required system.

Group norms and roles

Two concepts that are helpful in understanding the processes within groups are norms and roles. These, especially group norms, are discussed more fully in chapter 7. Here, they are briefly summarised to set the foundations for understanding group behaviour.

Group norms are a vital part of understanding group behaviour. They are the standards of behaviour that group members are expected to display. They are important in many ways, but particularly because a group may require everyone to maintain certain levels of performance. In some cases, members are discouraged from working too hard since it may make others look bad or force them to work harder. Norms can also relate to a range of other group behaviours such as greetings, breaks, dress codes and social participation. For example, it might be expected group members attend morning tea, or stick together in conflicts between ordinary workers and management. Group norms are not written down but can have an impelling effect on the behaviour of individuals.

The roles people play in groups are also important. **Group roles** are sets of expectations for the behaviour of a person holding a particular office or position. In groups, people often hold certain positions, such as group leader. Such roles are often explicitly defined in statements of duties, but may also be implicitly developed within the group by group members. The complexity and difficulties of roles in teams, including differences in the way roles are perceived by the role holder and by others, will be discussed further in chapter 7.

Group 'roles' sometimes refer more generally to how a person is expected to behave in order to achieve group goals, including task performance or group maintenance. We are able to use these expected roles to describe whether a person is helping or hindering the performance or continuation of the group. For example, in a group situation, whenever we make a suggestion or offer a comment in a meeting, we are playing a role. Because these types of roles are important in analysing the outputs of groups, in terms of whether they support the task performance or group maintenance, we consider these later in the chapter as 'task activities' and 'maintenance activities'.

Required behaviours are those contributions the organisation formally requests from group members as a basis for continued affiliation and support.

Emergent behaviours are tasks group members do in addition to, or in place of, what is formally asked of them by the organisation.

Group norms are the standards of behaviour that group members are expected to display.

Group roles are the sets of behaviours expected by the managers of the organisation and the group members for the holder of a particular position.

A mature group possesses:

1. Adequate mechanisms for getting feedback

Poor feedback mechanisms	1	2	3	4	5	Excellent feedback mechanisms
			Average			

2. Adequate decision-making procedure

Poor decision-making procedure	1	2	3	4	5	Very adequate decision making
			Average			

3. Optimal cohesion

Low cohesion	1	2	3	4	5	Optimal cohesion
			Average			

4. Flexible organisation and procedures

Very inflexible	1	2	3	4	5	Very flexible
			Average			

5. Maximum use of member resources

Poor use of resources	1	2	3	4	5	Excellent use of resources
			Average			

6. Clear communication

Poor communication	1	2	3	4	5	Excellent communication
			Average			

7. Clear goals accepted by members

Unclear goals — not accepted	1	2	3	4	5	Very clear goals — accepted
			Average			

8. Feelings of interdependence with authority persons

No interdependence	1	2	3	4	5	High interdependence
			Average			

9. Shared participation in leadership functions

No shared participation	1	2	3	4	5	High shared participation
			Average			

10. Acceptance of minority views and persons

No acceptance	1	2	3	4	5	High acceptance
			Average			

FIGURE 6.5 Ten criteria for measuring the maturity of a group

Source: E Schein, *Process consultation*, vol. 1, 2nd ed. 1998, figure 6.1, pp. 81 and 82. Reprinted by permission of Pearson Education Inc. Upper Saddle River, NJ.

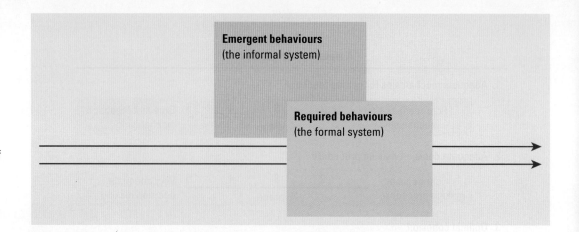

FIGURE 6.6 The two faces of group dynamics: emergent behaviours and the informal system as a 'shadow' for required behaviours and the formal system

Emotions in groups

The role of emotion in group dynamics has been a constant, although often only implicit, theme in the social psychological and organisational behaviour literatures.[39] Emotions are an essential and unavoidable element of group life. Disappointment, happiness, sadness, fear and dissatisfaction are just some emotions that can be found in a group situation. Because emotions are an inseparable part of task activity in group situations, managers must embrace them rather than preventing their expression. This approach will help improve group effectiveness and therefore organisational effectiveness. Given the pejorative view of emotion in group situations, only a limited range of emotional expression tends to be socially acceptable. Expressions of negative emotion, such as anxiety, fear or anger, tend to be unacceptable except under fairly circumscribed conditions. For example, it is frequently accepted a high-status group member can convey impatience with a low-status group member, but this is not generally accepted in reverse. Often, group tensions are fuelled by affective or expressive concerns that have little to do with task-focused issues, and minor disagreements can quickly escalate into major conflicts, with the group polarised into rival camps. In groups that are charged with negative emotions, intragroup conflict — whether over ends, means or resources — may generate distrust and hostility such that the conflict becomes the group's focal concern and initial goals are forgotten. Such emotions in groups can have negative effects on group performance as is discussed in the Ethical perspective.

ETHICAL
Perspective

Managing emotions and moods at work — how far can managers go?

Research by Jordan et al.[40] found negative moods in a group have negative effects on performance, but, in some cases, positive effects can also occur. While emotions are short-term in their duration, intense and usually directed towards someone or something, moods are experienced for a longer period with less intensity. Negative moods can impact on group social cohesion and increase group conflict. The research results suggest conflict related to *group processes* has a negative effect, while conflict relating to *group tasks* might sometimes improve performance (especially if it stimulates task completion). The authors argue managers need to understand the result of ambient mood within a group, and that the moods individual group members bring to work may affect other group members.[41]

The notion that the moods and emotions of individuals can impact on the whole group is not new. Sigal Barsade coined the term 'the Ripple effect'[42] to describe the transfer of moods among people in a group. Barsade has researched the influence that mood has on group dynamics. Perhaps not surprisingly, when group members experienced positive emotional contagion (excitement, happiness, contentment, and so on) the result for the work group was improved cooperation, decreased conflict, and increased perceived task performance.

So, managers may have some responsibility for managing the moods and emotions of their work group. While it is desirable for managers to work towards eliminating disruptive behaviours, the management of emotions and moods (of the group as a whole or individual members) is fraught with risk in terms of breaching privacy and/or the personal space of group members. For example, if two group members have a conflict generated by personality differences, the manager may not be successful in counselling them about their disruptive behaviours or helping them to identify and deal with their moods or emotions.

Individuals who are experiencing unpleasant situations at home (such as financial pressure, relationship breakdowns or custody battles) may bring their negative emotions to work. These cases are particularly difficult for managers to deal with. Unless the employee wishes to confide in the manager, the source of the employee's disruptive behaviour and negative emotions are likely to be unknown. Organisations often offer access to independent counselling services for employees, but there are many employees who do not use this service. Helen Carouzos-Antoniades, a counsellor, says managers often need to deal with an employee who is affected by a tragedy.[43]

Even more problematic might be cases in which the boundary between workplace and private lives becomes blurred, such as when individuals form romantic or sexual relationships with work colleagues. Such relationships can cause resentment from others — if the relationship is disruptive to group dynamics — or create problems between the individuals involved if they break up and must continue to work with each other. Because of this scenario, there is a trend for organisations in the United States to require employees who date one another to sign 'love contracts'. This guards the organisation against having responsibility for the separation and against sexual harassment suits.[44]

Group communication and decision making

Within groups, communication and decision making are important functions. However, they are also important processes in the organisation as a whole, and for this reason they are each the subject of a separate chapter in part 4. It is important to acknowledge the dynamics of groups will affect the quality of decision making and communication. Also, the functioning of groups (both in terms of task performance and group maintenance) will be affected by decision making and communication. One particular problem that can occur with group decision making is 'groupthink', when members of a highly cohesive group seek to conform, come to think alike and/or become unwilling to be critical of one another's ideas and suggestions. This can result in poor, and sometimes very costly, decision errors. This and other group decision-making issues are discussed at length in chapter 12. In terms of communication, the structure of groups and how group members work on tasks will relate closely to the way in which group members communicate.

OBinAction

Group problem solving

From business to science to government, teams of people are set to work solving problems. It makes sense to think that the smartest team would be one comprised of the smartest people together, but a recent study suggests that might not always be the case. Researchers have found that collaborative groups, where all group members participated equally, were more efficient at completing sets of given tasks, and produced better results, than groups comprised of dominant individuals.[45]

Anita Woolley, an Assistant Professor of organisational behaviour at Tepper School on Business in the United States has been studying what it means to say a group is 'intelligent'. Woolley and her colleagues formulated some brainstorming tasks, where the idea is for a group to form as many creative ideas as possible. The groups performed other tasks where there was only one right answer, or where the teams had to develop innovative solutions to a problem.

The researchers found that the groups were more collectively intelligent when the conversation was more evenly distributed and where there was roughly equal participation among all of the group members. Not only was it annoying to have one person dominate, but groups where this happened tended to come up with a less balanced and thoughtful result — that is, it wasn't as intelligent. When Woolley looked for the qualities that made groups successful, she found that the individual intelligence of group members was unrelated to the outcome. Interestingly, a higher level of social sensitivity and group intelligence was also found in groups with more females.[46]

Outputs of the group process — task performance and group maintenance

Group outputs are the results of the transformation of group inputs through group processes.

Earlier in the chapter, when groups were described as open systems, **group outputs** were described as the products of the group process. A formal group has the purpose in an organisation of fulfilling one or more organisational tasks, and managers are typically concerned with ensuring the group does so. From the perspective of group members (including leaders or managers within groups), groups need to enable them to fulfil these task needs and also to fulfil their human maintenance needs.[47] These are necessary group outputs if groups are to function successfully in organisations. Every member of a group can and must assist in the group's development by doing things that specifically respond to group task and maintenance needs. Although a person in a position of formal authority, such as chairperson or department head, should also do these things, the responsibility is shared by and distributed among all group members. Any and all group members should be able to recognise when task needs and/or maintenance needs must be met; they should also possess the skills needed to step in and help meet these needs at any time. This sharing of responsibility for fulfilling group task and maintenance needs is sometimes called **distributed leadership** in group dynamics. As this term suggests, all members of effective groups help lead these groups by contributing towards both task and maintenance activities in the group process.[48]

Distributed leadership is the sharing of responsibility for fulfilling group task and maintenance needs.

Group task performance

Group task performance is a vital output of the group process. It is expected groups use the resources they have (including group inputs like membership and emotions) to achieve their task goals effectively and efficiently. This is a major output of the group, but contributing to that will be task-oriented behaviours members of the group exhibit. So, all groups need members who are able and willing to perform task activities. These are the various things members do that directly contribute to the performance of important group tasks. As already mentioned, they are not tasks that only the leader, chair, head or manager of the group should do; rather, they are tasks all members should be doing. If task activities are not adequate, group process will suffer and the group will have difficulty accomplishing its objectives. In an effective group, members will enhance group process by performing important task activities as needed.[49]

- *initiating* — offering new ideas or ways of defining problems; suggesting solutions to group difficulties
- *seeking information* — attempting to clarify suggestions in terms of factual accuracy; asking for ideas of others
- *giving information* — offering authoritative and relevant information and facts
- *clarifying* — clarifying relations among various suggestions or ideas; attempting to coordinate member activities
- *summarising* — assessing group functioning; raising questions about the logic and practicality of member suggestions.

Task activities are the various things members do that directly contribute to the performance of important group tasks.

Group maintenance

Maintaining the group and the group members is another important group output and much group activity is directed towards that. Whereas task activities advance the task agenda of a group, maintenance activities support the social and interpersonal relationships among its members. 'Maintenance' activities do just that — they help maintain the group as an ongoing social system. If maintenance activities are not performed well, group processes will suffer as members become dissatisfied with one another and their group membership. In such cases, emotional antagonisms and conflicts may develop and drain energies that could otherwise help advance group purposes. Depending on the past experiences of the group and the problems to be solved, the proportion of maintenance roles to task roles will vary. Some groups, such as a bridge club, may only perform group maintenance roles. Their sole purpose is sociability. A church-building committee, on the other hand, has an assigned purpose and would probably show a preponderance of group task roles. The members of an effective group are aware of the need for maintenance activities and are able to provide them in ways that help build good interpersonal relationships and enhance the ability of the group to stay together over time.

Maintenance activities are activities that support the emotional life of the group as an ongoing social system.

At this point, it is important to introduce a key concept of groups. In a group, cohesiveness (or group cohesion) is the degree to which members are attracted to and motivated to remain part of the group. The cohesiveness of the group is useful in explaining group behaviour in many contexts (for example, its relationship to group diversity and group norms), but is mentioned here because it has direct relevance to the social and interpersonal relations of group members. The concept is so important it is discussed at length in chapter 7. Cohesiveness helps us to understand the following examples of important group maintenance activities. They include:

Cohesiveness is the degree to which members are attracted to and motivated to remain part of the group.

- *encouraging* — praising, accepting or agreeing with other members' ideas; indicating solidarity and warmth
- *harmonising* — mediating squabbles within the group; reconciling differences; seeking opportunities for compromise

- *compromising* — maintaining group cohesion by 'coming halfway' or admitting an error; sacrificing status to maintain group harmony (The major difference between the harmoniser and the compromiser is that the compromiser is one of the parties in a conflict.)
- *gatekeeping* — encouraging participation of group members; trying to keep some members from dominating
- *setting standards* — expressing standards for the group to achieve or use in evaluating group process
- *following* — going along with the group; agreeing to try out the ideas of others.[50]

Having considered the inputs, processes and outputs of groups, it is worth considering the usefulness of these concepts in a wider context.

Intergroup dynamics

Before leaving this discussion of group dynamics, we need to look once again at the organisation itself as a network of many interlocking groups. In this complicated setting, intergroup dynamics become very important. They are the dynamics that operate between two or more groups.

The organisation ideally operates as a cooperative system in which the various groups are willing and able to help one another as needed. An important managerial responsibility is to make sure groups work together to the benefit of the total organisation. Yet, by their nature, intergroup dynamics can be competitive as well as cooperative. Although there may be times when a bit of competition can help groups maintain their creative edge, too much competition can work to the detriment of the larger system. When intergroup rivalries and antagonisms detract from the ability of the groups to cooperate with one another, the organisation will lose the desired synergy. Progressive managers are able to build and maintain effective intergroup relations.[51]

Work flow interdependency and intergroup relations

The way in which work flows in an organisation from one group to the next — that is, the nature of work flow interdependency — affects intergroup dynamics. Figure 6.7 depicts how pooled, sequential and reciprocal interdependencies affect the ways in which groups work together to achieve their goals.

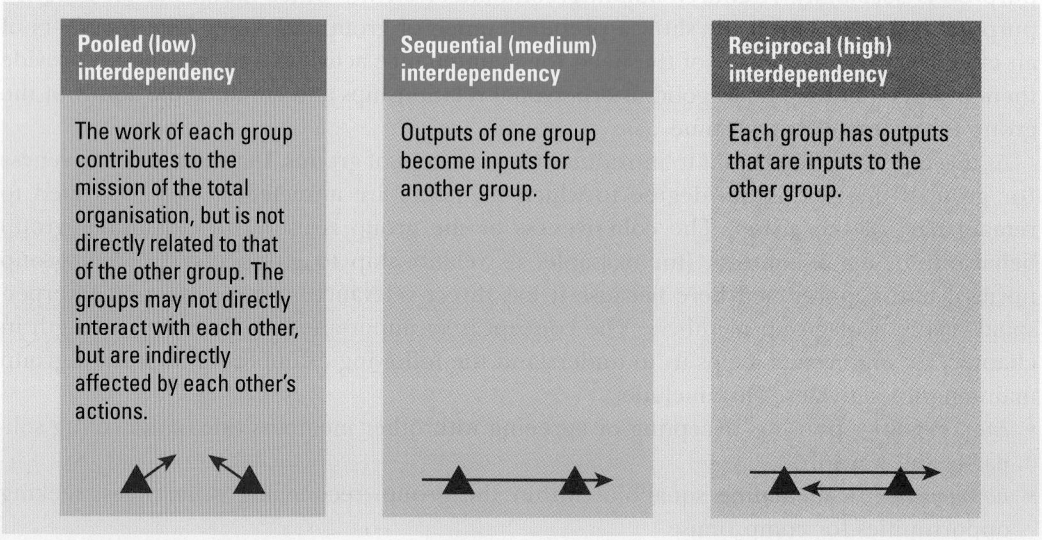

Intergroup dynamics are the dynamics that take place between groups, as opposed to within groups.

Work flow interdependency is the way work flows in an organisation from one group to the next.

Pooled (low) interdependency	Sequential (medium) interdependency	Reciprocal (high) interdependency
The work of each group contributes to the mission of the total organisation, but is not directly related to that of the other group. The groups may not directly interact with each other, but are indirectly affected by each other's actions.	Outputs of one group become inputs for another group.	Each group has outputs that are inputs to the other group.

FIGURE 6.7 Types of work flow interdependency and their impact on intergroup relationships

Not much attention to the management of intergroup relationships is needed in pooled interdependency. The groups seldom, if ever, meet and they perform their respective tasks quite independently. As long as each group does its job in accordance with organisational goals, the activities of other groups are of little concern.

What other groups do becomes more important when there is sequential interdependency of the work flows. This means one group's outputs become another group's inputs. The second group depends on the first group and cannot do its job unless the first group provides it with needed inputs in a timely and high-quality fashion. Naturally, this type of interdependency is prone both to more contact between the groups and to more potential problems in the intergroup relations. This creates a need for managerial attention to intergroup relations.

Things become even more complicated when there is *reciprocal interdependency* in the work flow. In this situation, many groups interact in input–output relationships. With frequent and varied interactions among many groups in the normal day-to-day course of work, the intergroup dynamics become complex. They are also extremely important because a breakdown at any point will have spillover effects to other points. Managers in such settings must be good at helping multiple groups build and maintain good working relationships with one another.

These interdependencies exist in all organisations in various combinations and to various degrees.

Other factors affecting intergroup relations

Many other factors may affect intergroup dynamics, some of which will now be discussed. The way in which they impact may vary according to the particulars of each situation.

The group status or prestige of one group compared with that of others may be important, particularly in sequential or reciprocal work flow interdependencies. For example, if a lower-status group must wait for the output of the higher-status group, the lower-status group may have little power to demand faster work from the other group. Groups may also differ in the ways in which they deal with time and goals. The time orientation of a group is based on the length of time needed to obtain necessary information and to accomplish tasks. When some groups are able to operate on shorter time horizons than other groups with whom work flow interdependencies exist, these differences can complicate intergroup relations. For example, nurses concerned for patient recovery may wish to extend the duration of patients' stay in hospital, while admissions staff, who focus mainly on the brief task of scheduling and admitting patients, may agitate for quicker discharges to free up beds.

The reward system under which a group performs can have a strong impact on intergroup relations. For example, if a group of concreters in a construction firm is being rewarded for the amount of concreting done per week (rather than its quality), that may cause potential problems for the group that is responsible for quality and safety of construction. The rewards are likely to reinforce the different goals of the two groups and exacerbate difficulties in intergroup relations.

Finally, groups differ in available resources. If a resource-rich group has frequent dealings with one that is, or perceives itself to be, resource poor, intergroup problems can easily arise. For example, if a research and design group is well resourced with funds and/or staff but must work with a poorly-resourced production unit to trial its designs, the production unit may be resistant to cooperating. The underlying issue has much to do with the equity theory of motivation discussed in chapter 3. Sometimes, groups need to share resources to get their jobs done. When the shared resource is in scarce supply and/or when there is no clear agreement on how it is to be allocated, intergroup problems are prone to develop.

Dynamics of intergroup competition

Earlier in the chapter, it was highlighted that the ideal organisation is a cooperative system in which people and groups always work together harmoniously. But, as the last two sections have indicated, the real world of the organisation as an interlocking network of groups may be far from perfect.

There are many ways and reasons for intergroup problems to develop. Competition occurs as well as cooperation. When this occurs, and it negatively affects performance, the dynamics depicted in figure 6.8 are also likely to occur.

There are two approaches to managing the dynamics of intergroup competition.[52] The first is to deal with the competition after it occurs. Recommended ways for controlling existing dysfunctional competition include:

- identifying a common enemy that can unite the groups
- appealing to a common goal that can unite the groups
- initiating direct negotiations between the groups
- training members of the groups to work cooperatively.

The second approach for managing intergroup competition is to take action before it occurs — that is, to prevent its occurrence in the first place. Recommended ways for preventing the emergence of destructive intergroup competition include:

- rewarding groups for their contributions to the total organisation
- avoiding win–lose competitions for important rewards
- rewarding groups for giving help to one another
- stimulating frequent interactions between members of different groups
- preventing groups from withdrawing and becoming isolated from one another
- rotating members among different groups.

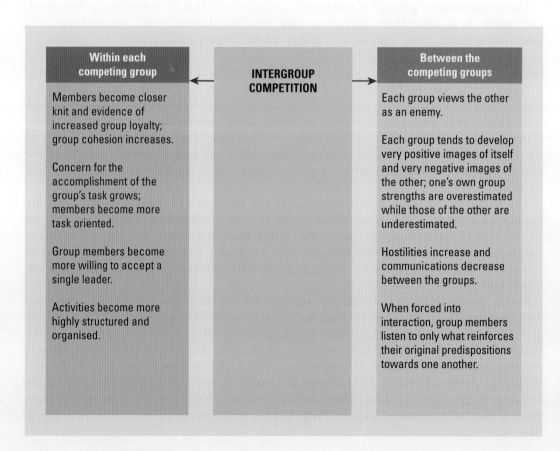

FIGURE 6.8 What happens within and between groups engaged in intergroup competition

Within each competing group

Members become closer knit and evidence of increased group loyalty; group cohesion increases.

Concern for the accomplishment of the group's task grows; members become more task oriented.

Group members become more willing to accept a single leader.

Activities become more highly structured and organised.

INTERGROUP COMPETITION

Between the competing groups

Each group views the other as an enemy.

Each group tends to develop very positive images of itself and very negative images of the other; one's own group strengths are overestimated while those of the other are underestimated.

Hostilities increase and communications decrease between the groups.

When forced into interaction, group members listen to only what reinforces their original predispositions towards one another.

The potential disadvantages of intergroup competition are numerous. The competition may divert energies away from the performance of important tasks, as members focus on dealing with the other groups. Also common is the emergence of grudges, animosities or biased and selective viewpoints of one group towards another. The result is poor intergroup coordination. Therefore, the suggestions listed become quite important. Managers at all levels in organisations walk a thin line as they try to avoid the disadvantages of intergroup competition while still enjoying its advantages.

Those managers who are successful with intergroup dynamics can tap the potential advantages of intergroup competition. When groups compete with others, they may work harder, become more focused on key tasks, develop more internal cohesion and satisfaction, and achieve a higher level of creativity in problem solving. When properly harnessed, such dynamics of intergroup competition can be strong assets for an organisation.

Summary

Groups and types of groups

A group is formally defined as a collection of people who interact with one another regularly to attain common goals. Groups in organisations fall into two major categories. Formal groups are 'official' groups — work units, task forces, committees and so on that are created by a formal authority to achieve a specific purpose. Many such groups can be identified on organisation charts. Informal groups are 'unofficial'. They emerge spontaneously and are not designated by the organisation to serve any purpose. They may work for or against organisational needs, but tend to satisfy important individual needs.

How groups meet individual and organisational needs

One way to view an organisation is as an interlocking network of groups. From this perspective, the results accomplished by each group should add up in building-block fashion to fulfil organisational needs for task accomplishment. Any group offers the potential to satisfy important individual needs for social interaction, security and so on.

Managing for group effectiveness

Group effectiveness occurs when groups are able to achieve high levels of both task performance and human resource maintenance. Within groups, synergy occurs when a group is able to accomplish more than its members would accomplish individually. However, disruptive or negative behaviours such as social loafing (when individual members do not work as hard as they might otherwise) sometimes occur. Groups can be viewed as open systems interacting with their environments. Group effectiveness involves success in transforming a variety of inputs to the group (such as organisational setting, nature of the task, group membership characteristics and size) into group outputs (task performance and human resource maintenance) through the group process. The group processes or group dynamics represent the internal processes of the group.

Group inputs and effectiveness

The foundations of group effectiveness begin with the presence of the right inputs. Group input factors set the stage for group action. Among the inputs of special managerial significance is the organisational setting, including available operating resources, spatial arrangements, technologies, rewards and goal systems, cultures and structures. Other important inputs are the nature of the task; general membership characteristics such as member compatibilities and homogeneity or heterogeneity; status; and group size. Optimum group size depends on the context and group goals. Highly effective groups use their inputs fully to achieve success.

Group processes and group dynamics

Group dynamics are the forces operating within groups that affect task performance and human resource maintenance. They are the internal processes through which members work together to accomplish the transformation of group inputs into group outputs. The terms 'group dynamics' and 'group processes' are often used interchangeably. The behaviours within groups may be required or they may be emergent, additional behaviours. All groups pass through various stages in their life cycles. Five different stages of group development pose somewhat distinct management problems. Groups in the forming stage have problems managing individual entry. The storming stage introduces problems of managing expectations and status. Groups in the initial integration stage have problems managing member relations and task efforts. Groups in the total integration stage encounter problems managing continual improvement and self-renewal. Groups in the adjourning stage have problems managing task completion and the process of disbanding. Group norms or standards of behaviour will impact upon the behaviour of all group members. Group roles relating to particular positions in the group describe the expected behaviours for individuals in those roles. Emotions and patterns of communication and decision making are also elements of group dynamics.

Groups' task and maintenance outputs

Groups have two broad sets of needs that must be met if they are to operate successfully. First, group members contribute a variety of task activities, such as initiating and summarising, that make direct contributions to the group's task performance. Second, group members must contribute to the fulfilment of maintenance needs. These include other activities, such as encouraging and gatekeeping, that specifically help to maintain the social fabric of the group over time. Both task activities and maintenance activities must be accomplished in any group. The principle of distributed leadership points out these activities can and should be provided, as needed, by all group members, not just by those formally designated as leaders. Groups are capable of providing many advantages to organisations but can also result in disadvantages.

Intergroup dynamics

Intergroup dynamics are the forces that operate between two or more groups. Although groups are supposed to cooperate in organisations, things do not always work this way. Groups can become involved in dysfunctional conflicts and competition. Sometimes, the origins of these conflicts lie in work flow interdependencies; at other times, the origins can be traced to differing group characteristics. Variables including status, time and goal orientations, reward systems and resource availabilities can all make a difference in the way groups work together. Managers must be aware of the potential for problems in intergroup relations and know how to deal with them, even as they recognise some competition can be good. The disadvantages of intergroup competition can be reduced through management strategies to direct, train and reinforce groups to pursue cooperative actions instead of purely competitive actions.

CHAPTER 6 study guide

Key terms

adjourning stage, *p. 229*
cohesiveness, *p. 235*
disruptive behaviour, *p. 217*
distributed leadership, *p. 234*
effective groups, *p. 218*
emergent behaviours, *p. 230*
formal groups, *p. 211*
forming stage, *p. 228*
friendship groups, *p. 213*
group dynamics, *p. 227*
group inputs, *p. 220*
group norms, *p. 230*

group outputs, *p. 234*
group roles, *p. 230*
groups, *p. 211*
heterogeneous groups, *p. 225*
homogeneous groups, *p. 225*
informal groups, *p. 213*
initial integration stage, *p. 229*
interest groups, *p. 214*
intergroup dynamics, *p. 236*
maintenance activities, *p. 235*
permanent formal work
groups, *p. 212*

required behaviours, *p. 230*
social loafing, *p. 217*
status, *p. 225*
status incongruence, *p. 225*
storming stage, *p. 228*
sub-goal optimisation, *p. 220*
synergy, *p. 217*
task activities, *p. 235*
temporary formal work groups, *p. 212*
total integration stage, *p. 229*
work flow interdependency, *p. 236*

Review questions

1. Summarise the reasons why groups fulfil individual and organisational purposes.
2. Explain how group heterogeneity might affect group processes and effectiveness.
3. What are the key outputs required for effective groups?
4. Explain what happens within groups and between groups when they are in competition with each other.

Application questions

1. If groups are to create positive synergy in the accomplishment of organisational tasks, what must managers do to overcome disruptive behaviours?
2. Your product marketing group consists of ten people who must work together to find the best ways to market your organisation's products. The group comprises of seven women (aged 52, 47, 33, 28, 26, 24 and 21) and three males (aged 39, 33 and 29). Two of the group members were born and raised in different countries (the 33-year-old woman is from Nigeria and the 52-year-old woman is from Lebanon). The 29-year-old male has a vision impairment. What aspects of group membership might have an impact on the likely effectiveness of the group?
3. Until recently, your group of seven members has been operating successfully and you felt it was achieving high levels of effectiveness. However, since two members left your team (and the organisation) to go to other jobs and you replaced them with two new

members (one from outside the organisation and one from another organisational section), there is less group cohesion and more conflict. Discuss the reasons why these changes might have occurred and use theories and concepts about groups to explain them.
4. Julia is managing a completely new group of five people, comprising two women and three men (not including Julia). The group is responsible for developing new and innovative work processes in the organisation to enhance the efficiency of operations. They have a year to introduce a series of key changes. Julia and two of the people in the group are completely new to the organisation but have strong backgrounds in change management, while the other three group members were already in the organisation and have a strong knowledge of the organisation and its current processes. How is the group likely to develop and what problems might eventuate?

5. The BluePot organisation is currently working on its enterprise agreement. The organisation has established a group of senior managers and employee representatives from various parts of the organisation to negotiate with the union representatives (employees of the organisation with help from the external union organisation) on the agreement. What types of groups are involved in this negotiation process?
6. In your organisation, the production, sale and delivery of products depends on three groups: (1) production (to manufacture goods), (2) marketing (to promote and sell goods) and (3) transport (to deliver products to buyers). Recently, the production section has been having problems achieving its targets, because of a shortage of skilled production workers. What are the likely workflow relationships between each group and why might they cause problems? What intergroup conflicts are likely to emerge and why? What can be done to overcome the problems?

Research questions

1. Investigate your own university or college and look for evidence of groups. They could be in the teaching faculty or department which manages your course or in other parts of the organisation, such as administrative sections or sections that support student activities. Find out what you can about the groups that exist by talking to people and investigating documents such as brochures, handbooks and web pages. You might also observe some groups who engage in non-work activities, or who work together on fundraising activities. You might find groups such as teaching staff and non-teaching staff, research teams or centres, groups from different disciplines (such as Economics, Management and Law) and various committees. Discuss your findings, noting:
   (a) the different types of groups that exist
   (b) how members of one group might also belong to another
   (c) what formal decision-making groups exist
   (d) what group member characteristics exist (for example, numbers of men and women, economists versus accountants, senior versus lower-level staff).
   Draw some conclusions about the nature of group behaviour in your university/college faculty or department.
2. Search the website of a major company looking for depictions of the company structure — either an organisational chart or lists of sections and departments in the company. Use this information to draw up a profile of *formal* groups within the organisation, labelling different types of groups and links between them. Analyse the groups, as much as you can from the information available, in terms of their likely features (size, homogeneity, position roles within them, resources, goals and decision-making functions). Repeat the process for another company and compare the two.

Running project

Complete the following tasks relating to your organisation.
1. Refer back to any earlier work you did on the structure of your organisation. Also try to obtain an organisational chart for the organisation. Describe how the organisation uses groups to structure the workplace.
2. If you have direct access to the organisation, try to find out about informal groups. Try to determine why these groups formed.
3. Choose one group in the organisation and draw a diagram of the group as an open system. List the most important outputs of the group and explain how the manager, group leader or group members would know whether the group is effective at any given time.
4. Choose two different groups within the organisation. Describe how these groups work with each other. If you have direct access to the organisation, ask management how it deals with intergroup conflict.

Analysing a group

Objective

To better understand the basic attributes of groups.

Activity

For this exercise, select a specific group with whom you work or have worked, or a group you are familiar with from an organisation in your local community. Answer the following questions as they relate to the group.

1. Is the group a formal or an informal group? Explain why.
2. Is the group an open system? Explain why, by discussing the following.

(a) Its inputs

What is the organisational setting (resources, technology, spatial arrangements, reward systems and goals, structure, size and culture)? What is the nature of the group task? What are general membership characteristics (interpersonal compatibilities, membership homogeneity–heterogeneity, status)? What is the group size?

(b) Its processes

What are some of the required and emergent behaviours of the group? How does communication occur? How are decisions made?

(c) Its outputs

How does it satisfy task and maintenance needs?

Analysing your groups

Objective

To show the relevance and pervasiveness of formal and informal groups within your lives:
- in your 'organisational' environment at university/college
- outside that environment (social and other organisations).

Procedure

Individually

List all of the various groups to which you currently belong.

In groups

1. Discuss the groups you have listed as individuals and place them into categories — formal or informal.
2. Are there some types of groups to which you all, or several of you, belong? Why?
3. What conclusions can you draw about the number of groups to which you individually and collectively belong?
4. Do you behave differently in different groups? If so, explain how and why you do so.

Case study: Workgroup behaviour in a New Zealand factory

The following is adapted from McLennan and Liew (1980)[53]

The site chosen for the research consisted of the 'water removing' section of the factory, which was part of its processed cheese-making operation. The task of the employees working in the section was to remove 7-kg blocks of cheese from a battery of vats, place them on a conveyor, squeeze water and chemicals out of them by rollers, and stack them in a cold room. Unloading the vats and cold room stacking was heavy, repetitive work; watching the conveyor and the rollers required steady observation, and occasional bursts of physical activity.

The five male employees in the section worked within a relatively confined space. They ranged in age from 18 to 25, four of them being between 18 and 22. Four had left school after two years of secondary education; one was a university dropout. All of them were single, except the 25 year old, and had worked in the section for a year or more.

A foreman was formally responsible for the work of the section and three other sections in the processed cheese department. He appeared in the section only once a day, and spent nearly all his time elsewhere. The factory manager showed the flag in [*walked around*] most sections of the factory twice a day. Low wages were paid to the workers, and there was no incentive scheme.

Interaction between the workers was easy, partly because of the low noise level, their proximity, their similarity on demographic variables, and the absence of supervisors.

There were strong opportunities to sanction [*give permission or approval for*] one another's behaviour. The workers operated a system of job rotation by which each member worked two days on each job in the section. The origins of this practice were unknown. They spent much of the day talking to each other about girls, sex, pool and drinking. One of them said that if they did not talk a lot they would 'go insane or quit'. Another said that 'If you were to keep dumb the whole day, by the time you finished . . . you'd really be buggered off'. They interacted very little with other workers in the factory, and were united in a strong dislike of them. The other workers were typically at least ten years older.

The group usually helped other workers when they were in trouble with their tasks. In addition, a 'mind your own business' attitude developed, a worker should not help another unless asked to do so. The group restricted

their expenditure of energy on the section's work. They handled five vat loads of cheese each day, even when a larger number awaited their attention. They anticipated work breaks by knocking off work ten minutes before lunch, and for morning and afternoon 'smokos', walked away from the section together, and sat together in the canteen. They manipulated the time they arrived at work by fiddling with the time-clock, and rested, read and smoked in the cold room. Smoking in work areas of the factory was against the rules. To protect the group from their supervisors they operated an early warning system to let them know when a supervisor approached. Members were posted on rotation as sentries, and sang loudly when a supervisor appeared. The group also observed norms concerning their off-job behaviour. They went frequently to a particular pub at lunch time, and gathered there in the evenings and at weekends. At the pub they drank, talked, and played pool. The group made up the factory's pool team in a local competition. The work group coextended to the leisure group and vice-versa.

Questions

1. Describe the norms that appear to exist in this group.
2. Explain why these norms arose.
3. Discuss how useful these norms are for: a member, the group, the factory.
4. Discuss how cohesive this group is and who benefits or loses from this level of cohesiveness.
5. What advice would you give to improve performance of the 'water removing' department?

End notes

1. S Cain, 'The Rise of the New Groupthink', *The New York Times* (15 January 2012) www.nytimes.com.
2. J Westbrook et al., 'Association of interruptions with an increased risk and severity of medication administration errors', *Archives of Internal Medicine*, vol. 170, no. 8 (2010), pp. 683–90.
3. J Westbrook et al., 'The impact of interruptions on clinical task completion', *Quality and Safety in Health Care*, vol. 19 (2010) pp. 284–9.
4. S Cain, *Quiet: The power of introverts in a world that can't stop talking* (Random House USA Inc.: New York, 2012).
5. S Cain, op. cit.
6. Little is written specifically on task forces, but one useful reference is W Alan Randolph and Barry Z Posner, *Getting the job done! Managing project teams and task forces for success* (Englewood Cliffs, NJ: Prentice Hall, 1992).
7. *The New Zealand Herald*, 'NZ air crew help seize tonnes of hashish off Somalian coast' (6 October 2014), www.nzherald.co.nz.

8. R Morrison, 'Informal relationships in the workplace: associations with job satisfaction, organisational commitment and turnover intentions', *New Zealand Journal of Psychology*, vol. 33, no. 3 (2004), pp. 114–28; RL Morrison, 'Organisational outcomes of friendships', in RL Morrison and S Wright (eds), *Friends and enemies in organisations: a work psychology perspective* (London: Palgrave Macmillan, 2009).
9. D Tannahill-Moran, 'No friends at work?', *Career rocketeer* (9 June 2011), www.careerrocketeer.com.
10. Harold J Leavitt, 'Suppose we took groups seriously' in Eugene L Cass and Frederick G Zimmer (eds), *Man and work in society* (New York: Van Nostrand Reinhold, 1975), pp. 67–77.
11. Bib Latane, Kipling Williams and Stephen Harkins, 'Many hands make light the work: the causes and consequences of social loafing', *Journal of Personality and Social Psychology*, vol. 37 (1978), pp. 822–32; E Weldon and GM Gargano, 'Cognitive effort in additive task groups: the effects of

12. R Birchfield, 'Information technology: improving care with technology', *New Zealand Management* (March 2011).

13. *Harrogate Informer*, 'Harrogate trust leaps ahead in patient safety with tech fund money' (16 September 2014), www.harrogate-news.co.uk.

14. For further insights see J Richard Hackman, 'The design of work teams' in Jay W Lorsch (ed.), *Handbook of organizational behavior* (Englewood Cliffs, NJ: Prentice Hall, 1987), p. 343.

15. Linda N Jewell and H Joseph Reitz, *Group effectiveness in organizations* (Glenview, IL: Scott, Foresman, 1981), pp. 149–50.

16. This discussion is developed from D Herold, 'The effectiveness of work groups' in Steven Kerr (ed.), *Organizational behavior* (Columbus, OH: Grid Publishing, 1979), pp. 99–103.

17. ibid.

18. See www.treehugger.com and www.seashepherd.org.

19. O Milman, 'Japan whaling push: Australia joins New Zealand in bid to curb 2015 hunt', *The Guardian* (September 2014), www.theguardian.com.

20. James Ware, 'Managing a task force', note 478002 (Boston: Harvard Business School, 1977).

21. Executive profile on Andrew McGregor in 'Doing business in China', *Management Today* (July 2006), p. 24.

22. Frank J Landy and Jeffrey M Conte, *Work in the 21st Century*, 2nd edn (Oxford: Blackwell Publishing, 2007), pp. 567–8.

23. Ruth Le Pla, 'The ties that bind', *Management* (New Zealand, June 2007), p. 49.

24. Ellen Read, 'Remote control', *Management* (New Zealand, October 2007), pp. 59–61.

25. William C Schutz, *FIRO: a three-dimensional theory of interpersonal behavior* (New York: Rinehart and Co., 1958).

26. William C Schutz, 'The interpersonal underworld', *Harvard Business Review*, vol. 36, no. 4 (July/August 1958), p. 130.

27. Michael A Hitt, J Stewart Black and Lyman W Porter, *Management*, international ed. (Upper Saddle River NJ: Pearson Prentice-Hall, 2005), pp. 456–7.

28. MA Campion, GJ Medsker and AC Higgs, 'Relations between work group characteristics and effectiveness: implications for designing effective work groups', *Personnel Psychology*, vol. 46 (1993) pp. 823–50.

29. See Jon R Katzenbach and Douglas K Smith, 'The discipline of teams', *Harvard Business Review* (March–April 1993), pp. 111–20.

30. EJ Thomas and CF Fink, 'Effects of group size', in Larry L Cummings and William E Scott (eds), *Readings in organizational and human performance* (Homewood, IL: Richard D. Irwin, 1969), pp. 394–408.

31. See Marvin E Shaw, *Group dynamics: the psychology of small group behavior*, 2nd ed. (New York: McGraw-Hill, 1976).

32. T Featherstone, 'Is group work overrated?', *The Age* (18 April 2011), www.theage.com.au.

33. David W Johnson and Frank P Johnson, *Joining together: group theory and group skills*, 7th ed. (Boston: Allyn & Bacon, 2000), p. 30.

34. This approach is based on J Steven Heinen and Eugene Jacobson, 'A model of task group development in complex organizations and a strategy of implementation', *Academy of Management Review*, vol. 1 (October 1976), pp. 98–111; Bruce W Tuckman, 'Developmental sequence in small groups', *Psychological Bulletin*, vol. 63 (1965), pp. 384–99; Bruce W Tuckman and Mary Ann C Jensen, 'Stages of small group development revisited', *Group and Organization Studies* vol. 2, (1977), pp. 419–27.

35. Tuckman, op. cit.; Tuckman and Jensen, op. cit.

36. Trevor Tyson, *Working with groups*, 2nd ed. (Melbourne: Macmillan, 1998), pp. 11–12.

37. Stephen Linstead, Liz Fulop and Simon Lilley, *Management and organization* (Basingstoke: Palgrave Macmillan, 2004), pp. 377–8.

38. George C Homans, *The human group* (New York: Harcourt Brace, 1950).

39. BE Ashforth and RH Humphrey, 'Emotion in the workplace: a reappraisal', *Human Relations*, vol. 48, no. 2 (1995), p. 97.

40. Peter J Jordan, Sandra A Lawrence and Ashlea C Troth, 'The impact of negative mood on team performance', *Journal of Management & Organization*, vol. 12, no. 2 (September 2006), pp. 131–45.

41. ibid.

42. SG Barsade, 'The Ripple effect: emotional contagion and its influence on group behavior', *Administrative Science Quarterly*, vol. 47, no. 4 (December 2002), pp. 644–75.

43. Ann-Maree Moodie, 'Calm in a storm', *The Sydney Morning Herald* (Career Section, 10–11 May 2008), p. 8.

44. '"Love contracts" on the rise', *Human Resources* (27 May 2008), p. 4.

45. J Palca, 'Collaboration beats smarts in group problem solving', *NPR* (30 September 2010), www.npr.org.

46. AW Woolley, CF Chabris, A Pentland, N Hashmi and TW Malone, 'Evidence for a collective intelligence factor in the performance of human groups', *Science*, vol. 330, no. 6004 (29 October 2010), pp. 686–8.

47. Robert F Bales, 'Task roles and social roles in problem-solving groups' in Eleanor E Maccoby, Theodore M Newcomb and EL Hartley (eds), *Readings in social psychology* (New York: Holt, Rinehart and Winston, 1958).

48. For a good description of task and maintenance functions see John J Gabarro and Anne Harlan, '*Note on process observation*', note 9477029 (Boston: Harvard Business School, 1976).

49. This discussion is developed from Edgar H Schein, *Process consultation*: vol. I, 2nd ed. (New York: Addison-Wesley, 1988), pp. 49–53; Rensis Likert, *New patterns of management* (New York: McGraw-Hill, 1961), pp. 166–9.

50. ibid.

51. For a good discussion of intergroup dynamics see Schein, op. cit., pp. 106–15.

52. Schein, op. cit.

53. R McLennan and T Liew, 'Work group behaviour in a New Zealand factory', *Journal of Sociology*, vol. 16, no. 84 (1980).

CHAPTER 7

TEAMWORK AND TEAM BUILDING

LEARNING OBJECTIVES

After studying this chapter, you should be able to:

1. define teams and explain the difference between teams and groups

2. explain how teams operate and what makes them effective

3. discuss a range of team-building activities and approaches

4. explain the factors that affect team performance and cohesiveness

5. describe the main types of teams that exist in organisations

6. list and explain some future challenges for work teams.

TEAMWORK IN THE DEFENCE FORCES — IS IT A MATTER OF LIFE OR DEATH?

While many organisations talk of the value and need for teamwork, there are some for whom it literally can be a matter of life and death — not for the organisation itself, but for the employees of the organisation. Covering jobs from fire fighting to the military, the concept of teamwork takes on a very clear focus but also raises questions as to how organisational teams operate effectively and what culture is required to allow them to do so?

While hiring and training are traditional strengths of many of the organisations such as the Defence Forces, they are being challenged by the demands of a world that increasingly sees the need for 'softer' skills. An address by the Chief of Army, Lieutenant General David Morrison, AO, at Lavarack Barracks, Townsville illustrates the complex nature of teamwork in such organisations:[1]

> We need to build toughness, cohesion and resilience in our teams, which in turn are the building blocks of our formations. In short, we need to mould soldiers who can display courage, initiative, respect and teamwork and if we fail in that task, then we fail as an Army. And the cost of failure in our calling is very high and irrecoverable.

Lieutenant General Morrison's speech came after recent comments he had made that were critical of the culture of the way teams operated in the army, and he noted that:

Over the past 16 years, there have been 13 major inquiries and reports into various aspects of the Australian Defence Force, its culture, its treatment of recruits, women, minorities, the abuse of alcohol and the way bullying emerges from our attempts to build small teams. Trust and shared values are brought together though the notion of respect as the answer to addressing these problems, as Morrison explained:

> That is why we are adding 'Respect' to our trio of existing values. It must be the glue that binds the other three together. It is the quality which will both temper, and sharpen the hard edge that must be a part of our service if we are to survive and prevail in war… And at a personal level — respect for who you are; for your self discipline; for the standards of your personal behaviour; for the respect you show to your mates and their respect for you — an expert in close combat; physically and mentally tough; compassionate and courageous; committed to learning and working for the team; a believer in trust, in loyalty and Country. An Australian Soldier.

Teamwork is essential but it is not easy and what we can learn from examples such as the military is that it can also be a challenge as well as providing opportunity.

Introduction

Many organisations are relying on their employees to work in teams to find solutions to productivity, innovation and customer service problems. From the opening vignette, it is clear that the role, composition and operation of teams is vital to their ongoing success. Teams are pervasive in organisations, with many companies putting their employees through team-building activities or adopting team approaches. Organisations often use teamwork as part of their employee involvement program.[2] The increase in the use of teamwork is evident in many countries and organisations of many kinds. For example, in New Zealand, whitegoods producer Fisher & Paykel has introduced 'everyday workplace teams', which support project teams to gain the benefits of greater employee involvement. In the public service in Singapore, there has been extensive use of teams for various activities, including problem solving and innovation.[3] In Korea, research has shown how teams have been used by a number of organisations within the fashion industry in successfully developing their own plans for safety improvement, efficiencies and activities to support business priorities.[4] Team approaches to work can foster top-quality products, individual employee concern for enhancing production, increased efficiency and high employee morale. Research has shown that teams consistently outperform individuals or random groups, especially when diverse skills, judgements and experiences can improve results. Teams generally work their magic by encouraging the individuals who comprise them to build new skills, and by raising organisational performance. Teams can add value to organisations committed to a set of core values that ensure quality performance. Teamwork is increasingly considered one of the benchmarks of a successful organisation, while the ability to build effective teams is increasingly considered one of the benchmarks of a successful manager.

Given the rise of teamwork and a shift to flatter management structures, communication, compassion and a 'sharing, caring' approach to business leadership are paramount. To enhance the contributions of teams, it is essential to understand teams and how to manage and lead them. This chapter introduces the concept of teams and their differences compared with groups. It examines a range of team-building approaches and goals, and several types of teams that exist in organisations.

What are teams?

Formally defined, a **team** is a small group of people with complementary skills, who work together as a unit to achieve a common purpose for which they hold themselves collectively accountable. In an employment situation or business setting, a team is a group of employees at any level in the organisation who are charged with working together to identify problems, form a consensus about what to do, and implement necessary actions in relation to a particular task or set of tasks. GM Design is an example of a workplace with a positive team environment.

Teams are small groups of people with complementary skills, who work together as a unit to achieve a common purpose for which they hold themselves collectively accountable.

Bain Southeast Asia: a great place to work

Bain Southeast Asia offices provide an open and fun atmosphere that encourages entrepreneurial thinking and action as well as advanced strategic and analytical learning. They have consistently been ranked as a 'best place to work' and have been ranked 'best consulting firm to work for' by *Consulting* magazine for 10 consecutive years, while in Asia they were recognised as 'best employer' in 2011 and again in 2013 by AON-Hewitt, the global human resources consulting firm.

As the company website proudly states:

Bain Southeast Asia works with ambitious business leaders to transform great companies into sharper, smarter, better

International
SPOTLIGHT

(continued)

versions of themselves. Our experts in Southeast Asia share a passion for results and bring a diverse set of skills and industry experience to each client engagement. We understand the complexities and challenges facing businesses operating in Southeast Asia — the diversity of languages, cultures, political systems and markets in the region. We look at businesses from a chief executive's perspective and we work together as 'one team' to achieve enduring results.[5]

Groups versus teams

The definition of teams above indicates that teams are groups. They are one type of group. In the previous chapter we saw that a group is made up of individuals who see themselves, and who are seen by others, as a social entity. The group is interdependent as a result of the tasks that the group members perform. The group is also embedded in one or more larger social systems, such as a community or an organisation, and it performs tasks that affect others, such as customers or coworkers. In recent years, the concept of the team has largely replaced that of the group in much organisational behaviour literature. Is this simply a matter of wording? Or are there more substantive differences between groups and teams?

As we saw in chapter 6, a **group** is a number of people who interact with one another for a common purpose. Teams are groups but they are groups that function as a unit. When we think of the word 'team', sporting teams may come to mind; for example, a football, netball or cricket team. But work groups can also be teams. Groups do not become teams because that is what someone calls them. Nor do teamwork values ensure team performance. The essence of a team is shared commitment. Without it, groups perform as individuals; with it, they become a powerful unit of collective performance. Another fundamental distinction between teams and other forms of working groups hinges on performance. A working group relies on the individual contributions of its members for group performance. However, a team strives for something greater than its members could achieve individually. An effective team is always worth more than the sum of its parts (refer to the concept of synergy, discussed in chapter 6). Some suggest that groups and teams form a continuum with groups at one end, being collections of people whose individual efforts combine 'additively' towards the achievement of a goal. Teams, at the other end, are collections of people whose efforts combine, synergistically, towards the achievement of the team's particular goals as well as the goals of the organisation.[6] Table 7.1 draws together some of the discussion so far, illustrating some of the common and distinct characteristics of teams and groups.

Groups are collections of two or more people who work with one another to achieve one or more common goals.

TABLE 7.1 Some common and distinct features of teams compared to groups

Groups	Teams (a particular kind of group)
Two or more people	Are 'small groups' (with two or more people but unlikely to be very large)
Have a common purpose	Have a common purpose for which they have a *shared commitment* and for which they hold themselves *collectively accountable*
Individuals who interact with each other	Team members work together with *complementary skills* and *function as a unit*
At one extreme of the continuum of groups, groups can comprise members whose individual efforts combine *additively* towards the achievement of a goal.	At the other extreme of the continuum of groups, team members' efforts combine *synergistically* to achieve team and organisational goals.

Teams can be extremely powerful when they work well, but transforming a group of individuals into a team can be hard work. The stages of group formation (forming, storming, initial integration, total integration and adjourning) discussed in chapter 6 also apply to the development of teams, and much of this chapter focuses on the building of teams.

Teams and their effectiveness

Teams operate on three levels.

1. *Team task level.* Teams are organised to carry out a specific task or to achieve a goal. Frequently, the team is so conscious of the need to accomplish this task that it is unaware of the other levels of need that operate simultaneously.

2. *Individual needs level.* Every individual member brings to the team a particular set of needs that impinge on the team and its task. Teams are most likely to be found wanting at this level, for individual needs are often well hidden behind the task drive of the team, or behind the personal drive of the team leader or facilitator. Each individual on a team — member or leader — has a responsibility to ensure the successful working of the team.

3. *Team maintenance level.* As people work together on a task, they also constantly interact in a shifting network of relationships. To accomplish its task, a team needs to have an awareness of itself as a team, and to recognise the need to maintain the relationships within it. Many of these responsibilities fall on the team leader or facilitator.

Note that these correspond to the purposes of groups (individual and organisational) and group outputs (group task performance and group maintenance) discussed in chapter 6.

Effective teams

Typically, *teams that make or do things* are the effective groups discussed in chapter 6. They perform ongoing tasks, such as marketing or manufacturing, and are considered permanent; that is, they operate without scheduled dates for disbanding. Members of these teams must have long-term working relationships as well as good operating systems and the external support needed to achieve effectiveness over a sustained period of time.

Teams that run things consist of the leaders at the top of an organisation or at the top of major organisational subunits. Although otherwise referred to as 'top management groups', these groups must also perform as true teams. Key issues for such teams include identifying overall organisational purposes, goals and values, and helping others fulfil them. It is increasingly common today to find such teams formally designated in the top management structure of organisations. This approach receives support from management consultants and scholars and also well-regarded executives.[7]

Organisational direction and purpose is a key value for teams. There must be clarity about the task, even if there is considerable latitude in the means of achieving it. Quality relationships exist only when people can argue without the team falling apart. They should be able to disagree without creating resentment. Each member must recognise that the team exists to complete a task that is more than an individual can manage. 'Pulling together' can be facilitated by developing and supporting a common language and culture. While individual goals are important, they must be compatible with the team's goals. To unify a team, members must know their goals and roles, and work out relationships with other team members. Some of the problems affecting group effectiveness, discussed in chapter 6, also apply to teams. Compared with employees who work individually, effective teams tend to have:

- higher morale
- higher productivity
- greater pride in the job
- greater pride in the company.

Effective teams understand the value of working together instead of against each other. For a team to be effective, its members must include the necessary experts or those most familiar with the problem, and any team needs members with the right mix of skills if it is to achieve high levels of performance. Skills are group input factors that can make a large difference in the ability of the team to accomplish its tasks properly.

The most effective teams have a blend of styles, strengths and skills — a blend that fosters interdependence. If team members are expected to believe the whole is greater than the sum of its parts (that is, synergy), then the leader must make each individual aware of the big picture by fostering pride not only in the individual job, but in the team's results and its impact on the overall success of the organisation.

Every team needs to have certain roles assumed by or assigned to its members. If team members' roles are well planned, participants will have a clear idea of what they are doing. Team meetings are one aspect of team activity where these principles apply. Some of the most frequent organisational barriers to team performance are:

- inadequate rewards and compensation systems
- inadequate personnel and human resources development systems
- a lack of appropriate information systems
- a lack of top management commitment
- an ambiguous organisational alignment
- difficulties in personal mind shift (or lateral thinking)
- inadequate individual abilities and characteristics
- an inadequate team size and other membership factors.

One way to increase team effectiveness is to encourage bonding outside the workplace, as the following example shows.

OBinAction

Sushi team bonding

An Auckland woman is offering something different in executive team building — Japanese cooking classes. Sachie Nomura-Siu (www.sachieskitchen.com) says cooking

together is a great way for teams to bond and get to know colleagues or clients better. And you can eat the results! She states 'It's not intimidating and much more appealing than climbing trees or sitting in a restaurant — and it's really creative, a great way to give the analytical brain a break'. The Auckland-based Japanese-born chef says there are always lots of laughs in her classes, as students discover rolling your own sushi in seaweed wrap is not as easy as it looks.[8]

The discussion so far has suggested that teams have special characteristics that enable them to be particularly effective and synergistic. Given the effectiveness of teams, work organisations will put considerable resources into building and improving teams — thus this chapter (in the next section) has a strong emphasis and extensive discussion on team building.

Another way to conceptualise team effectiveness is team IQ, as discussed in the following OB in action.

Team IQ is the ability of a group of individuals to tackle and manage complex and non-routine situations together.

Team IQ

Management consultant Bill Murray has been working with many of the top-ranking corporations and firms in Asia, Europe, the US and Australia for the last 20 years. Writing on the issue of high performance teams (HPTs), he examines the rhetoric versus reality with the example of an organisation where the vision was that 'By 2012, this company must be seen as "world class"', John Major, the CEO of Enthuse Logistics Inc. (ELI) (obviously not its real name), thundered at the AGM to rapturous applause. 'We will be a high performing corporation consisting of High Performing Teams (HPTs) in all areas of our business.'

Actually writing in 2012, Murray noted that not only has none of this happened, in fact:

ELI has slipped in the rankings of its peers, is losing its best people to rival organizations and its teams are not high performing in any of its business areas.

What went wrong? As Murray goes on to suggest:

… just putting a number of high-IQ people together does not make a HPT. Rather, what makes a team high performing is the team's ability to form a mutually supportive social group. The group IQ, and its overall performance, rises in line with its sociability… We tend to work best with people that we enjoy working with; it's really as simple as that.[9]

Foundations of the team-building process

Formally defined, team building is a sequence of planned activities designed to gather and analyse data on the functioning of a group, and to initiate changes designed to improve teamwork and increase group effectiveness.[10] The essence of the team-building process is teamwork. Formally stated, teamwork occurs when members of a team work together in a way that represents certain core values that promote the use of skills to accomplish common goals. These values have been described as 'listening and responding constructively to views expressed by others, giving others the benefit of the doubt, providing support and recognising the interests and achievements of others'.[11] Teamwork does not always happen naturally; it is something that team members and leaders must work hard to achieve. Also, it is a continuous process, so the effort of maintaining teamwork is ongoing. Efforts within the team must relate to team maintenance as well as task performance. Thus, the core values that underpin teamwork that is effective in accomplishing team goals should be clearly understood and communicated.

Successful team building and teamwork are assisted by clear goals, and are accomplished by members of the team and their leaders, sometimes with the assistance of facilitators. Teams need to work on their teamwork skills and can be assisted in this by training and team-building approaches that are designed to assist people operate as teams. These particular aspects of teams are now discussed in more detail.

> **Team building** is a sequence of planned action steps designed to gather and analyse data on the functioning of a group, and to implement changes to increase its operating effectiveness.

> **Teamwork** is when members of a team work together in a way that represents certain core values that promote the use of skills to accomplish certain goals.

Team-building goals

In addition to its general emphasis on improving teamwork and group effectiveness, team building is useful for:
- clarifying core values to guide the behaviour of members
- clarifying core values to direct the behaviour of members
- transforming a broad sense of purpose into specific performance objectives
- developing the right mix of skills to accomplish high-performance results
- enhancing creativity in task performance.[12]

Values are an important ingredient in the organisational or corporate culture, as discussed in chapter 9. The same holds true at the level of the work group or team. Good values help guide members' attitudes and behaviours in directions consistent with the team's common purpose. These values act as an internal control system for the group or team, and they can substitute for outside direction that a supervisor may otherwise have to provide.

Team building is one way in which core values can be identified, encouraging commitment on the part of group members. It can help the team to assess and develop the goals, values and skills of its membership and determine what must be done to maximise this input factor. Team building is also a way for ongoing groups to assess themselves periodically and to make the constructive changes necessary for the group to keep up with new developments.

Creating and sustaining a high-performing team is a challenging task in any setting. The effective manager 7.1 offers some guidelines for meeting this challenge.

How to build a high-performing team

1. Communicate clear high-performance standards.
2. Set the tone in the first team meeting.
3. Create a sense of urgency; set a compelling context for action.
4. Make sure team members have the right skills.
5. Establish clear rules for behaviour by the team.
6. As team leader, 'model' the expected behaviours.
7. Identify specific objectives that can be achieved to create early 'successes'.
8. Continually introduce new facts and information to the team.
9. Make sure the team members spend a lot of time together.
10. Give positive feedback; reward and recognise high-performance results.[13]

Effective team leadership

Skilled team leaders are essential to the operation of effective teams. While team leaders are involved in the day-to-day leadership of the team, they are also involved in team building, either at the time of establishment or when the team is endeavouring to refresh or renew its teamwork skills. Team leaders need competencies in a range of areas, including the ability to:

- build trust
- inspire teamwork
- facilitate and support team decisions
- expand team capabilities
- create a team identity
- make the most of team differences
- foresee and influence change.

While many of these leader competencies appear obvious, applying them in a real context may be more complex. For example, it may be difficult to work towards creating a team identity and inspiring teamwork, while at the same time, making the most of the differences between individuals. The Ethical perspective draws attention to some of these difficulties.

The team leader or manager's role is to make it easy for the team to define goals, develop plans and solve problems. Effective team leaders work to bring the team together and keep it focused on resolving one issue before moving on to the next. For teams to be effective, team leaders often need training in the right skills, roles and styles for teams as well as in conducting team development activities and meetings.

Leaders should be able to supply essential information and clarify issues. Awareness and self-assessment can enable team leaders to evaluate the way in which they communicate with team members. When team leaders listen attentively, they appear open and interested in what people are saying. By asking for and carefully considering advice, leaders allow employees to participate in decisions that affect them. Leaders should avoid domineering practices, such as being impatient with alternative views and interrupting people. However, avoiding arguments by not responding to disagreements could be misinterpreted as agreement, disregard or lack of fortitude. By merely listening during meetings, leaders send a message that they have nothing to contribute to the team and may fail to keep the team on track with their tasks.

Fair treatment of team members and perceptions of justice

ETHICAL **Perspective**

Research by Erdogan and Bauer builds on the concept of leader–member exchange (LMX), which suggests that leaders develop different relationships with each of their followers.[14] The particular focus was to consider the outcomes of those different relationships. One aspect of this differential treatment is the tangible and intangible rewards (such as the level of decision influence) given by the leader to some team members. In terms of procedural organisational justice, differential LMX can lead to perceptions of inconsistency in the treatment of team members. Organisational procedural justice can be understood as the 'fairness of formal organisational policies and leader enactment of these policies'.[15] The role of the leader in transmitting organisational policies fairly or unfairly (in the perception of those in the team) can have an important impact on team members.

Those team members who have the high-quality relationships with the team leader report positively on their perceptions of organisational justice. However, the overall results for the entire team may be worsened by the fact that others in the team (who do not have such favourable relationships) may perceive unfairness.

From their own research and earlier research, Hooper and Martin suggest that perceptions of variable LMX may affect team commitment and have effects on employee reactions including job satisfaction and wellbeing (the latter varying with perceptions of team conflict).[16] The researchers conclude that 'leaders may need to be cautious about fostering very high quality relationships with only a select subset of followers'.[17] Since team members have mutual accountability for achieving goals and should function together as a unit, these are important aspects for achieving effective team performance.

In teamwork, traditional top-down leadership is replaced by a situation in which:
- the team is an interacting and collective unit rather than a set of individuals
- responsibility for team performance and maintenance is shared by all team members
- position and power is diminished in team leadership
- expressions of members' needs and feelings are not discouraged, but dealt with openly in team meetings.

The effective manager 7.2 (overleaf) suggests ten rules for team leaders to follow to avoid needless mistakes.

Effective team facilitators

Facilitating team building is a challenging task and one that should not be taken lightly. Whether organisations use outside facilitators or internal facilitators (such as facilitators from the human resources area or from within the team itself), it is important that the facilitator is trained and competent to do the job. Facilitators who have team-building and development skills can help teams become more viable and productive organisational entities. Team-building facilitators structure their interventions to gain:

- appreciation and understanding of the complexity and dynamics of the team-building process
- identification of team needs in order to build greater proficiency in the approaches and skills necessary to help the team
- develop a safe and open forum for discourse in which team members can ask tough questions and share deep concerns that have been plaguing them and inhibiting their team's progress.

A trained facilitator or management consultant contributes to improving the corporate team process by fostering interdependence, leader support, willingness to try new ideas and to suggest new options, and open and improved communication.

A part of facilitating teamwork is encouragement to make the necessary choices, even if these are unpopular. There must be a belief by senior leaders and team members that the positive results of change are worth the challenge of disrupting the status quo.

While facilitators can work to encourage teamwork through playful and constructive activities (light-side team building), sometimes, there is a need to address the 'dark side' too. Real issues emerge and, sometimes, they are not pleasant to deal with and can frighten not only the participants but their team facilitators as well. If team members hear a facilitator sidestep real issues to stay positive, they may distrust the facilitator and the process. It is rare to find a team facilitator who feels equally comfortable and skilled at both the light side and the dark side of team building. What may work well in these situations is a partnership between two consultants — one who is skilled and comfortable with the light-side activities, and one who is effective on the dark side. Team members who work on both sides have a better chance to address their fears about working as a team.

Effective team facilitators observe and listen to the team, and assess its needs. They may then apply models and theoretical perspectives from a stock of models with which they are familiar. The What would you do? illustrates a situation where the senior executive team has problems.

When the senior executive team is to blame

There is a lot of talk about building and empowering teams to enhance innovation and/or organisational performance. Guidelines often place emphasis on what leaders should do to improve teamwork in their organisations. But, sometimes, it is the leaders themselves who are having a negative impact on performance in the organisation.

Professor Lynda Gratton, an academic and author, talks about organisations in terms of energy. High-energy organisations have 'hot spots' of creativity and innovation. She argues that smaller organisations are more likely to build hot spots, probably because they are less encumbered by slow and bureaucratic procedures.

Using the same type of metaphor, Gratton also speaks of 'the big freeze' — this indicates an organisation in which the executive team is choking off and chilling any 'heat' being generated in the organisation. The executive team, in effect, stifles the hot spots generating creativity and innovation. Regardless of how much enthusiasm and new ideas are being generated in the organisation, the senior executives somehow manage to affect others in the organisation negatively through their collective behaviour.

Even when it becomes apparent that the senior executive team is having such a significant effect on the organisation's workers, it is not easy to find a way to confront them or to work on changing the dynamics of the team. Working to change team dynamics needs to involve all team members (including the team leader) and the way in which they interact in order to accomplish effective transition to a more functional team. The change process can be so difficult that Professor Gratton recommends people avoid organisations with 'the big freeze' when making career moves. She estimates that around 30–40 per cent of people are working under such executive teams.[19]

Questions

1. If you were a human resources manager in such an organisation, what would you do to highlight the need to change the executive team and build a more effective team?
2. Who would be most effective in bringing about change to team dynamics in an organisation in which the executive team is not functioning well and so is impacting widely on organisational performance? Explain your answer.

Teamwork activities and training

There are numerous methods, games and training techniques that help teams, their leaders and/or their facilitators improve teamwork, broaden perspectives, maximise ideas and reach consensus. An organisation's training department and/or external consultants can provide managers with assistance for team building, whether it is when the team is first formed or later, when the team members need revitalisation with their teamwork.

Most of the many possible approaches to team building have the common steps shown in figure 7.1 (overleaf). In other words, someone in or out of the team notes a problem; then, team members work together to gather and analyse data about the problem — to plan actions for improvement, implement action plans, monitor and evaluate results and take further action if it is required.

The team-building process just described is a cooperative one. There is an emphasis on team members working together to accomplish various team-building tasks. Throughout the process, everyone is expected to participate, as group effectiveness is evaluated and decisions are made on what needs to be done to maintain or improve this effectiveness in the future. Then, everyone shares in the responsibility for implementing the agreed action plans and evaluating action results.

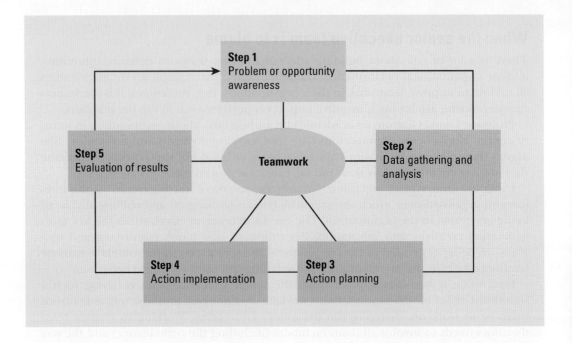

FIGURE 7.1 How team members work together in a typical team-building activity

Effective management principles and good team-building skills go hand in hand. The team's objectives should be defined and the team members should understand why they are important. In addition, the team members should understand how they benefit individually. Any team must be made up of members who feel responsible for actively working together to accomplish important tasks, whether those tasks involve recommending things, making or doing things, or running things; that is, the members must feel 'collectively accountable' for what they accomplish through 'teamwork'. Three of many possible types of teamwork activities are now described: (1) experiential activities, (2) challenging viewpoints and (3) reaching consensus through brainstorming. It is important to note that these methods are not exclusive of each other and different methods or approaches can accomplish similar outcomes.

OBin**Action**

Trust drives empowerment in Chinese hotels

Research from the School of Hotel and Tourism Management (SHTM) at the Hong Kong Polytechnic University has found that 'trust in individual employees and their merits lies at the heart of empowerment in Asian hotel management'.[20] While the role of trust is important in all organisations, the authors of this study (Dr Catherine Cheung and Dr Alan Wong) found an individual-centric conceptualisation of empowerment, which they suggest contrasts with the organisation-driven view that prevails in the West. The researchers suggested this difference can be overcome by a blend of practices. For instance, they advocate that 'managers must personally know staff members who are to be empowered, or a person whom the manager trusts must recommend them'. Finding that 'personal trust' was repeatedly linked with empowerment and explicitly tied to guanxi. Interestingly, those cited as most reliable and trustworthy were family members or other close relatives. The researchers provide clear insight into the notion that even well-accepted concepts, such as trust, cannot be simply and uncritically applied across cultures and contexts.

Experiential activities

To enhance the quick formation of teams, facilitators may resort to experiential approaches, including 'games'. The games are designed to encourage participants to process information actively, rather than receiving it passively. They are intended to build on the motivational qualities of cooperation and competition among team members, as well as trust. A good example is the game referred to as 'learning teams', which involves two types of activity: (1) the cooperative learning session and (2) the competitive tournament session.[21]

An example of a 'cooperative' learning session game involves the team receiving an identical set of 15 objects, which are arranged on a table and hidden from view. After viewing half of the objects, each team is asked to duplicate the exact arrangement of the objects, using its own set of matching objects. The team that accomplishes the task in the least amount of time wins a prize. Each group is told that either team might have one or two saboteurs who would work against their own team to keep it from winning. The deciding factor in the game is the amount of time and energy a team spends dealing with the idea of a saboteur in their midst. Teams that are most concerned with saboteurs always lose. The results of the game show that trust is critical for meeting team goals.[22] Even in day-to-day teamwork, trust is important for almost all teams.

The Pirates Dilemma

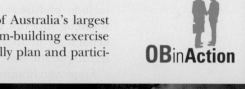

Teambuilding Australia (www.teambuildingaustralia.com.au) is one of Australia's largest and most experienced corporate training companies. They offer a team-building exercise called The Pirates Dilemma. In this exercise, teams need to successfully plan and participate in a mission to recapture gold stolen from the Queen by the pirates. All teams are successful, but some are more successful than others. What is emphasised is the overall results of the group, rather than individual teams.

Some key aspects of The Pirates Dilemma include:
- rewarding a moderate level of aggressiveness and risk-taking, while not rewarding excessive risk nor excessive competitiveness with other teams
- a balanced approach will result in maximum results
- planning — plan the work and work the plan
- flexibility — new information becomes available that needs to be integrated into the existing plan in a logical way
- training, which is optimising and beneficial, not a waste of time.

Challenging viewpoints

Some team-building approaches work on breaking down team members' viewpoints, either individually or collectively, since these may impede team performance. One approach is called the *devil's advocate* process, which helps team members overcome resistance to change. Playing the devil's advocate means taking an oppositional stance in an argument to force others to strengthen their position and clarify their reasoning. Other approaches can also help to shift people from their usual roles to look at the problem differently.

Reaching consensus through brainstorming

Team consensus is general agreement that all members of a team support. Consensual decision making is more effective than other types of decision making. It forces the team to consider more aspects of a problem and to be alert to objections. Team consensus does not just happen; it results from following careful guidelines, including:

- working towards a common goal through brainstorming
- using quiet time to allow for personal reflection
- avoiding voting
- not expecting unanimous agreement on all reasons for making a particular decision.

We discuss decision making in further detail in chapter 12, but the important issue here is that reaching consensus means that people are making a true team decision.

In **brainstorming**, team members actively generate as many ideas as possible, and they do so relatively quickly and without inhibitions. Members of a brainstorming team follow these four rules.

1. *All ideas are acceptable.* All criticism is ruled out. No-one is allowed to judge or evaluate any ideas until the idea-generation process has been completed.
2. *'Freewheeling' is welcomed.* The emphasis is on creativity and imagination; the wilder or more radical the idea, the better.
3. *Quantity is wanted.* The emphasis is also on the number of ideas; the greater the number, the more likely that a superior idea will be raised.
4. *'Piggy-backing' is good.* Everyone is encouraged to suggest how others' ideas can be turned into new ideas, or how two or more ideas can be joined into still another new idea.

The core of brainstorming rests with the ban on evaluation during the idea-generation process. This approach tends to reduce members' fears of criticism or failure. Typical results include enthusiasm, involvement and a free flow of ideas. Researchers consider brainstorming superior to open-group discussions when the goals are creative thinking and the generation of alternative solutions to identified problems. Therefore, this time-honoured technique still has important practical applications in the modern workplace.

Employee brainstorming sessions can be a valuable way in which to produce great ideas. But before convening a session, the group should establish goals. A goal may be to gather information, solve a problem, make a decision, deal with change or plan a project. Once the group decides on the goal, it should choose a specific agenda or topic. Participants should have time to think about the topic before the session. And a generous amount of time should be allowed for the actual session, which should take place in a comfortable, non-threatening setting. Brainstorming can go beyond discussions and can include creative activities, as the following example illustrates.

Brainstorming is a technique by which team members generate as many ideas as possible, without being inhibited by other team members.

Brainstorming is brilliant

Kevin Vincent is a Christchurch-based business consultant in New Zealand. He's a fan of brainstorming and, writing for *NZ Management Magazine*, he claims that teams will become more creative in their outlook by using brainstorming.[23] It is, however, essential that managers are open to the input of their team, and that that they don't dismiss any ideas that are generated.

Structured brainstorming is essential for bringing ideas to the table. Ideas that encourage participation, effective listening, thought sharing and the freedom to toss in 'crazy stuff' (or, as management guru Tom Peters might say, 'the wow') are critical. The process assists in the development of innovative solutions to existing problems; builds trust and confidence between colleagues; and generates a cooperative, collaborative and unified team environment.

Timing and location of teamwork activities

Some of the broad foundations and particular activities of team building have already been discussed. With these in mind, we can also talk about some different choices that are made about when to conduct team-building activities, and where to locate them. While many factors can impinge on these decisions, the following represent some common approaches. These are: formal retreats, continuous improvement and outdoor experiences.

Formal retreats

In the formal retreat approach, the team-building activities take place during a 'retreat' that is organised off-site. During this retreat, which may last from two to seven or more days, the members of a team work intensively on a variety of planning and experiential activities. These activities are often initiated by a review of data gathered through surveys, interviews or group activities such as the nominal group technique. Formal retreats are typically held with the assistance of a consultant who is either hired or made available by in-house staff. Team-building retreats offer opportunities for intense and concentrated efforts to examine team problems and future directions. In this context, organisations often seek the help of outside facilitators.

Continual improvement

Not all team building is done in a formal retreat format, or with the assistance of consultants. Indeed, in light of the new workplace's emphasis on teams, a continual improvement approach to team building is important. Here the manager, team leader and/or team members take responsibility for regularly engaging in the team-building process. This method can be as simple as periodic meetings that implement the team-building steps; it can also include self-managed retreats such as those just described. In all cases, team members are committed to monitoring team development and accomplishments continually, and to taking collective responsibility for making the day-to-day changes needed to ensure team effectiveness.

From a total quality management perspective, continual improvement of work teams through team building is certainly an important concept. Any informed manager should be able to assist teams in fulfilling this responsibility, and team building should become a regular element in the annual or semi-annual task agendas of any team. Many quality improvement programs rely on team efforts. The internal goals of such teams are for members to trust one another, work together to solve problems, help enhance one another's performance and aspire to feel like winners. The external goals are for these teams to identify their customers and suppliers, gain commitment from their customers and suppliers, focus on team performance and project the image of winners.

Outdoor experiences

The outdoor experience approach is an increasingly popular team-building technique that may be performed on its own or in combination with the data-feedback and continual improvement approach just described. For a group that has never experienced team building, an outdoor experience can be a high-powered way to begin the process; for teams experienced with team building, it can be a way of enriching and varying the process over time. The essence of any outdoor experience involves putting group members in a variety of situations in which they need to work collectively to overcome physical tests that may be beyond individual capabilities. By having to work together in the face of such obstacles, both individual character and commitments to teamwork can be developed. A popular sponsor of such team building is the Outward Bound Leadership School,[24] but many others exist.

Team performance and cohesiveness

While many factors will influence team cohesiveness and performance, norms and roles are two key areas for consideration. We will also examine the important relationship between norms, performance and team cohesion.

Team norms

Norms of behaviour can occur in many subsets of the organisation. For example, in chapter 6 we defined group norms, and in chapter 9 you will see that cultural norms of behaviour also operate in the organisation. So, the norms that occur in teams are defined in the same way. A team norm is an idea or belief about the behaviour that team members are expected to display. **Norms** are often referred to as 'rules' or 'standards' of behaviour that apply to team members.[25] They help clarify membership expectations in a team. Norms allow members to structure their own behaviour and to predict what others will do; they help members gain a common sense of direction; and they reinforce a desired team or organisational culture.

When a member of a team violates a team norm, other members typically respond in ways that attempt to enforce the norm. Time and energy can be saved if team members take the time in the beginning to write a code of conduct establishing the basic principles and rules that will determine the power, duties and rights of both the team and its members. Every team's code will be unique to the set of circumstances of its project. The code of conduct should deal with the 'soft' issues — philosophies, principles and values. These are difficult concepts to deal with and yet, if the team's views on them are resolved, this could yield the greatest payoff for the team in the long run. The code of conduct should also deal with organisational detail, and may include responses to direct criticisms, reprimands, expulsion, social ostracism and the like. For instance, Livia, an enthusiastic employee, may enter a team as a highly capable and highly motivated worker. But her efforts to achieve high performance are met with 'pressure' from other team members who want her to reduce her efforts and conform to the team's low-performance norm. Livia gives in to the pressure, accepts the norm, and agrees to work at far less than her true performance potential. Another example may be the subtle pressure by fellow team members to attend or participate in certain social functions.

Teams operate with many types of norm. Among these norms are those regarding expected performance, attendance at meetings, punctuality, preparedness, criticism, social behaviours and so on. Other common norms in work teams deal with relationships with supervisors, colleagues and customers, as well as honesty, security, personal development and change. Norms are essentially determined by the collective will of team members, so it is difficult for organisations and their managers to dictate which norms a given team will possess. The concerned manager must try to help team members adopt norms supportive of organisational goals. A manager or team leader can take a number of steps to encourage the development of positive team norms; some are shown in The effective manager 7.3.[26]

Norms are rules or standards about the behaviour that group members are expected to display.

THE EffectiveManager 7.3

Seven steps for leaders to encourage positive team norms

1. Act as a positive role model.
2. Hold team meetings to gain agreement on desired behaviours.
3. Recruit and select new members who can and will perform as desired.
4. Train and orient new members in the desired behaviours.
5. Reinforce and reward the desired behaviours.
6. Hold team meetings to discuss feedback and review performance.
7. Hold team meetings to plan ways to increase effectiveness.

Team roles and role dynamics

A **role** is a set of expectations for the behaviour of a person holding a particular office or position.

Roles were discussed in chapter 6, but here we extend this to a team context. Membership expectations can create problems for any member of any team. In teams, the term **role** describes a set of expectations for the behaviour of a person holding a particular office or position. Often these expectations are unclear, and this uncertainty raises anxieties and creates problems. This can occur in newly formed teams, when new members join an existing team, or in teams whose members have reached the total integration stage of development, as discussed in chapter 6.

In chapter 13, we discuss some of the issues involved in the communication of role expectations. In the specific context of a work group or team, role dynamics that involve uncertainties and stress can create problems. **Role ambiguity** occurs when a member of a work group or team is unsure about what other members expect of them. This uncertainty raises anxieties and creates problems. **Role conflict** occurs when a member is unable to respond to the expectations of one or more members. This conflict may be due to overload or incompatibility. Just as in the case of ambiguity, the stress and anxiety associated with role conflicts of both types can cause problems for both the individual member and the team as a whole. The team-building techniques discussed earlier are designed to address these types of problem.

Role ambiguity is the uncertainty about what other group members expect of a person.

Role conflict occurs when a person is unable to respond to the expectations of one or more group members.

Cohesiveness is the degree to which members are attracted to and motivated to remain a part of a team.

Team cohesiveness

The extent to which members of a team conform to the team's norms is strongly influenced by the level of **cohesiveness** in the team; that is, the degree to which members are attracted to, and motivated to remain part of, a team.[27] Cohesiveness tends to be high when:

- team members are homogeneous in age, attitudes, needs and backgrounds
- team members respect one another's competencies
- team members agree on common goals
- team tasks require interdependent efforts
- the team is relatively small
- the team is physically isolated from other groups
- the team experiences performance success
- the team experiences a performance crisis or failure.

Cohesive teams are good for their members. Members of highly cohesive teams are concerned about their team's activities and achievements. In contrast to persons in less cohesive teams, they tend to be more energetic when working on team activities, they are less likely to be absent, and they tend to be happy about performance success and sad about failures. Cohesive teams generally have stable memberships and foster feelings of loyalty, security and high self-esteem among their members; they satisfy a full range of individual needs. Sometimes, tough experiences and survival of them, as well as isolation, can be very influential in developing high team cohesiveness. For example, volunteer teams in the difficult situations in developing countries have been said to generate high cohesiveness in teams.[28]

Cohesive groups or teams may or may not be good for the organisation. The critical question is: 'How does cohesiveness influence performance?' Figure 7.2 (overleaf) helps answer this question by showing the relationship between team cohesiveness and team performance. Typically, the more cohesive the team, the greater the conformity of members to team norms. As you would expect, the performance norm is critical for any team. Thus, when the performance norm is positive, high conformity to it in a cohesive team should have a beneficial effect on task performance; when the performance norm is negative in a highly cohesive team, undesirable results may be experienced.

Notice in figure 7.2 (overleaf) the performance implications for various combinations of cohesiveness and norms. Performance is highest in a very cohesive team with positive performance norms. In this situation, members encourage one another to work hard on behalf of the team. The worst situation for a manager is a highly cohesive team with negative performance norms. Again, members will be highly motivated to support one another, but the organisation will suffer as the team restricts its performance, consistent with the negative norm. Between these two extremes are mixed situations, in which a lack of cohesion fails to ensure member conformity to the guiding norm. The strength of the norm is reduced, and the outcome is somewhat unpredictable but is most likely to be on the moderate or low side.

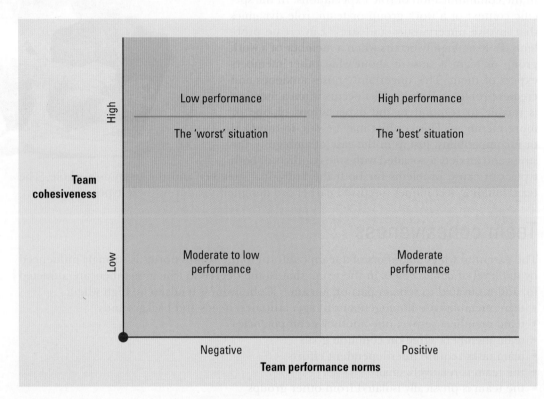

FIGURE 7.2 How team cohesiveness and performance norms can influence team performance

Influencing team cohesiveness

Look again at figure 7.2. How would you feel with a team that falls into any cell other than the high-performance one? To deal with these possibilities, a manager must recognise that there will be times when steps should be taken to build cohesiveness in a team, such as when the team has positive norms but low cohesiveness. There may be other times when steps must be taken to reduce cohesiveness, such as when the members of a highly cohesive team are operating with negative performance norms and when previous efforts to change these norms have failed. Managers must be prepared to deal with both situations. The fact that cohesive teams are not always good is highlighted in the Counterpoint opposite. As shown in figure 7.3, managers can take steps to increase or decrease team cohesiveness. These include making changes in team goals, membership composition, interactions, size, rewards, competition, location and duration.

Trust is a very important ingredient for team cohesiveness and performance. The higher the level of trust is in a team, the greater the cohesiveness, satisfaction and effectiveness. The genuine sharing of information can also greatly contribute to the building of trust; this simple act can demonstrate a strong commitment to the team.

Conflict is a frequently unavoidable part of teamwork. It is not necessarily detrimental and can lead to creative solutions. However, if not managed, it can destroy team cohesiveness. You can manage conflict by:

• giving ample recognition to each member of the team
• focusing on a win–win situation, in which both the individual and the team benefit

- establishing a team charter that states the responsibilities of each team member
- mediating personal differences, allowing all team members an opportunity to express their views
- finding areas of agreement to allow team members to focus on team goals rather than areas of conflict
- helping team members to address personal behaviours that will facilitate change.[29]

How to *decrease* cohesion	Targets	How to *increase* cohesion
Create *dis*agreement	Goals	Get agreement
Increase *hetero*geneity	Membership	Increase homogeneity*
Restrict within team	Interactions	Enhance within team
Make team bigger	Size	Make team smaller
Focus within team	Competition	Focus on other teams
Reward individual results	Rewards	Reward team results
Increase contact with other teams	Location	Isolate from other teams
Disband the team	Duration	Keep team together

*Increased homogeneity may result in other negative effects such as groupthink or lack of diverse opinions.

FIGURE 7.3 How to increase and decrease cohesiveness in a work team

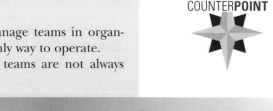

COUNTER**POINT**

When 'teams' do not work!

There are many guidelines for how to establish, build and manage teams in organisations and almost a belief that teams are 'it' — the best and only way to operate.

However, there is an emerging literature that suggests that teams are not always the answer or that some people simply cannot work in teams. Arnold provides a succinct overview of ten ways workplace teamwork should not be used.[30] From the 'one person is the hero' scenario to those 'out to achieve their own agenda' or 'to diffuse blame' the examples she cites focus on one simple rule — use teams where they make sense!

Ancona and Bresman, in their book *X-teams*, argue that most talk about teams is focused on the *internal dynamics* of teams with concern for achieving camaraderie, trust and internal working processes.[31] While this is beneficial, it means that we often fail to give enough consideration to how the team must operate and connect with outsiders. As Ancona and Bresman argue, we tend to have this limiting mindset when establishing and managing teams. As a result, teams become

(continued)

inwardly focused and team members miss seeing the bigger picture of what is required to be successful. The authors give an illustration of a team that was developing a new version of a software product. The team was so focused on its goals of continuous improvement and meeting deadlines that it chose to ignore information given to it by managers, about possible improvements to the product (these improvements were customer suggestions). In the end, due to this inward focus, the team went into a downward spiral and failed.

Successful X-teams have three features: (1) external activity, (2) extreme execution and (3) flexible phases. *External activity* includes seeking out information about technology, the market and the competition, as well as finding ways to work with others outside the team. Team members also make sure they understand what directions management is moving in and what other teams are doing; that is, they have an effective communication with other people outside the team. *Extreme execution* refers to the development and use of effective internal processes to achieve work, but it must be coordinated with the external activity. Finally, X-teams are also adaptable and are prepared to shift their activities over the team's lifetime. For example, they incorporate *flexible phases*, such as exploration, exploitation and exportation, in developing new products or services. Thus, the team work involves exploration of customer needs — for example, top management expectations — and exploitation of that learning to develop new products, and working with outsiders to transfer their new product, services or ideas to others. X-teams are also built on the principles of having *extensive ties* to useful outsiders, having *expandable tiers* to structure themselves to do the work, and having *exchangeable membership* to accommodate rotating leadership and the coming and leaving of team members over time (team members might come or leave through natural growth and attrition, or, to fulfil task requirements).

Just as Harris pointed to the situation in which single employees have full responsibility for a task, so the work of Ancona and Bresnan points to the idea that teams collectively have a mutual responsibility for tasks, which goes beyond developing healthy internal team dynamics. Regardless of how much trust and camaraderie exists in a team, the team will not be successful unless it can flexibly and fully engage with relevant outsiders to achieve its purposes.

Questions

1. Consider the software product development team that is discussed, and explain the nature of its cohesiveness and the problems this caused in terms of its long-term effectiveness.
2. What could the organisation's management do to turn around the problems identified in the software product development team?
3. One of the points in figure 7.3 suggests that increasing contact with other teams might decrease team cohesion. How does this fit with Ancona and Bresnan's idea of external activity, and what methods might be used to maintain team cohesion and also to encourage working with others to achieve team and organisational goals?

Types of workplace teams

There is no ready-reckoner to tell us exactly what category a particular team may fit into, or for giving a precise picture of the types of teams that operate in organisations and how successful they are. While some broad types of teams are recognisable, there are many subtle variants, many terms used to label them and many degrees of success. However, we do know that managers in contemporary organisations are adopting many innovative ways of better using teams as human resources of organisations. The watchwords of these approaches are empowerment, participation and involvement. More recently, technology enables physically remote membership of teams.

We cannot comprehensively cover all types of teams or all developments in team theory. However, for the rest of this section, four common types of teams are outlined: (1) employee involvement teams, (2) problem-solving teams, (3) self-managing teams (SMTs) and (4) virtual teams. Despite classifying them into types, it must be accepted that every team is different and may have features that overlap the types discussed here. For instance, it is possible to have a problem-solving team that is also an employee involvement team, or a SMT that is also a virtual team. You will come across many other terms to describe teams and/or types of teams, such as cross-functional teams and world-class teams.

Employee involvement teams

Many of the creative developments applied to the use of teams in organisations fall into the category of **employee involvement teams**. This term applies to a wide variety of settings in which teams of workers meet regularly outside their normal work units for the purpose of collectively addressing important workplace issues. The goals of an employee involvement team often relate to total quality concepts and the quest for continuous improvement in all operations. Typically consisting of five to ten members, these teams regularly spend time discussing ways to enhance quality, better satisfy customers, raise productivity and improve the quality of work life.

> **Employee involvement teams** are teams of workers who meet regularly outside their normal work units for the purpose of collectively addressing important workplace issues.

Employee involvement teams are mechanisms for participation. They allow workers to gain influence over matters affecting them and their work. They also allow the full advantages of team decision making to become a part of everyday organisational affairs. These advantages include bringing the full extent of worker know-how to bear on problems and gaining the commitment of these workers to implement fully any problem-solving approaches that may be selected.

For employee involvement to succeed, traditional managers must make sincere commitments to participation and empowerment. The opportunities for the workers to have an influence on what happens to them must be real. When accomplished, true employee involvement offers the potential for contributing positively to performance accomplishments in the new workplace. It also offers employees the advantages of filling higher-order needs such as achievement, recognition and growth (see chapter 3).

Problem-solving teams

Some teams are created for the specific purpose of generating solutions to problems — for example, quality circles, task forces and autonomous work teams. Developed as a means of generating ideas that would raise product quality by reducing defects and error rates, quality circles were a precursor to the total quality movement.[32] A **quality circle** is a small group of people who meet periodically (for example, for an hour or so once per week) to discuss and develop solutions for problems relating to quality, productivity or cost.

> **Quality circles** are groups of workers who meet periodically to discuss and develop solutions for problems relating to quality, productivity or cost.

For the circles to be successful, members should receive special training in information-gathering and problem-analysis techniques. Quality circle leaders should emphasise democratic participation in identifying and analysing problems and choosing action alternatives. After proposed solutions are presented to management, implementation should be a joint effort between the quality circle and management.

However, quality circles cannot be looked on as panaceas for all of an organisation's ills. Indeed, a number of conditions must be met to keep quality circles from becoming just another management 'gimmick'. These include the following:
- an informed and knowledgeable workforce
- managerial willingness to trust workers with necessary information
- the presence of a 'team spirit' in the quality circle group
- a clear emphasis on quality in the organisation's goals
- an organisation that encourages participation.

The task force is another kind of team created to solve problems. **Task forces** are temporary, created with a relatively well-defined task to fulfil. They have a more limited time horizon than that of quality circles; once the task is accomplished, the task force is disbanded.

Other 'teams' might include the 'Skunk Works™'[33] and 'hotgroups' that may be formed to solve important problems or to develop new ideas. The intention is to remove these teams from the pressures and demands of day-to-day work. However, it is important to acknowledge that some hotgroups or Skunk Works™ are so intensely involved in their task that individual needs and group maintenance activities are neglected. In this sense, they would fail to live up to the criteria of being high-performing and trusting over a long period. In other contexts, specific teams might be set up within an organisation, but with the task of investigating a problem in the society in which it operates.

Autonomous work teams perform highly related or interdependent jobs, and they are given significant authority and responsibility for many aspects of their work, such as planning, scheduling, assigning tasks to members and making decisions with financial consequences.[34] They were the precursor to the SMT, which we will examine in the next section.

Self-managing teams (SMTs)

Many companies across the world have moved towards the concept of SMTs in which employees work together as equals to solve problems and improve operations. Every SMT needs members with three different strengths:

1. technical or functional expertise
2. problem-solving and decision-making skills
3. interpersonal skills.[35]

Formally defined, **self-managing teams (SMTs)** are small groups of people empowered to manage themselves and the work they do on a day-to-day basis.[36] They are also referred to as 'self-directed teams'. Typically, a SMT is one in which the members:

- make decisions on how to divide up tasks within the team
- make decisions on scheduling work within the team
- are able to perform more than one job for the team
- train one another in jobs performed by the team
- evaluate one another's job performance on the team
- are collectively held accountable for the team's performance results.

What differentiates SMTs from more traditional work groups is the fact that their members have substantial responsibility for a wide variety of decisions involved in the accomplishment of assigned tasks. Indeed, the very purpose of the SMT is to take on duties previously performed by traditional supervisors — that is, things such as quality control, work scheduling and even performance evaluation. Google Australia uses the SMT approach.

At Google Australia, SMTs are a means to help staff handle the big objectives confronting them. Each SMT is focused on part of a larger, specific project. Team members are very project-focused and often decide their own goals. The hiring process is such that only self-driven, self-motivated people are recruited, who usually become enthusiastic team members.[37]

Well-designed, step-by-step methods of developing SMTs can move authority and responsibility to all levels, allow employees to manage their own activities, and help managers feel more comfortable with the process of empowering employees. This typically assumes that the proper foundations have been laid and the proper culture exists to allow an organisation to begin this process.[38]

The establishment and implementation of the concept requires a number of steps. These may include:

- learning about the SMT concept
- conducting a readiness assessment to determine if teams are right for the culture
- communicating the organisation's vision and values to employees, as they relate to empowerment and teams

- taking the organisation through the workplace redesign process
- implementing the redesign
- evaluating the progress of SMTs.

Organising into SMTs requires planning, selecting the right team members and leaders, designing teams for success, training continually, and carefully managing the shift of power and responsibilities from leaders to team members.

Self-managing teams operate with fewer layers of management than do traditional organisational structures. Research shows that, in comparison with individuals with no participation in a team, members of self-managed teams are significantly more likely (than non-members) to report that teams have increased profits, improved customer service and boosted the morale of both employees and management.[39]

When SMTs are added to an organisation, a number of benefits are expected. Among the advantages that may be realised are:
- improved productivity and production quality
- greater production flexibility
- faster response to technological change
- fewer job classifications and fewer management levels
- lower employee absenteeism and turnover
- improved work attitudes.[40]

Because a SMT really does manage itself in many ways, there is no real need for the former position of supervisor. Instead, a team leader usually represents the team when dealing with higher-level management. The possible extent of this change is shown in figure 7.4, where the first level of supervisory management has been eliminated and replaced by SMTs. Note also that many traditional tasks of the supervisor are reallocated to the team. Thus, for persons learning to work in such teams for the first time, and for those managers learning to deal with SMTs rather than individual workers, the implications can be substantial.

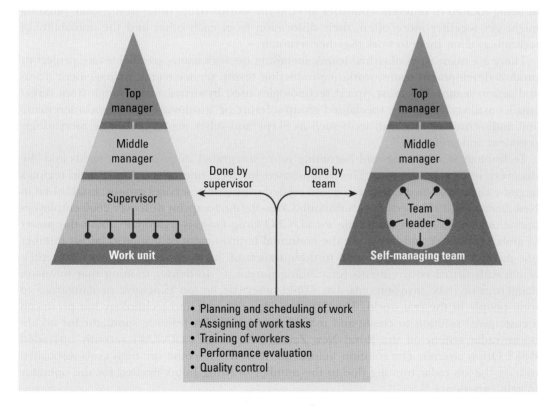

FIGURE 7.4 Organisational and management implications of self-managing work teams

Perhaps the most important prerequisite is for team members' jobs to be interdependent. Administrative systems must be able to record performance based on team accomplishments. At the same time, these systems should also enable rewards to be given to team members over time periods that may vary depending on the nature of team assignments. Self-managed work teams differ from traditional work groups in that the team, rather than the first-line supervisor, controls the critical management processes that typically include:

- planning
- organising
- directing
- staffing.

Typically, these teams move through five stages of development as they grow from new creations to mature, fully functioning groups over a period. To reach a fully functioning stage, teams may need to undergo training that includes communication, administrative and technical skills. Progressive levels of training in these areas through each of the stages of development become the driving force for team growth and development.

Virtual teams

A **virtual team** is one whose members work interdependently towards the achievement of a common goal across space and time.

Alongside the changing trends towards teamwork in organisations, other important developments have resulted in the emergence of virtual teams. A **virtual team** is one whose members work interdependently towards the achievement of a common goal across space and time.[41] Such teams can also work across organisational boundaries. They have developed in the context of new forms of organisational structure, the rapid and ongoing advances in information and communication technologies (ICTs), and globalisation. Virtual teams rely particularly on ICTs to enable communication and team activity, since they are physically separate.

The degree of separation may range from being on separate floors of a large building to being located in different countries around the world. While those in the same building might get together more often, their dislocation from each other and the availability of technology allow them to work together remotely.

There are many types of virtual teams, including network teams, parallel teams, project or product-development teams, work or production teams, service teams, management teams and action teams. The most typical technologies used by virtual teams range from direct email, email via list servers, specialised group software or 'groupware', to videoconferencing and audio-conferencing with tools such as Skype and other media becoming increasingly prevalent and preferred.[42]

Technology is advancing and becoming more integrated in response to needs and the discovery of new possibilities. This is illustrated by Beca, one of the Asia–Pacific region's largest employee-owned engineering and related consultancy services groups. Established in New Zealand in 1918, Beca has a substantial Asia–Pacific footprint with over 2600 employees operational in 18 offices across the world. CEO Greg Lowe is passionate about the power of global teamwork and has made the continual improvement of teamwork as his number one priority. Beca has applied itself to the question of 'how can technology facilitate interaction with virtual environments for training purposes?' to deliver training that simulates dangerous or risky environments that would otherwise be too expensive or dangerous to train people in the real world. Their cutting-edge research and technology has produced a customised solution to create and maintain a high-fidelity training simulator for an airborne radar system on the Royal New Zealand Air Force's (RNZAF) recently upgraded P-3K2 Orion aircraft. The solution helped the RNZAF overcome the high costs associated with on-the-job radar training due to the number of flying hours needed for the operator to gain experience.[43]

Virtual team intelligence

In the earlier OB in action about team IQ, we described characteristics of teams that would increase their 'intelligence'. These factors included group members speaking in turns, the proportion of females on a team, and social sensitivity. But are these initiatives more difficult in virtual teams? Given that many people work in virtual settings today, it is worthwhile considering how these recommendations influence team intelligence when team members are scattered in different locations.

There are reasons to believe that virtual team IQ may actually be higher — or, at least, equal to that of equivalent non-virtual teams. Depending on the richness of the media used for virtual meetings and other communication within the team, body language and facial expressions are, of course, harder to read, and social sensitivity requires more intuition. However, speaking in turns becomes easier when physical appearances matter less, and people tend to express their opinions more freely online than in face-to-face settings. Because status cues are less visible, the merit of an argument will trump charisma or enthusiasm in a virtual setting. An imposing physical appearance or a 'charming personality' may allow one individual to dominate a face-to-face meeting, but in a virtual setting these qualities are somewhat neutralised, thus allowing participants to flourish on the basis of the accomplishments and skills that they bring to the team.

With the above in mind, your team can increase its collective intelligence and, hopefully, take advantage of the complex challenges of globalisation. Far too often the potential of diverse teams is not reached. Team processes and culture hold the key to success. At the end of the day, it is all about identifying competencies to embrace differences rather than merely tolerating them.[44]

Relationships are clearly important in productive teams. Even more established technology is important as keeping 'connected' through emails, texts and phone calls (including teleconference or videoconference calls) can keep relationships alive between team members who are isolated, and just as importantly, with team leaders. This is essential if team members work together to achieve team goals. According to Georgia Tsamis, Regional Director of Learning and Development at Michael Page, who has over eight years of experience in looking after teams in Asia, while 'managing people remotely is hard work … because remote teams are isolated from the day to day communication that the rest of us take for granted', 'the secret to effectively managing teams remotely is simple: when in doubt, communicate!' 'Asia team, before we move on from this topic, do you have anything more to add?' This gives my remote team ample opportunity to have things repeated, clarified or explained. Meetings are minuted and distributed, then followed up with a personal phone call to ensure everything was understood, and to give them a chance to clarify things privately. It also means that as a manager all major announcements and changes are captured, should I need to refer to them down the track. When it comes to managing people remotely, out of sight doesn't need to mean out of mind. By making the effort to (over)communicate and include them as part of the team, we both win — the business leverages their talents, and they feel like an engaged and valued member of the team.[45]

Duarte and Snyder explain seven critical success factors for virtual teams:

1. supportive human resource policies including career development, rewards for cross-boundary work and results, and provision of resources for virtual work
2. training and on-the-job education and development, especially in the use of the communication technology
3. standard organisational and team processes including clarification of goals, costing, planning, reporting and controlling
4. provision and maintenance of necessary electronic collaboration and communication technology
5. organisational culture that allows free flow of information, shared leadership and collaboration
6. leadership support that values teamwork, communication, learning and capitalising on diversity
7. team-leader and team-member competencies for operating in a virtual and cross-cultural environment.[46]

In some ways, virtual teams are no different from other teams, and many teams may have elements of the 'virtual team' present. However, as we saw in the OB in action, virtual teams do face particular risks, because of the context in which they operate. The crucial areas in which they differ from other teams are as follows.

- *Dependence on technology.* Participation may be inhibited if a team member is uncertain of the technology or if equipment is inadequate.
- *Absence of non-verbal cues in communication.* For example, misunderstandings in communication may occur as words are read or heard in the absence of facial expression and body gestures.
- *Place of interaction.* Outside the context of a particular place, and often a particular culture or subculture, there may be fewer initial shared assumptions and values among team members.
- *Timing of interaction.* Communication may be synchronous (real time) or asynchronous as members respond in their own time.
- *Degrees of public and private communication.* In a team that physically meets, there is more chance that conflict, domination and other aspects of human interaction are visible and unavoidable; whereas in virtual teams, it is possible that private communications between some team members, in addition to full team shared communications, may influence behaviour.
- *Recording of the group process.* The electronic media used tend to record the group process automatically, whether or not the participants desire it, which may sometimes lead to team members exhibiting extra caution about what they are willing to 'say' in writing.[47]

Virtual teams can bring together a range of members with diverse contributions without requiring that those members be located in the same place. They have the ability to transcend borders and organisational structures. However, as for any other team, there are many other requirements for team success. Hackman argues that virtual teams have the same needs and potential problems as any other team (as discussed throughout this chapter), but that it is even harder to create the right conditions for success in virtual teams.[48]

Future challenges for work teams

Work teams will continue to present various challenges in organisations. These challenges relate to use of technology, trust, accountability, diversity and the nature of leadership within the teams. While challenges are likely to be applicable to teams of all kinds, sometimes, one is particularly relevant to a certain type of group, and this is reflected in the following discussion.

Empowerment through new technology

Empowerment strategies play a crucial role in team development and maintenance. A new technology, group support systems, can assist managers as they strive to improve team performance while fostering effective and productive team member behaviours. These systems involve software that supports activities, such as brainstorming, idea consolidation, alternative evaluation and voting. Status liabilities confronting those of lesser rank in corporate groups are diminished by input anonymity, concurrent access to participation, and the capability of the group support system's voting tool to promote and restrict decision making through group consensus. The structure of the electronic meeting room where the group support system technology is housed promotes equitable interaction and suggests a commitment to task. Because verbal discussion is an integral part of the group support system process, effective leadership is essential. The group support system's tools complement the session leader's facilitation activities by contributing directly to the management and automation of the meeting process.

Trust

To build trust, members usually need face-to-face contact. Trust is important in all teams but it can often be missing. For example, a SMT might be undermined by a lack of trust when team leaders or other groups within the organisation try to control their behaviour by resorting to hierarchical authority. Employee involvement teams may feel distrust if they have worked hard to provide a recommendation to solve a problem, only to find that it is ignored. There are particular issues for trust in virtual teams. Management author Charles Handy identified the issues nearly twenty years ago, suggesting that this is the challenge and key difficulty for virtual teams, because people develop trusting relationships mainly through personal interactions.[49] A lack of daily personal contact can heighten misunderstandings and undermine a team's effectiveness.[50]

Virtual teams, therefore, need to develop a high level of trust and work hard at maintaining it. Handy suggests that to build trust among dispersed team members, creating a shared sense of purpose is paramount. He also suggests that the first meeting of the team should occur face-to-face rather than online, if this is possible. As he notes, 'Virtuality requires trust to make it work — technology on its own is not enough'.[51]

Accountability

As more organisations adopt SMTs, autonomous work groups and cross-functional teams, the question of accountability often arises, and answers are usually difficult to find. Most managers have a good idea of what it means to hold an individual accountable, but they do not always know how to apply accountability to a team. As we have already shown, there is much evidence to suggest that work teams can accomplish far more than individuals working separately. However, unless it is harnessed through an appropriate structure and monitored through individual accountability, much of the potential of a team is wasted.

Diversity

There can be many difficulties in managing diverse teams in organisations. These occur whether the organisation is located in one country or transcends national borders. Diversity can occur across a range of criteria such as gender, profession and different religious, ethnic and national cultures. In the case of culture, the impact of diversity will depend in part on the balance of team membership. Some teams may have just one representative from a minority culture (for example, an Australian team may have one Aboriginal representative), some may have two distinct cultures (a New Zealand team may have a mix of representatives from European and Maori cultures), and yet others will embrace several cultures (a Malaysian team may include those from Malay, Chinese, Indian and European backgrounds). Other diversity issues are also important and may influence team management. The purpose of the team will be relevant, and the cohesiveness and performance of the team will be affected by these issues.

The relative numbers of women in senior teams is often discussed, even though women are not a minority group in society. In some teams, there may be an imbalance of representation by profession. For example, a strategic planning team may have two or three accountants but no human resource professionals. Even the age of team members may have an impact because of different attitudes and experiences, or when, for example, one young person feels out of place among much older team members.

While diversity can improve productivity, faulty processes can undermine diverse teams. Adler provides some common explanations for problems in multicultural teams (and, in many cases, these may apply equally well to teams with other types of diversity). They include the following.

- Different perspectives and behaviours can prevent people from seeing situations in common ways.
- Dislike and mistrust can occur between members through ignorance, stereotyping or misunderstanding.
- Language and cultural norms (for instance, about punctuality or presenting bad news or different jargons) may cause conflict.
- Communication inaccuracies are common and can cause stress.

Such teams have to spend more time on building cohesion and solidarity than homogeneous teams, but the research is clear in supporting that diversity, be it based on culture through to age, as scope is provided for a greater contribution of ideas, more creativity and overall synergy within teams.[52]

Team leadership

Contemporary research recommends moving beyond SMTs to self-leading teams. Self-leading team members should have more freedom and authority to make decisions, independent of external supervision. Leaders should not compromise team membership processes by imposing control, but rather encourage and facilitate the team's self-managing capacity.[53] This capacity for self-leading is not just anchored in the joint actions of team members but also rests on the development of individuals within the team who are better equipped to self-manage and self-lead. Such an approach appreciates that team members are competent individuals who may be willing and interested in playing a role in the strategic direction of the organisation as well as influencing their own specific work performance. If self-leading teams are also oriented towards the organisation's strategy, they will be able to operate effectively on the organisation's behalf without constant referral to higher-level leaders.

A distinguishing feature of self-leading teams is that workers perform work more for the natural (intrinsic) rewards that are built into the task than to receive externally administered rewards. However, self-leading, team-based work systems can only work under two fundamental conditions:

1. a significant involvement of the workforce in determining the direction of the organisation as well as pursuing that direction
2. an opportunity for the work teams to influence that direction, especially as it relates to their specific work performance.

Summary

Teams and groups

A group is a number of people who interact with one another for a common purpose, whereas a team is a group of people who function as a unit. A team is a small group of people with complementary skills who work together as a unit to achieve a common purpose for which they hold themselves collectively accountable.

Teams and their effectiveness

Teams operate on three levels so that members engaged in team tasks are also concerned with individual needs and the maintenance of the team. Teams can operate to make or do things, or to run things in an organisation. The most effective teams have members with a balance of complementary skills and strengths so that they can achieve synergy.

Team-building approaches

Team building is a series of planned action steps designed to gather and analyse data on the functioning of a team. It is also about implementing changes to increase the team's operating effectiveness. Teamwork occurs when members of a team work together in a way that represents certain core values, all of which promote the use of skills to accomplish common goals. Team building is thus a way of building the capacity for teamwork and high performance. The team-building process is participative and engages all team members in identifying problems and opportunities, planning appropriate actions, making individual commitments to implement these actions, and conducting appropriate evaluation and feedback activities. Team building can involve brainstorming to generate uninhibited ideas, facilitators to raise self-awareness and group awareness, and training to develop team skills. Some specific team-building processes are formal retreats, continual improvement and outdoor experiences.

Team performance and cohesiveness

An important aspect of any team is the set of norms within which it operates. Norms are rules or standards of member behaviour; they are ideas or beliefs about what is appropriate behaviour for team members. Norms identify the way in which 'loyal' members are supposed to behave. As such, they can exert a major influence on teams when members adhere to them. The clarification of roles is important for all members of work teams. Role ambiguities and conflicts create anxieties and stress, and can detract from performance and personal satisfaction. Cohesiveness is a measure of the attractiveness of a team for its members. In a highly cohesive team, members value their place in the team and are very loyal to it. Thus, an important rule of thumb is that members of highly cohesive teams conform to team norms. Consequently, the combination of the team performance norms and level of cohesiveness can reveal a lot about its performance potential. The most favourable situation for any manager or team leader is to be in charge of a highly cohesive team with positive performance norms; the positive norms point behaviour in desired directions, and the high cohesiveness creates desires to live up to the expectations set by these norms. Good managers are able to influence team cohesiveness in ways that support the accomplishment of long-term team effectiveness.

Types of teams

An employee involvement team is any team whose members meet regularly outside of their formal task assignments to address important work-related problems and concerns. Most typically, these teams deal with issues involving total quality management and the quest for continual improvement in operations. Popular types of problem-solving teams are the quality circle, the task force and the autonomous work team. The latter was the precursor to the SMT. A SMT is a work group whose members collectively take responsibility for performing the group task and making many of the 'supervisory' decisions relating to task performance on a day-to-day basis. The team members, in the full sense of the word, 'manage' themselves. The traditional level of supervisory management is eliminated, and in its place the work team agrees to accept responsibility for self-management. Members of this team will plan, complete and evaluate their own work; they will collectively train and evaluate one another in task performance; they will share tasks and responsibilities; and they may even determine one another's pay grades. Such teams are based on the concept of empowerment, and offer another creative way to allow people to become more involved in important decisions affecting their work. Under the right circumstances, SMTs can contribute to improved productivity for organisations and improved quality of working life for their members. Virtual teams have members who work interdependently towards common goals even though they are not together in the same place at the same time.

Future challenges for work teams

While teams potentially have many advantages, there are some challenges. New technology can enable more empowerment in teams and enhance decision making. However, the lack of face-to-face interaction can undermine levels of trust in virtual teams. Also, team decision making can lead to a diffusion of accountability for decisions. This may be a problem when quality needs to be monitored and improved or corrective action taken. Diversity in teams, encompassing factors from multiculturalism and religion to age and gender, may lead to problems such as conflict, misunderstanding, stress and mistrust. This complication is increasing with the growth in global and virtual teams. Finally, there is still debate about whether there should be team leaders or whether team members should be equipped to self-lead in teams.

CHAPTER 7 study guide

Key terms

autonomous work teams, *p. 268*
brainstorming, *p. 260*
cohesiveness, *p. 263*
employee involvement teams, *p. 267*
groups, *p. 250*
norms, *p. 262*

quality circles, *p. 267*
role, *p. 262*
role ambiguity, *p. 263*
role conflict, *p. 263*
self-managing teams (SMTs), *p. 268*
task forces, *p. 268*

team building, *p. 253*
team IQ, *p. 252*
teams, *p. 249*
teamwork, *p. 253*
virtual team, *p. 270*

Review questions

1. Explain the key differences between teams and groups and the reasons organisations might wish to instigate teams in their organisations.
2. Explain what makes an effective team.

3. What are the likely performance outcomes for a highly cohesive team and how can team cohesion be increased or decreased?
4. Explain the features of virtual teams and why technology is so important in operating them.

Application questions

1. Your team leader is always pushing your work group to work harder, be more productive and be the most successful production team in the company. You and your fellow team members just laugh at him and get on with your work. You feel you are all productive and there is no need to work any harder. You get your weekly pay and working harder will not change that. What is the likelihood that the team could be more productive and what can the leader do to improve productivity?

2. Your team members have been told you are to be taken to a formal retreat for some team-building activities. The members of your group have been working together for five years and are familiar with each other, though there are disagreements and conflict sometimes about who is doing the work. What benefits do you think may come from this facilitation, and why?

3. Your respected and successful team leader has left the organisation and your team is getting a new team leader. After years of being an effective team with this team leader, what are the likely challenges your team faces?

4. Your organisation produces linen household goods. In the production of those goods, groups of

15–20 employees typically work in a production unit with a supervisor, who gives them frequent directions about what is required. The organisation has decided to move towards a model of self-managing teams, after trialling it successfully in the finance and the human resources departments. What are the likely changes that employees will face in changing to this way of working, and how should management introduce the changes?

5. Your team is close and members of the team will do anything to help each other out, including covering up for each other if there is a crisis or poor performance. What issues are there for the performance of the group?

6. You have been assigned to lead a new team of five members with each member being located in a different global city (you work for a multinational company with offices in the United States, China, Malaysia, Brazil, Australia and New Zealand). Since the success of the team depends on using new technologies to communicate, what can you do to encourage full and equal participation by team members and what will you do to strengthen and enhance team behaviours?

Research questions

1. Find two local examples, and/or examples from journal articles, of organisations that have introduced teams. Investigate and compare the organisations in terms of:
   (a) the method of introducing the teams
   (b) the success of the teams
   (c) the perceived differences between team-based management and what existed before.

2. Search for at least two team-building consultants on the internet. Look for what sorts of team-building processes they offer. What do they promise for organisations that use their services? How do their programs compare with each other?

Running project

1. Look back at the tasks you completed for chapter 6. Now that you have studied teams, which of the groups you examined in chapter 6 could be described as teams and which could not?
2. Describe the team-building exercises your organisation undertakes.

3. Does the organisation use self-managing teams? Why?
4. Describe a virtual team in your organisation. Be sure to examine why it exists and how the team members work together.

Individual activity

Identifying norms that influence teams

Objectives
1. To help you determine the norms operating in an organisation
2. To assess the strength of response to particular norms
3. To help clarify the importance of norms as influences on team behaviour

Time: 60 minutes

Procedure
1. Choose an organisation about which you know quite a bit.
2. Insert each of the statements below into the following sentence: If an employee in your organisation were to [insert statement here], most other employees would, too.

   Statements
   1. show genuine concern for the problems that face the organisation and make suggestions about solving them (organisational/personal pride)
   2. set very high personal standards of performance (performance/excellence)
   3. try to make the work group operate more like a team when dealing with issues or problems (teamwork/communication)
   4. think of going to a supervisor with a problem (leadership/supervision)
   5. evaluate expenditures in terms of the benefits they will provide for the organisation (profitability/cost effectiveness)
   6. express concern for the wellbeing of other members of the organisation (colleague/associate relations)
   7. keep a customer or client waiting while looking after matters of personal convenience (customer/client relations)
   8. criticise another employee who is trying to improve things in the work situation (innovativeness/creativity)
   9. actively look to expand their knowledge to be able to do a better job (training/development)
   10. be perfectly honest in answering this questionnaire (candour/openness).

3. For each statement (within the question), indicate your response it terms of A, B, C, D or E.
   A. Strongly agree or encourage it
   B. Agree with it or encourage it
   C. Consider it unimportant
   D. Disagree with or discourage it
   E. Strongly disagree with or discourage it

Evaluation

Review your results to decide whether the organisation is likely to provide a suitable environment for effective teams.

Group activity

Brainstorming

Brainstorming really is a fairly simple concept to understand. Most people think they know it well, and they probably do. But even though they know it well, people struggle to demonstrate it in a small group. As outlined in the chapter, effective brainstorming is more than just following a simple set of rules and guidelines.

Objective

To practise your brainstorming skills
Time: 20–60 minutes

Process

Break into small groups. Discuss the concept of brainstorming, using material from the chapter. Review the following basic rules for brainstorming. Select a topic for brainstorming. Choose a topic that is a problem of real concern; for example, how can we get everyone to come to lectures on time? How can we get class members to participate more in class? What are the best criteria for evaluating students undertaking an organisational behaviour course? Begin the brainstorming period. When everyone has no more ideas, formally stop the brainstorming process and begin the closure discussion.

Some basic brainstorming rules
- Each group member is asked to contribute at least one idea.
- No member is allowed to dismiss or criticise the idea or suggestion of another member.
- List each idea, even if the same or similar idea has already been posted.
- Everyone should be explicitly asked to contribute; for example, 'David, do you have any idea to add?'
- Record ideas as quickly as they are stated.
- Encourage group members to contribute more ideas when their contributions slow.
- Encourage funny, silly or seemingly foolish ideas.
- Make sure, before stopping, that all possible ideas are heard and posted. Go around the room and ask everyone.
- Encourage group members to build on or add to ideas already suggested.
- Important: do not evaluate the ideas of others while they are being expressed or written down by the brainstorming facilitator or group leader. If this happens, in either a negative or a positive way, the leader should ask the person evaluating to add another idea to the list, thereby channelling such participation into a contribution. Every idea expressed by any member of the group counts. Every idea must therefore be included and added to the list.

Evaluation

At the end of this exercise evaluate how effectively you operated as a team.

Case study: Understanding the self

Mind Warriors (www.mindwarriors.com) is a company set up by Steve Hill and Wade Jackson, who have created JOLT Challenge — a nine-week self-intelligence program that focuses on developing self-awareness and self-management for people within teams. Its premise is that leaders cannot lead others until they can effectively lead themselves. Steve and Wade believe that everyone in business is a leader these days, even if it's just a leader of one — themselves. In a 2013 study by the Hay Group on Global top 20 Best Companies for Leadership, it was found that 90 per cent of the 'best companies' expect employees to lead, regardless of whether they have a formal position of authority, and that best companies give all employees the opportunity to develop and practise the capabilities needed to lead.[54] It is widely acknowledged that self-awareness is the cornerstone to emotional intelligence, but *knowing* is not enough — one must be able to *do* as well, and that is where self-management comes in.

Team work and team building are wonderful buzzwords often bandied around the corporate environment; however, it's important to keep in mind that a team is made up of a group of individuals who are working collaboratively towards a shared outcome. Since a team is a group of individuals, it's essential to look at the prerequisite elements that create the environment for these individuals to work together effectively. One of the most important elements is trust. In a low-trust environment, people are looking out for themselves, so there is little open communication or creativity. Teams need to build trust, and this takes time. It doesn't have to take a lot of time, but people have to feel they are in a safe environment. Once people feel they are in a safe environment, they are willing to share, take risks and make themselves vulnerable, which improves the team spirit. Individuals become more willing to sacrifice their personal goals for the sake of the team, in pursuit of their common goal.

Mind Warriors' JOLT Challenge has four components: a book, a work journal with over 150 transformation tools, 10 weekly sessions with a facilitator, and a measurement component. The program looks at all areas of one's life, including health, wealth and relationships, and has both professional and personal benefits. Wade and Steve believe that while you can measure and track the changes this program delivers to an individual, and that changes will also feed into the organisation in terms of socialisation, higher trust, better communication and enhanced creativity.

The Telecom Women In Leadership group were already incredible leaders; busy, successful women juggling work, full lives and families. However, one issue was remarkably consistent throughout the group. Many of the women in the group were perfectionists, no doubt this was one reason they were so successful. Yet, in some circumstances this was holding them back from achieving their leadership potential. They experienced this in the Mind Warriors' JOLT Challenge classes as the group struggled to come to grips

with new exercises that threw them into a state of chaos. Yet, once they had mastery, they inevitably performed the exercises with distinction. Participants also shared that this trait showed up in the work environment through lack of delegation and taking on excessive workload themselves, often impinging on their productivity and work/life balance. They developed the ability to welcome the state of chaos with the confidence they would get through that and eventually gain mastery. In the meantime, they embraced some of the failures that come with chaos and capitalised on the new ideas that often spring out of those failures. This was applied in the workplace through increased delegation and creating time to focus on the important, rather than the urgent stuff, which after all is what leaders should do. Teams need to embrace diversity because solutions seldom lie with one individual alone. However, it is a lack of appreciation for diversity that often creates problems for many teams. This lack of appreciation can result in individuals or cliques within teams playing office politics, patch protection, a silo mentality and, ultimately, preferring personal goals ahead of collective ones. Effective teams have self-aware individuals — people who are comfortable in their own skin.

Steve and Wade travelled to Singapore to initiate a project involving JOLT Challenge as part of the CLD (Centre for Leadership Development) with SAFTI (Singapore Armed Forces Training Institute). As a country with compulsory military training for youth, all male Singaporean citizens and second-generation permanent residents must enrol in the military for 2 years of training when they reach 18 years of age. Steve and Wade noted that, in a multi-cultural society like Singapore, it is a great way to bring people together under a set of common values, while providing skills, discipline and direction for many of their youth. A key feature of SAFTI is that it acknowledges self-intelligence (self-awareness and self-management) as a meta-competency among other core competencies in its leadership development. The JOLT Challenge content and methodology therefore aligns extremely well with its existing frameworks. When people better understand themselves, there is a higher likelihood they will accept and understand others better, having a higher propensity for diversity.[55]

Questions

1. Evaluate how developing the self-awareness of an individual can benefit the development of strong, cohesive teams.
2. How is self-intelligence (self-awareness and self-management) a meta-competency for leadership development?
3. What are the likely benefits to an organisation if they have self-aware leaders?
4. Why do you think it is important to have a time-spaced program to create behavioural change?

End notes

1. Address by the Chief of Army, Lieutenant General David Morrison, AO at the launch of the fourth value of the Australian Army, 'Respect', at Lavarack Barracks Townsville (Thursday 4 July 2013), www.army.gov.au.
2. A Wiewiora, B Trigunarsyah, G Murphy and V Coffey, 'Organizational culture and willingness to share knowledge: a competing values perspective in Australian contexts', *International Journal of Project Management*, vol. 31, no. 8 (2013), pp. 1163–74.
3. Various sites within the PS21, Office of Public Service Division, Singapore — see especially 'People-WITS', http://app.ps21.gov.sg.
4. B Kim, 'Competitive priorities and supply chain strategy in the fashion industry', *Qualitative Market Research: An International Journal*, vol. 16, no. 2 (2013), pp. 214–42.
5. ibid.
6. B Senior and S Swailes, 'The dimensions of management team performance: a repertory grid study', *Journal of Productivity and Performance Management*, vol. 53, no. 4 (2004), pp. 317–33.
7. D Garvin, 'The processes of organization and management', *MIT Sloan Management Review*, vol. 39, no. 4 (1998).
8. 'Sushi bonding', *NZ Management Magazine* (August 2010).
9. B Murray, '*What is a high performing team and what does it do differently?*' (2012), http://fortinberrymurray.com.
10. For a good discussion of team building see W Dyer, J Dyer and W Dyer, *Team building* (San Francisco: Jossey-Bass, 2013).
11. JR Katzenbach and DK Smith, 'The discipline of teams,' *Harvard Business Review* (March/April 1993), pp. 118–19.
12. Based in part on Katzenbach and Smith, op. cit., p. 113.
13. ibid., p. 115.
14. B Erdogan and T Bauer, *Leader-member exchange (LMX) theory: the relational approach to leadership, Oxford handbook of leadership and organizations* (Oxford: Oxford University Press, 2013).
15. DT Hooper and R Martin, 'Measuring perceived LMX variability within teams and its impact on procedural justice climate,' in AI Glendon, BM Thompson and B Myors (eds), *Advances in organisational psychology* (Brisbane: Australian Academic Press, 2007, p. 258 citing J. Lee (2001).
16. ibid, p. 255.
17. ibid, p. 249.
18. KE Hultman, 'The ten commandments of team leadership,' *Training and Development*, vol. 52, no. 2 (February 1998), p. 12.
19. Developed from material in P Wilson interviewing L Gratton, 'Heat treatment,' *HRMonthly* (April 2008), pp. 22–27.
20. C Heung and A Wong, 'Trust Drives Empowerment in Chinese Hotels', *Research Horizons*, vol. 6, no. 2 (2012), pp. 7–8.
21. S Thiagarajan, 'A game for cooperative learning,' *Training and Development*, vol. 46, no. 5 (May 1992), pp. 35–41.
22. G Thompson and PF Pearce, 'The team–trust game,' *Training and Development*, vol. 46, no. 5 (May 1992), pp. 42–3.
23. K Vincent, 'Brainstorming is brilliant', *NZ Management Magazine* (March 2010).
24. Outward Bound Leadership School, www.outwardbound.org.
25. See DC Feldman, 'The development and enforcement of group norms,' *Academy of Management Review*, vol. 9 (1984), pp. 47–53.
26. Developed from RF Allen and S Pilnick, 'Confronting the shadow organization: how to detect and defeat negative norms,' *Organizational Dynamics* (Spring 1973), pp. 6–10.
27. For a good summary of research on group cohesiveness, see ME Shaw, *Group dynamics* (New York: McGraw-Hill, 1971), pp. 110–12, 192.
28. 'Free spirits: volunteering to learn' (interview with D Snelson), *Management Woman* (July 2005), pp. 15–16.
29. RA Guzzo and E Salas (eds), *Team effectiveness and decision making in organizations* (San Francisco: Jossey-Bass, 1995); JR Hackman (ed.), *Groups that work and those that don't* (San Francisco: Jossey-Bass, 1990).
30. Arnold, '*Workplace teamwork: Where not to use teams*', pp. 40–42, www.sideroad.com.
31. D Ancona and H Bresnan, *X-teams: How to build teams that lead, innovate and succeed* (Boston, MA: Harvard Business School Press, 2013).
32. See K Ohmae, 'Quality control circles: they work and don't work,' *Wall Street Journal* (29 March 1982), p. 16; RP Steel, AJ Mento, BL Dilla, NK Ovalle and RF Lloyd, 'Factors influencing the success and failure of two quality circles programs,' *Journal of Management*, vol. 11, no. 1 (1985), pp. 99–119; EE Lawler III and SA Mohrman, 'Quality circles: after the honeymoon,' *Organizational Dynamics*, vol. 15, no. 4 (1987), pp. 42–54.
33. This term was specifically developed during World War II when British firm Lockheed Martin was contracted to design advanced jet engine technology to counter German developments. It did so in 143 days and Lockheed now holds the trademark. See Lockheed Martin, 2008, 'Skunk Works®', www.skunkworks.net.
34. AG Dobbelaere and KH Goeppinger, 'The right and wrong way to set up a self-directed work team,' *Human Resource Professional*, vol. 5 (Winter, 1993), pp. 31–35.
35. Katzenbach and Smith, op. cit., p. 112.
36. RS Wellins, WC Byham and J.M. Wilson, *Empowered teams* (San Francisco: Jossey-Bass, 1993).
37. C Rautenbauch, '*Employee involvement @ Google Australia*' (1 June 2014), http://prezi.com.
38. L Lacy, 'Self-managed work groups step-by-step,' *Journal for Quality and Participation*, vol. 15, no. 3 (June 1992), pp. 68–73.
39. RM Belbin, *Management teams*, (Oxford, UK: Routledge, 2012).

40. ibid.; Developed in part from RS Wellins, WC Byham and JM Wilson, 'Proactive teams achieve inspiring results,' *World Executive's Digest* (October 1992), pp. 18–24.

41. G Berry 'Enhancing effectiveness on virtual teams', *Journal of Business Communication*, vol. 48 no. 2 (2011), pp. 186–206.

42. D Leonard, P Brands and A Edmondson, 'Virtual teams: using communications technology to manage geographically dispersed development groups,' *Managing Knowledge Assets, Creativity and Innovation* (31 August 2011), p. 325.

43. Beca, '*Training for the real world in the simulation systems sandpit*', www.beca.com.

44. G. Tsamis, '*Are you getting the best from your remote staff? 6 tips to make it work*', http://blog.michaelpage.asia (New Zealand, April 2008), pp. 48–51.

45. ibid.

46. D Duarte and NT Snyder, *Mastering virtual teams*, 3rd ed. (San Francisco: Jossey-Bass, 2011), pp. 3–23.

47. G Elwyn, T Greenhalgh and F Macfarlane, *Groups: a guide to small group work in healthcare, management, education and research* (Abingdon, UK: Radcliffe Medical Press, 2001), pp. 206–14.

48. JR Hackman, *Leading teams: setting the stage for great performances* (Boston: Harvard Business School Press, 2002), pp. 130–2.

49. C Handy, 'Trust and the virtual organization,' *Harvard Business Review* (May/June 1995).

50. G Tsamis, '*Are you getting the best from your remote staff? 6 tips to make it work*, http://blog.michaelpage.asia.

51. Handy, op. cit.

52. Y Guillaume, J Dawson, S Woods, C Sacramento and M West 'Getting diversity at work to work: what we know and what we still don't know', *Journal of Occupational and Organizational Psychology*, vol. 86 (2013), pp. 123–141.

53. AJ Sylva, '*Are you a collaborative leader?*' (16 June 2011), http://blogs.hbr.org.

54. HayGroup website, '*Best companies for leadership*', www.haygroup.com/bestcompaniesforleadership.

55. W Jackson and S Hill, '*SAFTI first in Singapore*', www.joltchallenge.com.

MANAGING ORGANISATIONAL PROCESSES AND PERFORMANCE

CHAPTER 8

ORGANISATIONAL STRUCTURE AND DESIGN

LEARNING OBJECTIVES

After studying this chapter, you should be able to:

1. define and compare organisational design and structure and discuss the relationship between them

2. explain the basic factors that impact upon designing organisational structures and what organisational designs may emerge

3. describe the different types of organisational goals and different methods of controlling and coordinating the activities of organisational members

4. define vertical specialisation and explain what is meant by chain of command, unity of command and span of control

5. describe and compare different patterns of horizontal specialisation used by organisations

6. describe some of the emerging forms of organisation design and their implications for the individuals within them.

STRUCTURE, DESIGN AND PARTNERSHIPS

The way in which organisations can be structured is diverse. In addition, there is a complex web of inter-organisational partnerships or collaborations that also relate to organisational structure and design.

Businesses range from huge global corporations to one-person operations. An 'organisation' such as Lark Distillery, Tasmania's first licensed whisky distillery since 1939, started as a small family affair in 1992.[1] They filled their first barrel with spirit from a hobby-sized 75-litre still. 'When we started the idea was simply to see if we could make good malt whisky in Tasmania, not necessarily with the idea to establish an industry,' says founder, Bill Lark. 'The fact is that the whisky soon proved to be of such good character that the business quickly grew up around us.' The Lark Distillery quickly began to outgrow its modest set-up. In order to cater for a flood of orders and the possibility of commercial trade, the distillery moved to a more suitable site in the historic town of Richmond. With the first of Tasmania's malt whisky maturing in oak barrels, the Larks pursued the idea of diversifying their product range. Bill's daughter (one of the three co-founders, with Lyn Lark, her mother being the third), Kristy explains that, 'Our main focus was the single malt but to keep the business afloat while we waited for it to mature, we decided to do other products as well.'[2] Lark Distillery now runs an 1800-litre copper pot still along with a 500-litre spirit still, and produces ten to twelve 100-litre barrels per month, and has moved to premises on the Hobart waterfront — providing greater access to Tasmania's growing tourist market. The range of distilled products includes the flagship single malt whisky, premium vodka, gin, and TASI aromatica bush liqueur. The size of the operation has also grown in numbers, with 2014 seeing Lark Distillery winning Telstra's small business of the year award and employing staff from cellar door retailing, production, marketing, exporting and their new venture of whisky tourism. Bill sees a bright future for the distillery. 'The whisky market has been dominated by the large international whisky companies, but I believe the market for handcrafted whiskies will have the strongest growth into the foreseeable future. In ten years' time I see my daughter and General Manager, Kristy, taking the world by storm'.[3]

Collaborations have played a large part in the success of the distillery, from the maltings supplied by the local Cascade Brewery, locally produced stills and cut-down wine barrels by a local cooper, to Scottish whisky maker Glenfiddich's invitation to be a 'sister city distillery' (with plans for a work exchange).[4] These show how collaborations between organisations can be important in helping to achieve common goals, gain fresh perspectives, undertake vast projects, and move beyond entrenched approaches. Alternatively, an organisation might choose to outsource to another company in the same or another country. Employees within the organisations must liaise and work closely with each other. Public–private partnerships (PPPs) are often formed to work together on major physical infrastructure such as bridges, major roads and hospitals (the Sydney Cross City Tunnel is one example[5] and the designing, building, financing and running of the Singapore Sports Hub is another).[6] They can also involve social infrastructure and/or the development of social capital or a public–private community partnership (PPCP). One example is the Business Capability Partnership's (a group of public and private organisations) objective to build New Zealand's management and business capability into the future.[7] Another is the Byrraju Foundation's 'Model Schools' project, which partners the government, foundation partners and the village community to pool together resources and best practices for the benefit of rural children in India's Andhra Pradesh province.[8]

Organisations also form partnerships with other organisations for the purposes of fulfilling corporate social responsibility (CSR), which can benefit the bottom line of the organisation as well as benefiting the environment and society. For example, United Motor Works in Malaysia partners with the Malaysian Medical Relief Society (Mercy) as part of its CSR program. Besides donating vehicles for Mercy Malaysia to work in remote areas and setting up a community grant, the partnership also facilitates UMW staff to participate in training with Mercy Malaysia and to help in relief missions when disasters strike.[9]

Introduction

As the examples in the chapter opening show, there are many types of organisation and many options for organisational design. Every organisation must decide how to divide its work or activities, how to coordinate all work-related activities and how to control these activities to ensure that goals are achieved. When there are connections or partnerships with other organisations, these issues of managing, dividing, coordinating and controlling activities also apply and affect the people in the organisations. The organisation must consider its external environment and the internal systems and processes used to transform inputs to outputs. These differences help to explain, for example, why a sports club is different to a manufacturing company. A manager of any organisation must ensure consistency between the structure of the organisation, the scale of its operations, the tasks at hand, the needs of all stakeholders and the strategic direction of the organisation. This consistency between structure and operations distinguishes successful organisations from less successful ones.

In this chapter we will first explain the difference between organisational structure and organisational design and then consider the various factors that may impinge upon the design; that is, the scale of the organisation, the technology it utilises, its environment and its strategy. Collectively they will all influence how the structural elements are combined into a suitable design for the organisation. While certain emerging forms of organisational design are presented at the end of the chapter, we must remember that every organisation will be unique.

The basic structural attributes of organisations include the different types of goals that organisations develop and implement. They also involve the techniques used to effect control and coordination within organisations. Other structural considerations relate to how the organisation allocates authority and manages the chain of command and how labour is divided into organisational units. These elements are, in essence, the building blocks of structure. They reflect various choices that can be made when organising how work is to be done and goals are to be achieved. Understanding all these elements is necessary to predict how they affect employee behaviour.

Organisational structure and design

Organisational structure and organisational design are two different but closely related concepts. The process of choosing and implementing a structural configuration is referred to as organisational design.[10] Some researchers have recently argued that organisational design has been largely ignored, but is critical for organisational performance as it drives strategy formulation and implementation, as well as providing a framework for identifying and enabling organisational change.[11] Organisational executives should adjust the structural configuration of their organisations to best meet the challenges faced at any given point in time.

Formal structure shows the intended configuration of positions, job duties and lines of authority among different parts of the enterprise. This structure emerges from the process of designing the organisation. It reflects the goals of the organisation and also reflects the contingency factors that impact on the organisation design, such as the organisation's size, environment, technology and strategy. The formal structure also involves the decisions that

Organisational design is the process of choosing and implementing a structural configuration for an organisation.

The **formal structure** is the intended configuration of positions, job duties and lines of authority among the component parts of an organisation.

are made about who has authority, how the organisation and its members will be divided up to achieve tasks and how activities will be controlled and coordinated. We emphasise the word 'formal' simply because the intentions of organisational designers are not always fully realised. While no formal structure can provide the detail needed to show all the activities within an organisation, it is still important because it provides the foundations for managerial action; that is, it outlines the jobs to be done, the people (in terms of position) who will perform specific activities, and the ways in which the total task of the organisation will be accomplished.

Organisation charts are diagrams that depict the formal structures of organisations.

Organisation charts are diagrams that provide a visual representation of the formal structures of organisations. A typical chart shows the various positions, the position holders and the lines of authority that link them to one another. The top half of figure 8.1 is a partial organisation chart for a small regional university. The chart allows university employees to locate their positions in the structure and to identify the lines of authority linking them with others in the organisation. In this figure, the head of financial services reports to the registrar and secretary, who reports to the vice-chancellor (the chief executive officer of the university).

Such charts predominate in representing organisational structures. However, there has been some criticism that they show only lines of authority and the division of the organisation into different units. An alternative means of mapping organisational activities has been developed by Mintzberg and Van der Heyden. Their organigraphs show how an organisation works, what it does, and how people, products and information interact. This can bring more insight, or at least a different perspective, to explaining the behaviour of people in organisations. The bottom half of figure 8.1 shows a simple 'organigraph' for teaching in a university.

In summary, organisational design involves the choices made about how to structure the organisation, and the implementation of those choices. The formal structure explains in more detailed ways how the structural elements are configured. The terms 'organisational structure' and 'organisational design' are sometimes used interchangeably. Since organisational design is a structural configuration, the reasons for this are quite apparent.

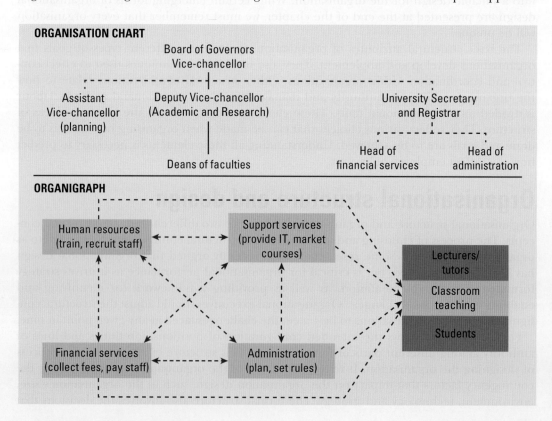

FIGURE 8.1 A partial organisation chart for a university and an organigraph for university teaching

Source: Organigraph developed from H Mintzberg and L Van der Heyden, 'Organigraphs: drawing how companies really work,' *Harvard Business Review* (September/October 1999), pp. 87–94.

In the following sections, we will examine basic ways of understanding the design choices and structural features of organisations.

Factors influencing organisational design

Some particular factors will have an impact on the choices made when designing the organisation: scale, technology, environment and strategy. This analysis will identify the way in which these factors impact and their implications on design. Some of the possible design outcomes that may emerge are described at the end of the chapter.

Scale

The more individuals in an organisation, the more possible interconnections there are among them and the less the likelihood of direct interpersonal contact between everyone. Thus, as organisations grow, their structure is likely to become more complex. More advanced electronic communication methods and policies, rules and procedures are used as substitutes for direct supervision, both to save money and to ensure consistency. Larger organisations can be more efficient, with potential economies of scale in production and services through repetition, but then there is more need to break tasks down into parts, to allocate authority and to make sure everything and everyone is acting in a coordinated way to achieve the organisation's goals. Larger organisations often have more products, production processes, geographic locations and so on. This additional complexity calls for more sophisticated organisational designs.

Technology

Organisations are said to arrange their internal structures to meet the dictates of their dominant 'technologies' or work flows; this is known as the **technological imperative**.[12] The importance of technology was identified back in the 1960s. **Technology** is the combination of resources, knowledge and techniques that creates a product or service output for an organisation. The match between structure and technology is important for the successful design of organisations. Thompson[13] and Woodward[14] present different classifications that illustrate the possible diversity in technology and these are shown in table 8.1. For example, Woodward's successful small-batch and continuous-process plants have flexible structures with small work groups at the bottom; more rigidly structured plants are less successful. In contrast, successful mass production operations are rigidly structured and have large work groups at the bottom.

The **technological imperative** is the idea that if an organisation does not adjust its internal structure to the requirements of the technology, it will not be successful.

Technology is the combination of resources, knowledge and techniques that creates a product or service output for an organisation.

TABLE 8.1 Thompson's and Woodward's classifications of technology

Sources: Developed from James D Thompson, *Organization in action* (New York: McGraw-Hill, 1967); and Joan Woodward, *Industrial organization: theory and practice* (London: Oxford University Press, 1965).

Thompson	
Intensive technology	Involves a team of highly interdependent specialists using a variety of techniques, but no certain techniques, to produce the desired outcomes for non-routine problems or situations. Because the problem is unique there are no standard operating procedures and there must be mutual adjustments to deal with it. Examples include the team in a hospital emergency room and a research development laboratory.
Mediating technology	Links parties that want to become interdependent, such as wholesalers who link producers and retailers. Also, banks link creditors and depositors, and store money and information to facilitate such exchanges. Interdependent depositors and creditors rely on each other through pooled activity of the bank. If one creditor defaults on a loan, no one depositor is injured.
Long-linked technology	The way to produce the desired outcomes is known so the task is broken into sequential, interdependent steps. An example is the high-volume car assembly line.

(continued)

TABLE 8.1 (*continued*)

Woodward	
Small-batch	A variety of custom products, such as tailored suits, are made to fit customer specifications. The machinery and equipment used are generally not elaborate, but considerable craftsmanship is often needed. For example, producing a unique marketing campaign or television movie.
Continuous-process	Producing a few products with considerable automation in an ongoing process. Examples include automated chemical plants and oil refineries.
Mass production	Similar to Thompson's long-linked technology; produces one or a few products using an assembly-line type of system. The work of one group depends on that of another, the equipment is typically sophisticated and the workers are given detailed instructions. Cars and refrigerators are produced in this way.

There are other possible technologies that can be described. For example, with more flexible manufacturing systems, there is a trend towards more 'mass customisation', where custom adjustments are possible, even in a mass production process. Such a process would allow an infinite variety of goods and services unique to customer requirements. For example, customers' preferences for colour and fabric could be accommodated, while otherwise, mass production occurs. Australian 'mass customisation' companies range from Sneaking Duck, which offers a pureplay concept to fit you with the perfect glasses frames for any prescription, to Rozibaby, which offers the world's first fully customisable pram. The concept is so unique that it's netted the company a coveted Product of the Year Award at a recent industry event night.[15]

Dell Corporation has also operated under a similar arrangement, with online customers being able to specify their particular computer requirements when buying their own personal computer, without the intervention of 'middlemen'. While Dell has always sold this way online, it has more recently had to surrender to market pressure to sell its products through retail stores such as Wal-Mart (in the United States) and Officeworks (in Australia).[16] Notwithstanding, the 'mass customisation' trend looks likely to gather more momentum with new technologies like three-dimensional printing, which makes it as cheap to create single items as it is to produce thousands, reducing the need for economies of scale in manufacturing.[17]

Environment

An effective organisational design reflects powerful external forces as well as the desires of employees and managers. There are two main sets of parameters we can use to explain the environment. First, as open systems, organisations need to receive various inputs from their environment and sell various outputs to their environment. Environments can be labelled as either:

- *general* — that is, the set of cultural, economic, legal–political and educational conditions found in the areas in which the organisation operates. These can include different global economies and markets
- *specific* — which involves the mix of owners, suppliers, distributors, government agencies and competitors with which it interacts.

Another basic concern in analysing the environment of the organisation is its complexity. **Environmental complexity** is the estimated magnitude of the problems and opportunities in the organisation's environment, as evidenced by the combination of the following three main factors that emerge uniquely, in the context of each organisation, from the general and specific environments.[18]

1. *Environmental richness.* The environment is *richer* when the economy is growing and improving, customers are spending more and investors investing more; when individuals are improving their education, and others the organisation relies upon are also

Environmental complexity is the magnitude of the problems and opportunities in the organisation's environment, as evidenced by the degree of richness, interdependence and uncertainty.

prospering. Organisational survival is easier, there is more dynamism and there are more opportunities for change. The opposite is *decline*, which occurs in economic recession. Typically, workers may be laid off and the number of working units and managers may be reduced.

2. *Environmental interdependence.* The link between external interdependence and organisational design is often subtle and indirect. The organisation may co-opt powerful outsiders onto its board of directors, and/or adjust its design strategy to absorb or buffer the demands of a more powerful external element. For example, it may include a public relations unit to deal with public pressures or to lobby government for policy change. Because of increasing internationalisation, many organisations face a number of 'general environments' and maintain highly complex and diffused interdependencies with them.

3. *Uncertainty and volatility.* In times of change, investments quickly become outmoded and internal operations no longer work as expected. The obvious organisational design response to uncertainty and volatility is to opt for a more flexible structure. However, these pressures may run counter to those that arise from large size and technology and the organisation may continue to struggle while adjusting its design a little at a time.

The global financial crisis and organisational design

OBinAction

Organisations around the world were hit badly hit by the 2007–2008 global financial crisis, and many embarked on major restructuring plans to help them overcome the subsequent global downturn. They included easily recognisable corporations like General Motors, Reebok, Samsung, United Airlines, Toshiba, Newsweek and Qantas. The Australian airline Qantas, like most of the major global air carriers, was hit by a combination of falling passengers due to the global recession, increased competition, and rapidly rising costs from rising fuel prices. This has resulted in Qantas cutting over 4000 jobs, including 1500 management roles, set to be shed by the end of June 2015 and reversing parts of its 'segmentation strategy' (where businesses such as engineering and catering operated on a stand-alone basis), by bringing these back under the Qantas Operations division. While the Australian public may be fixated on the competition between the airlines, the reality is that 'their futures will be determined within a global arena in which airline survival and success is determined by a vast array of economic, political, social and environmental factors'.[19]

Strategy

Organisational strategy is the process of positioning the organisation in its competitive environment and implementing actions to compete successfully.[20] The study of linking strategy, organisational design and performance has a long tradition in organisational analysis. While it cannot be covered extensively here, the important point is that the organisation's strategy will be driving its goals and vision, and an organisational design must be established to achieve the vision. For example, an organisation may be endeavouring to become a market leader by having the cheapest or best value-for-money product. Alternatively, it may be trying to differentiate its product from others. In other words, the degree to which the

Organisational strategy is the process of positioning the organisation in the competitive environment and implementing actions to compete successfully.

organisation's strategy is aiming to produce standardised products, and the narrow or broad scope of the organisation's business, may impact on the design choices that are made.

Another issue of strategy involves the organisation building on and refining its unique experience and competencies; that is, competency-based strategies. Business practices that have built up over time and proved a key to the success of a business or the competence of employees may well be factors upon which the business should focus and make design decisions. For example, the design may need to be flexible and allow employees the scope to make decisions, such as when the organisation is trying to capitalise on employee creativity in innovating new products. In other cases, it may be more important to have relatively rigid, formalised structures with more rules and controls.

Organisational goals, control and coordination

The first of the structural building blocks are organisational goals. In an organisation, people are organised into a structure in order to work together to achieve organisational goals. This involves breaking people and tasks up into units, allocating authority and making other decisions about how things are done. Two other components of structure are control and coordination, which provide ways of ensuring that these subdivided activities can be brought together to achieve the organisational goals.

Organisational goals

Organisations may be viewed as entities with goals.[21] The goals they pursue are multifaceted and often conflict with, or overlap, one another. These goals are common to individuals within an organisation though their reasons for involvement in the organisation are partly about serving their own individual interests. There are two types of organisational goals. The first centres on how the organisation intends to serve particular groups in society, or with social responsibility, serve society as a whole. The second focuses on organisational survival.

Output goals and serving society

Organisations are inevitably involved in some 'type of business', whether or not it is profit-oriented. They operate to provide products, services, infrastructure or wealth, for example. Output goals define the organisation's type of business, and are the basis of the mission statements that organisations often use to indicate their purposes. These can form the basis for long-term planning and strategies and may help prevent huge organisations from diverting too many resources to peripheral areas.

While some organisations may provide benefits to the society as a whole, most target their efforts towards a particular group or groups.[22] The main recipients of the organisation's efforts are the primary beneficiaries. Political organisations serve the common good, while culturally based organisations, such as churches, may emphasise contributions to their members. Social service organisations, such as hospitals, are expected to emphasise quality care to patients. In Australia and New Zealand, it is generally expected that the primary beneficiaries of businesses are the shareholders, but this is not the same everywhere. In Japan, long-time workers are typically placed at the centre of the organisation, with an expectation that through them and their secure employment there will be economic growth for the country. Many larger organisations have found it useful to review, clarify and state carefully their type of business.[23]

In the process of serving society, there is an expectation of corporate social responsibility (CSR); that is, the organisation or corporation has an obligation to behave in ethical and moral ways. There is some argument about whether this should be labelled corporate social responsibility or simply corporate responsibility (CR) since it involves not just 'social' issues and giving back to the community but also being concerned with the economic and environmental wellbeing of society.[24] For our purposes, since CSR is still the more widely used term,

Output goals are the goals that define the organisation's type of business.

Primary beneficiaries are particular groups expected to benefit from the efforts of specific organisations.

Corporate social responsibility (CSR) is the obligation of organisations to behave in ethical and moral ways. It generally refers to the notion that corporations have a responsibility to the society that sustains them.

'social' embraces those social, economic and environmental effects as they impact on the stakeholders and society or societies in which the organisation operates[25]. Organisations contributing to societal goals are given broader discretion and may obtain some control over resources, individuals, markets and products at lower costs. Organisations are typically expected to take action to improve society in a socially responsible way, or at least to avoid damaging it. Social responsibility is exhibited towards small and large social beneficiaries for a range of reasons, both altruistic and related to the organisation's reputation. It is important for organisations to maintain society's trust and confidence if they wish to avoid negative impacts on their operations.

Systems goals and organisational survival

Organisations also face the immediate problem of just making it through the coming years. Systems goals are concerned with the internal conditions that are expected to increase the organisation's survival potential. The list of systems goals is almost endless, because each manager and researcher links today's conditions to tomorrow's existence in a different way. However, for many organisations the list includes *growth, productivity, stability, harmony, flexibility, prestige* and, of course, *human resource maintenance*. For some businesses, analysts consider *market share* and *current profitability* to be important systems goals. Other studies suggest that *innovation* and *quality* also may be considered important.[26]

In a practical sense, systems goals represent short-term organisational characteristics that higher-level managers wish to promote. Systems goals must often be balanced against one another; for instance, a productivity and efficiency drive may cut the flexibility of an organisation. Different parts of the organisation may be asked to pursue different types of systems goal. Higher-level managers, for example, may expect to see their production operations strive for efficiency, while pressing for innovation from their research and development laboratory and promoting stability in their financial affairs. Systems goals provide a 'road map' to assist in linking together various units of an organisation to assure its survival. Well-defined systems goals are practical and easy to understand, focusing the manager's attention on what needs to be done.

> **Systems goals** are goals concerned with conditions within the organisation that are expected to increase its survival potential.

Australian wool exporter conquers Chinese market

OBin**Action**

Beginning as a family business in Adelaide, South Australia in 1870, Australian company Michell Group has been in the business of wool for 140 years. Back in 1949, with a booming Chinese market, company owner Ron Michell travelled to China to set up a network of local agents. For the next 55 years, Michell Group continued to trade wool with China and other parts of the world.[27] By 2004, the company had outgrown its local processing capacity and was unable to meet growing global demand. The grandsons of the founder, Peter and David Michell, followed in their grandfather's footsteps to China — but rather than seeking a market, it was to build a US$10 million scouring and carbonising plant. Aided by Austrade, who they acknowledged as 'vital in keeping the lines of communication open', the company found success as a buyer and exporter of Australian wool. Michell Group has steadily grown its footprint in China and the company's turnover is now around A$100 million.

Control

Control is one of the basic management functions and is involved with ensuring the organisation achieves what it is intended to achieve. **Control** is the set of mechanisms used to keep actions and/or outputs (based on predetermined organisational goals) within predetermined limits. Control deals with setting standards, measuring results against standards and instituting corrective action.

The control process that is used in activities such as accounting and production is depicted in figure 8.2. Note the iterative nature of the process; in other words, controlling activities within an organisation is an ongoing process. Note also that once the actual output is compared with the objective or standard that has been set, the manager may need to decide whether to adjust the standard (if it proves unrealistic or unachievable) or produce a different level of output in step with the standard. For a given project, actual expenditure (output) may be exceeding the budget (standard), so the manager will need to take measures to reduce ongoing costs for the project in some way.

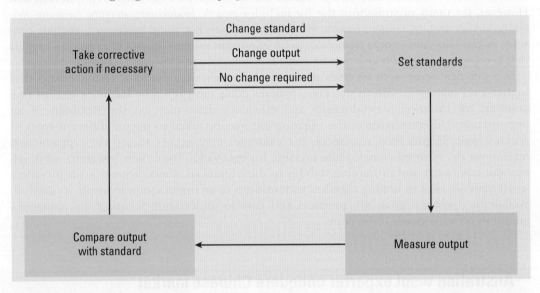

FIGURE 8.2 The business control process

While controls are needed in all organisations, just a few controls may go a long way. Astute managers need to be aware of the danger of too much control in the organisation, as noted in The effective manager 8.1.

THE **EffectiveManager** 8.1

Signs of too much control

One of the myths in management is the illusion of control. There are many variations of this, but one centres on the formal controls themselves. Many managers want to believe they can specify all of the relevant goals for subordinates as well as how they are to be accomplished. With too many output and process goals, subordinates have very little flexibility.

However, as the number of output and process controls escalates, so do the conflicts between the output and process controls. The result is that subordinates begin to pick and choose which controls they follow and managers only have the illusion that subordinates are reaching towards the specified goals.[28]

Astute managers look for the signs that too much control or inappropriate controls have been placed on their units. They look for:

* too much emphasis on one measured goal to the exclusion of all others
* too much emphasis on the quick fix, and an unwillingness to look for underlying causes of problems or new opportunities

- a tradition of across-the-board cuts rather than reductions linked to demands, constraints and opportunities
- too many vague and unrealistic expectations that breed defeat
- raising of quotas without reward for employees, particularly after employee suggestions for change are implemented.

Output controls

Developing targets or standards, measuring results against these targets and taking corrective action are all steps involved in developing output controls. Output controls focus on desired targets and allow managers to use their own methods for reaching defined targets. Most modern organisations use output controls as a part of an overall method of managing by exception; that is, when identification of a problem triggers corrective actions (see chapter 11). Such controls are popular because they promote flexibility and creativity, as well as facilitating dialogue about corrective action.

There is an important link between controls and goals but it is not necessarily simple or one-way. The links are complex and encompassing. Goals define what is to be achieved and influence the controls set in place to ensure the goals are met. Controls may also have an impact on goals. For example, output goals may be revised if targets cannot be realistically met. Controls over the manner in which tasks are done may also have an impact on an organisation's systems goals, especially if there is little choice over the controls. For example, an organisation may be obliged to comply with certain requirements of government legislation, such as workplace safety, or with the requirements of an allied organisation, such as a supplier, major customer or alliance partner.

Output controls are controls that focus on desired targets and allow managers to use their own methods for reaching defined targets.

Process controls

Few organisations run on output controls alone. Once a solution to a problem is found and successfully implemented, managers do not want the problem to recur, so they institute process controls. Process controls attempt to specify the manner in which tasks will be accomplished. There are many types of process control, but three groups have received considerable attention.

Process controls are controls that attempt to specify the manner in which tasks will be accomplished.

1. Policies, rules and procedures

Most organisations have a variety of policies, rules and procedures in place at any time. Usually, we think of a policy as a guideline for action that outlines important objectives and broadly indicates how an activity is to be performed. A policy allows for individual discretion and minor adjustments without direct clearance by a higher-level manager. Many organisations have a stated policy towards cultural diversity, for example, that not only outlines their goals for increasing the diversity of the workforce but also specifies the procedures to be used in recruiting staff.

Rules and procedures are more specific, rigid and impersonal than policies. They typically describe in detail how a task or series of tasks is to be performed. They are designed to apply to all individuals under specified conditions. Most car dealers, for example, have detailed instruction manuals for repairing a new car under warranty. They must follow strict procedures to obtain reimbursement from the manufacturer for warranty work that they have undertaken.

Other examples of rules and procedures include requirements for employees to:
- have someone countersign approval for payments
- wear certain apparel for certain jobs
- follow particular steps for cleaning equipment (such as coffee machines) or conducting regular maintenance checks (such as of electrical equipment).

A **policy** is a guideline for action that outlines important objectives and indicates how an activity is to be performed.

A **procedure** (or **rule**) is a more specific, rigid guideline that describes in detail how a task is to be performed.

Rules, procedures and policies are employed as substitutes for direct managerial supervision, leaving managers to focus on exceptional incidents or unique problems. Under the guidance of written rules and procedures, the organisation can specifically direct the activities of many individuals. It can ensure virtually identical treatment across even distant work locations. McDonald's hamburgers and fries, for example, taste much the same whether they are purchased in Hong Kong, Kuala Lumpur, Singapore or Sydney, simply because the ingredients and the cooking methods follow standardised written rules and procedures.

2. Formalisation and standardisation

Formalisation is the written documentation of work rules, policies and procedures.

Formalisation refers to the written documentation of rules, procedures and policies to guide behaviour and decision making. It is often used to simplify jobs: for example, written instructions allow individuals with less training to perform comparatively sophisticated tasks. Written procedures may also be available to ensure a proper sequence of tasks is executed, even if this sequence is performed only occasionally.

Standardisation is the degree to which the range of actions in a job or series of jobs is limited.

Most organisations have developed additional methods for dealing with recurring problems or situations. **Standardisation** is the degree to which the range of allowable actions in a job or series of jobs is limited. It involves the creation of guidelines so similar work activities are repeatedly performed in a similar fashion and employees know what they can and cannot do. Remember the example of McDonald's!

Formalisation and standardisation may have variable effects on behaviour, depending on the circumstances and the perceived need for consistency and fairness. In some cases, there may be no need for formalisation and standardisation, and rules and regulations may unnecessarily hinder workers' progress in their jobs. In other cases, they may be vital for ensuring equity, fair treatment of clients, or safety. Typically, a worker's job requirements and limits are clearly defined in a job description, and these often form part of a broad pattern of jobs. However, if you wanted highly creative workers to be innovative in the development of a new product, for example, putting them into straitjacketed jobs might not gain the desired behaviours from them. Sometimes, the formalisation of rules and procedures, and/or the clear definition of what a person can do in a job is important for preventing unethical activities in the organisation. For example, a rule makes it clear whether employees can use company software to do private work, and whether taking home company stationery is acceptable or not.[29]

3. Quality management

Another way to institute process controls is to establish a quality management process. Quality management emerged from the total quality management (TQM) movement founded by W Edwards Deming. The heart of Deming's approach is to institute a process approach to continual improvement based on statistical analyses of the organisation's operations.[30] All levels of management are to be involved in the quality program; managers are to improve supervision, train employees, retrain employees in new skills and create a structure that will push the quality program. The emphasis is on training, learning and consistency of purpose, which appear to be important lessons and all organisations need to be reminded of this constantly. One business understands well the critical part quality control plays in his success as the following example illustrates.

OBinAction

The Chinese perception of quality

Research by Cheng, Li and Luo (2014) provides an important contribution to our view of quality — the fact that it is dynamic and may be determined by context. They suggest that the evaluation of quality in China can only partly take into consideration existing mature quality evaluation models traditionally accepted by Western economies (particularly the methods of evaluating customer satisfaction) because there are conditions that are unique to China and the conditions it has experienced during its economic transition. While there is a general perception, both nationally and internationally that, overall, product quality is poor in China (with widespread media attention on the outbreak of serious product safety incidents such as milk powder and infant formula containing melamine), there is less recognition of quality indicators — such as that China is now the largest commodity exporter in the world, particularly to countries with strict quality standards such as the United States and European countries. Using four measures of quality: consumer satisfaction with quality; product safety; government regulations on quality; and citizens' concept of quality, Cheng, Ki and Luo suggest that the overall evaluation of quality in China is summarised as having just reached a general

standard. What is most revealing about the study is that they find that while product safety remains steady as a whole, government quality regulations are ineffective because it is Chinese citizens' perceptions about the concept of quality which are actually poor. Supporting this are their findings of a positive relationship between the effectiveness of government regulation on quality and Chinese citizens' concept of quality, consumer satisfaction with quality, and product safety. This shows it is not enough to simply have controls in place — it is also important to communicate them. This perspective adds a twist to our traditional notions of continuous improvement, with the authors calling not only for an emphasis on product safety during quality evaluation and quality improvement systems, but also for the constant enhancement of quality regulation effects on Chinese citizens' concept of quality, as the means to drive quality development.[31]

4. Security control

A growing area of concern for organisations is the security of their information. Not only must organisations protect their own business outcomes, businesses have legal obligations to protect the privacy of customers and staff. Growing threats in the information technology devices that organisations depend upon come from hacking, identity theft, viruses and other email and web threats. These have grown in volume with Kapersky, an IT security firm, reporting that in 2013, nearly 145 000 new malicious programs for mobile devices were detected, with approximately 4 million malicious applications used by cybercriminals to distribute mobile malware for Android-based devices and a total of 10 million malicious Android apps detected in 2012–2013.[32]

Coordination

In order to enhance the operation of the organisation, there must be ways to get all the separate activities, people and units working together. **Coordination** is the set of mechanisms that an organisation uses to link the actions of its units into a consistent pattern. The greater the specialisation in the organisation; the greater the need for effective coordination. Much of the coordination within a unit is handled by its manager. Smaller organisations may rely on their management hierarchy to provide the necessary consistency. But as the organisation grows, managers become overloaded. The organisation then needs to develop more efficient and effective ways of linking work units to one another. Coordination methods can be personal or impersonal.

Coordination is the set of mechanisms used in an organisation to link the actions of its subunits into a consistent pattern.

Personal methods of coordination

Personal methods of coordination produce synergy by promoting dialogue, discussion, innovation, creativity and learning, allowing the organisation to address the particular needs of distinct units and individuals simultaneously. Perhaps the most popular of the wide variety of personal methods is direct contact between and among organisational members. Typically, this involves the development of an effective informal network of contacts within the organisation; for example, direct personal communication and email. Committees, though generally costly and sluggish, are effective for mutual adjustment across unit heads, for communicating complex qualitative information, and for helping managers whose units must work together to adjust schedules, workloads and work assignments to increase productivity. Task forces are typically formed with limited agendas, and involve individuals from different parts of the organisation identifying and solving problems that cut across different departments. Another personal method of coordination involves developing a shared set of values that allows organisational members to predict accurately the responses of others to specific events.

There is no magic involved in selecting the appropriate mix of personal coordination methods and tailoring them to the individual skills, abilities and experience of employees. Managers need to know the individuals involved and their preferences. The effective manager 8.2 provides some guidelines for understanding how different personal methods can be tailored to match different individuals.

THE **EffectiveManager** 8.2

Selecting personal coordination styles

The astute manager must recognise the following important differences in matching up workers.
1. Individuals and representatives of departments often have their own views of how best to move towards organisational goals.
2. Some individuals emphasise immediate problems and move towards quick solutions; others stress underlying problems and longer term solutions.
3. Given that each department develops its own unique vocabulary and standard way of communicating, the coordination method chosen should recognise such potential differences and include many opportunities for direct exchange.
4. There are often pronounced departmental and individual preferences for formality.[33]

Impersonal methods of coordination

Impersonal coordination methods are often refinements and extensions of process controls, with an emphasis on formalisation and standardisation. Most larger organisations have written policies and procedures, such as schedules, budgets and plans, that are designed to mesh the operations of several units into a whole.[34] Some other examples of impersonal methods of coordination are:

- cross-departmental work units that coordinate the efforts of diverse functional units
- management information systems (MIS) that coordinate and control the operations of diverse subordinate units. These are computerised substitutes for schedules, budgets and the like. In some firms, MIS still operate as a combined process control and impersonal coordination mechanism. In the hands of astute managers, MIS become an electronic network, linking individuals throughout the organisation. Using decentralised communication systems, supplemented with the telephone, fax machine and email, a manager can greatly improve coordination. The following Counterpoint illustrates how social media can be integrated to bring about coordination in one organisation. It is also important to note that the same system, in an integrated manner, also connects the processes and productivity of the organisation.

Social media and workplace productivity

In the last few years, social media — including social networking websites such as Facebook and Twitter, as well as other tools like instant messaging, discussion forums and online chat programs — have exploded in popularity. Facebook claims to have over 13.4 million users in 2014 in Australia alone, and more than 1.3 billion registered accounts worldwide.[35] Similar to when the internet became common in the workplace, there have been concerns raised that allowing employees to use social media at work will result in lost productivity. The research thus far is inconclusive. For instance, while one study in North America found that Facebook users were less productive in their studies as well as in their workplaces, another study claims that it makes employees more productive.[36] This latter view is supported in a study conducted by the University of Melbourne which found that workers who spend no more than 20 per cent of their workplace time in online social networking are 9 per cent more productive than those who do not. Workers who engage in workplace internet leisure browsing (WILB), such as accessing Facebook, seemed to benefit by the short breaks by improving their concentration. According to Dr Brent Coker, who was involved in the study, 'People need to zone out for a bit to get back their concentration'.[37]

Other recent benefits of social media include the streamlining of internal communication by use of instant messaging as an alternative to emails, as well as better job satisfaction and staff retention. This is especially true among Gen Y employees (born after 1979), who consider the use of the internet and social media websites in the workplace to be an employment benefit.[38] Internal social media systems aim to spread knowledge and encourage employees to share 'tacit' knowledge (i.e. knowledge that may have remained hidden in old-fashioned, hierarchically managed, silo-based organisations). Yammer, an in-house social media tool currently used by more than 100 000 organisations, brings together all of a company's employees inside a private and secure enterprise social network. The system is based on an enterprise-class software built from the ground up to drive business objectives. It can create external networks to allow non-employees, such as clients, suppliers and customers to communicate directly with an organisation.[39] Initially begun as an unauthorised social media experiment, the National Australia Bank (NAB) implemented an internal social network in 2008, which by 2011 was an accepted part of its online academy as it was found to be positive in improving employee engagement, thereby allowing them to better realise their full potential.[40] Another perspective on the power of social media is seen in the move towards 'crowd sourcing', whereby a wide network of people are used to solve problems — for example, Airtasker is a website that allows people to outsource items on their to-do list through a simple process of posting a task, reviewing bids, review the runner and get the task completed.[41]

Questions

1. Do you think that the use of social media should be allowed or discouraged in the workplace?
2. If an organisation decides to allow the use of social media, what should it do to ensure that it can maximise the benefits of this technology to the organisation?
3. In particular, how do you think that use of social media can help with the coordination within an organisation?

Two broad types of organisational design that reflect the degree of control and coordination in an organisation (as well as the allocation of authority, which is considered in the next section) are mechanistic and organic design. A mechanistic design is an organisational structure that tends to emphasise authority and control, as well as specialisation in jobs. Organisations of this type stress rules, policies and procedures; specify

Mechanistic design emphasises vertical specialisation, hierarchical levels, tight control and coordination through rules, policies and other impersonal methods.

WhatWould
You**Do?**

Organic design is an organisational structure that emphasises horizontal specialisation, an extensive use of personal coordination, and loose rules, policies and procedures.

techniques for decision making; and emphasise well-documented control systems backed by a strong middle management and supported by a centralised staff. In an **organic design** there is more flexibility in how things are done, with fewer rules and procedures; there is even flexibility in how elements of the structure can change quickly in response to changing circumstances. More responsibility is placed in the hands of workers, who are seen as competent and/or expert at what they do. As the following What would you do? demonstrates, temporary workers often need to coordinate very quickly in order to get the job done.

Coordination in temporary organisations

In today's world, many individuals have jobs that take them to a number of different temporary settings, such as a corporate task force, an alliance, or a special project. Coordinating the actions of the members in these temporary arrangements is often a problem. However, research by Beth Bechky offers some insight. She studied the workers on a movie set — not the actors or producer, but the crew who set up and run the equipment, shoot the movie, and make sure the sound is perfect. These individuals are generally 'independent' contractors whose work must mesh quickly even though they have only been together a few hours.

How do they do it in the short-lived organisation of a movie set? According to Bechky, they negotiate their roles with each other. Each has his or her own specialisation and assignment, but these must be coordinated with all the others. While each recognises his or her and the others' career progression (some have more experience and they are looked to for help), all recognise that the current assignment is one among the many they want in the future. All are on their best behaviour so they will be hired for the next movie.

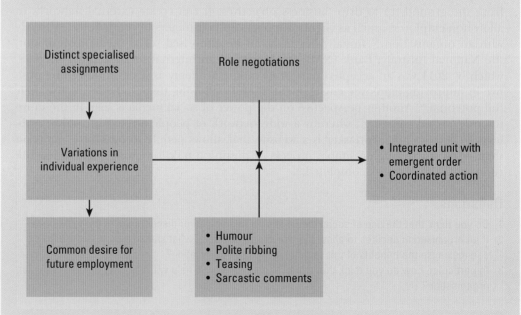

To coordinate successfully, Bechky found that the more experienced crew may provide enthusiastic thanks and very polite admonition to other less-experienced crew members. To enforce an emerging order and maintain coordination, all will use humour, polite ribbing, sarcastic comments and teasing. Public display of anger is rare and frowned upon. With these mechanisms, it only takes a few hours for the crew to emerge as an integrated unit.

To transfer findings to a student group, try and build a simplified model of the factors mentioned in the description. It might look somewhat like the figure opposite.

Pick a temporary student group to perform a team case study with majors in different areas (such as accounting, finance, management). See if the members self-assign to specialised areas based on their major. Look for variations in experience and check if there is a common desire for high performance. As the group starts work on the project, observe if they negotiate roles. Do they use humour, polite ribbing, teasing or sarcastic comments to coalesce? Do they form an integrated group with an identified order and coordinated action, or do just a few actually run the show?[42]

Questions

1. Would you expect a student group to form up much the way professionals do?
2. If the student group does not use humour or teasing, what do they use to gain coordinated action?

Vertical specialisation

In most larger organisations, there is a clear separation of authority and duties by hierarchical rank. This separation represents **vertical specialisation**, which is a hierarchical division of work that distributes formal authority and establishes where and how critical decisions will be made. This division creates a hierarchy of authority, and a chain of command, that arranges work positions in order of increasing authority. We will also discuss another form of division of labour in the next section on horizontal specialisation.

The distribution of formal authority is evident in the responsibilities typically allocated to managers. Top managers or senior executives plan the overall strategy of the organisation and plot its long-term future.[43] Middle managers guide the daily operations of the organisation, help formulate policy, and translate top-management decisions into more specific guidelines for action. Lower-level managers supervise the actions of employees to ensure implementation of the strategies authorised by top management and compliance with the related policies established by middle management.

When allocating authority or specialising vertically, one feature of organisational structure can be explained. That is, those organisations that have many levels in their hierarchies can be described as *tall*. Others that have very few levels can be described as *flat*.

We also consider organisations in terms of how centralised or decentralised they are. The degree of **centralisation** of decision-making authority is high if discretion to spend money, recruit people and make important decisions is retained further up the hierarchy of authority. The more such decisions are delegated, or moved down the hierarchy of authority, the greater is the degree of **decentralisation**.

Applying these characteristics to mechanistic and organic designs, we can make the following general (but not the only possible) observations about design. Visually, mechanistic organisations tend to have a tall hierarchy and may resemble a tall, thin pyramid with centralised decision-making senior staff at the top. Taller or more vertically specialised structures have more managers per worker. This may mean closer and tighter control over workers, with formal communication through several layers of hierarchy that can be slow and distorted. People might get frustrated waiting for approval in tall structures and feel unable to take responsibility for their own work.

Organic organisations are more likely to have a flatter structure, since more responsibility is delegated down to workers. Flatter organisations with fewer layers of hierarchy

Vertical specialisation is a hierarchical division of labour that distributes formal authority and establishes how critical decisions will be made.

Centralisation is the degree to which the authority to make decisions is restricted to higher levels of management.

Decentralisation is the degree to which the authority to make decisions is given to lower levels in an organisation's hierarchy.

and authority, and fewer managers, generally permit sub-managers and employees more discretion; they decentralise decision making and loosen control. Generally speaking, greater decentralisation provides higher subordinate satisfaction and a quicker response to problems, and may give workers a sense of ownership and greater levels of motivation in their work. Decentralisation also assists in the on-the-job training of employees for higher-level positions.

Two other organisational characteristics that emerge from vertical specialisation (though other factors might also contribute) are unity of command and span of control.

Unity of command and span of control

As already indicated, with vertical specialisation, executives, managers and supervisors are hierarchically connected through the 'chain of command'. Individuals are expected to follow their supervisors' decisions in the areas of responsibility outlined in the organisation chart. Traditional management theory suggests that each individual should have one supervisor and each unit should have one leader. Under these circumstances, there is a **unity of command**. Unity of command is considered necessary to avoid confusion, to assign accountability to specific individuals, and to provide clear channels of communication up and down the organisation. Unity of command, in a traditional hierarchy, is a readily understood approach for employees. A single boss makes life easier and less ambiguous but it could mean more hierarchical control, impersonality and rigid communication channels.

When vertically specialising the organisation, decisions are made about the number of individuals that each manager directly supervises. To reduce the costs of having many managers, as is the case in flatter organisations, a manager may be given many employees to supervise, though the number any single manager can realistically manage is obviously limited. The concept of the number of individuals reporting to a supervisor is called the **span of control**.

Span of control may have a considerable impact on both manager behaviour and employee behaviour. If a supervisor has a *wide* span of control with many subordinates to supervise, it is more likely that the employees will have freedom to do the job their own way (autonomy). This may be suitable if they are highly experienced and/or in a very creative role. Control may be looser and people may have a higher satisfaction level (but not necessarily performance level).

Narrower spans of control are expected when tasks are complex, when employees are inexperienced or poorly trained, and/or when tasks call for team effort.[44] Unfortunately, narrow spans of control yield many levels in the organisational hierarchy. The excessive number of levels is not only expensive (typically requiring more managers), but also makes the organisation unresponsive to necessary change. A research study based on data collected in China found that product customisation correlates with more formal control, fewer layers and narrower spans of control.[45]

Horizontal specialisation

Control, coordination and vertical specialisation are only part of the picture. Managers must divide the total task into separate duties, and group similar people and resources.[46] Different groups or people do different parts of the larger operation. Look again at figure 8.1 and note the two work groups reporting to the university secretary and registrar. **Horizontal specialisation** is the division of labour that establishes work units or groups within an organisation; it is often referred to as the process of departmentalisation. In the following section we will examine three forms of horizontal specialisation — by function, division and matrix — and also look at some 'mixed' or 'hybrid' forms that can emerge.

Prior to doing this it is valuable to consider the difference between the terms 'line' and 'staff'. In an organisation **line personnel** conduct the major business that directly affects

Unity of command is the situation in an organisation where each worker has a clear reporting relationship to only one supervisor.

The **span of control** is the number of individuals reporting to a supervisor.

Horizontal specialisation is the division of labour through the formation of work units or groups within an organisation.

Line personnel are work groups that conduct the major business of the organisation.

the organisation. The academic staff in universities and the workers who make the goods in factories are line workers. In contrast, staff personnel assist the line units by providing specialised expertise and services, such as accounting, human resources and public relations. The dotted lines on the organisation chart depicted in the top of figure 8.1 (on p. 288) denote staff relationships, whereas the solid lines denote line relationships (teaching in the faculties is the major business of the university).

Line personnel are likely to feel more directly involved with the operations of the organisation, especially if they can clearly see their part in achieving the organisation's goals (task significance and task identity from the job characteristics model are particularly relevant). However, a common behavioural consequence is that there tend to be different perspectives between the line and staff groups. Staff personnel are often accused of interfering with line work with their unnecessary forms and procedures (although often they are trying to accomplish important things such as financial audits, legal compliance, payrolls and so on). Line personnel say they just want to get on with the job, and lower-level managers, in particular, resent the demands or requirements of staff personnel. Intergroup and interpersonal conflict can be common. The Ethical perspective illustrates how these conflicts might occur in the health services.

> **Staff personnel** are groups that assist the line units by performing specialised services for the organisation.

**ETHICAL
Perspective**

Health check

According to experienced commentators and experts, there is an eternal dilemma in the management of public hospital systems. The clinicians (doctors, nurses, therapists) and the administrators have different views on what should be done. As the cost of health continues to rise steadily in Australia (as in many countries around the world), the government is increasingly worried about how this level of public spending will be sustained. While ways to contain the growth in health care expenditure are fiscally important, there are a myriad of factors driving up health costs — many of which, such as an ageing population and improving life expectancies, are beyond the reach of government or even the hospital administrators to control.[47]

As Campbell (2014) notes, the typical response in most hospital reforms has been on efficiency gains, 'doing more with less'. But he also notes that this alone is not enough and that a redesign of the workforce is needed. This means hospitals staffed by general physicians and nurses who take on more complex roles.[48] While notions such as up-skilling hospital-based nurses to ease the pressure on hospitals, employing nursing assistants to undertake more administrative tasks, and freeing up nurses to take on more complex roles seem sensible, the reality is that they are seen as highly contentious. Campbell suggests that disruptive innovation will need to challenge professional silos built around specialisation as well as stereotypes. While this debate appears to offer some solutions, the reality of increasing numbers of older patients with more complex medical issues is creating what Chief Executive of the Consumers Health Forum of Australia Carol Bennett says is a 'two tiers of system for those that can afford care. The out-of-pocket costs is one, but there are rationing systems in place that mean that people who can least afford care and are most likely to experience illness are

(continued)

missing out'.[49] She says people who can afford to pay are bypassing public hospital elective surgery lists by going to a private hospital.

(The term 'elective surgery' is also a misnomer as it catches anything that is not emergency surgery, including surgery for broken bones.) Canberra's two major hospitals are failing to meet targets on waiting times in their emergency departments and semi-urgent elective surgeries. Ms Bennett says more funding for public hospitals and more money for surgery would help those figures and give disadvantaged patients such as the elderly and indigenous Australians better care. 'Waiting times are a really good indicator and what we've seen in recent times is that waiting times for elective surgery have really gone up, particularly in disadvantaged areas where people are waiting 11 days longer for elective surgery than a well-off suburb.'[50]

Departmentalisation by function

Functional departmentalisation is the grouping of individuals and resources by skill, knowledge and action.

Grouping individuals by skill, knowledge and action yields a pattern of **functional departmentalisation**, and represents the most commonly used arrangement.[51] Figure 8.3 shows the organisation chart for a supermarket chain, where each department has a technical specialty considered necessary for efficient operation. The organisation is divided into four main functional groups — financial services, customer and marketing services, distribution and logistics, and company support services — and within each of these groups employees in different sections or departments undertake separate and specialised tasks. In business organisations generally, marketing, finance, production and personnel are important functions. In many small organisations, this functional pattern dominates; for instance, Apple Computer used this pattern early in its development. Functional units or departments are often criticised as encouraging functional 'silos' that stand alone for too much of the time and discourage cooperative and coordinated behaviours. People working in functional departments tend to develop narrow interests, limited perspectives, competitive behaviours, unique language and cultures, and a propensity to pass problems on to other sections.[52]

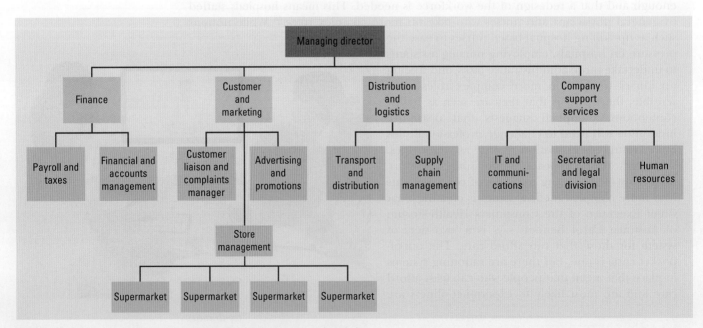

FIGURE 8.3 A functional pattern of departmentalisation for a supermarket chain

Table 8.2 summarises the advantages (and disadvantages) of a functional pattern. With all these advantages, it is not surprising that the functional form is extremely popular, being used in most organisations, despite some disadvantages. Organisations that rely on functional specialisation may expect the following tendencies to emerge over time:

- an emphasis on quality from a technical standpoint
- rigidity with respect to change, particularly if change within one functional area is needed to help other functional areas
- difficulty in coordinating the actions of different functional areas, particularly if the organisation must continually adjust to changing external conditions.

Advantages	Disadvantages
1. It can yield clear task assignments that are consistent with an individual's training.	1. It may reinforce the narrow training of individuals and lead to boring and routine jobs; for example, accounts processing. Communication across technical areas is difficult, and conflict between units may increase. Lines of communication across the organisation can become complex.
2. Individuals within a department can easily build on one another's knowledge, training and experience. Facing similar problems and having similar training facilitates communication and technical problem solving.	2. Complex communication channels can lead to 'top management overload'. Top management may spend too much time and effort dealing with cross functional problems.
3. It provides an excellent training ground for new managers, who must translate their academic training into organisational actions.	3. Individuals may look up the organisational hierarchy for direction and reinforcement rather than focusing on products, services or clients. Guidance is typically sought from functional peers or superiors.
4. It is easy to explain. Most employees can understand the role of each unit, even though many may not know what individuals in a particular function do.	

TABLE 8.2 Major advantages and disadvantages of functional specialisation

Departmentalisation by division, geography and customer

Alternatively, a **divisional departmentalisation** groups individuals and resources by products, services and/or clients/customers. Figure 8.4 (overleaf) shows a divisional pattern of organisation grouped around products (automotive parts such as transmissions and engines), regions (Asia–Pacific, South American and European) and customers (government accounts, corporate accounts and university/college accounts) for three divisions of a large international organisation. This pattern is often used to meet diverse external threats and opportunities.

Many larger, geographically dispersed organisations that sell to national and international markets use **departmentalisation by geography**. The savings in time, effort and travel can be substantial, and each territory can adjust to regional differences. The National Australia Bank is partly structured on a regional basis to embrace banks and finance organisations in the United Kingdom, Asia, the Americas and New Zealand, as well as geographically dispersed banks across Australia (it also partly structures based on the type of product or customer it has with its Business and Private Banking, Retail Banking and Wealth Management entities).[53] Organisations that rely on a few major customers may organise their people and resources by client. The idea is to focus attention on the needs of the individual customer. To the extent that customer needs are unique, **departmentalisation by customer** can also

Divisional departmentalisation is the grouping of individuals and resources by product, service and/or client.

Departmentalisation by geography is the grouping of individuals and resources by geographical territory.

Departmentalisation by customer is the grouping of individuals and resources by client.

reduce confusion and increase synergy. Organisations expanding internationally may also divisionalise to meet the demands of complex host-country ownership requirements. NEC, Sony, Nissan and many other Japanese corporations, for example, have developed Australasian divisional subsidiaries to service their customers in the Australasian market. Some huge Europe-based corporations, such as Philips and Nestlé, have also adopted a divisional structure in their expansion to the Asia–Pacific region.

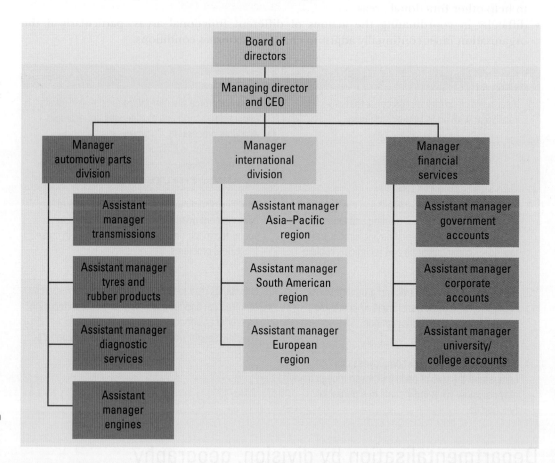

FIGURE 8.4 A divisional pattern of departmentalisation for a large international organisation

In organisations in which satisfying the demands of outsiders is particularly important, the divisional structure may provide the desired capabilities. This pattern can help improve customer responsiveness for organisations that operate in many territories, produce quite different products and services, serve a few major customers or operate internationally, as the following International spotlight demonstrates.

International
SPOTLIGHT

Fonterra: from local prominence to global reach

On 3 July 2008, Fonterra Co-operative Group, New Zealand's largest company, conducted the world's first global internet trading of dairy products.[54] Although the company was only formed through a merger in 2001 between the New Zealand Dairy Board and the country's two largest dairy cooperatives, it continues to grapple with the paradox of New Zealanders' popular perception of the firm as a national company (as it is still owned cooperatively by its 10 600 farmer shareholders). Yet, inside Fonterra, the management and employees have seen themselves as international for some time (in 2013, the company was responsible for 30 per cent of the world's dairy exports).[55]

While Fonterra has been successful at developing an extensive network of international processors and distributors, many companies are realising that widely dispersed, low-cost supply chains make them very vulnerable to protectionism, rising transportation costs and quality issues.[56] To overcome increasing competition and the problems of government-imposed barriers to trade (e.g. tariffs) in overseas markets, Fonterra is increasingly focused on developing milk locally in overseas locations, thereby reducing its dependence on New Zealand.[57]

Advantages	Disadvantages
1. It provides adaptability and flexibility in meeting the demands of important external groups.	1. It does not provide a pool of highly trained individuals with similar expertise to solve problems and train new employees.
2. It allows for spotting external changes as they are emerging.	2. It can lead to a duplication of effort as each division attempts to solve similar problems.
3. It provides for the integration of specialised personnel deep within the hierarchy.	3. Divisional goals may be given priority over the health and welfare of the overall organisation; divisional organisations may have difficulty responding to corporation-wide threats.
4. It focuses on the success or failure of particular products, services, clients or territories.	4. Conflict problems may arise when divisions attempt to develop joint projects, exchange resources, share individuals or 'transfer price' one another for goods and services.
5. To the extent that this pattern yields separate 'business units', top management can pit one division against another; for instance, Procter & Gamble has traditionally promoted friendly competition among product groups.	

TABLE 8.3 Major advantages and disadvantages of divisional specialisation

Organisations that rely on divisional specialisation can generally expect the following tendencies to occur over time:
- an emphasis on flexibility and adaptability to the needs of important external units
- a lag in the technical quality of products and services compared with that of functionally structured competitors
- difficulty in achieving coordination across divisions, particularly where divisions must work closely or sell to each other.

Departmentalisation by matrix

From the aerospace industry, a third, unique form of departmentalisation was developed; it is now called a **matrix structure**.[58] In the aerospace industry, projects are technically complex, and they involve hundreds of subcontractors located throughout the world. Precise integration and control is needed across many sophisticated functional specialties and corporations. This is often more than a functional or divisional structure can provide. Thus, departmentalisation by matrix uses both the functional and divisional forms simultaneously. Figure 8.5 (overleaf) shows the basic matrix arrangement for an aerospace program. Note the functional departments (production, marketing and engineering) on one side and the project efforts on the other. Workers and supervisors in the middle of the matrix have

A **matrix structure** is a combination of functional and divisional patterns in which an individual is assigned to more than one type of unit.

two bosses — one functional and one project. For example, if you are one of the people in the marketing function and in the Vulcan project, you would report to the marketing manager, but you would also report to your Vulcan project manager. Thus, the matrix breaks the 'unity of command' principle that is central to bureaucratic hierarchy. Each person in a project team has two bosses. The project manager will be responsible for the person's contribution to the project. The department manager will be responsible for the person's:

- general career development
- pay
- promotion prospects within the organisation
- contributions to the work of the department if/when there are gaps in their project team duties.[59]

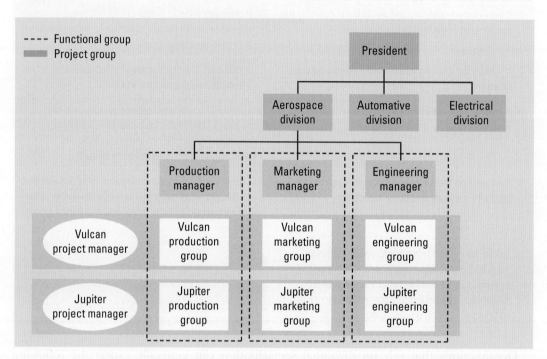

FIGURE 8.5 A matrix pattern of departmentalisation in an aerospace division

It is also possible that some people in such an industry work outside this matrix structure. As you can see from the figure, there may be some people who work in the functional departments (production, marketing and engineering) but who are not necessarily also in a project team.

The major advantages and disadvantages of the matrix form of departmentalisation are summarised in table 8.4. The key disadvantage is the loss of unity of command. Individuals can be unsure as to what their jobs are, who they report to for specific activities, and how various managers are to administer the effort. It can also be an expensive method because it relies on individual managers to coordinate efforts deep within the organisation. In figure 8.5, note that the number of managers almost doubles compared with the number in either a functional or a divisional structure. Despite these limitations, the matrix structure provides a balance between functional and divisional concerns.

Many organisations also use elements of the matrix structure. Special project teams, coordinating committees and task forces, for example, can be the beginnings of a matrix. A large advertising firm could use project teams for major client contracts. Yet, these temporary structures can be used within a predominantly functional or divisional form without upsetting unity of command or recruiting additional managers.

Advantages	Disadvantages
1. It combines strengths of both functional and divisional departmentalisation.	1. It is expensive.
2. It helps to provide a blending of technical and market emphasis in organisations operating in exceedingly complex environments.	2. Unity of command is lost (because individuals have more than one supervisor).
3. It provides a series of managers able to converse with both technical and marketing personnel.	3. Authority and responsibilities of managers may overlap, causing conflicts and gaps in effort across units and inconsistencies in priorities.
	4. It is difficult to explain to employees.

TABLE 8.4 Major advantages and disadvantages of a matrix structure

Many problems can be resolved at the working level, where the balance between technical, cost, customer and organisational concerns can be rectified. However, introducing such a structure may not be easy, as the Sustainability feature illustrates.

Organisational structures for sustainability

Sustainability

Making recommendations for designing an organisation can be very attractive in theory; but, in practical application, recommendations can go very wrong. Organisations need more than a formulaic approach to ideal design as the following extract illustrates.

In recent years, sustainability has become a 'hot topic' and something most organisations would like to be associated with. Some years ago, Sharma argued that it is important to visualise 'organisational forms, structures, strategies and outcomes as firms travel on the path to sustainability'.[60] However, while academic and practitioner publications have focused on strategies for sustainability and sustainability reporting, there is a clear gap in terms of what organisational structures or 'architectures' are best for delivering these sustainable strategies.[61]

Griffiths and Petrick[62] suggest that existing organisational structures impede both ecological and human sustainability in three ways.

1. They insulate organisational systems and processes from a broad range of environmental information.
2. The established organisational systems and routines aim to maintain the status quo and hence obstruct new ways of working.
3. They limit or even prevent access to wider stakeholders whose involvement is crucial for implementing sustainability strategies.

They propose that there are three 'ideal-type' structures that may be appropriate alternative structures for sustainability as follows:

1. *Network organisations.* These organisations rely on networks to execute strategies, while the centre retains only key areas of decision making. They are a major source of innovation, and facilitated by the new developments in information technology. (See Other Structural Arrangements further in the chapter for details.)
2. *Virtual organisations.* These are organisations that can be interpreted to have a limited life and/or operate globally with a very small number of employees. They tend to leave a very small environmental footprint. (See Other Structural Arrangements further in the chapter for details.)
3. *Communities of practice.* These are not clearly defined entities and may have amorphous, fluid structures that are developed around an area of common interest, expertise or project.

Benn, Dunphy and Griffiths argue that the move to these 'ideal types' is a process that may take organisations some time to achieve.[63] Stubbs and Cocklin go further, arguing that the existing

(continued)

model of organisations must be transformed in order for sustainability to be institutionalised.[64] In a case study of Millenium3 Financial Services, an Australian-based private company in the financial services sector, Pederson and Nagengast find evidence that supports the proposition that virtual and networked organisations are viable alternative forms of sustainable organisations.[65]

Questions

1. What are the problems with existing organisational structures, and why might some of the alternative organisational forms overcome some of these problems?
2. If the senior management of an organisation decides to change the structure as part of its adoption of sustainable strategies, what factors might interfere with the effectiveness of the changed structure?
3. Can you think of other possible structures or 'architectures' that will promote sustainability?

Mixed forms of departmentalisation

As the matrix concept suggests, it is possible to departmentalise by two different methods at the same time, but the matrix form is not the only possibility. Organisations often use a mixture of departmentalisation forms; it may be desirable to divide the effort (group people and resources) by two methods at the same time to balance the advantages and disadvantages of each.

Consider the example in figure 8.6. Notice that this organisation has overall functional units (that is, production, marketing and finance) but that work is divided on a divisional basis (that is, domestic and foreign) within each functional area. Thus, departmentalisation can take different permutations. Another example might be a geographically departmentalised organisation that has functional departments within each major geographical area. Various permutations of departmentalisation can be found. Sometimes, the way in which functional activities are divided (into functional departments or divisions) is a matter of degree, as the following example illustrates.

OBinAction

Breaking the silos at Sony and the New Zealand public sector

Organisations need to make many decisions about their structure, such as whether functions like human resource management would be better handled by a central group of functional experts, or spread out among various divisions. With rapid advances in technology and globalisation, companies like Sony have to innovate faster and produce better products and services to satisfy increasingly demanding consumers. Sony has traditionally been a conservative, engineering-led multinational firm with very disparate divisions. Such a structure and culture is not well suited to the market conditions that it faces in the contemporary business environment. Sony has attempted to respond through various measures designed to motivate its staff and divisions to cooperate and work together more closely than they ever have in the past. In other words, Sony is trying to facilitate a collaborative approach within its organisation.

A powerful example of this can be seen in the New Zealand public sector where the quest for 'more and better' public services for less money put the focus on outcomes and empowered public servants to work together.[66] The desired result is an increasingly joined-up government. It has been driven by the goal of aligning with the changing expectations of citizens for 'better public services, delivered to them in more immediate, responsive and flexible ways'. Deputy State Services Commissioner Ryan Orange can already point to success with examples such as eight agencies working together to develop efficient 'wrap-around' services, which will make it simpler for citizens to interact with government at key points in their lives like childbirth or retirement. While collaboration is mostly being driven by shared cross-agency goals, he says functional leadership serves 'an important catalytic role' by helping establish a shared vision of the future. Another very visible example is the 'all-of-government website' at www.govt.nz, which has been redeveloped to connect New Zealanders directly with government services and information from a citizen-centric, not agency-centric, perspective.

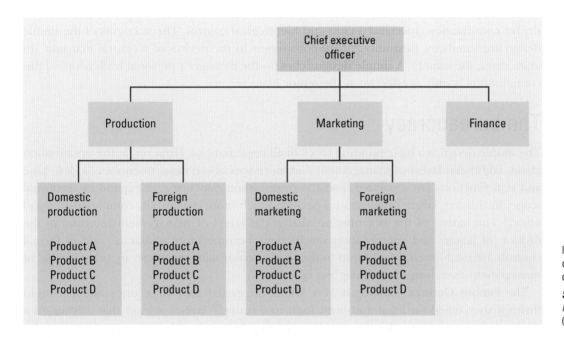

FIGURE 8.6 Partial organisation chart showing a mixed form of departmentalisation

Source: R Hodgetts and F Luthans, *International management* (New York: McGraw-Hill, 1997).

Emerging forms of organisational design and workforce implications

Every organisation will develop a unique design in response to its scale, technology, environment and strategic aims, and in terms of the choices it makes about goals, control, coordination, and vertical and horizontal specialisation. Other factors may also have an impact on design, such as the history of the organisation, sudden changes, mergers and acquisitions, and geographical locations.

In this section, we will consider some recognisable types of organisational design in the contemporary world. While they are not necessarily new or unimagined, they do illustrate some generally occurring design trends for organisations. Common forms are the simple design, the bureaucracy, the divisionalised organisation and the conglomerate. However, there are distinctions in the design of organisations even within these categories; for example, variations in the degree of organic or mechanistic design in bureaucracies. Figure 8.7 (overleaf) illustrates these popular basic designs. Other forms of organisation design also emerge, such as alliances, virtual organisations, core–ring designs and adhocracies. These, and their impact on the people working within such organisations, will be briefly examined.

The simple design

A **simple design** is a configuration involving one or two ways of specialising individuals and units.

The **simple design** is a configuration involving the specialisation of individuals and units. That is, vertical specialisation and control typically emphasise levels of supervision without elaborate formal mechanisms (such as rule books and policy manuals), and the majority of the control based with the manager. One or two ways of organising departments are used, and coordination mechanisms are often personal. The organisation visually resembles a 'pyramid' with few staff individuals or units (see the simple design at the top of figure 8.7).

The simple design is appropriate for many small organisations, such as family businesses, retail stores and small manufacturing companies,[67] since these have few people, little necessity for coordination, specialised tasks and hierarchical control. The strengths of the simple design are simplicity, flexibility and responsiveness to the desires of a central manager (in many cases, the owner). A simple design relies on the manager's personal leadership, so this configuration is only as effective as the senior manager.

The bureaucracy

A **bureaucracy** is an ideal form of organisation whose characteristics include a division of labour, hierarchical control, promotion by merit with career opportunities for employees, and administration by rule.

The simple design is a basic building block of all organisations. However, as the organisation grows, additional layers of management and more specialised departments are added. Line and staff functions are separated, and the organisation may begin to expand its territorial scope. In this way, larger organisations become much more structurally complex than small ones.[68] The nature of the organisation changes as layers of management increase, as the division of labour and coordination mechanisms become more elaborate, and as formal controls are established. In addition to the single, senior manager there are other 'levels' of management exercising varying degrees of authority.

The famous German sociologist Max Weber suggested that large organisations would thrive if they relied on legal authority, logic and order.[69] Weber argued that relying on a division of labour, hierarchical control, promotion by merit with career opportunities for employees, and administration by rule was a superior option to the simple design. While Weber knew the **bureaucracy** he was designing was an ideal type and that it could not always be perfect, he believed that efficiency, fairness and more freedom for individual expression within the organisation would be important outcomes. Bureaucracies are often criticised for being too rule-bound and procedural and some organisations seek to reduce the impact of this, as the following example illustrates. The effective manager 8.3 also indicates some of the dysfunctional tendencies of bureaucracies.

THE EffectiveManager 8.3

The natural dysfunctional tendencies of a bureaucracy

All large organisations must systematically work to minimise the dysfunctional characteristics of the modern bureaucracy. Among these dysfunctions are tendencies to:

1. overspecialise and neglect to mitigate the resulting conflicts of interest resulting from specialisation
2. overuse the formal hierarchy and emphasise adherence to official channels rather than problem solving
3. assume senior managers are superior performers on all tasks and rulers of a political system, rather than individuals who should help others reach goals
4. overemphasise insignificant conformity that limits individual growth
5. treat rules as ends in and of themselves rather than as poor mechanisms for control and coordination.

All large organisations are bureaucratic to some extent, though there are variations in the ways they are designed. The following discussion shows some possible variations to bureaucratic design.

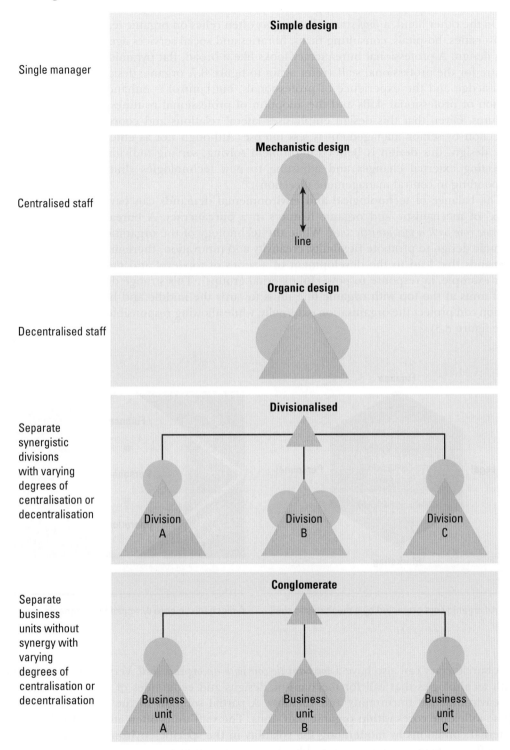

Single manager

Simple design

Centralised staff

Mechanistic design

line

Decentralised staff

Organic design

Separate synergistic divisions with varying degrees of centralisation or decentralisation

Divisionalised

Division A

Division B

Division C

Separate business units without synergy with varying degrees of centralisation or decentralisation

Conglomerate

Business unit A

Business unit B

Business unit C

FIGURE 8.7 Visual depiction of different design options

Machine bureaucracies (characterised by mechanistic design features, as in figure 8.7) are popular in industries with large-scale operations, such as banks, insurance companies and government offices. However, when the organisation is viewed as too rigid and centralised, employees may feel constrained and the organisation may be hindered in its capacity to adjust to external changes or new technologies. The inherent problems of such mechanistic command-and-control type structures are often overlooked by companies that try to resolve problems by frequent restructuring instead of fundamental changes in design.

On the other hand, a *professional bureaucracy* often relies on organic features in its design.[70] Universities, hospitals, consulting firms, libraries and social services agencies typically adopt this design. A professional bureaucracy looks like a broad, flat pyramid with a bulge in the centre for the professional staff (refer again to figure 8.7, organic design). Power rests with knowledge and the experience of professionals, but control is enhanced by the standard-isation of professional skills and the adoption of professional routines, standards and pro-cedures. Given that this design emphasises lateral relations and coordination, centralised direction by senior management is less intense. Although not as efficient as the mechan-istic design, this design is better for problem solving, serving individual customer needs, detecting external changes and adjusting to new technologies (but at the sacrifice of responding to central management direction).[71]

The balance of technological and environmental demands can have an impact on the 'mix' of mechanistic and organic features in a bureaucracy. A bureaucracy can have an *organic core with a mechanistic shell*. While the technology of the organisation may call for an organic design to promote flexibility, creativity and innovation, there may be environmental demands that lead to the development of a series of top-level and mechanistic staff units (for example, in response to powerful external groups). This strange design of mechanistic staff units at the top with organic line units towards the middle and bottom of the organ-isation can protect the organisation externally, while allowing responsible internal operations (see figure 8.8).

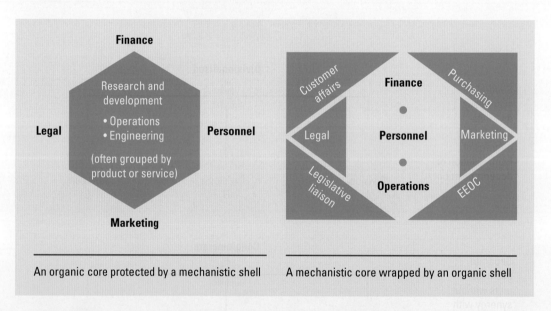

FIGURE 8.8 Two design hybrids

A bureaucracy can also have a *mechanistic core with an organic shell*. Very large organisations with technologies that call for mechanistic designs and economies of scale are vulnerable to environmental uncertainty and volatility. A partial solution to the problem is to wrap these inflexible cores within organic staff units. The staff units often attempt to change the external conditions by moderating the volatility in the specific environment and to absorb or buffer as many changes as possible. This latter option is found most often in organ-isations that must balance efficient production with flexible marketing and design oper-ations. The assembly line is mechanistically structured, yet products may be designed by more organically structured teams.

Divisionalised organisations

Many very large organisations find that neither the mechanistic nor the organic designs are suitable for all their operations. Adopting a machine bureaucracy would overload senior management and yield too many levels of management,[72] but adopting an organic design would mean losing control and becoming too inefficient. Even in the same industry, some business activities may call for an organic structure, while others call for a mechanistic one. The solution is the divisionalised design, by which the organisation establishes a *separate structure for each business or division*. The classic divisional organisation was created for General Motors by Alfred Sloan, who divided the company's operations into divisions for designing and producing Chevys, Oldsmobiles, Pontiacs, Buicks and Cadillacs.[73] Each division was treated as a separate business; each business competed against the others.

In the divisionalised organisation, all the businesses are coordinated by a comparatively small centralised team that provides support, such as financial services and legal expertise. Senior line management provides direction and control over the presumably 'autonomous' divisions. In very large organisations, this approach can free top management to establish strategy and concentrate on large, long-term problems. Divisional heads run their own businesses and compete for resources, yet each enjoys the support (financial, personnel, legal and so on) of the larger parent.

While this structure is expensive, because many similar staff and support units must be developed for each division, it allows the organisation greater flexibility to respond to different markets and customers. However, tension between divisional management and senior management is often apparent. It is difficult for corporate executives and corporate staff to allow the divisions to operate as independent businesses. Over time, senior staff may grow in number and force 'assistance' on the divisions. Further, because divisions compete for common resources, coordination across divisions is also often difficult.

> **Divisionalised design** is an organisational structure that establishes a separate structure for each business or division.

The conglomerate

Organisations that own several unrelated businesses are known as conglomerates. The line between the divisionalised form and the conglomerate can often be confusing. For our purposes, the key question is whether there is synergy among the various businesses owned by the corporation. Synergies are potential links, as between computers and information systems,or between financing and vehicle rentals, that create an entity with an output greater than its individual parts. If there is synergy, we would call the organisation divisionalised; if there is little synergy, the organisation is a conglomerate.

Pure conglomerates have not done particularly well in the United States, mainly because substantive knowledge of the various businesses is often needed for them to be successfully managed.[74] While most scholars would argue against conglomerates, and for a more synergistic approach, organisational survival might depend on other factors, as the What would you do? demonstrates.

> **Conglomerates** are organisations that own several unrelated businesses.

The pros and cons of growth and acquisition

Organisations typically begin their lives as providers of one or few products or services. Over time, growth and acquisition can result in a business expanding in the same areas. A very high profile Australian example, which is still current in the minds of many, is ABC Learning Centres. Characterised by an approach that involved relentless acquisition — in 2001 it owned just 94 centres, by 2008, it had 1084 centres in Australia alone, with more in New Zealand, the United States and the United Kingdom. However,

(continued)

WhatWould YouDo?

a wave of negative publicity about the ABC group's financial position (focusing on high debt levels after the rapid offshore expansion) rocked the business in early 2008 and it sold a 60 per cent stake in its US operations. At this stage, CEO Eddy Groves believed the brand's reputation was not irreversibly damaged. It was still Australia's biggest childcare centre operator, with 16 000 employees in 1100 centres caring for 100 000 children. However, by late 2008, with more than 1200 centres in Australia, ABC Learning Centres was in crisis and was moved into the hands of administrators. With high debt levels, when the company was delisted from the Australian Securities Exchange, the federal government put $22 million into ABC Learning to keep its childcare centres open for the short term.[75] About 570 of its childcare centres were taken over by Goodstart, a non-profit consortium consisting of Mission Australia, the Benevolent Society, the Brotherhood of St Laurence and Social Ventures Australia.[76] The firm was eventually wound up in 2010, with creditors owed almost $2 billion.[77]

Other organisations expand and grow but all or some of their acquisitions or new businesses have some synergy with aspects of their broad business operations. For example, in 1899, Sir Sidney Kidman founded S Kidman & Co., a cattle business.[78] Through acquisition of other cattle stations and related farming businesses, the business now controls about 3.5 per cent of the land in Australia (about 11 million hectares of agricultural land in Queensland, South Australia, Western Australia, the Northern Territory and New South Wales).[79] The consolidation and aggregation of agricultural businesses has been ongoing for many years, driven by the goal of farmers to achieve economies of scale and diversification in terms of climate and usage. This has been especially the case among farming families and, as the Australian *Farm Journal* editor Patrick France notes, 'There's a growing number of larger-scale, multiple-property family farms now, brothers owning and operating them as a conglomerate'.[80] In the business services sector, the Citadel Group, established in 2002, has followed a mergers and acquisitions strategy that offers a good strategic fit that does not distract from their core business. This saw the business growing its revenue at a phenomenal rate of 246 per cent over the course of three years.[81] In 2010, Citadel Group was the twentieth fastest growing private company in Australia and by 2014 it could claim over 200 staff nationwide, a $100 million market capitalisation, and an ability to 'reach back' and draw on the expertise of over 1500 people.[82]

Wesfarmers is one of Australia's largest public companies and one of Australia's largest retailers. Its headquarters are in Perth, Western Australia and it has become well known as a vast conglomerate that incubates many businesses. It has successfully 'parented' many different businesses, while maintaining a centralised control through an integrated system focused on shareholders. Later, interested buyers may come along who can take advantage of the synergistic opportunities with their own, existing, businesses.[83] Wesfarmers is a corporate company with multiple business units in diverse and unrelated areas. For example, it established the Coles Division when it acquired Coles in 2007 (including Bi-Lo, Coles Liquor, Liquorland and Coles Express fuel and convenience stores). It also acquired Officeworks and grouped it with its own established business, Bunnings, in the Home Improvement and Office Supplies division. Kmart was also acquired in the 2007 acquisition. Other divisions include Insurance (three general insurance companies, three insurance brokers, and premium funding and superannuation activities included), Industrial & Safety (several businesses involved in industrial consumables, packaging, materials handling and lifting products), Chemicals & Fertilisers (for mining, industrial and agricultural sectors), Energy (including four gas businesses, a power generation business and support services) and several other businesses (such as investment banking, an equity business, a plantation softwood sawmill and a property trust).[84] Across this diversity of business interests, there may be several opportunities to create synergy, but there other areas where there is no apparent advantage, meaning there are fewer opportunities to capitalise on common areas of competency and expertise.

However, with the advent of new technologies like the internet and wireless broadband, globalisation, deregulation and the rate of change of some industries means that big is not always better. Some firms choose to remain deliberately small. The unbundling of financial institutions, which used to write all their own loans, has meant that small independent mortgage brokers, like New South Wales company Investors Choice Mortgages, have benefited. Founder Jane Slack-Smith has found a niche by 'sitting down with really experienced investors … and finding a solution for them', and, as such, has brokered more than $75 million worth of property loans over the past five years.[85] Similarly, companies that develop applications (or Apps) for the Apple iPhone and iPad have benefited from Apple's changed business model, leaving the creation of applications for the smartphone and tablet to thousands of independent small businesses for the more than 40 million potential buyers worldwide.[86]

Questions

1. What are the potential pros and cons of a conglomerate like Wesfarmers owning unrelated businesses?
2. If you were managing a small business like Investors Choice Mortgages, explain the possible advantages or disadvantages of remaining small as opposed to growing.
3. How might employees in large, divisionalised or conglomerate organisations be affected by the structure of their organisations and new acquisitions (both within their specific division and in the wider organisation)?

The core–ring organisation

The pressure to enhance productivity in the last decades of the twentieth century encouraged many organisations to 'downsize', or reduce their number of employees. While this trend slowed in the early 2000s, the global financial crisis led to a resurgence of retrenchments in 2009.

The widespread practice of downsizing has led to the increased popularity of an organisational design known as the core–ring organisation. The major driver behind this new core–ring organisation is the greater need for flexibility in production. An organisation adopting a core–ring design (figure 8.9, overleaf) takes on a two-tiered structure, in which the inner core workforce represents the high value-adding members of the organisation. These employees often have higher job security, higher salaries and better career paths.

The second tier of this structure is also known as the flexible ring, and it is made up of a contingent workforce. Contingent workers in this outer ring may supply specialised services to the organisation on an ongoing basis and, as a result, have a relatively stable employment relationship with the core organisation (as least for the duration of their contracts). Traditionally, such services would be contained within the core of a large bureaucratic organisation, but in the core–ring organisation services such as cleaning, information technology and specialist consultants can be more cost-effectively contracted or outsourced. For example, almost all large corporations outsource at least one function and, in Australia, most outsourcing spending comes from companies with 500 or more employees. While it is hard to quantify, about two thirds of the outsourcing spending comes from banking, insurance and financial services, telecommunications and government organisations. Functions outsourced include applications management and network management[87] but can also include accounting, customer service, technology support and cleaning.[88]

The largest component of the outer ring consists of lower-skilled, casual employees. Statistics show that approximately 20.8 per cent of the Australian workforce is casual.[89] Such employees typically experience lower job security, relatively lower pay and a lack of available career paths.[90] Workers in this peripheral category may actually receive a higher hourly rate of pay than that of some core workers in the organisation, but on-costs, such as holiday loadings, training costs, sick leave and other fringe benefits, do not apply to them because they are employed on a just-in-time basis. From the casual employee's point of view, their employment can be 'precarious', with little certainty about having a steady income, where the next day's work is coming from, and whether the family can enjoy a holiday together (as they may be called in for work).

Such workers are temporary; fluctuations in the size of this outer ring depend on prevailing levels of demand for the organisation's products. These fluctuations may be due to changes in economic prosperity, market competition or other factors.

For the organisation, the core–ring design offers a flexible and cost-effective structure to adapt quickly to such variations in demand for a particular product. When product demand rises, the ring or contingent workforce can be rapidly expanded at short notice, given the high levels of unemployment in most OECD countries over the past decade. Given that organisations no longer expect demand patterns to be constant throughout the year, if demand falls, the contingent workforce can be cut back at short notice depending on the nature and the level of the work required.

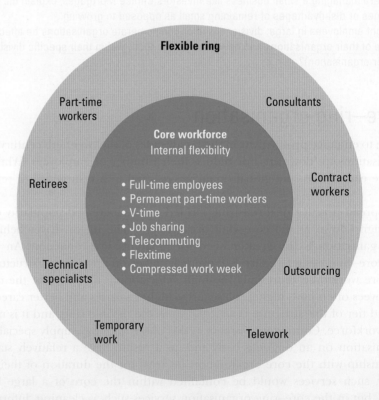

FIGURE 8.9 Core and peripheral workforce employment options

The adhocracy

The influence of technological considerations can be clearly seen in small organisations and in specific departments within large ones. In some instances, managers and employees simply do not know the appropriate way in which to service a client or to produce a particular product. This is the extreme of Thompson's intensive type of technology and may be found in some small-batch processes where a team of individuals must develop a unique product for a particular client. Mintzberg suggests that the 'adhocracy' may be an appropriate structure at these technological extremes.[91] An **adhocracy** is characterised by:

- few rules, policies and procedures
- high level of decentralisation, shared decision making among members
- extreme horizontal specialisation, because each member of the unit may be a distinct specialist
- few levels of management
- virtually no formal controls.

The adhocracy is particularly useful when an aspect of the organisation's technology presents two problems: first, the tasks facing the organisation vary considerably and provide many exceptions, as in a hospital; and second, problems are difficult to define and resolve.[92] The adhocracy places a premium on professionalism and coordination in problem solving, especially in solving technical problems. As such, adhocracies are often used as a supplement to other designs to offset their dysfunctional effects.[93] Organisations use temporary task forces, special committees and even contracted consulting firms to provide the creative problem identification and problem solving that the adhocracy promotes. Lotus Development Corporation, for instance, creates autonomous departments to encourage talented employees to develop software programs. Allied Chemical and 3M also set up quasi-autonomous groups to work through new ideas.

> An **adhocracy** is an organisational structure that emphasises shared, decentralised decision making, extreme horizontal specialisation, few levels of management, the virtual absence of formal controls, and few rules, policies and procedures.

Other structural arrangements

Many other forms of organisational design are emerging or exist. They often involve alliances of two or more organisations, or networks of several organisations or of businesses within larger organisations. Some of these are now discussed, and may be useful in describing some organisational or part-organisational designs.

Strategic alliances are announced cooperative agreements or joint ventures between two independent organisations. Often these agreements involve corporations that are headquartered in different nations.[94] In high-technology areas, such as robotics, semiconductors, advanced materials (ceramics and carbon fibres) and advanced information systems, a single company often does not have all the knowledge necessary to bring new products to the market. Often the organisations with the knowledge are not even in the same country. In this case, the organisational design must go beyond the boundaries of the organisation into strategic alliances. Another purpose for alliances is to provide goods in the supply chain, an activity common for major retailers and supermarkets.[95]

> **Strategic alliances** are announced cooperative agreements or joint ventures between two independent organisations.

Alliances exist in other forms in other countries. In Europe, for example, they are called informal combines or cartels; competitors work cooperatively to share the market, decrease uncertainty and create more favourable outcomes for all. The legality of such arrangements may vary between countries, depending on trade practices laws and other regulations. For example, in Australia, collusion or collaboration in markets is generally illegal (as it is in New Zealand), although in 2003, the Dawson Report suggested that small businesses be given limited rights to join forces for collective negotiations with larger customers or suppliers in order to give them some competitive capacity.[96] From July 2009, cartel conduct became a criminal offence in Australia. The campaign by the Australian Competition and Consumer Commission (ACCC) against cartels was a 2012–2013 priority and, as at September 2012, the ACCC reported that there were 10 cartel prosecutions before the Federal Court of Australia and a number of active cartel investigations under way.[97] In 2014, the ACCC developed a policy to encourage cooperation and, in the case of cartels, an immunity policy to encourage whistleblowers.

In Japan, strategic alliances among well-established organisations in many industries are quite common and linked in a network of relationships called a Keiretsu. For example, organisations may be linked to each other directly via cross-ownership and through historical ties to one bank, such as with the Mitsubishi group. Alternatively, a key manufacturer

A **network organisation** is a de-layered organisation aligned around the complementary competencies of players in a value chain.

may be at the hub of a network of supplier organisations, with long-term supply contracts and cross-ownership ties, such as with Toyota. Similar arrangements exist elsewhere.

The **network organisation** involves a central organisation that specialises in a core activity, such as design and assembly. It works with a comparatively small number of participating suppliers on a long-term basis for both component development and manufacturing efficiency. Google is a leader in the development of these relationships[98]. More extreme variations of this network design are also emerging to meet apparently conflicting environmental, size and technological demands simultaneously. Organisations are spinning off staff functions to reduce their overall size and concentrate their internal design on technological dictates. Network organisations are de-layered and flexible, with freer and less formal communication, control and coordination. Activities are geared towards alignment with the value chain in the industry, with an array of complementary competencies and resources brought together to achieve the objectives of the network.[99]

Virtual organisations comprise individuals, groups and businesses that work together across time and space.

Virtual organisations or virtual alliances emerge from the environment of networks but they are also distinctly dependent on the ready connections gained by information and communications technology. Virtual organisations comprise a range of individuals, groups and businesses who work together in a diversity of working arrangements across space and time. They are characterised by their shared vision; clustering of activities around core competencies; teamwork to implement activities throughout a value chain and to coordinate and make decisions in real time through information technology; and a tendency to empower members at the bottom levels when it serves the needs of the whole group. They tend to be focused on the sharing and processing of knowledge and information through electronic mediums rather than transforming physical resources in physical places. These features enable a high degree of responsiveness to environmental change.[100] Control in virtual organisations occurs through extensive use of videoconferencing and the internet.[101]

Franchises do not fit neatly into a design category but are worth mentioning here. A successful organisation often allows other organisations to buy a franchise to run a 'relatively' independent business using the name, reputation and business product and/or procedure of the parent organisation in return for some payment or fee. While franchises are often thought to be mostly 'imports' (such as KFC, Pizza Hut and McDonald's), there are home-grown franchises as well. In Australia, there are around 1025 franchise systems with about 91 per cent of these being Australian-based. Individual franchise business units number around 69 900 and about 690 000 employees including full-time, permanent part-time and casual employees.[102]

In New Zealand, the number of franchisors grew from 350 in 2003 to around 485 in 2012 — with 22 400 franchisees — giving it the highest proportion of franchises per capita in the world. About 70 per cent of these systems are locally-bred (with almost a quarter of them franchising internationally, with Australia as the most popular destination), but New Zealanders have also given a warm welcome to appropriate franchise systems from all over the world such as Anytime Fitness, Snap-on Tools, Speedy Sign A Rama (Speedy Signs), Jani-King and, of course, McDonald's.[103] An important feature of franchises is that they typically need controls — franchise owners, managers and employees need to operate using the successful system the franchise offers.[104]

Summary

Formal structure and organisational design

Organisational design is the process of choosing and implementing a formal structural configuration (that is, a formal structure) for an organisation. The structure is typically represented on an organisational chart. Structure defines the configuration of jobs, positions and lines of authority of the various component parts of the organisation.

Factors for organisational design

Four main factors can be said to affect organisational design — scale, technology, environment and strategy. Scale is important since the number of people and the degree of division of labour and authority will have an impact on the complexity of the organisation and the need for compensatory control and coordination mechanisms. Major distinctions in technology are the Thompson (intensive, long-linked, mediating) and Woodward (small batch, mass production, continuous processing) classification systems. The technology of the organisation will have some impact on the chosen structure. Environmental differences have a large impact on the type of organisational design that works best. Both the general environment (background conditions) and specific environment (key actors and organisations) are important, as is the environmental complexity (richness, interdependence, and uncertainty and volatility in the organisation/environment). The organisational design must support the strategy if it is to prove successful. Strategy positions an organisation in its competitive environment. Strategies such as differentiating the business, or leading the market in price and value, or strategies based on competency, can have an impact on the organisational design.

Goals, control and coordination

Organisational goals include both output and systems goals. Output goals relate to the type of business the organisation is engaged in; they are concerned with satisfying primary beneficiaries and corporate social responsibility. Systems goals establish a basis for organisational survival and prosperity. Control is the set of mechanisms the organisation uses to keep action and/or outputs within predetermined levels. Output controls focus on desired targets and allow managers to use their own methods for reaching the desired target. Process controls (such as policies, rules, procedures, formalisation and standardisation, quality and security) attempt to specify the manner in which tasks will be accomplished. Coordination is the set of mechanisms that an organisation uses to link the actions of separate units into a consistent pattern. Coordination methods can be impersonal (such as centralised staff units) or personal (such as network development and task forces). Organisational designs, overall, can be said to be mechanistic (involving many levels of authority, high levels of control and impersonal coordination) or organic (breakup of work horizontally; personal coordination and loose control).

Vertical specialisation

Vertical specialisation is the hierarchical division of labour that specifies formal authority and a chain of command. The organisation's hierarchy can be said to be tall or flat, relating to the number of levels of management or authority in the organisation. Organisational authority can also be centralised (concentrated at the top or centre or the organisation) or decentralised (where decision making is pushed down to lower levels of the organisation). Unity of command defines the situation in which each worker has a clear reporting relationship to only one supervisor. It lessens confusion and provides clear channels of communication. Span of control indicates the number of individuals reporting to a supervisor. Wide spans of control mean the supervisor supervises many people, whereas a supervisor with a narrow span of control will have few employees.

Horizontal specialisation

Horizontal specialisation is the division of labour that results in various work units or groups in the organisation. The distinction between line and staff units can be particularly relevant to horizontal departmentalisation. Line personnel conduct the major business of the organisation while staff personnel assist in performing specialised supportive services. Three main types of 'departmentalisation' are: functional, divisional and matrix departmentalisation. Each structure has advantages and disadvantages. Organisations may successfully use any type, or a mixture, as long as the strengths of the structure match the needs of the organisation's goals.

Implications of emerging forms of work organisation

Each organisation's design will be unique. Smaller organisations often adopt a simple structure; larger organisations often adopt a bureaucratic form. The bureaucracy is an ideal form based on legal authority, logic and order rather than on individual supervision or tradition. While most larger corporations are bureaucracies, they differ in the degree and combination of mechanistic and organic features. Divisionalised organisations establish a separate structure for each business or division in the organisation so that there is emphasis on coping with the particular aspects of that part of the business, but also overall synergy. Conglomerates are organisations that own several unrelated businesses that do not have inherently synergistic advantages. Within divisionalised or conglomerate organisations each business can develop different design features. The core–ring organisation involves an inner core, relatively permanent, workforce with higher job security, higher salaries and better career paths. There is also a flexible outer ring of workers employed on a part-time or casual basis as required. They tend to have lower job security, lower pay and a lack of career paths. This approach enables the organisation to achieve economies by adapting its employment levels to suit the circumstances. The adhocracy is a structural form that emphasises shared, decentralised decision making, extreme horizontal specialisation, few levels of management and few formal controls. Other organisation designs include strategic alliances, networked organisations, virtual organisations and franchises.

CHAPTER 8 study guide

Key terms

adhocracy, *p. 319*
bureaucracy, *p. 312*
centralisation, *p. 301*
conglomerates, *p. 315*
control, *p. 294*
coordination, *p. 297*
corporate social responsibility (CSR), *p. 292*
decentralisation, *p. 301*
departmentalisation by customer, *p. 305*
departmentalisation by geography, *p. 305*
divisional departmentalisation, *p. 305*
divisionalised design, *p. 315*
environmental complexity, *p. 290*

formal structure, *p. 287*
formalisation, *p. 296*
functional departmentalisation, *p. 304*
horizontal specialisation, *p. 302*
line personnel, *p. 302*
matrix structure, *p. 307*
mechanistic design, *p. 299*
network organisation, *p. 320*
organic design, *p. 299*
organisation charts, *p. 288*
organisational design, *p. 287*
organisational strategy, *p. 291*
output controls, *p. 295*
output goals, *p. 292*
policy, *p. 295*

primary beneficiaries, *p. 292*
procedure (rule), *p. 295*
process controls, *p. 295*
simple design, *p. 312*
span of control, *p. 302*
staff personnel, *p. 303*
standardisation, *p. 296*
strategic alliances, *p. 319*
systems goals, *p. 293*
technological imperative, *p. 289*
technology, *p. 289*
unity of command, *p. 302*
vertical specialisation, *p. 301*
virtual organisations, *p. 320*

Review questions

1. Explain how control relates to organisational goals.
2. Explain the difference between mechanistic and organic organisations.
3. What roles do size, technology, environment and strategy play in organisational design?
4. What is a core–ring organisation and why does it have an impact on the workforce?

Application questions

1. Demonstrate the purpose of an organisational chart in terms of depicting horizontal and vertical specialisation in an organisation. What are some of the things that an organisation chart may not reveal about an organisation?
2. From the perspective of an employee, how might it be to work in the following situations (compare the choices in each of a, b and c):
   (a) a functionally departmentalised organisation compared to a functionally departmentalised organisation with project teams in a matrix structure
   (b) an organisation that is highly decentralised compared with one that is highly centralised
   (c) an organisation that is very mechanistic compared to one that is very organic?
3. In a large organisation employing mostly highly educated professionals, what do you think might be the best approaches to achieving control over those professionals? Explain your answers.
4. Many organisations are becoming flatter, reducing levels of hierarchy and widening the span of control. What advantages and disadvantages would there be in this approach for an organisation that relied on its employees to make judgements on customers' requests (for example, for loans, insurance claims or special consideration of circumstances in social welfare cases)?

5. What form of hybrid design might be necessary for an organisation that is very large and must reach economies of scale, but also needs to adapt to environmental uncertainty? Explain your answer.
6. How would you describe the technology and organisational forms used in the following? (It is acceptable to describe a mix of technologies and forms.) Explain your reasons.

(a) An organisation designing a major television ad campaign for health awareness issues.
(b) A large company providing 'new' kitchens for established homes that manufactures units in the factory to custom fit the house, and later installing them in customers' homes.
(c) A firm of accountants.
(d) A multinational mining organisation.

Research questions

1. Find two local organisations. Try to choose two different-sized organisations that have different processes; for example, retail and service industries. It would be best to avoid organisations that are branches of a bigger organisation, as this would complicate your research. Give a brief overview of these two organisations and what they do and then compare and contrast them in terms of the following criteria: goals, control methods, vertical specialisation, horizontal specialisation and coordination methods. Also assess and compare the scale, environment, technology and strategy of the organisations to consider how this may have affected the design of the organisations.
2. Search the website of a major organisation you are familiar with, analysing the organisation in terms of the following elements of organisational structure:
   - statements of goals (output/system goals)
   - explanations or diagrams of the formal structure of the organisation (organisational charts, number of layers in the hierarchy, span of control, apparent centralisation/decentralisation)
   - different groups/sections in the organisation (type of specialisation into divisions or departments, line and staff personnel, casual and permanent components of the staff).

If there are different business units within the organisation, analyse the range of businesses or business units in the 'organisation' and draw conclusions based on whether you find them synergistic (or not synergistic) in the design of the entire organisation.

Running project

Complete the following activities for your chosen organisation.
1. Identify the organisation's goals. These might include formal, written goals as well as less obviously stated goals. Try to identify output goals and systems goals.
2. Refer to the organisational chart for your organisation. From this chart, and from everything else you know about how the organisation functions, construct an organigraph for the organisation. Do you think the organisational chart or the organigraph is most useful in understanding the structure of the organisation? Why?
3. How is the organisation departmentalised? Explain how and why this is appropriate (considering types of departmentalisation and issues such as line and staff personnel).
4. How does technology and environment affect the organisational design of your organisation?
5. What are the likely implications of the design and structure of the organisation on the employees?

Vertical and horizontal specialisation: organising XYZ Paper Company

XYZ does not have an organisational chart. The following is a list of its management position titles. Develop an organisational chart by dividing the total task into separate duties, grouping similar people and resources together in a division of labour that establishes specific work units/ departments. Draw your organisational chart using both the title and the letter in each box.

A sales manager
B accountants
C engineering department
D vice-president of personnel
E president
F credit manager
G product A manager (facial tissue, paper towels, napkins, etc.)
H product B supervisor
I vice-president of finance
J advertising manager
K vice-president of manufacturing
L quality-control manager
M product A supervisor
N product A sales supervisor
O purchasing manager
P training manager
Q data-processing manager
R vice-president of marketing
S product B manager (writing paper, envelopes etc.)
T sales supervisor product B
U assistant to the president

After completing the organisational chart, answer the following questions.

1. What is the span of control for the president and each vice-president? Is it broad or narrow?
2. Identify the line and staff units and consider whether XYZ uses standardisation.
3. What type of departmentalisation does your organisational chart have?
4. Use the following criteria to consider whether the organisational design tends towards being organic or mechanistic.

Mechanistic	*Organic*
Stable predictable environment	Innovative unpredictable environment
Strict formal lines of authority	Flexible informal lines of authority
Centralised authority	Decentralised authority
Extensive use of managerial techniques	Minimal use of managerial techniques
Many rules and procedures	Few rules and procedures
Specialist jobs	Generalist jobs
Formal and impersonal coordination and control	Informal and personal coordination and control
Large batch or mass production technology	Made-to-order or long-run process technology
Functional departmentalisation	Divisional departmentalisation

Assessing organisational structure and design

Objectives

To develop and refine your understanding of the basic design and structural characteristics of various organisations
Total time: 60–90 minutes

Procedure

1. In groups of five, choose an organisation with which you are reasonably familiar. Develop a list of its basic structural elements using a chart or table to record all discussion on each of the attributes.
2. Address the following concerns.[105]
   (a) Product. What is the core business and the products/services that your organisation provides to customers (or clients, members)? Are its products of real social value? What technologies are used to produce its products/services?
   (b) Workplace. Is the workplace safe? Is the business finding ways to involve workers in the decision-making process?

(c) Environment. For example, if you have chosen a manufacturer, does the business protect air, water and so on? If you have chosen a financial business, does it use environmental responsibility when investing or underwriting?

(d) Community. What kind of commitment does it have to its local and national community? Does it apply some standards to immigrant workers?

3. Suggest an organisational design that best suits your organisation. Discuss why you chose it over other designs (it could be an improved design, or if you think the existing design is best you need to justify it).

Wrap up
Present your team findings to the class.

Case study: Why do bosses need to go 'undercover'?

Undercover boss is a reality TV show about corporate executives who go 'undercover' to observe, in person, what is really happening on the front lines of their businesses and to discover how their management decisions are actually being implemented.

In the 2010 premiere of the Ten Network Australian version, *Undercover boss Australia*, Don Meij, chief executive of Domino's Pizza, disguised himself with a cap and some glasses to take on a variety of frontline jobs across the business he had been with for over 20 years, including delivery driver, human billboard and pizza-maker. He was surprised by the labour-intensive dishwashing process that wasted water, and was also given incorrect pizza preparation instructions from a staff member who was not trained properly. Meij said the experience was 'definitely worthwhile … the way that I was treated was extremely positive. I wouldn't have picked some things up without doing the task over and over'.[106]

Among the other executives that went undercover included Director of Operations at Veolia Environmental Services, Peter Murray; founder and Chief Executive of Boost Juice, Janine Allis; Chief Executive of Big 4 Holiday Parks, Ray Schleibs; Toga Hospitality's Rachel Argaman; and Chief Executive of Ritchies IGA, Fred Harrison. As Ray Schleibs noted:

> It was a great chance for me, from day one, to get a real insight into the numerous jobs that park owners and staff do on a daily basis … From a business perspective, I now have some great ideas as to how to make this already successful group even better, and I am really looking forward to getting behind the desk and putting them into practice.[107]

This reveals the paradox of why leaders have to resort to these measures to find out what really goes on in their organisations, and why they are unable to just sit behind a desk to manage effectively. As Julian Birkinshaw and Stuart Crainer, writing for *Business Strategy Review*, note:

> The clean and orderly, even elegant, surroundings of a company's headquarters often do not resemble much

of the sites where products are manufactured or services are provided. Often geographically removed from the workplace, the upper levels of an organization are also distanced from information about worker attitudes, values and priorities. Unfortunately, the higher one rises in an organization, the more difficult it is to know what's happening on the loading dock, shop floor or sales counter.[108]

This dysfunctionality provided the genesis for the idea of the original *Undercover boss* series in the United Kingdom in 2008, when British Airways opened its new multi-billion-dollar terminal at Heathrow Airport to massive chaos, caused by the breakdown of the baggage system. When questioned by reporters on 'When was the last time he travelled as a punter [paying customer]?', British Airways CEO Willie Walsh responded that 'I can't because people in BA recognise me'. So, Stephen Lambert and Eli Holzman, the original producers of *Undercover boss*, wondered whether this was true, and set out to test their theory:

> Would ordinary workers in large corporations recognise their big boss if he or she were dressed like them and they were told that here was a new trainee trying out their kind of job? We suspected that they wouldn't.[109]

Vice versa, as Stephen Xavier notes:

It's impossible for a CEO to understand everyone's situation or story, considering that companies can have thousands of employees ... For anyone who has watched *Undercover boss*, there are several simple yet critical takeaways ... the Undercover CEOs and other corporate leaders have strayed too far away and become too out-of-touch with who their people are and what makes their companies function effectively.[110]

Questions

1. Based on the case, in what way can organisational design hamper the 'real' picture that leaders need to have in order to manage effectively?

2. Do you think that organisations that grow beyond a certain size (in terms of employee numbers) will face similar problems? Why or why not?
3. Some people have criticised the 'undercover bosses' for sending the message that they don't trust their staff by using disguise and deception. Do you agree? Why or why not?
4. The 'undercover bosses' have invariably been affected by their experiences and have implemented changes to ensure that organisational structure does not get in the way of effective management. What do you think are some of these changes? (You can check online for episodes to see what these changes were, and conduct further research to evaluate how effective they have been.)

End notes

1. Lark Distillery, 'About', www.larkdistillery.com.au.
2. Family Business Australia 'Back the Lark Distillery', http://peak.fambiz.org.au; Nicks Wine Merchants (Doncaster) Pty Ltd, 'The Lark Distillery', www.nicks.com.au.
3. ABC News, 'Tasmanian whisky maker Lark Distillery takes small business top gong' (8 August 2014), www.abc.net.au; Cooperative Business New Zealand, 'The Top 40', http://nz.coop; K Scherer, 'Big two supermarket chains locked in fierce food fight', *The New Zealand Herald* (12 April 2010), www.nzherald.co.nz.
4. Dan Murphy's, 'Q&A with Lark Distillery' (2014), www.danmurphys.com.au.
5. Deloitte, 'UK and Australia world leaders in use of PPPs', press release for global Deloitte study 'Closing the Infrastructure Gap: The Role of Public-Private Partnerships', www.deloitte.com.
6. Singapore Ministry of Finance, 'Public Private Partnership', http://app.mof.gov.sg/ppp.aspx.
7. G Clydesdale, 'Capabilities and industrial policy: lessons from the New Zealand movie industry', *Industrial and Corporate Change*, vol. 24, no. 3 (2014), pp. 1–29.
8. Byrraju Foundation, 'The Model School Programme: An initiative in rural transformation', www.byrrajufoundation.org.
9. UMW news release — UMW & MERCY Malaysia in Community Service Programme, www.umw.com.my/community.php.
10. RN Osborn, JG Hunt and LR Jauch, *Organization theory: integrated text and cases* (Melbourne, FL: Krieger, 1984), pp. 123–215.
11. R Greenwood and D Miller, 'Tackling design anew', *Academy of Management Perspectives*, vol. 24, no. 4 (2010), pp. 78–88.
12. J Woodward, *Industrial organization: theory and practice* (London: Oxford University Press, 1965).
13. JD Thompson, *Organization in action* (New York: McGraw-Hill, 1967).
14. Woodward, op. cit.
15. C Phillips, 'Exploring the pureplay mass customisation field by product category', *Power Retail* (18 February 2014), www.powerretail.com.au.
16. C Williams, 'How Dell became yesterday's tech giant', *The Telegraph* (7 February 2013), www.telegraph.co.uk.
17. '3D printing scales up', *The Economist* (7 September 2013), www.economist.com.
18. See RN Osborn and CC Baughn, 'New patterns in the formation of US/Japanese cooperative ventures,' *Columbia Journal of World Business*, vol. 22 (1988), pp. 57–65.
19. 'Latest cuts to cause Qantas delays: union', *News.com.au* (08 July 2014), www.news.com.au; J Cairns, 'Aussie airlines feel the pressure as international competition strengthen', *The Conversation* (2 September 2013), http://theconversation.com.
20. LR Jauch and RN Osborn, 'Toward an integrated theory of strategy', *Academy of Management Review*, vol. 6 (1981), pp. 491–8; AD Chandler, *The visible hand: the managerial revolution in America* (Cambridge, MA: Bellknap, 1977); Karen Bantel and RN Osborn, 'The influence of performance, environment, and size on firm strategic clarity', working paper (Detroit, Michigan: Department of Management, Wayne State University, 1990).
21. See RM Cyert and JG March, *A behavioral theory of the firm* (Englewood Cliffs, NJ: Prentice Hall, 1963). A discussion of organisational goals is also found in Charles Perrow, *Organizational analysis: a sociological view* (Belmont, CA: Wadsworth, 1970) and in RH Hall, 'Organizational behavior: a sociological perspective' in JW Lorsch (ed.), *Handbook of organizational behavior* (Englewood Cliffs, NJ: Prentice Hall, 1987), pp. 84–95.
22. See, for instance, IC MacMillan and A Meshulack, 'Replacement versus expansion: dilemma for mature US businesses,' *Academy of Management Journal*, vol. 26 (1983), pp. 708–26.

23. WH Starbuck and PC Nystrom, 'Designing and understanding organizations' in PC Nystrom and WH Starbuck (eds), *Handbook of organizational design: adapting organizations to their environments* (New York: Oxford University Press, 1981).

24. StarBiz.Icr (Corporate Social Responsibility Awards, Malaysia citing John Zinkin, Institute Corporate Social Responsibility, Malaysia), http://thestar.com.my.

25. J Schermerhorn, P Davidson, D Poole, P Woods, A Simon and E McBarron, *Management*, 5th Asia-Pacific ed. (Milton, Qld: John Wiley & Sons, 2014).

26. See PR Lawrence and JW Lorsch, *Organization and environment* (Homewood, IL: Richard D. Irwin, 1969).

27. 'Australian wool exporter conquers Chinese market — Australian outward investment case study', www.austrade.gov.au.

28. JR Schermerhorn Jr, JG Hunt, RN Osborn and M Uhl-Bien, *Organizational behavior*, 11th ed. (Hoboken, NJ: John Wiley & Sons, 2010), p. 398.

29. A Heathcote, 'To catch a thief', *BRW* (3–9 February, 2005), pp. 70–71.

30. Adapted from W Edwards Deming, 'Improvement of quality and productivity through action by management', *Productivity Review* (Winter 1982), pp. 12–22; W Edwards Deming, *Quality, productivity and competitive position* (Cambridge, MA: MIT Center for Advanced Engineering, 1982).

31. H Cheng, D Li and L Luo, 'The Chinese perception of quality: model building and analysis based on consumers' perception', *Journal of Chinese Management*, vol. 1, no. 3 (May 2014), http://link.springer.com.

32. F Hsu and D Marinucci, *Advances in cybersecurity: technology, operation, and experiences*, (Bronx, NY: Fordham University Press, 2013).

33. Adapted from PR Lawrence and JW Lorsch, *Organization and environment: managing differentiation and integration* (Homewood, IL: Richard D. Irwin, 1967).

34. J Thill, C Bovee, R Chatterjee, K Subramanian 'Excellence in business communication', Pearson (2013).

35. Facebook: figures of monthly active users 2008–2014, www.statista.com.

36. Facebook: figures of monthly active users 2008–2014, www.statista.com.

37. P Cohan 'Is Facebook Slicing $1.4 trillion out of U.S. GDP?', Forbes (2 June 2012), pp. 1–2; D Mielach 'No, really, Facebook makes employees more productive', *Business News Daily* (13 April 2012), http://businessnewsdaily.com.

38. C Hadley and K Chambers, 'Networking vs notworking', *Charter* (2011).

39. Yammer website, https://www.yammer.com.

40. B Chacos 'What the heck is Yammer?' *PCWorld* (7 August 2012), www.pcworld.com.

41. 'The Yammer journey so far at NAB', *IDM*, www.idm.net.au.

42. 'Top 10 movers & shakers in Australian crowdsourcing', *Business Review* (20 February 2014), www.businesreviewaustralia.com.

43. For a review see RN Osborn, JG Hunt and LR Jauch, op. cit.

44. R Davis, *Fundamentals of top management* (New York: Harper & Row, 1951); David Van Fleet and Arthur Bedeian, 'A history of the span of management,' *Academy of Management Review* (1977), pp. 356–72.

45. E Fang, Q Wu, J Xia and D Chen 'The impact of new product & operations technological practices on organizational culture', *International Journal of Production Economics*, vol. 145, no. 2 (2013), pp. 733–42.

46. This section is based on Osborn, Hunt and Jauch, op. cit., pp. 273–303.

47. A Boxall, 'What are we doing to ensure the sustainability of the health system?', House of Representatives Committee Research Paper, no. 4 (2011–12), www.aph.gov.au.

48. D Campbell, 'Why hospitals need more generalist doctors and specialist nurses', *The Conversation* (9 October 2014), http://theconversation.com.

49. E Kretowicz, 'Our failing health', *The Canberra Times* (11 August 2013), www.canberratimes.com.au.

50. DI Ben-Tovim, JE Bassham, DM Bennett, ML Dougherty, MA Martin, SJ O'Neill, JL, Sincock, and MG Szwarcbord, 'Redesigning care at the Flinders Medical Centre: clinical process redesign using "lean thinking"', *Medical Journal of Australia*, vol. 188, no. 6 (2008), pp. 27–31.

51. D Twomey, F Scherr and W Hunt, 'Configuration of a functional department: a study of contextual and structural variables', *Journal of Organizational Behavior*, vol. 9 (1988), pp. 61–75.

52. P Herbert 'HR, knock down those office silos', Symbolist (May 2012), www.symbolist.com.blog.

53. NAB, 'Shareholders/Company Overview', www.nab.com.au.

54. A Fox, 'Price falls linked to Fonterra auctions', *New Zealand Herald* (13 July 2009); A Fox, 'Fonterra turns up heat on farmers', *New Zealand Herald* (21 September 2009).

55. Fonterra Co-operative Group Limited, *Annual report 2013*, www.fonterra.com.

56. P Ghemawat, 'The cosmopolitan corporation', *Harvard Business Review*, vol. 89, no. 5 (2011), pp. 92–9.

57. C Stringer, C Tamasay, R Le Heron, and S Gray, 'Growing a global company from New Zealand: the case of dairy giant Fonterra', C Stringer and R Le Heron (eds), *Agri-food commodity chains and globalising networks* (Surrey: Ashgate Publishing, 2008).

58. For a discussion of matrix structures see S Davis, P Lawrence, H Kolodny and M Beer, *Matrix* (Reading, MA: Addison-Wesley, 1977).

59. Open University, *The effective manager. Unit 9: organisations* (United Kingdom, 1984), p. 19.

60. S Sharma, 'Research in corporate sustainability: what really matters?', S Sharma, and M Starik (eds), *Research in corporate sustainability: the evolving theory and practice of organizations in the natural environment* (Cheltenham: Edward Elgar Publishing, 2002), p. 2.

61. W Zhu and H Li, 'CSR based on game theory', American *Journal of Industrial and Business Management*, vol. 3, no. 7, (2013), pp. 610–13.

62. A Griffiths and JA Petrick, 'Corporate architectures for sustainability', *International Journal of Operations & Production Management*, vol. 21, no. 12 (2001), pp. 1573–85.

63. S Benn, D Dunphy and A Griffiths, 'Enabling change for corporate sustainability: an integrated perspective', *Australasian Journal of Environmental Management*, vol. 13, no. 3 (2006), pp. 156–65.

64. W Stubbs and C Cocklin, 'Conceptualizing a "sustainability business model"', *Organization & Environment*, vol. 21, no. 2 (2008), pp. 103–27.

65. C Pedersen and J Nagengast, 'The virtues of the virtual organization', *Strategic HR Review*, vol. 7, no. 3 (2008), pp. 19–25.

66. S Easton, 'More, better with less: inside NZ's silo-breaking service reform', *The Mandarin*, www.themandarin.com.au.

67. See Henry Mintzberg, *Structure in fives: designing effective organizations* (Englewood Cliffs, NJ: Prentice Hall, 1983).

68. For a comprehensive review see W Richard Scott, *Organizations: rational, natural, and open systems*, 2nd ed. (Englewood Cliffs, NJ: Prentice Hall, 1987).

69. Max Weber, *The theory of social and economic organization*, AM Henderson and HT Parsons trans (New York: The Free Press, 1947).

70. Mintzberg, op. cit.

71. See Osborn et al., op. cit., for an extended discussion.

72. See P Clark and K Starkey, *Organization transitions and innovation-design* (London: Pinter Publications, 1988).

73. Osborn et. al., op. cit.

74. ibid.

75. C Nader, 'ABC gets $22m in state aid to stay open', *The Age* (7 November 2008), www.theage.com.au.

76. 'Goodstart takes on ABC Learning centres', *Sydney Morning Herald* (31 May 2010), www.smh.com.au.

77. D Clark, 'ABC learning to be wound up', *ABC News* (3 June 2010), www.abc.net.au.

78. S Kidman & Co., www.kidman.com.au.

79. 'Kidman', *Dynasties* (8 December 2003), www.abc.net.au.

80. M Kelly, 'Pastoral holdings remain a family affair', *The Weekend Australian* (30–31 October 2010), p. 6.

81. J-V Douglas, 'Strike up the brands: acquisitions produce a robust portfolio', *BRW*, vol. 31, no. 43 (2009), p. 31.

82. Citadel Group, 'About us', www.citadelgroup.com.au.

83. P Kerin, 'The gold Wesfarmers,' *BRW* (1–7 September 2005), p. 32.

84. Wesfarmers website, www.wesfarmers.com.au.

85. A Sibillin, 'Why it's great to be small', *BRW*, vol. 32, no. 10 (2010), pp. 20–5.

86. A Sibillin, 'The iPhone Apps model', *BRW*, vol. 32, no. 10 (2010), p. 23.

87. C Body, 'Remote control,' *HR Monthly* (February 2008), pp. 14–19.

88. 'Why offshore outsourcing is the next big industry trend', *B&T Magazine* (29 July 2014), www.bandt.com.au.

89. Australian Bureau of Statistics, *Employee Earnings and Hours, Australia, May 2012*, cat. no. 6306.0 (Canberra: ABS).

90. J Champy, *Reengineering management* (Glasgow: HarperCollins, 1995); M Hammer and S Stanton, *The reengineering revolution: a handbook* (New York: HarperCollins, 1995); R Morgan and J Smith, *Staffing the new workplace* (Chicago, IL: CCH, 1996).

91. Mintzberg, op. cit.

92. C Perrow, *Complex organizations: a critical essay*, 3rd ed. (New York: Random House, 1986).

93. Osborn et. al., op. cit.

94. See J Ettlie, 'Technology drives a marriage', *Journal of Commerce* (16 March 1990), p. 6.

95. E Knight, 'Solly Lew lines up a few more brands', *The Sydney Morning Herald* (27 July 2005), p. 20.

96. M Davis and F Buffini, 'Sector "betrayed" by inquiry', *The Weekend Australian*, Financial review section (17–21 April 2003), p. 6.

97. *Annual report 2011–12: Australian Competition and Consumer Commission and the Australian Energy Regulator* (Canberra, Australian Government, 2012), www.accc.gov.au.

98. D Dubios, 'Google, the network company: from theory to practice' (11 September 2013), http://knowledge.insead.edu.

99. F Luthans, *Organizational behavior*, 9th ed. (Boston: McGraw-Hill, 2002), pp. 117–19.

100. Derived from Z Rahman and SK Bhattachryya, 'Virtual organisation: a strategem,' *Singapore Management Review*, vol. 24, no. 2 (2002), pp. 29–45; C Barnatt, 'Virtual organisation in the small business sector: the case of Cavendish Management Resources', *International Small Business Journal*, vol. 15, no. 4 (1997), pp. 36–47.

101. ibid.

102. L Frazer, S Weaven and K Bodey, *Franchising Australia 2010 survey* (Brisbane: Griffith University, 2010).

103. S Lord, 'An introduction to franchising in New Zealand' (17 July 2013), www.franchise.co.nz.

104. J Cherrington, 'Franchising success,' *Management Today* (September 2005), pp. 28–30.

105. Exercise adapted from *Mother Jones Magazine* (June 1985).

106. T Boreham, 'Bosses benefit by getting up close on personnel', *The Australian* (4 January 2011), www.theaustralian.com.au.

107. 'Big4 Holiday Parks new CEO spends one day undercover', *e-Travel Blackboard* (13 October 2010), www.etravelblackboard.com.

108. S Martin, J Birkinshaw and S Crainer, 'Covert operations', *Business Strategy Review*, vol. 20, no. 3 (2009), pp. 76–80.

109. S Lambert and E Holzman, *Undercover boss: inside the TV phenomenon that is changing bosses and employees everywhere* (San Francisco: Jossey-Bass, 2010).

110. S Xavier, 'CBS reality show Undercover Boss sends a wake-up call to America's CEOs', *America's Top Coach* (7 April 2010), www.americastopcoach.com.

CHAPTER 9

ORGANISATIONAL CULTURE

LEARNING OBJECTIVES

After studying this chapter, you should be able to:

1. define the concept of organisational culture and explain its relationship to national culture

2. explain the levels of cultural analysis in organisations and the notions of subcultures and cultural diversity

3. explain the idea of observable aspects of organisational culture and describe stories, rites, rituals and symbols

4. explain how shared values are central in understanding organisational culture and how they relate to organisational action

5. explain how common assumptions comprise the deepest level of organisational culture and how they contribute towards that culture

6. discuss what organisational researchers investigate

7. discuss alternative perspectives on organisational culture and the functions of culture for members of an organisation

8. outline some hints for managing culture

9. summarise the link between ethics and organisational culture.

ORGANISATIONAL CULTURE AND VALUES

Organisational culture brings together individual and organisational values. Individual values are the concepts, activities and relationships that an individual relates to most. They are highly influential as to how the individual makes interpretations, is responsive and behaves in the work environment. In contrast, organisational values are the collective roles, functions and goals that are necessary for the organisation to be successful. Often these are delineated through corporate strategies, annual reports or press releases. An operational culture is generated when there is an alignment between these two sets of values. Values also

change, dependent on shifting personal values and influences on the organisation.[1] As personal values and organisational influences also fluctuate through time, organisations are in a constant state of change, the rate of which varies from organisation to organisation. Importantly, at the centre of this change are people and it is the people in organisations who, therefore, 'do' the actual changing.[2] Employee satisfaction is, therefore, critical in aligning individual and organisational values and in managing changing cultures in the modern era.

In a global survey, global consulting firm Regus found that Australian workers valued character aspects of culture, like showing respect towards all members of staff, as the most important ingredient to creating a happy business culture.[3] As William Willems, Regus Regional Vice President for Australia, New Zealand and South-East Asia notes:

> As work pressures and hours expand further into people's personal lives, Australian workers are ever more aware of the importance that the character of the people they work and spend so many hours of their day with has on job satisfaction.[4]

The challenge for organisations in Australia and elsewhere is to implement strategies that will enable individuals to perform, while not ignoring important ethics, norms and attitudes that their employees value in their quest for performance and excellence.

Introduction

Most people have a basic notion of what culture is. The suggestion would probably be that culture studied by anthropologists and sociologists represents the belief systems, values and specific human behaviours that distinguish one society from another. The same can be said of organisations, because they are one significant subsystem within any society. Thus, it is important to have a firm understanding of the elements of organisational culture, what they represent and how some may be used.

Many managers believe that a sound organisational culture is the key to competitive advantage for leading corporations. There is evidence that some successful organisations sustain continued growth and development by 'implanting' a strong culture that is shared and acted on by all members of the organisation.[5] However, others express concerns about striving for a strong organisational culture, because of the difficulties associated with strongly integrated belief systems and the need for creative thinking, innovations and the ability to cope with change.[6] The old methods of command and control are being replaced by methods of participation and involvement, and managers are becoming facilitators, helpers, guides and coaches. These changes require adjustment of individual, group and overall organisational value systems and affect an organisation's culture.

This chapter considers the concept of organisational culture, how it manifests itself within organisations, and its functions. We look at the observable aspects and values of organisational cultures, and common assumptions about organisational culture, and discuss the importance of subcultures, countercultures and the diversity of organisational cultures. Finally, we discuss the link between organisational culture and ethical behaviour.

The concept of organisational culture

In chapter 1, we examined 'culture' as it applies internationally and ethnically to the various nations and peoples of the world; that is, we looked at national culture. Here, we are concerned with **organisational culture**. Organisational culture is defined as the system of shared beliefs and values that develops within an organisation and guides the behaviour of its members.[7] Later in this chapter we will add to this definition to make explicit the complexities associated with the notion of organisational culture and cultural research.

Organisational culture is a system of shared beliefs and values that guides behaviour.

Just as no two individual personalities are necessarily the same, no two organisational cultures are identical. Most significantly, management scholars and consultants increasingly believe that cultural differences can have a major impact on the performance of organisations and the quality of work life experienced by their members.

Understanding the connections between organisational and national cultures

It is important to clarify the distinction between organisational culture and national culture. Only then is it possible to understand the connections between the two. The major reason that there is a strong connection is that organisational culture frequently derives from national culture. In other words, many of the shared beliefs and values that develop in organisations can be traced to commonly held assumptions in society.

However, despite being embedded in a national or host culture, organisations will still develop their own individual cultures. Every organisation in Australia, Japan, Ireland, France or Indonesia has a culture that is unique to that organisation. It is influenced by the national culture and frequently mirrors many aspects of it, but it also derives from the particular characteristics and experiences unique to the organisation.

It is important that we do not stereotype organisations in other national cultures as all sharing the same organisational culture; in the same way that not all organisations in our own country share the same organisational culture, neither will all organisations in other countries have similar values and beliefs. Indeed, globalisation makes the distinctions and the connections between national culture and organisational culture even more interesting, as large multinational corporations with an individual organisational culture, bearing some marks of the national culture that spawned them, will have to absorb and consider different national cultures that host their many branches across the world.

Maintaining creativity in times of organisational growth

OBinAction

As Google grows, its initial innovative culture is being challenged as a burgeoning bureaucracy arises. To thwart this threat, Google began holding regular meetings in which staff members were able to offer novel concepts to Eric Schmidt, Google CEO (2009), as well as Larry Page and Sergey Brin (Google's co-founders). In an attempt to prevent a conservative culture arising, as the organisation matures, some projects had more resources dedicated to them. In 2009, this new organisational arrangement had allowed for the roll out of Google Wave, a new software application to facilitate online collaboration and allow users to create shared content hosted on Google's cloud facilities.

(continued)

Google Wave would enable users to interact between emails, folders, address books, text posts, photographs and web feeds. Although the project had been enthusiastically received by some employees, it created quite a stir among others. The Wave team purposely created distance from Google's headquarters, setting up its offices in Sydney. Insistence on secrecy by the Wave team, in an attempt to avoid scrutiny, however, began to create cultural tensions within Google. For example, Lars Rasmussen, one of the project leaders, admitted openly that not all employees were supportive of this approach — some Googlers believed it was a betrayal of Google's open culture.[8] On 4 August 2010, Google announced it was halting development of Google Wave and would not say what would happen to the Sydney team.[9] This event instigated a move for Lars Rasmussen to join Facebook, which he believed did not have the same cultural challenges he has experienced at Google.[10] The case of Google reveals that keeping small, close-knit cultures is important for the innovation process that generated the products and services that originally put Google on the map. Keeping this culture alive as functional needs arise, due to the growth of Google's business, is a tricky affair that all organisations in the twenty-first century need to balance.

Levels of cultural analysis

Figure 9.1 graphically depicts three important levels of cultural analysis in organisations: observable culture, shared values and common assumptions. These may be envisioned as layers; the deeper we get, the more difficult it is to discover the phenomenon from the surface.

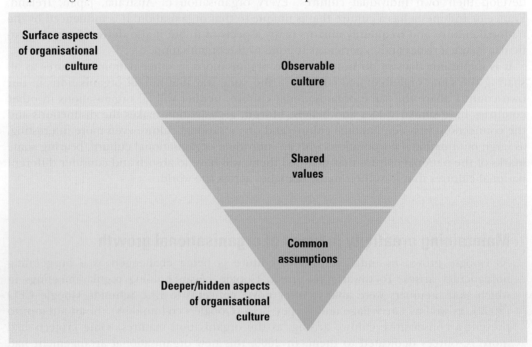

FIGURE 9.1 Three levels of analysis in studying organisational culture

Observable culture is behavioural patterns that a group displays and teaches to new members.

The first level relates to **observable culture**, or 'the way we do things around here'.[11] These are the methods that the group has developed and teaches to new members. The observable culture includes the unique stories, ceremonies and corporate rituals that make up the history of a successful work group or the organisation as a whole. It also includes symbols such as physical design, dress codes, logos and badges. Organisational cultural researchers look for patterns *for* behaviour or espoused cultural forms.

The second level of analysis recognises that **shared values** (for example, 'Quality in this organisation is our cornerstone to success', or 'We value innovative ideas', or 'We will provide the best possible care') can play a critical part in linking people and can provide a powerful motivational mechanism for members of that culture. Organisational values underpin the patterns for behaviour in observable cultural analysis. Many consultants suggest that organisations should develop a 'dominant and coherent set of shared values'.[12] The term 'shared' in cultural analysis implies that the group is a whole. Every member may not agree with the shared values, but they have all been exposed to them and have often been told they are important. Hence, many managers believe that cultivating a strong organisational culture will have a positive effect in gaining a competitive advantage.

> **Shared values** are the set of coherent values held by members of the organisation and that link them together.

Corporate clothing gives a sense of unity

OBinAction

The corporate uniform is one example of a clearly visible organisational cultural form. In particular, uniforms are an extremely effective indicator of the codification of appropriate rules of conduct.[13] Some companies can capitalise on the fact that every member of staff is a potential brand ambassador who can reflect the professional values of the organisation, as well as encourage team spirit and productivity.[14] Many companies require staff wear corporate uniforms that display the company logo and colours.[15]

In the United Kingdom, a 2014 National Health System (NHS) industry research report has shown that uniforms are becoming increasingly equated with professional behaviours. The research has revealed that the culture has shifted in the NHS with views being expressed such as, 'I wouldn't dream of now going into the NHS and turning up in a pair of jeans and a t-shirt and treat somebody, it's just not something you would think of'. It is not just in wearing the uniforms; the research also shows that uniforms need to be up-to-date and worn properly to maintain the image of professionalism in line with the branding of the NHS.[16]

Shared values, such as wearing a uniform with pride, have ties to the important values in society. Unique and shared values can provide a strong identity, enhance collective commitment, provide a stable social system and reduce the need for controls. However, we also need to acknowledge the individual differences within a collective and the value of individuality to the overall organisational culture.

At the deepest level of cultural analysis are **common assumptions**, or the taken-for-granted truths that collections of organisational members share, as a result of their joint experience. In most organisational cultures, there are a series of common assumptions known to everyone in the organisation. For example, 'we are progressive' or 'we are better at …' Such assumptions become reflected in the organisation's culture. These common assumptions may surface in an organisational crisis. 'We are different' is a common assumption that permeates the practices of some organisations.

> **Common assumptions** are the collection of truths that organisational members share as a result of their joint experiences and that guide values and behaviours.

Subcultures and countercultures

It is important to recognise distinct groups within a culture. **Subcultures** represent groups of individuals with a unique pattern of values and philosophy that are not necessarily inconsistent with the organisation's dominant values and philosophy.[17] Strong subcultures are often found in high-performance task forces, teams and special project groups

> **Subcultures** are unique patterns of values and philosophies within a group that are not inconsistent with the dominant culture of the larger organisation or social system.

in organisations. In addition, subculture formation has also been linked to educational background, professional identity and distinctive work paradigms.[18] The culture emerges to bind individuals working intensely together: organisational values and assumptions are shared, but actions can be influenced differently by distinct occupational tasks. For example, at a hospital, the common assumption of 'doing things better' underpins the common value of providing the best possible care. However, the expressed 'care' is performed differently by different occupational groups, each with distinctive interpretations of what 'best care' means. For catering staff, this may be providing a meal at the correct temperature; for surgeons, this may mean removing the cause of illness; and for occupational therapists, this may mean helping patients and their relatives to achieve an improved quality of life. Because 'providing the best care' means different things to different individuals and groups, we must expect that conflict arises between occupational subcultures and that this conflict is normal. In contrast, **countercultures** have a pattern of values and a philosophy that reject the surrounding culture.[19]

Countercultures are the patterns of values and philosophies that outwardly reject those of the larger organisation or social system.

Within an organisation, mergers and acquisitions may produce countercultures. Employers and managers of an acquired organisation may hold values and assumptions that are quite inconsistent with those of the acquiring organisation. This is often referred to as the 'clash of corporate cultures'.[20]

Fortunately, not all mergers and acquisitions cause cultural clashes, although this may be a matter of opinion among different subcultures within the new organisation. Understanding the importance of culture can also help a company to absorb or accommodate the cultures within the organisations that are acquired or merge, or to manage the complex interplays in alliances, company formations and employment relations.[21] There is a need to evaluate the 'fit' between the acquirer and the target, and, given that this is never perfect, the buyer needs to consider the trade-off between integrating the acquired firm and leaving it autonomous — the so-called integration vs. autonomy dilemma.[22] Balancing integration and autonomy is especially critical in the technology industry. Because the industry is characterised by tacit, socially complex forms of knowledge that are difficult to transfer, a high degree of post-deal integration may be required to realise an acquisition's potential value.[23] On the other hand, too much integration may result in the destruction of the acquired firm's knowledge-based resources and innovation capability if it leads to employees leaving, the disruption of highly effective organisational routines, or the stifling of entrepreneurial culture.[24]

Subculture formation may be different according to where the organisation is located in the world. For example, in Japan subcultures may be formed on the basis of date of graduation from university. In Europe, subcultures may exist on the basis of language and in North America on locational similarities. Other subculture formations may be influenced by ethnicity, gender, generational differences, socioeconomic status, place within the organisation, political and religious beliefs, and so forth.

OBin**Action**

Organisational culture and customer service at GASP clothing

Is putting down customers and being disrespectful of them acceptable in any organisational culture? Apparently so, in the often snobbish, snooty and 'bitchy' world of high fashion. This was experienced by GASP customer Keara O'Neil, who visited the clothing store in Melbourne to shop for bridesmaid dresses. The store assistant, who was initially helpful, soon turned nasty, making comments about her dress size and yelling at her as she left the store.[25] This was not just an individual staff member's action; nor was it just particular to that store. Rather, it was reflective of the organisational culture of the company.

In its response to Ms O'Neil's complaint, GASP lauded the sales assistant as a 'retail superstar', and the anonymous sender goes on to take grammatically challenged swipes at Ms O'Neil:

[The person] whom served you is a qualified stylist whom has a sixth sense for fashion, and [his] only problem is that he is too good at what he does, and as I am sure you are aware, people whom are talented, generally do not tolerate having their time wasted, which is the reason you were provoked to leave the store.[26]

This was further reinforced when the email exchange between the customer and GASP clothing went viral on social media, with the bulk of the comments posted online being negative ones by people who had shopped at GASP clothing stores. Maybe this behaviour is 'normal' on TV shows and Hollywood movies. GASP claims that its clothing range is 'worn by A list celebrities to the likes of Kim Kardashian, Selena Gomez and Katy Perry to name only a few'.

In 2012, the company was Victoria's most complained about frock shop,[27] which you would assume would be bad for business. In stark contrast, Matt Chidley, the GASP area manager, considered the coverage that had erupted since the event as 'the best thing that has ever happened to our business'.

Imported subcultures and cultural diversity

Every large organisation imports potentially important subcultural groupings when it recruits employees from the larger society. The difficulty with importing groupings from the larger society lies in the relevance these subgroups have to the organisation as a whole. At one extreme, senior managers can merely accept these divisions and work within the confines of the larger culture. However, there are three primary difficulties with this approach. Firstly, subordinated groups, such as members of a specific religion or ethnic group, are likely to form into a counterculture and to work more to change their status than to better the organisation. Secondly, the organisation may find it extremely difficult to cope with broader cultural changes. Thirdly, organisations that accept and build on natural divisions from the larger culture may find it extremely difficult to develop sound international operations. For example, many Japanese organisations have had substantial difficulty adjusting to the equal treatment of women in their US and European operations.

A recent study found that people from different ethnic and gender groups filter and process information about organisational culture differently. This means that they may interpret the same cultural messages differently. Thus, attempts by management to manipulate cultural elements may need to take account of the fact that they will not be universally and consistently understood. Management efforts to homogenise culture will almost inevitably result in subunit variations in interpretation, and this is likely to contribute to the development of subcultures.[28]

Australia is a multicultural society, with a population that has people speaking almost 400 languages, including Indigenous languages, identifying with more than 270 ancestries and observing a wide variety of cultural and religious traditions.[29] By 2010, of its 22.3 million population, 27 per cent of the population was born overseas (6.0 million people).[30] Therefore, it has become important for organisations to manage this multiculturalism effectively. Robin Ely and David Thomas[31] discuss three paradigms for an organisation's level of openness to multiculturalism.

Firstly, the 'discrimination and fairness' paradigm looks at multiculturalism with respect to equal opportunity, fair treatment, recruitment, and compliance with legislation by ensuring certain numbers of staff from ethnically diverse backgrounds are employed. This paradigm insists that individuals assimilate into the existing organisational culture, and tends to lead to the development of potentially destructive subcultures (as ethnic differences are ignored or suppressed).

Secondly, the 'access and legitimacy' paradigm for an organisation's level of openness to multiculturalism emphasises gaining access to new and diverse markets by using cultural diversity within the organisation. This may create a feeling of exploitation in staff as they are the 'token representative of their culture'. In addition, this differentiation of individuals from the group can lead to subculture development as differences are highlighted.

Thirdly, the 'learning and effectiveness' paradigm for an organisation's level of openness to multiculturalism incorporates elements of the other two paradigms. Additionally, this paradigm firmly connects diverse ethnicity to diverse approaches to work. According to Ely and Thomas, by creating openness, organisations will find that individuals from different national cultures do not feel devalued by assimilation into the existing organisational culture, nor will subcultures along ethnic lines be created.

Managing cultural diversity in organisations is a skill that contemporary managers must acquire. Many organisations run courses on multiculturalism to ensure knowledge and understanding of national and cultural differences. In addition, many organisations have courses for ethnically different groups and individuals, including English language for the workplace. For example, Medibank Private, Deakin University and the Construction, Forestry, Mining and Energy Union run English language courses that are funded by the Department of Education, Science and Training.[32]

OBinAction

Ethical dilemmas and the workplace

The workplace can challenge our assumption that we would always be ethical in any circumstance. Our ethical boundaries are not often well defined in the workplace. For example, while covering for a colleague who needs to be out of the office for the afternoon, you hear your boss discussing particulars about your friend. You must decide whether or not to inform your friend. What do you do in these circumstances? As another

example, you have a long-standing friend who works for a company that deals with your company. You go out to lunch and claim it on expenses. Was this the right thing to do? So, as you can see, ethical dilemmas can really challenge what we believe to be right and wrong.[33]

Simon Longstaff, Head of the St James Centre based in Sydney, believes that employees and employers need to have mutually aligned ethical principles and values to avoid people being asked to undertake work activities that are clearly unethical. He believes that employees need to carefully choose companies whose ethics are harmonious with their own. Equally, employers have the right to expect employees to behave according to the company's ethical framework.[34]

Observable aspects of organisational culture

Look again closely at figure 9.1. Because we are viewing organisational culture from a social constructivist point of view, we assume important aspects of an organisation's culture emerge from the collective experience of its members. These emergent aspects of the culture help make it unique and may well help provide a competitive advantage for the organisation. Some of these features may be directly observed in day-to-day practices. Others may have to be discovered; for example, by asking members to tell stories of important incidents in the history of the organisation. We often learn about the unique aspects of the organisational culture through descriptions of very specific events.[35] By observing organisational symbols and rituals, listening to stories and asking organisational members to interpret what is going on, you can begin to understand the organisation's culture.

Stories, rites, rituals and symbols

Stories indicate the state of an organisation's health. Stories offer evidence of unique qualities and characteristics that an organisation is proud of. A story may be as simple as telling a new employee about the rookie who stood up to the chief executive officer (CEO) of the company, and progressed quickly through the company because the CEO admired his or her courage (which may be something that is considered to be an important quality of the company in question).[36] Perhaps one of the most important stories concerns the founding of the organisation. The **founding story** often contains the lessons learned from the efforts of an embattled entrepreneur whose vision may still guide the firm. The story of the founding may be so embellished that it becomes a **saga**, a heroic account of accomplishments.[37] Sagas are important because they are used to tell new members the real mission of the organisation, how the organisation operates and how individuals can fit into the company. Rarely is the founding story totally accurate, and it often glosses over some of the more negative outcomes along the way.

> The **founding story** is the tale of the lessons learned and efforts of the founder of the organisation.

> A **saga** is an embellished heroic account of the story of the founding of an organisation.

If you have job experience, you may well have heard stories concerning the following questions: How will the boss react to a mistake? Can someone move from the bottom to the top of the company? What will get me dismissed? These are common story topics in many organisations.[38] Often, the stories will provide valuable hidden information about who is 'more equal' than others, whether jobs are secure and how things are really controlled. The stories suggest how organisational members view the world and live together.

Among the most obvious aspects of organisational culture are rites and rituals. **Rites** are standardised and recurring activities that are used at special times to influence the behaviours and understanding of organisational members. **Rituals** are systems of rites. Rituals serve to establish boundaries and relationships between the stakeholders of an organisation through the repetition of events, such as staff meetings or how long people take for lunch. In Japan, for example, it is common for workers and managers to start their work days together with group exercises and singing the 'company song'. Separately, the exercises and song are rites. Collectively, they form part of a ritual.

> **Rites** are standardised and recurring activities used at special times to influence the behaviours and understanding of organisational members.

> **Rituals** are systems of rites.

Rituals and rites may be unique to particular groups within the organisation. Subcultures often arise from the type of technology deployed by the unit, the specific function being performed and the specific collection of specialists in the unit. The boundaries of the subculture may well be maintained by a unique language. Often, the language of a subculture, as well as its rituals and rites, emerges from the group as a form of jargon. In some cases, the special language starts to move outside the organisation and enter the larger society. For example, the information technology (IT) industry is renowned for its use of technical language and, slowly, terms such as software, download, floppy, desktop, browser, hyperlink, icon, multimedia and online have become part of mainstream language. On the other hand, many of the IT industry's plentiful jargon terms have yet to find wide acceptance.

One such term, used by personnel manning an IT help desk to point to a *user* problem, is 'PEBKAC': problem exists between keyboard and chair.

Language is used to convey the meaning of an organisational culture, with particular words and phrases either being unique to an organisation or having a particular meaning in the organisation. It has been suggested that many conversations in organisations are making cultural statements when they convey what the company expects and wants to occur;[39] for example, language can convey meaning about daily routines and habits of employees. It can also be a valuable measure in highlighting possible subcultural differences within an organisation.

Of course, no discussion of corporate culture would be complete without mentioning the symbols found in organisations. A **cultural symbol** is any object, act or event that serves to transmit cultural meaning. Symbols can include the architecture of a building, the layout of offices and space assigned to employees, the décor of the offices, and the general impression that is communicated to visitors by way of company name and size of the establishment. Although many such symbols are quite visible, their importance and meaning may not be. Other symbols include badges, prizes, organisational branding and stationery.

> A **cultural symbol** is any object, act or event that serves to transmit cultural meaning.

OBinAction

Coworking around the world

The internet and the associated knowledge management applications have spawned a virtual world of work opportunities. No longer bound by geography and locality, tele-working has evolved into virtual teamwork, and new challenges have emerged regarding how to achieve tasks in a non-physical environment (as discussed in chapter 8). However, research on virtual teams has found that virtual workers face unique challenges, especially

in terms of building trust, cohesion and team identity, as well as overcoming isolation.[40] As such, recently, a large segment of virtual workers has begun to seek out the tra-ditional office-based experience. The growing phenomenon of coworking was conceived in the United States, but has quickly spread around technologically enabled parts of the world. The coworking office is not one overseen by one company but one that is shared by workers from different kinds of organisations. Although set free by technology and able to work from anywhere, coworkers find they are less effective when sitting home alone. Office coworking is something like a community version of corporate business centres. People can come and work and have meetings that serve the social function of community.

The coworking phenomenon has spread across the world, and there are now coworking locations in Australia, New Zealand and many parts of Asia. One example is BizDojo, which was launched in Auckland, New Zealand, in 2009.[41] It provides a collaborative working space for virtual staff who are 'Fed up with working from home', and advances the valued proposition that:

> It's time to get out there and seek your fortune. Increase your productivity, motivation, and networks. Say goodbye to the call of the fully-stocked fridge, and say hello to social business. There is a better way to work.[42]

BizDojo offers different subscription and support models for different types of virtual workers, from full-time dedicated desks and office storage to hot desks for people who only come in once a week. The success of the scheme has seen 35 companies working from the same office and, in 2011, a second BizDojo location was opened in Wellington.[43] By 2014, BizDojo had expanded to include a location in Auckland.[44]

Does the virtual worker concept, however, mean the end of office-based employees and effective collaboration? Not for Michael Bernd Bayer, communications technology expert and president at Avaya, Global Growth Markets.[45] Michael believes that there are misconceived ideas that office work has become less productive than working remotely. He identifies a contrasting position, that with the introduction of a new wave of communication technologies, the office environment is going to become even more productive and collaborative. The new office environment will be able to monitor individuals' locations and facilitate more effective collaboration. Michael believes the office environment will become increasingly important as sophisticated technologies transform what can be achieved in business offices.

Cultural rules and roles

Organisational culture often specifies when various types of actions are appropriate and where individual members stand in the social system. These cultural rules and roles are part of the normative controls of the organisation and emerge from its daily routines.[46] For instance, the timing, presentation and methods of communicating authoritative directives are often quite specific to each organisation. In one organisation, meetings may be forums for dialogue and discussion, where managers set agendas and then let others offer new ideas, critically examine alternatives and fully participate. In another organisation, the 'rules' may be quite different. The manager goes into the meeting with fixed expectations. Any new ideas, critical examinations and the like are expected to be worked out in private before the meeting takes place. The meeting is a forum for letting others know what is being done and for passing out instructions on what to do in the future. Cultural rules and roles can become deeply ingrained in organisational behaviour, as they influence 'the way things are done around here', but sometimes, they need to be changed. The What would you do? looks at dress standards in the workplace.

WhatWould **You**Do?

Dress to express

Decades ago, dress codes were fairly straightforward; employees wore either a uniform or business attire. These days, an organisation's dress code is one way of defining who and what the organisation stands for. If an organisation is trying to promote a sharp, sleek, professional image, then it is likely that individuals will need to dress in a smart manner. On the other hand, if the organisation is trying to foster a relaxed atmosphere of creativity and individualism, then it is likely that the dress code will be far more relaxed and casual. Dress codes are a cultural form. For example, at White Lady Funerals, an Australian all-female funeral parlour, all staff that meet the public are dressed in white suits and carry a white rose to symbolise purity.[47]

The problem may be in defining 'professional dress' and 'casual dress', and whether the same rules apply for men and women. An unfortunate consequence of the new workplace phenomenon, where different organisations require different attire, is that industrial tribunals are increasingly being asked to adjudicate matters that relate to appropriate attire in the workplace. For example, a male console operator at a petrol station was found to have been unfairly dismissed for refusing to take out an earring he was wearing, even though women were allowed to wear such adornments.[48] In another example, a woman at Star City Casino, a 5-star facility in Sydney, Australia, was found

(continued)

to have been unfairly dismissed for refusing to take out a tongue stud that was against the luxury casino's dress policy.[49]

Any workplace dress codes should be reasonable and applicable to men and women and must not breach any antidiscrimination legislation. Further, undesirable items must be clearly stated. For example, if midriff tops or thongs are unacceptable, the organisation needs to specifically state this in their policy, along with the reasoning for unacceptability.

Dress codes can also be extended to customers of an organisation. For example, the Bank of New Zealand recently introduced a customer dress code that involved the banning of hoods and sunglasses inside branches. In this case, the right for staff to feel safe and secure was deemed to be more important than the right for customers to wear anything that they liked into a bank branch.[50]

Dress codes are best determined in a collaborative effort between managers and their staff and communicated effectively to all in the organisation.[51] A Melbourne call centre made an attempt to remind staff about their dress code by emailing a poem outlining the appropriate attire for their workplace.[52]

Questions

1. Why would wearing a tongue stud be unacceptable to a 5-star organisation? Is there a difference in the acceptability of tongue studs, earrings, nose studs or eyebrow rings?
2. What would you do if your employee was wearing gaudy or provocative clothing?
3. How would you define 'gaudy' or 'provocative' in a dress code? Compare your definitions with the answers given by other class members. Are there distinct differences between your answers and the answers of your class members; if so, why?
4. How would you communicate the dress code message in a creative but effective way to others in an organisation?

Values and organisational culture

Consider figure 9.1 again. In order to describe fully the culture of an organisation, it is necessary to go deeper than the observable aspects. To many researchers and managers, shared values lie at the heart of organisational culture. Shared values:

- help turn routine activities into valuable, important actions
- tie the corporation to the important values of society
- may provide a very distinctive source of competitive advantage.

Linking actions and values

Individuals collectively learn behaviours and concepts to help them deal with problems. In organisations, what works for one person is often taught to new members as the correct way to think and feel. Important values are then attributed to these solutions to everyday problems. By linking values and actions, the organisation taps into some of the strongest and deepest realms of the individual. The tasks a person performs are not only given meaning but value; what one does is not only workable but correct, right and important.

Some successful organisations share some common cultural characteristics. Figure 9.2 provides a list suggested by two well-known US management consultants, Terrence Deal and Allan Kennedy.[53] As is shown in the figure, organisations with 'strong cultures' possess a broadly and deeply shared value system. Increasingly, organisations are adopting values statements that express their commitment to such areas as customer service, product and service quality, creativity and innovation, and social responsibility.

However, a strong culture can be a double-edged sword. Unique, shared values can:

- provide a strong corporate identity
- enhance collective commitment
- provide a stable social system
- reduce the need for formal and bureaucratic controls.

Conversely, a strong culture and value system can reinforce a view of the organisation and its environment. If dramatic changes are needed, it may be very difficult to change the organisation.

A *widely shared philosophy*. This philosophy is not an abstract notion of the future but a real understanding of what the organisation stands for, often embodied in slogans.

A *concern for individuals*. This often places individual concerns over rules, policies, procedures and adherence to job duties.

A *recognition of heroes*. Heroes are individuals whose actions illustrate the shared philosophy and concerns of the company.

A *belief in ritual and ceremony*. Management understands that rituals and ceremonies are real and important to members and to building a common identity.

A *well-understood sense of informal rules and expectations*. Employees understand what is expected of them.

A *belief that what employees do is important to others*. Networking in order to share information and ideas is encouraged.

FIGURE 9.2 Elements of strong corporate cultures

Common assumptions and organisational culture

At the deepest level of organisational culture (see figure 9.1), there are common understandings known to almost everyone in the corporation: 'we are different', 'we are better at …' and 'we have unrecognised talents'. These shared truths, or common assumptions, often lie dormant until actions violate them.

Common assumptions and management philosophy

If culture is considered a variable that can be changed to affect an organisation's competitive advantage, managers need to recognise what can and what cannot be changed in the organisation's culture. The first step is to recognise the group of managers as a subculture in itself. Senior managers often share common assumptions, such as 'we are good stewards', 'we are competent managers' or 'we are practical innovators'. In many organisations, broadly shared common assumptions of senior management go even further. The organisation may have a well-developed management philosophy.

A **management philosophy** links key goal-related issues with key collaboration issues and comes up with a series of general ways in which the organisation will manage its affairs. A well-developed management philosophy is important, because it establishes generally understood boundaries for all members of the organisation; it provides a consistent way of approaching novel situations; and it helps hold individuals together by assuring them of a known path towards success. In other words, a well-developed management philosophy is important because it links strategy with how the organisation operates and thus helps

A **management philosophy** links key goal-related issues with key collaboration issues to come up with general ways by which the organisation will manage its affairs.

an organisation adapt to its environment. For example, Cisco Systems' strategy of growth, profitability and customer service is linked to empowering employees to generate best ideas quickly; hiring the best people, with ideas and intellectual assets that drive success; and disseminating information to compete in an 'ideas world'.

Elements of the management philosophy may be formally documented in a corporate plan, a statement of business philosophy or a series of goals. Yet, it is the unstated but well-understood fundamentals these written documents signify that form the heart of a well-developed management philosophy.

What do organisational culture researchers investigate?

Organisational culture researchers are interested in researching cultural manifestations, while attempting to gather meaning about the patterns that link these manifestations. Studying manifestations includes researching the working environment of a culture; for example, the décor of the office, hierarchical structures and money earned by employees,

as well as relationships between organisational members. Joanne Martin identifies four types of cultural manifestations, including cultural forms, formal practices, informal practices and content themes.

Cultural forms are manifestations of organisational culture conveyed to employees. Tools used to convey observable culture include symbols, rituals, stories and language. For example, the 'employee of the month' award or the story of how the company was founded help employees to identify with the organisation's culture, as these rituals and stories are all part of 'the way things are done here'. Symbols, such as branding — for example, the golden arches of McDonald's — have meaning. What does your company or university brand symbol on the top of any letterhead convey to you? This is a cultural form!

Formal practices are written down and are, on the surface, easily controllable by management. These can include structure, task and technology, policies and procedures, and financial controls. The formal practices are all expressions of an organisational culture. Therefore, formal practices need to be observed when studying organisational culture.

Informal practices evolve through interaction, are not written down and take the form of *social rules*. Informal practices can include the time used for tea breaks throughout the day and arriving at work a few minutes late or leaving work a few minutes earlier at the end of the day. Such informal practices serve to highlight possible contradictions within the formal practices that are written down and not always adhered to.

Content themes are considered common threads of concern that underlie *interpretations of several organisational cultural manifestations*. Top companies may try to impress certain images on stakeholders and the general public; for example, by promoting respect of the environment in all business pursuits. Companies that include such values in the mission statement or on company websites are attempting to create positive associations with their brands. Often, the way that managers behave in organisations, such as showing a friendly yet competitive nature to the outside world, will communicate to observers the content themes (or the images the organisation is attempting to create in an audience's mind) of a company being studied.[54]

The majority of cultural studies within organisations take place via information obtained from the views of those members in management. However, it is now widely recognised that organisational culture researchers must also extract information about how the organisation works by providing members of the organisation who do not hold managerial positions with a tool through which to express their opinions. This ensures the organisational cultural research is conducted from multi-perspectives (see the section on alternative perspectives of culture later in this chapter) and is more complete.

Quantitatively, cultural forms, formal practices and content themes can be measured by way of asking questions about the organisation. This might take the form of an assessment of the general feelings and beliefs participants hold about the organisation, their sense of affiliation with the organisation, and so on.[55] Content themes can be examined by questioning organisational/supervisory characteristics, and by ranking the importance of organisational goals, reputation, engagement with community and service quality. Formal practices are studied by analysing policies and procedures and how these are put into operation. Informal practices are slightly more difficult to measure via questionnaire and are best revealed through interview and observation. Quantitative methods can include survey questionnaires.

Qualitatively, manifestations of organisational culture can be observed by participant observers, who have discussions with organisational members via formal and informal interviews and focus groups. The researcher examines patterns of behaviour, looks at consistencies and inconsistencies in behaviours, and is particularly interested in patterns of behaviours that are more covert. The interviews can include questions about organisational reputation before and after employment. What has changed? This is important as inconsistencies in what is reported to members outside an organisation and what members inside an organisation actually experience may reveal important information about the covert behaviours. Furthermore, the way an employee portrays the organisation to outsiders may differ, depending on the position or the occupational group that the organisational member belongs to. This may reveal patterns of inconsistencies between occupational groups, or subcultures. Interview questions can also examine 'accountability' in terms of who sets standards formally and what happens informally. This may highlight the importance of informal practices for the day-to-day functioning of an organisation. Observations can reveal a great deal about the organisation's reliance on formal and informal practices, and organisational content themes. Interpretations help to make sense of interactions between organisational actors and occupational groups, and, ultimately, the relations between organisational culture and overall organisational performance.

Many organisational culture researchers use a mix of quantitative and qualitative methods to obtain a complete of 'what is going on' in the organisation.

Different perspectives on organisational culture

Organisational culture is a complex system that does not always respond to management decisions and actions as anticipated. It is useful to take a variety of perspectives on culture to move closer to a pragmatic understanding of the forces at play. This section looks briefly at the different perspectives we can take, including the integration perspective, the differentiation perspective, and the ambiguity/fragmentation perspective.

The integration perspective

Many studies of organisational culture adopt only one perspective of culture, the integration perspective, which investigates organisational culture in terms of harmony and a supposed organisation-wide consensus.[56] The integration perspective views organisational culture as a system of shared meanings, unity and harmony. Dunphy suggests that the way we understand the pattern formed by the elements of organisational culture (the pattern of values, common assumptions, and visible elements or artefacts) can vary.[57] Organisational members, as directed by their leaders, jointly agree on 'the way we do things around here'. This cohesiveness is considered to be a variable that managers can use to adjust organisational

The **integration perspective** views organisational culture as a system of shared meanings, unity and harmony.

culture, when change is required. This perspective is characterised by assimilation through unity and harmony, among organisational members. They reinforce, integrate and bind people together and core values pervade and characterise the organisation as a whole. Socialisation helps to maintain this consistency.

We need to have more than one perspective, and be inclusive of views of members throughout the organisation, rather than presuming an occupational group, a profession or a functional level represents all organisational voices. Although the integration perspective is most commonly researched and published, there are additional perspectives: the differentiation and ambiguity perspectives.

The differentiation perspective

The differentiation perspective views an organisation's culture as a compilation of diverse and inconsistent beliefs that are shared at group level.

The **differentiation perspective** views organisational culture as a system of shared beliefs in different groups (often differentiated by location, division, gender, ethnicity and so on). Sometimes, these group values are in tune with the dominant culture. Some researchers believe that a distinction can be made between corporate culture and organisational culture. *Corporate* culture is devised by management and sold to — or imposed upon — the rest of the organisation. Rituals, stories and values are offered to organisational members as part of seducing them into membership of and identification with the organisation, and of gaining their commitment and behavioural compliance. This perspective is not only characterised by harmony, but also by diversity and inconsistency. *Organisational* culture is culture that grows or emerges from within the organisation and emphasises members as culture makers, perhaps resisting the dominant culture. Organisational culture takes into account the beliefs and values of organisational members. The overall organisational culture is shared and unique as a result of the patterns of interaction between and within groups.

Individuals develop differences in perception and opinion because of social bondings. Some of these relationships can span organisations. For example, plumbers in a large engineering factory can develop a shared relationship through their membership of a plumbing staff association. In contrast to the integration perspective, the differentiation perspective sees organisations as characterised not just by harmony and unity, but also by diversity and inconsistency. It accepts the possibility and value of internal conflict and suggests that this normally occurs due to the processes of differentiation and specialisation that are common in modern organisations.

Ambiguity/fragmentation perspective

The fragmentation perspective views organisational culture as lacking any form of pattern as a result of differing meanings between individuals and within individuals over time.

The ambiguity or **fragmentation perspective** does not see clear-cut cultural groupings within organisations as the normal state; rather it sees a normal state in organisations as one of ambiguity, because meanings differ between individuals and within individuals over time. The normal state for meanings, values and behavioural norms is diverse, because each individual independently assesses his or her environment. If consensus is observed then it is only momentary and such groupings soon dissolve.[58]

The fragmentation perspective sees attempts at cultural change along normative lines as having no effect, because the impact of any change will be absorbed. You cannot change the culture, because change is continual. However, current followers of alternative perspectives on organisational culture acknowledge that these patterns of culture can be found at any given time within the organisation.[59]

Hence, understanding multiple perspectives of culture goes beyond instilling shared values and beliefs in organisational members, as proposed by integration; it is having an in-depth insight into patterns of overt and covert behaviour that link patterns of integration, differentiation and ambiguity perspectives. Each of these perspectives can operate at any one time or at the same time.[60] Thus, by adding different perspectives, organisational culture can be more comprehensively defined as 'the socially constructed patterns of behaviours that link expressions of organisational integration, group differentiation and individual ambiguities together. These patterns of behaviour reflect individual, group and organisational values and beliefs.'[61] The Counterpoint discusses the role of culture in adopting sustainability in business.

COUNTERPOINT

The role of culture in adopting sustainability in business

The corporate world is becoming increasingly concerned about sustainability. How corporations adopt sustainability practices has been shown by researchers at the University of New South Wales and the University of Melbourne to be highly dependent upon local culture and institutional settings. Cultures with more flexibility (giving people more choice) enable alternative approaches to adopting sustainability, such as adopting sustainability practices that have an economic benefit and entrepreneurial solutions to sustainability. In contrast, adoption of sustainability practices in tight cultures where conformance to traditional conventions is very strong may build on pre-existing cultural norms.[62]

Questions

1. What may be the challenges in adopting corporate sustainability practices in countries with either flexible or traditional cultures?
2. Why may the differentiation perspective provide insight into the challenges global corporations face in adopting unified solutions to sustainability?
3. Do you believe the culture in which you live hinders or promotes the adoption of sustainability practices by business?

The functions of organisational culture for its members

Our discussion pointed to the importance of acknowledging multiple perspectives of organisational culture. However, it is undeniable that organisational cultures have an element of functionality. In other words, organisational culture may be influenced by top management, in order to achieve a competitive advantage. For example, in your first managerial job one of the 'old hands' on the job will ideally sit down with you and explain exactly what is to be done and how and why it is to be done. Experienced individuals know what to do and are aware of all the informal rules surrounding their roles in the organisation. These 'old hands' bring all sorts of benefits — they possess years of both formal and informal knowledge, and are repositories of an organisation's core values.[63] Australian and New Zealand bank Westpac has dubbed some older staff 'sages', and asked them to codify the firm's informal knowledge.[64]

Through their collective experience, members of an organisation resolve two types of extremely important survival issues. The first is the question of external adaptation: what precisely needs to be accomplished and how can it be done? The second survival issue is the question of internal integration: how do members solve the daily problems associated with living and working together?

External adaptation

External adaptation involves reaching goals and dealing with outsiders. These issues involve the tasks to be accomplished, the methods used to achieve the goals, and the methods of coping with success and failure.

Through their shared experiences, members develop common views that help guide their day-to-day activities. Organisational members need to know the real mission of the

External adaptation is the process of reaching goals and dealing with outsiders.

organisation, not just the pronouncements to key constituencies, such as shareholders. Members will naturally develop an understanding of how they contribute to the mission via interaction. This view may emphasise the importance of human resources, or it may emphasise the role of employees as cogs in a machine or a cost to be reduced.

Closely related to the organisation's mission and its view of staff contribution are the questions of responsibility, goals and methods. These need to be translated into specific contributions, identifying clearly what the organisation is endeavouring to achieve in its external environment. Organisations often present numerous goals; for example, in relation to strategy or corporate social responsibility and establishing procedures and methods, including the selection of the 'right people' to achieve their aims. They will also define jobs and procedures that reflect their approaches to external adaptation.

The final issues in external adaptation deal with two important, but often neglected, aspects of coping with external reality. Firstly, individuals need to develop acceptable ways of telling outsiders just how good they really are. For example, at 3M, the company most famous for its Post-it Notes, employees talk about the quality of their products and the many new and useful products they have brought to the market. Secondly, employees must know collectively when to admit defeat. The answer is easy for new projects: for example, at the beginning of the development process, 3M members establish 'drop' points at which to abandon the development effort and redirect it.

In summary, external adaptation involves answering important instrumental or goal-related questions concerning coping with reality, such as: What is the real mission? How do we contribute? What are our goals? How do we reach our goals? What external forces are important? How do we measure results? What do we do if specific targets are not met? How do we tell others how good we are? When do we abandon and move on to something else?

Internal integration

While the questions of external adaptation help a collection of individuals cope with a changing environment, the organisational culture also provides answers to the problems of internal integration. Internal integration deals with the creation of a collective identity and with finding ways of matching methods of working and living together.

Through dialogue and interaction, organisation members begin to characterise their world. They may see it as malleable or fixed, filled with opportunity or threatening. For instance, real progress towards innovation can begin when group members collectively believe that they can change important parts of the world around them and that what appears to be a threat is actually an opportunity for change.

Three important aspects of working together are:
1. deciding who is a member and who is not
2. developing an informal understanding of acceptable and unacceptable behaviour
3. separating friends from enemies.

To work together effectively, individuals need to decide collectively how to allocate power, status and authority, and to establish a shared understanding of who will get rewards and sanctions for specific types of actions.

Managers often fail to recognise these important aspects of internal integration. For example, a manager may fail to explain the basis for a promotion and to show why this reward, the status associated with it and the power given to the newly promoted individual are consistent with commonly shared beliefs. For example, at AstraZenica, a pharmaceutical company, the human resource managers surveyed employees' values in regard to affiliation with the company. They found that important items to the employees include: learning and development opportunities, competitive rewards, an energising work environment and a successful business. So the HR department works in accord with building a capable, talented team with the potential for growth; building credibility by getting the fundamentals right;

Internal integration is the creation of a collective identity and the means of matching methods of working and living together.

aligning the HR strategy with the business strategy; and understanding, communicating and measuring the return on investment (ROI) for HR initiatives. HR is committed to constantly reviewing and changing in response to business needs.[65] Although these don't seem to be unusual features, they are applied in the organisation in a way that reveals real commitment to the values and principles that underpin them.

We have seen how organisational culture helps members by providing answers to important questions of external adaptation and internal integration. However, there is often an important difference in the answers to these questions between executives towards the top of the organisation and members at the bottom. This may be because senior executives may owe their primary allegiance to their position in the organisation. They may identify with the organisation as a whole and may equate organisational and individual success; and they may want all others in the organisation to believe much the same. Naturally, they expect to be handsomely rewarded. On the other hand, employees may see themselves as part of a larger, more varied and complex network of relationships. The job may be just an instrumental mechanism, such as a means of getting the financial rewards necessary to live. The distance between the values and beliefs of employees and those of their managers, expressed in the formation of distinct subcultures, may in itself be a cultural construct of an organisation.

Some organisations encourage their middle and senior managers to 'stay in touch with their floor workers' by taking on tasks usually done by employees. This is in an effort to facilitate integration between managers and their employees. However, in practice, employees express a level of discomfort working closely with their managers on their own routine tasks. For example, research found that employees were reluctant to share a task or convey criticism directly to the manager when needed. In addition, managers felt isolated in performing their tasks and expressed discomfort changing roles. The research concluded that in this organisation, efforts to facilitate boundary crossing were not very successful and may have reinforced occupational boundaries between managers and their employees.[66]

This finding signifies that, when attempting to manage organisational culture, different perspectives need to be considered. Approaching organisational culture from a multicultural perspective will be more complex, but that is the true nature of organisational cultural research. Nevertheless, we cannot deny that most research accounts for the integration perspective, giving direction and prescriptions on how to manage an organisation's culture. The next section deals with how a manager might want to manage, reinforce and change culture.

Managing organisational culture: building, reinforcing and changing culture

Managers and researchers agree that strong cultures and shared values and beliefs characterise an organisational setting in which people are committed to one another and to an overriding sense of mission. This commitment can be a source of competitive advantage over such an organisation's rivals. Other organisations, however, resemble a collection of separate units and people who do not seem to have much in common. The organisation may also have a strong culture that does not meet the needs of a changing environment. It is important that managers are able to analyse the nature of an organisation's culture if they seek to manage it. If the culture cannot meet the needs of a changing environment, the very strength of the organisation's culture becomes a liability; any change program that seeks to develop a different set of shared values and assumptions will constantly be opposed from within the organisation. An organisation may be a mix of subcultures and countercultures. Here, rivalries and value differences may create harmful conflicts.

International
SPOTLIGHT

Dover Park Hospice: embracing volunteers into its culture

Hospices exist to provide palliative care for patients who are terminally ill and going through the final stages of their lives. They aim to provide all physical, emotional, psychosocial and spiritual needs so as to alleviate suffering and maximise quality of life for patients and their loved ones.[67] However, hospices, especially those in Asia, face major difficulties in the context of the dominant culture, whereby the superstitions surrounding death are highly significant and death is seen as something that should not be associated with.[68] This is evidenced in recent research that has shown that these taboos often get in the way of minimising suffering as death approaches, with a 2006 survey finding that only 40 per cent of people in Singapore were aware of hospice services and palliative care.[69] Hospices that are run as not-for-profit institutions rely significantly on volunteers to provide much-needed human resources, energy and spirit. However, in most developed economies (Singapore included), volunteer participation levels have been declining.[70]

Dover Park Hospice (DPH) was founded in the early 1990s to provide palliative care to the terminally ill, and was Singapore's first dedicated palliative care institution.[71] It aimed to change the prevailing attitudes towards hospice and palliative care by creating a very bright and happy place and focusing on easing the pain of the dying, thereby also easing the anxiety of patients' friends and relatives.[72] And, despite the trends highlighted above, and the difficulties associated with caring for terminally ill patients, DPH has managed to not only win over its employees, but, also, those so-called 'elusive' volunteers. By 2012, the hospice had been established 20 years. While the focus on palliative care remains, the hospice has extended its reach out to the community at large too. This has included collaboration with four other organisations on Project SilverCare, which provides free community health-screening and a blood donation drive. In 2011, the hospice set up its new Dover Park Home Care, accepting 271 patients into the new program. Together with the other members of the Hospice Care Association, DPH is also involved in increasing awareness of the importance of hospice care and reinforcing the message that hospices are not death houses, but places where people can appreciate life much more when confronted with death.[73] The new home care program has been successful in combating the pervasive culture concerning death with only 5 per cent of deaths of patients in the hospices' care occurring in hospitals.[74]

Managers can help foster a culture that provides answers to important questions concerning external adaptation and internal integration. Recent work on the links between corporate culture and financial performance reaffirms the importance of an emphasis on helping employees to adjust to the environment. It also suggests that this emphasis alone is not sufficient. Nor is an emphasis solely on shareholders or customers associated with long-term economic performance. Instead, managers must work to emphasise all three issues simultaneously. Managers are also challenged to consider whether it is possible to manage culture in the same ways for both core and peripheral workforces. Peripheral workers often spend too little time in the company to be socialised into the culture, and core workers may resent peripheral workers experiencing the same positive treatments that they receive. Sometimes, managers adopt a two-tier approach to managing culture to deal with these differences.[75] Sometimes, however, managers attempt to revitalise an organisation by dictating major changes, rather than by building on shared values. While things may change a bit on the surface, a deeper look often shows whole departments resisting change and many key people who do not want to learn new ways. Such responses may indicate that the responsible managers are insensitive to the effects of their proposed changes on shared values. They fail to ask if the changes are:

- contrary to important values held by participants within the organisation
- a challenge to historically important organisation-wide assumptions
- inconsistent with important common assumptions derived from the national culture outside the organisation.

All too often, executives are unable to realise that they too can be captured by the broadly held common assumptions within their organisations (see The effective manager 9.1).[76] Top management may, for example, take a decision to introduce autonomous working teams to improve productivity and innovation, yet not face the reality that the organisational culture invests all authority in the executive management team. In such circumstances, the introduction of autonomous working teams will be disastrous, as decision-making responsibility will not be devolved to the team. Culture influences managerial behaviour as much as that of everyone else in the organisation, and astute managers who seek to manage culture will seek to understand it first.

THE **EffectiveManager** 9.1

Using organisational culture to help the organisation compete

As more organisations are moving into volatile industries using advanced technology and confronting international competitors, managers may need to help their corporate culture adjust. Here are some pitfalls to avoid and some factors to emphasise when entering and competing in highly volatile, high-technology markets, such as computing and biotechnology.

1. When entering the market early, do not allow employees to become disenchanted when facing initial technical barriers and skill development challenges.
2. When entering slowly, do not give competitors too big a lead; keep stressing to all employees the necessity of building technical and market skills.
3. When adding new products to an existing market, take the opportunity to reassess approaches to decision making and management for both new products and old ones; challenge old routines.
4. When adjusting to new markets with new products, avoid using 'conventional wisdom' and stress the development of new ways to compete.
5. When entering the market, foster the internet culture by embracing all forms of open communication in all possible media.

Ethics and organisational culture

We have already talked quite a lot about ethics in this book and we will continue to do so. For now, the issue is framed in a question: 'Do organisations vary in the "ethical climates" they establish for their members?' The answer to this question is yes. To many researchers, it is clear that the ethical tone or climate of an organisation is set at the top; that is, what top managers do, and the culture they establish and reinforce, makes a big difference to the way lower-level personnel act and to the way the organisation as a whole acts when faced with ethical dilemmas. What is needed in today's complicated times is for more organisations to step forward and operate with strong, positive and ethical cultures.[77] However, instilling ethical behaviour is not just a manager's responsibility; the behaviour of employees can resonate throughout the organisation to set an ethical culture organisation-wide. The **ethical climate** of an organisation is the shared set of understandings about what is correct behaviour and how ethical issues will be handled. This climate sets the tone for decision making at all levels and in all circumstances.

In some organisations, the ethical climate supports doing the right thing; though often, in other organisations (perhaps too many) concerns for operating efficiency may

The **ethical climate** is the shared set of understandings in an organisation about what is correct behaviour and how ethical issues will be handled.

outweigh social considerations when staff face difficult decisions. Along with other aspects of organisational culture, therefore, the ethical climate will be an important influence on the behaviour of individual members and the organisation as a whole. When the ethical climate is clear and positive, people know what is expected of them when inevitable ethical dilemmas occur. They can then act confidently, knowing they will be supported by top management and the other members of the organisation.

In the Australian Defence Force example in the case study at the end of the chapter, there was a reference to 'toxic' culture in the armed forces. Recent research has attempted to show how toxic organisational cultures can lead people to override basic morals and engage in unethical behaviour. Miguel Pina e Chunha, Armenio Rego and Stewart Clegg have argued that organisational cultures, especially those that are not transparent and allow leaders to rule by fear, contribute significantly to employees submitting to unconditional obedience and engaging in inappropriate behaviour.[78] While organisations may be engaging in corporate ethics programs, ethical theory may not be enough to promote ethical behaviour, because, in certain contexts, individuals lose autonomy in decision making.[79] Leaders and organisational members need to understand how the features of the situation may capture their ethical reasoning, thereby making them more aware of the situations conducive to the 'banalisation of evil'.

Climate versus culture

Given that we have used both the terms 'climate' and 'culture' here, it is appropriate to clarify the differences and/or similarities between the terms. In the past, some scholars have used the terms interchangeably, noting that the differences are insignificant.[80] Others claim that while they are different, there is a significant overlap between the two terms.[81] However, over time, this has resulted in significant confusion and, in recent years, there have been concerted attempts and research approaches to untangle the concepts, resulting in a growing clarity of the differences between the terms.[82] In organisational climate, 'the focus is on the organisational members' agreed to perceptions of their organisational environment' (i.e. that which can be locally created in an organisation). In organisational culture, 'the focus is on judgement and values, rather than perceived practices and procedures', with the term being a broader one that can be applied to larger units, such as industries and even countries.[83] While these differences are important at the theoretical level, there is acknowledgement that, at the practical level, they may not be critical.[84]

ETHICAL
Perspective

Ethical cultural change at Siemens

Cultural change was brought upon Siemens following a series of corrupt practices such as bribes contracts for power generation equipment in Italy, telecommunications infrastructure in Nigeria and national identity cards in Argentina. Serious irregularities in the financial, legal and corporate management areas have led to what became the highest recorded Foreign Corrupt Practices Act (FCPA) fine globally, worth US$450m (2008). The crisis began emerging in 2006 with approximately A$3.6bn being paid out in fines which affected 60 per cent of Siemens markets globally. In mid 2007, Peter Losher was recruited as the new CEO to bring a new era of ethics to the organisation and offered an amnesty to corrupt staff members: come forward now or be fired later. One hundred and thirty people ventured forward. The entire governance structure of the company was also completely changed. This included a new climate of communication between all company members from top to bottom. For example, Siemens have implemented 'integrity dialogues', which are integrated into all sales meetings so that there is an open forum for discussion on ethical issues.[85] The failing of Siemens from the outset was not to fully understand the changing world of transparency that is being demanded of organisations in the modern era.

Amod Choudhary claims that the lesson to be learned from the Siemens bribing experience is that culture plays a crucial role in organisations.[86] If it was not for a new regulatory environment, a bribing culture that may have existed since the Second World War may have gone unnoticed. Choudhary illuminates further that when unethical practices are so engrained in the culture an outside influence is needed — in this instance, the new CEO Peter Losher. Importantly too, Choudhary uses the Siemens case to show us that illegal and unethical behaviour end up costing companies money and culture becomes an important part of managing corporate risk.

In summary, this chapter has introduced you to the elements of organisational culture, organisational subcultures and how an organisation's culture is formed and researched. It also dealt with how culture is often seen as a function to improve competitive advantage and how it may be managed. In addition, this chapter emphasised the complex nature of an organisation's culture, as organisations are socially constructed by the people in them.

Summary

Organisational culture and national culture

The concept of organisational culture is as important to the management of an organisation as are strategy and structure. As the system of shared beliefs and values that guide and direct the behaviour of members, culture can have a strong influence on day-to-day organisational behaviour and performance. There are connections between organisational culture and national culture, but each organisational culture is unique despite being embedded in a national culture.

Cultural levels, subcultures and diversity

Culture can be analysed through its three components: observable culture, which is the behaviours that can be seen within an organisation; shared values held by members of an organisation; and, at the deepest level, common assumptions or truths developed and shared by members through their joint experiences in the organisation. Organisations can also experience the strains of dealing with subcultures among various work units and subsystems, as well as possible countercultures, which can be the source of potentially harmful conflicts. There are also challenges for managing different national groupings within the organisation.

Observable aspects of organisational culture

Observable aspects of organisational culture include the stories, rites, rituals and symbols that are shared by organisational members. These are powerful aspects that can be important in helping to establish and maintain a certain culture. Shared meanings and understandings help everyone in a strong culture know how to act and to expect others to act in various circumstances. They provide a common orientation to decision making and action that can facilitate performance. Cultural rules and roles similarly define expectations for behaviour within an organisation and lend consistency to the behaviour of its members.

Shared values and their importance

Values and organisational culture are highly intertwined. Clearly articulated organisational values — such as quality, customer service and innovation — help guide and direct action. When in place and understood, clear and positive values can create a competitive advantage for organisations. They can be a unifying force that brings efforts to bear on highly desirable outcomes.

Common assumptions contributing to culture

Common assumptions and organisational culture are also highly interrelated. Common assumptions are the taken-for-granted truths that are shared by collections of organisational members. Some organisations express these truths in a management philosophy that links key goal-related issues with key collaboration issues into a series of general ways the organisation will manage its affairs. In many cases, the management philosophy is supported by a series of corporate myths.

Organisational culture research

Organisational culture researchers investigate cultural forms, formal and informal practices and content themes. These manifestations can be measured quantitatively and/or qualitatively.

Different perspectives on organisational culture

Considering different perspectives of culture gives a more complete picture of what is going on in the organisation. A combined view of the integration, differentiation and fragmentation perspective is needed. A well-developed culture can assist in responding to internal and external problems. Through common shared behaviours, values and assumptions, organisational members will clearly understand the organisation's mission, strategies and goals in relation to the external environment. Culture also helps to achieve internal adaptation — the ability of members to work together effectively on organisational activities. A third function of culture is to help bring management and employees much closer together in their respective goals.

Managing culture

Managing organisational culture is considered a top management task in organisations. A strong culture can be a competitive advantage, and managers can try to create such cultures where none previously existed and/or change existing cultures to become more productive ones. In order to manage organisational culture effectively, the foundations must be established in the management of culture's observable aspects and in the belief systems that are sponsored from the top. Managers need to understand the culture in order to manage it.

Ethics and organisational culture

Ethics and organisational culture must be considered in today's demanding times. The ethical climate of an organisation is the shared set of understandings about what is correct behaviour and how ethical issues will be handled. When properly established, a positive and clear ethical climate can help all organisation members make good choices when faced with ethical dilemmas. It can give them the confidence to act with the understanding that what they are doing is considered correct and will be supported by the organisation.

CHAPTER 9 study guide

Key terms

common assumptions, *p. 335*
countercultures, *p. 336*
cultural symbol, *p. 340*
differentiation perspective, *p. 346*
ethical climate, *p. 351*
external adaptation, *p. 347*

founding story, *p. 339*
fragmentation perspective, *p. 346*
integration perspective, *p. 345*
internal integration, *p. 348*
management philosophy, *p. 343*
observable culture, *p. 334*

organisational culture, *p. 333*
rites, *p. 339*
rituals, *p. 339*
saga, *p. 339*
shared values, *p. 335*
subcultures, *p. 335*

Review questions

1. What is organisational culture and what are the levels of analysing culture in organisations?
2. What functions do organisational cultures serve, and how do subcultures and cultural diversity help in this?
3. Why is it important to study organisational culture? What implications of studying organisational behaviour are relevant for the twenty-first century?
4. What are some ethical issues when managing organisational culture?

Application questions

1. You are a manager who wishes to encourage employees to make suggestions and contribute to new ideas. What aspects of culture could be manipulated to try to encourage this?
2. What observable elements of organisational culture can you identify from your own organisation or an organisation with which you are familiar?
3. Give examples of both formal and informal processes that occur in your organisation or at your university. What can you say about the non-observable culture in your organisation?
4. In a small organisation with 50 employees, senior management has espoused values of equality, respect and high performance for employees and customers. When the latest performance figures for the company are released, management's response is to call the staff to a general meeting and tell them they all have to 'lift their game' if they expect to retain their jobs. What comments can you make on the cultural features of the organisation?
5. Your company has just merged with another that provides a similar service. What issues will emerge in

relation to the merging of two organisational cultures and what can managers do to deal with them?
6. Examine the following values and visible elements of culture. What underlying assumptions do you think might exist 'beneath' these aspects of culture?
   • Organisation A values new ideas and selects its highest-performing employees for special monthly creative workshops. Organisation B values new ideas and promises a prize of $4000 to any employee whose idea contributes clearly to increasing profits. Organisation C values new ideas and encourages employees, as owners of shares in the company, to contribute ideas in their day-to-day work.
   • Organisations D, E and F express the importance of high-performing employees. Organisation D conducts annual performance reviews between supervisor and worker, and if workers perform according to requirements, they are given an incremental increase in wages. Organisation E conducts six-monthly reviews and more regular 'chats' between supervisor and worker. If the workers are not performing according to requirements, they are asked to account for their low performance.

- In Organisation F, no reviews are conducted, but workers and supervisors work closely together. If employees are demonstrating outstanding performance, their work is commended and publicised in the company newsletter. They also receive a bonus.
- In Organisations G and H, an employee makes a significant mistake. In Organisation G, the manager speaks to the employee and tries to analyse the problem and find ways to overcome it. In Organisation H, the manager discusses the employee's mistake at a team meeting in front of all members of the group and expresses disappointment at their poor behaviour. The incident is also reported to senior management and recorded on the employee's file.

Research questions

1. Search the internet, newspapers and business magazines for news of the launch of a new internet-driven services company. Find out what you can about this organisation and compare the culture of the new enterprise to similar companies initiated 10 years ago.
   (a) What differences do you think there are between the culture of the new and older companies?
   (b) Why do you think the cultures may be different? Are there any defining new cultural aspects evident in the new company?
2. Search the internet for two different organisations in the same industry — for example, two insurance companies, two major retail chains or two universities. It is especially valuable if you understand the type of activity the organisation carries out and/or if you have had some experience with at least one of them as a customer. Set yourself a purpose for your inquiry to give it some focus. For example, look at the website and ask questions such as:
   (a) As one of your customers, will I expect customer-focused service?
   (b) Will your employees be helpful?
   (c) Will it be easy for me to do business with your organisation?

(d) Will you have up-to-date technological interfaces for customers?

Try to assess the answers to these questions at three levels, in the following order (remember, you are looking for information about underlying assumptions, shared values and observable symbols of the culture):
- by looking at the images
- by looking at the structure and layout of the website
- by looking at the information available to answer these questions.

The order is important, since you will be looking to see how compatible different aspects of the culture are and how they may vary or conflict with each other.

An example of conflict might be an organisation's claim that 'we put our customers first', while its website is very difficult for a customer to navigate. An example of compatibility might be if an organisation using the same slogan has a website that is extremely easy to navigate, with clear, simple, easy-to-understand navigation tools.

Evaluate both websites and compare the two in the context of your focus question. What observations can you make from this study of the two organisations about the nature of their particular organisational cultures? Does the exercise give you any insights into how easy or difficult it might be to investigate organisational culture?

Running project

Complete the following activities for your chosen organisation.

1. Outline what you consider the key parts of your organisation's observable and non-observable culture (shared values and common assumptions) and give examples.
2. What does your organisation do to manage the organisational culture?
3. To what extent do management's preferred culture and the observable culture correlate? Do any countercultures exist within the organisation?

Which culture fits you?

Identify which of the following organisation 'cultures' closely represents the way you feel most comfortable working.

1. A culture that values talent, entrepreneurial activity and performance over commitment; one that offers large financial rewards and individual recognition.
2. A culture that stresses loyalty, working for the good of the group and getting to know the right people; one that believes in 'generalists' and step-by-step career progress.
3. A culture that offers little job security; one that operates with a survival mentality, stresses that every individual can make a difference, and focuses attention on 'turnaround' opportunities.
4. A culture that values long-term relationships; one that emphasises systematic career development, regular training, and advancement based on gaining functional expertise.

Scoring

These labels identify the four different cultures: 1 = 'the cricket team', 2 = 'the club', 3 = 'the fortress', and 4 = 'the academy'.

Interpretation

To some extent, your future career success may depend on working for an organisation in which there is a good fit between you and the prevailing corporate culture. This assessment can help you learn how to recognise various cultures, evaluate how well they can serve your needs, and recognise how they may change with time. A risk taker, for example, may be out of place in a 'club' but fit right in with a 'cricket team'. Someone who wants to seek opportunities wherever they may occur may be out of place in an 'academy' but fit right in with a 'fortress'.

Source: Reproduced from JR Schermerhorn, JG Hunt, RN Osborn and M Uhl-Bien, *Organizational behavior*, 11th ed. (Hoboken: John Wiley & Sons, 2010), p. W-53.

Your university culture

Preparation

Select a university or college, or a department within this institution, to analyse its culture. Answer the following questions.

1. How many stories do you know about it?
2. How many sagas do you know about it?
3. How many myths do you know about it?
4. Identify as many rites and rituals that are used as you can.
5. Identify as many cultural symbols that are used as you can.
6. Identify as many shared meanings that are used as you can.
7. Identify as many rules and roles that are used as you can.
8. Identify as many shared values that are used as you can. Do these values give the organisation or department a competitive advantage?

Objectives

1. To understand the elements of organisational culture
2. To understand how to analyse and manage organisational culture

Total time: 15–45 minutes

Procedure

1. The lecturer or tutor calls on students to give their answers to the eight preparation questions.
2. The more information you have for each question, the stronger is the culture at your university/college or its department. Based on your answers, do you believe the organisation or its unit has a strong or a weak culture?
3. How could the organisational culture be managed to make it stronger?
4. What is the down side of having a strong culture?

John Leonard reported that in 1989, authority holders at the Australian Defence Force Academy (ADFA) routinely abused their authority. The dominance of legal authority that was expected in such an organisation was often replaced by gratuitous or illegal use of power. Leonard reported that by 1998, authoritarian methods remained; but these were allied with a concern for the welfare of subordinates. There was no dominating disparity between civilian and academy values; female cadets seemed to have achieved greater equality; and discrimination and harassment were not noted as before. The relationship between senior and junior cadets was based on a model of leadership and mutual respect, rather than one of fear and intimidation. Leonard indicated that the source of these changes was a deliberate and comprehensive program of change that was carefully sequenced over time. Those responsible for implementing the program were trained, and 'backsliders' who were found to work against the new approach were stripped of their power and privileges. The structure was also drastically altered to avoid power acquisition through control of substantial aspects of the culture.[87]

Despite Leonard's report on apparent cultural change between 1989 and 1998, there is evidence that the ADF (Australian Defence Force) continues to foster a culture of illegal power. In recent years, there have been a series of rolling inquiries (six being major parliamentary ones). A 20-month Senate inquiry found that there was still widespread abuse in the ADF, and it had a defective military justice system that was incapable of performing adequately. The inquiry recommended that parts of the military justice system be handed over to the civilian authorities.[88]

Over 150 submissions were made to the inquiry about 'recent events including suicides, deaths through accident, major illicit drug use, serious abuses of power in training schools and cadet units, flawed prosecutions and failed, poor investigations' and included complaints from all ranks.[89]

In 2008, Air Marshal Angus Houston, the recently appointed Chief of the Australian Defence Force, reaffirmed his commitment to fix the military system.[90] However, this remains a very difficult task, and the ADF was subsequently criticised in the commission of inquiry into a soldier's suicide. Some parents of ADF soldiers who have committed suicide have claimed that their sons were victims of a 'toxic culture' of bullying and victimisation that pervades the armed forces.[91] The ADF was also rocked by incidents on the Royal Australian Navy's HMAS *Success* during its tour of Asia between March and May 2009. Members of the crew engaged in predatory sexual and drunken behaviour amidst what has been described as a 'tribal culture of alcohol misuse, leadership failure and cover-up'.[92]

Despite an extensive and very public commission of inquiry which saw many embarrassing details revealed (and which led to the ADF chief re-emphasising the need to 'cut out this cancer'), the ADF was again in the news in April 2011. This time, it involved allegations that a male cadet had transmitted a video of consensual sex at the college over the internet without the female cadet's knowledge. This prompted Defence Minister Stephen Smith to launch a wide-ranging review on the way women are treated at ADFA, led by the Australian Sex Discrimination Commissioner Elizabeth Broderick. The review will also consider strategies for encouraging women into ADF's leadership.[93] The Minister stated that:

> The time has come for external review. We need to drive home that inappropriate conduct in uniform or as a representative of the Defence Force brings with it serious adverse consequences. [This includes] the treatment of women, alcohol use and use of social media and representational behaviour more generally.[94]

One of the first actions as part of this review has been the freeing up of restrictions to allow for female front-line combat roles by the year 2016.[95] While women have been working in traditionally male-oriented roles in many conflict zones and in the mining and farming industries, Australia has lagged behind some developed countries in allowing women to serve in combat roles. It may be that this is partly a reflection of wider society values and culture;[96] however, given the progress women have had in other aspects of Australian life (e.g. work, politics, education etc.), it is likely that organisational culture plays a significant role in this. A soldier from front-line Afghanistan noted:

> It was … the fact that they believed if a woman was in a patrol, that whole patrol would become a higher-value target purely because of the way women are viewed by the Taliban and the locals here, but also because of the press they believe it would generate if a woman was killed or captured in combat.[97]

This is echoed by former senior military leaders like retired Major General Morlan, who commented that:

> It complicates the issues … One was men were overly protective of wounded women, the second was an extraordinary reluctance to surrender to women, which meant you had to kill more people.[98]

Ironically, these comments were made just after the passing away of Australia's most decorated World War II female veteran, Nancy Wake, in August 2011, who was involved in very close combat as part of the resistance against the Nazis, and even killed an SS sentry with her bare hands during an assault on the Gestapo headquarters.[99]

In the long run, it is unclear how successful the Defence Minister and the senior military officers will be in creating real cultural change. Even the newly appointed ADF chief General David Hurley has admitted that 'The challenge today is to continue to deliver a high-quality combat force while implementing fundamental changes to Defence culture and practices'.[100] There is a shortage of labour within the ADF, and unless the problem of illegal authority changes, it remains a challenge for the ADF to attract new members to its ranks.[101] As Stephen Bartos from the ABC notes:

> Organisational cultures are resilient and elastic — even where temporary progress can be made they tend to rebound to their former state. It can take a decade before the fruits of a change effort are harvested, and in the meantime the enemies of change will use whatever means at their disposal to undermine those efforts. This applies to all organisations, but even more so in Defence because it is larger and more conservative.[102]

Questions

1. Identify the subcultures and countercultures that exist within the ADF. How might these impact (either positively or negatively) on the organisation as a whole?
2. Which perspective do you think would be most useful to take in understanding the culture at the ADF (integration, differentiation or ambiguity/fragmentation). Explain the reasoning for your choice.
3. Refer back to the section on managing organisational culture. What obstacles might the ADF face in changing its culture, and how might these potentially be overcome?

End notes

1. State Services Authority, *Organisational culture: an ideas sourcebook for the Victorian public sector*, State of Victoria Government Victoria (2013), p. 6, www.ssa.vic.gov.au.
2. E Goodman and L Loh, Organizational change: A critical challenge for team effectiveness, *Business Information Review*, vol. 28, no. 4 (2011), pp. 242–50.
3. Regus website, 'Aussie workers secretive with skills but generous with respect' (18 August 2011), www.regus.presscentre.com.
4. ibid.
5. D Den Hartog and RM Verburg, 'High performance work systems, organisational culture and firm effectiveness', *Human Resource Management Journal*, vol. 14, no. 1 (London, 2004), pp. 55–78.
6. ibid.
7. E Schein, 'Organisational culture', *American Psychologist*, vol. 45, no. 2 (1990), pp. 109–19.
8. *The Economist*, Google's corporate culture: creative tension (17 September 2009), www.economist.com.
9. ibid.
10. L Whitney, *Rasmussen: Why I left Google for Facebook* (2 November 2010), www.cnet.com/au.
11. T Deal and A Kennedy, *Corporate culture* (Reading, MA: Addison-Wesley, 1982).
12. T Peters and R Waterman, *In search of excellence* (New York: Harper & Row, 1982).
13. S Peoples, 'Dress, moral reform and masculinity in Australia', *Grainger Studies: An Interdisciplinary Journal*, vol. 1 (2011), pp. 115–35.
14. P Moore, 'A uniform approach to business', *NZ Business*, vol. 18, no. 1 (2004), pp. 33–5.
15. ibid.
16. Health & Care Professions Council, *Professionalism in healthcare professionals* (2014), www.hcpc-uk.org.
17. G Hofstede and MH Bond, 'The Confucius connection: from cultural roots to economic growth', *Organisational Dynamics*, vol. 16, no. 4, pp. 4–21.
18. JA Fitzgerald and G Teal, 'Health reform and occupational sub-cultures: the changing roles of professional identities', *Contemporary Nurse*, vol. 16, nos 1–2 (2004), pp. 9–19; JA Fitzgerald and A Van Marrewijk, 'Redefining organisational control in changing organisations: Two cases of social construction of professional identity in organisations — engineering and medicine', paper

presented to 6th international conference on organisational discourse: Arte*facts*, Arche*types and* Archi*texts*, Amsterdam (28–30 July 2004); K Hayes and JA Fitzgerald, 'Preliminary findings of an investigation into interactions between commercial and scientific occupational cultures', paper presented to the 6th international CINet conference, Brighton, United Kingdom (4–7 September 2005).

19. R Jones, B Lasky, H Russell-Gale and M le Fevre, 'Leadership and the development of dominant and countercultures: a narcissistic perspective', *Leadership & Organisation Development Journal*, vol. 25, no. 1/2 (2004), p. 216.

20. J Martin and C Siehl, 'Organisation culture and counterculture', *Organisational Dynamics*, vol. 12 (1983), pp. 52–64.

21. G McColl, 'Toll's takeover touch', *Business Review Weekly* (12–18 December 2002), pp. 40–1; N Way and J Walker, 'Railway gamble', *Business Review Weekly* (17–23 December 2002), pp. 60–3.

22. ME Graebner, KM Eisenhardt and PT Roundy, 'Success and failure in technology acquisitions: lessons for buyers and sellers', *The Academy of Management Perspectives*, vol. 24, no. 3 (2010), pp. 73–92.

23. P Puranam, H Singh and S Chaudhuri, 'Integrating acquired capabilities: when structural integration is (un) necessary', *Organization Science*, vol. 20, no. 2 (2009), pp. 313–28.

24. AL Ranft and MD Lord, 'Acquiring new technologies and capabilities: a grounded model of acquisition implementation' *Organization Science* (2002), pp. 420–41; Graebner, Eisenhardt and Roundy (2010), op. cit.

25. A Burns, 'Customer complaint email and response by GASP clothing goes viral', *Herald Sun* (29 September 2011), www.heraldsun.com.au.

26. N Haddow, 'Service to make you gasp', *Sydney Morning Herald* (29 September 2011), www.smh.com.au.

27. *News.com*, 'Frock shoppers flock to consumer affairs with Gasp gripes' (13 June 2012), www.news.com.au.

28. MM Helms and R Stern, 'Exploring the factors that influence employees' perceptions of their organisation's culture', *Journal of Management in Medicine*, vol. 15, issue 6 (Hong Kong, 2001), pp. 415–25.

29. Australian Bureau of Statistics, 'Yearbook Australia, 2009–10', www.abs.gov.au.

30. Australian Bureau of Statistics, 'Migration, Australia, 2009–10', www.abs.gov.au.

31. R Ely and D Thomas, 'Cultural diversity at work: the effects of diversity perspectives on group processes and outcomes', *Administrative and Science Quarterly*, vol. 46, no. 2 (Ithaca, 2001), pp. 229–74.

32. Workplace Diversity Corporate website, http://diversityatwork.com.au; Department of Education, Employment and Workplace Relations Corporate website, www.deewr.gov.au.

33. L Gettler, 'An ethical dilemma', *The Sydney Morning Herald* (3 November 2011), www.smh.com.au.

34. ibid.

35. E Schein, 'Organisational culture', *American Psychologist*, vol. 45, no. 2 (1990), pp. 109–19; E Schein, *Organisational culture and leadership* (San Francisco: Jossey-Bass, 1985), pp. 52–7.

36. J Martin, *Cultures in organisations* (New York: Oxford University Press, 1992); J Martin, *Organisational culture: mapping the terrain* (Thousand Oaks, CA: Sage, 2002).

37. C Geertz, *The interpretation of culture* (New York: Basic Books, 1973).

38. JM Byer and HM Trice, 'How an organisation's rites reveal its culture', *Organisational Dynamics* (Spring 1987), pp. 27–41.

39. K McManus, 'The challenge of changing culture', *Industrial Engineer*, vol. 35, no. 1 (2003), pp. 18–19.

40. BL Kirkman, B Rosen, CB Gibson, PE Tesluk and SO McPherson, 'Five challenges to virtual team success: lessons from Sabre, Inc.', *The Academy of Management Executive* (2002), pp. 67–79.

41. BizDojo website, http://bizdojo.com.

42. ibid.

43. 'The business gymnasium', *Capital Times* (27 July 2011), www.capitaltimes.co.nz.

44. The BIZ DOJO website, http://bizdojo.com/coworking.

45. MB Bayer, 'The modern working environment: have we become a nation of office phobes?', *Huffington Post*, (1 October 2013), www.huffingtonpost.co.uk.

46. DN Den Hartog and RM Verburg, 'High performance work systems, organisational culture and firm effectiveness', *Human Resource Management Journal*, vol. 14, no. 1 (London, 2004), pp. 55–79.

47. White Lady Funerals corporate website, www.whitelady funerals.com.au.

48. *Bree v Lupevo Pty Ltd* [2003] NSWADT 47 (11 March 2003).

49. *Fairburn v Star City Pty Ltd*, PR931 032 (6 May 2003).

50. *TV3 New Zealand*, Dress-code for customers introduced at Bank of New Zealand, www.3news.co.nz.

51. M Wearring, 'Casual office, work harder?', *News.com.au* (10 March 2008), www.news.com.au.

52. 'HR uses poetry to address staff', *News.com.au* (21 November 2007), www.news.com.au.

53. Developed from T Deal and A Kennedy, *Corporate cultures: the rites and rituals of corporate life* (Reading, MA: Addison-Wesley, 1982).

54. J Martin, *Organisational culture: mapping the terrain* (Thousand Oaks, CA: Sage, 2002), pp. 87, 88.

55. P Degeling, J Kennedy, M Hill, M Carnegie and J Holt, *Professional sub-cultures and hospital reform* (Sydney: Centre for hospital management and information systems research, University of New South Wales, 1998).

56. J Martin, *Organisational culture: mapping the terrain* (Thousand Oaks, CA: Sage, 2002).

57. RW Dunphy, 'Organisational culture', *Organisational behaviour: an organisational analysis perspective* (Sydney: Addison-Wesley, 1992), pp. 163–91.

58. J Martin, op. cit.

59. JA Fitzgerald, '*Managing health reform: a mixed method study into the construction and changing of professional identities*',

unpublished PhD thesis (2002); J Martin, op. cit.; J Martin, *Cultures in organisations: three perspectives* (New York: Oxford University Press, 1992); D Meyerson and J Martin, 'Cultural change: an integration of three different views', *Journal of Management Studies*, vol. 24, no. 6 (1987), pp. 623–47.

60. J Martin, op. cit.

61. JA Fitzgerald, 'Managing health reform: a mixed method study into the construction and changing of professional identities', unpublished PhD thesis (2002).

62. DV Caprar and BA Neville, '"Norming" and "conforming"?: integrating cultural and institutional explanations for sustainability adoption in Business', *Journal of Business Ethics*, vol. 110, no. 2 (2012), pp. 231–45.

63. P Cappelli and B Novelli, *Managing the older worker: how to prepare for the new organizational order* (Boston: Harvard Business Press, 2010).

64. 'Age shall not wither them', *The Economist*, vol. 331, no. 9 (April 2011).

65. C Donaldson, 'AstraZenica HR: a study in strategic people management', *Human Resources* (November 2002), pp. 12–14.

66. JA Fitzgerald and B Hinings, 'Changing professional identities: adjusting professional delineations in health', paper presented at the International Federation of Scholarly Associations of Management (IFSAM) VIIth world congress, Goteburg, Sweden, 2004.

67. 'Hospice and palliative care' [brochure], Singapore Hospice Council, www.singaporehospice.org.sg.

68. P-S Seet, *Entrepreneurial dilemmas and resolutions: the experience of singapore's knowledge-based entrepreneurs*, PhD Thesis, University of Cambridge, 2005.

69. J Tan, 'Debunking the "death house" myth about hospices', *Straits Times* (5 September 2011), www.straitstimes.com.

70. L Lien, 'Matching the supply and demand of volunteers' in W Cheng And S Mohamed (eds.), *The world that changes the world: how philanthropy, innovation and entrepreneurship are transforming the social system* (Singapore: John Wiley & Sons, 2010), pp. 191–207.

71. HCA Hospice Care website, www.hca.org.sg.

72. Seet (2005), op. cit.

73. Tan (2011), op. cit.

74. Dover Park Hospice, *Annual report 2012—2013* (2013), www.doverpark.org.sg.

75. E Ogbonna and LC Harris, 'Managing organisational culture: insights from the hospitality industry', *Human Resource Management Journal*, vol. 12, no. 1 (2002), pp. 33–53.

76. AC Cooper and CG Smith, 'How established firms respond to threatening technologies', *Academy of Management Executive*, vol. 6, no. 2 (1992), pp. 56–69.

77. SLS Nwachukwu and SJ Vitell, Jr, 'The influence of corporate culture on managerial ethical judgements', *Journal of Business Ethics*, vol. 16, no. 8 (June 1997), pp. 757–76.

78. M Pina e Cunha, A Rego and Clegg, 'Obedience and evil: from milgram and kampuchea to normal organizations', *Journal of Business Ethics*, vol. 97, no. 2 (2010), pp. 291–309.

79. R Card, 'Individual responsibility within organizational contexts', *Journal of Business Ethics*, vol. 62, no. 4 (2005), pp. 397–405.

80. D Katz and RL Kahn, *The social psychology of organizations*, 2nd ed. (New York: Wiley, 1978).

81. D Denison, 'What is the difference between organizational culture and organizational climate? A native's point of view on a decade of paradigm wars', *The Academy of Management Review*, vol. 21, no. 3 (1996), pp. 619–54.

82. EH Schein, 'Preface', in NM Ashkanasy, CPM Wilderom and MF Peterson (eds), *The handbook of organizational culture and climate* (Thousand Oaks, CA: Sage Publications, 2010), pp. xi–iii.

83. N Ashkanasy, 'Organizational climate', in S Clegg and J Bailey (eds.), *International encyclopedia of organizational studies*, vol. 3 (Thousand Oaks, CA: Sage Publications, 2007), pp. 1028–30.

84. Ashkanasy, Wilderom and Peterson (2010), op. cit.; N Nicholson, RS Schuler and AH Van de Ven, *The Blackwell encyclopedic dictionary of organizational behavior* (London: Blackwell, 1995).

85. Chartered Global Management Accountant, *CGMA briefing: rethinking the value chain: ethical culture change at Siemens: a case study*, (May 2014), www.cgma.org.

86. A Choundhary, 'Anatomy and impact of bribery on Siemens AG, *Journal of Legal, Ethical and Regulatory Issues*, vol. 16, no. 2 (2013).

87. From J Leonard, based on his personal studies and written in 'From transformation to transcendence', *Management Today* (April 2001), pp. 20–3.

88. T Harris, 'Military justice missing in action', *The Australian* (17 June 2005), p. 1.

89. Senate Standing Committees on Foreign Affairs, Defence and Trade, 'Inquiry into the effectiveness of Australia's military justice system' executive summary, para. 10 (16 June 2005), www.aph.gov.au.

90. Department of Defence, 'New Defence Leadership Team Announced', www.defence.gov.au.

91. R Viellaris, 'Soldier suicide report criticises ADF', *Courier-Mail* (9 January 2011), www.couriermail.com.au; M Edwards, 'Suicide soldier's dad decries "toxic" ADF', *ABC News* (12 April 2011), www.abc.net.au/news.

92. HMAS *Success* Commission of Inquiry, www.defence.gov. au/coi/success/index.htm; K Landers, 'Navy inquiry unvails "cancer" on HMAS Success', *Lateline* [transcript] (22 February 2011), www.abc.net.au/lateline.

93. J Thompson, 'Smith orders review of Defence culture', *ABC News* (11 April 2011), www.abc.net.au/news.

94. S Smith, 'Largs Bay and C-17 acquisition; ADFA Skype incident', Press conference transcript (6 April 2011), www.defence.gov.au/minister.

95. 'Defence Force changes will see women in frontline combat', *ABC News* (27 September 2011), www.abc.net.au.

96. ibid.

97. B Nicholson, 'Diggers in Afghanistan voice concerns women in combat added attraction for enemy', *The Australian* (5 October 2011), www.theaustralian. com.au.

98. 'Defence Force changes will see women in frontline combat', op. cit.

99. N Keene, 'The Mouse that roared — tributes flow for war heroine Nancy Wake', *The Telegraph* (9 August 2011), www.dailytelegraph.com.au.

100. S Balogh, 'Defence culture has to change, says new chief', *The Australian* (19 August 2011), www.theaustralian.com.au.

101. T Allard, 'New defence chief vows to treat his people right', *The Sydney Morning Herald* (5 July 2005), p. 4.

102. S Bartos, 'Changing Defence culture will take time' *The Drum Opinion* (14 April 2011), www.abc.net.au/ unleashed.

CHAPTER 10

POWER, POLITICS AND INFLUENCE IN ORGANISATIONS

LEARNING OBJECTIVES

After studying this chapter, you should be able to:

1. discuss the meaning of power and explain the sources of power available to managers and employees

2. explain the relationship between power, authority and obedience

3. explain how managers acquire power

4. discuss the meaning and importance of empowerment in organisations

5. explain organisational politics and its dual faces in organisations

6. explain various kinds of political behaviours in organisations

7. discuss the ethical implications of politics in organisations.

ORGANISATIONAL POLITICS, POWER AND CORRUPTION

Individuals seeking power and financial opportunities, through corrupt practices, may heavily influence the political scene of organisations. Calculated crime, for economic gain, may not be the actual end game but may be the instrument of power within organisations.[1] This is evidential in one of Australia's most recent and significant corruption cases. With the Victorian desalination plant, Sydney's ABC studios and Townsville's Ross River Dam under its belt, Leighton Holdings has a reputation as one of the largest construction companies in Australia — worth almost $7 billion. Behind this guise, bribery, corruption and cover-ups had become part of the political scene within the organisation — well known to Leighton's previous CEO Wal King and successor David Stewart.

A six-month investigation by Fairfax Media indicated that Leighton was involved allegedly in multi-million dollar paybacks in Iraq and South-East Asia and exposed the organisation as the most corrupt Australian company in recent times. Wal King had been CEO of Leighton for 23 years and had elevated the company to be a $13 billion global construction player. The revelations came at a time when David Stewart took over the reigns as CEO and there was a wrangle between Leighton's key shareholders — Hochtief of Germany and ACS of Spain.

Particularly damaging was a 2010 handwritten memo that suggested that Wal King was aware of a $42 million payment to Iraqi officials in Monaco, who then provided Leighton with a $750 million oil pipeline contract. Similar corruption scandals were also emerging about Leighton's Asian activities. Even though legal advice informed the company of the inherent risks that these activities could represent for the organisation, key files and memos were protected from scrutiny by authorities. In addition, the Australian Securities and Investments Commission had failed to conduct serious investigations following Leighton's report to Federal police that they may have broken foreign bribery laws in Iraq. The leaked files also indicated that Wal King and other key executives were emailed by an informant who advised that corrupt payments were being made to a Leighton employee in association with an Indian barge-building contract as well as systemic fraud occurring across a range of countries. A Sydney lawyer, who warned the organisation of its poor governance behaviour and reputational risk, was particularly damning of Leighton.[2]

Former Leighton's chief Wal King.

Introduction

No discussion of organisations would be complete without a study of power and politics. To succeed, managers and entrepreneurs need to acquire many skills. In particular, they need to understand the meaning of power and how it is acquired. Furthermore, their long-term success and the survival of their organisations depend on their ability to network with external economic, social and political players. In addition to their involvement in the business life of their organisation, they are increasingly required to show concerns for social issues as they emerge in their social sphere. This means that the acquisition and maintenance of power within organisations is not a simple process. It depends on a range of internal and external factors.

By virtue of their social dynamics, organisations are the arenas in which power and politics are most frequently found. Every day, in every kind of situation, managers and employees alike use power and politics to achieve their personal goals and do their jobs. A manager hires a personal assistant, a finance manager audits an entire department, a senior manager sacks his personal adviser, a board of directors forces a subsidiary into liquidation, shareholders sack a chief executive officer, a political leader is forced out of office for fraud or sexual misbehaviour — all of these are instances of the use of power, and they often entail politics. Power and politics may be the source of solutions as well as problems in organisations. They are important but remain quite elusive as concepts in organisational behaviour. This is because managers' actions often take place with varying and, sometimes, contradictory objectives in mind. For instance, a manager may be seeking to maximise profits and dividends to please shareholders, while at the same time attempting to fulfil requests for cost adjustments made by employees, unions and other stakeholders. To be effective, managers need to know how power is acquired and exercised. They also need to know why political behaviours are common in organisations and what may prompt such behaviours.

In this chapter we examine the meaning of power and politics, as well as their effects at both the interpersonal and organisational levels. We outline and discuss some fundamental theoretical contributions to the field. We also investigate practical and contemporary issues that are relevant to managers.

Some of the management activities most commonly affected by politics, power and influence are budget allocations; facilities/equipment allocations; changes to rules and procedures; reorganisation changes; delegation of authority; personnel changes such as promotions and transfers, recruitment and selection, pay and work appraisals; and interdepartmental coordination.[3]

On the one hand, power and politics represent the less desirable side of management. On the other, they can be the essence of what happens in organisations on a daily basis. This is because organisations are not democracies composed of individuals with equal influence. Some organisations are more akin to medieval feudal states, in which managers believe they can rule because they have some divine right. Any attempt to undermine the role of politics in the daily life of managers and employees would be erroneous. In essence, people are political animals. Some organisations have become so political that organisational interests are completely subordinated to individual interests.

Clearly, power and politics are important organisational tools that managers use to get the job done. In effective organisations, astute individuals delicately develop, nurture and manage power and politics. Power is usually a self-centred and individualistic endeavour. Yet there are instances where individual and organisational interests are compatible. The astute manager knows how to find such instances and capitalise on the opportunities. In other words, power and politics may be unsavoury notions to some, but when used with care, they can bring together individual desires for joint accomplishment.[4] They may be the source of solutions as well as problems in organisations.

Power and influence

Power may be defined as 'the potential ability to influence behaviour, to change the course of events, to overcome resistance, and to get people to do things that they would not otherwise do. Politics and influence are the processes, the actions, the behaviours through which this potential power is utilized and realized.'[5] In simpler terms, **power** may be defined as the ability to get someone to do something you want done or the ability to make things happen in the way you want. The essence of power is control over the behaviour of others.[6] Power is the force that makes things happen in an intended way; **influence** is a behavioural response to the exercise of power — that is, influence is an outcome achieved through the use of power. Managers use power to achieve influence over other people in the work setting.

Power is the ability to get someone else to do something you want done, or the ability to make things happen or get things done in the way you want.

Influence is a behavioural response to the exercise of power.

Figure 10.1 summarises the link between power and influence. It also identifies the key bases of power that managers can use to influence the behaviour of other people at work. Managers derive power from both organisational and individual sources. We call these sources position power and personal power, respectively.[7] French and Raven first raised this distinction in their landmark study, and it underpins our discussion on the subject.

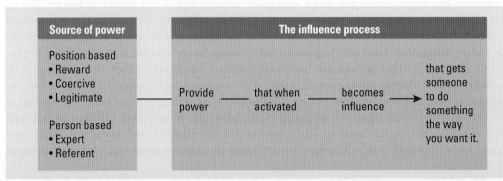

Source of power	The influence process			
Position based • Reward • Coercive • Legitimate **Person based** • Expert • Referent	Provide power	that when activated	becomes influence	that gets someone to do something the way you want it.

FIGURE 10.1 Power sources and the influence process

OBinAction

Empowering employees

The empowerment of employees that enables ownership of tasks and activities in an organisation has, in the last few decades, become important in the service industry. Critical to the working empowerment process is a working environment that is conducive to self-motivation, that enhances personal control and improves the level of customer service.[8] For example, the need for a shift to empowering employees in the Hilton chain of hotels emerged from the merger and acquisition that formed 'Hilton Worldwide'. At the time, the organisation was deemed to be highly dysfunctional and not well aligned. In particular, performance, brand and growth were targeted as problem areas, even though there was

strong customer awareness of the brand. So, the key priority then became how to stimulate growth in the newly formed entity. In 2007, the former CEO of Host Hotels and Resorts, Christopher J. Nassetta, was brought in to transform the organisation. He targeted four key concerns: aligning the culture and organisation, lifting baseline performance, consolidating and developing the brands, and promoting growth. Central to this revolution, and in a sustainable way, was the creation of an organisational culture that all 300 000 employees would embrace. In 2007, however, Nassetta explained that the culture was fractured, and to bring cultural alignment required a simple approach that is in practice difficult to implement. The simplicity of the approach was to align who you are as an organisation with the behavioural expectations of the organisation and to promote intensely the key priorities to every single person in the organisation. Together, he explains, a mass of people heading in the same direction is a 'power of force' and this means aligning mission, vision, values and important priorities, and diffusing these aspects across the organisation. Decision making is moved away from central control, which allows teams associated directly with customers to impart their knowledge, and information, and make good decisions that really serve customers and fundamentally drives the business. Shifting the organisation in this direction means that employees take ownership of the way the company operates and they feel a part of the business.[9]

Position power

Three bases of power are available to managers solely as a result of their position in the organisation: reward, coercive and legitimate power.

Reward power

Reward power is the extent to which a manager can use extrinsic and intrinsic rewards to control other people. Managers usually hold power in organisations by virtue of their ability to reward. This power is one aspect of motivation, as we saw in chapter 3. The strength of the power differs depending on the rewards that the manager controls and the strength of the employee's desire for the rewards.

Examples of such rewards include money, promotions, compliments or enriched jobs. These types of rewards are discussed in detail in chapters 3 and 4. Although all managers have some access to rewards, success in accessing and using rewards to achieve influence varies according to the skills of the manager.

> **Reward power** is the extent to which a manager can use extrinsic and intrinsic rewards to control other people.

Coercive power

Power can also be founded on punishment rather than reward. Managers can cause others to have unpleasant experiences. In such circumstances, coercive power is thought of as a form of punishment for failing to complying with the wishes of the power holder. A manager may threaten, for example, to withhold a pay raise, or to transfer, demote or even recommend the firing of an employee who does not act as desired. The manager could also allocate the least desirable task to a person as a form of punishment, or deliberately overlook the employee's good performance. Such **coercive power** is based on the extent to which a manager can deny desired rewards or administer punishments to control other people.

The availability of coercive power also varies from one organisation and manager to another. It should be noted that this type of power may have negative effects and should be used with caution. For this reason, most organisations devise rules and principles to guide rewards and punishment. Rules may be established to govern, for example, how supervisors may use coercive power to prevent them from using their formal authority arbitrarily to benefit some employees at the expense of others. Most organisations also have a system of 'appeal' to protect employees against coercion and various illegitimate acts, such as harassment in the workplace. Such organisational policies on employee treatment, and the presence of unions, for example, can weaken this power base considerably. Unions point out that when unemployment is high and job insecurity is rampant, employees may feel less able to confront coercive power; further, employees may not seek the assistance of unions for fear of further unpleasant consequences. Power and bullying are discussed in the Ethical perspective.

> **Coercive power** is the extent to which a manager can deny desired rewards or administer punishment to control other people.

Power and bullying

Workplace bullying is a major source of employee discontent and lost productivity. Both employers and employees are threatened by its presence and have an equal interest in its eradication. As a form of employee abuse it has unfortunately become commonplace in organisations.[10] The power to bully can be derived from various sources. Bullying is seen as an abuse of the power relationship between the bully and the victim.[11] Workplace bullying is defined as bullying in the workplace that involves the inappropriate use of coercion. It can also be described as a form of degradation, humiliation, intimidation and unfavourable treatment.[12] The office playground can be compared with the school playground. In the office playground, 'power is the chief perk in most companies …

(continued)

ETHICAL
Perspective

offices can bring out the bully in people'.[13] It seems that bullying tends to be more prevalent in times of restructuring and downsizing. Bullying may be used as a tactic in downsizing to force unwanted employees to leave.[14] It appears coercive power is the preferred type of power among bullies. With coercive power, an individual uses their ability to influence others' behaviour by punishing undesirable behaviour. Some forms of bullying also manifest from legitimate or expert power. Examples of such behaviour include verbal reprimands or abuse, allocation of undesirable work duties and tighter and closer supervision. These types of behaviours are seen by the victim as inappropriate.

On the other side of the continuum is the maxim that in the course of employment, it is imperative to treat others with respect and courtesy and to refrain from harassment. These issues are linked to valuing and encouraging diversity in the workplace, which needs to be an environment that is based on respect for differences between employees. This type of environment operates in tandem with protections for employees under federal anti-discrimination legislation and relevant state legislation. Bullying and harassment are evident in all types of workplaces. The Australian House of Representatives' Education and Employment Committee has recently produced a workplace bullying report. The report shows that, in one study, 6.8 per cent of Australian workers were bullied in the workplace over the last six months. A key problem for victims of workplace bullying is the lack of protection provided by Australian law and scarce examples of psychological bullying being brought to the courts. There are also significant overlapping gaps across a variety of legislation including: work health and safety law, industrial relations law and worker's compensation law. The committee has made recommendations to create a national advisory service for employers and employees, and for organisations to consider workplace bullying as a health and safety issue, as continuous unreasonable behaviour toward an employee may impair health and safety in the workplace. The report also urges for a Code of Practice and national training program to be established.[15]

As a method of pursuing organisational interests, it seems bullying is not a good use of power or influence. Therefore, it is essential that private and public sector organisations of all sizes develop codes of conduct and educate managers and employees on suitable workplace behaviours. Such behaviours should include problem-solving methods for addressing cases of workplace bullying, as well as mediation techniques. Furthermore, appropriate procedures should also be established in organisations to report and investigate allegations of workplace bullying.

Legitimate power and formal authority

The capacity to command does not always mean the right to command. They should not be equated. Legitimate power relates to the right (rather than capacity) to command. As the third base of power, **legitimate power** stems from the extent to which a manager can use the internalised belief of employees that the 'boss' has a 'right of command' to control their behaviour. Legitimate power provides an organisationally or culturally afforded right to direct the actions of others, and it is based on a mutually accepted perception that the power holder (in this case, the manager) has the right to influence the employee. In this context, managers are the bosses, their employees are the subordinates, and many routine instructions and requests are accepted simply because everyone agrees that employees should do what managers say. Legitimate power allows a manager to approve or deny employee requests for such things as job transfers, equipment purchases, personal time off or overtime work.

Legitimate power is the extent to which a manager can use the internalised belief of an employee that the 'boss' has a 'right of command' to control other people.

Legitimate power is often used interchangeably with the term *formal authority*. The two terms represent a special kind of managerial power that exists because employees believe it is legitimate for a person occupying the managerial role to have the right to command. Companies as entities need to consider that they hold considerable position power.

Legitimate power confers on an individual the legal authority to control and use organisational resources to accomplish organisational goals. For example, the organisation's board of directors grants the legitimate power of a chief executive officer, which gives him or her authority over all organisational resources. In turn, the chief executive officer has the right to confer legitimate power upon managers lower down in the organisation's hierarchy. Supervisors, too, have legitimate power over their employees.

Questioning the legitimacy of people in senior positions is, in general, a separate matter. This involves challenging fundamental organisational principles, such as management prerogative. So, when a challenge to legitimacy occurs, it tends to be with regard to specific issues rather than as a pervasive challenge to this basis of power.

An important part of legitimate power is **process power**. Process power is acquired when individuals are put in positions that allow them to influence how inputs are transformed into outputs. In their endeavour to meet production targets, organisations often establish positions for process specialists, who work with managers to ensure production targets are met. The specialists may sometimes turn into analysts or have to work with analysts. The analysts are individuals who are given control over the analytical process used to make decisions. For instance, an organisation may nominate a financial controller to monitor the efficiency of a production process. Another example is where an organisation uses business process re-engineering systems. Such systems are typically designed to empower workers and supervisory staff by giving them responsibility for entire processes. Hence, they overturn traditional management techniques that call for processes to be dissected and managed from the top, with workers trained to complete localised, repetitive tasks.

> **Process power** is the control over methods of production and analysis.

Information is also an important source of power. Managers with legitimate authority who do not have control over information they need in their role, would most likely be dependent on those who hold such information. Hence, in order for managers to effectively exercise their legitimate power, they need to secure control over information that is vital to their day-to-day managerial activities. Without such control, they are dependent on others who may manipulate such information to suit their own personal interests and agendas. This is often referred to as 'restrictive control', which is 'a form of power exertion in which one actor pushes his wishes through against the interests of another actor'.[16] In essence, **information power** constitutes an important part of legitimate power.

> **Information power** is the extent to which individuals have control over information needed by others.

Empowering women

OBinAction

In 1886, the California Perfume Company was established when very few women worked outside of the home. In the spirit of the founder David H. McConnell, the company that became 'Avon' has become a company totally committed to empowering women. As a result, many of the 6 million sales representatives working across 100 countries, are women. Avon is one of the world's major contributors in helping women both to support their families financially and to work flexibly. These attributes have become especially important as the World Bank and the International Labour Organization have forecast that women's unemployment will remain higher than men's through the continuing economic recession. It is not only Avon's sales force that is empowering to women. In 2013, four of Avon's executive committee and the Chief Scientific Officer were women. Globally, women represent 34 per cent of the vice president and higher positions and 44 per cent of director roles. As a result, Avon has been ranked amongst the top companies by the US National Association of Female Executives.[17]

Personal power

Personal power resides in the individual and is independent of the position the individual holds. However, the management literature considers that, in essence, the two main bases of personal power are expertise and reference.

Expert power

Expert power is the ability to control another person's behaviour through the possession of knowledge, experience or judgement that the other person does not have but needs. Employees would obey a supervisor possessing expert power because they feel the boss knows more about what is to be done or how it is to be done. Similarly, patients would typically listen to their doctor's recommendation because the doctor is more knowledgeable about medicine than they are. Computer specialists can influence non-technical staff behaviour because they have special knowledge that may be critical to the rest of the staff.

Access to or control over information is an important element in this particular power base. However, the proliferation of information technology means expert power is more likely to be challenged as individuals gain access to specialist knowledge. Patients, for example, are increasingly seeking medical information on the internet and challenging decisive expert decisions by their doctors.

'Expertise' is potentially a multifaceted concept that may include many areas of knowledge and information. Even those who know how to manage knowledge or know what knowledge is needed may be called 'experts'. Chapters 1 and 2 referred to the importance of knowledge management in our organisations and how it is necessary to gain knowledge, share it and use it for the benefit of the organisation. In that context, we should see experts as those who have any knowledge, judgement or experience that is required. For this reason a low-level employee without specialist training who has been in the organisation a considerable period may have experience or knowledge that is needed and that, therefore, may potentially influence the behaviour of others. Other sorts of knowledge also fit into this category. Gossip, for example, can be a form of knowledge or expertise with which a person may potentially influence the behaviour of others.

Access to key organisational decision makers is another element in expert power. A person's ability to contact key people informally can allow for special participation in the definition of a problem or issue, alteration in the flow of information to decision makers, and lobbying for use of special criteria in decision making. However, individuals with expert power do not always have the desire to exercise influence over others. In this case, managers with legitimate power have to develop good working relationships with employees who hold expert power. The power struggles in play at an immigration detention centre are discussed in the What would you do? that follows.

WhatWould
You**Do?**

Working in the Woomera detention centre

The following is an extract of Margot O'Neill's interview with Dr Simon Lockwood on the ABC's *Lateline* program. Lockwood was the longest serving medical officer at the Woomera detention centre, which was closed in 2003.

MARGOT O'NEILL: Dr Lockwood watched Woomera descend into a living hell, and it wasn't just detainees who were broken.

The trauma of the families locked inside spread to the Australian officers paid to guard them.

DR SIMON LOCKWOOD: A lot of the officers would cope with the stress by going to the pub and drinking themselves into oblivion or gambling on the pokies, so there was a lot of social problems in the town.

MARGOT O'NEILL: But did the Government know that it had a mass psychiatric disaster on its hands inside the detention centre?

DR SIMON LOCKWOOD: They did know.

They definitely knew that a major amount of the population were very sick.

MARGOT O'NEILL: And they just decided not to do anything about it?

DR SIMON LOCKWOOD: Well, they must have, because they didn't do anything about it.

MARGOT O'NEILL: Unlike many of his medical colleagues, Dr Lockwood decided not to go public.

Instead, Simon Lockwood took his case directly to Canberra, addressing a meeting of officials from the Immigration Department, or DIMIA.

For more than two hours Dr Lockwood told a room full of bureaucrats about the detention centre's catastrophic impact on families, on children.

DR SIMON LOCKWOOD: And then towards the end of the meeting one of the bureaucrats said to me, in front of everyone there, 'That sounds all well and good to us, Simon, but we don't want to make it so nice for them in detention that they won't want to leave'.

I knew that I'd spoken for two hours probably for nothing.

MARGOT O'NEILL: By now Woomera was the country's most controversial detention centre, attracting violent protests, which Simon Lockwood says only made camp life even more difficult.

DR SIMON LOCKWOOD: They never helped, because I always thought that it would be better for those protesters to go to [then Immigration Minister] Philip Ruddock's office and protest there, because the amount of distress and tension in the camp that was brought on by those protests lingered for months.

MARGOT O'NEILL: Dr Lockwood tried to get the worst-affected people, including children, out of the detention centre.

But he was often blocked by DIMIA.

DR SIMON LOCKWOOD: The problem that I had with DIMIA was that they're not doctors, they're not nurses, they're not psychologists, and yet they would do the opposite of what was recommended by an expert in child psychiatry, for example.

On what basis?

Because no-one died, DIMIA or the bureaucrats believed that no-one made genuine attempts, but I can tell you being the doctor that was looking after those people and saving their lives, that that wasn't the case.

(continued)

I look back on it now and I find it hard to believe that it was in Australia that we had a place like that, that it couldn't have been better designed to break people down, detainees and staff.[18]

Questions
1. Describe the types of power that would be at work in the management of an institution such as Woomera.
2. What would you have done in Dr Lockwood's position?

Referent power

Referent power is the ability to control another's behaviour because that person wants to identify with the power source. In this case, employees would obey the boss because they want to behave, perceive or believe as the boss does. This might occur, for example, because the employee likes the boss personally and, therefore, tries to do things in the way the boss wants them done. In a sense, the employee behaves to avoid doing anything that would interfere with the pleasing boss–employee relationship.

Individuals may have one or more such sources of power, to varying degrees and in varying combinations. It is important that managers do not rely on a single source of power, as this may limit their effectiveness. For example, managers who rely only on legitimate power may have very limited ability to influence the behaviour of others, and their efforts may be undermined by the referent power of informal leaders.

Power, authority and obedience

Power is the potential to control the behaviour of others; formal authority is the potential to exert such control through the legitimacy of a managerial position. Yet, we also know that people who seem to have power do not always get their way. This leads us to the subject of obedience. Why do some people obey directives while others do not? More specifically, why should employees respond to a manager's authority, or 'right to command', in the first place? Further, given that employees are willing to obey, what determines the limits of obedience?

The Milgram experiments

These last questions point to Stanley Milgram's seminal research on obedience.[19] Milgram designed an experiment to determine the extent to which people obey the commands of an authority figure, even if they believe they are endangering the life of another person. The subjects were forty males, ranging in age from twenty to fifty years and representing a diverse set of occupations (engineers, salespeople, school teachers, labourers and others). They were paid a nominal fee for participation in the project, which was conducted in a laboratory at Yale University.

The subjects were told (falsely) that the purpose of the study was to determine the effects of punishment on learning. The subjects were to be the 'teachers'. The 'learner', an associate of Milgram's, was strapped to a chair in an adjoining room with an electrode attached to his wrist. The 'experimenter', another confederate of Milgram's, was dressed in a grey laboratory coat. Appearing impassive and somewhat stern, the experimenter instructed the teacher to read a series of word pairs to the learner and then to re-read the first word along with four other terms. The learner was supposed to indicate which of the four terms was in the original pair by pressing a switch that caused a light to flash on a response panel in front of the teacher.

The teacher was instructed to administer a shock to the learner each time a wrong answer was given. This shock was to be increased by one level of intensity each time the learner made a mistake. The teacher controlled switches that ostensibly administered shocks ranging from 15 to 450 volts. In reality, there was no electric current in the apparatus, but the learner purposely and very frequently 'erred', responding to each level of 'shock' in progressively distressed ways. A summary of the switch markings and the learner's fake responses to the various levels of shock is shown in figure 10.2.

Switch voltage marking	Switch description	'Learner's' response
15–60	Slight	No sound
75–120	Moderate	Grunts and moans
135–180	Strong	Asks to leave
195–240	Very strong	Cannot stand the pain
255–300	Intense	Pounds on wall
315–360	Extreme intensity	No sound
375–420	Danger: severe shock	No sound
435–450	XXX	No sound

FIGURE 10.2 Shock levels and set learner responses in the Milgram experiment

If a teacher proved unwilling to administer a shock, the experimenter used the following sequential prods to get him to perform as requested.
1. 'Please continue' or 'Please go on'.
2. 'The experiment requires that you continue.'
3. 'It is absolutely essential that you continue.'
4. 'You have no choice, you must go on.'

Only when the teacher refused to go on after the fourth prod would the experiment be stopped. When would you expect that the 'teachers' would refuse to continue?

Milgram asked some of his students and colleagues the same question. Most felt that few, if any, of the subjects would go beyond the 'very strong shock' level. But 26 subjects (65 per cent) continued to the end of the experiment and shocked the 'learner' to the XXX level! None stopped before 300 volts — the point at which the learner pounds on the wall. The remaining 14 subjects refused to obey the experimenter at various intermediate points.

Most people are surprised by these results, as was Milgram. The question is: why would other people have a tendency to accept or comply with authoritative commands under such extreme conditions? Milgram conducted further experiments to try to answer this question. The subjects' tendencies towards compliance were somewhat reduced when:
• experimentation took place in a rundown office (rather than a university lab)
• the victim was closer
• the experimenter was farther away
• the subject could observe other subjects.

The level of compliance was still much higher than most of us would expect. The results of this experiment are useful and informative. However, the conduct of this type of experiment would probably not be permitted under today's more demanding guidelines for research. Social scientists now abide by increasingly stringent rules on research ethics.

Obedience and the acceptance of authority

As the Milgram experiments suggest, there are strong tendencies among individuals to follow the instructions of the boss. Direct defiance within organisational settings is quite rare. If the tendency to follow instructions is great and defiance is rare, then why do so many organisations appear to drift into apparent chaos? The answer to this question lies at the heart of the contribution made by the well-known management writer Chester Barnard.[20] Essentially, Barnard's argument focused on the 'consent of the governed' rather than on the rights derived from ownership. He argued that employees will accept or follow a directive from the boss only under special circumstances, and all four must be met.

1. The employee can and must understand the directive.
2. The employee must feel mentally and physically capable of carrying out the directive.
3. The employee must believe the directive is not inconsistent with the purpose of the organisation.
4. The employee must believe the directive is not inconsistent with his or her personal interests.

These four conditions are carefully stated. To accept and follow an order, employees do not need, for instance, to understand how the proposed action will help the organisation; they only need to believe the requested action is not inconsistent with the purpose of the organisation. The astute manager will not take these guidelines for granted. In giving directives, the astute manager recognises that the acceptance of the request is not assured. If the directive is routine, then it is not surprising that the employee may merely comply without enthusiasm. The manager needs to understand what employees consider acceptable or unacceptable actions.

International SPOTLIGHT

The challenge of managing across cultures

Managing in an international environment is a significant challenge for organisational leaders in multinational corporations. Managing across cultures is never easy, and undertaking international leadership roles can be particularly difficult. Global supply chains, marketing strategies and human resource management approaches require constant coordination and fine-tuning. Whether you wish to lead a global corporation one day, or simply hope to develop international leadership skills, an overseas job assignment can provide an array of new skills and experiences. The twenty-first century also presents challenges as BRIC (Brazil, Russia, India and China) and other emerging economies join traditional Western economic powerhouses to form a dynamic global trading environment. Working across a myriad of diverse cultures is, therefore, becoming increasingly important in conducting global business.

The emergence of China, India and Indonesia, as well as other strong economies in South-East Asia, will challenge the predominance of global trade by Western economies. Regional knowledge and culture have implications for management theory and, at the same time, there is a lack of management theories and knowledge based on the uniquely differing contexts across these nations. Some early insight towards understanding the Asian mindset was put forward by Gunnar Myrdal in the 1960s. He described the diverse array of Asian mindsets as the 'Asian Drama'. In particular, he identified key structural and religion-based obstacles generally across the Asian region, independent of the size of the country; for example, China, India, Singapore, Indonesia and Malaysia. This may provide a real barrier to these countries developing management capabilities that are suitable to reflect the cross-cultural contexts of managing in a global community. However, countries such as India have shown that they are able to overcome these hurdles and develop as a global player.

Obedience and the zone of indifference

Most people seek a balance between what they put into an organisation (contributions) and what they get from an organisation in return (inducements). Within the boundaries of the psychological contract (see chapter 1), therefore, employees will agree to do many things in and for the organisation because they think they should; that is, in exchange for certain inducements, employees recognise the authority of the organisation and its managers to direct their behaviour in certain ways. Based on his acceptance view of authority, Chester Barnard calls this area in which directions are obeyed the 'zone of indifference'.

The **zone of indifference** is the range of authoritative requests to which employees are willing to respond without subjecting the directives to critical evaluation or judgement — that is, the range in which they are indifferent. Directives falling within the zone are obeyed; requests or orders falling outside the zone of indifference are not considered legitimate under terms of the psychological contract. The latter directives may or may not be obeyed. This link between the zone of indifference and the psychological contract is shown in figure 10.3.

The **zone of indifference** is the range of authoritative requests to which an employee is willing to respond without subjecting the directives to critical evaluation or judgement — that is, the requests to which the employee is indifferent.

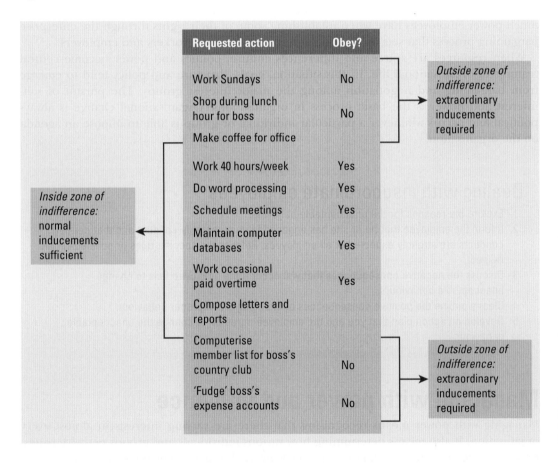

Requested action	Obey?
Work Sundays	No
Shop during lunch hour for boss	No
Make coffee for office	
Work 40 hours/week	Yes
Do word processing	Yes
Schedule meetings	Yes
Maintain computer databases	Yes
Work occasional paid overtime	Yes
Compose letters and reports	
Computerise member list for boss's country club	No
'Fudge' boss's expense accounts	No

Outside zone of indifference: extraordinary inducements required

Inside zone of indifference: normal inducements sufficient

Outside zone of indifference: extraordinary inducements required

FIGURE 10.3 Hypothetical psychological contract with a secretary showing zone of indifference

The secretary whose psychological contract is shown in figure 10.3 may be expected to perform a number of activities falling within the zone of indifference with no questions asked. Examples include scheduling meetings and maintaining computer databases. But there may be times when the boss would like the secretary to do things falling outside the zone, such as running personal errands for the boss on the secretary's lunch hour. This requires efforts to enlarge the zone to accommodate additional behaviours. In these attempts, the boss will most likely have to use more incentives than pure position power. In some instances, such as Sunday work and 'fudging' of expense accounts, no power base may be capable of accomplishing the desired result. Before leaving this discussion, there is another side to power, authority and obedience with which you should be familiar as a manager. That side is your own zone of indifference and tendency to obey. When will you say 'no' to your boss? When should you be willing to say 'no'? At times, the situation may involve ethical dilemmas, where you may be asked to do things that are illegal, unethical or both. Research on ethical managerial behaviour shows that supervisors are singled out by their employees as sources of pressure to do such things as support incorrect viewpoints, sign false documents, overlook the supervisor's wrongdoing and do business with the supervisor's friends.[21]

Most of us will occasionally face ethical dilemmas during our careers. Saying 'no' or 'refusing to keep quiet' can be difficult and potentially costly, as many whistleblowers discover. But it may still be the right thing to do.

It is possible to say 'no' and to air issues, however, without going as far as whistleblowing the whole issue in the courts, the media or elsewhere. In such cases, other measures can be tried. Employees may have recourse to the law, for example, in cases of occupational health or safety, workers compensation, unfair dismissal or discrimination. The 'legitimate power' of managers may be countered by the employees' knowledge of their rights. However, contesting the power of a manager may not always be easy. It is also important to question how much power employees have when establishing some of their rights through the enterprise bargaining process that sets up working agreements between workers and employers.

When resources are scarce and differences endure, politics and power become central features of organisational life. In this situation, goals, structure and policy tend to emerge from bargaining and negotiation among the major interest groups. The pursuit of self-interest and power is the basic process in organisations. Organisational change is always political and occurs whenever a particular individual or group is able to impose an agenda on the organisation.

Dealing with insubordinate employees

1. Explore the reasons for the unacceptable behaviour.
2. Inform the employee that he or she has engaged in unacceptable conduct and that certain conducts are strongly expected of all employees. Refer to the specific rules or policies in that respect.
3. Discuss the negative consequences that will occur if the employee fails to change unacceptable behaviours.
4. Clearly outline the positive consequences of changing the improper behaviour.
5. Develop an action plan that you and the employee agree on to change the unacceptable behaviour.

Managing with power and influence

Managing with power means recognising that there are varying interests in almost every organisation. It also means determining how various individuals and groups perceive issues. Further, it means understanding that power is needed to get things done, and that sources of power must be developed. Managing with power also requires an understanding of the strategies and tactics through which power is developed and used in organisations. By learning to manage with power, managers are able to achieve both their own goals and the goals of their organisation.

A considerable part of any manager's time will be directed towards what is called 'power-oriented' behaviour — that is, behaviour directed primarily at developing or using relationships in which other people are to some degree willing to defer to your wishes.[22] Figure 10.4 shows three basic dimensions of power and influence with which a manager will become involved in this regard: downward, upward and lateral. Also shown in the figure are some preliminary ideas for achieving success along each of these dimensions.

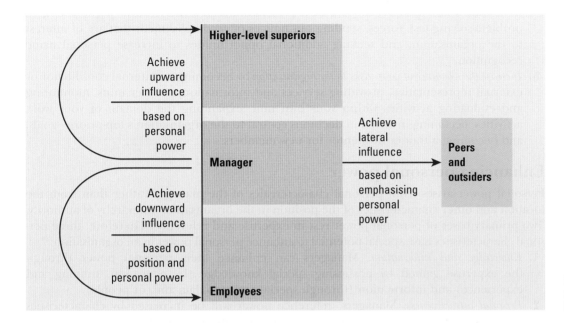

FIGURE 10.4 Three dimensions of managerial power and influence

When 'facing upwards', managers must rely on the use of personal power to achieve influence over higher-level superiors. In contrast, when 'facing downwards', managers can mobilise both position and personal power in dealing with employees. In lateral relations with peers and outsiders, the manager must again emphasise personal power to achieve the desired influence.

Acquiring managerial power

The effective manager is one who, over time, succeeds in building and maintaining high levels of both position and personal power. Only then will sufficient power of the right types be available when the manager needs to exercise influence on downward, lateral and upward dimensions.

Enhancing position power

As we mentioned earlier, position power is based on formal authority and the legitimacy of a manager's location in the organisation's hierarchy of authority. Position power can be enhanced when managers are able to demonstrate to others that their work units are highly relevant to organisational goals, and are able to respond to urgent organisational needs. In addition, there are five general guidelines for enhancing position power.[23]

1. *Increase your centrality and critical role in the organisation* by acquiring a more central role in the work flow, having information filtered through you, making at least part of your job responsibilities unique, expanding your network of communication contacts, and occupying an office convenient to main traffic flows.

2. *Increase the personal discretion and flexibility of your job* by removing routine activities, expanding task variety and novelty, initiating new ideas, getting involved in new projects, participating in the early stages of the decision-making process, and avoiding 'reliable performance criteria' for judging your success on the job.

3. *Build tasks into your job that are difficult to evaluate* by creating an ambiguous job description, developing a unique language or set of labels in your work, obtaining

advanced training, becoming more involved in professional associations, and exercising your own judgement.

4. *Increase the visibility of your job performance* by expanding the number of contacts you have with senior people, making oral presentations of written work, participating in problem-solving task forces, sending out notices of accomplishment that are of interest to the organisation, and seeking additional opportunities to increase personal name recognition.

5. *Increase the relevance of your tasks to the organisation* by becoming an internal coordinator or external representative, providing services and information to other units, monitoring and evaluating activities within your own unit, expanding the domain of your work activities, becoming involved in decisions central to the organisation's top-priority goals, and becoming a trainer or mentor for new members.

Enhancing personal power

Personal power arises from personal characteristics of the manager rather than from the location and other characteristics of the position in the organisation's hierarchy of authority. Two primary bases of personal power rest in expertise and reference. Therefore, three personal characteristics have special potential to enhance personal power in an organisation.[24]

1. *Knowledge and information.* Managers can enhance their personal power through the expertise gained by possessing special knowledge (by education, training and experience) and information (through special access to data and/or people).

2. *Personal attractiveness.* Managers' reference power will be increased by characteristics that enhance their 'likeability' and create personal attraction in their relationships with other people. These include pleasant personality characteristics, agreeable behaviour patterns and attractive personal appearance.

3. *Effort.* The demonstration of sincere hard work in task performance can also increase personal power by enhancing both expertise and reference. A person who is perceived to try hard may be expected to know more about the job and thus be sought out for advice. Managers who try hard are also likely to be respected for the attempt, and others may even come to depend on them to maintain that effort.

While all of these methods may have merit in some contexts, and may increase the power of individuals, there is no guarantee that such approaches will not be utilised unethically — this is something that will be a matter of judgement and/or analysis in each case. It is also possible that some of these approaches may work against the principles of empowerment to a greater or lesser extent. Empowerment is discussed later in the chapter.

Turning power into influence

The acquisition of power is certainly an important task for any manager. Actually using this power well to achieve the desired influence over other people is another challenge.

Consider the following examples of how some managers attempt to exercise influence.

- 'I voice my wishes loudly.'
- 'I offer a *quid pro quo* — that is, I offer to do for them if they do for me.'
- 'I keep at it and reiterate my point over and over again until I get my way.'
- 'I have all the facts and figures ready, and I use them as necessary.'
- 'I go over the boss's head to higher levels when I get turned down.'

Practically speaking, there are many useful ways of exercising influence. The most common strategies involve:[25]

- *reason* — using facts and data to support a logical argument
- *friendliness* — using flattery, goodwill and favourable impressions
- *coalition* — using relationships with other people for support
- *bargaining* — using the exchange of benefits as a basis for negotiation
- *assertiveness* — using a direct and forceful personal approach

- *higher authority* — gaining higher-level support for requests
- *sanctions* — using organisationally derived rewards and punishments.

Research on this particular set of strategies for achieving managerial influence suggests that reason is the most popular strategy overall.[26] In addition, friendliness, assertiveness, bargaining and higher authority are used more frequently to influence employees than to influence supervisors. This pattern of 'influence attempts' is consistent with our earlier contention that downward influence generally includes the mobilisation of both position and personal power sources, while upward influence will more likely draw on personal power. Other influence tactics have also been studied. The following list is drawn from the work of Gary Yukl and his colleagues. The tactics are:
- *rational persuasion* — using logical arguments and factual evidence
- *consultation* — seeking a person's involvement in an activity in which you require their support or assistance
- *inspirational appeals* — appealing to a person's values, ideals or aspirations to arouse enthusiasm and confidence to carry out the task
- *personal appeals* — appealing to a person's feelings of loyalty and friendship
- *ingratiation* — trying to get a person in a good mood or thinking of you favourably before making a request
- *exchange* — offering an exchange of favours, or a willingness to exchange favours, or a share in the benefits of an action
- *pressure* — using demands, threats, frequent checking or constant reminders
- *legitimating tactics* — claiming the authority or right to make your request by showing how it links with organisational rules, policies, practices or traditions
- *coalition tactics* — seeking the aid of others to help persuade a target person to do what you request.[27]
- The researchers found, consistent with earlier studies of the same set, that consultation, inspirational appeals and strong rational persuasion are the most effective tactics. However, variation could be expected based on the context, the direction of the influence attempt and the objectives of the influence attempt. They suggest that managers diagnose their power relationships carefully in order to be able to use the tactics effectively.[28]

Little research is available on the specific subject of upward influence in organisations. This is unfortunate because truly effective managers are able to influence their boss as well as their employees. One study reports that both supervisors and employees view reason, or the logical presentation of ideas, as the most frequently used strategy of upward influence.[29] However, when queried on reasons for success and failure, both groups exhibit similarities and differences in their viewpoints. Table 10.1 shows that the perceived causes of success in upward influence are similar for both supervisors and employees, and involve the favourable content of the influence attempt, the favourable manner of its presentation, and the competence of the employee.[30] The two groups disagree on the causes of failure, however. Employees attribute failure in upward influence to the closed-mindedness of the supervisor, the unfavourable content of the influence attempt, and unfavourable interpersonal relationships with the supervisor. In contrast, supervisors attribute failure to the unfavourable content of the attempt, the unfavourable manner in which it was presented, and the lack of competence of the employee.

Supervisor's views	Employee's views
Favourable content of influence attempt; favourable manner in which attempt was made; competency of employee	Agreement with supervisor's views
Unfavourable content of influence attempt; lack of competence of employee; poor manner in which attempt was made	Unfavourable content of influence attempt; closed-mindedness of supervisor; poor interpersonal relations with supervisor

TABLE 10.1 Perceived causes of success and failure in upward influence attempts

However, power and influence do not just work up and down within the organisation; customers also have the opportunity to exert influence over various processes and decisions in the organisation, They do so through increasing consumer demands, greater concern for and response to consumer feedback, and the increasing availability of information on-line. Shareholders, and people in wider society, may also have some potential to influence decisions and behaviours in organisations. Such influence is not necessarily intentional, and typically not as strong as power sources inside the organisation. This shows that power and influence do not just emerge and function within the organisation, but come from outside as well.

Exercising upward influence

Power and influence may also be exercised upward. Research indicates that a number of upward influence tactics may be used. The most common tactics are:

- *rationality* — refers to the use of facts and data to support a logical argument or to alter the thinking of a supervisor or manager
- *coalition* — involves making claims about support for your position from others in the organisation
- *ingratiation* — use of impression management, flattery and goodwill, and the promotion of a pleasant relationship when making a request
- *exchange of benefits* — pertains to negotiating by means of bargaining or favours
- *assertiveness* — a direct and forceful approach
- *upward appeal* — involves gaining the support of those higher up in the organisation to back your requests.[31]

Empowerment

Empowerment is the process by which managers help others acquire and use the power needed to make decisions affecting themselves and their work (chapter 3). More than ever before, managers in progressive organisations are expected to be good at — and highly comfortable with — empowering the people with whom they work. Rather than considering power as something to be held only at higher levels in the traditional 'pyramid' of an organisation, this view considers power to be something that everyone working in flatter and more collegial structures can share. Empowerment is a key foundation of the increasingly popular self-managing work teams and other creative worker involvement groups. Despite this, there are limits to the process of empowerment, which we will discuss in some detail soon.

Power keys to empowerment

One base for empowerment is a radically different view of power itself. Our discussion so far has focused on power exerted over other individuals. In contrast to this, the concept of empowerment emphasises the ability to make things happen. Cutting through all the corporate rhetoric on empowerment is difficult because the term has become fashionable in management circles. However, each individual empowerment attempt needs to be examined in the light of how power in the organisation will be changed.

Expanding the zone of indifference

When embarking on an empowerment program, management needs to recognise the current zone of indifference and systematically move to expand it. All too often, management assumes that its directive for empowerment will be followed; however, managers often fail to show precisely how empowerment will benefit the individuals involved.

Power as an expanding pie

Along with empowerment, employees need to be trained to expand their power and their new influence potential. This is the most difficult task for managers and a difficult challenge

Empowerment is the process by which managers delegate power to employees to motivate greater responsibility in balancing the achievement of both personal and organisational goals.

for employees, because it often changes the dynamic between supervisors and employees. The key is to change the concept of power within the organisation — from a view that stresses power over others to one that emphasises the use of power to get things done. Under the new definition of power, all employees can be more powerful.

In practical terms, empowerment means that all managers will need to emphasise different ways of exercising influence. Appeals to higher authority and sanctions will need to be replaced by appeals to reason, friendliness and bargaining. More than a few employees will be uncomfortable when asked to be assertive or to engage in bargaining. Yet, these influence techniques are likely to become more important with the spread of empowerment. Special support may be needed for these individuals so that they can become comfortable in developing their own power.

Empowering others

When an organisation attempts to move power down the hierarchy, it also needs to alter the existing pattern of position power. Changing this pattern raises important questions. Can 'empowered' individuals give rewards and sanctions? Has their new right to act been legitimised with formal authority? All too often, attempts at empowerment disrupt well-established patterns of position power, and threaten middle and lower-level managers. As one supervisor said, 'All this empowerment stuff sounds great for top management. They don't have to run around trying to get the necessary clearances to implement the suggestions from my group. They never gave me authority to make the changes, only the new job of asking for permission.'

When all goes well, everyone can gain from empowerment. To keep the organisation competitive, top management must attend to a variety of challenging and strategic forces in the external environment. While top management tends to concentrate on decisions about strategy and dynamic change, others throughout the organisation must be ready and willing to make critical operating decisions. By providing these opportunities, empowerment increases the total power available in an organisation. In other words, the top levels do not have to give up power for the lower levels to gain it. The same basic argument holds true in any manager–employee relationship. Following is a list of some emerging guidelines for managing the empowerment of others.

THE **EffectiveManager** 10.2

Guidelines for implementing empowerment

1. Encourage creative decision making by allowing employees ample flexibility in how they achieve company objectives.
2. Provide all the necessary information to assist employees to make informed decisions.
3. Communicate openly with employees on the organisation's activities, performance and long-term goals. Let them know how the organisation is doing and how their roles and actions affect the bottom line.
4. Employee training on problem solving, time management and decision making can help prepare them for increased responsibility.
5. Run regular meetings between employees and management, staff surveys — even a traditional suggestion box can be effective.
6. Be sure to respond swiftly to input and suggestions from employees, since lengthy silence can lead to discouragement.
7. Allow room for error; encouraging employees to be more involved inevitably entails some risk taking. Hence, a certain amount of error is likely to occur. Allow for this and put in place an action plan to address errors.

Empowerment varies in the degree to which it is applied and accepted in any organisation. Empowerment can range from the addition of extra small tasks to full involvement and responsibility for important decision making or project completion. Clearly, quantifying the degree of empowerment is a difficult and complex task. In the United Kingdom an empowerment audit (EA) was developed to try to measure the degree of empowerment, resulting in a matrix of 15 major indicators, each with a five-point scale of traditional, participative, involved, early self-directed and mature self-directed.[32] Empowerment involves the development of all employees, including managers. There is a significant risk that trying to introduce the highest degrees of empowerment too quickly will fail to give people time to develop and adjust to new demands. The result may be that they conclude that empowerment can not or did not work, when a slower, steadier program of introduction may have allowed individuals to adapt to empowerment over time.

The limits of empowering others

Empowerment programs can transform a stagnant organisation into a vital one by creating a shared purpose among employees, encouraging greater cooperation and, most importantly, delivering enhanced value to customers. Despite that potential, empowerment programs often fall victim to the same structural and cultural problems that made them desirable in the first place. On the one hand, many managers may view empowerment as a threat, and may continue to measure their personal status and value in terms of the hierarchical authority they wield. These managers perceive the shift of responsibility for work assignments and output evaluation to employees as a loss of authority and a change to a less satisfying role. As a result, they may resist empowerment efforts. On the other hand, some employees mistake empowerment for discretionary authority — the power to decide things unilaterally — and lack necessary cooperative skills in which managers neglect or refuse to train them. Most employees define power in terms of discretion — that is, the ability to make unilateral decisions — and expect an empowerment program to increase their personal decision-making ability. This expectation can lead to conflicts between employees and managers about the limits of power and the actions that violate accepted practice. Employees need to be coached that being empowered does not mean having more personal discretion. It means having an increased ability to create value for customers. A key element of this concept is the belief that effective value creation depends on interdependence and cooperation, with corresponding limits on personal discretion.

Organisational politics

Any study of power and influence inevitably leads to the subject of 'politics'. Political processes form the dynamic that enables the formal organisation to function. In a sense, power and politics act as the lubricant that enables the interdependent parts of the organisation to operate smoothly together.

The word 'politics' may conjure up thoughts of illicit deals, favours and special personal relationships. Politics is a common game played in business organisations. How well the game is played depends on the skill of the political players and how well they choose and use the organisation. This image of organisational politics whereby shrewd, often dishonest, practices are used to obtain influence is reflected in Machiavelli's classic sixteenth-century work, *The prince*, which outlines how to obtain and hold power via political action. For that reason, political actions are also referred to in terms of 'Machiavellianism'.

Politics may also be described as the art of using influence, authority and power to achieve goals. These goals may be self-interested for an individual, group or department, for example. Political skills, like technical skills, are a tool for getting things done. Managers must develop an understanding of the concepts of influence, power and authority before they can use politics effectively. If managers have an understanding of these concepts, along with an awareness of the self-interest barriers (departmental, personal, corporate and group self-interest), then they are able to present views or decisions to the self-interest group in the least threatening manner possible. Managers should frequently and openly discuss the political ramifications of all decisions confronting a department. They can use this to illustrate political realities, and to explain the many nuances of good political planning.

The two traditions of organisational politics

To survive in a highly political environment requires particular skills, including the ability to recognise those who are playing political games despite surface appearances of openness and cooperation. It also requires the ability to identify the power sources of the key players, and to build your own alliances and connections. There are two quite different traditions in the analysis of organisational politics.

Politics as unsanctioned and self-interested

This first tradition builds on Machiavelli's philosophy and defines politics in terms of self-interest and the use of non-sanctioned means. In this tradition, **organisational politics** may be formally defined as the management of influence to obtain ends not sanctioned by the organisation, or to obtain sanctioned ends through non-sanctioned means of influence.[33] Managers are often considered political when they seek their own goals or use means not currently authorised by the organisation. It is also important to recognise that where there is uncertainty or ambiguity it is often extremely difficult to tell whether a manager is being political in this self-serving sense.[34]

> **Organisational politics** is the management of influence to obtain ends not sanctioned by the organisation, or to obtain sanctioned ends through non-sanctioned means of influence.

In politics, contesting forces compete for favourable outcomes on decisions involving who gets what and how. Political activity is usually stronger where there are no prescribed routine answers or no stated policy. It also centres around the interpretation of existing policies and those situations involving value judgements. Any organisation that attempts to totally reduce these arenas of political activity by instituting rules, regulations and policies from the top would quickly be strangled in its own red tape.

Politics as a compromise between competing interests

The second tradition treats politics as a necessary function resulting from differences in the perceived self-interest of individuals. Organisational politics is viewed as the art of compromise among competing interests. In a heterogeneous society, individuals will disagree on whose self-interest is most valuable and whose concerns should be bounded by collective interests. Politics arise because individuals need to develop compromises, avoid confrontation and live together. The same holds true in organisations, where individuals join, work and stay together because their self-interest is served. Further, it is important to remember that the goals of the organisation are established by organisationally powerful individuals in negotiation with others. Thus, organisational politics is also about the use of power to develop socially acceptable ends and means that balance individual and collective interests.

The belief that everything that happens in the organisation is the result of human beings pursuing their rational self-interest implies that ideas do not matter at all. People are often taught that arguments and theories will have no impact on them because they will just do whatever is in their rational self-interest. Within the liberal tradition, the fundamental power of ideas is often denied. This thesis, which has become especially prominent in public sector organisations, holds that starting with standard economic assumptions, it is possible to explain behaviours within public sector organisations. Of course, the behaviour of all public officials is guided by ideas. The difference is that some keep tabs on their ideas, others do not, and others do it in a perverse way. Therefore, one cannot deny that people are motivated by ideas — small ones, borrowed ones, scrutinised ones. This is indeed paradoxical.

The important point here is that if you go to work expecting other people in the organisation to behave rationally and logically at all times, then you will be surprised. Self-interest, or the pursuit of ideas, will be present. Perceptions about personal behaviour are discussed in the Counterpoint.

COUNTERPOINT

Managing up: exercising personal power

Employees are increasingly taking their career progression in their own hands and ensuring they use their personal power to influence their superiors. 'Managing up' is the polite term for the art of getting along with your boss at all costs.[35] Many employees are increasingly deciding that this is an effective way of getting ahead, according to a poll of 5000 people carried out by jobs website Reed. The survey shows that the vast majority of staff who have been promoted up the career ladder have used the 'managing up' approach.

The key to employees 'managing up' is ensuring supervisors with the reward power are made aware of their extra efforts, and they may even take on additional responsibilities to demonstrate their worth. Networking with managers and key decision makers is cited as another key strategy, as well as using every possible chance to show off their potential and untapped skills. In addition, undertaking extra training and actively sharing personal successes with decision makers prove to be popular choices in securing promotion.[36] Even though these types of actions are sometimes classified as brownnosing, grovelling or crawling, it is clear that they could have a positive effect on employees' career progression. In a recent study involving 1000 senior-level American managers in the manufacturing and services sectors (134 CEOs and 765 board directors), Professors Ithai Stern (Kellogg School of Management, Northwestern University) and James Westphal (University of Michigan) examined their appointments to these positions and what they have done to achieve them. The results of the study showed that corporate leaders were successful in being named to boards of directors when they used subtle forms of flattery, and indicated their agreement on issues with those involved in the selection process. In other words, implied conformity was a key strategy in obtaining these corporate positions.[37]

Within the general work situation, it could even be argued that maintaining good relations with your boss is absolutely crucial, as has been demonstrated by an unfair dismissal case in Melbourne where Bruce Guthrie, the former editor-in-chief of the *Herald Sun*, sued News Limited for sacking him 15 months before his three-year contract was due to expire.[38] One of the reasons for his dismissal was the allegedly poisonous relationship he had with his boss, Peter Blunden, the Managing Director of the *Herald* and *Weekly Times*, with whom he is said to have clashed from day one. According to the *Sydney Morning Herald*, even though Guthrie argued that the problem was no more than the usual difficulty of newspaper men in such positions, he did tell the court that he had been warned to 'never go up against' Blunden.[39] Even though Guthrie won the case and was awarded $580 808 plus costs,[40] the case demonstrates the impact that a negative relationship between an employee and management can have on one's career.

Questions

1. Describe the types of power that would be at work where an employee is engaged in managing-up behaviour.
2. What do you think are the pitfalls of 'managing-up' behaviours?
3. Have you tried to 'manage-up' to your boss? What have been the consequences?

Organisational politics in action

Political action is a part of organisational life; it is best to view organisational politics for its potential to contribute to managerial and organisational effectiveness. It is in this spirit that we now examine political action in organisations from the perspectives of managers, subunits and chief executives. Organisational politics occurs in different ways and across different levels in the organisation.

Office politics and the informal network

An organisational chart can show who is the boss and who reports to whom. However, this formal chart will not reveal which people confer on technical matters or discuss office politics over lunch. Much of the real work of an organisation is achieved through this informal organisation with its complex network of relationships that cross functions and divisions.

As companies in Australasia continue to flatten their structures and rely on teams, managers tend to rely less on their authority and more on understanding these informal networks. However, whether the organisation is flat or tall, one aspect of politics will always prevail — 'office politics'.

Office politics is as prevalent today as it ever was. The person who knows just when and whom to flatter, or the person who can befriend the boss, or the one who knows everyone's business — they all carry considerable clout and they know it. Most people who fall victim to the ravages of office politics fall into one of two basic categories — the innocents who unwittingly offend the wrong people, and the savvy players who let their defences down too soon. To thrive in the political landscape of the office, it is a good idea to become allied with admirable people, to be concerned primarily with your own business, not to overdo politics and to strive for trust.

Political action and the manager

Managers may gain a better understanding of political behaviour by placing themselves in the positions of other people involved in critical decisions or events. Each action and decision can be seen as having benefits and costs to all parties concerned. Where the costs exceed the benefits, the manager may act to protect their position.

Figure 10.5 (overleaf) shows a sample payoff table for two managers, Lee and Leslie, in a problem situation involving a decision about whether to allocate resources to a special project. If both managers authorise the resources, the project gets completed on time, and their company keeps a valuable client. Unfortunately, by doing so, both Lee and Leslie will overspend their budgets. Taken on its own, a budget overrun would be bad for the managers' performance records. Assume that the overruns will be acceptable only if the client is retained. Thus, if both managers act, both they and the company win, as depicted in the upper left block of the figure. Obviously, this is the most desirable outcome for all parties concerned.

Assume that Leslie acts, but Lee does not. In this case, the company loses the client, Leslie overspends the budget in a futile effort, but Lee ends up within budget. While the company and Leslie lose, Lee wins. This scenario is illustrated in the lower left block of the figure. The upper right block shows the reverse situation, in which Lee acts but Leslie does not; in this case, Leslie wins, while the company and Lee lose. Finally, if both Lee and Leslie fail to act, they each stay within the budget and gain, but the company loses the client.

The company clearly wants both Lee and Leslie to act. But will they? Would you take the risk of overspending the budget, knowing that your colleague might refuse? The question of trust is critical here, but building trust among comanagers and other workers takes time and can be difficult. The involvement of higher-level managers may be needed to set the stage better. Yet, we would predict that both Lee and Leslie would fail to act because the 'climate' or 'culture' in many organisations too often encourages people to maximise their self-interest at minimal risks. What we need are more settings in which people are willing to take a chance and are rewarded for doing so.

Power, or the ability to obtain, retain and move resources, requires two sets of attributes: competence and political intelligence. The first, and probably most important, strategy for improving an individual's political intelligence is to be able to read the work climate, preferably before beginning work.

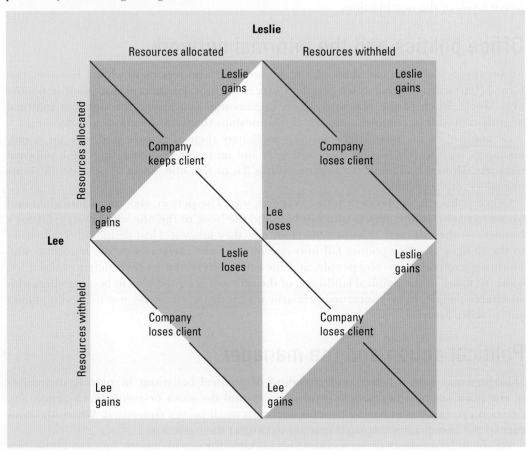

FIGURE 10.5 Political payoff matrix for the allocation of resources on a sample project

Political action and subunit power

Political action links managers more formally to one another as representatives of their work units. In chapter 7 we examined the group dynamics associated with such intergroup relationships. Table 10.2 highlights five typical lateral and intergroup relationships in which you may engage as a manager: work flow, service, advisory, auditing and approval relationships.[41] The table also shows how lateral relationships further challenge the political skills of a manager; each example requires the manager to achieve influence through some means other than formal authority.

TABLE 10.2 Relationships of managers and associated influence requirements

Type of relationship	Sample influence requirements
Work flow — contacts with units that precede or follow in a sequential production chain	An assembly-line manager informs another line manager responsible for a later stage in the production process about a delay.
Service — contacts with units established to help with problems	An assembly-line manager asks the maintenance manager to fix an important piece of equipment as a priority.

Type of relationship	Sample influence requirements
Advisory — contacts with formal staff units that have special expertise	A marketing manager consults with the personnel manager to obtain special assistance in recruiting a new salesperson.
Auditing — contacts with units that have the right to evaluate the actions of others	A marketing manager tries to get the credit manager to retract a report criticising marketing's tendency to open bad-credit accounts.
Approval — contacts with units whose approval must be obtained before action may be taken	A marketing manager submits a job description to the company affirmative action officer for approval before recruiting for a new salesperson can begin.

To be effective in political action, managers should understand the politics of subunit relations. Line units are typically more powerful than are staff groups, and units towards the top of the hierarchy are often more powerful than are those towards the bottom. In general, units gain power as more of their relations with others are of the approval and auditing types. Work flow relations are more powerful than advisory associations, and both are more powerful than service relations. Units can also increase power by incorporating new actions that tackle and resolve difficult problems. Certain strategic contingencies can often govern the relative power of subunits. For a subunit to gain power, it must increase its control over the following.

- *Access to scarce resources.* Subunits gain in power when they obtain access to, or control, scarce resources needed by others.
- *The ability to cope with uncertainty.* Subunits gain in power when they are able to cope with uncertainty and help solve problems that uncertainty causes for others.
- *Centrality in the flow of work.* Subunits gain in power when their position in the work flow allows them to influence the work of others.
- *Substitutability of activities.* Subunits gain in power when they perform tasks or activities that are non-substitutable — that is, when they perform essential functions that others cannot complete.[42]

Political action in the chief executive suite

From the Holmes à Courts to the Murdochs and to the Packers, Australians have been fascinated by the politics of the chief executive suite. An analytical view of executive suite dynamics may lift some of the mystery behind the political veil at the top levels in organisations.

Resource dependencies

Executive behaviour can sometimes be explained in terms of **resource dependencies** — that is, an organisation's need for resources that others control.[43] Essentially, the resource dependence of an organisation increases as:

- needed resources become more scarce
- outsiders have more control over needed resources
- there are fewer substitutes for a particular type of resource controlled by a limited number of outsiders.

Thus, one political role of chief executives is to develop workable compromises among the competing resource dependencies facing the organisation — compromises that enhance the executive's power. To create such compromises, executives need to diagnose the relative power of outsiders and to craft strategies that respond differently to various external resource suppliers.

For larger organisations, many strategies may centre on altering the organisation's degree of resource dependence. Through mergers and acquisitions, an organisation may bring key

Resource dependencies occur when the organisation needs resources that others control.

resources within its control. By changing the 'rules of the game', an organisation may also find protection from particularly powerful outsiders; for instance, trade barriers may protect markets, or labour unions' 'right to work' laws may check union activity. Yet, there are limits on the ability of even our largest and most powerful organisations to control all important external contingencies. International competition has narrowed the range of options for chief executives; they can no longer ignore the rest of the world. Some may need to redefine fundamentally how they expect to conduct business. Once, many large firms in the Asia–Pacific region could go it alone without the assistance of foreign corporations. Now, chief executives are increasingly leading them in the direction of joint ventures and strategic alliances with foreign partners from around the globe. Such 'combinations' provide access to scarce resources and technologies among partners, as well as new markets and shared production costs.

Organisational governance

Organisational governance is the pattern of authority, influence and acceptable managerial behaviour established at the top of the organisation.

Organisational governance refers to the pattern of authority, influence and acceptable managerial behaviour established at the top of the organisation. This system establishes what is important, how issues will be defined, who should and should not be involved in key choices, and the boundaries for acceptable implementation. Those studying organisational governance suggest that a 'dominant coalition' comprising powerful organisational actors is a key to its understanding.[44] While you might expect many top officers within the organisation to be members of this coalition, the dominant coalition occasionally includes outsiders with access to key resources. Thus, analysis of organisational governance builds on the resource dependence perspective by highlighting the effective control of key resources by members of a dominant coalition.

OBinAction

The nasty side of office politics

According to New Zealand law firm Simpson Grierson, by far the majority of intimidation claims are made against supervisors. Partner John Rooney argues that there are two kinds of bullies — those who don't realise they are making other people's lives hell, and those who enjoy it.[45] Intriguingly, recent research has shown the dichotomy between the bully and the victim is not so clear-cut. According to Linton and Power, a significant

majority of bullies (89.7 per cent) and a significant number of victims (41.7 per cent) were both perpetrators and victims at least once a week, over the course of six months (known as bully/victims).[46] Following their research, Linton and Power have advised employers to be aware of the bully/victim syndrome in an effort to reduce workplace bullying.

What can managers do to minimise destructive office politics? They can be role models in how they conduct themselves: delegate tasks without being too much of a 'control freak', make sure accountability for tasks is clarified, let staff know that bad behaviour is unacceptable, and ensure staff feel safe to discuss any issue in confidence with them.

The acceptability of workplace bullying across countries has been the focus of recent workplace studies. The findings of Power et al., for example, reveal that workplace bullying has been found to be more acceptable than intimidating someone physically.[47] The same was found across both culture groups as well as globally. They also found that cultures that focused on future and human values were less tolerant of bullying than high performance cultures. Across the globe, the research also showed that 'Confucian Asia' was more accepting of workplace bullying than Anglo-Latin America and Sub-Saharan Africa, and more accepting of physically intimidating bullying than Anglo-Latin America.

OBinAction

Boys' clubs alive and well

In Australia, Victoria's Chief of Police has expressed his concerns regarding a 'secret' group called The Brotherhood. He argues that the group has members from a range of professions, including serving and former police officers, lawyers and public servants. The founder of The Brotherhood describes the group as a lunch club of 'men of good ilk'. Following a whistleblower's complaint about the group, Ombudsman George Brouwer found that The Brotherhood commenced its activities in 2003 (unlike most men-only clubs that have been operating for decades or centuries), met every six weeks for lunch at Melbourne restaurants, and counted hundreds of people on its 'circulation list'. It is reported that at these lunches the founder would start the meetings by saying 'We are all members of the Brotherhood and we must assist each other', and that 'Chatham Rules apply, in other words, what's said in the room stays in the room'. The Ombudsman expressed his concern about fostering a culture that allows for inappropriate networking and improper exchange of favours and information.[48] The male dominance of police forces is shown to be a phenomenon globally, but recent police gender and diversity studies suggest a shift in attitudes to women in police forces. For example, in US police SWAT (special weapons and tactical) teams evidence exists that shows men are open to having women team members, but, nevertheless, hold the perception that women are not strong or skilled enough. Female members, however, view that they are worthy team members.[49] The lack of equity toward women police officers is also evidenced in a 2012 study of diversity in European police forces revealing that European women police officers never achieve 50 per cent of the workforce, even at the most basic policing level. Likewise, with rank, opportunities for diverse groups including women are shown to diminish.

Furthermore, a study commissioned by the federal government's Equal Opportunity for Women in the Workplace Agency[50] also found boys' clubs may still be alive and well in the workplace. The survey, which tested more than 1600 people, found there is widespread concern about how Australian bosses handle promotions. Based on the results, working women aged 16 to 65 — dubbed 'Generation F' — still battled unfair obstacles at work. More than a third of the women thought females had to work much harder to prove themselves, and that male colleagues were often promoted more promptly. Such obstacles would have negative implications, including encouraging a sense of exclusivity and fostering workplace alienation.

What is your view on 'boys' clubs and the impact they can have on political dynamics in contemporary organisations?

There is another new wrinkle in the discussions of organisational governance and executive pay. When corporations downsize, when they ask employees to take on new responsibilities in the form of empowerment initiatives, and when they start cutting such benefits as health care, employees begin to ask some serious questions about excessive executive compensation.

The politics of empire building

Executives are increasingly thinking in terms of kinship and are paying more attention to personal networks to enhance their individual value, power and influence. This is a logical reaction to the rapid increase in the pace of business that can encourage an executive to focus on short-term results. Many executives see their career prospects in terms of 'success today or gone tomorrow'.

Under such circumstances, executives may be inclined to recruit a 'mate' (someone they know well) as the best candidate for a position. When executives are judged on short-term achievements, their success depends on assembling an effective team quickly. It often can seem a rational choice for managers to bring in people they know, but the downside is that the lack of formal recruitment processes may mean the wrong people are hired. Morale may also suffer as existing staff see the boss's 'mates' moved into managerial positions ahead of them. Another risk is that people may start to believe the new executive is building a protective power base rather than developing a high-performance team. It is important for managers to realise that a good working relationship is only one element in achieving high performance. They also need to ensure any new employees are adding value to the organisation.

Another important consideration is that focusing on short-term financial results alone means a loss of focus on the deeper values of an organisation, such as its long-term relationship with the community or its distinctive values that attract both employees and customers. A perception of nepotism can be harmful to an executive.

The forces of extreme competition and globalisation are leading to the formation of executive teams — teams of managers that move as units to set up new businesses or turn around poorly performing ones. When large executive salaries are involved, and the time frames of organisational commitment are shortened, such teams may be seen as executive mercenaries. Such team movements can be a natural progression from forming good alliances, and introducing a team with good working relationships already in place can enhance performance. However, a lack of conflict in an executive team does not always guarantee high performance. Conflict is part of working in a team, and if managed well can add to its creativity and problem-solving skills (see chapter 7). Thus, there are benefits from hiring and sustaining diversity in executive teams as well as in organisations overall.

Many organisations believe they are reducing risk by hiring a complete executive team comprising individuals who have previously worked together. However, existing employees may perceive such a hiring policy as an exercise in empire building, and it may be difficult to attract employee commitment to the new team when employees question the organisational equity and fairness of such a team. Mistrust can result in a severe loss of morale in the company, and it may be difficult to convince employees that the organisation still rewards according to merit, and that promotions are earned through high performance. If the organisation introduces an empowerment program, employees may see the potential benefits but feel apprehensive about the likelihood of added opportunities if they no longer believe that merit will secure advancement. Under such circumstances, employees' immediate reaction to any change program may be one of guarded optimism, cynicism or mistrust. These reactions will inhibit the change process.

The consequences of power and politics

Whether or not organisational politics is good or bad may be a matter of perspective and depend on each situation. It may be good for an individual but not for the organisation, or individuals might suffer but the organisation might be better off.

The double-edged sword of organisational politics

The two different traditions of organisational politics (as described in this chapter) are reflected in the ways in which executives describe their effects on managers and their organisations. In one survey, 53 per cent of those interviewed indicated that organisational politics enhanced the achievement of organisational goals and survival.[51] Yet, 44 per cent suggested that it distracted individuals from organisational goals. In this survey, 60 per cent of respondents suggested that organisational politics was good for career advancement; 39 per cent reported that it led to a loss of power, position and credibility.

Organisational politics is not automatically good or bad. It can serve a number of important functions, including helping managers to do the following.

- *Overcome personnel inadequacies.* As a manager, you should expect some mismatches between people and positions in organisations. Even in the best-managed organisations, mismatches arise among managers who are learning, burned out, lacking in needed training and skills, overqualified, or lacking the resources needed to accomplish their assigned duties. Organisational politics provides a mechanism for circumventing these inadequacies and getting the job done.
- *Cope with change.* Changes in the environment and technology of an organisation often come more quickly than an organisation can restructure. Even in organisations that are known for detailed planning, unanticipated events may occur. To meet unanticipated problems, people and resources must be moved into place quickly before small headaches become major problems. Organisational politics can help to identify such problems, and to move ambitious, problem-solving managers into the breach.
- *Substitute for formal authority.* When a person's formal authority breaks down or fails to apply to a particular situation, political actions can be used to prevent a loss of influence. Managers may use political behaviour to maintain operations and to achieve task continuity in circumstances in which the failure of formal authority may otherwise cause problems.

Politics pervades most commercial and industrial organisations, and the organisation is frequently the loser. The varying political tactics can be highly counterproductive because they may be used to discredit and disable often more able colleagues.[52]

If political behaviour is effective in achieving organisational goals and overcoming the weaknesses of managers or of the system and processes in the organisation, then it *may* be highly beneficial. There may be cases in which politics dominates organisational activity to an extent that the activity is dysfunctional. Alternatively, it is unlikely that political behaviour never occurs, and if such a case existed, it might be equally dysfunctional. The following sections on ethics and trust give further insight into political behaviour.

The ethics of power and politics

All managers use power and politics to get their work done, but every manager also bears a responsibility to do so in an ethical and socially responsible fashion. By recognising and confronting ethical considerations, each of us should be better prepared to meet this important challenge. No treatment of power and politics in organisations is complete without considering the related ethical issues. We can begin this task by clarifying the distinction between the non-political and political uses of power.[53] Power is non-political when it remains within the boundaries of usually formal authority, organisational policies and procedures, and job descriptions, and when it is directed towards ends sanctioned by the organisation. When the use of power moves outside the realm of authority, policies, procedures and job descriptions, or when it is directed towards ends not sanctioned by the organisation, that use of power is said to be political.

When the use of power moves into the realm of political behaviour, important ethical issues emerge. It is in this context that a manager must stop and consider more than a pure 'ends justify the means' logic. These issues are broader and involve distinctly ethical questions, as the following example shows.[54] When the role and importance of political actions is overemphasised and upheld, employees may be discouraged and may be led to slacken or to underperform. This is because they come to realise that their effectiveness is limited not by knowledge of their own technical field, but by organisational and political factors, in the settings in which they operate. When prolonged, the situation will lead them to think that they have little direct control over events and must make progress by influencing others.

Chan is the production manager of a work group responsible for meeting a deadline that will require coordinated effort among her employees. Believing that the members of the work group will pull together and meet the deadline if they have a little competition, Chan decides to create the impression that members of the sales department want the group to fail to meet the deadline so sales can gain an edge over production in upcoming budgetary negotiations.

Think about what Chan's decision means. On the one hand, the action may seem justifiable if it works and the group gets its assigned job done on time. On the other hand, there may be negative side effects. What about the possibility that the sales and production departments will lose trust in one another and so find it difficult to work together in the future? Also, consider the fact that Chan was 'creating an impression' to achieve her goal. Isn't this really 'lying'? And, if it is, can we accept lying as an ethical way for a manager to get a job done?

Work in the area of ethical issues in power and politics suggests the usefulness of the integrated structure for analysing political behaviour depicted in figure 10.6. This structure suggests that a person's behaviour must satisfy the following criteria to be considered ethical.

1. *Utilitarian outcomes.* The behaviour results in optimisation of satisfactions of people both inside and outside the organisation; that is, it produces the greatest good for the greatest number of people.
2. *Individual rights.* The behaviour respects the rights of all affected parties; that is, it respects basic human rights of free consent, free speech, freedom of conscience, privacy and due process.
3. *Distributive justice.* The behaviour respects the rules of justice; that is, it treats people equitably and fairly, as opposed to arbitrarily.[55]

The figure also indicates that there may be times when a behaviour is unable to pass these criteria but can still be considered ethical in the given situation. This special case must satisfy the criterion of overwhelming factors, in which the special nature of the situation results in:

- conflicts among criteria (for example, a behaviour results in some good and some bad)
- conflicts within criteria (for example, a behaviour uses questionable means to achieve a positive end)
- an incapacity to employ the criteria (for example, a person's behaviour is based on inaccurate or incomplete information).

Choosing to be ethical often involves considerable personal sacrifice. Four rationalisations are often used to justify unethical choices.

1. Individuals feel the behaviour is not really illegal and could be moral.
2. The action appears to be in the organisation's best interests.

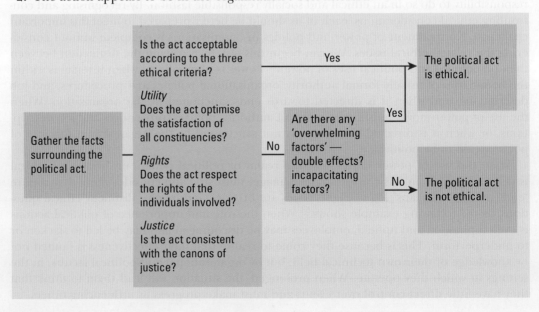

FIGURE 10.6 An integrated structure for analysing political behaviour in organisations

Source: Manuel Velasquez, Dennis J Moberg and Gerald F Cavanagh, 'Organizational statesmanship and dirty politics: ethical guidelines for the organizational politician', *Organizational Dynamics*, vol. 11 (August 1983), p. 73. Used by permission.

3. It is unlikely the action will ever be detected.

4. The action appears to demonstrate loyalty to the organisation.

While these rationalisations may appear compelling at the moment of action, each deserves close scrutiny. The individual must ask: 'How far is too far?', 'What are the long-term interests of the organisation?', 'What will happen when (not if) the action is discovered?', and 'Do individuals, groups or organisations that ask for unethical behaviour deserve my loyalty?'[56]

Trust and managerial influence

Earlier in the chapter we looked at how critical trust is to managerial influence.[57] Generating trust in relationships involves taking an ethical stance. In a general sense, trust is the level of confidence you feel when you think about a relationship. Managers increase their influence when they build high-trust relationships with their employees. This influence does not operate through the manager, but through the common principles and values on which both parties have agreed, and through the past experience of keeping promises.

Any relationship in which employees find it difficult to trust their managers is troublesome. Managers experiencing a low-trust relationship with their employees are more likely to experience problems of harmonious and effective control in their day-to-day management. Managers vary in their predisposition to trust their employees. As we saw in chapter 2, individuals have personality differences. Distrustful managers tend to perceive their employees as self-centred, uncaring, intolerant, unmotivated and unresponsive. Their perceptions of employee behaviours and motives are biased by their initial suspicion.

Once trust has been violated it is doubly difficult to re-establish it. Even if a manager introduces change and tries to improve workplace relations, employees will tend to perceive positive actions in a negative light. This occurs, for example, when employees have undergone a series of downsizing decisions in a betrayal of earlier promises and yet are asked to retain faith in managerial promises for the future. In this situation, most employees would be unwilling to accept the promises in good faith because their trust has been violated. Further, every error, however unintentional, becomes one more piece of evidence that the new promise will also be betrayed and that nothing in workplace relations will change. It is not impossible to begin to repair the damage inherent in such a cycle, but the potential for rebuilding a relationship is fragile, especially when uncertainty and job insecurity continue to be part of organisational life. For these reasons, trustworthiness is a distinctive trait of an effective manager, and essential for effective influence. Managers who are considered untrustworthy will find it difficult to influence employees from either a position or personal power base.[58]

Summary

Power and its sources

Power is an essential managerial resource. It is demonstrated by the ability to get someone else to do what you want them to do. Power vested in managerial positions derives from three sources: rewards, punishments and legitimacy. Legitimacy, which is the same as formal authority, is based on the manager's position in the hierarchy of authority. Personal power is based on a person's expertise and reference; it allows managers to extend their power beyond that which is available in their position alone.

The relationship between power, authority and obedience

Power, authority and obedience are interrelated. Obedience occurs when one individual responds to the request or directive of another person. In the Milgram experiments, it was shown that people may have a tendency to obey directives coming from others who appear powerful and authoritative, even if these directives seem contrary to what the individual would normally consider to be 'right'. A zone of indifference defines the boundaries within which people in organisations will let others influence their behaviour without questioning it. Ultimately, power and authority work only if the individual 'accepts' them.

Managerial power and influence

Managerial perspectives on power and influence must include the practical considerations of how to obtain the power needed to get the job done. Managers can pursue various ways of acquiring both position and personal power. They can also become skilled at using various tactics, such as reason, friendliness, ingratiation and bargaining, to influence superiors, peers and employees.

Empowerment

Empowerment is the process through which managers help others acquire and use the power needed to make decisions that affect themselves and their work. Clear delegation of authority, integrated planning and the involvement of senior management are all important to implementing empowerment. However, the key to success lies in redefining power so everyone can gain. The redefinition emphasises power as the ability to get things done rather than to get others to do what you want.

Dual faces of politics

Organisational politics are inevitable. Managers must become comfortable with political behaviour in organisations and then use that behaviour responsibly and to good advantage. Politics involve the use of power to obtain ends not officially sanctioned, or to achieve sanctioned ends through unsanctioned means. Organisational politics is also use of power to find ways of balancing individual and collective interests in otherwise difficult circumstances.

Types and levels of political behaviour

Political action in organisations can be examined at the managerial, subunit and chief executive levels. It may also occur widely throughout the organisation's informal networks. For the manager, politics often occur in decision situations in which the interests of another manager or individual must be reconciled with their own. Politics also involve subunits that jockey for power and advantageous positions. For chief executives, politics that come into play as resource dependencies with external environmental elements must be strategically managed, and as organisational governance is transacted among the members of a 'dominant coalition'. To minimise their risks when assembling teams to meet short-term objectives, managers may resort to hiring people with whom they have previously worked. This may be perceived as nepotism or an attempt at empire building. Managers need to be aware of the challenges of using teams of people they know well, who may be seen as 'mates' rather than as the best people for the job.

The ethics of power and politics in an organisation

Organisational politics can be effective in getting things done in an organisation. It is not necessarily good or bad. Political behaviour can be especially useful in overcoming personnel inadequacies, in coping with change and in substituting for formal authority when it breaks down or does not cover a particular situation.

The ethics of power and politics are common to those found in any decision situation. Managers can easily slip into questionable territory as they resort to power plays and politics to get their way in situations where resistance exists. While this behaviour may be 'rationalised' as acceptable, it may not meet the personal test of ethical behaviour established in chapter 1. When political behaviour is ethical, it will satisfy the criteria of utilitarian outcomes, individual rights, distributive justice and/or overwhelming factors. Managers need to develop high-trust relationships and understand that trust involves taking an ethical stance. If they do not keep promises, or if they betray trust, then employees will be less likely to accept managerial influence from either a position or a personal power base.

CHAPTER 10 study guide

Key terms

coercive power, *p. 367*

empowerment, *p. 380*

expert power, *p. 370*

influence, *p. 365*

information power, *p. 369*

legitimate power, *p. 368*

organisational governance, *p. 388*

organisational politics, *p. 383*

power, *p. 365*

process power, *p. 369*

referent power, *p. 372*

resource dependencies, *p. 387*

reward power, *p. 367*

zone of indifference, *p. 375*

Review questions

1. Explain how power is acquired.
2. Explain some of the ethical implications of power and politics.
3. How might personal power differ from authority?
4. Explain the meaning and importance of empowerment in an organisational context.
5. Why is process power associated with legitimate power?

Application questions

1. Under what circumstances would managers increase their power and influence over other managers?
2. Why would organisations wish to empower their employees? Describe some of the risks associated with excessive empowerment?
3. How would a manager work to acquire greater levels of power, and is it ethical to do so? Explain your response, giving reasons and examples to support your point of view.
4. Describe some of the political tactics and tricks that an employee may use to gain influence and some power advantage over his or her manager.
5. Personal assistants and secretaries of people in power tend to have much influence in organisations. Explain the reasons and rationales for such influence.
6. Your lecturer asks you to complete and submit an assignment. Explain the various bases of power that she or he would be utilising to influence you and ensure your compliance.
7. 'Bullying should not be tolerated in the workplace.' 'Some people are oversensitive to the autocratic managerial styles of their supervisors.' Are both these statements true and can they be reconciled?

Research questions

1. Find out what you know about 'emotional intelligence' and use that information to address the following questions. You may like to add specific examples to support your answers.
   (a) What is emotional intelligence, and how might it be used as a source of power for managers in an organisation?
   (b) Explain ways in which emotional intelligence might help managers engage in successful political behaviours?
   (c) What are the likely implications for ethics, trust and organisational effectiveness if managers are able to draw upon their emotional intelligence for political behaviours?
2. Think of a position you might have held (or currently hold) in an organisation, or as a member of a sporting or past-time organisation. What kind of referent power existed (or exists)? What is the effect of the kind of referent power that you have experienced upon your own behaviour? In what ways do you think referent power can be beneficial to organisations or hinder performance?

Complete the following activities for your chosen organisation.

1. Choose a manager in your organisation and explain the various types of power that he or she holds.
2. Try to identify others who hold various types of power (for example, referent power or expert power).
3. Assess the level to which your organisation empowers its employees. What has motivated this level of empowerment? What are the outcomes?
4. Identify recent examples of political behaviour in your organisation. Briefly assess them against figure 10.6 to determine whether they were ethical or unethical according to the model offered by Velasquez, Moberg and Cavanagh.
5. Try to identify an example of misuse of power in your organisation.

If you are studying an organisation to which you have direct access, exercise careful discretion in finding information for and answering questions 4 and 5.

Influence tactics

Objective

To check your understanding of influence tactics and when they may be most useful

Procedure

Read each of the following 11 statements made by Jackie to Lee and, by applying them to the given scenario:

(a) decide which influence tactic is being used and briefly explain your reasoning
(b) rank each statement from 1 to 11 in terms of how effective it might be in influencing Lee (although you have limited information, consider how you might feel and react if you were Lee)
(c) decide whether and why you think the approach is ethical and briefly explain your reasoning.

Scenario

The senior management of the organisation is developing a new proposal to introduce performance pay into the organisation. Jackie and Lee are managers at the same level in the organisation but in different sections. Jackie is seeking Lee's support to fight the proposal.

1. Come on, Lee. You've got to accept that this is the worst thing the company can do — look at the figures and how they show it won't work.
2. Lee, you've got to join me in fighting this proposal. I have to have your help.
3. I know you've always believed that performance pay will only ever advantage senior management while the rest of us are left carrying the workload. This is the only way our department is going to get ahead, and you're so good at speaking in public.
4. Lee, you need to help me fight this. If you don't, I'll have to reconsider the special arrangements I have for your staff when they want something from my department.
5. We need to get together to fight this proposal before it gets approved and ruins our operations.
6. Come on, Lee. The manager of Finance agrees with me that this proposal won't work.
7. I'd like you to help me fight this proposal. I'd help you out in the same situation, just as I did last year when you needed help with your upgrading application.
8. An intelligent person like you will immediately see that this proposal won't work.
9. Hi, Lee, you're looking bright and healthy today. That was a great job you did on last month's report.
10. If you support me on fighting this, I'll support you in your promotion application.
11. Lee, would you look at this memo I've prepared to present a counter-argument to the performance pay proposal. I'd value your opinion.

Evaluation

Once you have ranked your responses, compare them to the information in the chapter that explains which influence tactics are likely to be most effective.

Machiavellianism

Objectives
1. To assess individual Machiavellianism (Mach) scores
2. To explore the dynamics of power in a group environment
3. To develop an understanding of the rewards and frustrations of held power
4. To analyse behaviours of various Mach personality types

Total time: 45–60 minutes

Procedure
1. Complete the following ten-item Mach assessment instrument.[59] Follow directions for scoring your instrument individually.
2. Form a group of five to seven persons, and designate one individual as the official group 'observer'.
3. The observer will not participate in any of the discussion but will take notes on the activities of the group and later report to the class.
4. Your lecturer will announce the topic to be discussed. The topic should be highly controversial and stimulating, and one that encourages different viewpoints.
5. The observer will begin by handing a specific textbook or magazine to one member of the group. Only that member of the group may speak. The textbook or magazine will be held by that person until another member of the group signals, nonverbally, that they wish to have it. The person with the textbook or magazine may refuse to relinquish it, even when signalled. The group discussion has a time limit of 15 minutes.
6. Following the controversial discussion period, the group observer leads a group discussion on what they observed and learned about power phenomena, frustrations, feedback and so on.
7. Each group observer then presents what the group has learned to the entire class.

Mach assessment instrument
For each of the following statements, circle the number that most closely resembles your attitude.

Statement	DISAGREE			AGREE	
	A lot	A little	Neutral	A little	A lot
1. The best way to handle people is to tell them what they want to hear.	1	2	3	4	5
2. When you ask someone to do something for you, it is best to give the real reason for wanting it rather than reasons that may carry more weight.	1	2	3	4	5
3. Anyone who completely trusts someone else is asking for trouble.	1	2	3	4	5
4. It is hard to get ahead without cutting corners here and there.	1	2	3	4	5
5. It is safest to assume that all people have a vicious streak, and that it will emerge when they are given a chance.	1	2	3	4	5
6. You should take action only when it is morally right.	1	2	3	4	5
7. Most people are basically good and kind.	1	2	3	4	5
8. There is no excuse for lying to someone.	1	2	3	4	5
9. Most people forget more easily the death of their father than the loss of their property.	1	2	3	4	5
10. Generally speaking, people will not work hard unless forced to do so.	1	2	3	4	5

Scoring key and interpretation

This assessment is designed to compute your Machiavellianism (Mach) score. Mach is a personality characteristic that taps people's power orientation. The high-Mach personality is pragmatic, maintains emotional distance from others, and believes that ends can justify means. To obtain your Mach score, add up the numbers you circled for questions 1, 3, 4, 5, 9 and 10. For the other four questions, reverse the number you have circled, so 5 becomes 1, 4 is 2, and 1 is 5. Then total both sets of numbers to find your score. A random sample of adults found the national average to be 25. Students in business and management typically score higher.

Research using the Mach tests has found the following results.

- Men are generally more Machiavellian than women.
- Older adults tend to have lower Mach scores than those of younger adults.
- There is no significant difference between high Machs and low Machs on measures of intelligence or ability.
- Machiavellianism is not significantly related to demographic characteristics such as educational level or marital status.
- High Machs tend to be in professions that emphasise the control and manipulation of people — for example, managers, lawyers, psychiatrists and behavioural scientists.

Case study: When leadership brawls become ugly

The issue of leadership styles hit the Australian news headlines in early 2012, with a public battle for the leadership of the parliamentary Labor party between former prime minister Julia Gillard and former prime minister Kevin Rudd. The seething tensions between the two political veterans exploded into open warfare between the two competing camps of Rudd and Gillard.

Camp Rudd argued that their leader was visionary, that he had the popular support of the Australian people, and that only he could lead the party to victory at the next election. Camp Gillard fired back with accusations that while in the role of prime minister, Kevin Rudd became increasingly autocratic; that he exhausted the people around him with his chaotic, 24/7, workaholic lifestyle; that in private he was rude and contemptuous of others; and that he dithered on important policy reforms. Camp Gillard also argued that their leader had achieved significant policy reform during her time in office, that she was consultative and widely respected by her parliamentary colleagues, and that she was as decent to others in private as she was in public. Camp Rudd responded with accusations that she was poor in convincing the public of the value of her reforms, that she had lost the trust of the Australian people after breaking a number of promises, and that she could not win the next election due to her poor showing in public opinion polls.

During the national debate, the two styles of leadership were presented in dramatic contrast. Rudd had the support of the voters, whereas Gillard had the support of the Labor party. Rudd was an effective public communicator, whereas Gillard could not sell her message. One leader was autocratic (Rudd), whereas the other was consultative (Gillard). One achieved the goals of policy reform (Gillard), whereas the other (Rudd) backed down on issues such as an emissions trading scheme and could not gain support for a new mining tax.

Eventually Julia Gillard triumphed on 27 February 2012, with federal Labor parliamentarians voting 71 to 31 in her favour. Julia Gillard pledged to improve her style of communicating with the Australian public and to present a stronger style of leadership into the future. Federal Labor ultimately rejected the style of the visionary autocrat in favour of the consultative mediator. The public saw the ugly side of their leaders; however, the opinion polls at that time continued to indicate that they still favoured Rudd over Gillard. In mid 2013, in line with the opinion polls, Rudd reclaimed the leadership from Gillard to become prime minister yet again.[60]

Questions

1. Considering managers increase their influence by building high-trust relationships with their employees, how do you think Julia Gillard's bid for the leadership affected her influence within the Labor party?
2. What do you think is more important for a manager: to achieve reform, or to lead people towards achieving a vision? Give reasons for your answer.

End notes

1. O Agatiello, 'Corruption not an end', *Management Decision*, vol. 48, no. 10 (2010), pp. 1456–68.
2. M McKenzie and R Baker, 'Building giant Leighton at centre of bribery scandal', *The Sydney Morning Herald* (3 October 2013), www.smh.com.au.
3. WN Shaw, 'Politics and management services', *Management Services*, vol. 30, no. 12 (December 1986), pp. 8–12.
4. R Moss Kanter, 'Power failure in management circuit', *Harvard Business Review* (July/August 1979), pp. 65–75.
5. J Pfeffer, 'Understanding power in organizations', *California Management Review*, vol. 34, no. 2 (1992), p. 45.
6. JRP French and Bertram Raven, 'The bases of social power' in Dorwin Cartwright (ed.), *Group dynamics: research and theory* (Evanston, IL: Row, Peterson, 1962), pp. 607–23.
7. See French and Raven, op. cit.
8. H Moradi and MR Fallah, 'Empowering service employees: a case study of banking industry', *Management Science Letters*, vol. 4 (2014), pp. 1381–4.
9. 'Hilton CEO talks about building company culture that empowers employees' (4 May 2014), *Arabian Business.com Staff*, HotelierMiddlejEast.com, http://skift.com.
10. Office of the Ombudsman website, www. employeeombudsman.sa.gov.au.
11. C Spiers, 'Bullying at Work: The Cost to Business', *Training Officer*, vol. 32, no. 8 (1996), pp. 236–8.
12. *Queensland Chamber of Commerce & Industry*, 1998, Bullying Information Sheet.
13. HE Marano, 'When the Boss is a Bully', *Psychology Today*, vol. 28, no. 5 (1995b), pp. 58–60.
14. Smith, cited in R Kiesker and T Marchant, '*Workplace bullying in Australia: a review of current conceptualisations and existing research*', www.usq.edu.au.
15. M McCarthy, 'Industrial, workplace bullying', *Australian Nursing Journal*, 13 February, vol. 20, no. 7.
16. W Scholl, 'Restrictive control and information pathologies in organizations. Social influence and social power: using theory for understanding social issues', *Journal of Social Issues*, vol. 55, no. 1 (Spring 1999), p. 101(1).
17. Avon, *Committed to empowering women*, http://avoncompany. com.
18. M O'Neill, 'Woomera detention centre doctor speaks out' [transcript], *Lateline* (27 October 2004), www.abc.net.au.
19. S Milgram, 'Behavioral study of obedience' in DW Organ (ed.), *The applied psychology of work behavior* (Dallas: Business Publications, 1978), pp. 384–98. Also see the following works by Stanley Milgram: 'Behavioral study of obedience', *Journal of Abnormal and Social Psychology*, vol. 67 (1963), pp. 371–8; 'Group pressure and action against a person', *Journal of Abnormal and Social Psychology*, vol. 69 (1964), pp. 137–43; 'Some conditions of obedience and disobedience to authority', *Human Relations*, vol. 1 (1965), pp. 57–76; *Obedience to authority* (New York: Harper & Row, 1974).
20. C Barnard, *The functions of the executive* (Cambridge, MA: Harvard University Press, 1938).
21. See SN Brenner and EA Mollander, 'Is the ethics of business changing?', *Harvard Business Review*, vol. 55 (February 1977), pp. 57–71; BZ Posner and W H Schmidt, 'Values and the American manager: an update', *California Management Review*, vol. 26 (Spring 1984), pp. 202–16.
22. JP Kotter, 'Power, success, and organizational effectiveness', *Organizational Dynamics*, vol. 6 (Winter 1978), p. 27.
23. DA Whetten and KS Cameron, *Developing managerial skills* (Glenview, IL: Scott, Foresman, 1984), pp. 250–9.
24. Whetten and Cameron, op. cit., pp. 260–6.
25. D Kipinis, SM Schmidt, C Swaffin-Smith and I Wilkinson, 'Patterns of managerial influence: shotgun managers, tacticians, and bystanders', *Organizational Dynamics*, vol. 12 (Winter 1984), pp. 60, 61.
26. ibid., pp. 58–67; D Kipinis, SM Schmidt and I Wilkinson, 'Intraorganizational influence tactics: explorations in getting one's way', *Journal of Applied Psychology*, vol. 65 (1980), pp. 440–52.
27. Adapted from G Yukl, PJ Guinan and D Sottolano, 'Influence tactics used for different objectives with subordinates, peers, and superiors', *Groups & Organization Management*, vol. 20, no. 3 (September 1995), p. 275.
28. ibid, pp. 294–5.
29. WK Schilit and EA Locke, 'A study of upward influence in organizations', *Administrative Science Quarterly*, vol. 27 (1982), pp. 304–16.

30. ibid.

31. Kipinis, Schmidt, Swaffin-Smith and Wilkinson (1984 & 1980), op. cit.

32. M Dufficy, 'The empowerment audit-measured improvement', *Industrial and Commercial Training*, vol. 30, no. 4 (1998), pp. 142–6.

33. BT Mayes and RW Allen, 'Toward a definition of organizational politics', *Academy of Management Review*, vol. 3, no. 4 (1977), p. 675.

34. J Pfeffer, *Power in organizations* (Marshfield, MA: Pitman, 1981), p. 7.

35. A Horin, 'Managing up: the disturbing rise of office brown-nosers', *Sydney Morning Herald* (1 May 2010), www.smh.com.au.

36. R Wigham, 'Bossing the bosses helps to boost career prospects', *Personnel Today* (2 March 2004), www.personneltoday.com.

37. J Taggard, 'Is sucking up to your boss the way to get ahead? What would Machiavelli think?', *Open Salon* (31 January 2011), http://open.salon.com.

38. A Crook, 'Guthrie wins out, judge slams Harto & Blunden', *Crikey* (14 May 2010), www.crikey.com.au.

39. Horin, op. cit.

40. Crook, op. cit.

41. Developed from JL Hall and JL Leldecker, 'A review of vertical and lateral relations: a new perspective for managers', in P Connor (ed.), *Dimensions in modern management*, 3rd ed. (Boston: Houghton Mifflin, 1982), pp. 138–46, which was based in part on L Sayles, *Managerial behavior* (New York: McGraw-Hill, 1964).

42. See J Pfeffer, *Organizations and organization theory* (Boston: Pitman, 1983); J Pfeffer and GR Salancik, *The external control of organizations* (Englewood Cliffs, NJ: Prentice Hall, 1978).

43. ibid.

44. JD Thompson, *Organizations in action* (New York: McGraw-Hill, 1967).

45. J Barratt, 'Office politics turn nasty', *New Zealand Herald* (21 February 2010), www.nzherald.co.nz.

46. DK Linton and JL Power, 'The personality traits of workplace bullies are often shared by their victims: is their a dark side to victims?', *Personality and Individual Differences*, vol. 54 (2013), pp. 738–43.

47. JL Power, CM Brotheridge, J Blenkinsopp et al, 'Acceptability of workplace bullying: a comparative study on six continents', *Journal of Business Research*, vol. 66 (2013), pp. 374–80.

48. M Rout, 'Victoria Police chief Simon Overland warns against The Brotherhood', *The Australian* (3 March 2011), www.theaustralian.com.au.

49. M Dodge, L Valcore and F Gomez, 'Women on SWAT teams:separate but equal?', *Policing: An International Journal of Police Strategies and Management*, vol. 34, no. 4 (2011), pp. 699–712.

50. *Equal opportunity for women in the workplace agency annual report 2007–08* (Equal Opportunity for Women in the Workplace Agency: Sydney, 2010), www.eowa.gov.au.

51. BE Ashforth and RT Lee, 'Defensive behavior in organizations: a preliminary model', *Human Relations* (July 1990), pp. 621–48; personal communication with Blake Ashforth, December 1992.

52. A Drory and T Romm, 'The definition of organizational politics: a review', *Human Relations*, vol. 43, no. 11 (1990), pp. 1133–54.

53. This discussion is based on G Cavanagh, D Moberg and M Velasquez, 'The ethics of organizational politics', *Academy of Management Review*, vol. 6 (1981), pp. 363–74; and M Velasquez, DJ Moberg and G Cavanagh, 'Organizational statesmanship and dirty politics: ethical guidelines for the organizational politician', *Organizational Dynamics*, vol. 11 (1983), pp. 65–79, both of which offer a fine treatment of the ethics of power and politics.

54. Adapted from G Cavanagh, D Moberg and M Velasquez, 'The ethics of organizational politics', *Academy of Management Review*, vol. 6 (1981), pp. 363–74.

55. These criteria are developed from Cavanagh, Moberg and Velasquez.

56. SW Gellerman, 'Why "good" managers make bad ethical choices', *Harvard Business Review*, vol. 64 (July/August 1986), pp. 85–97.

57. RM Zeffane and DE Morgan, 'The implication of change strategies on organisational trust: evidence from Australia' in T Taillieu (ed.), *Organisational partnerships and cooperative strategies* (Leuven: Garant, 2001); Rachid M Zeffane and David E Morgan, 'Organisational change and trust: can management be trusted to change', *International Journal of Human Resource Management*, vol. 14, no. 1 (2003), pp. 55–75.

58. FL Flores and RC Solomon, 'Rethinking trust', *Business and Professional Ethics Journal*, vol. 16, no. 1 (Spring 1997), p. 47; BF Meeker, 'Cooperative orientation, trust and reciprocity', *Human Relations* (March 1984), pp. 225–43; DJ Moberg, 'Trustworthiness and concientiousness as managerial virtues', *Business and Professional Ethics Journal*, vol. 16, no. 1 (Spring 1997), p. 171; E Soule, 'Trust and managerial responsibility', *Business Ethics Quarterly*, vol. 8, no. 2 (April 1998), p. 249.

59. Exercise adapted from R Christie and FL Geis, *Studies in machiavellianism* (New York: Academic Press, 1970). Reproduced by permission.

60. Ben Packham and Lanai Vasek, 'Julia Gillard to win Caucus vote, but Kevin Rudd has not ruled out being drafted as leader later', *The Australian* (27 February 2012), www.theaustralian.com.au.

CHAPTER 11

LEADERSHIP

LEARNING OBJECTIVES

After studying this chapter, you should be able to:

1. explain the difference between leadership and management

2. understand and evaluate trait and behavioural theories of leadership

3. understand and evaluate situational contingency theories of leadership

4. discuss charismatic leadership and transformational leadership

5. explain emerging perspectives on leadership

6. outline some of the current diversity issues in leadership.

PAVING THE WAY FOR INNOVATION

A leader who is paving the way for innovation in Australian safety is Loren Murray from Pacific Brands. Workplace injury costs Australia $60 billion a year (6 per cent of GDP). In a market place where margins are shrinking and productivity is key, Australia collectively spends tens of thousands of hours working on the same pervasive problems.

The safety leader is trail blazing a new paradigm in how safety is approached in Australian firms and is a living example of lateral leadership. Instead of viewing safety from predominantly a compliance perspective, Loren believes that forcing employees to follow rules to work safe is not having the desired effect and that a new approach is needed where employees are inspired to make safe choices. She believes that new, bold, unique and progressive behavioural-based safety approaches are needed that leverage choice, self-direction, and autonomy to create not only the context in which employees want to work safely but also lead to exceptional and sustainable business and cultural performance outcomes. She

says that in order to create extraordinary safety performance, a fresh approach is needed where employees self-organise, make their own decisions and self-implement safety solutions. One such approach is the PEER (performance, engage, enable, research) approach. In collaboration with the University of Southern Queensland, she first trialled this approach in her previous role at Linfox, one of Australia's largest privately owned Transport Logistics organisations, with the aim to explore how the creation of peer teams and peer effect could change safety behaviour from the inside out instead of mainly relying on a compliance approach to safety. This approach not only achieved a significant reduction in safety incidents but had an overwhelming positive impact on cultural key performance indicators (KPIs) such as improved motivation, morale, job satisfaction, employee engagement and improved perception about the company, to name just a few. Loren is now employing this approach in Pacific Brands to not only improve safety and productivity outcomes but also to a wider range of positive cultural KPIs in the company. Loren's passion for shared leadership is expressed in her view that successful initiatives happen when each and every member is engaged and connected. She argues that 'to achieve this kind of engagement you have to leverage individuals' potential and strengths'. Her passion for creating positive safety outcomes through employee engagement is influencing other safety leaders to think about safety in a new and different way.

Introduction

As the chapter opening shows, regardless of their rank, senior managers are expected to play a leadership role. As leaders, they are expected to foster work environments conducive to learning and self-renewal. They need to develop a capability to create an appetite and agility for continuous change. They must encourage relationships and be able to build trust across the organisation. In fact, for most organisations to prosper and perform nationally and internationally, their managers need strong leadership skills. While the importance of leadership is indisputable, there is no singular type or style of leadership that works in all situations. Yet, the kind of leadership that is vital for organisational success is not a phenomenon that develops magically on its own.[1]

Continuing the discussions of power and influence, this chapter focuses on the topical issue of leadership — a special form of influence and the subject of enduring interest in organisational behaviour. Most attention has been focused on answering the central question — what makes a good leader? Is it personality characteristics, a set of behaviours, or the ability to adapt leadership style to different followers and situations? Can effective leadership be taught or is it something a person is born with?

Some people have posed an even more fundamental question — are leaders always accountable for failures or lack of achievement of their group or organisation? Let us think of a professional sports team that has had a bad season and the likelihood of the coaches taking the blame for the bad performance. This is a recurrent phenomenon. Yet it is hard to believe that coaches are always to blame for the failure of a team.

In this chapter, we first examine the traditional approaches to leadership.[2] We will differentiate between notions of leadership and management, and summarise and evaluate the major theories of leadership. The essential elements of 'new leadership theory', particularly charismatic and transformational ideas, will then be identified. We will also discuss the issue of diversity as it poses a challenge to leadership.

Until recent years, little leadership research had been undertaken in Australia and New Zealand. More recently, a few projects on leadership were initiated which include data from Australia and New Zealand. Among others, the works of Ken Parry and Neal Ashkanasy are to be noted.[3] The more recent empirical research on leadership in the Australian context, co-led by James Sarros from Monash University, reinforced the importance of this topic both in theory and in practice.

Leadership and management

In earlier chapters of this book we often referred to 'managers' and to 'management functions'. A fundamental question is whether leadership and management are (or can be) separated. There is often heated controversy over whether leaders are different from managers, and whether management is different from leadership.

A simple distinction would be to say that leadership is more concerned about doing the right thing while management is about doing things right Another way to make the same distinction is to argue that management is more concerned with promoting stability and enabling the organisation to run smoothly, while the role of leadership is to promote adaptive and long-term change. Managers see and solve problems, while leaders see possibilities to overcome these by going beyond them.

Hence, leaders' roles are distinguishable from those of managers.

- **Managers** are concerned with making things happen and keeping work on schedule, engaging in routine interactions to fulfil planned actions.
- **Leaders** provide inspiration, create opportunities, coach and motivate people to gain their support on fundamental long-term choices.

Leadership is all about using appropriate interpersonal styles and methods in guiding individuals and groups towards task accomplishment.

In practice, however, most managers are expected to be leaders or to play leadership roles as well. They are expected to be able to influence and inspire the people in their organisation to work willingly towards organisational goals, and to encourage high-quality results. What is often required of them, in the same way as it is for leaders, is a balanced and strong concern for both people and task.

In the main, **leadership** is a special case of interpersonal influence that gets an individual or group to do what the leader wants them to do.

Leadership may take two forms:

1. **formal leadership**, which is exerted by individuals appointed to or elected to positions of formal authority in organisations
2. **informal leadership**, which is exerted by individuals who become influential because they have special skills that meet the needs and resources of others.

Both types of leadership are important in organisations.

Managers are concerned with making things happen and keeping work on schedule, engaging in routine interactions to fulfil planned actions.

Leaders provide inspiration, create opportunities, coach and motivate people to gain their support on fundamental long-term choices.

Leadership is a special case of interpersonal influence that gets an individual or group to do what the leader wants done.

Formal leadership is the process of exercising influence from a position of formal authority in an organisation.

Informal leadership is the process of exercising influence through special skills or resources that meet the needs of other people.

Traditional leadership approaches: trait and behavioural theories

All the trait and behavioural approaches assume, in one way or another, that selected personal traits or behaviours have a major impact on leadership outputs. According to these theories, leadership is central and other variables are relatively less important. However, the various approaches offer different explanations for leadership results.

Trait theory

Trait theory is the earliest approach used to study leadership and dates back to as early as the turn of the twentieth century. The early studies attempted to identify those traits that differentiated the 'great person' in history from the masses (for example, how did Peter the Great differ from his followers?).[4] This approach led to a research emphasis that tried to separate leaders from non-leaders, or more effective leaders from less effective leaders. The argument was that certain traits are related to success and that these traits, once identified, could be used to select leaders. This argument is made in chapter 2, concerning individual attributes, except that this earlier research concentrated on leaders and looked for general traits, cutting across groups and organisations. Thus, researchers looked at traits such as height, integrity, intelligence and the like. Proof of this theory lies in predicting and finding a set of traits (charisma, intelligence and so on) that differentiates effective leaders from ineffective ones — that is, it is derived from whether a set of traits distinguishes leaders from non-leaders (followers).

For various reasons, including inadequate theorising, inadequate measurement of many traits and failure to recognise possible differences in organisations and situations, the studies were not successful enough to provide a general trait theory.[5] But they laid the groundwork for considering certain traits, in combination with other leadership aspects (such as behaviours), that forms the basis for some of the more current theories.

Behavioural theories

By the 1940s attention had turned towards a behavioural position about leadership. In essence, the focus changed from attempting to identify the inner traits of leaders to one of examining their behaviour.

Like the trait approach, the behavioural theories approach assumes that leadership is central to performance and human resource maintenance. However, instead of dealing with underlying traits, it considers behaviours or actions. Two classic research programs at the University of Michigan and Ohio State University provide useful insights into leadership behaviours.

The Michigan studies

In the late 1940s researchers at the University of Michigan introduced a program of research on leadership behaviour. The researchers were concerned with identifying the leadership pattern that results in effective performance. From interviews of high- and low-performing groups in different organisations, the researchers derived two basic forms of leader behaviours: employee-centred and production-centred.

Employee-centred supervisors are those who place strong emphasis on the welfare of their employees. In contrast, *production-centred supervisors* tend to place a stronger emphasis on getting the work done than on the welfare of the employees. In general, employee-centred supervisors were found to have more productive work groups than those of the production-centred supervisors.[6]

These behaviours may be viewed on a continuum, with employee-centred supervisors at one end and production-centred supervisors at the other. Sometimes, the more general terms 'human relations oriented' and 'task oriented' are used to describe these alternative leader behaviours.

The Ohio State studies

An important leadership research program was started at Ohio State University at about the same time as the Michigan studies. A questionnaire was administered in both industrial and military settings to measure subordinates' perceptions of their superiors' leadership behaviour. The researchers identified two dimensions similar to those found in the Michigan studies: *consideration* and *initiating structure*.[7] Highly considerate leaders are sensitive to people's feelings and, much like employee-centred leaders, try to make things pleasant for their followers.

In contrast, leaders who are high in initiating structure are more concerned with spelling out task requirements and clarifying other aspects of the work agenda; they may be seen as similar to production-centred supervisors, emphasising getting the work done above the needs of their employees. These dimensions are related to what people sometimes refer to as socioemotional and task leadership, respectively. They also encompass what we discussed in chapter 8 as group maintenance and task activities.

At first, the Ohio State researchers thought that a leader high on consideration, or socioemotional warmth, would have more highly satisfied and/or better performing employees. Later results indicated that leaders should be high on both consideration and initiating structure behaviours. This dual emphasis is reflected in the Leadership Grid® approach.[8]

The Leadership Grid®

Robert Blake and Jane Mouton developed the Leadership Grid® perspective.[9] It measures a manager's:
- *concern for people*
- *concern for production.*

The results are then plotted on a nine-position grid that places these concerns on the vertical axis and horizontal axis, respectively (figure 11.1, overleaf). A person with a 9/1 score is a 'country club manager' (9 on concern for people; 1 on concern for production). Some other positions are 1/1 — impoverished management style — and 1/9 — task management style. A 5/5 style, in the middle of the grid, is a middle-of-the-road management style. The ideal position is a 9/9 'team manager' (high on both dimensions).

The behavioural approaches discussed share a common emphasis on the importance of people-oriented and production- or task-oriented behaviours in determining outputs. But how well do these behaviours transfer internationally? Research in the United States, the United Kingdom, Hong Kong and Japan shows that the behaviours, although they seem to be generally important in all these countries, must be carried out in different ways in different cultures. UK leaders, for instance, are seen as considerate if they show employees how to use equipment, whereas in Japan the highly considerate manager helps employees with personal problems.[10]

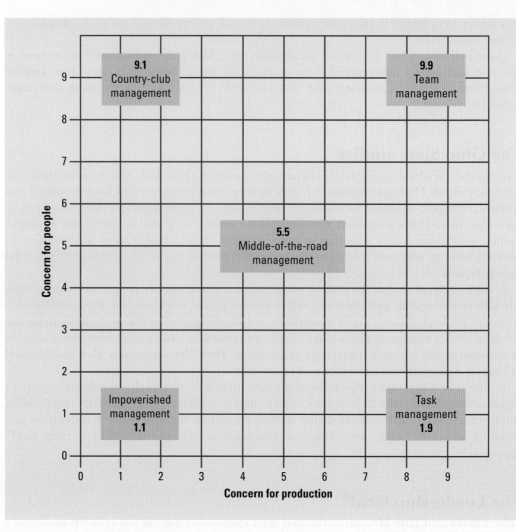

FIGURE 11.1 The Leadership Grid®

COUNTER**POINT**

Reality check: the perils of leadership

Being a leader certainly has its fair share of perks, such as being in the driver's seat of creating a big and inspiring vision, having a sense of deep accomplishment when the vision and goals turn into achieved goals, having the opportunity to serve others, steering a creative process and being part of building a sustainable future, to name just a few.

However, anybody going into a leadership position to earn more, have more power and prestige and work less is naïve and ignorant. Accompanying leadership are perils that the leader needs to navigate on a daily basis. For example, there is no escaping pressure. Pressure has an impact upon a leader's personal values, positions and philosophies and too much pressure experienced by an unwilling, unprepared, ill-equipped, or incapable leader results in flawed thinking, bad decisions, and wrong actions. How leaders deal with pressure could mean the difference between rapidly progressing an organisation towards success, or contributing to its demise.[11]

Another peril leaders don't always anticipate is that they will never have everybody's approval and they need to be prepared to be hated. If a leader cannot deal with disapproval, then leadership probably isn't for them. Furthermore, part of the job description is being 'uncomfortable' and the sooner they get comfortable with discomfort and vulnerability, the better.[12]

Questions

1. What other perils of being the leader can you identify?
2. What strategies would be effective in dealing with the perils outlined above and the ones you have identified?

Situational contingency theories of leadership

Despite their usefulness, behavioural theories of leadership proved difficult to justify. Leaders with the same behavioural tendencies could find success in one situation and not in another. This led researchers to propose that perhaps the leader's situation is a critical contributor to the likelihood of success. Adding situational characteristics underlined the fact that leadership is more complex than isolating a set of unique traits or behaviours. This led to the emergence of the contingency approach to leadership, which encompasses a number of theories.

Some of the main contributions of these theories include the work of Fred Fiedler, Robert House, Paul Hersey and Kenneth Blanchard, and Steven Kerr and John Jermier.

Fiedler's leadership contingency theory

The first situational contingency approach we consider is Fred Fiedler's, because his work essentially started the situational contingency era in the mid 1960s.[13] Fiedler's approach predicts work group effectiveness. His theory holds that group effectiveness depends on an appropriate match between a leader's style and the demands of the situation. Specifically, Fiedler considers the amount of control the situation allows the leader. **Situational control** is the extent to which leaders can determine what their group is going to do, and what will be the outcomes of the group's actions and decisions. Where control is high, leaders can predict with a good deal of certainty what will happen when they want something done.

Fiedler uses an instrument called the **least preferred coworker (LPC) scale** to measure a person's leadership style. Respondents are asked to describe the person with whom they are able to work least well (their least preferred coworker, or LPC), using a series of adjectives such as these:

Unfriendly	.....	.....	.....	.....	.....	.....	.....	.....	Friendly
	1	2	3	4	5	6	7	8	
Pleasant	.....	.....	.....	.....	.....	.....	.....	.....	Unpleasant
	1	2	3	4	5	6	7	8	

Fiedler argues that high LPC leaders (those describing their LPC very positively) have a relationship-motivated style, while low LPC leaders have a task-oriented style. In other words, relationship-oriented leaders describe more favourably the person with whom they are least able to work than do task-oriented leaders.

Fiedler considers this task or relationship motivation to be a trait that leads to either directive or nondirective behaviour, depending on whether the leader has high, moderate or low situational control (as already described).

Situational control is the extent to which leaders can determine what their group is going to do and what the outcomes of their actions and decisions are going to be.

Least preferred coworker (LPC) scale is a measure of a person's leadership style based on a description of the person with whom respondents have been able to work least well.

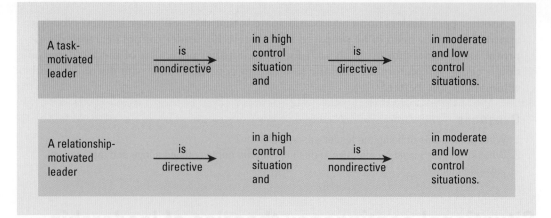

Let us now elaborate on Fiedler's situational control concept and its match with task- and relationship-oriented styles. Figure 11.2 shows the task-oriented leader as having greater group effectiveness under high and low situational control, while the relationship-oriented leader has a more effective group under a moderate control situation.

The figure also shows that Fiedler measures high, moderate and low control with the following three variables arranged in the situational combinations indicated:
- *leader–member relations* (good/poor) — member support for the leader
- *task structure* (high/low) — spelling out of the leader's task goals, procedures and guidelines in the group
- *position power* (strong/weak) — the leader's task expertise and reward/punishment authority.

Following are some examples showing how different combinations of these variables provide differing amounts of situational control. First, consider the experienced and well-trained supervisor of a group that manufactures a part for a car engine. The leader is highly supported by his group members and can grant raises and make hiring and firing decisions. This supervisor would have high situational control and would be operating in situation I in figure 11.2. Likewise, those leaders operating in situations II and III would have high situational control, although not as high as that of our production supervisor. In any of these three high-control situations, a task-oriented leader behaving nondirectively would have the most effective group.

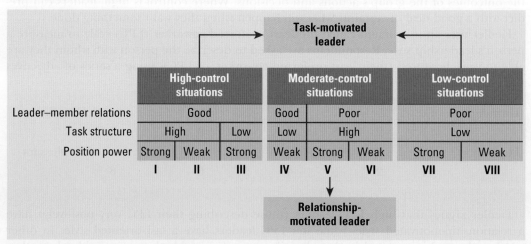

FIGURE 11.2 Predictions from Fiedler's contingency theory of leadership

Contrast the previous example with the chair of a student council committee of volunteers who are not happy about this person being the chair and who have the low-structured task of organising a Parents' Day program to improve school–parent relations. Here we have a low-control situation (situation VIII) calling for a task-motivated leader who would need to behave directively. In other words, Fiedler argues that the leader must act directively in this situation to keep the group together and focused on the ambiguous task; the situation demands it.

Finally, let us consider a well-liked academic department head with a tenured lecturing staff. Fiedler argues that this is a moderate-control situation (IV) with good leader–member relations, low task structure and weak position power, calling for a relationship-motivated leader. The leader should emphasise nondirective and considerate relationships with the lecturing staff. Can you develop one or two moderate-control relationships for situation V?

To summarise, Fiedler's model links effectiveness with the match between the leader's style of interacting with employees and the extent to which the leader has control over the situation. Put simply, this theory predicts leadership effectiveness as a function of these two factors. Using Fiedler's developed LPC (least preferred coworker) questionnaire, it is possible to identify a person's style (person or task oriented) and then assess the situational component through three criteria — leader–member relations, task structure and position power.

Fiedler's cognitive resource theory

Fiedler has since moved beyond his contingency theory by developing the cognitive resource theory.[14] Cognitive resources are abilities or competencies. According to this approach, whether a leader should use directive or nondirective behaviour depends on the following situational contingencies: the leader's or subordinate group member's ability/competency; stress; experience; and group support of the leader. Basically, cognitive resource theory is most useful because it directs us to leader or subordinate group member ability, which other leadership approaches typically do not consider.

The theory views directiveness as most helpful for performance when the leader is competent, relaxed and supported. In this case, the group is ready and directiveness is the clearest means of communication. When the leader feels stressed, they are diverted. In this case, experience is more important than ability. If group support is low, then the group is less receptive and the leader has less impact. Group member ability becomes most important when the leader is nondirective and there is strong support from group members. If group support is weak, then task difficulty or other factors have more impact than either the leader or the followers do.

More recent studies have verified and extended Fiedler's contingency model of leadership effectiveness to followers' behaviour. For instance, a recent study of personnel serving with the US army in Europe re-examined the relationship between followers' motivational disposition, situational favourability and followers' performance. That study found that, in accordance with Fiedler, relations-oriented followers performed better in moderately favourable situations while task-oriented followers performed better in highly unfavourable situations.[15]

Although there are still unanswered questions concerning Fiedler's contingency theory (especially concerning the meaning of LPC), the theory continues to receive relatively strong support both in academia and in practice.

House's path–goal theory of leadership

Another well-known approach to situational contingencies is one developed by Robert House based on the earlier work of others.[16] This theory has its roots in the expectancy model of motivation (chapter 3). The term 'path–goal' is used because it emphasises how a leader influences employees' perceptions of both work goals and personal goals and the links or paths found between these two sets of goals.

The theory assumes that a leader's key function is to adjust his or her behaviours to complement situational contingencies, such as those found in the work setting. House argues that when the leader is able to compensate for things lacking in the setting, employees are likely to be satisfied with the leader. The leader could, for example, help remove job ambiguity or show how good performance could lead to more pay. Performance should improve as leaders clarify the paths by which effort leads to performance (expectancy) and performance leads to valued rewards (instrumentality). Redundant behaviour by the leader will not help, and may even hinder, performance. People do not need a boss telling them how to do something that they already know how to do!

House's model represents a process approach to leadership that takes into account three interrelated variables. The overall process in sequential order is:

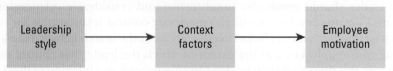

Details of House's approach are summarised in figure 11.3.[17] The figure shows four types of leader behaviours — directive, supportive, achievement-oriented and participative — and two categories of situational contingency variables — employee attributes and work-setting attributes. The leader behaviours are adjusted to complement the situational contingency variables to influence employee satisfaction, acceptance of the leader and motivation for task performance.

- **Directive leadership** has to do with spelling out the what and how of employees' tasks; it is much like the initiating structure mentioned earlier.
- **Supportive leadership** focuses on employee needs and wellbeing, and promotes a friendly work climate; it is similar to consideration.
- **Achievement-oriented leadership** emphasises setting challenging goals, stressing excellence in performance and showing confidence in the group members' abilities to achieve high standards of performance.
- **Participative leadership** focuses on consulting with employees and seeking and accounting for their suggestions before making decisions.

The contingency variables include employee attributes and work-setting or environmental attributes. Important employee characteristics are authoritarianism (closed-mindedness, rigidity), internal–external orientation (for example, locus of control) and ability. The key work-setting factors are the nature of the employees' tasks (task structure), the formal authority system and the primary work group.

Directive leadership is leadership behaviour that spells out the what and how of employees' tasks.

Supportive leadership is a leadership style that focuses on employee needs and wellbeing, and promotes a friendly work climate; it is similar to consideration.

Achievement-oriented leadership is leadership behaviour that emphasises setting challenging goals, stressing excellence in performance and showing confidence in the group members' abilities to achieve high standards of performance.

Participative leadership is a leadership style that focuses on consulting with employees, and seeking and accounting for their suggestions before making decisions.

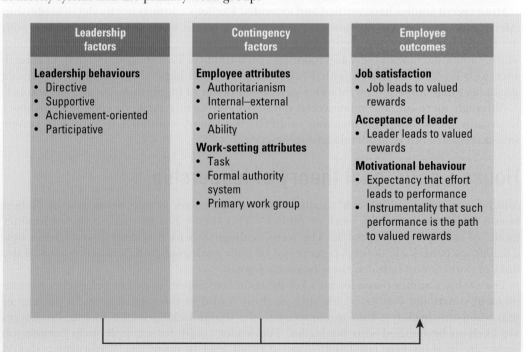

FIGURE 11.3 Summary of major path–goal relationships in House's leadership approach

House's path–goal approach has attracted considerable research, and there is support for the theory in general as well as for the particular predictions discussed earlier.[18] Not all aspects shown in figure 11.3 have been tested, and few applications have been reported in the literature. The path–goal approach lends itself to at least a couple of possibilities, however. First, training could be used to change leadership behaviour to fit the situational contingencies. Second, the leader could be taught to diagnose the situation and to learn how to change the contingencies (employee attributes and work-setting attributes).

Leadership across the generations

A recent Bankwest business leaders report outlines the views of senior leaders about a range of leadership issues. More than 60 per cent of leaders view being a role model to enhance ownership of a common vision and goals as an effective strategy but that a leader's leadership approach ought to adapt to different generations of staff. This is essential since younger people are predominantly looking for leadership, mentoring, coaching and promotion prospects while baby boomers seek stability, flexibility, and have a preference for higher salaries and bonuses in their performance arrangements.[19] Mark McConnell, a serial entrepreneur, a mid-market expert and former member of the BRW Young Rich, is an example of adapting his leadership to fit with different groups.[20] He argues that simply dangling carrots and rewards, and kudos or uniform strategies to motivate people does not equate to leadership and that there is no one style fits all. He argues a leader ought to tailor her/his leadership style to the individual and understand the division of the workforce. His five tips for becoming an adaptable leader include the following.[21]

- Identify the types of staff you wish to attract to your company and engage them in an active talent management program and leadership training.
- Investment in staff is just as important as investment in product.
- Learn from your previous unsatisfactory work experiences to ensure your organisation doesn't repeat these mistakes.
- Adapt your leadership style to meet the unique needs of each stage of a firm's maturation, including the start-up, growth and maturity stage.

Hersey and Blanchard's Situational Leadership® model

The Situational Leadership® model developed by Paul Hersey and Kenneth Blanchard is similar to the other situational approaches in its view that there is no single best way to lead.[22] Like the approaches discussed earlier, Situational Leadership® emphasises situational contingencies. Hersey and Blanchard focus on the readiness of followers, in particular. Readiness is the extent to which people have the ability and willingness to accomplish a specific task. Hersey and Blanchard argue that 'situational' leadership requires adjusting the leader's emphasis on task behaviours (for example, giving guidance and direction) and relationship behaviours (for example, providing socioemotional support) according to the readiness of followers to perform their tasks.

The model identifies four leadership styles:
- delegating
- participating
- selling
- telling.

Each emphasises a different combination of task and relationship behaviours by the leader. The model suggests a particular leadership style for followers at each of four readiness levels.

A telling style is best for low follower readiness. The direction provided by this style defines roles for people who are unable and unwilling to take responsibility themselves; it eliminates any insecurity about the task that must be done.

A selling style is best for low to moderate follower readiness. This style offers both task direction and support for people who are unable but willing to take task responsibility; it involves combining a directive approach with explanation and reinforcement to maintain enthusiasm.

A participating style is best for moderate to high follower readiness. Able but unwilling followers require supportive behaviour to increase their motivation; by allowing followers to share in decision making, this style helps enhance the desire to perform a task.

A delegating style is best for high readiness. This style provides little in terms of direction and support for the task at hand; it allows able and willing followers to take responsibility for what needs to be done.

This Situational Leadership approach requires the leader to develop the capability to diagnose the demands of situations and then to choose and implement the appropriate leadership response. The theory gives specific attention to followers and their feelings about the task at hand. It also suggests that an effective leader reassess situations over time, giving special attention to emerging changes in the level of readiness of the people involved in the work. Again, Hersey and Blanchard advise that leadership style should be adjusted as necessary to remain consistent with actual levels of follower readiness. They further suggest that effectiveness should improve as a result.[23]

The Situational Leadership® approach has a great deal of intuitive appeal for managers but little systematic research support. What support is available is not very strong, and the theory still needs systematic empirical evaluation.[24]

The approach does include an elaborate training program that has been developed to train leaders to diagnose and emphasise appropriate behaviours. Internationally, this program is particularly popular in Europe, where an organisation headquartered in Amsterdam provides Situational Leadership® training for leaders in many countries.

Substitutes for leadership

The 'substitutes for leadership' perspective argues that sometimes hierarchical leadership makes essentially no difference. John Jermier and others contend that certain individual, job and organisational variables can either serve as substitutes for leadership or neutralise a leader's impact on employees.[25] Examples of these variables are shown in figure 11.4. Experience, ability and training, for example, can serve as individual characteristics; a highly structured or routine job can serve as a job characteristic; and a cohesive work group can serve as an organisational characteristic.

Substitutes for leadership make a leader's influence both impossible and unnecessary. *Neutralisers* make a leader's influence impossible but not unnecessary; substitutes replace a leader's influence. As you can see in figure 11.4[26] it will be difficult, if not impossible, for a leader to provide the kind of task-oriented direction already available to an experienced, talented and well-trained employee. Further, such direction will be unnecessary, given the employee's characteristics. The figure shows a similar argument for a highly structured task.

Now let us look at a couple of neutralising examples in the figure. If leaders have low position power or formal authority, their leadership may be negated, even though task structuring and supportiveness are still needed. If leaders are physically separated from employees, their task-oriented and supportive leadership may be negated but still necessary.

The substitutes for leadership perspective is a more generalised version of the situational contingency approaches mentioned earlier, particularly House's path–goal theory. However,

Substitutes for leadership are organisation, individual or task-situational variables that substitute for leadership in causing performance/human resource maintenance.

the substitutes perspective goes further by assuming that leadership, in some cases, has no impact on outputs because it is replaced by other factors. The earlier situational approaches argued that both leadership and other factors are needed.

Research on the substitutes theory has shown mixed results. Some work comparing Mexican and US workers suggests both similarities and differences between various substitutes in the two countries.[27] Within the United States, some early work appeared to support the theory, but two later, comprehensive studies (covering 13 different organisations) provided little support.[28]

Despite this last finding, given the emerging importance and popularity of work teams, leadership substitutes are likely to be important and need to be tailored to the team-oriented workplace. Thus, in place of a leader specifying standards and ways of achieving goals (task-oriented behaviours), the team will set its own standards and substitute these for the leader's standards.

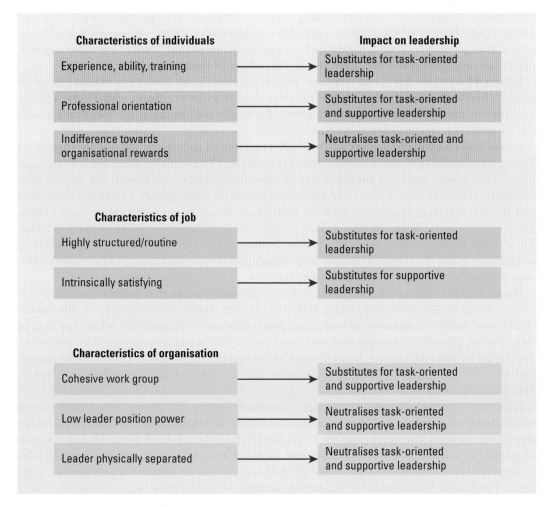

FIGURE 11.4 Example leadership substitutes and neutralisers

Inspirational leadership perspectives

So far, we have taken a well-trodden path in presenting theories of leadership from a historical perspective. However, no building-block progression of knowledge is assumed, and you should be careful not to jump to the conclusion, for example, that most recent is necessarily best!

More recent ideas are attribution theory of leadership, charismatic leadership, transaction versus transformational leadership, and leading through empowerment. The more recent inspirational approaches to leadership have tended to move right away from traditional leadership characteristics and endorse charisma, vision and transformation as catalysts to effective leadership.

The general notion that leadership is largely symbolic or 'in the eye of the beholder' has carried over to a related set of research directions. Ironically, the first of these argues that leadership makes little or no real difference to organisational effectiveness. The second tends to attribute greatly exaggerated importance to leadership and leads us into charisma and other aspects of the new leadership. Let us briefly examine each of these two directions.

Charismatic approaches

Charismatic leadership[29] uses attribution theory to suggest that we make attributions of heroic leadership competencies or personal characteristics when we see good leaders in action. Conger and Kanungo, for example, assert that charismatic leaders are self-confident, display an articulate vision and have strong conviction of their vision.[30]

Robert House and his associates have produced some work based on extensions of an earlier charismatic theory that House developed (not to be confused with House's path–goal theory, discussed earlier in the chapter). Especially interesting is the fact that House's theory uses both *trait* and *behaviour* combinations.

Charismatic leaders are those leaders who, by force of their personal abilities, are capable of having a profound and extraordinary effect on followers.

House sees charismatic leaders as those 'who by force of their personalities are capable of having a profound and extraordinary effect on followers'. Essentially, these leaders are high in need for power and have high feelings of self-efficacy and conviction in the moral rightness of their beliefs; that is, the need for power motivates these people to want to be leaders and this need is then reinforced by their conviction of the moral rightness of their beliefs. The feeling of self-efficacy, in turn, makes people feel that they are capable of being leaders. These traits then influence such charismatic behaviours as role modelling, image building, articulating goals (focusing on simple and dramatic goals), emphasising high expectations, showing confidence and arousing follower motives.

House and his colleagues also summarise several other studies that support aspects of the theory. Some of the more interesting related work has shown that negative, or 'dark-side', charismatic leaders emphasise personalised power (focus on themselves), while positive, or 'bright-side', charismatics emphasise socialised power that tends to empower their followers. This helps explain differences between dark-side leaders such as Adolf Hitler, David Koresh and Reverend Jim Jones and bright-side leaders, such as Martin Luther King Junior,[31] Nelson Mandela or Gandhi.

Jay Conger has developed a four-stage charismatic leadership theory based on his work with Rabindra Kanungo.[32] In the first stage, the leader develops a vision of idealised change that moves beyond the status quo; for example, US President John F Kennedy had a vision of putting a man on the moon by the end of the 1960s. In the second stage, the leader communicates the vision and motivates the followers to go beyond the status quo. In stage three, the leader builds trust by exhibiting qualities such as expertise, success, risk taking and unconventional actions. In the final stage, the leader demonstrates ways to achieve the vision by means of empowerment, behaviour modelling for followers and so forth. Conger and Kanungo have argued that if leaders use behaviours, such as vision and articulation, environmental sensitivity and unconventional behaviour, rather than maintaining the status quo, followers will attribute charismatic leadership to them. Such leaders are also seen as behaving quite differently from those labelled 'noncharismatic'.[33]

Recent research on leadership involving three countries in Asia (Singapore, New Zealand and India) showed that charisma and vision were made up of two charismatic factors (social sensitivity and persuasive personality traits) and two visionary factors ('expert and analytical' and 'visionary and futuristic'). Tests across the three countries showed that the two visionary factors influenced reported performance and the two charismatic factors influenced employee commitment. Only social sensitivity predicted both performance and commitment of employees.[34]

Another important leadership researcher, Gary Yukl, has addressed the issue of whether charismatic and transformational leadership are compatible — can a leader be both highly transformational and highly charismatic at the same time? This issue concerns the role of followers. Transformational leadership usually involves empowering followers and making them partners in the change process, whereas charismatic leadership is more likely to require followers to place their trust in the leader's special expertise to achieve radical change. While these leadership approaches are often grouped together, Yukl's work directs us to consider this aspect of leadership behaviour more closely.[35]

Another recent empirical study involving 180 participants (51 managers and 129 employees) from 37 large-scale companies in Taiwan examined the interface between value and charisma and the inherent value intervening mechanism: the fit between the person's and organisation's values. One of its main findings was that CEO charismatic leadership had both direct and indirect effects on employees' extra effort to work, and satisfaction with the CEO, as well as their commitment to the organisation. However, that study also found that these relationships were mediated by employees' perceived person–organisation values fit.[36]

Transactional and transformational leadership approaches

We made the point earlier that transformational leadership has many similarities to charismatic leadership but involves the followers as partners. Building on notions originated by James MacGregor Burns, as well as ideas from House's work, Bernard Bass has developed an approach that focuses on both transformational and transactional leadership. The high points are summarised in figure 11.5.

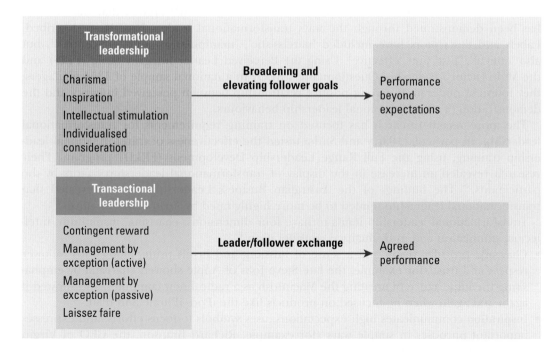

FIGURE 11.5 High points of Bass's transformational/ transactional leadership approach

Transactional leadership
involves daily exchanges
between leaders and followers,
and is necessary for achieving
routine performance on which
leaders and followers agree.

Contingent rewards are
rewards that are given in
exchange for mutually agreed
goal accomplishments.

**Active management by
exception** involves watching
for deviations from rules
and standards and taking
corrective action.

**Passive management by
exception** involves intervening
with employees only if
standards are not met.

Laissez faire leadership
involves abdicating
responsibilities and avoiding
decisions.

Transformational leadership is
a leadership style by which the
followers' goals are broadened
and elevated, and confidence
is gained to go beyond
expectations.

Charisma is a dimension of
leadership that provides vision
and a sense of mission, and
instils pride, respect and trust.

Inspiration is the
communication of high
expectations, the use of
symbols to focus efforts, and
the expression of important
purposes in simple ways.

Let's start by discussing Bass's transactional category. **Transactional leadership** involves daily exchanges between leaders and employees, and is necessary for achieving routine performance on which leaders and employees agree. It is based on transactions that occur between leaders and followers. These transactions may include agreements, contingent rewards, communications or exchanges between leaders and followers. There are many dimensions of transactional leadership.

- **Contingent rewards** involve providing various kinds of reward in exchange for accomplishing mutually agreed goals (for example, your boss pays you a $500 bonus for completing an acceptable article by a certain date). Conversely, you could be subject to disciplinary action for failing to achieve the goals.
- **Active management by exception** involves concentrating on occurrences that deviate from expected norms, such as irregularities, mistakes, exceptions and failures to meet standards. This means watching for deviations from rules and standards, and taking corrective action (for example, your boss notices that you have an increasing number of defects in your work and helps you adjust your machine to correct these).
- **Passive management by exception** involves intervening only if standards are not met (for example, your boss comes to see you after noticing your high percentage of rejects in the weekly production report).
- **Laissez faire leadership** involves abdicating responsibilities and avoiding decisions (for example, your boss is seldom around and does not follow through on decisions that need action).

Transformational leadership might go beyond this routine accomplishment, however. For Bass, transformational leadership occurs when leaders broaden and elevate the interests of their followers; when they generate awareness and acceptance of the purposes and mission of the group; and when they stir their followers to look beyond their own self-interest for the good of others.

Transformational leadership is a leadership style by which the followers' goals are broadened and elevated, and confidence is gained to go beyond expectations. This approach to leadership is based on motivating followers to do more than they originally intended, and often more than they thought possible. It involves guiding, influencing and inspiring people to excel and to contribute towards the achievement of organisational goals.

In recent times, the ethical nature of transformational leadership has been the subject of much debate and controversy. Parry and Proctor-Thomson[37] argued that such debate has been demonstrated through the ways transformational leaders have been described. Labels and descriptors have included 'narcissistic', 'manipulative' and 'self-centred', but also 'ethical', 'just' and 'effective'. Using the Perceived Leader Integrity Scale (PLIS) and the Multi-Factor Leadership Questionnaire (MLQ) in a national sample of 1354 managers, they found a moderate to strong positive relationship between perceived integrity and the demonstration of transformational leadership behaviours.

The more recent research has focused on training requirements for transformational leadership. In particular, Parry and Sinha tested the effectiveness of transformational leadership training, using the Full Range Leadership Development (FRLD) program. Their research revealed an increase in the display of transformational leadership factors by the participants.[38] The findings of the Australian Business Leadership Survey revealed that transformational leadership tended to be more highly rated by Australian executives.[39]

Transformational leadership tends to have four dimensions: charisma, inspiration, intellectual stimulation and individualised consideration.[40]

- **Charisma** provides vision and a sense of mission, and instils pride, along with follower respect and trust (for example, the late Steve Jobs of Apple showed charisma by emphasising the importance of creating the Macintosh as a radical new computer, and showed it again and again when he focused on products like the iPod, iPhone and iPad.
- **Inspiration** communicates high expectations, uses symbols to focus efforts, and expresses important purposes in simple ways (for example, Richard Branson, the CEO of Virgin

Airlines, has been known to personally greet passengers on flights that have experienced difficulties or been delayed, and when in Australia he actually travels alongside passengers commuting from state to state).[41]

- **Intellectual stimulation** promotes intelligence, rationality and careful problem solving (for example, your boss encourages you to look at a difficult problem in a new way).
- **Individualised consideration** provides personal attention, treats each employee individually, and coaches and advises (for example, your boss drops by and makes remarks reinforcing your worth as a person).

Together, charisma and inspiration transform follower expectations, but intellectual stimulation and individualised consideration are also needed to provide the necessary follow-through.

Bass concludes that transformational leadership is likely to be strongest at the top management level, where there is the greatest opportunity for proposing and communicating a vision. But it is by no means restricted to the top level; it is found throughout the organisation. Further, transformational leadership operates in combination with transactional leadership. Transactional leadership is similar to most of the traditional leadership approaches mentioned earlier, and leaders need both transformational and transactional leadership to be successful, just as they need both leadership and management. The effective manager 11.1 looks at the four 'I's of transformational leadership.

The four 'I's of transformational leadership

The following useful pointers about transformational leadership are given by Bruce Avolio and his associates:[42]

- *Individualised consideration* — pay attention to individual employees
- *Intellectual stimulation* — be concerned with helping people to think through new ways
- *Inspirational motivation* — inspire people to give their best
- *Idealised influence* — engender respect and trust that gives power and influence over people.

THE **EffectiveManager** 11.1

Leadership at The Physio Co

The Physio Co is an Australian small business offering physiotherapy to aged care residents. Since commencement of operation in 2004, The Physio Co has been ranked in the top 50 Best Places to Work in Australia for 5 years in a row, and ranked in the top 5 in 2013. Founder and CEO Tristan White emphasises the importance of a strong workplace culture. According to Tristan, recruiting and embedding great staff into a strong workplace culture has also helped the business to be additionally ranked as one of the fastest growing businesses in Australia for the past 5 years consecutively.

Along with strong leadership, a clear vision, and a strong set of guiding principles, Tristan believes The Physio Co's constant growth has resulted from years of refinement of the recruitment process and a focus on attracting, nurturing and retaining staff who are the best positive, active, and independent thinkers. The Physio Co operates on mottos such as 'innovate, grow and succeed', and 'the best way to ensure the future happens is to create it'. Staff are inspired to give their best through a values-driven modus operandi that ensures all employees receive individual attention, provide feedback, fit the culture, share a common passion, and ultimately recognise how their individual roles contribute to bringing the company's vision to life.[43]

OBinAction

To summarise, transactional leaders guide employees in their tasks towards the achievement of pre-stated goals, whereas transformational leaders inspire their employees to transcend individual interest for the sake of their organisation.

Bryman has summarised a large number of studies using Bass's approach, ranging from six studies on the extra effort of followers to 16 studies on performance or effectiveness, to nearly a dozen covering various aspects of satisfaction. Still other studies cover outcomes such as burnout and stress and the predisposition to act as innovation champions. The strongest relationships tend to be associated with charisma or inspirational leadership, although in most cases the other dimensions are also important. These findings are impressive and broaden leadership outcomes beyond those used in the traditional leadership studies.[44]

Bernard Bass has also recently reviewed the two decades of research into transformational leadership. Recent findings in the field include evidence of why transformational leadership is more effective than transactional leadership, and of why female leaders may be more transformational than their male counterparts. Bass concluded, despite an abundance of applied research, that more basic research and theory development is needed. More work needs to be done, for example, on how context affects transactional and transformational leadership, and on how transformational leadership moves followers from compliance to the identification and internalisation of values and beliefs beyond their own self-interest.[45]

OBinAction

Exerting influence without authority

Congratulations — you've been chosen to lead a change initiative in your organisation! But there's a catch — the success of this initiative depends upon the cooperation of several people across your organisation over whom you have no formal authority. This is the type of challenge a greater number of managers face every day, owing to flatter management structures, having to get things done through peers inside and outside the organisation and virtual teams. More and more leaders have to exert influence over peers in other organisations and the traditional notion of 'I am the leader and you the follower' won't get you very far.

Influencing without authority or lateral leadership is an essential skill all contemporary leaders have to have in their leadership toolbox. If you have acquired the skill of getting things done through other people who are not your followers, your championing of the change initiative stands a far better chance of being implemented quickly and effectively.

Conger argues that this skill comprises four main interconnected capabilities. First, through networking you will be able to develop a broad network of relationships with people you wish to influence both inside and outside the organisation. It is about finding those people who could be portals to others and bigger networks and actively building relationships with them. When conducted through the lens of mutual benefit, your influence can be significantly enhanced. Second, through consultation and seeking the opinions of others about the initiative you are championing, you can gauge their ideas and reactions to your ideas. By advocating the desired outcome, you are seeking and inviting peers to participate in defining the process for achieving that outcome and you are likely to set the initiative up for success. Third, through coalition building and onboarding others to collectively advocate your initiative, you are likely to exert more influence than advocating the initiative by yourself. It is about gathering influential people around your cause and forming a single collective voice. The trick is to begin by asking yourself who's most likely to be affected by the change you're proposing and whose blessing you need to successfully progress your initiative and then to follow through on gaining that 'buy-in.' Finally, leaders can also significantly enhance their influence through using constructive persuasion and negotiation as a way to achieve mutual benefit instead of using it as a tool for manipulation.[46]

Emerging leadership perspectives

In the previous sections we have covered contemporary leadership approaches. In this section we are covering emerging leadership perspectives. Some of these are recent extensions of contemporary approaches, while others are quite new. These emerging leadership approaches are mostly still in relatively early stages of development, regardless of their link to contemporary approaches that was discussed earlier. This section begins with an outline of some of the emerging theoretical leadership themes in the leadership discipline. A discussion of more practical leadership issues for Australian leaders follows.

Integrative leadership

We start our discussion of these emerging leadership perspectives with integrative leadership. We call this integrative because of the broad scope of perspectives treated and the way they tie together. These approaches range from full-range leadership theory, which involves nine dimensions covering both transformational and transactional leadership, to shared leadership, cross-cultural leadership, and, finally, strategic leadership.

Full-range leadership theory

Beyond the generally promising results of transformational leadership theory and some attempts to consider it along with transactional leadership, has been an attempt to systematically extend the approach into what is called **full-range leadership theory (FRLT)**.[47] Some consider this an approach that ultimately could serve as a general leadership model that would reduce or eliminate the numerous models now emphasised. The theory currently consists of nine factors: five transformational, three transactional, and one nontransactional factor. The charismatic dimension has been divided into socialised charisma–labelled 'idealised influence (attributed)' and 'idealised influence (behaviour),' respectively.

Laissez-faire is dealt with as a nonleadership dimension. There are transformational, transactional, and nontransactional laissez-faire components to the model.

The approach is built around revisions to Bass's Multifactor Leadership Questionnaire. It is designed to recognise what are called **contextual variables** that link observations to a set of relevant facts, events, or points of view, such as organisational characteristics, work functions, external environment factors, and demographic variables. So far, environmental risk, leader hierarchical level, and leader–follower gender have received some consideration.

Current empirical work is quite promising and suggests that the FRLT can serve as a baseline for pointing out the systematic treatment of context on leadership and vice versa. Such results can help drive future leadership development approaches, among other things.

Shared leadership

Leadership can be treated as a vertical influence. The white-hatted rider on a white horse is contacted, comes into town, saves the day, and says: 'My work here is done.'

More and more, however, those concerned with leadership are seeing it as *not* being restricted to the vertical influence of the lone figure in a white hat. Leadership is not

Full-range leadership theory (FRLT) involves nine dimensions covering both transformational and transactional leadership, *especially emphasising contextual variables.*

Contextual variables link observations to a set of relevant facts, events, or points of view, such as organisational characteristics, work functions, external environment factors, and demographic variables.

restricted simply to the vertical influence of a single individual but extends to other people as well.

One name for this alternative conception is the label 'shared leadership'. **Shared leadership** is defined as a dynamic, interactive influence process among individuals in groups for which the objective is to lead one another to the achievement of group or organisational goals or both. This influence process often involves peer or lateral influence; at other times, it involves upward or downward hierarchical influence. The key distinction between shared leadership and traditional models of leadership is that the influence process involves more than just downward influence on subordinates by an appointed or elective leader. Rather, leadership is broadly distributed among a set of individuals instead of centralised in the hands of a single individual who acts in the role of a superior.[48]

We can more specifically illustrate shared and vertical leadership in terms of self-directing work teams.

Leadership in self-directing work teams
This type of leadership can come from outside or inside the team. Within a team, such leadership can be assigned to one person, rotated across team members, or even shared simultaneously as different needs arise across time.

Outside the team, the leaders can be traditional, formally designated vertical first-level supervisors, or foremen or an outside vertical leader of a self-managing team whose duties tend to be quite different from those of a traditional supervisor. Often, these nontraditional leaders are called 'coordinators' or 'facilitators'. A key part of their job is to provide resources to their unit and serve as a liaison with other units, all without the authority trappings of traditional supervisors. Here, team members tend to carry out traditional managerial/leadership functions internal to the team along with direct performance activities.

The activities or functions vary and could involve a designated team role or even be defined more generally as a process to facilitate shared team performance ('whatever it takes'). In the latter case, you are likely to see job rotation activities, along with skill-based pay, where workers are paid for the mix and depth of skills they possess as opposed to the skills of a given job assignment they might hold. If we argue that a key contribution to team performance (regardless of who provides it) is to create and maintain conditions for that performance, then the following are important considerations.[49]

Efficient, goal-directed effort
The key is to coordinate the effort both inside and outside the team. Team leaders can play a crucial role. It is harder than it looks because you need to coordinate individual efforts with those of the team, and team efforts with those of the organisation or major subunit. Among other things, such coordination calls for shared visions and goals, and the like.

Adequate resources
Teams rely on their leaders to obtain enough equipment, supplies and so on to carry out the team's goals. These are often handled by the outside facilitator and almost always involve internal and external negotiations so the facilitator can then do his or her negotiating outside the team.

Competent, motivated performance
Team members also need the appropriate knowledge, skills, abilities and motivation to perform collective tasks well. Leaders may be able to influence team composition so as to enhance shared efficacy and performance. We often see this demonstrated with short-term teams such as task forces. Sometimes student teams are selected with this very point in mind.

A productive, supportive climate
Here, we are talking about high levels of cohesiveness, mutual trust and cooperation among team members. Sometimes, these kinds of aspects are part of a team's 'interpersonal climate'. Team leaders contribute to this climate by role-modelling and supporting relationships that

Shared leadership is a dynamic, interactive influence process among individuals in groups for which the objective is to lead one another to the achievement of group or organisational goals or both.

build the high levels indicated. Team leaders can also work to enhance shared beliefs about team efficacy and collective capability.

Commitment to continuous improvement and adaptation
A really good team should be able to adapt to changing conditions. Again, both internal and external team leaders may play a role.

Self-leadership activities
These shared and vertical self-directing team activities tend to encourage self-leadership activities, which in turn can help individuals and the team. *Self-leadership* represents a portfolio of self-influence strategies that are believed to positively influence individual behaviour, thought processes, and related activities. Often, self-leadership activities are divided into three broad categories: behaviour-focused, natural-reward, and constructive-thought-pattern strategies.[50]

Behaviour-focused strategies tend to increase self-awareness, leading to the handling of behaviours involving necessary but not always pleasant tasks. These strategies include *self-observation, self-goal setting, self-reward, self-correcting feedback*, and *practice.* Self-observation involves examining your own behaviour to increase awareness of when and why you engage in certain behaviours. Such examination identifies behaviours that should be changed, enhanced or eliminated. Poor performance could lead to informal self-notes documenting the occurrence of unproductive office behaviours. Such heightened awareness is a first step towards behaviour change.

Self-rewards, in conjunction with behaviour-focused strategies, can be quite useful in moving behaviours towards goal attainment. Self-rewards can be real (for example, a steak dinner) or imaginary (for example, imagining a steak dinner). Also, such things as the rehearsal of desired behaviours before actual performance can prove quite useful.

Constructive thought patterns focus on the creation or alteration of cognitive thought processes. Self-analysis and improvement of belief systems, mental imagery of successful performance outcomes, and positive self-talk can all help. As a package these three activities can influence and control team members' own thoughts through the use of specific cognitive strategies designed to facilitate habitual ways of thinking that can positively affect performance. Where the three above activities occur, they tend to serve as partial substitutes for hierarchical leadership even though they may be encouraged in a shared, in contrast to a vertical, leadership setting.

To summarise, in leaving this section on shared and vertical leadership, a final thought is in order. While you no longer want to restrict your leadership simply to the white-hat style of vertical leadership, neither is shared leadership the *only* way to go. As we have seen, shared leadership appears in many forms. In addition, it often is used in combination with vertical leadership. As with a number of the leadership approaches discussed in this chapter, various contingencies operate that influence the emphasis that should be devoted to each of the leadership perspectives.

Strategic leadership

We now move to strategic leadership. Strategic leadership is identified by concern for the advancement of the organisation, including its evolving capabilities and goals. There is not yet an overarching strategic leadership approach. Thus, we discuss three different perspectives, each of which considers strategic leadership in a somewhat different way. The first of these is termed multiple-level leadership. To this we add a top management teams (TMT) approach, and finally we focus on a strategic leadership approach developed by Boal and Hooijberg.

Strategic leadership is identified by concern for the advancement of the organisation, including its evolving capabilities and goals.

Multiple-level leadership
The multiple-level perspective argues that there are three different organisational domains from the bottom to the top of the organisation, typically made of no more than

two managerial levels within a domain: (1) the *production domain* at the bottom of the organisation, (2) the *organisation domain* in the middle levels, and (3) the *systems domain* at the top.[51] Each domain and level gets more complex than those beneath it in terms of its leadership and managerial requirements. But even the largest and most complex organisations can be designed to require no more than seven levels, from the lowest level to the highest top management level.

One way of expressing the increasing complexity is in terms of how long it takes to see the results of the key decisions required at a given domain and level. These roughly range from three months or so at the lowest level, which emphasises hands-on work performance and practical judgment to solve ongoing problems, to 20 years or more at the top.

Since the problems become increasingly complex, you can expect that managers at each domain and level must demonstrate increasing cognitive and behavioural complexity in order to deal with increasing organisational complexity. One way of measuring a manager's cognitive complexity is in terms of how far into the future he or she can develop a vision. Notice that this measure is trait oriented, similar in some ways but different in others from intelligence. In other words, using an intelligence measure instead of a complexity measure will not do. Accompanying such vision should be increasing sophistication across a wide range of the kinds of leader behaviours described in this chapter. Thus, successful leaders at each domain and level are expected to think and act more complexly as they move up the organisation.

This approach, or extensions of it, is now beginning to pick up momentum, although its underlying roots have been with us for many years. It is notable for emphasising the impact of top leadership as it cascades deep within the organisation. Leadership-at-a-distance is one example of such cascading, indirect leadership. One way of thinking about such cascading is in terms of a *leadership of* emphasis at the top and much more of a *leadership in* emphasis as the cascading moves down the organisation.

The systems domain *leadership of* at the top is normally responsible for creating complex systems, organising acquisition of major resources, creating vision, developing strategy and policy, and identifying organisational design. These functions call for a much broader conception of leadership than does the lower-level *leadership in*. Of course, *leadership in* is also exercised in the systems and organisation domains and involves the much more face-to-face approach stressed in that type of leadership. One example of *leadership of* is the indirect, cascading effects of an upper-domain decision concerning, say, leadership development programs to be implemented down the organisation. Of course, upper-domain executives also exercise *leadership in* as well, as they interact with top management teams and their own direct reports. Indeed, the previously discussed shared leadership is an important consideration for these teams, as it is for the top management teams to be discussed next.

Top-management teams

Top-management teams (TMTs) use demographic characteristics as proxies for harder-to-obtain psychological variables. Such variables as age, tenure, education, and functional background are used in this perspective. Researchers typically attempt to link such variables to various kinds of organisational outcomes, including sales growth, innovation, and executive turnover.[52]

Because of conflicting research findings, there has been recent work to enrich this approach. One such particularly important review argues that a given TMT is likely to face a variety of different situations over time. Demographic composition may be relatively stable but the tasks are dynamic and variable. Sometimes team members have similar information (symmetric) and interests, and sometimes not (asymmetric). The researchers argue that group process must be handled differently and effectively for dynamic and less-dynamic tasks, and that group process can vary depending on dynamism along such lines as information, interests, power asymmetries, and selected combinations of these.

One example covering information asymmetry can be seen in a merger. Here, each team member is likely to have different unshared and distinct information about the strategy, organisation and finances of potential partner organisations. The researchers ultimately developed a process-oriented model to deal with predicted information, interests, and power asymmetries. They argue that such a model integrates insights from research on leadership, TMTs, small group process, and negotiation and has practical implications for how top-level executives can improve TMT effectiveness through appropriate process choices.

Boal and Hooijberg's strategic leadership perspective

Let us start with a figure to help interpret the Boal and Hooijberg perspective.[53] Notice especially the charismatic, transformational, and vision leadership block. We will also discuss emotional intelligence (complexity). We will briefly discuss these as they apply to figure 11.6.

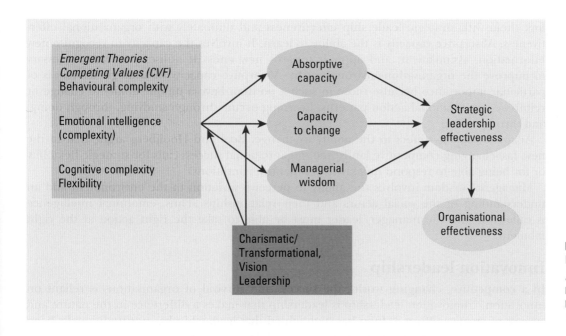

FIGURE 11.6 Boal and Hooijberg perspective

Source: Kimberly B. Boal and Robert Hooijberg, 'Strategic Leadership Research: Moving On', *The Leadership Quarterly* 11 (2009).

We start with the Emergent Theories and the Competing Values Framework (CVF).[54] CVF emphasises flexibility versus control and internal focus versus external focus. The internal versus external focus dimension distinguishes between social actions, emphasising internal effectiveness measures, such as employee satisfaction and focusing on external effectiveness measures such as market share and profitability. The control versus flexibility dimension contrasts social actions focused on goal clarity and efficiency and those emphasising being adaptive to people and the external environment. As a whole, the two focus dimensions define four quadrants and eight leadership roles that address these distinct organisational demands.

Thus, CVF recognises leaders often face competing requirements in meeting the competing demands of stakeholders. Top-level managers/leaders, for example, constantly need to balance demands from direct reports and other employees because doing so highlights executives' ability to change. Therefore, executives who have a large repertoire of leadership roles available and know when to apply these roles are more likely to be effective than leaders who have a small role repertoire and who indiscriminately apply these roles. This repertoire and selective application is termed *behavioural complexity*. To exhibit both repetitive and selective application, managers/leaders need cognitive and behavioural complexity as well as flexibility. Of course, they may understand and see the differences between their subordinates and superiors but not be able to behaviourally differentiate so as to satisfy the demands of each group. *Emotional intelligence*, the ability to manage oneself and one's relationships effectively, calls for both discernment and appropriate action at the right time.

In terms of cognitive complexity, the underlying assumption is that those high in cognitive complexity process information differently and perform certain tasks better than less cognitively complex persons because they use more categories to discriminate. In other words, such complexity taps into how a person constructs meaning as opposed to what he or she thinks.

Figure 11.6 (p. 423) shows CVF, behavioural complexity, and emotional complexity and cognitive complexity as directly associated with *absorptive capacity*, *capacity to change*, and *managerial wisdom* as well as with *charismatic/transformational leadership*, and *vision*. The association between CVF and the above complexities and the capacities differs according to how well the charismatic/transformational and visionary leadership is carried out.

Finally, Boal and Hooijberg briefly discuss what they mean by each of the capacities and link them with strategic leadership effectiveness and ultimately with organisational effectiveness. Absorptive capacity is the ability to learn. It involves the capacity to recognise new information, assimilate it, and apply it towards new ends. It utilises processes necessary to improve the organisation-environment fit. Absorptive capacity of strategic leaders is of particular importance because those in such a position have a unique ability to change or reinforce organisational action patterns. Learning occurs through studying, through doing, and through using.

Adaptive capacity refers to the ability to change. Boal and Hooijberg argue that in the new, fast-changing competitive landscape, organisational success calls for strategic flexibility or for being able to respond quickly to competitive conditions.

Managerial wisdom involves the ability to perceive variation in the environment and an understanding of the social actors and their relationships. Thus, emotional intelligence is called for and the manager/leader must be able to take the right action at the right moment.

Innovation leadership

In a competitive, changing world, the success and survival of organisations is reliant on innovation.[55] Innovation leadership is leadership that makes a difference in the nature and success of creative efforts.[56] Jung has highlighted that leadership has not traditionally been perceived to have a significant influence on creativity and innovation.[57]

Studies have pointed to two theories. Firstly, that leadership, or at least certain types of leadership, is related to creativity and innovation in 'real-world' settings; and secondly, that the influence tactics used by leaders affect people's willingness to engage in, and the likely success of, creative ventures.[59]

The multilevel approach proposed by Mumford, Ginamarie, Scott, Gaddis and Strange[60] is used to discuss individual, group and organisational pressures on requirements for the effective exercise of influence in creative efforts. A substantial proportion of relevant research was completed between 1955 and 1975 on the impact of leadership on creative ventures. There was a 20-year research hiatus, before a renewal in efforts during the mid-1990s. Since then, research has advanced an understanding of creative performance[61] and importantly, organisations have gone through a radical set of changes.[62]

Leadership of creative efforts calls for an integrative style — a style that permits the leader to orchestrate expertise, people and relationships in a way that brings new ideas into being.[63] This integrative style involves three crucial elements.

The first major element of an integrative style of leadership is *idea generation*. Most of the available research on creative leadership stresses the role of the leader in facilitating idea generation. The leader should apply creative problem-solving techniques or embrace intellectual stimulation as they look towards guiding others. They should also support new ideas, become involved with people who are developing ideas and grant these people freedom to pursue their ideas.

Cognitive complexity is the underlying assumption that those high in cognitive complexity process information differently and perform certain tasks better than less cognitively complex people.

Absorptive capacity is the ability to learn.

Adaptive capacity refers to the ability to change.

Managerial wisdom is the ability to perceive variations in the environment and having an understanding of social actors and their relationships.

Innovation leadership is leadership that makes a difference in the nature and success of creative efforts.[58]

Leaders should also construct an environment that is conducive to idea creation. They must ensure diversity in the group and open communications. Through role modelling, crisis management and policy decisions, they should seek to create a climate and a culture where people are likely to generate and pursue new ideas. One of the more important findings that has emerged from recent studies on creativity is that ideas — especially a plethora of diverse ideas — are a mixed blessing in organisational settings.[64]

Idea structuring is the second major element of an integrative style of leadership. It refers to guidance about the technical and organisational merits of work and involves setting output expectations and identifying and integrating projects to be pursued. It does not entail day-to-day direction or close supervision of work, since research indicates this kind of leadership inhibits innovation.[65] Idea structuring activities — in contrast to the idea generation process — tend to be indirect and to entail the creation of action or project frameworks that maximise worker autonomy. For example, it may be more useful to set a deadline than to show someone how to meet this deadline.

The third component of an integrative style of leadership is *idea promotion*. This involves gathering support from the broader organisation for the creative enterprise 'as a whole' as well as the implementation of a specific idea or project. For leaders of creative people, promotional activities are essential, primarily because they ensure resources needed to carry out work are available. Idea promotion places the leader in a persuasive mode where ideas must be placed in the context of broader organisational strategies if they are to succeed.[66]

One attractive feature of the multilevel approach is that it acknowledges the complex — and perhaps somewhat contradictory — nature of creative leadership. However, a question remains. How can any one person effectively pursue three distinct types of activities at the same time? Casimir[67] proposes a response to this query. Leaders might stress idea generation when addressing issues early on in cycle projects, before becoming more concerned with idea structuring and idea promotion as projects reach later phases of development. As attractive as this shift strategy might be, it may not always prove effective.[68] For example, a leader who is working on a highly complex project may not be able to acquire the relevant advanced technical expertise that is needed to appraise new ideas and the practical production expertise that is needed to structure production activities related to the project.

Gronn[69] and Kidder[70] suggest leaders may cope with these competing demands by forming leadership teams. Indeed, by applying a team approach to cope with these multiple, potentially competing aspects of creative leadership, the diversity needed for effective internal and external interaction is assured. For example, to encourage idea generation, leaders of creative ventures may select assistants who have a different technical background and approach to the leader. This is an uncommon strategy, but one that is suited to the demands of creative leadership. Moreover, the leader of creative people may need to give more attention to issues of climate and culture as these issues provide a context for idea generation.

Mumford, Scott, Gaddis and Strange have developed two theories about the indirect nature of leaders structuring activities.

1. Change in creative groups is most likely to be brought about by defining new projects for which support is needed, or by providing support to existing projects with people from different technical backgrounds.
2. Leaders will prove more effective if they are actively engaged in the initial project definition. This is because early involvement reduces ambiguity and allows the leader to frame the problem in terms of organisational needs.

The authors assert it may be impossible for leaders to promote idea generation or to effectively integrate projects if high levels of personalised conflict exist in groups. An implication of this is that successful leaders of creative ventures may go to unusual lengths to minimise disruptive interpersonal conflict — while simultaneously creating technical conflict. Mumford, Scott, Gaddis and Strange also argue that while leaders must encourage diversity and technical debates in idea generation, that idea promotion — vis-à-vis persuasive requirements — needs to have a common, consistent message. Because of this, leaders of creative people may have different expectations for internal and external interactions, with debate encouraged internally but not outside the creative group.[71]

Crisis leadership

Catastrophic events and unforeseen disasters — such as 9/11 in the United States, severe floods and fires in Australia, earthquakes in New Zealand and the multiple Malaysia Airlines disasters in 2014 — have brought crisis leadership to the fore. Although leader cognition has been studied widely,[72] it is important to appreciate studies examining the 'thinking' of leaders under conditions of crisis or change are rare.[73] In recent years, scholars have begun to ask 'When does leadership make a difference towards group and organisational performance?' The answer appears to be straightforward. Leadership makes a difference under conditions of crisis.

Previous theoretical and empirical work suggests the occurrence of a crisis may significantly affect the relationship between leaders and their followers.[74] The plethora of emotions felt in the aftermath of a crisis — including shock, confusion, fear, anger, sorrow, and anxiety — can have a potentially devastating effect on individual self concepts as well as on collective organisational or even national identity. Times of crisis enhance the likelihood followers:

1. will want to invest increased faith in leaders
2. will view their leaders as more powerful
3. will identify more with their leaders as a coping mechanism.[75]

A crisis is a low-probability, high-impact event that threatens the viability of an organisation. It is characterised by ambiguity of cause, effect and means of resolution; as well as by a belief decisions must be made swiftly.[76] A crisis implies a change from standard operating procedures. This 'change' has significant implications for performance and people and may potentially have both positive and negative consequences.

A study has found crises have an effect on peoples' perceptions of and need for leadership. The findings suggested peoples' perceptions of leaders and leader-impact on group performance are heightened in crisis conditions.[77] Other research indicates the emergence of a charismatic or visionary leader during a crisis has an impact on organisational performance.[78]

Research shows leaders play a central role in crises through the sensemaking and the viable mental models.[79] In *sensemaking*, leaders create a structure (a cognitive structure) for understanding and responding to the high stakes change events broached by crisis situations. The articulation of the sensemaking system reduces stress, clarifies the causes and goals operating in the situation, and provides a basis for integrating actions among multiple parties. Furthermore, the fundamental importance of leaders' formulation of viable mental models provides a basis for sensemaking.[80] This is noteworthy, because research suggests that underlying leader vision, and leader sensemaking activities, is the formation of a prescriptive mental model.

The prescriptive mental model articulates an idealised state for understanding the nature and significance of crisis or change events. The prescriptive mental model in essence provides the 'solution' to the problems broached by crisis. It serves to identify critical goals and key causes, it provides a structure around which followers can interpret the change event and the desirability of various actions. And, it, by creating understanding, both reduces stress and bounds the problem. Thus, the basis of 'solutions' to crises lies in the leaders' formulation of a viable prescriptive mental model.[81] Prescriptive mental models — models bounded by a crisis — may be seen to be an overarching template plan[82] that provides a framework for understanding and acting on the crisis event through sensemaking.

Emerging research also examines the role of knowledge structures in **crisis leadership**. It has been suggested case-based or autobiographical knowledge is likely to equip a leader with the best basis for problem solving under crisis conditions.[83] There are several reasons case-based knowledge may be applied by a leader who is attempting to solve a crisis. Case-based knowledge represents information elicited from past experience. Case-based knowledge structures are typically held to be complex, including information about goals, outcomes, critical causes, contingencies, and restrictions.[84] Case-based knowledge is also interpersonal. So, it may include information about people in a situation as well as details on how they are affected by it, what their involvement is and what their goals are. Information about both the 'objective' and 'subjective' aspects of a situation are embedded in case-based knowledge structures. Case-based knowledge appears most applicable in crisis leadership for the following three reasons.

Crisis leadership is leadership during a traumatic period or event.

1. *Case-based knowledge is known to be integral to planning.*[85] Leaders — in thinking about crises — must formulate a plan.
2. *Case-based knowledge is contextually based.* It provides information that is relevant (at least in principle) to generating viable responses to crisis situations.
3. *It incorporates models.* Embedded in case-based knowledge are models that might be used to understand and respond to the crisis at hand.

Some support for the application of case-based knowledge in resolving change events has been provided in studies.[86] Hershey et al.[87] obtained 'think aloud' protocols from financial experts preparing retirement plans. The content analysis of this protocol data indicated that plans tended to be based on experiential cases. In fact, errors arose from the imposition of prototype cases in the formulation of these plans. Other work by Isenberg[88] compared managers with varying levels of experience as they progressed through a case study. Isenberg's findings indicated more experienced leaders (for example, senior managers) differed from their less experienced counterparts (for example, business students) by virtue of the application of general case models and the analysis of conditions bearing on the application of these models.[89] Further evidence is needed on leaders' use of case models in resolving crises or change events. However, the foregoing studies indicate the assumption that leaders' thinking about crises is case-based is plausible.

In crises, leader actions are not always steady and consistently directed towards a clear objective. At any time, leader actions may appear erratic, halting, and incomplete — as leaders stumble towards what they hope is at least a slightly better future. However, patterns emerge over time. In a crisis, it is never only a leader standing above subordinates. Leaders are always also involved with superiors, peers and subordinates in a collective influence to cope with a crisis and to change the context in which it occurs. While conventional leadership dimensions have been shown to be important, it is increasingly assumed these do not have to be provided by a single leader.[90] Osborn, Hunt and Jauch offer a specific proposition. They argue in an organisational crisis, both individual and collective leadership are needed to improve the situation.[91]

Researchers have demonstrated situational variables (such as a crisis) may make the emergence of charismatic leadership more or less likely to occur.[92] In these studies, a crisis has been defined as a situation in which necessary resources are in short supply, and so threaten organisational standing.[93] An early empirical study found that in a crisis situation; groups are more likely to be influenced by their leaders and to replace unsuccessful leaders.[94] Moreover, the mere presence of a crisis has caused followers to choose leaders based on charisma and to attribute charisma to leaders.[95] So, a leader's effectiveness is more likely to be attributed to their charisma in a crisis situation.

While there is no doubt leader affect, emotional support and vision are important aspects of leadership in a crisis; research suggests information also plays a key role.[96] Two informational dimensions of leadership are *the patterning of attention* and *network development*. The patterning of attention involves subtle dialog by leaders concerning the interpretations of a crisis as well as definitions of success and relevant processes for change. The patterning of attention is more mundane than the emphasised transformational, visionary, or charismatic aspects of leadership. Transformational leadership involves using values, visions and emotions to evoke unusual effort.[97] These appeal to hopes, dreams and to the 'right-brain'.[98] In a crisis, the patterning of attention involves more of a left-brain linear type of thinking that is typical of the way an engineer or organisational scientist might think.

The patterning of attention involves not telling others what to do — unlike the methodology that is consistent with leadership dimensions such as initiating structure and directiveness. A relatively clear idea of what others should be doing and how individual actions fit into a 'whole' is needed to initiate structure. Directiveness is appropriate in settings where the leader knows where the system is going and how to get there; while subordinates do not. In contrast to these approaches, the patterning of attention involves isolating and communicating information that is important and is given attention from an endless stream of events, actions, and outcomes. It calls on leaders to separate the more important from the less important. Osborn, Hunt and Jauch[99] suggest *all* leaders involved in complex organisations practise the patterning of attention; however, they argue it is most important in crises and most applicable at the top of complex systems.

Network leadership is the establishment of direct and indirect interpersonal communication and information patterns of influence by a leader or group of leaders. The prior work by Hunt and Ropo[100] shows that there are dialogs up, down and across the organisation as to what are the really important aspects of a crisis. Established interpersonal network connections influence the patterning of attention, as individuals seek understanding via dialog and discussion. Networks are also altered when those defining a crisis and the processes towards a solution seek out individuals who are in a position to resolve uncertainty. Osborn, Hunt and Jauch suggest that leaders interpret the crisis in developing meaningful targets for improvement.[101]

OBin**Action**

Preparing for a crisis

Even though it is impossible to anticipate a crisis, crisis management expert Michael Regester says there are steps a company can take to prepare for one. The founding partner of a London-based crisis and issues management consultancy, Regester summarises the critical success factors for planning for a crisis as:

- cataloguing potential crisis situations
- devising policies for their prevention
- formulating strategies and tactics for potential crises
- identifying who will be most affected by crises
- devising effective communication channels to those affected to limit damage to the organisation's reputation
- testing everything.[102]

Moral leadership

All of us are currently aware of recent concerns with various moral leadership problems, such as those with Enron and those in various government, religious and other organisations. As these problems have gained increasing attention, there has also been a stronger emphasis in the literature on topics such as ethical leadership, authentic leadership, servant leadership and spiritual leadership. These are the topics covered in our treatment of moral leadership.

Ethical leadership

Figure 11.7 summarises the similarities and differences among ethical, authentic, spiritual and transformational leadership. A key similarity cutting across all these dimensions is role modelling, which is important in social learning theory. Altruism, or concern for others, and integrity are also important similarities. In terms of differences, authentic leaders stress authenticity and self awareness and tend to be more transactional than do the other leadership aspects. Ethical leaders emphasise moral concerns, while spiritual leaders stress visioning, hope, and faith, as well as work as a vocation. Transformational leaders emphasise values, vision and intellectual stimulation. Related literature specifies a number of ethical leadership propositions and suggests a number of topic areas particularly important for ethical leadership. In addition, some preliminary work has been done on measuring ethical leadership. Taken as a whole, it is obvious that any of these related approaches are important and ripe for systematic empirical and conceptual development. Even servant leadership would lend itself to further developments if those most strongly emphasising it were so inclined.[103]

> **Ethical leadership** is leadership that abides by core values and standards acceptable to both the institution and society.

	Key similarities with ethical leadership	Key differences from ethical leadership
Authentic leadership	• Concern for others (altruism) • Ethical decision making • Integrity • Role modelling	• Ethical leaders emphasise moral management (more transactional) and 'other' awareness • Authentic leaders emphasise authenticity and self-awareness
Spiritual leadership	• Concern for others (altruism) • Integrity • Role modelling	• Ethical leaders emphasise moral management • Spiritual leaders emphasise visioning, hope/faith; work as vocation
Transformational	• Concern for others (altruism) • Ethical decision making • Integrity • Role modelling	• Ethical leaders emphasise ethical standards and moral management (more transactional) • Transformational leaders emphasise vision, values and intellectual stimulation

FIGURE 11.7 Similarities and differences between ethical, spiritual, authentic and transformational theories of leadership

Source: Michael E Brown and Linda K Trevino, 'Ethical Leadership: A Review and Future Directions', *The Leadership Quarterly 17.6* (December 2006) p. 598.

Authentic leadership

Authentic leadership essentially argues 'know thyself'.[104] It involves both *owning* one's personal experiences (values, thoughts, emotions and beliefs) and acting in accordance with one's true self (expressing what you really think and believe, and acting accordingly). Although no one is perfectly authentic, more authenticity is something to strive for. It reflects the unobstructed operation of one's true or core self day-to-day. It also underlies virtually all other aspects of leadership, regardless of the particular theory or model involved.

Those high in authenticity are argued to have optimal self-esteem — or genuine, true, stable and congruent self-esteem — as opposed to the fragile self-esteem based heavily on outside responses. Consider the psychological wellbeing emphasised in the positive psychology literature: there is self-efficacy, which you will recall is an individual's belief about the likelihood of successfully completing a specific task; *optimism*, which is the expectation of positive outcomes; *hope*, which is the tendency to look for alternative pathways to reach a desired goal; and *resilience*, which is the ability to bounce back from failure and keep forging ahead.[105] An increase in any one of these is seen as increasing the others. These are important for a leader to demonstrate, and such demonstration is believed to positively influence his or her followers. The modelling in social learning is quite relevant here. Indeed, some

> **Authentic leadership** involves both owning one's personal experiences (values, thoughts, emotions and beliefs) and acting in accordance with one's true self (expressing what you really think and believe, and acting accordingly).

have termed the positive modelling behaviour of followers as authentic followership to accompany authentic leadership.

Authentic leadership is now beginning to generate conceptual and empirical work, with more of the former than the latter. Therefore, it is difficult to go much further in the current discussion. However, there does appear to be enough interest so that the idea is more than a fad. Furthermore, as mentioned, it appears to bear a family resemblance to concepts such as servant leadership, spiritual leadership, and ethical leadership in general. We now turn to servant and spiritual leadership.

Servant leadership

Servant leadership involves deliberately choosing to serve others and prioritising other people's needs, aspirations and interests.

In recent times, some researchers have attempted to rejuvenate a relatively old concept of leadership: servant leadership. **Servant leadership** involves leaders making a deliberate choice to serve others and to put other people's needs, aspirations and interests above their own.[106] The servant leader operates on the assumption that 'I am the leader, therefore I serve' rather than 'I am the leader, therefore I lead', which could be seen as more characteristic of most of the other perspectives on leadership.[107] People follow servant leaders freely because they trust them. One of the tests of servant leadership is how those served (led) benefit. Servant leadership is usually seen as a philosophical movement and it has not been systematically empirically tested, nor are its proponents interested in such testing. Regardless, its guiding philosophy is consistent with that of the other moral leadership family members discussed here.

Spears identified ten critical characteristics of the servant leader. Many are similar to the characteristics identified in other models but with a very strong focus on the followers.

1. Servant leaders must reinforce their communication skills by *listening* to others.
2. Servant leaders strive to understand and *empathise* with others.
3. Learning to *heal* oneself and others is a unique characteristic.
4. Self-*awareness* strengthens the servant leader — as it does all leaders.
5. Servant leaders rely on *persuasion* rather than positional authority.
6. Servant leaders are able to *conceptualise*, to see beyond the day-to-day and to dream great dreams.
7. *Foresight* is the characteristic that enables servant leaders to understand the lessons of the past, the realities of the present, and the likely consequences of a decision for the future.
8. In these days of corporate distrust, *stewardship* is a most attractive element of servant leadership, particularly if it can be combined with foresight.
9. Servant leaders are *committed* to the personal, professional and spiritual growth of each individual in the organisation.
10. Servant leaders seek to identify means for *building community* among those who work within any given institution.[108]

Spiritual leadership

Spiritual leadership is inclusive of religious and ethically based values, attitudes, and behaviours.

Spiritual leadership can be seen as a field of inquiry within the broader setting of workplace spirituality.[109] Neither of these fields currently has a strong research base. Western religious theology and practice and leadership ethics and values provide much of the organisational base. In addition, the literature does not agree on whether spirituality and religion are the same. When they are seen to differ, organised religions provide rituals, routines, and ceremonies that can provide a vehicle for achieving spirituality. Of course, one could be religious by following religious rituals but lack spirituality, or one could reflect spirituality without being religious.

Even though we have argued that spiritual leadership does not yet have a strong research base, there has been some recent work with the beginnings of such a base. Not surprisingly, the work is termed Spiritual Leadership Theory, or SLT. It is a causal leadership approach for organisational transformation designed to create an intrinsically motivated, learning organisation. Spiritual leadership includes values, attitudes and behaviours required to intrinsically motivate self and others to have a sense of spiritual survival through calling and membership. In other words, self and others experience meaning in their lives, believe they make a difference, and feel understood and appreciated. Such a sense of leader and follower survival tends to create value congruence across the strategic, empowered team and at the individual level; it ultimately encourages higher levels of organisational commitment, productivity and employee wellbeing.

Some key terms in figure 11.8 are considered qualities of spiritual leadership: *vision* defines the destination and journey, reflects high ideals and encourages hope and faith; *altruistic love* involves trust or loyalty, as well as forgiveness, acceptance, gratitude, honesty, courage and humility from the organisation and its followers; and *hope/faith* includes endurance, perseverance, doing what it takes and having stretch goals.

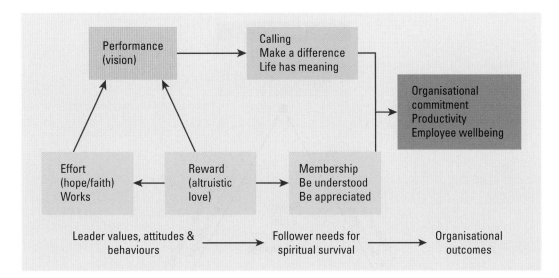

FIGURE 11.8 Causal model of spiritual leadership theory

Source: Lewis W Fry, Steve Vitucci and Marie Cedillo, 'Spiritual Leadership and Army Transformation Theory, Measurement, and Establishing a Baseline', *The Leadership Quarterly* 16.5 (2005) p. 838.

Sustainability leadership

Sustainability leadership, as proposed here, goes well beyond currently accepted views of leadership. 'Sustainability leaders take conscious actions, individually and collectively, leading to outcomes that nurture, support and sustain healthy economic, environmental and social systems.'[110] Furthermore sustainability leadership doesn't have to be centered on the leader(s) of the organisation. Any person who takes on responsibility for understanding and taking sustainability actions qualifies as a sustainability leader. Hence, sustainability leadership is not dependent upon the formal position of an individual, nor the acknowledgement of political and social–economic influence. A sustainability leader has an understanding of interconnectivity, and that people and organisations function within a dynamic, ever-changing environment. Sustainability leadership reflects an emerging awareness among people who select to lead their organisations in a manner that accounts for its impact on the environment, people and society, including the health of local and global communities. The concept of 'sustainability' tends to be a personal value of the sustainability leader, and their actions are generally grounded in these personal values.

Sustainability leaders are very good at creating opportunities for individuals and teams to come together and produce their own answers and to learn, explore and develop appropriate actions to address sustainability challenges. Therefore, they engage actively in actions 'with' others. They are very effective as participants in collaborative experiences — without drawing on their formal positions of power — to find solutions to sustainability challenges.[111]

The 'triple bottom line' comprises socially and environmentally responsible and economically viable strategies, which are critical elements of sustainable business. Individuals in sustainable organisations (including leaders) tend to have primary interest in one of these areas: environmental awareness and actions; social consciousness service activities including a regard for human resources; and responsible economic and business actions and activities. For example, an environmental friendly initiative could create significant financial saving in the organisation and also inspire staff morale. Business leaders are increasingly finding that by focusing on one of the three elements, the other two elements are also enhanced. Munasinghe visualised the integration of these activities as a triangle (figure 11.9).[112]

Each element is indicated on a corner of the triangle, although each corner is also an integral part of a holistic approach to sustainability. Therefore, it is essential that leaders should understand the impact of changing one of the elements.

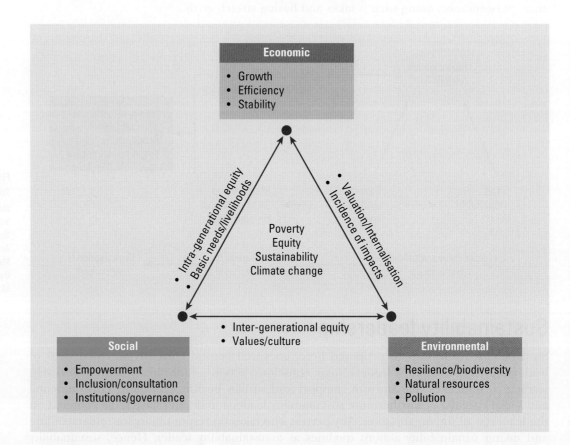

FIGURE 11.9 Sustainable development triangle

Source: Munasinghe (2007).

Sustainability

Views from a sustainability leader

The list of sustainability awards Rockcote, an Australian-owned, multi-award-winning company, has won is impressive. Employing about 60 staff, the company is recognised as a leader in the development, manufacture and distribution of environmentally friendly coloured renders, paints and coating systems for the residential and commercial market. The company boasts an impressive 18 per cent market share of the national exterior render market, with clients ranging from individual homeowners to multimillion-dollar companies. Owned and managed by Bob Cameron and his wife Chris Cameron (Chris won the 'business entrepreneur' title at the inaugural national 100 women of influence awards), the company has been on a journey of reducing its environmental footprint and having a significant impact upon its community over a

Questions and answers concerning the emerging leadership perspectives

In addition to examining and contrasting the core themes of traditional and new leadership approaches, it is important to answer questions concerning the role of more recent leadership approaches in the workplace. It seems all the new and emerging leadership approaches include vision in one way or another.

Can people be trained in new leadership? Research in this area argues that training in new leadership is possible. Bass and his colleagues have put a lot of work into such training efforts. They have created one workshop that lasts from three to five days, with later follow-up. Initially, leaders are given feedback on their scores on Bass's measures. Then the leaders devise improvement programs to strengthen their weaknesses and work with the trainers to develop their leadership skills. Bass and Avolio report findings that demonstrate beneficial effects from this training. They also report on team training and programs tailored to individual organisations' needs.[113] Similarly, Conger and Kanungo propose training to develop the kinds of behaviour summarised in their model.[114]

Regional leadership development in the Pacific

OBinAction

An example of how government and the private sector can collaborate on leadership development is the Emerging Pacific Leaders' Dialogue (EPLD). This regional leadership development initiative is funded by both government agencies and the private sector across the Pacific. It is committed to inspire and uplift proven leaders, as well as those with high leadership potential. EPLD participants are high-calibre, mid-career men and women who are drawn from business, government, trade unions, education, and the community service sector. With the aim of promoting regional understanding and cooperation through fostering important relationships across sectors, nations and territories, the initiative focuses on themes such as 'Navigating our Future Together'. The significance of leadership is central to economic and social development, regional cooperation, the environment, business and industry, and the strengthening of communities. Supported in particular by Australia and New Zealand, the EPLD aims to develop participants' leadership skills and promote a culture of leadership across the Pacific that is driven by an alignment of values and good governance.

Finally, a couple of approaches with a special emphasis on vision emphasise training. Kouzes and Posner report the results of a week-long training program. The program involved training of leaders on five dimensions oriented around developing, communicating and reinforcing a shared vision. According to Kouzes and Posner, leaders showed an average 15 per cent increase in these visionary behaviours ten months after participating in the program.[115] Similarly, Sashkin has developed a leadership approach that emphasises various aspects of vision and organisational culture change. Sashkin discusses ways to go about training leaders to be more visionary and to enhance the culture change.[116] Many of the new leadership training programs involve a heavy, hands-on workshop emphasis so leaders do more than just read about vision.

- *Is new leadership always good?* No. Dark-side charismatics, such as Adolf Hitler, can have negative effects on the population of followers.
- *Is new leadership always needed?* No. Sometimes emphasis on a vision diverts energy from more important day-to-day activities.
- *Is new leadership by itself sufficient?* No. New leadership needs to be used in conjunction with traditional leadership.
- *Is new leadership important only at the top?* Probably not. While generally considered most important at the top levels, new leadership is considered by some experts to apply at all organisational levels.

Table 11.1 discusses themes in the new leadership literature. After this, the Ethical perspective looks at the integrity of company leaders and The effective manager 11.2 outlines 20 characteristics of strong leaders.

TABLE 11.1 Themes in the new leadership literature

Less emphasis needed on	Greater emphasis needed on
Planning	Having a vision/mission
Allocating responsibility	Infusing vision
Controlling and problem solving	Motivating and inspiring
Creating routine and equilibrium	Creating change and innovation
Retaining power	Empowering others
Creating compliance	Creating commitment
Emphasising contractual obligations	Stimulating extra effort
Exhibiting leader detachment and rationality	Exhibiting interest in others and intuition
Taking a reactive environmental approach	Taking a proactive environmental approach

THE **EffectiveManager** 11.2

20 characteristics of a strong leader

1. *A sense of mission.* They have clarity of vision and mission, which provides the foundation to excite and inspire others in the team and organisation.
2. *Values-based measurable goals.* They have clear understanding of the values of both the organisation and individuals and these form the foundations enabling them to meet clear objectives. At their instigation the concept of ownership of goals unifies members of the team and organisation and continues to provide everyone involved with a clear sense of direction towards a common cause.
3. *Action orientation.* They are entrepreneurial, innovative and forward in their thinking, and they launch quickly. An attitude of 'we can do it!' prevails.
4. *Courage.* They are initiators of action and attack, they persistently stay the course, believing that the future belongs to the risk-taker.
5. *Planners and strategists.* They are big-picture thinkers, taking the long view, looking at all options and outcomes. Concentrating on personal strengths and weaknesses, always aware of what could be the worst possible outcome, in order to avoid it.

6. *Inspiring and motivational.* They have an ability to draw out additional capacity within others, to arouse enthusiasm with total commitment. High levels of regular encouragement establish trust, confidence and loyalty.

7. *Committed to success.* They are future oriented, never thinking of failure, always learning from mistakes. They display a commitment to excellence and quality performances from products, services and people within the organisation.

8. *Communicators.* They have the ability to delegate with agreed clear responsibilities. Everyone in the team knows what is expected of him/her, consequently instilling meaning and purpose into a task.

9. *Low pressure salespeople.* They possess a sound knowledge of the 'relationship' selling process and how to apply it in daily interactions with customers and members of the organisation to make them feel significant. They have excellent presentation and negotiation skills, and are prepared to compromise, always looking for a win–win solution.

10. *Visibility.* Never hiding behind a desk, they are always available to meet and talk with customers and team members. They actively seek responses to improve products, services and leadership style and achieve targets.

11. *Team builder.* They demonstrate clear coaching skills, which enables them to determine ineffective team members. Only quality people are hired and continually developed via appropriate training strategies. Tasks are distributed to most suited individuals where they can make a major contribution. Open communication abounds.

12. *Prioritising.* They ensure measurable and prioritised key result areas are known by all.

13. *Love of leadership.* They are self-reliant with a strong desire to be in charge. If asked, they like to make their own decisions and to be in control; however, they also recognise that in order to lead, an individual must first be a good follower.

14. *High self-esteem and positive self-image.* They gain self-knowledge via introspection and this provides sensitivity towards the feelings of others in the team and organisation. Strong leaders know their limitations and honestly evaluate themselves.

15. *Self-motivated.* They have a strong vision, which provides them with the ability to continually set higher goals and gain commitment from others.

16. *Ask advice.* They are able to build upon their known strengths. They are prepared to seek advice from others in order to discover and compensate for any weaknesses.

17. *Power through cooperation.* They are always seeking talented people and developing relationships with key people. They understand and appreciate that if others are first helped to achieve their goals, they will in return assist you towards achieving your goals.

18. *Listening.* They learn to listen without interrupting, understanding that the more people are allowed to discuss an idea the more likely they will be committed towards its implementation.

19. *Integrity.* They understand that trust and credibility are the foundation of strong leadership. They always keep promises and are prepared to stand up for their beliefs, knowing that those beliefs are based upon sound personally-owned values.

20. *Continual personal growth.* They have a strong commitment towards life-learning and ensure their own self-improvement through reading, study and personal development courses.[117]

Since the recent exposure of so many unethical practices, much has been written about the need for more stringent corporate governance. Surely the ultimate onus should be on the organisations, their boards of directors and even the shareholders to exert pressure to ensure that those in a position of power are not given the opportunity to abuse that power. The question is 'how?' One suggestion is to hire leaders who practise honourable principles and live by the highest standards of honesty and integrity. Then, once such leaders are in place at all levels of the organisation; there needs to be an emphasis on 'frequent, candid information'. Continued sharing of both good and bad news builds trust — the other key to effective organisations. Employees are well aware everything won't always be rosy. From the launching pad of honest exchange between leader and follower, an organisation can do the 'right things right' and prosper in the process.[118]

The cost of absenteeism

Absenteeism in the Australian workplace has been estimated to cost Australian business up to $30 billion per year, according to Paul Dundon, managing director of Direct Health Solutions. Paul describes high absenteeism as a point of failure between the employee, their manager, and the organisation. The issue of workplace absenteeism was highlighted by Max Yasuda, president and chief executive of Toyota Motor Corporation Australia, when he lamented that as many as 30 per cent of employees in some sections of the Toyota plant would claim a 'sickie' when a Friday followed a Thursday public holiday. Australian Human Resource Institute president Peter Wilson recommends thoughtful

introspection for organisations with high absenteeism in order to identify signs of bad leadership that inevitably results in employees' reluctance to go to work.[119] With Toyota confirming that the company will cease its vehicle and engine production in Australia by the end of 2017, signalling the end of automotive manufacturing in Australia, the company argues that 'various negative factors, such as an extremely competitive market and a strong Australian dollar, together with forecasts of a reduction in the total scale of vehicle production in Australia have forced us to make this painful decision'.[120] It does make one wonder what role absenteeism has played in the mix of factors leading to its decision to cease vehicle production in Australia.

Gender, age and cultural diversity — current issues in leadership

Much of the leadership theory and research has been conducted within a North American context and has focused primarily on masculine models of leadership. Given the globalisation of business, the increasing cultural diversity of domestic societies, the ageing of the workforce, and the importance of women in the workforce and the community, this is a significant gap in leadership studies.

Gender and leadership

Women are increasingly accessing leadership roles that have traditionally been occupied by men. In reviewing recent research on transformational leadership, we mentioned that Bass indicates that women are more disposed towards transformational leadership than are men. This tendency is illustrated by female leaders who are vision driven, and who emphasise both the importance of empowering employees and participative forms of leadership, and the links between business and the community.

ETHICAL
Perspective

Companies with few females in governing positions may be short-changing their investors

Asian societies have made a lot of progress towards educating and offering opportunities to women; however, when it comes to the emotional issue of wealth succession and distribution in family businesses, it often becomes clear that the lack of women participation in family business governance is a still a major problem.[121] However, companies with few females in governing positions may actually be short-changing their investors. A recent study, which created some controversy with regard to its findings, compared what males and females bring to firm governance. It was found that female directors achieved significantly higher scores than their male counterparts with regard to making consistently fair decisions when competing interests are at stake. Since directors are responsible for making decisions in the best interest of the organisation while taking into account the perspectives of multiple stakeholders, females would appear to be an important resource for making these types of decisions and making them more effectively. The researchers support the view that women will be most effective in the boardroom if they are simply authentic and do not try to model their behaviour after men.[122]

Research on the difference between women and male leaders is mixed. Gary Yukl has reviewed the research on leadership and gender differences, and concludes that it is 'inconclusive'.[123] Others argue that, rather than a focus on gender differences, the gender blindness of leadership models needs a fundamental re-examination. Sinclair argues that we need to review the relationship between heroic masculinity and corporate leadership, and that if this is not done, leadership will remain the privilege of a homogeneous elite. Such homogeneity in leadership, in the face of dramatic changes in workforce and customer diversity, is a potential liability.[124]

In Australia, recent findings from the Australian Business Leadership Survey revealed that female executives tended to record significantly higher mean scores on all aspects of transformational leadership. They also tended to score higher on effectiveness and satisfaction in their leadership approach, compared to male executives.[125]

The difficulties women still face in progressing up the corporate hierarchy (referred to as the 'glass ceiling') may have led to the unique and diverse paths women have taken to leadership positions. Some transfer into leadership positions from other fields (rather than rising within a corporate structure); others become leaders of organisations through succession in family business. Still others start their own small businesses, which may then grow into substantial corporations.[126]

On a wider international scale, a recent study on Arab women's conceptions of leadership compared women's leadership authority values in Oman, the United Arab Emirates and Lebanon. It found evidence of common leadership authority values in the Gulf countries (Oman and the UAE). Lebanon, meanwhile, was distinguished by relatively low levels of 'traditional' authority, and very high levels of 'charismatic' authority. The findings demonstrate important regional similarities and difference in leadership authority values in the 'Arab world'.[127]

Age and leadership

As we grow older, our leadership skills change; however, do they improve or deteriorate? Generally speaking, our slowing cognitive ability and other signs of ageing start to affect the supposed worth of our judgement and decision making. Others contend that as we age, we tend to become naturally experienced and wise. We tend to have a better understanding of the 'workings' of the world, and seem more capable of drawing on our life experience in making more effective decisions and providing better leadership.

What Would You Do?

The trust predicament

One of the best examples of how trust can impact both speed and cost is when Berkshire Hathaway, CEO Warren Buffett acquired McLane Distribution — a $23 billion company — from Wal-Mart in 2003. Typically, this type of deal would take months to finalise and cost millions to complete due diligence processes. In this case, both parties operated with high trust and the deal was made in one two-hour meeting and a handshake and finalised in less than a month. Management guru, Stephen Covey, argued trust is what separates leaders from managers and that the first job of any leader is to inspire trust and secondly to extend it. When trust goes down, speed goes down along with

it, and cost goes up. When there is a trust problem, relationships suffer, production is slow, customers leave, employee turnover goes up, stocks plummet and the costs are enormous. The negative effects of trust in organisations, or as Covey so eloquently put it 'trust taxes' are: redundancy in the form of unnecessary duplication; bureaucracy in the form of complex and cumbersome rules and policies; disruptive office politics that divide the culture of the organisation; disengagement in the form of withholding talent, energy and passion; employee turnover in the form of losing value people in the organisation; churn in the form of other stakeholders aside from employees leaving the organisation; and fraud in the form of dishonesty, sabotage and disruption. All of these are tremendously costly to an organisation. Covey reflected on the question of what is the role of leaders with respect to trust? He came to the conclusion that first, the leader needs to recognise the business case for trust and avoid being an obstacle in the process; second, the leader needs to personally model trust through character competence and behaviour, hence achieving results in a manner that inspires trust; and third, the leader needs to work hard to align organisational systems and structures around trust.[128]

Questions

1. Consider the perils (or taxes) of trust outlined above and consider what the benefits of a leader inspiring high trust in an organisation would be.
2. Discuss some examples of the impact low trust has had on you in the past.

Cultural differences

Arguably, the worth with which the supposed benefits of age are seen is culturally determined. Africans generally ascribe higher status to their older citizens; the average age of African leaders tends to be significantly higher than in the West.[129] The Chinese and other Asian countries tend to have a similar view of age, but with markedly different economic fortunes. Table 11.2 below shows this comparison of African and Western leaders as recorded during July 2014.

TABLE 11.2 Themes in the new leadership literature

Africa	The West
Ibrahim Mahlab (Egypt): age 65	Barrack Obama (United States): age 53
Robert Mugabe (Zimbabwe): age 90	David Cameron (UK): age 47
Hage Geingob (Namibia): age 73	Vladimir Putin (Russia): age 61
Michael Sata (Zambia): age 77	Stephen Harper (Canada): age 55
Raila Odinga (Kenya): age 69	Tony Abbott (Australia): age 56
Ellen Johnson Sirleaf (Liberia): age 75	Manuel Valls (France): age 52
Jacob Zuma (South Africa): age 72	

Taking the age issue one step further, the important question is: Does maturity in years in a leader represent valuable experience, or does it suggest it's time to make way for someone younger with fresh ideas? A fair answer would be to judge each individual on his or her merits, rather than fall into the trap of stereotyping.

The issue of age and experience versus youth and energy will always be a challenge in leadership, yet the collaboration of executives at both ends of the age spectrum can bring a variety of qualities and perspectives to the organisation.

Leadership and culture

Using a similar approach to that of Geert Hofstede,[130] Robert House and his colleagues embarked on an ambitious research project involving 62 countries. The GLOBE project investigated how cultural values are related to organisational practices, conceptions of leadership, the economic competitiveness of societies, and the human condition of an organisation's members. More than 17 000 managers participated worldwide. Some of the main results of the project indicated that cultural values contributed either positively or negatively to the leadership profiles. For example, power-distance values were found to be a negative predictor of charismatic/value-based and participative leadership, but gender egalitarianism proved to be a positive predictor of the same. One of the key recommendations of the project was that leaders need to be aware of the links between cultural values and leadership practices.[131] Other recent cross-national comparative studies have also reinforced the relevance of culture in leadership.[132]

International
SPOTLIGHT

The challenges of leading cross-cultural virtual project teams

Working in geographically distributed project teams within a matrix organisation is a norm in many organisations these days. For example, the project leader may lead the team from Malaysia, but the rest of the team may be scattered across Australia, New Zealand, Hong Kong, Singapore, South Africa and other parts of the globe. The team may work together virtually for say three to five years and only meet face to face about once a year. The team may consist of managers across several functions such as marketing, sales, technical development, and so on. Leaders in this situation tend to experience a range of challenges.[133] First, often they have to lead people over which they have no real authority. In doing so, they have to develop trust and respect to enable them to interact successfully with each other and provide each other with what they need to develop the product. Second, the virtual nature of communication makes aligning time zone differences very problematic and a lack of face-to-face contact brings its own challenges. Navigating the problems of inadequate technologies such as breakdowns in video conferencing could pose a problem, which makes face-to-face communication once every so often essential. Third, managing the task is key in ensuring everyone possesses the same level of information, particularly when things are moving fast in a certain stage of the project. Finally, managing language and cultural issues could be problematic and the leader needs to be aware that different patterns of recognition and interpretation exist; for example, learning to read between the lines in meetings becomes an essential skill.[134]

Question

If you were leading a virtual cross-cultural project, explain what skills you need to cope effectively with the challenges outlined above.

Summary

Differences between leadership and management

Leadership and management differ in that management is designed to promote stability or to make the organisation run smoothly, while the role of leadership is to promote adaptive change. A leadership function corresponds to each of the management functions but is carried out differently.

Traditional and new leadership differ. Traditional leadership approaches range from trait and behaviour approaches that give leadership a central role in performance and human resource maintenance outputs to various approaches that combine leadership with situational contingencies to predict outputs. The new leadership differs from traditional leadership primarily in that it emphasises vision and change, and focuses on attribution, charisma, transformation and related concepts.

Trait and behavioural theories of leadership

Trait and behavioural leadership approaches argue that leader traits or behaviours have a major impact on leadership outcomes. Traits are more innate and harder to change than behaviours. They are also often used with behaviours in a situational contingency or new leadership approach.

Situational contingency theories of leadership

Leader situational contingency approaches argue that leadership, in combination with various situational variables, has a major impact on outcomes. Sometimes, as in the case of the substitutes for leadership approach, the role of the situational variables replaces that of leadership to the point that leadership has little or no impact in itself. Fiedler's contingency theory, House's path–goal theory, and Hersey and Blanchard's Situational Leadership® theory are other approaches that consider the impact not just of leadership but of various situational contingencies.

Charismatic leadership and transformational leadership

Attribution theory overlaps traditional and new leadership by emphasising the symbolic aspects of leadership. These aspects are an especially important part of the new leadership, charismatic, transformational and related perspectives, according to which followers tend to attribute heroic or extraordinary leadership abilities to a leader when they observe certain behaviours from that leader. These attributions can then help transform followers to achieve goals that go beyond their own self-interest and, in turn, help transform the organisation.

Charismatic leadership approaches emphasise the kind of leader–follower social relationship summarised above. Two of these approaches emphasised earlier are House and associates' approach and the work of Conger and Kanungo.

Transformational leadership approaches are typically broader than charismatic ones. Bass and associates' transformational approach is a particularly well-known theory that includes charisma as one of its dimensions. It separates vision-oriented transformational leadership from day-to-day transactional leadership, and argues that the two work in combination. Transformational and charismatic leadership, and the new leadership in general are important because they facilitate change in our increasingly fast-moving world.

Emerging perspectives in leadership

Some of the emerging theoretical leadership themes are recent extensions of the contemporary approaches mentioned above, while others are quite new. These emerging leadership themes are mostly still in relatively early stages of development, regardless of their linkage to contemporary approaches. Full-range leadership theory, self leadership, shared leadership, strategic leadership, innovation leadership and crisis leadership can be classified as forms of *integrative leadership*. In contrast, ethical leadership, authentic leadership, servant leadership and spiritual leadership are types of *moral leadership*.

Diversity issues in leadership

Western, masculine models have dominated leadership theory and research. Such a limitation is significant given the increasing diversity of the workforce and society in general. In Australia, the progress of women's representation in organisational leadership positions at executive and board level has been slow, but recently women have gained a greater presence in leadership roles across many industries, some of which were traditionally male dominated. We are also seeing much younger company leaders, both male and female, who are excelling in their field. Recent research has explored the need to recognise the impact of culture on leadership styles and the appropriateness of approaches across different cultures.

CHAPTER 11 study guide

Key terms

absorptive capacity, *p. 424*

achievement-oriented leadership, *p. 410*

active management by exception, *p. 416*

adaptive capacity, *p. 424*

authentic leadership, *p. 429*

charisma, *p. 416*

charismatic leaders, *p. 414*

cognitive complexity, *p. 424*

contingent rewards, *p. 416*

contextual variables, *p. 419*

crisis leadership, *p. 427*

directive leadership, *p. 410*

ethical leadership, *p. 429*

formal leadership, *p. 403*

full-range leadership theory (FRLT), *p. 419*

individualised consideration, *p. 417*

informal leadership, *p. 403*

innovation leadership, *p. 424*

inspiration, *p. 416*

intellectual stimulation, *p. 417*

laissez faire leadership, *p. 416*

leaders, *p. 403*

leadership, *p. 403*

least preferred coworker (LPC) scale, *p. 407*

managerial wisdom, *p. 424*

managers, *p. 403*

participative leadership, *p. 410*

passive management by exception, *p. 416*

servant leadership, *p. 430*

shared leadership, *p. 420*

situational control, *p. 407*

spiritual leadership, *p. 430*

strategic leadership, *p. 421*

substitutes for leadership, *p. 412*

supportive leadership, *p. 410*

transactional leadership, *p. 416*

transformational leadership, *p. 416*

Review questions

1. Review and discuss the pros and cons of the trait and behavioural approaches to leadership.
2. Discuss the reasons for the popularity of the contingency approach to leadership.
3. Explain how leadership and trust may be related.
4. Discuss the contemporary inspirational approaches to leadership.
5. Review and explain each of the emerging leadership approaches.

Application questions

1. You will recall that we discussed that leadership appears in two forms, *formal leadership* and *informal leadership*. Think of a situation in which you have been part of a group or a team, maybe at work or in your recreational time. Reflect on that situation — its actual dynamics and the outcome. Identify the *formal* and *informal leadership* roles and how they played out in your example. How did each of the leaders contribute to the outcome? Who was the most effective? What did you learn from that?
2. You have recently formed a new consulting business with three colleagues whom you met while studying at university. Explain the process you will go through to establish the leadership role for the business.

    For example, would the role of leader automatically be given to the person who initiated the consulting idea or would you consider another method of selection?
3. Using an example of a situation you are familiar with, ideally in the workplace, identify and explain the different dynamics between *leadership* and *management*.
4. Your company has offered you a promotion as head of a division in a country that has a very different culture from that of your native country. While you are excited by the new challenge, you are also aware that you need to consider whether your leadership style will be effective or appropriate for the new location. Using two countries of your choice (your native country and one with a different culture), outline

four of the most important factors relating to the style of leadership you should adopt when considering the offer of promotion into the new culture.

5. In this chapter we discussed the concept of new leadership training. Prepare a two-page case either for or against the following statement:

   People can be trained in new leadership.

   This exercise could provide an opportunity for an interesting debate among several groups in your organisational behaviour class.

6. Imagine you have been asked to address a class of high-school students who are in their final year and looking forward to graduating. Their social studies teacher did not provide you with much information other than that she wanted you to deliver a ten-minute speech on how the students can develop their leadership potential. Prepare a list of the things you would include in your speech. Be sure to make the content relevant for the group you are speaking to — that is, young adults who are about to embark on their individual career journeys. Rather than past or current leaders, you may want to consider what the future might demand of leaders and what attributes they will need to cater to that demand. You should consider issues at a macro as well as micro level. This exercise will be interesting as a class discussion, and your lecturer may want to expand the topic into an assignment.

Research questions

1. Some scholars have argued that the new leadership style in its various forms involves mystical qualities that few people possess. Others have argued that it can be readily identified and that people can be trained to display it.

   You are required to prepare two scripts. The first is a script for the CEO of a major telecommunications company to present to a small group of junior managers who show great leadership potential. In this case, the CEO is emphasising the need for new leadership approaches to be adopted by the junior managers. The second is a script for a leader supporting the case for a more traditional leadership approach to a particular situation. This might be a one-off situation in which a more directive leadership style is appropriate.

   Following are several questions you may want to consider, but you may prepare your own topics if you wish.

   (a) How mystical is the new leadership? How desirable is it?

   (b) How successful do you think leaders who use your new leadership script might be in convincing followers that they are charismatic or transformational?

   (c) Do you think one particular leadership style is more appropriate than another when considering the gender of a particular group — for example, men leading women or women leading men?

   (d) Do you think leadership approaches should change depending on the circumstances, the industry or the current environment?

2. Leadership is a topical and controversial subject in the global business arena. Using the internet, search through leadership links on sites, such as the Australian Institute of Management, www.ceoforum. com.au; the Australian Institute of Company Directors; the *New Zealand Management* journal; or *The British Journal of Administrative Management*. When your search is complete, and as a result of the information you have compiled from your search, compose a list of five common characteristics that successful leaders are currently perceived to display.

Running project

Complete the following activities for your organisation.

1. Choose a few of the most senior people in the organisation and assess whether they are leaders, managers or both, according to the descriptions given in this chapter. Do you think there is a genuine difference?

2. Try to identify the leadership traits of the leaders in the organisation. Do the traits vary between the top managers of the organisation and lower-level managers?

3. Choose one of the leadership models discussed in this chapter and use it to analyse the leadership of one of the leaders in your organisation.

4. How important is the top manager or other top leader in your organisation? Do they individually make a difference? Would you expect the overall

performance of the organisation to change if a new leader took over? Why or why not?

5. What degree of diversity is there among the leaders in your organisation? Explain, specifically for your organisation, why the diversity or lack of diversity has occurred.

6. Evaluate whether the CEO of the organisation inspires trust or mistrust in the organisation. Explain your answer.

Individual activity

Survey of leadership

Objective
To develop your ability to assess leadership styles
Total time: 15 minutes

SURVEY OF LEADERSHIP

The following ten questions ask about your supervisor's leadership behaviour and practices. Try to respond on the basis of your actual observations of your supervisor's actions; tick the box that corresponds to your observations.

To a great extent
To a considerable extent
To a moderate extent
To a slight extent
To almost no extent

To what extent:

	To a great extent	To a considerable extent	To a moderate extent	To a slight extent	To almost no extent
1. is your supervisor easy to approach?	☐	☐	☐	☐	☐
2. does your supervisor encourage people to give their best effort?	☐	☐	☐	☐	☐
3. does your supervisor show you how to improve your performance?	☐	☐	☐	☐	☐
4. does your supervisor encourage people to work as a team?	☐	☐	☐	☐	☐
5. does your supervisor pay attention to what you say?	☐	☐	☐	☐	☐
6. does your supervisor maintain high standards of performance?	☐	☐	☐	☐	☐
7. does your supervisor provide the help you need so you can schedule work ahead of time?	☐	☐	☐	☐	☐
8. does your supervisor encourage people to exchange opinions and ideas?	☐	☐	☐	☐	☐
9. is your supervisor willing to listen to your problems?	☐	☐	☐	☐	☐
10. does your supervisor offer new ideas for solving job-related problems?	☐	☐	☐	☐	☐

Scoring

Score 1 for almost no extent, 2 for slight, 3 for moderate, 4 for considerable and 5 for great. Now fill in the following boxes.

Interpretation

Support (S) and *interaction facilitation (IF)* are the two dimensions that define interpersonal or relationship-centred leadership behaviours. Support refers to the leader's personal concern for employees, while interaction facilitation measures how the leader encourages teamwork among employees. The two scores, S and IF, can be added to yield an overall interpersonal relationship score.

Goal emphasis (GE) and *work facilitation (WF)* both centre on task-oriented leader behaviour. Goal emphasis simply refers to the degree to which the leader emphasises the importance of achieving high goals, while work facilitation measures the degree to which the leader engages in behaviour that helps employees to get their jobs done effectively. The two scores, GE and WF, can be added to yield an overall task orientation score.[135]

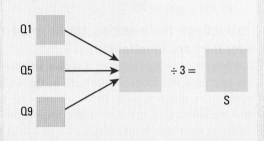

Support

Q1 → □
Q5 → □ ÷ 3 = □
Q9 →   S

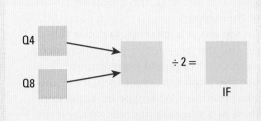

Interaction facilitation

Q4 → □
Q8 → □ ÷ 2 = □
    IF

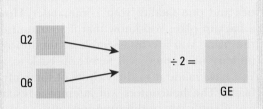

Goal emphasis

Q2 → □
Q6 → □ ÷ 2 = □
    GE

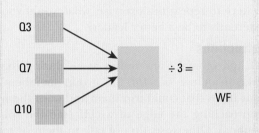

Work facilitation

Q3 → □
Q7 → □ ÷ 3 = □
Q10 →   WF

Group activity

Leadership in action

Objectives

1. To provide an opportunity to observe different types of leadership
2. To examine the link between leadership and situational contingencies
3. To develop your understanding of your own leadership behaviour
4. To develop your ability to analyse leadership in action
   Total time: 90 minutes

Procedure

1. Form a circle of 8–18 people in a large area of empty space where you can spread out without running into chairs or walls.
2. Ask for a volunteer(s) to be an observer: if your group is small, one observer will do; if your group has 18 people, you can have three observers. The observers should withdraw from the circle and read the observer instructions.
3. Everyone in the circle should put on a blindfold. (If you wear glasses, place them in your pocket or give them to an observer to hold.)

4. The instructor will read you the instructions for the exercise. You have 20 minutes to complete the assigned task.
5. Please answer the following questions individually in the next ten minutes.
   (a) What types of leadership emerged in this exercise? In your opinion, who were the leaders? Why? What leader behaviours did they exhibit?
   (b) What occurred in the group to help you solve the problem?
   (c) What occurred in the group that hindered you from solving the problem or from solving it quickly?
   (d) What did you learn about leadership from this exercise?
   (e) What did you learn about yourself as a leader in this exercise?
6. Discuss the questions in step 5 in smaller groups (four to six people). Ask the observers what they observed. Choose a representative to report to the entire class a summary of your observations.
7. Undertake a plenary debriefing session.

(a) The observer(s) briefly and objectively describe what happened when their group did the blindfold exercise. Next, the group representatives present their report.

(b) Can you see any relationships between this exercise and the 'real world' you experience at work or in other organisational settings?

(c) What are the important contingencies in this particular situation? What type of leadership works best in a situation like this? What leader behaviours are needed?

(d) There are no leaders without followers. In this exercise, what were the characteristics of a good follower?

(e) If you were to repeat this exercise, what would you do differently to be a better leader?

Observer instructions

Do not talk, laugh or make any noises at all during the exercise. Do keep an eye out for the group members' safety; move any items that could trip them and warn them if they are approaching the edge of a cliff (see the following instructions). Otherwise, do not talk to them or to the other observers.

Please undertake the following tasks based on your observations.

1. Look for leadership behaviour in the group. Who emerged as leaders? What did they do to become leaders?
2. Please observe and describe the group's communication patterns and nonverbal language.

3. Describe how the group made decisions. Be prepared to share these observations in the group discussion of the exercise.[136]

Instructions for exercise (to be read to the group after they are blindfolded)

You are the last survivors of a secret intelligence unit that has just escaped from an ambush at the local airport. You were on a mission to a small country to rescue a high-ranking official of great strategic importance to your own country, who was being held as a political prisoner. The operation was successful and the official made it onto the last plane, but your unit was left behind; you were all occupied defending the airport against local militia. Unfortunately, you sustained a number of minor casualties and one fatality, your commander. However, there is a backup plan. You know that if your unit does not make the plane you are to assemble at the top of a cliff where military helicopters will ferry you back to a waiting ship. You have made it to the vicinity of the cliff, but it is pitch black. The helicopters will attempt a rescue only if they can identify you as the stranded unit.

Before the mission it was agreed that the signal would be established by your unit forming a square on the top of the cliff; if at night, special heat-detecting radar would be used to locate you. Somehow you have to form this square in the dark, on the edge of a cliff with a 50-metre drop to rocks and the ocean. Time is not on your side. Your unit succeeded in destroying five local militia vehicles back at the airport, but this delaying tactic will not hold the enemy for more than 20 minutes.

Case study: Sustainability leadership is alive and well at the Good Guys

The Good Guys is one of Australia's leading consumer household appliance retailers, delivering quality electronics at competitive prices. The retailer was rebranded from 'Mighty Muirs' to The Good Guys in 1998 to become the retail icon The Good Guys is known for today. Since its inception in 1952, the organisation has grown to a geographical footprint of 98 stores across Australia. The Good Guys is a responsible retailer, operating with the vision to always delight customers. One of its stores, the Good Guys, Capalaba, is leading the way in environmental sustainability within the company, but also the Redlands community in which it operates. Its director/proprietor, James Brockhurst, recipient of the Ministerial Climate Smart Leadership Award argues that, 'As far as sustainability, culturally we wanted to make a positive difference and I personally want to make a positive difference. I think everyone is motivated by something whether it is money, position or

whatever it is, so for me it is I wanted to leave a legacy. I think sustainability has always run through my veins'.

One way in which the Good Guys Capalaba achieved significant environmental sustainability outcomes was through participative-shared leadership. When the company started the sustainability process, James didn't realise that there were two staff with environmental degrees (environmental strategic planning and one in environmental science). These individuals were very passionate and enthusiastic to be involved because they were able to put their degrees to use. These employees were approached to fulfil the role of eco-champions in the company and they were to be a conduit between James and other staff allowing brainstorming and communication bottom–up and top-down.

James and his eco-champions asked themselves, 'How do we make the biggest difference in our community?' There are a lot of appliances that use a lot of water and energy, so the company commenced a training program to enable staff to educate consumers on their purchases because more and more consumers were asking what they could do for the environment. James and the eco-champions approached Redland City Council and the Department of Heritage and Environment to develop a program for staff on eco-efficient appliances and eco-efficient practices. This resulted in an electronic tool that is used to punch in the model number of that item based on the WELS labelling (WELS is Australia's water efficiency labelling scheme that requires certain products to be registered and labelled with their water efficiency in accordance with the standard set under the national *Water Efficiency Labelling and Standards Act 2005*) and the cost for energy and water is then calculated for that particular product. This enables them to tell a consumer what cost is associated with using an appliance; for example, a fridge will cost them $69.00 to run. This also enabled the sales team to incorporate this information in their sales equation. The company started with the front load washing machine in a time of drought when there was no rebate in existence. That was their first win — the business had a win, the environment had a win and the consumer had a win.

Progressively, they extended this approach to other products such as air conditioning where they recommended inverter air conditioning. Their environmental sustainability journey kept evolving to a number of projects. To enhance their change journey an external sustainability coach who worked with the internal eco-champions was also engaged as a staff educator and motivator. James and the eco-champions developed their sustainability vision by running several vision day sessions over a period of six months. They created a 'man on the moon' vision statement which represented 'thinking big', but which is also tangible, specific and motivating. Staff are also trained in early morning sessions prior to starting work for the day to enable them to educate the consumer; for example, to complement the company's focus on standby power. Together, James, the internal eco-champions, and sustainability coach came up with fun ways to engage staff.

In the early part of the company's sustainability journey, there was some resistance from staff because initially they couldn't understand the reasons behind the changes; however, through actively engaging staff they also became excited about the positive changes and feedback from the community and resistance fell over naturally.

The company has an active business plan with a sustainability focus. The majority of staff are actively engaged in the sustainability initiatives and vision of the firm. James uses the analogy of a train to demonstrate that there are passengers on the train who have a choice to get off the train if they don't feel their own values align with the sustainability vision of the firm. Staff use this analogy with each other demonstrating a cultural shift.

James's advice to other business managers wanting to achieve environmental sustainability is to:
- get to know the business first and then see what would engage staff optimally in sustainability measures
- engage an internal eco-champion(s) to ensure a main focus on sustainability
- make it simple for people
- make it a shared experience.[137]

Questions

1. What lessons can you draw from the Good Guys, Capalaba regarding sustainability leadership?
2. Suppose you are one of the key management staff in one of this company's stores. What other leadership theories could you draw on to enhance your capabilities as a sustainability leader? Explain your answer.

End notes

1. K Kahler, 'Leadership: different venues, common themes', *Financial Executive International* (July/August 2001), www.fei.org.
2. See A Bryman, *Charisma and leadership in organizations* (London: Sage, 1992), ch. 5.
3. NM Ashkanasy and MT Dasborough, 'Emotional awareness and emotional intelligence in leadership teaching', *Journal of Education for Business*, vol. 79, no. 1 (September–October 2003), pp. 18–22; KW Parry, 'The new leader: a synthesis of leadership research in Australia and New Zealand', *Journal of Leadership Studies*, vol. 5, no. 4 (Fall 1998), p. 82.
4. RM Stogdill, *Handbook of leadership* (New York: The Free Press, 1974).
5. ibid; BM Bass, *Bass and Stogdill's handbook of leadership* (New York: The Free Press, 1990).
6. R Likert, *New patterns of management* (New York: McGraw-Hill, 1961).
7. Bass, op. cit., ch. 24.
8. *Leadership dilemmas — grid solutions* (Houston, TX: Gulf Publishing Company, 1995). Reproduced by permission. All rights reserved.
9. RR Blake and JS Mouton, *The new managerial grid* (Houston: Gulf, 1978).
10. See MF Peterson, 'PM theory in Japan and China: what's in it for the United States?', *Organizational Dynamics* (Spring 1988), pp. 22–39; J Misumi and MF Peterson, 'The

performance-maintenance theory of leadership: review of a Japanese research program', *Administrative Science Quarterly*, vol. 30 (1985), pp. 198–223; PB Smith, J Misumi, M Tayeb, MF Peterson and M Bond, 'On the generality of leadership style measures across cultures', paper presented at *the International Congress of Applied Psychology*, Jerusalem, July 1986.

11. M Myatt, '6 ways to hack the leadership pressure gap', *Entrepreneur Handbook* (30 June 2014), www.entrepreneurhandbook.co.uk.

12. MA Smith, 'The 5 perils of leadership' (16 November 2012), www.greatleadershipbydan.com.

13. This section is based on FE Fiedler and MM Chemers, *The leader match concept*, 2nd ed. (New York: John Wiley & Sons, 1984).

14. This section is based on FE Fiedler and JE Garcia, *New approaches to effective leadership* (New York: John Wiley & Sons, 1987).

15. RL Miller; J Butler and CJ Cosentino, 'Followership effectiveness: an extension of Fiedler's contingency model', *Leadership and Organization Development Journal*, vol. 25, no. 4 (2004), pp. 362–8.

16. This section is based on RJ House and TR Mitchell, 'Path–goal theory of leadership', *Journal of Contemporary Business* (Autumn 1977), pp. 81–97.

17. Adapted from RN Osborn, JG Hunt and LR Jauch, *Organizational theory: an integrated approach* (New York: John Wiley & Sons, 1980), p. 464. Reprinted with permission.

18. House and Mitchell, op. cit.

19. Bankwest, *Future of business: business leaders report* (May 2014), www.bankwest.com.au.

20. P Pryo, 'How I made my millions: Mark McConnell', *The Sydney Morning Herald* (25 March 2012), www.smh.com.au.

21. M McConnell, 'How mid-market bosses can be more adaptable leaders', *BRW* (17 June 2014), www.brw.com.au.

22. See the discussion of this approach in P Hersey and KH Blanchard, *Management of organizational behavior* (Englewood Cliffs, NJ: Prentice Hall, 1988).

23. ibid.

24. For some criticisms see CL Graeff, 'The situational leadership theory: a critical view', *Academy of Management Review*, vol. 8 (1983), pp. 285–91.

25. The discussion in this section is based on S Kerr and J Jermier, 'Substitutes for leadership: their meaning and measurement', *Organizational Behavior and Human Performance*, vol. 22 (1978), pp. 375–403; JP Howell, DE Bowen, PW Dorfman, S Kerr and PM Podsakoff, 'Substitutes for leadership: effective alternatives to ineffective leadership', *Organizational Dynamics* (Summer 1990), pp. 21–38.

26. Based on S Kerr and J Jermier, 'Substitutes for leadership: their meaning and measurement', *Organizational Behavior and Human Performance*, vol. 22 (1978), p. 387; and F Luthans, *Organizational behavior*, 6th ed. (New York: McGraw-Hill, 1992), ch. 10.

27. PM Posakoff, PW Dorfman, JP Howell and WD Todor, 'Leader reward and punishment behaviors: a preliminary test of a culture-free style of leadership effectivess', *Advances in Comparative Management*, vol. 2 (1989), pp. 95–138; TK Peng, '*Substitutes for leadership in an international setting*', unpublished manuscript (Texas: College of Business Administration, Texas Tech University, 1990).

28. Based on 'The Columbus effect: unexpected findings and new directions in leadership research', presentation made at annual meeting, Academy of Management, Las Vegas, August 1992.

29. Bass, op. cit., ch. 12.

30. JA Conger and RN Kanungo, *Charismatic leadership, the elusive factor in organizational effectiveness* (San Francisco: Jossey-Bass, 1988).

31. See JM Howell and BJ Avolio, 'The ethics of charismatic leadership: submission or liberation', *The Academy of Management Executive*, vol. 6, no. 2 (May 1992), pp. 43–54.

32. Conger and Kanungo, op. cit.

33. ibid.; JA Halpert, 'The dimensionality of charisma', *Journal of Business and Psychology*, vol. 4, no. 4 (Summer 1990).

34. See A Hwang, N Khatri and ES Srinivas, 'Organizational charisma and vision across three countries', *Management Decision*, vol. 43, issue 7/8 (2005), pp. 960–74.

35. G Yukl, 'An evaluation of conceptual weaknesses in transformational and charismatic leadership theories', *Leadership Quarterly*, vol. 10, no. 2 (1999), pp. 285–305.

36. See M-P Huang, B-S Cheng, L-F Chou, 'Fitting in organizational values: the mediating role of person-organization fit between CEO charismatic leadership and employee outcomes', *International Journal of Manpower*, vol. 26, issue 1 (January 2005), pp. 35–49.

37. KW Parry and SB Proctor-Thomson, 'Perceived integrity of transformational leaders in organisational settings', *Journal of Business Ethics*, vol. 35, no. 2 (15 January 2002), pp. 75–96.

38. K Parry and P Sinha, 'Researching the trainability of transformational organizational leadership', *Human Resource Development International*, vol. 8, no. 2 (June 2005), p. 165–83.

39. Australian Institute of Management — Monash University, '*Key findings, Australian Business Leadership Survey*', www.aim.com.au.

40. See BM Bass, *Leadership and performance beyond expectations* (New York: The Free Press, 1985); A Bryman, *Charisma and leadership in organizations* (London: Sage, 1992), pp. 98–9.

41. K de Vries, 'Charisma in action: the transformational abilities of Virgin's Richard Branson and AAB's Percy Barnevik', *Organizational Dynamics* (Winter 1998), p. 18.

42. B Avolio, D Waldman and F Yammarino, 'Leading in the 1990s: the four Is of transformational leadership', *Journal of European Industrial Training*, vol. 15, no. 4 (1991), pp. 9–16.

43. T While, '*Culture is everything*', http://tristanwhite.com.au.

44. Bryman, op. cit., ch. 6; K Inkson and AT Moss, 'Transformational leadership — is it universally applicable?', *Leadership and Organizational Development*, vol. 14, no. 4 (1993), pp. 1–11; MS Frank, 'The essence of leadership', *Public Personnel Management*, vol. 22, no. 3 (Fall 1993).

45. BM Bass, 'Two decades of research and development in transformational leadership', *European Journal of Work and Organizational Psychology*, vol. 8, no. 1 (1999), pp. 9–32.

46. CL Pearce and JAA Conger, '*Shared leadership: reframing the hows and whys of leadership*', Sage Publications (2002) in 'Exerting influence without authority', *Harvard Management Update* (28 February 2008), http://blogs.hbr.org.

47. This discussion is built primarily upon J Antonakis, BJ Avolio, and N Sivasubramaniam, 'Context and leadership: an examination of the nine-factor full-range leadership theory using the multi-factor leadership questionnaire,' *The Leadership Quarterly*, vol. 14 (2003), pp. 261–296.

48. CL Pearce and JA Conger, eds, *Shared leadership* (Thousand Oaks, CA: Sage Publications, 2003), ch. 1.

49. This discussion relies heavily on that of KA Zalatan and G Yukl, 'Team Leadership', in GR Goethals, GJ Sorenson, and J McGregor Burns, *Encyclopedia of leadership*, vol. A (Great Barrington, MA, Berkshire/Sage, 2004), pp. 1529–52.

50. JD Houghton, CP Neck, and C C Manz, 'Self Leadership and Super Leadership', in CL Pearce and JA Conger (eds), *Shared leadership*, pp. 123–140 (Thousand Oaks, CA: Sage Publications, 2003).

51. This discussion of the multiple-level perspective is based primarily on JG Hunt, *Leadership: A New Synthesis* (Thousand Oaks, CA: Sage Publications, 1991) and K Shepard, JL Gray, JG Hunt & S McArthur (eds), *Organization Design, Levels of Work and Human Capability* (Ontario, Canada, Global Organization Design Society, 2007), p. 534.

52. This discussion of top-management teams is based primarily on AC Edmonson, MA Roberto and MD Watkins, 'A Dynamic model of top management team effectiveness: matching unstructured task streams,' *The Leadership Quarterly*, vol. 14 (2003), pp. 297–325.

53. This discussion of Boal and Hooijberg's strategic leadership perspective is based primarily on KB Boal and R Hooijberg, 'Strategic Leadership Research: Moving On', *The Leadership Quarterly* 11 (2000), pp. 515–550.

54. RE Quinn, SR Faerman, MP Thompson and MR McGrath, *Becoming a master manager*, 4th ed. (Hoboken, NJ: Wiley, 2006).

55. GG Dess and JC Pickens, Changing roles: leadership in the 21st century, *Organizational Dynamics*, vol. 28 (2000) pp. 18–34; ML Tushman and CA O'Reilly, *Winning through innovation* (Cambridge, MA: Harvard Business School Press, 1997).

56. MD Mumford and B Licuanan, 'Leading for innovation: Conclusions, issues, and directions', *The Leadership Quarterly*, vol. 15 (2004) pp. 163–71.

57. DI Jung, Transformational and transactional leadership and their effects on creativity in groups, *Creativity Research Journal*, vol. 13 (2001) pp. 185–97.

58. Mumford and Licuanan, op. cit.

59. MD Mumford, GM Scott, B Gaddis and JM Strange, 'Leading creative people: Orchestrating expertise and relationships', *The Leadership Quarterly*, vol. 13 (2002) pp. 705–50.

60. ibid.

61. MD Mumford, 'Social innovation: ten cases from Benjamin Franklin', *Creativity Research Journal*, vol. 14 (2002).

62. A Howard, *The changing nature of work* (San Francisco, CA: Jossey-Bass, 1995).

63. Mumford, Scott, and Strange, op. cit.

64. MD Mumford, JM Feldman, MB Hein and DJ Nago, 'Tradeoffs between ideas and structure: individual versus group performance in creative problem-solving', *Journal of Creative Behavior*, vol. 35 (2001), pp. 1–23; S Taggar, 'Group composition, creative synergy, and group performance', *Journal of Creative Behavior*, vol. 35 (2001), pp. 261–86.

65. LB Cardinal, 'Technological innovation in the pharmaceutical industry: the use of organizational control in managing research and development', *Organizational Science*, vol. 12 (2001), pp. 19–36.

66. MA Hitt, RE Hoskisson, RA Johnson and DD Moesel, 'The market for corporate control and firm innovation', *Academy of Management Journal*, vol. 39 (1996) pp.1084–1196.

67. G Casimir, 'Combinative aspects of leadership style: the ordering and temporal spacing of leadership behaviors', *Leadership Quarterly*, vol. 12 (2001), pp. 245–78.

68. ibid.

69. P Gronn, 'Substituting for leadership: the neglected role of the leadership couple', *Leadership Quarterly*, vol. 10 (1999), pp. 41–62.

70. T Kidder, *The sole of a new machine*, 1981, New York: Avon.

71. Mumford, Scott, Gaddis and Strange, op. cit.

72. Lord and Hall, op. cit.; MD Mumford and JJ Caughron, 'Neurology and creative thought: Some thoughts about working memory, the cerebellum and creativity,' *Creativity Research Journal*, vol. 19 (2007), pp. 49–54; Mumford, Campion, and Morgeson, op. cit.; Sternberg, 2007, op. cit.

73. FE Fiedler and JE Garcia, *New approaches to effective leadership: cognitive resources and organizational performance* (Oxford, England: John Wiley & Sons, 1987); KE Weick, *Sensemaking in organizations* (Thousand Oaks, California: Sage, 1995).

74. RJ House, WD Spangler and J Woycke, 'Personality and charisma in the US presidency: a psychological theory of leader effectiveness', *Administrative Science Quarterly*, vol. 36 (1991) pp. 364–95; JG Hunt, KB Boal and GE Dodge, 'The effects of visionary and crisis-responsive charisma on followers: an experimental examination of two kinds of charismatic leadership', *The Leadership Quarterly*, vol. 10 (1999), pp. 423–48; R Pillai, 'Crisis and the emergence of charismatic leadership in groups: an experimental investigation', *Journal of Applied Social Psychology*, vol. 26, no. 6 (1996). pp. 543–62; R Pillai and JR Meindl, 'Context and charisma: A "meso" level examination of the relationship of organic structure, collectivism, and crisis to charismatic leadership', *Journal of Management*, vol. 24, no. 5 (1998), pp. 643–64.

75. D Madsen and PG Snow, *The charismatic bond: Political behavior in time of crisis* (Cambridge, MA: Harvard University Press, 1991).

76. CM Pearson and JA Clair, 'Reframing crisis management', *Academy of Management Review*, vol. 23, no. 1 (1998), pp. 59–76.

77. JG Hunt, KB Boal and GE Dodge, 'The effects of visionary and crisis-responsive charisma on followers: an experimental examination of two kinds of charismatic leadership', *The Leadership Quarterly*, vol. 10, no. 3 (1999), pp. 423–48.

78. ML Tushman and CA O'Reilly, 'Ambidextrous organizations: managing evolutionary and revolutionary change', *Management Review*, vol. 38 (1996), pp. 8–30.

79. KE Weick, *Sensemaking in organizations* (Thousand Oaks, California: Sage, 1995).

80. JM Strange and MD Mumford, 'The origins of vision: Effects of reflection, models and analysis', *The Leadership Quarterly*, vol. 16 (2005), pp. 121–48.

81. Mumford, 2006, op. cit.

82. Mumford, Scott, Gaddis and Strange, op. cit.

83. CK Riesbeck and RC Schank, *Inside case-based reasoning* (Hillsdale, New Jersey: Lawrence Erlbaum Associates, 1989).

84. Hammond, 1990.

85. CR Berger and JM Jordan, 'Planning sources, planning difficulty, and verbal fluency', *Communication Monographs*, vol. 59 (1992), pp. 130–48; AL Patalano and CM Seifert, 'Opportunistic planning: Being reminded of pending goals', *Cognitive Psychology*, vol. 34 (1997), pp. 1–36.

86. DA Hershey, DA Walsh, SJ Read and AS Chulef, 'Effects of expertise on financial problem-solving: evidence for goal-directed, problem-solving scripts', *Organizational Behavior and Human Decision Processes*, vol. 46 (1990), pp. 77–101.

87. ibid.

88. DJ Isenberg, 'Thinking and managing: a verbal protocol analysis of managerial problem solving', *Academy of Management Journal*, vol. 29 (1986), pp. 775–88.

89. ibid.

90. JG Hunt and A Ropo, 'Multi-level leadership: grounded theory and mainstream theory applied to the case of General Motors', *The Leadership Quarterly*, vol. 6, no. 3 (1995), in F Dansereau and FJ Yammarino (eds), *Leadership: the multiple-level approaches* (Westport, CT: JAI Press), pp. 289–328.

91. Osborn, Hunt and Jauch, op. cit.

92. B Shamir, RJ House and MB Arthur, 'The motivational effects of charismatic leadership: A self-concept based theory', *Organization Science*, vol. 4, no. 4 (1993), pp. 577–594.

93. KB Boal and JM Bryson, 'Charismatic leadership: a phenomenological and structural approach', in JG Hunt, BR Baliga, HP Dachler and CA Schriesheim (eds), *Emerging leadership vistas* (Lexington, MA: DC Heath, 1987), pp. 11–28.

94. RL Hamblin, 'Leadership and crisis,' *Sociometry*, vol. 21 (1958), pp. 322–35.

95. R Pillai and JR Meindl, 'Context and charisma: A "meso" level examination of the relationship of organic structure, collectivism, and crisis to charismatic leadership', *Journal of Management*, vol. 24, no. 5 (1998), pp. 643–64; R Pillai, 'Crisis and the emergence of charismatic leadership in groups: an experimental investigation,' *Journal of Applied Social Psychology*, vol. 26, no. 6 (1996), pp. 543–62.

96. JG Hunt, KB Boal and GE Dodge, 'The effects of visionary and crisis-responsive charisma on followers: An experimental examination of two kinds of charismatic leadership', *The Leadership Quarterly*, vol. 10, no. 3 (1999) pp. 423–48.

97. BM Bass, *Leadership and performance beyond expectations* (New York: Free Press, 1985).

98. See RN Osborn and B Ashforth, 'Investigating the challenges to senior leadership in complex, high-risk technologies', *The Leadership Quarterly*, vol. 1 (1990), pp. 147–63.

99. Osborn, Hunt and Jauch, op. cit.

100. JG Hunt and A Ropo, 'Multi-level leadership: grounded theory and mainstream theory applied to the case of General Motors', *The Leadership Quarterly*, vol. 6, no. 3 (1995), in F Dansereau and FJ Yammarino (eds.), *Leadership: the multiple-level approaches* (Westport, CT: JAI Press), pp. 289–328.

101. Osborn, Hunt and Jauch, op. cit.

102. Ml Regester and J Larkin, *Risk issues and crisis management: a casebook of best practice* (London: Kogan Page Publishers, 2002).

103. Michael E Brown and Linda K Trevino, 'Ethical Leadership: A Review and Future Directions', *The Leadership Quarterly*, vol. 17 (2006), pp. 595–616.

104. Based on BJ Avolio and WL Gardner, 'Authentic leadership development: getting to the root of positive forms of leadership', *The Leadership Quarterly*, vol. 16 (2005), pp. 315–38; WL Gardner, B J Avolio, F Luthans, DR May and FO Walumba, '"Can you see the real me?" A self-based model of authentic leader and follower development', *The Leadership Quarterly*, vol. 16 (2005), pp. 343–72; B George, P Sims, AN McLean and D Mayer, 'Discovering your authentic leadership', *Harvard Business Review* (February 2007), pp. 1–9.

105. JA Ross, 'Making every leadership moment matter', *Harvard Management Update* (September 2006), pp. 3–5.

106. RK Greenleaf, *Servant leadership: a journey into the nature of legitimate power and greatness* (New York: Paulist Press, 1977).

107. S Sendjaya and JC Sarros, 'Servant leadership: its origin, development, and application in organizations', *Journal of Leadership & Organizational Studies*, vol. 9, no. 2 (Fall 2002), p. 57.

108. LC Spears (ed.), *Reflections on leadership* (New York: John Wiley & Sons, 1997).

109. Based on LW Fry, 'Toward a paradigm of spiritual leadership', *The Leadership Quarterly*, vol. 16 (2005), pp. 619–22; LW Fry, S Vitucci and M Cedillo, 'Spiritual leadership and army transformation: theory, measurement, and establishing a baseline', *The Leadership Quarterly*, vol. 16, no. 5 (2005), pp. 835–62.

110. MA Ferdig, 'Sustainability Leadership: co-creating a sustainable future, *Journal of Change Management*, vol. 7, no. 1, pp. 25–35.

111. MA Ferdig and JD Ludema, 'Transformative interactions: qualities of conversation that heighten the vitality of self-organizing change', in W Pasmore and R Woodman (eds),

Research in organizational change and development (Stamford: JAI Press, Inc., 2005).

112. M Munasinghe, *Making development more sustainable: sustainomics framework and practical applications* (Colombo, Sri Lanka: Mind Press, 2007), p. 34.

113. See BM Bass and BJ Avolio, 'The implications of transactional and transformational leadership for individual team, and organizational development', *Research in Organizational Change and Development*, vol. 4 (1990), pp. 231–72.

114. See JA Conger and Rabindra N Kanungo, 'Training charismatic leadership: a risky and critical task' in Conger and Kanungo, op. cit., ch. 11.

115. See JR Kouzes and BF Posner, *The leadership challenge: how to get extraordinary things done in organizations* (San Francisco: Jossey-Bass, 1991).

116. M Sashkin, 'The visionary leader' in Conger and Kanungo, op. cit., ch. 5.

117. NSW Business Chamber, 'Leadership — do you have what it takes?', www.nswbusinesschamber.com.au.

118. FA Manske Jr., *Secrets of Effective Leadership: A Practical Guide to Success* (Memphis, Tennessee: Leadership Education and Development, 1987).

119. J Murphy, F Smith and P Roberts, 'Absenteeism reflects sick organisation', *Australian Financial Review* (7 February 2012), www.afr.com.

120. S Davidson, A Beer, P Gollan, P Toner, R Davison, 'Toyota names 2017 end, Australian car making to cease: experts react', *The Conversation* (2014), http://theconversation.com.

121. Lee Woon Shiu in G Cua, 'Women's say in family businesses', *BT Invest* (28 May 2014), www.btinvest.com.sg.

122. C Bart and G McQueen, 'Why women make better directors', *International Journal of Business Governance and Ethics*, vol. 8, no. 1 (2013), pp. 93–9.

123. G Yukl, *Leadership in organizations*, 4th ed. (Englewood Cliffs, NJ: Prentice Hall, 1998).

124. A Sinclair, *Doing leadership differently* (Melbourne: Melbourne University Press, 1998), p. 13.

125. Australian Institute of Management–Monash University, 'Key findings, Australian Business Leadership Survey', www.aim.com.au (viewed 15 January 2009).

126. Nancy J Adler, 'Global women leaders: a dialogue with future history' in David L Cooperrider and Jane E Dutton (eds), *Organizational dimensions of global change* (Thousand Oaks, CA: Sage, 1999), p. 327; Sinclair, op. cit., p. 7.

127. See M Neal, J Finlay and R Tansey, 'My father knows the minister: a comparative study of Arab women's attitudes towards leadership authority', *Women in Management Review*, vol. 20, issue 7 (October 2005), pp. 478–97.

128. SMR Covey, 'The business case for trust', *Chief Executive Magazine* (June 2007), pp. 38–40.

129. 'Age and leadership: Africa versus the West', *My Weku* (22 November 2011), www.myweku.com.

130. See G Hofstede, *Culture's consequences: international differences in work-related values* (Beverly Hills, CA: Sage, 1980).

131. R House, Mansour Javidan, Paul Hanges and Peter Dorfman, 'Understanding cultures and implicit leadership theories across the globe: an introduction to project GLOBE (global leadership and organizational behavior effectiveness)', *Journal of World Business*, vol. 37, no. 1 (Spring 2002), p. 3(8); RJ House, PJ Hanges, M Javidan, PW Dorfman and V Gupta (eds), *Culture, leadership and organizations: the GLOBE study of 62 societies* (Thousand Oaks, CA: Sage, 2004).

132. See for example H Zagorsek, M Jaklic, SJ Stough, 'Comparing leadership practices between the United States, Nigeria, and Slovenia: does culture matter?', *Cross Cultural Management: An International Journal*, vol. 11, issue 2 (June 2004), pp. 16–34.

133. M Oertig and T Buergi, 'The challenges of managing cross-cultural virtual project teams', *Team Performance Management*, vol. 12, no. 1/2 (2006), pp. 23–30, University of Applied Sciences, Basel, Switzerland.

134. ibid.

135. Adapted from *The survey of organizations*, © 1980 by the University of Michigan and Rensis Likert Associates. Reprinted by permission of the Institute for Social Research.

136. Group procedure/process adapted from DA Kolb, JS Osland and IM Rubin, *Organizational behavior: an experiential approach*, 6th ed. (Englewood Cliffs, NJ: Prentice Hall, 1995). Adapted with permission of Prentice Hall, Inc.

137. R Wiesner, D Chadee and P Best, *A research report on developing a best practice framework for managing environmental sustainability in Australian small and medium size enterprises (SMEs)* (CPA Australia, January 2010).

CHAPTER 12

DECISION MAKING

LEARNING OBJECTIVES

After studying this chapter, you should be able to:

1. understand decision making in organisations, including the broad types of decisions made by managers and the potential environments in which they are made

2. outline the sequential steps in the decision-making process

3. summarise and contrast the classical, behavioural and garbage can decision-making models

4. explain why intuition, judgement and creativity are essential aspects of quality decision making

5. state the conditions under which individuals or groups are best placed to make and take decisions in organisations

6. discuss some of the issues facing managers who have to make decisions in today's highly competitive and global organisations.

HOW TOP CEOS MAKE DECISIONS

Decision-making styles vary greatly amongst business leaders. For Steve Jobs (former Apple CEO), good decision making was inherent in the quality of employee's ideas, whilst Amazon's Jeff Bezos believes that providing reading time during meetings ensures that decisions are fully informed.[1] Whatever the decision-making style, however, the engagement of employees is an important element in gaining their trust and increases employee willingness to input into the decision-making processes.[2] In turn, this leads to higher employee motivation and trustworthy employee–manager relationships.[3] This dynamic has been recognised

by Stephen Borg, global director of strategy and market development, at the electronics company AOPEN. He explains that decision making should be a collaborative approach between internal and external stakeholders of the company. He also identifies that although the way decisions are made depends on the expediency and significance of the decision, it is important not to make instant decisions based on emotions. Ultimately, though, as Gary Swart, CEO of oDesk, the largest global online workplace, says decisions do need to be made and the whole organisation needs to back the decision.[4] In a survey by *Management Today*, the recent appointment of Milward Brown, CEO of Travyn Rhall, identified the making and quick implementation of decisions as 'the biggest challenges'.

Introduction

In today's global and highly competitive markets, organisations live and die on the choices made by their members (managers and others) and the extent to which these members can effectively learn to define and make better choices. Decision making really does lie at the heart of successful organisations.

We start the chapter with a formal definition of decision making, linking it to the nature of problem solving. This is followed by a short discussion on the kind of decisions and decision environments that managers typically face in modern organisations. We then contrast models of decision making, together with their sequential steps. Some important ingredients of quality decision making, including the skilful use of intuition, judgement and creativity, are also presented. The chapter concludes with a short discussion on current issues that are influencing decision making in today's organisations, and presents a model for ethical decision making.

Decision making in organisations

Henry Mintzberg is famous for his work on managerial roles. His research — based on recording the work of senior managers — suggests that in performing their tasks, they fulfil ten distinct roles broadly classified into interpersonal roles, informational roles and decision roles.

Mintzberg defined **decision making** as the process of choosing a course of action for solving a problem or seizing an opportunity.[5] The choice usually involves two or more possible alternatives. Considered diagrammatically, it looks like figure 12.1.

Decision making is the process of identifying a problem or opportunity and choosing among alternative courses of action.

Solving a
problem or seizing
an opportunity

Decision making

FIGURE 12.1 Defining decision making — getting things done

Types of decisions made by managers

Two basic types of managerial decisions relate to the presence of both routine and non-routine problems in the work situation. **Routine problems** arise regularly and can be addressed through standard responses, called **programmed decisions**. These responses simply implement solutions that have already been determined by past experience as appropriate for the problem at hand. Examples of programmed decisions are reordering inventory automatically when stock falls below a predetermined level, and issuing a written reprimand to someone who violates a personnel procedure.

Non-routine problems are unique and new. When standard responses are not available, creative problem solving is called for. These **crafted decisions** are specifically tailored to a situation. Senior managers generally spend a greater proportion of their decision-making time on non-routine problems. An example is the marketing manager faced with countering a competitor's introduction of a new product from abroad. Although past experience may help, the immediate decision requires a solution based on the unique characteristics of the present market situation.

The types of problems and decisions can be summarised as:

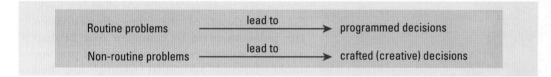

Routine problems   lead to →   programmed decisions

Non-routine problems   lead to →   crafted (creative) decisions

> **Routine problems** are problems that arise routinely and that can be addressed through standard responses.
>
> **Programmed decisions** are decisions that implement specific solutions determined by past experience as appropriate for the problems at hand.
>
> **Non-routine problems** are unique and new problems that call for creative problem solving.
>
> **Crafted decisions** are decisions created to deal specifically with a situation at hand.

Decision environments of managers

When making either programmed or crafted decisions, managers confront decision environments that affect the kinds of decisions made. Problem-solving decisions in organisations are typically made under three different conditions or environments: certain, risk and uncertain.[6]

Certain environments exist when information is sufficient to predict the results of each alternative in advance of implementation. When a person invests money in a savings account, for example, absolute certainty exists about the interest that the money will earn in a given period of time. Certainty is an ideal condition for managerial problem solving and decision making. The challenge is simply to locate the alternative offering a satisfactory or even ideal solution. Unfortunately, certainty is the exception rather than the rule in managerial decision environments.

Risk environments involve a lack of complete certainty regarding the outcomes of various courses of action, but some awareness of the probabilities associated with their occurrence. A *probability*, in turn, is the degree of likelihood that an event will occur. Probabilities can be assigned through objective statistical procedures or through managerial intuition. For example, statistical estimates of quality rejects in production runs can be made, or a senior

> **Certain environments** are decision environments in which information is sufficient to predict the results of each alternative in advance of implementation.
>
> **Risk environments** are decision environments that involve a lack of complete certainty but that include an awareness of probabilities associated with the possible outcomes of various courses of action.

production manager can make similar estimates based on past experience. Risk is a fairly common decision environment faced by managers. Managers often need to weigh up *likelihood* of an event versus the *consequence* of the event. Risks can then be assessed to be high, medium or low. Refer to the scenario at the beginning of this chapter. If you were one of the car company executives, how would you have assessed the risk associated with your travel decision at the time?

Uncertain environments exist when managers are unable to assign probabilities to the outcomes of various problem-solving alternatives. This is the most difficult of the three decision environments. Uncertainty forces managers to rely on individual and group creativity to succeed in problem solving. It requires unique, novel and often totally innovative alternatives to existing patterns of behaviour. Responses to uncertainty are often heavily influenced by intuition, educated guesses and hunches, which in turn are heavily influenced by perception.

> **Uncertain environments** are decision environments in which managers are unable to assign probabilities to the possible outcomes of various courses of action.

OBinAction

BP risks safety and environment in Gulf of Mexico

April 20, 2010 witnessed the explosion of the US$560-million Deepwater Horizon oil drilling rig. Fifteen crew members had gone missing, and the ensuing fire took two days to extinguish, and, finally the rig sunk. It was confirmed eventually that 11 people were killed and 17 people were injured. Furthermore, 4.2 million barrels of oil poured into the Gulf of Mexico, representing the worst ever environmental disaster in the history of the United States. As a result, BP may potentially have to pay an additional US$18 billion in fines on top of an existing US$42 billion. Carl Barbier, the Federal court judge, indicated that the event occurred due to a lack of care while drilling a well prone to blowouts. Not only did the judge proportion 67 per cent of the responsibility to BP, but also 30 per cent to Transocean and 3 per cent to Halliburton's, the sub-contractors involved in the drilling of the well.[7]

The judge also said that BP had been made aware of the dangerous implications of various unexpected pressures on the so-called Macondo 252 well ahead of the impending disaster. The judge went on to comment that BP had continued to drill even though normal practice would demand additional testing, and had thusly put profit before risk.[8]

Jesse Gagliano, who worked for Halliburton at the drill site, reported in court that he had informed BP by email of the risks associated with gas leaks.[9] But the setting for such a culture was underpinned by the risky decision-making approach of Peter Sutherland, BP Chairman 1997–2009, who said, 'No business can be without risk. Indeed, it is by taking strategic and commercial risks that we earn a return'. This is further supported by a report by US Coast Guard and Bureau of Ocean Energy Management who also suggest that BP put time and money above and beyond risk assessment.[10] Recent research has shown that everyone is involved in risk decisions, to some degree, and that risk taking is an adaption to changing environmental and social conditions. This adaption has harmful consequences such as gambling and crime.[11] Certainly in BP's case, this natural phenomenon of human risk taking demonstrates the consequences of uninformed risk.

Steps in the decision-making process

Managers make decisions throughout their working day. Many of these involve relatively unimportant matters that are resolved quickly. Prioritising the daily tasks and authorising project expenditure are typical examples. Other decisions are more complex, requiring careful consideration of the problem or opportunity, and the formulation and analysis of alternative solutions. Decision making is a process that contains several important steps; the final choice is simply one step along the way.

The four basic steps in systematic decision making are shown in figure 12.2. The first step is to recognise that a problem or opportunity exists and that something must be done about it. But, more than this, the real nature of the problem or opportunity has to be defined and assessed. A human resource manager investigating the low levels of job satisfaction indicated in an employee survey must first determine the root cause of the problem (low wages, poor physical conditions and so on) before making any attempt to solve the problem. The key is accurate information that is carefully evaluated.

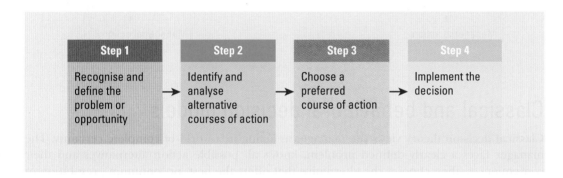

FIGURE 12.2 The decision-making process

The next step is to pose alternative courses of action to remedy the situation. The criteria to be used when assessing the relative merits of these alternatives are also selected. Relevant criteria might include ceilings on costs, industry specifications, work experience, ease of use, maintenance requirements and so on. Usually, two or more alternatives are available, and they measure up against the assessment criteria in different ways. If poor physical conditions are found to be the root cause of the problem just mentioned, then the alternative solutions might include moving to a new factory site or refitting the existing facility. Minimising the cost and production time lost is among the criteria important to management in their search for a solution.

The choice is made during step 3, after analysing the various alternatives. Here, the manager has to assess the consequences of choosing one option over another. But, as you now know, there is usually an element of risk or uncertainty in making any choice. Implementation of the decision occurs during step 4. Let us assume that the manager chooses to refit the existing facility because this appears to be the least costly and inconvenient alternative. Unfortunately, an unforeseen shortage of precision instruments needed for production is identified, increasing costs and extending the period of lost production. This is an often-repeated story in the complex world of managers. One reason decision making is often complex is because managers are faced with an ever-expanding amount of available knowledge.

Approaches to decision making

Organisational behaviour theorists have historically maintained that there are two alternative approaches to decision making (figure 12.3, overleaf) — classical and behavioural. A discussion of each will help you further understand the processes through which managers can and do make decisions.[12]

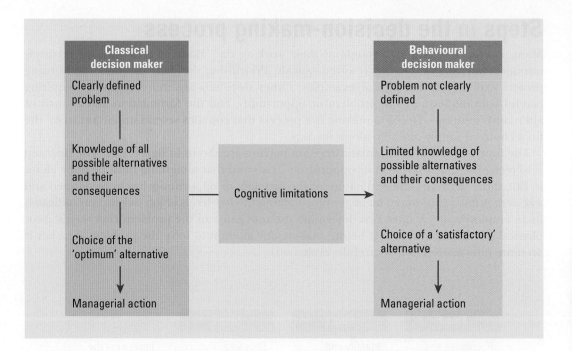

FIGURE 12.3 Managerial decision making viewed from the classical and behavioural perspectives

Classical and behavioural decision models

Classical decision theory
views the manager as acting in a world of complete certainty.

Classical decision theory views the manager as acting in a world of complete certainty. The manager faces a clearly defined problem, knows all possible action alternatives and their consequences, then chooses the alternative that offers the best, or 'optimum', resolution of the problem. Clearly, this is an ideal way to make decisions. Classical theory is often used as a model for how managers should make decisions.

Behavioural scientists are cautious about classical decision theory. They recognise that the human mind is a wonderful creation, capable of infinite achievements, but they also recognise that human beings have cognitive limitations. The human mind is limited in its information-processing capabilities. Information deficiencies and overload compromise the ability of managers to make decisions according to the classical model. As a result, behavioural decision theory gives a more accurate description of how people *actually* make decisions in work situations.

Behavioural decision theory
refers to the idea that people act only in terms of what they perceive about a given situation.

Behavioural decision theory states that people act only in terms of what they perceive about a given situation. Rather than facing a world of complete certainty, the behavioural decision maker is seen as acting under uncertainty and with limited information. Managers make decisions about problems that are often ambiguous; they have only a partial knowledge about the available action alternatives and their consequences; and they choose the first alternative that appears to give a satisfactory resolution of the problem. This model is referred to by Herbert Simon as a **satisficing** style of decision making.[13] Simon and a colleague state:

Satisficing means choosing the first satisfactory alternative rather than the optimal decision.

> Most human decision making, whether individual or organisational, is concerned with the discovery and selection of satisfactory alternatives; only in exceptional cases is it concerned with the discovery and selection of optimal decisions.

The key difference between a manager's ability to make an optimum decision in the classical style and the tendency to make a satisfying (or good enough) decision in the behavioural style is the presence of cognitive limitations and their impact on our perceptions. Cognitive limitations impair our abilities to define problems, identify action alternatives and choose alternatives — the key steps in the decision-making process.

Garbage can decision model

In the **garbage can decision model**, the main components of the decision-making process — problems, solutions, participants and situations — are all mixed up together in the 'garbage can' of the organisation. In many organisations where the setting is stable and the technology is well known and fixed, tradition, strategy and the administrative structure help order the contents of the garbage can. Specific problems can be matched to specific solutions, an orderly process can be maintained, and the behavioural view of decision making may be appropriate. But when the setting is dynamic, the technology is changing, demands are conflicting, or the goals are unclear and things can get mixed up. More action than thinking can take place. Solutions emerge as 'potential capabilities' — capabilities independent of problems or opportunities. Solutions emerge not so much in relationship with specific problems but as lessons learned from the experiences of others. Many solutions get implemented without being tied to a specific problem; they are just done for the sake of doing something. Although such actions may change things in some ways, they are unlikely to solve persistent problems.

The garbage can model highlights an important feature of decision making in many large organisations. Often the jobs of individuals and teams are to do things that make decisions already made by senior managers' work. This means they must interpret the intentions of their bosses as well as address local problems. Lots of agendas operate at once. Also, many problems go unsolved and organisations end up with chronic, persistent deficiencies that never seem to get much better. In a garbage can view, this is because decision makers cannot agree to match chronic problems with solutions, make choices, and implement them in a timely and consistent manner. Something happens, in a sense, only when a problem and a solution 'bump into one another'.[14]

> **Garbage can decision model** views problems, solutions, participants and choice situations as all mixed together in a dynamic field of organisational forces.

The precautionary principle

The precautionary principle works on the basis that it is better to be safe than sorry. In a way, the principle limits personal perception of scientific data, and directs decision makers to err on the side of caution if the consequences of making the wrong decision are serious or irreversible.[15] For example, lack of scientific certainty should not be used as a reason for failing to take measures to prevent degradation of the environment when there are threats of serious or irreversible damage.

The Garnaut Review generated a lot of debate amongst politicians and business managers in Australia regarding the extent to which the recommended carbon dioxide emissions reduction targets, designed to ensure effective global environmental protection, would balance with the needs of human development.[16] Only a year earlier in the United Kingdom, the Stern Review had sparked similar ruminations.[17] However, the problems in reaching a political and policy action consensus at the Copenhagen summit on climate change combined with the so-called 'Climategate' controversy (whereby the computer server at the Climate Research Unit at the University of East Anglia was hacked). Various emails were subsequently leaked, and climate sceptics claimed they demonstrated that climate scientists were manipulating research data.[18] Despite this, the follow-on investigations have found that despite the imperfection, modern science on climate change has held up well (i.e. the evidence of environmental degradation is mounting and the precautionary principle is garnering more consideration).[19]

In this context, in November 2010, Ross Garnaut was commissioned by the Australian Government to provide an independent update to his 2008 Climate Change Review,

(continued)

International **SPOTLIGHT**

which he completed in May 2011.[20] In this update, Ross Garnaut attacked the Business Council of Australia (BCA) for 'elevating the cause of narrow business interests' above the battle against climate change, and claimed the BCA was skewing the debate by calling for a system in which no-one would pay the cost of carbon reduction. Responding to the criticism, BCA deputy chief executive Maria Tarrant said it was essential that carbon reduction policies did not drive investors from Australia, and that 'the BCA has sought to engage constructively with Government and others in what is a complex debate on how to reduce global greenhouse gas emissions'.[21] In November 2011, the minority Australian Labor Government successfully passed the carbon price bill, which started off as a fixed price at A$23 per tonne of carbon pollution with the intention of converting to an emissions trading scheme in 2015. The bill stipulated an increase in the emissions reduction target to 80 per cent by 2050, the establishment of an independent climate authority to advise government on the effectiveness of the carbon price, and the establishment of the Clean Energy Fund.[22] Its passage left a nation deeply divided.

Environmentalists embraced the carbon price, but big business argued that the only certainty it would deliver would be higher electricity prices, less competitiveness and job losses.[23] In 2014, the newly elected Liberal government moved to repeal the carbon price through the Australian lower house, and prevent an automatic shift to an emissions trading scheme in the following year. The agreement required the backing of the Palmer United Party whose leader, Clive Palmer, only 14 hours before had stood with Al Gore, the former US vice-president, advocating that he would vote against scrapping the carbon price. Nevertheless, the Palmer United Party was instrumental in preventing the Liberal government from scrapping the Labor–Greens key institutions, namely the Climate Change Authority, the Clean Energy Finance Corporation and the Renewable Energy Target.[24] Towards the end of 2014, the Liberal Party had passed through the Senate its Direct Action Plan, which aims at unleashing A$2.55 billion to fund emission reductions in companies and reduce their carbon footprint.[25] The Direct Action approach of the Liberal Party has been criticised for being too short-term and damaging to the long-term reduction of CO_2 emissions, as well as prone to market distortions created by self-interest.[26]

In contrast, the United States is moving to reduce CO_2 emissions by 30 per cent, based on 2005 levels compared to the 5 per cent reduction (by 2000 levels) supported by both the Australian Labor and Liberal parties.[27] Comparison too with China represents a challenge for Australia to become more engaged with taking action on climate change. China committed to a 17 per cent cut in CO_2 emissions from 2010 levels by 2015 and is now the world's largest investor in renewable energy capacity.[28]

The intuitive decision model

Intuition is the ability to know or recognise quickly and readily the possibilities of a given situation.

A key element in successfully making non-programmed decisions is intuition. **Intuition** is the ability to know or recognise quickly and readily the possibilities of a given situation.[29] Intuition adds an element of spontaneity to managerial decision making and, as a result, it offers the potential for greater creativity and innovation. Especially in risky and uncertain environments, successful managers are probably using a good deal of intuition in problem solving. It is a way of dealing with situations in which precedents are unclear, 'facts' are limited or tenuous, and time is of the essence.

The role of intuition

A debate among scholars regarding how managers really plan highlights the importance of intuition for the practising manager. On one side of the issue are those who believe that planning can be taught and carried out in a systematic step-by-step fashion. On the other side are those who believe that the nature of managerial work makes this hard to do in practice. The ideas of Henry Mintzberg illustrate this.

* *Managers favour verbal communications.* Thus, they are more likely to gather data and to make decisions in a relational or interactive way than in a systematic step-by-step fashion.
* *Managers often deal with impressions.* Thus, they are more likely to synthesise than analyse data as they search for the 'big picture' to make decisions.
* *Managers work fast, do a variety of things and are frequently interrupted.* Thus, they do not have a lot of quiet time alone to think, plan or make decisions systematically.[30]

Indeed, managers should systematically plan in a step-by-step manner, but they should also recognise the job demands noted by Mintzberg and others, and hone their intuitive skills. Intuitive decision making is discussed in the Counterpoint.

COUNTER**POINT**

Asian leaders value creativity and intuition more than New Zealand leaders

A 2014 study by Grant Thornton found that business leaders in South-East Asian countries place a greater emphasis on creativity and innovation than leaders in New Zealand.[31] Whilst 90 per cent of leaders in South-East Asia responded that creativity is important and 85 per cent recognised the importance of intuition, only 62 per cent of New Zealand leaders valued creativity and 66 per cent intuition. The National Managing Partner at Grant Thornton New Zealand describes how this survey reveals how South-East Asian leaders take a 'modernist' approach that emphasises creativity and intuition in the coaching of team members, compared to the 'traditionalist' management philosophy of more developed economies. Although Quinn Mills from Harvard Business School has predicted that emerging economies will become more like developed countries as they mature, Tim Downes believes that leaders in South-East Asia will develop responsive solutions relevant to local markets. Shedding more light as to how the future of Asian leadership may look, another Grant Thornton study amongst Chinese leaders suggests that although analytics has become more prominent, the role of intuition will still have a role to play in a new 'Chinese way' of leadership. Certainly, in a swiftly changing and digital world, creativity and intuition will play an important role in leveraging innovation as a competitive market tool. This view of the future of Asian leadership styles is supported by recent research findings that show that intuition has a role to play in strategic decision making, positively impacting organisational performance.[32] Furthermore, a study of Singaporean and Malaysian companies demonstrates that intuition plays a significant purpose when making decisions in uncertain environments.[33]

(continued)

1. What are the advantages and disadvantages of introducing Eastern 'modernist' styles into contemporary Western management practices?
2. Why may increasingly complex twenty-first century business environments benefit from intuitive decision making?

The use of judgement heuristics

Judgement is the use of the intellect in making decisions.

Heuristics are simplifying strategies or 'rules of thumb' that people use when making decisions.

Judgement, or the use of the intellect, is important in all aspects of decision making. Analysing alternative courses of action and choosing one course (steps 2 and 3 in the decision-making process) involve making judgements.

Research shows that managers and others use **heuristics** — simplifying strategies or 'rules of thumb' — when making decisions. Heuristics can make it easier for managers to deal with uncertainty and limited information, and can prove helpful on certain occasions.[34] If they have accurate mental models, this has been found to lead to better decision rules and higher performance.[35] But heuristics can also lead to systematic errors that affect the quality of any decisions made.[36]

Managers often use heuristics when making decisions about expenditures. For example, the Australian government, like many organisations, uses budget forecasting based on events that happened in the past few years.[37] Heuristics are often used in making decisions about pay increases for staff. The negotiations start from an initial value that represents the responsibility of workers in the past. This leads to offers of pay increases being provided that are influenced by a mutual understanding of workers' increased responsibilities and customer demands.[38] The problem is that regardless of the basis of the initial value, adjustments from the initial value tend to be insufficient. If the initial value of the pay is deemed to be too low, the adjustment from the value is also likely to be too low. As a result, workers are still underpaid (despite having received a pay rise) considering the increase in responsibility they now carry. Thus, as a result of using heuristics, different *initial* values can yield a different decision for similar problems.[39]

It is inevitable that people will adopt some way of simplifying decisions, usually producing correct or partially correct judgements. A decision maker should be aware of the following common judgemental heuristics.[40] One involves assessing an event based on past occurrences that are easily available in your memory; for example, the product manager who bases a decision not to fund a new product on his or her recollection of the recent failure of a similar product. In this case, the existence of a past product failure has negatively, and perhaps inappropriately, biased the manager's judgement of the new product.

What about a situation in which you assess the likelihood of an event occurring based on the similarity of that event to your stereotypes of such occurrences? An example is the supervisor who takes on a new employee not because that person has any special personal qualities but because they have a degree from a university known to have produced high performers in the past. In this case, the individual's alma mater — and not their job qualifications — is the basis for the decision to recruit.

In addition to using these judgemental heuristics, managers are prone to two more general biases in decision making:
- the confirmation trap, whereby managers seek confirmation for what is already thought to be true and neglect opportunities to look for disconfirming information
- the hindsight trap, whereby managers overestimate the degree to which they could have predicted an event that has already taken place.

Reducing bias can make a difference. A recent study by McKinsey involving more than 1000 major business investments showed that when organisations worked at reducing the effect of bias in their decision-making processes, they achieved returns of up to seven percentage points higher than normal.[41] As Daniel Kahneman and his co-authors note:

> the real challenge for executives who want to implement decision quality control is not time or cost. It is the need to build awareness that even highly experienced, superbly competent, and well-intentioned managers are fallible.[42]

Creativity

Creativity in decision making involves the development of unique and novel responses to problems and opportunities. In a complex and dynamic environment, creativity in making 'crafted decisions' often determines how well organisations and their members respond to important challenges.

Creativity is the development of unique and novel responses to problems and opportunities.

New Zealander creates Unified Inbox

In 2010, Tony Ruckert recognised a need for an integrated approach to online communication and collaboration. He saw that people needed a way to manage their inbox more effectively and created an inbox dashboard launched through 'Unifiedinbox.com'.[43] Creativity does not just happen, however, it is an integration of personal and contextual factors, the nature of the work environment and job characteristics.[44] For Tony, the critical elements to the creative process began in the early 1990s when he was testing software for IBM and created a mailbox known as the 'Bulletin Board System'. With early access to a mobile phone, he then saw how online communication would be likely to develop. With the onset of the Internet, his mailbox started to crash and the computer failed to back up too. This taught him ways to improve synchronous online communication with digital communication channels. In 2003, he started to realise the significance of using smart approaches to global online communication and collaboration. Between 2007 and 2009, he began to optimise emails at a time that investors were supporting the growth of social networking and customer-focused solutions, rather than business-to-business start-ups. The concept of 'Unified Inbox' was created with the ascendancy of social media. Tony describes how the idea of having all of his information organised through one medium created the vision of a personal dashboard that would prevent losing information through other communication channels and browser tabs. Tony Ruckert's idea became a feasible business proposition because the integration of his personal desires, characteristics and operating environments eventuated over time. This case study, therefore, demonstrates that ideas that may not be possible may in the future become realised. It also shows that an incubation period may be necessary for the idea to be distilled by the mind and that a 'snowball effect' may motivate new ideas. Over time, these ideas will build exponentially and be developed.[45]

OBinAction

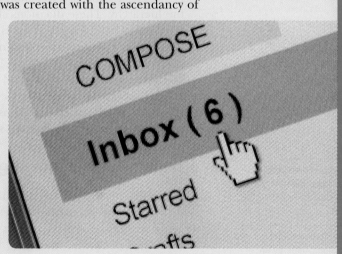

Making a choice and implementing a decision

Now we turn our attention to steps 3 and 4 in our model. Look back again at figure 12.2 (p. 457). Once alternative solutions to a problem or opportunity have been developed, a preferred course of action must be chosen and that decision needs to be implemented, because management is about action! The overall aim is to achieve the best result using the least resources, and creating the least amount of risk and uncertainty (if that is possible).

However, managers working at all levels, in all areas and in all types and sizes of organisation are not supposed to just make decisions. They are supposed to make good decisions. Sometimes, this means being willing to override previous commitments and to discontinue a course of action that is not working out the way it should. Frequently, it means crafting a creative solution to a non-routine problem. In all cases, successful managers make the right decisions in the right way at the right time. When it comes to managing the decision-making process, we can say that an effective manager is one who is able to pick precisely which problems are amenable to managerial decision making.

There are two important aspects of deciding to decide. The first step is selecting the problems and opportunities that deserve managerial attention. We talked about this earlier (step 1 in the model), but it requires more comment at this point. The second step is choosing a strategy for involvement.

Selecting problems carefully

Managers are too busy and have too many things to do with their valuable time to respond personally by making decisions on every problem or opportunity that comes their way. The effective manager knows when to delegate decisions to others, how to set priorities and when to abstain from acting altogether. When confronted with a problem, therefore, they ask themselves the following questions.

- *Is the problem easy to deal with?* Small and less significant problems should not get as much time and attention as bigger ones. Even if a mistake is made, the cost of decision error on small problems is also small.
- *Might the problem resolve itself?* Putting problems in rank order leaves the less significant for last. Surprisingly, many of these less important problems will resolve themselves or will be solved by others before the manager gets to them. One less problem to solve leaves decision-making time and energy for other purposes.
- *Is this my decision to make?* Many problems can be handled by people at lower levels in the hierarchy. These decisions should be delegated. Other problems can and should be referred to higher levels. This is especially true for decisions that have consequences for a larger part of the organisation, more so than for those under a manager's immediate control.[46]

To these three questions we add one of our own.

- *Is this a solvable problem within the context of the organisation?* The astute manager recognises the difference between problems that are amenable to solutions within the context of the organisation and those that are simply not solvable on a practical level.

Strategies for involvement — who decides?

One mistake made by many new managers is to presume that they must solve the problems and make the decisions themselves. In practice, managers end up making decisions in any or all of the following ways.

- **Individual decisions.** Managers make the final choice alone based on information that they possess and without the participation of others. Sometimes called an authority decision, this approach often reflects the manager's position of formal authority in the organisation.
- **Consultative decisions.** The manager solicits inputs on the problem from other people. Based on this information and its interpretation, the manager then makes a final choice.
- **Group decisions.** The manager not only consults with others for information inputs but asks them also to participate in problem-solving discussions and in making the actual

Individual decisions are decisions made by one individual on behalf of the group.

Consultative decisions are decisions made by an individual after seeking input from or consulting with members of a group.

Group decisions are decisions made by all members of the group, ideally with consensus being achieved.

choice. Although sometimes difficult, the group decision is the most participative of the three methods of final choice and the one that seeks true group consensus.

Good managers know when and how to use each of these methods. The basic goal, of course, is always to make a 'good' decision — that is, one that is high quality, timely and both understandable and acceptable to those whose support is needed for implementation. Further, good decisions can be made by each method — individual, consultative or group — if the method fits the needs of the situation (see The effective manager 12.1, overleaf).

OBinAction

Dealing with a flood of decisions

At 12.26 pm on Wednesday 5 January 2011, operations personnel at Brisbane's Wivenhoe Dam received a timely alert from Wivenhoe Dam engineering officer Graham Keegan. It was entitled 'Bureau of Meteorology (BOM) severe weather warning — dam flood operations', and warned that significant rainfall of 100 mm to 200 mm 'may occur during the next few days' and that:

> Somerset and Wivenhoe Dams are still above (full supply level) and rising slowly due to continuing base-flows from their catchments. As the catchments are still wet it is likely that we will be releasing floodwaters in the near future if BOM's forecasts are accurate. Please be prepared. We will keep you up to date with our plans as this event develops.[47]

Instead of draining the dam's flood compartment as the waters rose due to the heavy rainfall on 9–10 January 2011, the water levels were permitted to rise, eroding the dam's capacity for flood storage. This delay resulted in an emergency release of water on 11 January when the levels became so high that they threatened the stability of the dam. It may be that the engineers and dam managers were, under Queensland legislation, merely following the operating manual in order to avoid any liability for losses resulting from water releases from the dam. An initial investigation found that a lot of rain, not human errors, was the primary cause of one of Australia's worst disasters. However, follow-on investigations with expert studies and complex hydrology have found that massive releases of water from Wivenhoe Dam on 11 January did likely contribute to the flooding in the Brisbane River the following afternoon (which peaked early on 13 January). Even the dam operator, SeqWater, which insists it performed well, concedes as much in a carefully qualified part of its 1180-page report.[48]

Generally, good decisions are consultative decisions, but when is consultation finite, and who decides that? For example, Queensland Water Minister Stephen Robertson was briefed in October 2010 by the Bureau of Meteorology that the impending wet season would be 'unusually intense'. He then sought advice from the water grid manager, who had no direct role in managing the dams — but not from the government department responsible for flood mitigation and dam safety. In January 2011, the water grid manager did not advise a major drawdown of the dams, but pointed out that pre-emptive releases of about 16 per cent of dam storage would be needed to have an impact on medium and major flood events. In March 2012, the Flood Commission handed down its findings, which included a recommendation that the Crime and Misconduct Commission investigate the conduct of the

(continued)

dam operators.[49] In July 2014, lawyers Maurice Blackburn, supported by the litigation financier Bentham IMF, lodged a class action in the NSW Supreme Court, alleging that the Brisbane and Ipswich floods would have been avoided if the engineers managing the Wivenhoe and Somerset dams had been properly operated.[50] The action is being conducted through the NSW Supreme Courts as a class action cannot be launched in the State of Queensland.[51] In a quest to retrieve hundreds of millions of dollars for over 4000 victims of the floods, insurers too have joined the class action. The claim was filed against Seqwater, SunWater and the Queensland government. With the insurance industry already paying out over $1 billion to those affected by the floods, John Walker, Director Bentham IMF, describes how there is interest by the insurance industry to join the action to claim back more than $500 million. One insurer, Suncorp, who are not party to the class action, however, paid out $686 million, recouping $570 million from re-insurers. The saga continues with an expected hearing date in mid-2015.[52]

THE
EffectiveManager 12.1

Improving organisational problem-solving skills

- Believe that most problems can be solved.
- Ensure there is organisational commitment to solving problems. If top management is committed to continual improvement, then a strong message is sent to the rest of the organisation.
- Let people know that solving problems is part of their jobs, and that they are accountable for solving their day-to-day problems.
- Ensure employees receive training in problem solving.
- Recognise when problems have been solved and praise successful problem solving.
- Ensure teams communicate their successful problem solving so other teams benefit from their experience.
- Work towards problem solving becoming a habit of every employee.[53]

Managing participation in decision making

Victor Vroom, Philip Yetton and Arthur Jago have developed a framework for helping managers to choose which of the three decision-making methods is most appropriate for the various problem situations encountered in their daily work efforts.[54] Their framework begins by expanding the three basic decision-making methods just discussed into the following five forms.

- AI (*first variant on the authority decision*). The manager solves the problem or makes the decision alone, using information available at that time.
- AII (*second variant on the authority decision*). The manager obtains the necessary information from employees or other group members, then decides on the solution to the problem. The manager may or may not tell employees what the problem is before obtaining the information from them. The employees provide the necessary information but do not generate or evaluate alternatives.
- CI (*first variant on the consultative decision*). The manager shares the problem with relevant employees or other group members individually, collecting their ideas and suggestions without bringing them together as a group. The manager then makes a decision that may or may not reflect the employees' input.
- CII (*second variant on the consultative decision*). The manager shares the problem with employees or other group members, collectively obtaining their ideas and suggestions. The manager then makes a decision that may or may not reflect the employees' input.
- G (*the group or consensus decision*). The manager shares the problem with the employees as a total group and engages the group in consensus seeking to arrive at a final decision.

The central proposition in this model is that the decision-making method used should always be appropriate to the problem being solved. The challenge is to know when and how to implement each of the possible decision methods as the situation requires.

Vroom and Jago use a flow chart to help managers analyse the unique attributes of a situation and use the most appropriate decision method for the problem at hand. Key issues involve the quality requirements of a decision, the availability and location of the relevant information, the commitments needed for follow-through and the amount of time available.

The Vroom and Jago model at first seems complex and cumbersome, yet, there is a useful discipline in the model: it helps you recognise how time, quality requirements, information availability and employee acceptance issues can affect decision outcomes. It also helps you to remember that all of the decision methods are important and useful. The key to effectively managing participation in decision making is evident: know how to implement each decision method in situations for which it is most suited, and then do it well.

How groups make decisions

Edgar Schein, a noted scholar and consultant, has worked extensively with groups to analyse and improve their decision-making processes. He observes that groups may make decisions through any of the following six methods.

1. *Decision by lack of response*. A course of action is chosen by default or lack of interest.
2. *Decision by authority rule*. One person dominates and determines the course of action.
3. *Decision by minority rule*. A small subgroup dominates and determines the course of action.
4. *Decision by majority rule*. A vote is taken to choose among alternative courses of action.
5. *Decision by consensus*. Not everyone wants to pursue the same course of action, but everyone agrees to try it.
6. *Decision by unanimity*. Everyone in the group wants to pursue the same course of action.[55]

As you read more about these alternative decision methods, think how often you encounter them in your own group activities. Think, too, about the consequences resulting from each. In *decision by lack of response*, one idea after another is suggested without any discussion taking place. When the group finally accepts an idea, all others have been bypassed and discarded by simple lack of response rather than by critical evaluation. In *decision by authority rule*, the chairperson, manager or some other authority figure makes a decision for the group. This can be done with or without discussion and is time efficient. Whether the decision is a good one or a bad one depends on whether the authority figure has the necessary information, and on how well this approach is accepted by other group members. In a *decision by minority*, two or three people are able to dominate or 'railroad' the group into making a decision with which they agree. This is often done by providing a suggestion and then forcing quick agreement by challenging the group with statements such as: 'Does anyone object? … Let's go ahead then.'

One of the most common ways in which groups make decisions, especially when there are early signs of disagreement, is *decision by majority rule*. Here, formal voting may take place, or members may be polled to find the majority viewpoint. This method parallels the democratic political system and is often used without awareness of its potential problems. The very process of voting can create coalitions; that is, some people will be 'winners' and others will be 'losers' when the final vote is tallied. Those in the minority — the 'losers' — may feel left out or discarded without having had a fair say. As a result, they may be less committed to implementing the decision of the 'majority' and may carry lingering resentments that will impair group effectiveness in the future.

Another alternative is *decision by consensus*. Formally defined, a consensus exists after discussion leads to one alternative being favoured by most members and the other members agreeing to support it. When a consensus is reached, even those who may have opposed the chosen course of action know that they have been heard and have had a fair chance to influence the decision outcome. Consensus, therefore, does not require unanimity.

A *decision by unanimity* may be the ideal state of affairs. Here all group members agree totally on the course of action to be taken. This is a 'logically perfect' group decision method that is extremely difficult to attain in practice. Groups sometimes turn to authority decisions, majority voting or even minority decisions because managing the group process to achieve consensus or unanimity is difficult. Another useful typology of decision making in group situations is that proposed by the US Center for Rural Studies (shown in table 12.1). The effective manager 12.2 lists guidelines for members in consensus-seeking groups.[56] In this typology, six types of decision-making processes are identified, each with its advantages and disadvantages.

TABLE 12.1 Decision making in groups

Source: Adapted from Lois Frey, Bob Biagi and Duane Dale, '*Decisionmaking methods: advantages and disadvantages*', http://crs.uvm.edu/gopher/nerl/group/b/g/Exercise11.html.

Type of decision process	Meaning of process	Advantages	Disadvantages
1. *Individual/ autocratic*	Designate a leader to make all the decisions without consulting the group in any way.	Applies to administrative needs; useful for simple, routine decisions; should be used when little time is available to make the decision, or when group members lack the skills and information to make the decision any other way.	One person is not a good resource for every decision; advantages of group interaction are lost; no commitment to implementing the decision is developed among other group members; resentment and disagreement may result in sabotage and deterioration of group effectiveness; resources of other members are not used.
2. *Authority/ expert based*	Select the most expert member of the group and abide by his or her decision.	Useful when the expertise of one person is so far superior to that of all other group members that little is to be gained by discussion; should be used when the need for membership action in implementing the decision is slight.	It is difficult to determine who the expert is; no commitment to implement the decision is built; advantages of group interaction are lost; resentment and disagreement result in sabotage and deterioration of group effectiveness; resources of other members are not used.
3. *Average of members' opinions*	Poll members of the group, and then average the results.	Useful when it is difficult for group members to meet, when the decision is so urgent that there is no time for group discussion, when member commitment is not necessary for implementing the decision, or when group members lack the skills and information to make the decision any other way; applicable to simple routine decisions.	There is not enough interaction among group members for them to gain from each other's resources and from the benefits of group discussion; the group does not develop a commitment to implement the decision; unresolved conflict and controversy may damage group effectiveness in the future.
4. *Majority control*	Discuss an issue, then vote when 51 per cent or more accept the course of action.	Can be used when sufficient time is lacking for decision by consensus, when the decision is not so important that consensus needs to be used, or when complete member commitment is not necessary for implementing the decision; closes discussion on issues that are not highly important for the group.	Usually leaves an alienated minority, which damages future group effectiveness; relevant resources of many group members may be lost; full commitment to implement the decision is absent; full benefit of group interaction is not obtained.

Type of decision process	Meaning of process	Advantages	Disadvantages
5. *Minority control*	Allow two or more members to serve as an executive, with committee authority to make decisions.	Can be used when everyone cannot meet to make a decision, when the group is under such time pressure that it must delegate responsibility to a committee, when only a few members have any relevant resources, or when broad member commitment is not needed to implement the decision; useful for simple, routine decisions.	Does not use the resources of many group members; does not establish widespread commitment to implement the decision; unresolved conflict and controversy may damage future group effectiveness; not much benefit from group interaction.
6. *Consensus*	Discuss until the group arrives at a collective opinion acceptable to all members of the group.	Produces an innovative, creative and high-quality decision; elicits commitment by all members to implement the decision; uses the resources of all members; enhances the future decision-making ability of the group; useful in making serious, important and complex decisions to which all members are to be committed.	Takes a great deal of time and psychological energy and a high level of member skill; time pressure must be minimal; not useful in an emergency.

Guidelines for achieving group consensus

THE **EffectiveManager** 12.2

1. Avoid blindly arguing your case. Present your position clearly and logically, but listen to others' reactions; consider them carefully before pressing your point.
2. Do not change your mind just to reach agreement and avoid conflict. Yield to or support only those positions you believe have merit and sound foundations.
3. Avoid using 'conflict-reducing' procedures, such as holding a majority vote, tossing a coin, averaging or bargaining in reaching decisions.
4. Try to involve everyone in the decision process. Seek out and respect differences of opinion. Allow disagreements to bring a wide range of information and opinions to the deliberations.
5. Do not assume that someone must win and someone must lose when discussions reach a stalemate. Keep pressing to find an alternative acceptable to all members.
6. Discuss the assumptions underlying positions, listen carefully to one another, and encourage the participation of all members.

Groupthink

Social psychologist Irving Janis defines **groupthink** as the tendency of members in highly cohesive groups to lose their critical, evaluative capabilities.[57] Janis believes that because highly cohesive groups demand conformity, there is a tendency for their members to become unwilling to criticise one another's ideas and suggestions. Desires to hold the group together and to avoid unpleasant disagreements lead to an overemphasis on concurrence and an underemphasis on realistically appraising alternative courses of action.

Groupthink is a rationalisation process that develops when group members begin to think alike. It can be encouraged by leaders who do not tolerate dissent, and it can develop when employees underestimate potential problems. While some recent studies have found that strongly identified members do challenge group norms when they are perceived as

Groupthink is the tendency of members in highly cohesive groups to lose their critical, evaluative capabilities.

collectively harmful,[58] in most situations weakly identified group members kept their qualms to themselves, unless they were confident that their concern about the problem would be matched by their other team members.[59]

Groupthink is also a mode of thinking that people engage in when they are deeply involved in a cohesive in-group, when the quest for unanimity overrides their motivation to realistically appraise alternative courses of action. During groupthink, small groups develop shared illusions and related norms that interfere with critical thinking and reality testing. Some symptoms of groupthink are arrogance, over-commitment and excessive loyalty to the group. Other symptoms of groupthink are found in The effective manager 12.3. They can be used to help spot this phenomenon in practice.

OBinAction

Groupthink involved in space shuttle tragedy

Seventy-three seconds after its launch on 28 January 1986, the *Challenger* space shuttle exploded, killing the seven astronauts aboard. The cause of the explosion was found to be the failure of the O-ring seals on the solid rocket booster joints on the space shuttle. In the year prior to the *Challenger* launch, test launches and numerous investigations had shown that in low temperatures the O-ring seals failed to seal the joints, leaving them vulnerable to the high temperatures created at launch and, thus, increasing the possibility of explosion.

The day before the *Challenger* launch, managers were made aware of the low temperature forecast for the launch date and a meeting was called between managers and senior engineers. The engineers presented compelling data that a launch with an outside temperature of −7.8°C was dangerous and strongly recommended against launching *Challenger*. NASA managers, burdened by the economic consequences of the delayed launch, argued for continuation of the mission.

Eventually the engineers' concerns were dismissed as the head of the management team, Jerry Mason, turned to Bob Lund, vice-resident of engineering, and asked him to 'take off his engineering hat and put on his management hat'. After some discussion, it was unanimously recommended that the *Challenger* mission go ahead as scheduled.[60] Further information and an analysis of groupthink symptoms in this case can be obtained by watching the video *A major malfunction*.[61]

Worryingly, the other major space shuttle tragedy, the loss of *Columbia* in 2003, has also been linked to the effects of groupthink.[62] The post-incident investigation following the *Columbia* space-shuttle explosion found that the culture at NASA was one in which 'it is difficult for minority and dissenting opinions to percolate up through the agency's hierarchy'.[63] Collective decision-making failures are often attributed to group members' unwillingness to express unpopular opinions, and after-action investigations often find that the lack of dissent is a causal factor.[64]

More recently, the housing bubble and market failures present further examples of how groupthink can manifest within the society. The established wisdom, for example, that housing prices would always go up is not easily challenged. During the housing crisis especially, groupthink existed across all economic and financial institutions. Furthermore, the effect of 'groupthink' may cause decision makers to ignore negative market indicators. For example, in their efforts to compete and not miss out on market share, the banks continued to write bad home loans, even though the whole herd was heading towards disaster. The problem is that markets do not account for the possibility of groupthink, as all actors are assumed rational and independently motivated. The outcome of groupthink in the finance and housing sector has resulted in severe market failures in recent years with people losing their jobs and savings.[65]

It is one thing to identify the potential negative power of groupthink and another to accede to that power on more than one occasion. Managers need constant diligence and development of the appropriate culture to overcome problems in an effort to capitalise on the advantages of group decision making.

Janis suggests the following action guidelines for dealing with groupthink.
- Assign the role of critical evaluator to each group member; encourage a sharing of objections.
- Have the leader avoid seeming partial to one course of action.
- Create subgroups operating under different leaders and working on the same problem.
- Have group members discuss issues with employees and report back on their reactions.
- Invite outside experts to observe group activities and to react to group processes and decisions.
- Assign one member of the group to play a 'devil's advocate' role at each meeting.
- Write alternative scenarios for the intentions of competing groups.
- Hold 'second-chance' meetings after consensus is apparently achieved on key issues.[66]

Spotting the symptoms of 'groupthink'

THE **EffectiveManager** 12.3

- *Illusions of group invulnerability.* Members believe the group is beyond criticism or attack.
- *Rationalising unpleasant data.* Members refuse to accept or thoroughly consider contradictory data or new information.
- *Belief in inherent group morality.* Members believe the group is 'right' and above reproach by outsiders.
- *Negative stereotyping of outsiders.* Members refuse to look realistically at other groups; they may view competitors as weak, evil or stupid.
- *Applying pressure to deviants.* Members refuse to tolerate anyone who suggests that the group may be wrong; every attempt is made to get conformity to group wishes.
- *Self-censorship by members.* Members are unwilling to communicate personal concerns or alternative points of view to the group as a whole.
- *Illusions of unanimity.* Members are quick to accept consensus; they do so prematurely and without testing its completeness.
- *Mind guarding.* Members of the group keep outsiders away and try to protect the group from hearing disturbing ideas or viewpoints.

Techniques for improving decision making in groups

As you can see, the process of making decisions in any group is a complex and even delicate one. Group dynamics must be well managed to balance individual contributions and group operations. The following equation helps keep this point in mind:[67]

$$\begin{array}{ccccc} \text{Group decision} \\ \text{effectiveness} \end{array} = \begin{array}{c} \text{individual} \\ \text{contributions} \end{array} + \begin{array}{c} \text{group process} \\ \text{gains} \end{array} - \begin{array}{c} \text{group process} \\ \text{losses} \end{array}$$

Over the years, social scientists have studied ways of maximising the assets of the group decision-making process while minimising its liabilities to take full advantage of the group as a decision-making resource. A particular point of concern is with the process losses that are often associated with free-flowing open group meetings, such as a committee deliberation or a staff meeting to address a specific problem.

The advantages in using committees or groups for decision making or developing recommendations for a decision maker include collective wisdom or combined expertise, motivation, individual development and decision acceptance. The pitfalls that beset group or committee decision making can be roughly classified as human limitations and procedural problems. Among the human limitations are the fatigue factor, dominant personalities in the group and a lack of information. Procedural problems include procedures adopted, the time element and a lack of authority. Understanding the players and the process is the first step in making group decision making more effective.

Free-flowing open group meetings are settings in which the risk of social pressures to conform, domination, time pressures and even highly emotional debates may detract from the purpose at hand. It is precisely in such situations that special group decision techniques may be used to ensure that everyone gets a chance to participate and that the creative potential of the group is tapped to the fullest. Good examples are the brainstorming, nominal group and Delphi techniques, discussed shortly.[68]

When a department is not operating at an acceptable or desired level, the symptoms can often be found in meetings, memoranda and other forms of interaction. Many would say that a quantifiable reduction in trust — for instance, writing a memo to confirm a discussion — shows that people are looking out for themselves and are not at ease. Experiential techniques, by use of which groups complete physical events and group games and relate their experiences back to the work environment, have become increasingly popular methods of reinvigorating work groups. Once a department is sold on the idea of changing through group dynamics, an assessment can be made of the group's productivity and internal ability to function. The group then decides on the goals it wants to accomplish in the future. By giving groups experiences that encourage them to raise their benchmarks, experiential programs seek to instil new expectations in members.[69] If they are run on a regular basis, experiential programs may also contribute to building and/or reinforcing a 'group culture'.

Another technique for contributing ideas for decision making is brainstorming. In brainstorming, group members actively generate as many ideas and alternatives as possible, and they do so relatively quickly and without inhibitions. Brainstorming is discussed in detail in chapter 7.

The nominal group technique is a group decision technique that uses structured rules for minimising interactions to facilitate decision making on potentially controversial subjects. Participants are given a 'nominal question' and asked to generate ideas in response to it. The ideas are recorded, and group members vote on the best idea.[70] The structured nature of the nominal group and the voting procedure allows ideas to be evaluated without risking the inhibitions, hostilities and distortions that may occur in an open meeting. This makes the nominal group technique very useful in otherwise difficult or unwieldy group decision situations.

A third group decision approach, the Delphi technique, was developed by the Rand Corporation for use in situations in which group members are unable to meet face to face. In this procedure, a series of questionnaires is distributed to a panel of decision makers, and responses are summarised by the decision coordinator. The process is repeated until consensus is reached and a clear decision emerges.

One of the problems with the Delphi technique relates to the complexity and cost of administering this series of questionnaires. However, the technique does make group decision making possible in circumstances in which it is physically impossible to convene a meeting. A natural extension of the technique is the application of group decision software in computer network groups.

The problem of escalating commitment

We mentioned at the beginning of this section that effective managers should be making *good* decisions, and that they should be prepared to override previous commitments and discontinue courses of action that are just not working. Often, this means being bold and decisive! However, many managers fall into the trap of escalating commitment. Recognised by social psychologists as common and potentially dysfunctional, it is the tendency to continue with a previously chosen course of action even though feedback indicates that it is not working.[71]

Escalating commitment is encouraged by the popular adage: 'If at first you don't succeed, try, try again.' Current wisdom in organisational behaviour supports an alternative view: good decision makers know when to call it quits. They are willing to reverse previous decisions and commitments, and thereby avoid further investments in unsuccessful courses of action. However, the self-discipline required to admit mistakes and change courses of action is sometimes difficult to achieve. Often the tendency to escalate commitments to previously chosen courses of action outweighs the willingness to disengage from them. This occurs as decision makers:

- rationalise negative feedback as simply a temporary condition
- protect their egos and avoid admitting the original decision was a mistake
- use the decision as a way of managing the impressions of others, such as a boss or peers
- view the negative results as a 'learning experience' that can be overcome with added future effort.[72]

Escalating commitment is a form of decision entrapment that leads people to do things that are not justified by the facts of the situation. Managers should be proactive in spotting 'failures' and open to reversing decisions or dropping plans that do not appear to be working.

This form of decision making has been often linked to 'rogue traders' who make lots of money for banks but eventually lose them billions of dollars when they make illegal trades. For example, Nick Leeson caused the downfall of Barings Bank with illegal speculative trades amounting to US$1.8 billion in 1995. More recently, Jerome Kerviel lost French bank Societe Generale almost US$7 billion, and Kweku Adoboli lost UBS more than US$2 billion.[73] As the following What would you do? illustrates, research has focused on whether some measures that banks take (e.g. increased monitoring) can have an impact on controlling escalating commitment.

> **Escalating commitment** is the tendency to continue with a previously chosen course of action even when feedback suggests that it is failing.

WhatWould **You**Do?

Escalation of commitment by bank loan officers and university students

Study 1: bank loan officers

Some individuals escalate commitment to a losing course of action when it is clear to others they should quit. McNamara, Moon and Bromley asked whether monitoring by more senior management would help stop escalating commitment in a group of bank loan officers.

At first glance, their data seem to suggest that monitoring worked. When individual clients were put in high-risk categories, the loan officers on these accounts were monitored more closely. Undue overcommitment to these higher risk individuals was apparently reduced. But, on closer examination, the researchers found that loan officers showed 'intervention avoidance' and were reluctant to place clients with deteriorating credit into a higher risk category which would subject the officers to greater monitoring. For this group of clients, there was overcommitment by the loan officers.

(continued)

McNamara et al. use their data to argue that the question of escalation is more complex than traditionally recognised, and may involve a host of other organisational factors that directly influence the tendencies of individuals to make undesirable decision commitments.

Study 2: university students

Escalating commitments breed unethical behaviour. That's the conclusion reached in an empirical study by Marc and Vera L Street. They conducted an experiment with 155 undergraduate students working on a computerised investment task. Results showed that exposure to escalation situations increases tendencies towards unethical acts, and that the tendencies further increase with the magnitude of the escalation. Street and Street explain this link between escalation and poor ethics as driven by desires to get out of and avoid the increasing stress of painful situations.

Additional findings from the study showed that students with an external locus of control had a higher propensity to choose an unethical decision alternative than their counterparts with an internal locus of control.[74]

Questions

1. What role does escalating commitment play in the day-to-day performance of your work and class teams?
2. If you were in charge of hiring and training bankers, what would you do to instil in them the self-awareness necessary to counter the effects of escalating commitment?
3. Design a study that might identify when and why escalation is likely.

Current issues in organisational decision making

In today's environments, the problems facing organisational decision makers seem to get harder and more complex. We face difficult stresses and strains as the quest for higher productivity challenges the needs, talents and opportunities of people at all levels of responsibility. Prominent among the current issues relating to decision making in today's workplace are those dealing with culture and technology.

Culture and decision making

The forces of globalisation and workforce diversity have brought increased attention to how culture may influence decision making.

The cultural dimensions of power–distance and individualism–collectivism have special implications for decision making. Workers from high power–distance cultures may expect their supervisors to make the decisions and may be less inclined than individualists to expect or wish to be involved in decision making processes. Signs of good managers in cultures emphasising and respecting status differences may include a willingness to act as an expert in problem solving and to be decisive; a manager who seems uncomfortable making decisions without group involvement and consensus may be less favourably viewed.

Values relating to individualism–collectivism also affect cultural tendencies towards participation in decision making. Decision making in collectivist cultures tends to be time consuming, with every effort being made to gain consensus. The results are slower decisions but smooth implementation. Decision making in individualist cultures, by contrast, is oriented more towards being decisive, saving time and using voting to resolve disagreements. The results are often implementation problems and delays.[75] In collectivist Japan, for example, many companies use the *ringi* system — a group decision approach by which workers indicate written approval of proposals prior to their acceptance and implementation.[76] In more individualist France, it is common for decisions made at higher corporate levels to be passed down the hierarchy for implementation.[77]

Culture may even play a role in determining whether a decision is necessary at all — in other words, whether the situation should be changed. North Americans tend to perceive situations as problems to be solved and want to do something about them. Other cultures, such as Thai and Indonesian societies, are more prone to accept the status quo.[78]

Technology and decision making

There is no doubt that today's organisations are becoming more sophisticated in applying computer technologies to facilitate decision making. Developments in the field of **artificial intelligence** — the study of how computers can be programmed to think like the human brain — are many and growing. Nobel laureate and decision scientist Herbert Simon is convinced that computers will someday be more intelligent that humans. Already the applications of artificial intelligence to organisational decision making are significant. We have access to decision-making support from *expert systems* that reason like a human expert and follow 'either/or' rules or heuristics to make deductions, *fuzzy logic* that reasons beyond either/or choices in more[79] imprecise territory, and *neural networks* that reason inductively by simulating the brain's parallel processing capabilities. Uses for such systems may be found everywhere from banks, where they may help screen loan applications, and hospitals, where they check laboratory results and possible drug interactions, to the factory floor, where they schedule machines and people for maximum production efficiencies.

Artificial intelligence, or AI, studies how computers can be made to think like the human brain.

Computer support for group decision making, including developments with the internet and intranets, breaks the decision-making meeting out of the confines of face-to-face interactions. With the software now available, people working in geographically dispersed locations can define problems and make decisions together and simultaneously. Research confirms that group decision software can be especially useful for generating ideas, such as in electronic brainstorming, and improving the time efficiency of decision making.[80] People working under electronically mediated conditions tend to stay focused on tasks and avoid the interpersonal conflicts and other problems common in face-to-face deliberations. On the negative side, decisions made by 'electronic groups' carry some risk of being impersonal and less compelling in terms of commitments to implementation and follow-through. Further, there is evidence that the use of computer technology for decision making is better accepted by today's university or college students than by people who are already advanced in their organisational careers.[81]

Virtual teamwork is discussed in detail in chapter 7, and virtual organisations and co-working are discussed in chapters 8 and 9.

Ethical decision making

The nature and extent of ethical decision making is subject to ongoing debate. Some scholars profess that ethics have no role to play in organisational decision making: for example, economist Milton Friedman said that making decisions on purely ethical grounds may not be in the interest of organisational profit making and responsibility to shareholders.[82] Despite such views, contemporary managerial attitudes towards ethics and social responsibility suggest that ethics are a relevant and important aspect of management function in contemporary managerial decision making.[83] Organisations constantly influence what we do and have influenced the changes that have taken place within society over time. Therefore, large and complex organisations can be regarded as moral entities in their own right. Organisational operators solve economic problems by distributing goods and services across society in the best possible way, but the purpose of industry is not just profit making; it is also to serve the general welfare.[84] Therefore, in contemporary organisations, making ethically and socially responsible decisions is considered 'worthy' for both organisations and society as a whole.

To 'be ethical' you need to determine whether your *actions* are ethical or not. These determinations, according to Gregory Foster, can be based on numerous theoretical underpinnings.

- A *principle, rule, law or regulation*. For example, if the law states it is wrong to discriminate on the basis of race or gender, then it is unethical to break this law. This is known as *deontology*.
- *Behavioural or ethics codes*. For example, it would be unethical for a Christian to break the Ten Commandments, or for a Hindu to break the rules of Dharma. Similarly, it is considered unethical for workers to break a code of ethics that the organisation has in place.
- *The consequences of our proposed actions or utilitarianism*. When making decisions, the ethical choice is the one that has the outcome of the greatest good for the greatest number. It is this theory that states that the end justifies the means. Utilitarianism is commonly used in business in the form of a cost–benefit analysis.
- *The rights of the stakeholders involved and what obligations we owe*. This is also known as Kant's theory of deontology. Kant's work is complex and tests whether something is ethical or not via his 'categorical imperative'. The categorical imperative says that an action is only ethical if it can become universal law, if it treats individuals as an ends not a means, and if it applies to all other individuals.
- *Values, traits, and behaviours or virtues we consider worthy*. Virtue ethics dates back to the Eastern and Western philosophies of Confucius and Aristotle. For example, Aristotle's philosophy indicates that the virtuous path is the middle path between two undesirable attributes; so between recklessness and cowardice is courage. Therefore, to be courageous when making ethical decisions is the virtuous and right thing to do.[85]

It is important to note that all these theories have weaknesses; for example, deontology does not allow for exceptions — it is very black and white. Utilitarianism can result in unjust outcomes because it is dependent on what is good for the majority. Virtue ethics and other self-awareness theories rely heavily on individual perception; for example, what one individual sees as entrepreneurial, another may see as high risk taking.

The dominance of economics, based on the free market; increasing competition; and quests for corporate and organisational survival, nationally and internationally, have had an impact on the extent to which individuals and organisations are prepared to act ethically when making decisions. The simplest way of making decisions would be to use a tool or algorithm that produces a flowchart showing how to come to the most ethical decision. Unfortunately, ethical decision making is extremely complex. Before moving on to an ethical decision-making framework, it is important to reflect on the determinations already mentioned and what it is that influences our judgement about what is right or wrong.

The classical approach to decision making tends to preclude the use of judgement and intuition and determines that decisions are made through *deductive* reasoning. However, the information required to make a rational decision is often not available and judgement has to be exercised. Judgement is effectively dependent on previous experience, and how these experiences have shaped the person's paradigm or 'world view'. This method of learning by experience is also called heurism (as discussed earlier), or one for which no algorithm exists and which therefore depend on *inductive* reasoning — building upon past experiences of similar problems.

Ethical decisions are rarely black and white. This is because ethical decision making generally involves numerous, often conflicting, morals. The difficulty of reconciling these conflicting morals leads to ethical dilemmas.

An **ethical dilemma** occurs when a person must decide between competing values and beliefs, often in complex and value-laden contexts.[86] In organisations, ethical dilemmas occur when a person's behaviour or the behaviour of others conflict with personal beliefs and values. Organisations need to make their ethical principles known to their staff. When organisational and individual values differ it causes stress and this is difficult to remove. An employee suffering an ethical dilemma has only three choices: he or she can change the behaviour, change their personal beliefs or rationalise the behaviour. Most rationalise the behaviour, as this is obviously the simplest option.

People in organisations tend to use after-the-fact rationalisations to 'excuse' or 'explain' unethical behaviour. The common rationalisations include:
- pretending the decision is not really unethical or illegal
- excusing the intended behaviour by saying it really is in the organisation's or your own best interests
- assuming the decision is acceptable because no-one else would ever find out about it
- expecting your superiors to support and protect the decision if anything should go wrong.[87]

Ethical decision-making framework

It is clear that personal reflection and critical analysis are needed in order to introduce some measure of objectivity into discussions that are essentially subjective due to our own bias (brought about by experience and socialisation).[88] This is where an ethical decision-making model can be useful as it forces us to look beyond our preconceived ideas and judgements.

Making ethical decisions is not easy — this framework is not a 'one best way' solution. Indeed, there is no such thing when discussing ethics; nor is there any clear right or wrong decision. However, applying the framework may improve the prospects of making a sound decision,[89] because a framework allows for eclectic theories to be used and assists in structuring thought processes.

An ethical decision-making framework is a series of steps designed to ensure that ethical theory is applied properly and appropriately. Its aim is to identify important ethical considerations so they can be fully thought through. The steps in the following framework are an adaptation of work done by John Harrison[90] and Simon Longstaff.[91]

1. Identify all the stakeholders that will be affected by the decision.
2. State the facts of the decision to be made without making any statement as to their rightness or wrongness. Many issues create controversy; you need to take the emotion out of the decision and look at the facts.
3. Highlight the principles, values and codes relevant to the decision, in particular, those that appear to be in conflict. Occasionally things may appear to be in conflict initially, but upon further investigation can actually be reconciled.
4. Investigate all the possible options available to resolve the decision.
5. Assess all the options identified in step 4, in line with the various ethical theories and while making sure that the duties and/or responsibilities of all parties are recognised; for example:
   - Apply deontology to identify the legal, moral and equitable rights of all affected parties and which option will best protect those rights.
   - Apply utilitarianism to identify all the benefits and harms each option will produce; in particular, identify which option will produce the best outcome.
   - Apply virtue ethics to identify which course of action develops moral virtue.
6. Ask yourself the following questions to 'road test' the decision:
   - If the decision goes on the public record, how would I feel? If you would not be happy then that is your inner-self telling you that you are about to break your own moral code.
   - How would you vindicate the decision to your close family members (also called 'the double check'[92])?

An **ethical dilemma** occurs when a person must make a decision that requires a choice among competing sets of principles.

- What will this proposed course of action do to your character or the character of your organisation? Reputation is a key businesses asset; making a decision that will irreparably damage that reputation is not a sound decision.
- Will everyone around you respond to the decision in the same way? If they cannot, then why should you be able to respond in that way?
- How would you like it if someone did this to you? If you would feel bad, then clearly others would probably not like it either.
- Will the proposed course of action bring about a good result for all involved? If the result is not good for all, then why are you doing it?
- Is the proposed course of action consistent with your espoused values and principles? Individuals make up an organisation. In business life or personal life, individuals should always be true to their own values.

7. Make your decision and implement it, accepting responsibility for the outcome; stand by your decision and be prepared to justify it.

Balancing stakeholders' interests is arguably the most critical of managerial tasks, as it represents the principal mechanism by which managers 'pay attention to', elicit and maintain the support of stakeholder groups with disparate needs and wants. As a decision-making process, it involves assessing, weighing and addressing the competing claims of those who have a stake in the actions of the organisation.[93] All stakeholders need to be taken into account and they should all be involved with modern business decision making. Often, an assumption is made that stakeholder groups are in opposition to each other; for example, tensions between shareholders' interests and community interests. However, stakeholders are often members of more than one group. For example, an employee may also be a shareholder and a member of the community.[94] Therefore, using a decision-making approach that applies several ethical perspectives ensures that the decision taken will be one that is 'ethical' according to the views of all stakeholders, irrespective of the theoretical evaluation.

ETHICAL
Perspective

Discrimination evident in employers' recruitment decisions

The newspaper headline read: 'Racism rife as Irish twice as likely to be given job'. The report was on a study conducted in Ireland by the Economic and Social Research Institute, which found high levels of discrimination in recruitment decisions by

Irish employers. Researchers distributed pairs of résumés identical in all respects except for the job applicant's name, which looked and sounded Irish, African, Asian or German. Results showed:
- overall: 78 Irish and 38 minority applicants were called to interview
- Irish vs. African: 18 Irish and 5 African applicants were called
- Irish vs. Asian: 19 Irish and 7 Asian applicants were called
- Irish vs. German: 18 Irish and 3 German applicants were called.

In one case, an Irish applicant received a telephone call to discuss her résumé, and an African applicant received an email stating that the job had already been filled. Researchers concluded that the pattern of discrimination in the data was so strong it was only 'a one in a million chance' that the preferences shown Irish applicants were accidental.[95]

Ethical decision-making standards and practices are part of an organisation's culture, and often permeate the organisation from the top down. The following OB in action shows organisations can damage their reputational capital by making unethical choices.

Bendigo and Adelaide Bank consider stakeholder interests in decision making

OBinAction

Bendigo Bank is committed to meeting the needs of its stakeholders and in particular the community it serves. As Managing Director, Mike Hirst, explains, 'One of the things we are always keen to do is make sure the results of our business provide equity for all of our stakeholders, whether that be customers, staff or shareholders too'.[96] Recent research has shown that including citizens as stakeholders of the business (such as responsible consumers and ethical employees) adds to value-creating activities of corporations.[97]

A recent poll, for example, revealed that three quarters of Australians recognise the association between extreme weather events, climate change and the need to divest investments away from coal.[98] Bendigo and Adelaide Bank have been swift to react to such sentiments, becoming the first big bank to divest from the coal and gas industry. Marne Baker, executive at Bendigo Bank, describes how the bank has a clear commitment to minimise environmental impacts including the companies it invests in. Specifically she says, 'the bank does not lend to companies for whom the core activity is the exploration, mining, manufacture or export of thermal coal or coal seam gas'. The bank's decision to divest from the coal and gas industry follows similar moves by the superannuation industry.

Complexity, chaos, chance and conundrums in decision making

At the start of this book, we highlighted the increasingly rapid nature of change in the workplace, and also the growing complexity of work. This has had a significant impact on decision making and practice (as shown in the examples in this chapter), and research has found that some of the simpler models elaborated on earlier in the chapter are increasingly limited in helping managers and employees make better decisions. For example, Henry Mintzberg, in a recent reflection on the changes to his thinking since he wrote his first book on management in the 1970s notes:

> the rational approach (define->diagnose->design->decide) turns out to be uncommon ... Perhaps, then, decision making means periods of groping followed by sudden sharp insights that lead to crystallisation. Or perhaps it is a form of 'organised anarchy' ... Maybe messy, real-life decision making makes more sense than we think, precisely because so much of it is beyond conscious thought.[99]

One area that has traditionally been neglected is that of decision making in complexity. While collectively, most people acknowledge that the world has become more complex, there is an acknowledgement that the ability and knowledge to navigate complexity has not permeated the thinking of most of today's executives and tomorrow's managers.[100] Sargut and McGrath suggest various methods for leaders to be more effective decision makers in complex organisations. This includes using better tools for understanding how complex systems behave, taking steps to mitigate risks, making measured trade-offs that keep early failures small, and gathering diverse thinkers who can deal creatively with variation.[101]

Building on complexity approaches to decision making are approaches focusing on chaos, whereby the appearance of complete unpredictability, randomness, luck or chance actually belies the interactive effects of a small number of critical forces, and perhaps hidden effects of a few important variables. Ralph Stacey has conducted research in this area, and one method that he claims is effective is 'random opportunism'. This is the idea of strategy being a process of seizing random opportunities as they arise, and taking advantage of the unexpected fortuitous circumstances.[102] This is perhaps more appropriate for entrepreneurs, but the concept comes from studies into established organisations, with the most famous example being Honda's experience of selling motorcycles in the United States. When Honda executives realised the interest of passers-by in the mini-cub motorcycles that they were riding to one of their meetings, they dramatically shelved all existing plans of entering the US market with mainstream models. Instead, they opted to break into the market with these smaller, non-standard motorcycles, which were sold in outlets as diverse as department stores and supermarkets.[103]

Social scientists have long recognised that an uneasy tension between choice and chance or serendipity exists, especially in business.[104] However, despite rapid technological changes and increasingly complex organisational environments, most management researchers still assume a largely predictable world and a deterministic context to allow them some form of structure and to give their research some form of 'causal sufficiency'.[105] De Rond and Thietart argue that in the field of strategy, while 'determinism' is increasingly used in a weaker sense, a multi-level theory of strategic choice that is related to chance, and causal background would give greater explanatory power especially in complex and chaotic contexts. In a detailed investigation of the 'discovery' of Viagra by the pharmaceutical firm Pfizer, de Rond and Thietart argue that many successful drug discoveries did not come out of well-constructed and well-planned drug development projects, but that serendipity played a significant role.[106]

One approach to try to understand these dynamic, non-linear approaches to decision making is based on paradoxes and dilemmas,[107] or what Mintzberg has recently referred to as conundrums.[108] As Mintzberg notes, 'Managing is rife with conundrums. Every way a manager turns, there seems to be some paradox or enigma lurking'.[109] He goes on to outline five types of conundrums that managers face when making decisions — namely, thinking conundrums, information conundrums, people conundrums, action conundrums and overall conundrums. Despite some researchers showing that these paradoxes and conundrums are reconcilable,[110] Mintzberg is unconvinced, and notes that the 'managers ultimate conundrum [is] — how to deal with all these conundrums concurrently — remains'.[111]

Whatever approach taken, it is evident that the increasingly dynamic and complex context of decision making will make managing in the future an even more challenging task.

Summary

Decision making and the types of decisions and decision environments

Decision making in organisations is a continuing process of identifying problems and opportunities and then choosing among alternative courses of action for dealing with them successfully. According to classical decision theory, managers seek 'optimum' solutions, while behavioural decision theory recognises that managers 'satisfice' and accept the first available satisfactory alternative.

Routine problems arise on a regular basis and can be resolved through standard responses called programmed decisions. Non-routine problems require tailored responses referred to as crafted decisions. Managers make decisions in three different environments: certain, risk and uncertain. Under certainty, everything about the alternative solutions is known and a choice will lead to an outcome that is highly predictable. Under risk, the manager can estimate the probability that particular outcomes will result from the choices made, but there are no guarantees. In uncertain environments, the choice is made with little real knowledge of what might eventuate.

Steps in the decision-making process

The decision-making process involves four sequential steps: recognise and define a problem; identify and analyse alternative courses of action; choose a preferred course of action; and implement the decision.

Classical, behavioural and garbage can decision-making models

In classical decision theory the manager operates in a world of complete certainty and always knows what will happen if a certain choice is made. Under behavioural decision theory, the manager is normally faced with risk or uncertainty when making decisions because of incomplete knowledge, ambiguity in the situation, lack of time to continue collecting and analysing information, and other constraints.

Intuition, judgement and creativity

Intuition, judgement and creativity are all critical in effective managerial decision making. Intuition — the ability to recognise the possibilities of a situation quickly — is increasingly considered an important managerial asset. Judgement is the use of cognitive skills to make choices among alternatives, but heuristics (or simplifying rules of thumb) can potentially bias decision making. Creativity limitations can be overcome, and decision making improved, through individual awareness and a good use of groups as problem-solving resources.

Conditions for decision making

Managers must know how to involve others in decision making and how to choose among individual, consultative and group decision methods. This is often a complex process. The Vroom–Jago model identifies how decision methods can be varied to meet the unique needs of each problem situation. Key issues involve quality requirements, information availability and time constraints. Groups can make decisions in different ways: decisions by lack of response, authority rule, minority rule, consensus and unanimity. There are potential benefits to making decisions in a group. Typically, a group decision is based on more information and results in better member understanding and commitment. The liabilities include greater time requirement and the dangers of groupthink.

Issues facing today's managers

Globalisation and workforce diversity have brought into play the significance of culture in managerial decision making. Culture can dictate, for example, who should make the decision and the speed of the decision-making process within the organisation.

Computers are being used more and more to facilitate decision making, but it is important to recognise both the benefits and the limitations of these sophisticated artificial intelligence initiatives.

Ethical issues in decision making are extremely relevant in today's organisations. Managers are often faced with critical ethical dilemmas — situations in which a preferred, particular decision may lead to an outcome that could be perceived as unethical or even illegal by others inside and outside of the organisation. Using a decision-making model can assist managers in this regard.

CHAPTER 12 study guide

Key terms

artificial intelligence, *p. 475*

behavioural decision theory, *p. 458*

certain environments, *p. 455*

classical decision theory, *p. 458*

consultative decisions, *p. 464*

crafted decisions, *p. 455*

creativity, *p. 463*

decision making, *p. 454*

escalating commitment, *p. 473*

ethical dilemma, *p. 477*

garbage can decision model, *p. 459*

group decisions, *p. 464*

groupthink, *p. 469*

heuristics, *p. 462*

individual decisions, *p. 464*

intuition, *p. 460*

judgement, *p. 462*

non-routine problems, *p. 455*

programmed decisions, *p. 455*

risk environments, *p. 455*

routine problems, *p. 455*

satisficing, *p. 458*

uncertain environments, *p. 456*

Review questions

1. Explain how three types of environments can have an impact on the decision-making process.
2. Why is identification of the problem (step 1 in the decision-making process) so important and how does this step relate to ethical decision making?
3. How does heurism relate to the general biases that many managers have with respect to decision making?
4. What can an organisation do to improve its creativity?

Application questions

1. Often at university, students are required to work in groups with people they have never met before. When choosing potential group members, how do you make the decision on who you are going to work with? In your answer please explain the decision-making environments.
2. A member of your staff has put together a business plan to produce and market a new product. The plan is comprehensive, and conservative figures estimate that the new product would be highly profitable for your organisation. However, your previous experience with this particular staff member has caused you to not fully trust him. Despite having no tangible reason for your lack of trust, you decide not to go ahead with the project. Your board of directors now wants an explanation for your decision. How do you justify and explain your behaviour? In your answer, comment on rational, intuitive, heurisistic and ethical considerations.
3. You have been working within a group on a large project that has taken six months. Unfortunately, a crisis occurs just prior to the project's completion date, signifying a significant delay in finalisation. Redirection decisions must be made immediately to salvage any losses. In your opinion, and considering what you have learnt in this chapter, who should make decisions in such a crisis: the manager accountable for project outcomes or the group responsible for the project, or should this be a consultative process for decision making? Explain the reasons for your choice.
4. Decisions on whether or not to grant finance credit to an individual are often made using decision-making software. What are the advantages and disadvantages of using such technology?
5. You have recently been sent to a regional office to help implement much-needed organisational changes. You have been told that some of the day-to-day operating decisions are to be made collectively by the workers and that you will be informed of their decisions when you get there. Upon arrival you discover that no decisions have been made, and you are working to a deadline to complete implementation of change. Using what you have learnt in this chapter, explain what you will do from here.
6. What career path have you chosen? How did you arrive at this important decision? Please use what you have learnt in this chapter to explain your answer.

1. As corporations move to coordinate operations that are spread across various nations, senior executives are realising that there are often substantial differences in the decision-making styles in different countries. Systematically review the recent scholarly and practitioner literature on decision making to answer the following questions, then write a report that summarises the most recent thinking on the issues raised. You must reference your work. Your lecturer may ask you to present a formal 'executive-style' five-minute summary of your findings.
   (a) What are some of the major decision-making styles typically found in corporations headquartered in Asia and New Zealand?
   (b) How compatible are the styles in Asia and New Zealand with those typically found in Australia?

2. One visible guideline for organisational behaviour is an organisation's code of ethics. Search the Internet and compare and contrast codes of ethics of either two large organisations — one in the private sector (for example, a bank), and one in the public sector (for example, a health service) — or the code of one of these organisations and a professional code of ethics (for example, a code of ethics for accountants). How do these codes assist the decision-making practices of staff? How do you interpret these codes and is your interpretation the same as that of other members in your class? What are the implications of the different interpretations, if any?

3. Research the current status of the Crime and Misconduct Commission inquiry into the conduct of the dam engineers during the Queensland floods and write a 500-word report on your findings.

Complete the following activities for your chosen organisation.
1. Try to identify several examples of routine problems and programmed decisions and non-routine problems and crafted decisions at your organisation. If you cannot access this information directly, consider the way the organisation works and some of the internal and external factors affecting the organisation to identify the types of decisions facing the organisation.
2. Compare the extent to which the organisation relies on (a) heuristics and (b) creativity in its approach to decision making.
3. What arrangements does the organisation have in place to ensure ethical decision making?

Decision-making biases

Instructions

How good are you at avoiding potential decision-making biases? Test yourself by answering the following questions:
1. Which is riskier?
   (a) Driving a car on a 1000 km trip
   (b) Flying on a 1000 km commercial airline flight
2. Are there more words in the English language:
   (a) that begin with 'r'?
   (b) that have 'r' as the third letter?
3. Mark is finishing his MBA at a prestigious university. He is very interested in the arts and at one time considered a career as a musician. Is Mark more likely to take a job:
   (a) in the management of the arts?
   (b) with a management consulting firm?
4. You are about to hire a new central-region sales director for the fifth time this year. You predict that the next director should work out reasonably well since the last four were poor performers and the odds favour hiring at least one good sales director in five tries. Is this thinking:
   (a) correct?
   (b) incorrect?
5. A newly hired engineer for a computer company in Perth has four years experience and good all-round qualifications. When asked to estimate the starting salary for this employee, a chemist with very little knowledge about the profession or industry guessed

an annual salary of $45 000. What is your estimate? $_____ per year

Scoring

Your instructor will provide answers and explanations for the assessment questions.

Interpretation

Each of the preceding questions examines your tendency to use a different judgemental heuristic. In the third edition of his book, *Judgment in managerial decision making*, (New York: Wiley, 1994, pp. 6–7), Max Bazerman calls these heuristics 'simplifying strategies, or rules of thumb' used in making decisions. He states: 'In general, heuristics are helpful, but their use can sometimes lead to severe errors … If we can make managers aware of the potential adverse impacts of using heuristics, they can then decide when and where to use them.' This assessment offers an initial insight into your use of such heuristics. An informed decision maker understands the heuristics, is able to recognise when they appear, and eliminates any that may inappropriately bias decision making.

Write down a situation that you have experienced in which some decision-making bias may have occurred. Be prepared to share and discuss this incident with the class.

Source: Adapted from Max H. Bazerman, *Judgment in managerial decision making*, 3rd edn (New York: Wiley, 1994), pp. 13–14. This material is used by permission of John Wiley & Sons, Inc.

Group activity

The fishing trip

Objectives

1. To help you experience both individual and group work when confronting a non-routine problem situation
2. To show you the advantage of assessing and analysing differences between individual decision-making methods and group decision-making methods; and also to give you some insight into the processes used to make decisions

Total time: 60–75 minutes

Procedure

1. Read the following story, 'The fishing trip'.[112]
2. Assume you are a member of the group in the story, and rank the items in order of importance under column A on the form provided.
3. Form groups of four to six people and rank the items again, this time placing your group rankings under column B.
4. Obtain the ranking information of an experienced sea captain, record it in column X, and then follow further direction from your lecturer or tutor.

The fishing trip

It was the first week in August when four friends set out on an overnight fishing trip in the Gulf of Carpentaria. Everything went well the first day — the sea was calm, they caught fish and later they camped out on a lovely little island. However, during the night a very strong wind pulled the anchor free and drove their boat ashore, and the pounding waves broke the propeller. Although there were oars in the boat, the motor was useless.

A quick review of the previous day's journey showed that the group was about 100 kilometres from the nearest inhabited land. The small deserted island they were on had a few scrub trees and bushes but no fresh water. They knew from their portable AM–FM radio that the weather would be hot and dry, with daytime temperatures expected to be above 38°C for the rest of the week. They were all dressed in light clothing, but each had a windbreaker for the cool evenings. They agreed that whatever happened they would stick together.

Their families back on shore expected the group to return from their trip that evening and would surely report them missing when they did not return. However, they realised that it might take time for someone to find them because they had gone out further than anyone might have expected.

Although some members of the group were quite concerned about this predicament, there was no panic. To help keep the group calm, one member, Jim, suggested that they take an inventory of the food and equipment available to them, just to be safe. 'It may be several days before we are rescued,' Jim said, 'and I think we should prepare for that'. Kate, Tom and Ann agreed, and their effort produced the list of items that follows.

After the list was completed, Jim suggested that every person independently rank each item according to its importance to the survival of the group. They all agreed to do this.

Items available	A	B	X	Items available	A	B	X
Each person has:							
(a) one windbreaker	_____			(h) fishing equipment	_____		
(b) one poncho	_____			(i) matches, rope and a few tools	_____		
(c) one sleeping bag	_____			(j) one compass mounted on the boat	_____		
(d) one pair of sunglasses.	_____			(k) two rear-view mirrors that can be removed from the boat	_____		
The boat contains:							
(e) a cooler with two bottles of soft drink per person and some ice	_____			(l) one 'official' navigational map of the gulf area where the friends are	_____		
(f) one large flashlight	_____			(m) one salt shaker (full)	_____		
(g) one first-aid kit	_____			(n) one bottle of liquor.	_____		

Case study: Decision making in the Victorian bushfires

Following a long period of drought conditions, on 7 February 2009 — what has now become known as 'Black Saturday' — a series of uncontrollable bushfires burned through 4500 square kilometres of the Australian state of Victoria, resulting in 173 deaths (the highest number of deaths in any Australian bushfire).[113] In addition, about 5000 people were injured, 2029 homes were destroyed, and countless animals died. The official 2009 Victorian Bushfires Royal Commission noted in its final report that:

> The response to the fires on 7 February was characterised by many people trying their best in extraordinarily difficult circumstances. There were many examples of people who met the challenge admirably. Nevertheless, some poor decisions were made by people in positions of responsibility and by individuals seeking to protect their own safety.[114]

The commission devoted some analysis on individual decision making. It found that people underestimated the threat posed by the bushfires on 'Black Saturday' and appeared reluctant to change their plans, sometimes with fatal consequences. Further, the experience of facing a bushfire can be very stressful, which can lead to poor decision making at the time. Bushfires also interrupt personal plans and create dilemmas. When making the decision to stay and defend their properties, some people were influenced by their attachment to their pets or their home. Their decision making was often further complicated by insufficient warnings about the danger of the situation. Even with better warnings, however, these personal dilemmas are not trivial or easily resolved.

At the operational level, the commission praised many on-ground operations on Black Saturday, noting that firefighting equipment and operational systems worked well in many circumstances, even when there were there were problems with radios and phones (which made it hard to track firefighters and trucks). The frontline decisions, training and safety awareness of the Country Fire Authority (CFA) and the Department of Sustainability and Environment (DSE) staff was highlighted and praised.

At the management level, the commission noted that the sound preparation and effective responses on the part of the state, municipal councils, the community and individuals will collectively help to minimise harm. The report made it clear that one of key problems was that on Black Saturday there was no single person or agency in control of the situation. It also found that 'some elements of leadership were wanting' on the day, identifying former CFA chief officer Russell Rees and DSE chief fire officer Ewan Waller, both of whom should have done more about fire warnings; and former police chief Christine Nixon, whose approach to emergency coordination was 'inadequate'.

Evidence before the commission has revealed that during the peak of the bushfires, the state's top two emergency response coordinators were out of the office. Victoria's Emergency Services Minister Bob Cameron, the chief coordinator of emergency management, was still at home. The deputy coordinator, then–police chief Christine Nixon, had left the state control centre and later had dinner at a pub with friends.[115] In its summary, the Royal Commission was told that Victorians were abandoned during the state's worst disaster by catastrophic failures in leadership on Black Saturday. Emergency services chiefs were concerned with coordination rather than command, focused on overseeing their troops rather than supervising the firefight, and issuing warnings to people in the path of the inferno.[116] There is evidence to support this type of behaviour, in that research has shown that in hostile environments, managers make more erratic strategic decisions.[117]

Questions

1. Use concepts covered in this chapter to explain the flaws in the past and even current decision-making process.
2. What remedies would you suggest to individuals, councils and the emergency management departments to ensure 'good' decisions are made?

End notes

1. Australian Institute of Management, 'How top CEOs make decisions', *Management Today* (19 September 2013), www.mtmag.com.au.
2. G Tecker, 'The essence of trust in decision-making', *Tecker International* (4 March 2013), www.tecker.com.
3. SH Appelbaum, D Louis, D Makarenko, J Saluja, O Meleshko and S Kulbashian, 'Participation in decision making: a case study of job satisfaction and commitment (part three)', *Industrial and Commercial Training*, vol. 45, no. 7 (2013), p. 412–19.
4. Australian Institute of Management, op cit.
5. For an excellent overview see George P Huber, *Managerial decision making* (Glenview, IL: Scott, Foresman, 1980).
6. See also John R Schermerhorn, Jr, *Management for productivity* (New York: John Wiley & Sons, 1989), pp. 70–1.
7. 'BP found grossly negligent over 2010 Deepwater Horizon oil spill in Gulf of Mexico', *ABC News* (5 September 2014), www.abc.net.au.
8. ibid.
9. D Hammer, 'Warnings of gas-leak risk at BP well described at Gulf of Mexico oil spill hearings', *The Times-Picayune* (24 August 2010).
10. 'Poor risk assessment contributed to BP spill: federal report', *Safety & Health*, vol. 184, no. 5 (November 2011), p. 20.
11. S Mishra, Decision-making under risk: integrating perspectives from Biology, Economics, and Psychology, *Personality and Social Psychology Review*, vol. 18 (2014), p. 280, originally published online 25 April 2014.
12. This discussion is based on James G March and Herbert A Simon, *Organizations* (New York: John Wiley & Sons, 1958), pp. 137–42.
13. ibid. See also Herbert A Simon, *Administrative behavior* (New York: The Free Press. 1947).
14. Adapted from 'Garbage can decision model', in JR Schermerhorn, JG Hunt, RN Osborn & M Uhl-Bien, *Organizational behavior*, 11th ed. (Hoboken: John Wiley & Sons, 2010), p. 214.
15. N Ashford, 'Incorporating science, technology, fairness, and accountability in environmental, health, and safety decisions', *Human and Ecological Risk Assessment*, vol. 11, no. 1 (2005), pp. 85–96.
16. ABCNews, 'Rudd Unconcerned by Garnaut Report Criticism', *ABC News*, 2008.
17. N. Stern, *The Economics of Climate Change: The Stern Review* (Cambridge: Cambridge University Press, 2007), p. 692.
18. L Hickman and J Randerson, 'Climate sceptics claim leaked emails are evidence of collusion among scientists', *The Guardian* (20 November 2009), www.guardian.co.uk.
19. 'Part 1 the global shift: 1 beyond reasonable doubt', *Garnaut Climate Change Review*, www.garnautreview.org.au.
20. *Garnaut Climate Change Review*, www.garnautreview.org.au.
21. J Whalley, 'Climate change adviser Ross Garnaut chides Business Council over carbon tax debate', *Adelaide Now* (31 May 2011), www.adelaidenow.com.au.
22. M Farr, 'FAQ: What the carbon price means for you', News.com.au (8 November 2011), www.news.com.au.
23. L Wilson and M Chambers, 'Julia Gillard seals carbon tax but Greens want more', *The Australian* (9 November 2011), www.theaustralian.com.au.
24. M Kenny, 'Liberals rejoice as carbon tax repeal passes lower house', *The Sydney Morning Herald* (27 June 2014), www.smh.com.au.

25. 'Direct Action climate plan passes the Senate with help from Palmer United Party', *The Sydney Morning Herald* (31 October 2014), www.smh.com.au.

26. B Naughten, 'Emissions pricing, "Complementary Policies" and "Direct Action" in the Australian electricity supply sector: some conditions for cost-effectiveness', Economic Papers, vol. 32, no. 4 (December 2013), pp. 440–53.

27. G Jericho, 'Climate change: Australia and US are moving in opposite directions', *The Guardian* (30 June 2014), www.theguardian.com.

28. L Williams, 'China's climate change policies: actors and drivers', *Lowy Institute for International Policy*, 24 July 2014, www.lowyinstitute.org.

29. Weston H Agor, *Intuition in organizations* (Newbury Park, CA: Sage, 1989).

30. Henry Mintzberg, 'Planning on the left side and managing on the right', *Harvard Business Review*, vol. 54 (July/August 1976), pp. 51–63; H Minzberg, 'Decision making: it's not what you think', *MIT Sloan Management Review*, vol. 42, no. 3 (2001), pp. 89–93.

31. G Ramirez, 'Asian leaders value creativity and intuition more than New Zealand leaders', Grant Thornton (23 June 2014), www.grantthornton.co.nz.

32. V Cheng, J Rhodes and P Lok, 'A framework for strategic decision making and performance among Chinese managers', *The International Journal of Human Resource Management*, vol. 21, no. 9 (2010), pp. 1373–95.

33. S Chie-Ming Ko, 'A study on the strategy decision making process of ethnic Chinese companies in Singapore and Malaysia', Thesis (D.B.A.), University of Western Australia (2009), https://repository.uwa.edu.au.

34. CB Bingham and KM Eisenhardt, 'Rational heuristics: the 'simple rules' that strategists learn from process experience', *Strategic Management Journal*, vol. 32, no. 13 (2011), pp. 1437–64.

35. MS Gary and RE Wood, 'Mental models, decision rules, and performance heterogeneity', *Strategic Management Journal*, vol. 32 (2011), pp. 569–94.

36. The classic work in this area is found in a series of articles by D Kahneman and A Tversky: 'Subjective probability: a judgement of representativeness', *Cognitive Psychology*, vol. 3 (1972), pp. 430–54; 'On the psychology of prediction', *Psychological Review*, vol. 80 (1973), pp. 237–51; 'Prospect theory: an analysis of decision under risk', *Econometrica*, vol. 47 (1979), pp. 263–91; 'Psychology of preferences', *Scientific American* (1982), pp. 161–73; 'Choices, values, frames', *American Psychologist*, vol. 39 (1984), pp. 341–50.

37. Commonwealth Treasury, '*2004–2005* Budget paper no. 1, statement 11: statement of risks', www.budget.gov.au.

38. J Maley, 'Train drivers not to blame, say tetchy commuters', *The Sydney Morning Herald* (9 November 2004), www.smh.com.au.

39. M Bazerman, *Judgement in managerial decision-making*, 5th ed. (New York: Wiley & Sons, 2002).

40. Definition and subsequent discussion based on Max H Bazerman, *Judgement in managerial decision making*, 2nd ed. (New York: John Wiley & Sons, 1990), pp. 11–39.

41. D Lovallo and O Sibony, 'The case for behavioral strategy', *McKinsey Quarterly* (2011).

42. D Kahneman, D Lovallo and O Sibony, 'Before you make that big decision', *Harvard Business Review*, vol. 89, no. 6 (2011), pp. 50–60.

43. '10 questions with Toby Ruckert of Unified Inbox', *NZ Entrepreneur*, issue 7 (May 2013), http://nzentrepreneur.co.nz/issue-7.

44. B Joo, GN McLean and B Yang, 'Creativity and human resource development: an integrative literature review and a conceptual framework for future research', *Human Resource Development Review*, vol. 12, no. 4 (2013), pp. 390–421.

45. 'Creating an innovative culture', Business Planning, SmallBiz Connect, http://toolkit.smallbiz.nsw.gov.au/part/14/71/300.

46. James AF Stoner, *Management*, 2nd ed. (Englewood Cliffs, NJ: Prentice Hall, 1982), pp. 167–8.

47. H Thomas, 'The great avoidable flood: an inquiry's challenge', *The Australian* (22 January 2011), www.theaustralian.com.au.

48. H Thomas, 'Engineer bores a hole in dam untruths', *The Australian* (19 March 2011), www.theaustralian.com.au.

49. Queensland Floods Commission of Inquiry, *Interim Report* (2011, p. 62); *Complete list of Final Report recommendations* (2012, p. 15), www.floodcommission.qld.gov.au.

50. Reinsurers, insurers join Wivenhoe class action (14 July 2015), http://insurancenews.com.au/local/reinsurers-insurers-join-wivenhoe-class-action.

51. J Sturmer, 'Brisbane floods class action: victims claim Wivenhoe Dam operators liable for compensation bill' (8 July 2014), www.abc.net.au.

52. Insurance news, op cit.

53. CC Harwood, 'Solving problems', *Executive Excellence*, vol. 16 (9 September 1999), p. 17.

54. See Victor H Vroom and Philip W Yetton, *Leadership and decision making* (Pittsburgh: University of Pittsburgh Press, 1973); Victor H Vroom and Arthur G Jago, *The new leadership* (Englewood Cliffs, NJ: Prentice Hall, 1988).

55. This discussion is developed from Edgar H Schein, *Process consultation*, vol. I, 2nd ed. (New York: Addison-Wesley, 1988), pp. 69–75.

56. Developed from guidelines presented in the classic article by Jay Hall, 'Decisions, decisions, decisions', *Psychology Today* (November 1971), pp. 55, 56.

57. Irving L Janis, 'Groupthink', *Psychology Today* (November 1971), pp. 43–6; Irving L Janis, *Groupthink*, 2nd ed. (Boston: Houghton Mifflin, 1982). See also J Longley and DG Pruitt, 'Groupthink: a critique of Janis' theory' in L Wheeler (ed.), *Review of personality and social psychology* (Beverly Hills, CA: Sage, 1980); Carrie R Leana, 'A partial test of Janis's groupthink model: the effects of group cohesiveness and leader behavior on decision processes', *Journal of Management*, vol. 11, no. 1 (1985), pp. 5–18.

58. DJ Packer and AL Chasteen, 'Loyal deviance: testing the normative conflict model of dissent in social groups', *Personality and Social Psychology Bulletin*, vol. 36, no. 1 (2010), pp. 5–18.

59. DJ Packer, 'Avoiding groupthink', *Psychological Science*, vol. 20, no. 5 (2009), pp. 546–8.

60. R Boisjoly, E Curtis and E Mellican, 'Roger Boisjoly and the *Challenger* disaster: the ethical dimensions', cited in T Beauchamp and N Bowie (eds), *Ethical theory and business*, 7th ed. (New Jersey: Prentice Hall, 2004), pp. 123–36 at p. 128; *A major malfunction*, BBC Education & Training videorecording (1998).

61. *A major malfunction*, BBC Education & Training videorecording (1998).

62. C Ferraris and R Carveth, 'NASA and the Columbia Disaster: Decision-making by Groupthink?' Proceedings from the 68th Annual Convention of The Association for Business Communication, 22–25 October 2003, Albuquerque, New Mexico.

63. *Report of Columbia Accident Investigation Board, Volume I* (Washington, DC: NASA, 2003), www.nasa.gov.

64. CR Sunstein, *Infotopia: how many minds produce knowledge* (New York: Oxford University Press, 2006).

65. S Sorscher, 'Group-think caused the market to fail', *Huffington Post Business* (25 May, 2011), www.huffingtonpost.com.

66. Developed from Irving Janis, *Victims of groupthink*, 2nd ed. (Boston: Houghton Mifflin, 1982).

67. See Gayle W Hill, 'Group versus individual performance: are N + 1 heads better than one?', *Psychological Bulletin*, vol. 91 (1982), pp. 517–39.

68. These techniques are well described in George P Huber, *Managerial decision making* (Glenview, IL: Scott, Foresman, 1980); Andre L Delbecq, Andrew L Van de Ven and David H Gustafson, *Group techniques for program planning: a guide to nominal groups and Delphi techniques* (Glenview, IL: Scott, Foresman, 1975); William M Fox, 'Anonymity and other keys to successful problem-solving meetings', *National Productivity Review*, vol. 8 (Spring 1989), pp. 145–56.

69. Robert Carey, 'Is your team tired?', *Successful Meetings*, vol. 41, no. 12 (November 1992), pp. 97–100.

70. See Delbecq et al., op. cit.; Fox, op. cit.

71. Barry M Staw, 'The escalation of commitment to a course of action', *Academy of Management Review*, vol. 6 (1981), pp. 577–87; Barry M Staw and Jerry Ross, 'Knowing when to pull the plug', *Harvard Business Review*, vol. 65 (March/April 1987), pp. 68–74. See also Glen Whyte, 'Escalating commitment to a course of action: a reinterpretation', *Academy of Management Review*, vol. 11 (1986), pp. 311–21.

72. Bazerman, op. cit., pp. 79–83.

73. T Fullerton, 'A rogue trader, a Swiss bank and another financial scandal', *ABC News* (5 October 2011), www.abc.net.au.

74. Adapted from 'Escalation of commitment by bank loan officers and college students', in JR Schermerhorn, JG Hunt, RN Osborn & M Uhl-Bien, *Organizational behavior*, 11th ed. (Hoboken: John Wiley & Sons, 2010), p. 221.

75. See Fons Trompenaars, *Riding the waves of culture* (London: Nicholas Brealey, 1993).

76. J Tang, 'It's payback time', *Asia Computer Weekly* (11 April 2005), p. 1.

77. J Schramm-Nielsen, 'Cultural dimensions of decision making: Denmark and France compared', *Journal of Managerial Psychology*, vol. 16, no. 5/6 (2001), pp. 404–24.

78. Nancy J Adler, *International dimensions of organizational behavior*, 2nd ed. (Boston: PWS-Kent, 1991).

79. See 'Computers that think are almost here', *Business Week* (17 July 1995), pp. 68–73.

80. AR Dinnis and JS Valacich, 'Computer brainstorms: two heads are better than one', *Journal of Applied Psychology* (February 1994), pp. 77–86.

81. B Kabanoff and JR Rossiter, 'Recent developments in applied creativity', *International Review of Industrial and Organizational Psychology*, vol. 9 (1994), pp. 283–324.

82. M Friedman, 'The social responsibility of business is to increase its profits', *New York Times Magazine* (13 September 1970), reprinted in S Collins-Chobanian, *Ethical challenges to business as usual* (New Jersey: Prentice Hall, 2005), pp. 224–9.

83. J Kujala, 'Understanding managers' moral decision-making', *International Journal of Value-Based Management*, vol. 16, no. 1, (2003), pp. 37–52; P Ulrich and U Thielemann, 'How do managers think about market economy and morality? Empirical studies into business-ethical thinking patterns', *Journal of Business Ethics*, vol. 12 (1993), pp. 879–98.

84. D Lee, P Newman and R Price, *Decision making in organisations* (London: Pitman Publishing, 1999).

85. GD Foster, 'Ethics: time to revisit the basics', *The Humanist* vol. 63, no. 2 (2003), pp. 30–7.

86. L Ehrich, N Cranston and M Kimber, 'Public sector managers and ethical dilemmas', *Journal of The Australian And New Zealand Academy Of Management*, vol. 10, no. 1 (2004), pp. 25–37.

87. Saul W Gellerman, 'Why "good" managers make bad ethical choices', *Harvard Business Review*, vol. 64 (July/August 1986), pp. 85–90. See also Barbara Ley Toffler, *Tough choices: managers talk ethics* (New York: John Wiley & Sons, 1986) and Shari Collins-Chobanian, *Ethical challenges to business as usual* (New Jersey: Prentice Hall, 2005).

88. GD Foster, 'Ethics: time to revisit the basics', *The Humanist*, vol. 63, no. 2 (2003), pp. 30–7.

89. GD Foster, op. cit.

90. J Harrison, *Ethics for Australian business* (Sydney: Prentice Hall, 2001).

91. S Longstaff, 'Ethical issues and decision-making', www.ethics.org.au.

92. J Schermerhorn, J Campling, D Poole and R Wiesner, *Management: an Asia–Pacific perspective* (Milton, QLD: John Wiley & Sons Australia Ltd, 2004).

93. SJ Reynolds, FC Schultz and DR Hekman, 'Stakeholder theory and managerial decision-making: constraints and implications of balancing stakeholder interests', *Journal of Business Ethics*, vol. 64, no. 3 (2006), pp. 285–301.

94. TJ Radin, 'To propagate and to prosper: a naturalistic foundation for stakeholder theory', *Ruffin Series in Business Ethics*, Business, science and ethics (1 January 2004), pp. 289–310.

95. Adapted from 'Discrimination evident in employers' recruitment decisions', in JR Schermerhorn, JG Hunt, RN Osborn & M Uhl-Bien, *Organizational behavior*, 11th ed. (Hoboken: John Wiley & Sons, 2010), p. 209.

96. M Winnes, 'Bank committed to needs of stakeholders', *Bendigo Advertiser* (11 August 2014), www.bendigoadvertiser.com.au.

97. D Nyberg, A Spicer and C Wright, 'Incorporating citizens: corporate political engagement with climate change in Australia', *Organization*, vol. 20, no. 3 (2013), pp. 433–53.

98. 'Link between rise in insurance premiums and extreme weather', *Lonergan Research* (3 September 2014), www.lonerganresearch.com.au.

99. H Mintzberg, BW Ahlstrand, and J Lampel, *Management? It's not what you think!* (New York: Pearson Financial Times, 2010).

100. G Sargut and RG McGrath, 'Learning to live with complexity', *Harvard Business Review*, vol. 89 no. 9 (2011), pp. 68–76.

101. ibid.

102. RD Stacey, *Dynamic strategic management for the 1990s: balancing opportunism and business planning* (London: Kogan Page, 1990).

103. RT Pascale, 'Perspectives on strategy: the real story behind Honda's success', *California Management Review*, vol. 26, no. 3 (1984), pp. 47–72; C Hampden-Turner & F Trompenaars, *Mastering the infinite game: how East Asian values are transforming* (Oxford: Capstone, 1997).

104. CI Barnard, *The functions of the executive* (Cambridge, MA: Harvard University Press, 1938); I Berlin, *The hedgehog and the fox: an essay on Tolstoy's view of history* (London: Weidenfeld & Nicolson, 1953).

105. M de Rond and R-A Thietart, 'Choice, chance, and inevitability in strategy', *Strategic Management Journal*, vol. 28, no. 5 (2007) pp. 535–51.

106. ibid.

107. MW Lewis, 'Exploring paradox: toward a more comprehensive guide', *Academy of Management Review*, vol. 25, no. 4 (2000), pp. 760–76; WK Smith and MW Lewis, 'Toward a theory of paradox: a dynamic equilibrium model of organizing', *Academy of Management Review*, vol. 36, no. 2 (2011), pp. 381–403; C Hampden-Turner, *Charting the corporate mind: from dilemma to strategy* (Oxford, Blackwell, 1994); Seet and Ahmad (2009), op. cit.

108. H Mintzberg, *Managing* (San Francisco, CA.: Berrett-Koehler, 2009).

109. ibid.

110. A Trompenaars and C Hampden-Turner, *21 leaders for the 21st century: how innovative leaders manage in the digital age* (Oxford: Capstone, 2001); P-S Seet, 'The creativity paradox', Monash Business Review, vol. 4, no. 1 (2008), pp. 25–6.

111. Mintzberg, op. cit.

112. Exercise developed from Charles Wales and Robert Stages, 'The fishing trip', under an Exxon Guided Design IMPACT Grant.

113. 'Black Saturday', ABC website, www.abc.net.au/innovation/blacksaturday.

114. *2009 Victorian Bushfires Royal Commission: final report*, www.royalcommission.vic.gov.au.

115. M Papadakis, 'More quizzing for CFA chief Russell Rees at bushfires royal commission', *Herald Sun* (1 May 2010), www.heraldsun.com.au.

116. N Ross, 'Christine Nixon to give speech on leadership after commission criticism', *Herald Sun* (28 May 2010), www.heraldsun.com.au.

117. J Robert Mitchell, DA Shepherd and MP Sharfman, 'Erratic strategic decisions: when and why managers are inconsistent in strategic decision making', *Strategic Management Journal*, vol. 32 (2011), pp. 683–704.

CHAPTER 13

COMMUNICATION, CONFLICT AND NEGOTIATION IN ORGANISATIONS

LEARNING OBJECTIVES

After studying this chapter, you should be able to:

1. define communication and discuss its role in organisations

2. define conflict and explain how it may affect organisational effectiveness

3. explain how managers may deal with conflict effectively

4. explain the role of negotiation in organisations

5. discuss managerial issues in negotiation.

THE CHANGING SOCIAL MEDIA FACE OF ORGANISATIONS

New technology and an increasing demand for new emerging social media technologies are changing the way organisations communicate forever — from everyday communication channels and interaction, to the recruitment process in organisations. Relying on local newspapers and advertising agencies to recruit employees is fast becoming a practice of the past as more jobseekers turn to social networks for their hiring and job finding needs. A study in understanding the social media landscape in Australia and New Zealand found LinkedIn to be the most popular site for jobseekers, with 74 per cent of respondents having a LinkedIn profile. Facebook was second, with 69 per cent having a Facebook profile, Twitter at 18 per cent, Instagram 11 per cent and 3 per cent of people have a MySpace account. Of all respondents, only 9 per cent didn't have any presence on social media. When analysing the use of organisations' use of social media, 63 per cent of employers have a company LinkedIn page, 55 per cent a Facebook page, 35 per cent have a Twitter account, 1 per cent a MySpace page, 2 per cent an Instagram account and only 22 per cent of organisations have no social media presence at all.

Ninety-one per cent of professionals and 85 per cent of employers agreed that the only social media site that is acceptable to be classed as professional is LinkedIn and that other social media such as Facebook, Twitter and Instagram should be regarded as personal.[1] Whether this perception is held with the younger generation is a different story. Reprezent, a radio station that represents youth culture, young opinion and young voices in London, spoke with 110 young people to find out how much young people were making use of social media to look for employment opportunities. They found that 80 per cent of 18–24 year olds have used social media to look for work, one in six visited social media first when searching for employment opportunities, and Twitter was the most popular form of social media for this purpose.[2]

Organisations such as the Marriott embrace technologies such as Facebook in finding suitable staff. Marriott has four times more likes and followers than even Facebook's own careers page and allows visitors to apply for any one of thousands of jobs, broken down and easily searchable by location and specialty.[3] These types of communication offer new ways of accessing information. However, even though many organisations have a strong presence on career sites and job boards, they often also still use more traditional ways to communicate with prospective employees, such as through print publications, university networks and career fairs. The main objective in using a range of communication channels is to enhance the 'personal touch' approach, and to convey intended messages in a clear way that is suitable to an organisation's various clients. Therefore, it is essential to ensure that whatever the communication technology, it is used in an appropriate and professional manner.

Introduction

The study of communication encompasses nearly all of the critical topics that are basic to understanding human behaviour in general and human functioning within organisations in particular. In fact, communication and organisational success are directly related. Good communication can have a positive and mobilising effect on employees. Poor communication can produce powerful negative consequences, such as distortion of goals and objectives, conflict, misuse of resources and inefficiency in performance of duties. Collaboration requires effective communication, especially in the age of communicating through social media. Effective communication is the glue that holds everything together.

The ability to manage good communication and handle conflict effectively is a necessary skill in all management roles. In any situation where people interact, there is potential for disagreement, challenge and conflict. No area of an organisation is devoid of conflict, and in some cases, conflict can be a good and healthy thing. Constructive conflict can promote creativity, and make people reassess situations, identify problems and find new solutions. However, when conflict in the workplace becomes chronic or disproportionate, or leads to lost productivity and stress, then managers must deal with the problem. In some instances it can indicate that organisational members are seeking more effective means of communication that will help resolve the conflict. In other instances, organisational members could be challenging normal processes and procedures in an effort to improve productivity or introduce innovative systems. Hence, in order to resolve conflict, managers are increasingly required to possess negotiating skills. Such skills may in turn be used as a vehicle to create change or develop new opportunities.

In this chapter we will cover the basic process of communication and related issues in organisations. Also, because the daily work of people in organisations is based on communication and interpersonal relationships, conflict situations often arise and managers need to understand these and know how to deal with them. Hence, the chapter will also introduce you to conflict and negotiation as key processes of organisational behaviour.

Communication in organisations

Communication is the way we share information, ideas, goals, directions, expectations, feelings and emotions in the context of coordinated activities. We can think of interpersonal communication as a process of sending symbols with attached meanings from one person to another. These interpersonal foundations form the basis for discussing the larger issue of communication within the organisation. **Organisational communication** is the process by which members exchange information and establish a common understanding.

When we communicate with others, we are usually trying to influence other people's understanding, behaviour or attitudes. We are trying to share meaning in some way. As Mintzberg stresses, we are communicating with others to inform, instruct, motivate or seek information.

For example, you may wish to inform your human resource manager that staff turnover is up 5 per cent this month, or instruct your assistants to clean up their desks and work more methodically. Perhaps you want to have an informal chat with Janine to let her 'get things off her chest' in the hope that she will be happier and thus be more motivated to work effectively. Or, perhaps, you are going to call a staff meeting to gather information on a particular problem.

While the function of interpersonal communication is really to share meaning, effective organisational communication can provide substantial benefits to the organisation's members. Four functions are particularly important: achieving coordinated action, developing information, expressing feelings and emotions, and communicating roles.

From a top-management perspective, a primary function of organisational communication is to achieve coordinated action. The collection of individuals that make up an organisation remains an unfocused group until its members are in effective communication with one another. It is important that managers and individuals are aware of techniques in communication that are appropriate for their organisation's structure.

Organisational communication is the process by which entities exchange information and establish a common understanding.

Interpersonal communication

The key elements in the interpersonal communication process are illustrated in figure 13.1. They include a source (a person who is responsible for encoding an intended meaning into a message) and a receiver (a person who decodes the message into a perceived meaning). While the process may appear to be elementary, it is not quite as simple as it looks. Let us examine the model in some detail to identify the main elements in the process, the sequencing of these elements, and weaknesses in the process that can lead to communication problems or distortions.

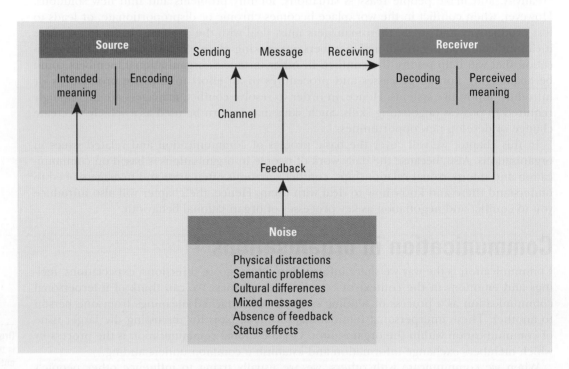

FIGURE 13.1 The communication process and possible sources of 'noise'

The conventional communication process is made up of the following essential components: the information source, the encoding of a message, the selection of a channel, the transmission of the message, the decoding of the message, feedback from the receiver of the message and any 'noise' (or interference) that may have affected accurate decoding (or interpretation of the message).

The **information source** is a person or group of persons with a reason to communicate with some other person(s), the receiver(s). The reasons for the source to communicate include changing the attitudes, knowledge or behaviour of the receiver. A manager, for example, may want to communicate with the boss to make him or her understand why the manager's work unit needs more time to finish an assigned project. Of course, the manager will want to do so in such a way that indicates respect for the receiver and an understanding that the job is important, among other factors.

The next step in the process is **encoding** — the process of translating an idea or thought into meaningful symbols. This translation, or encoding, process results in the **transmission** of a message via a channel that may consist of verbal, written and/or nonverbal symbols (such as gestures or body language), or some combination of all three. The message is what is communicated. A **channel** is the medium through which the message may be delivered in organisational communication. The choice of channels may alter the effectiveness of the intended message. For many people, it is easier to communicate verbally and face to face, for example, than in a letter or memo. On the other hand, perhaps our manager would prefer to carefully

An **information source** is a person or group of persons with a reason to communicate with some other person(s), the receiver(s).

Encoding is the process of translating an idea or thought into meaningful symbols.

Transmission is the actual communication of a message from one person to another through a chosen channel.

Channels are the media through which the message may be delivered.

construct a formal memo to his or her boss to set out the reasons why the work unit needs more time. Our manager should consider whether the boss might interpret the choice of a memo rather than a face-to-face meeting as avoidance. Alternatively, the boss might give the matter more weight if a letter arrives in an envelope in the in-tray than if the issue is briefly mentioned in an email. The manager's message is simple: 'Our work unit needs more time to complete this task', but there are many ways to try to communicate that message.

The process of communication does not stop with the sender. The **receiver** is the individual who hears (or reads or sees) the message. The receiver may or may not attempt to decode the message. **Decoding** involves interpreting or translating the symbols sent. This process of translation may or may not result in the assignment of the same meaning intended by the source. Frequently, the intended meaning of the source and the meaning perceived by the receiver differ, or the receiver may have difficulty interpreting the message. Our manager wants the boss to understand that the work unit needs more time to complete a task. Will the boss interpret the message this way? Alternative interpretations could be that the work unit is underperforming, that the manager is underperforming, or that the manager is seeking the appointment of more staff.

Most receivers are well aware of the potential gap between an intended message that was sent and the message that is received. **Feedback** is the process by which receivers acknowledge the communication and return a message concerning how they feel about the original message. Throughout the process, there may be any number of disturbances. **Noise** is the term used to indicate any disturbance within the communication process that disrupts the matching process between sender and receiver.

> The **receiver** is the individual or group of individuals that hear or read or see the message.
>
> **Decoding** is the interpretation of the symbols sent from the sender to the receiver.
>
> **Feedback** is the process of telling someone else how you feel about something the person did or said, or about the situation in general.
>
> **Noise** is anything that interferes with the effectiveness of the communication attempt.

Eliminating noise in communication

OBinAction

Consider an example of noise. A Singapore student in organisational behaviour is interviewing senior partners in a well-known accounting firm in Australia as part of a research project. The first day she went out on the job wearing casual clothes with sandals and making little eye contact because she felt shy. She got little cooperation from the senior partners. She spoke to a fellow student who advised her to dress quite formally because it is an accounting firm and to ensure she makes eye contact because it would show her level of involvement, interest and warmth. The senior partners became much more cooperative. This illustrates that even non-verbal communication cues can interfere with the effectiveness of the communication process.

It is a challenging task to communicate accurately. Managers and employees alike can make mistakes. As a study by Thomas Dahle clearly indicates, some forms of exchange between superiors and employees must be handled with great care.[4]

Effective and efficient communication

Effective communication occurs when the intended meaning of the source and the perceived meaning of the receiver are the same. This should be the manager's goal in any interpersonal communication attempt. However, it is not always achieved. Even now, we worry whether you are interpreting our written words as we intend. Our confidence would be higher if we were face to face in class together and you could ask clarifying questions. This opportunity to offer feedback and ask questions is one way of increasing the effectiveness of communication.

Efficient communication occurs at minimum cost in terms of resources expended. Time is an important resource in the communication process. Picture your lecturer taking the time to communicate individually with each student in your class. It would be virtually impossible to do so. And even if it were possible, it would be costly in terms of time. Managers often choose not to visit employees personally to communicate messages. Instead, they rely on

> **Effective communication** is communication in which the intended meaning of the source and the perceived meaning of the receiver are one and the same.
>
> **Efficient communication** is communication at minimum cost in terms of resources expended.

the efficiency of telephone conversations, memos, posted bulletins, group meetings, email, teleconferencing, videos and sometimes even text messages. However, efficient (economical) communications are not always effective. A low-cost communication, such as email, may save time for the sender, but it does not always achieve the desired results in terms of the receiver's perceived meaning. Similarly, an effective communication may not be efficient. For a manager to visit each employee and explain a new change in procedures may guarantee that everyone truly understands the change, but it may also be prohibitively expensive in terms of the required time expenditure.

Managers are busy people who depend on their communication skills to remain successful in their work. You need to learn how to maximise the effectiveness of your communications with others and to achieve reasonable efficiency in the process. These goals require the ability to overcome a number of communication barriers that commonly operate in the workplace. Such barriers may include cultural differences, defensiveness, misreading of non-verbal communication, and stereotyping.[5]

Communication channels

In a very important sense the organisation is a network of information and communication channels. Traditionally, there were formal and informal channels, but the electronic age has added a third category — quasiformal channels. While comparatively few managers are in a position to establish organisation-wide communication channels, all managers should understand and be able to use each of the multiple channels for communication within their organisation.

Formal communication channels follow the chain of command established by an organisation's hierarchy of authority. An organisation chart, for example, indicates the proper routing for official messages passing from one level or part of the hierarchy to another. Because formal communication channels are recognised as official and authoritative, written communication in the form of letters, memos, policy statements and other announcements typically adheres to these channels.

Although necessary and important, formal channels constitute only one part of a manager's overall communication responsibilities. Interpersonal networks represent the use of the formal channels just described as well as a wide variety of **informal communication channels** that do not adhere to the organisation's hierarchy of authority. These informal channels coexist with the formal channels but frequently diverge from them by skipping levels in the hierarchy and/or cutting across vertical chains of command.

In addition, there are many instances of chief executive officers and chairpersons of contemporary organisations who go to great lengths to improve communication with the entire staff. In some organisations managers may prefer to walk around to meet with and talk to floor employees as they do their jobs. 'Management by wandering around' can help develop trust in working relationships with employees and can avoid barriers caused by status effects. Managers who spend time walking around can greatly reduce the perceived 'distance' between themselves and their employees. Management, by wandering around, can also reduce selective perception biases by reducing the gap between what individuals want to hear and see and what is actually occurring. Managers can also create an atmosphere of open and free-flowing communication. As a result, more and better information is available for decision making, and the relevance of decisions to the needs of lower level personnel increases. Of course, the wandering around must be a genuine attempt to communicate; it should not be perceived as just another way to 'check up' on employees.

While formal channels conform to the organisation's chain of command and informal channels emerge from day-to-day activities, a set of quasiformal channels also exists in most corporations today. **Quasiformal channels** are planned communication connections between holders of various positions within the organisation. They are part of the organisation's overall management information system.

Formal communication channels are communication channels that follow the chain of command established by the organisation's hierarchy.

Informal communication channels are communication channels that do not adhere to the organisation's hierarchy.

Quasiformal channels are planned communication connections between holders of the various positions within the organisation.

Communication and sustainability

Forward-looking businesses are determined to lead the way with regard to environmental sustainability. Communication technology has a major role to play in reducing the carbon footprint of organisations. For example, teleworking (or telecommuting) enables employees to work from home, thus reducing commuter numbers, pollution and petrol use. Virtual technologies are also used increasingly by organisations wishing to reduce travel needs, aviation fuel consumption and air pollution. One firm with a strong commitment to environmental performance is Accounting North, a Chartered Accounting firm that is leading the way in the accounting industry by being virtually a paperless office. Another is Manpower Australia and New Zealand, which hosts its Global Leadership Meeting 'virtually'. The leaders are able to interact with colleagues, which is vital to their strategic planning and execution, and by holding the meeting virtually they eliminated nearly one million miles of air travel or 180 tonnes of CO_2 emissions.

Low richness							High richness
• Impersonal • One-way • Fast	• Postings • E-bulletins • Reports	• Memos • Letters • Blogs • Text messages	• Email • Wikis • Intranets • Voicemail	• Telephone • Instant messaging	• Meetings • Video conferences		• Personal • Two-way • Slow

An organisation exists and must be managed as a system of interdependent parts performing distinct but coordinated functions. When work flow interdependence is such that a person or group must rely on task contributions from one or more others to achieve its goals, the circumstances are ripe for developing a quasiformal communication link. In small organisations, these work flow relationships often evolve into important informal communication links. However, in large organisations, management must often plan quasiformal links to connect individuals and groups.

With the aid of computers and electronic mail systems, it is now possible to connect work flow related units across the globe. The Ethical perspective looks at controlling communication access and flow.

Organisational control and social media

A question often being debated is: where is the line between the use of social media and how the workplace reacts to it? Two issues are pertinent here. First, the use of social media by the workplace in the hiring process, and second, how the workplace controls the communication access of its employees. With regard to the first issue, both the lives of Gen Ys and Gen Xs are increasingly on public display (including to employers) as they use social media as a modern-day scrapbook — complete with captions and status updates. Two relevant questions here are: is it ethical for employers to research a prospective candidate using social media; and is it ethical to base their recruitment decision on the information they find on the candidate, even when a résumé and interview are also considered in the process? Carey Eaton, CIO from Seek Limited, argues that because it is public domain, there is nothing wrong with reading information on social media sites about the candidate; however, what the employer does with the information and the actions that follow could pose an ethical problem. Is the employer making unfair, discriminatory and even potentially illegal judgements about the candidate that would have a negative impact on the potential candidate?[6]

(continued)

With regard to the second issue, recent press has reported that the risks of giving employees access to social media outweigh the benefits of providing employees with access to this popular communication tool. However, some have argued that controlling employees' access to social media during work time could damage their overall sense of wellbeing, since engaging socially during the day could make for happy and more productive employees. Many organisations also monitor the content of employee emails. Some employees would classify this type of 'blocking' of communication flow as unethical behaviour by the organisation.

The argument against control of communication access and flow emphasises that if knowledge is power, it is reasonable to propose that knowledge should be continually channelled to employees to give them the power to develop the organisation. Employers should set clear guidelines for acceptable use while adopting social media for a productive, internal purpose. Michael Rudnick, global intranet and portal leader at Watson Wyatt, argues:

> Employers that avoid social media altogether are missing an important opportunity and running the risk of alienating generation Xers and millennials [generation Yers]. Embracing the technology with proper planning, guidelines and change management for its use are effective approaches to ensuring success.[7]

These measures, along with strong firewalls, could go a long way to ensuring social media is used in a productive way and information of a sensitive nature is not inadvertently disseminated. Educating employees regarding security implications, while still enabling reasonable access, might create a healthy environment of education and social responsibility.

Questions

1. What is your view on an employer researching a prospective candidate using social media; and is it ethical in your view to base their recruitment decision on the information they find on the candidate?
2. What is your view on monitoring the electronic communication of employees?

Barriers to interpersonal communication

Look back now to figure 13.1 (p. 494). Communication is not always perfect. Interference of some sort in the telecommunication process is called 'noise'. Given the rapid developments in telecommunications over the past 30 years, 'noise' due to technical faults is diminishing. Nonetheless, even today things can go wrong: telephone equipment does not always work; lines to exchanges still need to be repaired after underground flooding; calls can be misrouted through exchanges; and, sometimes, we need to redial because there is hissing or crackling on the line. Several less tangible barriers to communication relate directly to those people in the communication channel. For example, you will remember that earlier in the chapter we referred to the ever-increasing number of incoming and outgoing emails a manager is subjected to each day. While the development of technology can enhance the opportunity to communicate faster, particularly in a global market, this might not always be ideal. Therefore, managers should select the most appropriate channel of communication to get each message across to the recipient without distortion. For example, a recent survey found that few managers from the sample researched agreed that email was more persuasive than a face-to-face meeting, yet two-thirds of the same group researched reported that face-to-face communication skills had decreased as a result of email use.[8]

Noise still occurs in interpersonal communication in today's organisation; so to improve communications, it is important to understand the sources of noise. The most common sources of noise are physical distractions and cultural differences. Physical distractions include such things as a competing conversation being held in the office while you are trying to concentrate on an important telephone call. Environmental factors, such as too much noise in open-plan offices, construction work going on outside the building or uncomfortable temperatures, all fall into this category. Cultural differences can present a number of complications or obstructions to effective communication between individuals. The problems these blocks pose to managers are usually compounded by managers' deeply rooted orientations to life according to the pattern of their own society. While they may recognise that people from other cultures are different, they may find it hard to understand and adjust to the great variety of ways in which this difference manifests itself.

We need to recognise these sources of noise and to subject them to special managerial control. They are included in figure 13.1 (p. 494) as potential threats to any communication process.

Effective communicators not only understand and deal with communication barriers; they are also exceptionally good at active listening. Effective communicators recognise that being a good receiver is just as important, and often even more important, than being an accurate sender.

The habits of good communicators

For good interpersonal communication to occur, people need to:
- speak clearly
- write clearly
- be aware of cultural differences
- listen attentively
- question precisely
- answer honestly
- pause for feedback signals.

THE **EffectiveManager** 13.1

Social media and the workplace

Social media are changing contemporary workplaces on a number of fronts. No longer are we questioning whether firms should have a social media presence, but, rather, what channels and media are the best options, and what department of the company should claim ownership. Many firms use Facebook, Twitter, LinkedIn, blogs and even YouTube to source and attract candidates. Where communication, speed and collaboration are critical, a wiki page allows a group of people to create and edit documents together, making it an excellent tool for implementing new programs and processes for the workplace. Once programs are finalised, an organisation's CEO can make a vodcast or podcast, making it available on the corporate blog.

In contrast to traditional emailing and posting of information on an intranet, social media tools are useful in helping employees actively participate in creating and sharing information. One of the benefits is greater engagement of employees online;[9] for example, by creating a corporate blog and inviting employees to leave comments, or targeting specific managers to write posts for the blog. It could be a very useful portal for employee recognition, contests, or could serve as a suggestion box, an employee recruitment tool, and source of information about social events in the firm.[10]

Social media represents a powerful shift in favour of stakeholders, enabling employees to share their grievances with an unlimited audience as soon as the grievance occurs. However, this quick spread of individual voices and opinions and the potential to generate influential groups is one of the main risks of social media.[11] How could this be managed? A tailor-made policy to establish clear standards of online behaviour is crucial depending on the type of organisation, its objectives and type of workforce. Specifying the boundaries of social media usage in the organisation is important. This includes, for example, specifying the extent of personal use by employees; whether employees are allowed to comment on issues impacting on the organisation, its clients and employees; how the policy will be communicated, enforced; and ways in which the organisation will deal with the consequences of breaching the policy. Apart from a clear policy, it is essential to control the outflow of official social media content, including issues such as controlling account passwords and levels of permissions. Specific communications strategies ought to be in place when organisational social media is abused or something goes wrong to ensure public relations issues are handled effectively.[12] James Field, Managing Director of CompliSpace, argues that to accommodate these issues, individual authorisations could be tied to specific forms of social media used by staff. For example, permission could be given to one employee to publish on blogs and another could publish on Twitter only. In his view a good old-fashioned register of these types of authorisations could ensure the organisation maintains control of its branded social media sites.[13]

Conflict

Conflict is a universal phenomenon. It can facilitate learning, creativity and change, but for some people it makes their work day less enjoyable. For others, the frequency and intensity of workplace conflict makes them uncomfortable and impedes their effectiveness. Workplace conflict may reach such levels that people consider leaving the organisation.

Few people welcome conflict and many managers do not know how to manage it effectively. Yet, successful conflict management is at the root of organisational effectiveness. Whether in the boardroom or at the 'coalface', conflict situations, infighting and internal disputes are commonplace. Conflict in the workplace can erupt at any time and at any level of the organisation. While much of the focus is on how to resolve conflict among employees at the lower levels of the hierarchy, just as many conflict situations can erupt in the boardroom. It is not uncommon to read in mainstream media about disputes and conflict among top managers in major organisations. Rational people, who otherwise appear to model appropriate managerial conduct, sometimes descend into brawls that take on a life of their own.[14]

What is conflict?

Conflict occurs when two or more people disagree over issues of organisational substance and/or experience some emotional antagonism with one another.

Conflict occurs whenever disagreements exist in a social situation over issues of substance, or whenever emotional antagonisms create frictions between individuals or groups.[15] Managers are known to spend up to 20 per cent of their time dealing with conflict, including conflicts in which managers are themselves directly involved.[16] In other situations managers may act as mediators, or third parties, whose job is to try to resolve conflicts between other people. In all cases, managers must be skilled participants in the dynamics of interpersonal conflict. They must also be able to recognise situations that have the potential for conflict, and deal with these situations to best serve the needs of both the organisation and the people involved.

Conflict subscribes to no rules. Petty disputes are common occurrences in all workplaces. Full-scale discord can always occur. Such conflicts cannot be predicted, nor can they be prevented, but they can be managed. Among the common reasons for conflict are differences in personal styles, values and job perspectives. Differing needs for personal success and variations in skill level can also cause conflict. Individuals in a conflict need to be listened to, because their anger is frequently a desire to see change effected. A manager needs to know how to resolve such interpersonal conflicts effectively. Where tension develops between individual managers or different management functions, the conflict can have a dramatic impact on organisational performance. Managers who understand the fundamentals of conflict and negotiation will be better prepared to deal with such situations.

If you listen in on some workplace conversations, you might hear the following:

'I don't care what you say, I don't have time to do it and that's that!'

'I no longer open my emails when I first get to the office. I get so many "fwd", it's an annoying start to the day.'

'The lines of communication are pretty bad around here.'

The very words used in these statements are important. They convey a sense of discord in the workplace and 'frame' the thinking of the people making them in a negative or adversarial way. This way of thinking is bound to affect the speakers' working relationships with the other people involved. It is also likely to affect their attitudes and work behaviours. At issue in each case is conflict. The ability to deal with such conflict successfully is a key aspect of a manager's interpersonal skills. Conflict must be effectively managed for an organisation to achieve its goals. Before it can be managed, conflict must be acknowledged and defined by the disputants. However, it may be difficult for the parties involved to agree on what is in dispute in a shared conflict, because they may experience, or frame, the same conflict in different ways.[17]

Substantive and emotional conflicts

Conflict in organisations can be as diverse as the people working there. While interpersonal conflict is natural and can actually spur creativity, the objective for managers is to manage it, often by preventing interpersonal differences from culminating in confrontations. As rational adults, we tend to expect that when we present an idea we will achieve consensus. We believe others will see the logic of our views and support them, even when different cultures and backgrounds are apparent. However, because each of us has a different perspective we tend to support only those ideas and views that align with our own. To deal with conflict effectively, both objective and subjective elements contributing to the conflict need to be examined and addressed.

Two common examples of workplace conflict are a disagreement with your boss over a plan of action to be followed (for example, a marketing strategy for a new product); and a dislike for a coworker (for example, someone who is always belittling the members of an ethnic or identity group). The first example is one of substantive conflict — that is, a conflict that usually occurs in the form of a fundamental disagreement over ends or goals to be pursued and the means for their accomplishment.[18] When people work together day in and day out, it is only normal that different viewpoints on a variety of substantive workplace issues will arise. It is common for people to disagree at times over such things as group and organisational goals, the allocation of resources, the distribution of rewards, policies and procedures, and task assignments. Dealing successfully with such conflicts is an everyday challenge for most managers. The second example is one of emotional conflict — that is, a conflict

Substantive conflict is conflict that occurs in the form of a fundamental disagreement over ends or goals to be pursued and the means for their accomplishment.

Emotional conflict is conflict that involves interpersonal difficulties that arise over feelings of anger, mistrust, dislike, fear, resentment and the like.

that involves interpersonal difficulties that arise over feelings of anger, mistrust, dislike, fear, resentment and the like.[19] It is commonly known as a 'clash of personalities'. Emotional conflicts can drain people's energies and distract them from other important work priorities. They can emerge from a wide variety of settings and are common among coworkers as well as in superior–employee relationships. The latter is perhaps the most upsetting emotional conflict for any person to experience. Unfortunately, competitive pressures in today's business environment and the resulting emphasis on downsizing and restructuring have created more situations in which the decisions of a 'tough' boss can create emotional conflict.

Both types of conflict can have a positive influence on management performance. However, substantive (or task-oriented) conflict is likely to have the most positive effect, depending on how it is managed. Performance is what we typically think about when we consider effectiveness; it constitutes the decisions or solutions that affect productive output. Conflict can force managers to address some of their assumptions and override their attempts to achieve premature unanimity, thus leading to better performance. Managers engaged in substantive (task-oriented) conflict tend to direct their actions to their work, because the conflict forces them to concern themselves with task functions and related issues. By contrast, emotional conflict, although it affects the organisation's development and survival, is inward looking and, thus, offers a less positive effect on management performance. During such conflict, management actions are directed towards members' relations with each other, rather than with the organisation or the team agenda.

Communication that can lead to conflict

The conflict911.com 'conflict help centre' warns that there are five types of communication that can lead to conflict. Managers should avoid the following.

- *Negative communication.* We all know a 'Negative Nigel/Nancy' in every team — they exist and we find it near impossible to remove them. But constant negativity drains the other team members of enthusiasm, energy and self-esteem.
- *Blaming communication.* Blamers spray blame around, effectively stopping reflection and scrutiny of their performance and behaviour. However, their impact can be reduced by fostering a learning environment, as well as the use of 'I messages', peer pressure and individual feedback.
- *Superior communication.* 'Superiors' frequently order people about, direct, advise and moralise. They are also very skilled at withholding information.
- *Dishonest communication.* Dishonest communicators frequently fail to practise listening to understand and fail to display empathy. They also display circumlocutory communication — also known as 'talking around the issue, not addressing it'.
- *Selective communication.* Selective communicators only tell what they think others need to know, hence keeping themselves in a position of power over the other team members. Such behaviour can be effectively addressed through assertive requests for having access to all the information.

Source: Extracts from Lee Hopkins, 'Minimising conflict with effective communication', www.leehopkins.com/conflict.html

Levels of conflict

It is possible to examine conflict from a number of different communication levels. In particular, people at work may encounter conflicts at four levels:
1. intrapersonal, or conflict within the individual
2. interpersonal, or individual-to-individual conflict
3. intergroup conflict
4. interorganisational conflict.

When it comes to dealing personally with conflicts in the workplace, how well prepared are you to encounter and deal with various types of conflict?

Intrapersonal conflict

Among the significant conflicts that affect behaviour in organisations are those that involve the individual alone. These intrapersonal conflicts often involve actual or perceived pressures from incompatible goals or expectations of the following types. *Approach conflict* occurs when a person must choose between two positive and equally attractive alternatives. An example is having to choose between a valued promotion in the organisation or a desirable new job with another organisation. *Avoidance conflict* occurs when a person must choose between two negative and equally unattractive alternatives. An example is being asked either to accept a job transfer to another town in an undesirable location or to have your employment with an organisation terminated. *Approach–avoidance conflict* occurs when a person must decide to do something that has both positive and negative consequences. An example is being offered a higher paying job, but one with responsibilities that will make unwanted demands on your time.

Intrapersonal conflict is conflict that occurs within the individual as a result of actual or perceived pressures from incompatible goals or expectations.

Interpersonal conflict

Interpersonal conflict occurs between two or more individuals who are in opposition to one another; the conflict may be substantive or emotional in nature, or both. Two people debating aggressively over each other's views on the merits of hiring a job applicant is an example of a substantive interpersonal conflict. Two people continually in disagreement over each other's choice of work attire is an example of an emotional interpersonal conflict. Everyone has had experience with interpersonal conflicts of both types. It is a major form of conflict that managers face, given the highly interpersonal nature of the managerial role. We will address this form of conflict in more detail when we discuss conflict management strategies later in the chapter.

Interpersonal conflict is conflict that occurs between two or more individuals.

Intergroup conflict

Another level of conflict in organisations occurs between groups. Such intergroup conflict can also have substantive and/or emotional underpinnings. Intergroup conflict is quite common in organisations, and it can make the coordination and integration of task activities very difficult. Consider this example of conflict between sales and production personnel in two plants of the same manufacturing company.[20] In one, a conflict relationship exists between the two departments; in another plant, the working relationship is cooperative. These differences are most apparent in terms of how group goals and the handling of information affects decision making in each setting.

Intergroup conflict is conflict that occurs between groups in an organisation.

Interorganisational conflict

Conflict may also occur between entire organisations or independent units in large organisations. Such interorganisational conflict most commonly reflects the competition and rivalry that characterises organisations operating in the same markets. However, interorganisational conflict is really a much broader issue than that represented by market competition alone. Consider, for example, disagreements between unions and the organisations employing their members; between government regulatory agencies and the organisations subject to their surveillance; between organisations and those who supply them with raw materials; and between units within an organisation competing for organisational resources. If conflict between divisions in a company is ignored, the organisation will often be more concerned with internal competition than with external competition.

Interorganisational conflict is conflict that occurs between organisations.

New organisational structures, such as joint ventures, strategic alliances and networks, have the potential to release conflicts, both between the new partners and also within the participating organisations. These latter conflicts were contained within the old structure or resolved by rules. The changes inherent in restructuring bring them to the surface, and such conflicts within the organisation and between organisations may result in the dissolution of partnerships.

The etiquette of email communication

Communication via email is the most used communication medium in organisations today. However, because this method of communication lacks emotional and non-verbal cues, it is crucial to pay attention to the tone conveyed in the email. The best way to explain the concept of 'tone' within the context of email communication is that it is the way you 'say' something — your choice of words, and how your message may come across to the recipient. One's tone is easily controllable in verbal communication, and can be corrected easily; however, it's very difficult to correct it in writing.

It's advisable to do a bit of self-reflection before you send an email, especially when the content has an emotional connotation. Ensure that you come across respectful, approachable and friendly rather than demanding. Refrain from typing in CAPS, as this can be interpreted as YELLING in an email. Read your message several times before sending it, and try and ensure you send the right message with the right words. Similarly, when you receive an angry email from someone, wait 24 hours before responding — don't let it provoke an immediate angry response. Never say in an email what you aren't willing to say in person, and always consider the future of the relationship before clicking the send button.[21]

Conflict and culture

Culturally diverse countries, such as Australia and New Zealand, are characterised by a wide range of traditions, languages, beliefs, values, ideas and practices. In addition, the increasingly international nature of organisations' operations brings people of diverse backgrounds together. As the Queensland University of Technology acknowledges:

> Diversity is both an opportunity and challenge … Cultural, social and linguistic diversity are assets in an internationally competitive market and can broaden and enrich all teaching, research, curricula, community service, administrative activities and daily life, giving rise to new ways of conceptualising and addressing issues … It can be a source of tension, division or conflict within the University if difference is associated with exclusion, disadvantage or racism.[22]

In a multinational context, one of the key reasons for the early return of expatriates is the uncertainty and frustration resulting from poor cross-cultural adaptation. The result of this is an increase in the interpersonal conflict expatriates experience in the workplace abroad, caused by cultural differences.[23]

Constructive and destructive conflicts

Conflict in organisations can be dangerous. It is often upsetting both to the individuals directly involved and to others who may observe it or be affected by it. On an emotional level at least, many of us are more aware of its perils than its possibilities. A common byproduct of conflict is stress. It can be uncomfortable, for example, to work in an environment in which two coworkers are continually hostile towards each other. However, organisational behaviour recognises two sides to conflict — the constructive side and the destructive side (figure 13.2).

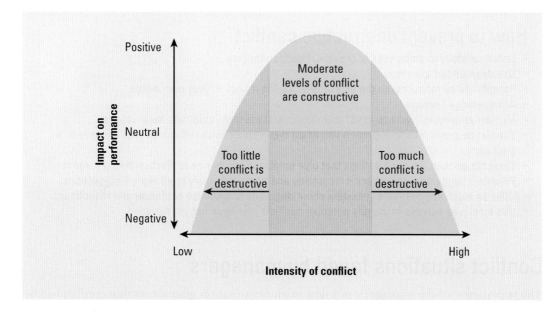

FIGURE 13.2 The two faces of conflict: constructive and destructive conflict

Constructive conflict results in benefits to the group or organisation. It offers the people involved a chance to identify otherwise neglected problems and opportunities; performance and creativity can improve as a result. Indeed, an effective manager is able to stimulate constructive conflict in situations in which satisfaction with the status quo inhibits necessary change and development. Such a manager is comfortable dealing with both the constructive and the destructive sides of the conflict dynamic. Another value of conflict is that it can prevent stagnation, stimulate interest and curiosity, and foster creativity.

When conflict arises, most people's first reaction is to become angry or distressed, and to seek to eliminate the problem. However, managers need to realise that if they can understand the issues that are causing the disagreement they will be in a better position to minimise the anger and distress and to use the conflict to the organisation's advantage. Conflict presents an opportunity for managers to become aware of substantive issues and to think of ways in which to resolve them. Members of a cross-functional team may have different information, ideas and perspectives about how the team should proceed, what the important issues are, how to solve problems facing the team and even what role each team member should play. An effective manager will seek to deal with these issues and the conflict will diminish.

Positive conflict can also help organisations become more innovative. Innovation can occur when different ideas, perceptions and ways of processing and judging information collide. Creative thinking can be a powerful tool in managing conflicts that result from personal disagreements and cognitive differences. Such conflict nurtures creativity. Various organisational members who see the world differently need to cooperate. Even when the parties have different viewpoints, managing those differences can be productive.[24]

Destructive conflict works to the group's or organisation's disadvantage. It occurs, for example, when two employees are unable to work together as a result of interpersonal hostility (a destructive emotional conflict), or when the members of a committee fail to act because they cannot agree on group goals (a destructive substantive conflict). Destructive conflict of these types can decrease work productivity and job satisfaction and contribute to absenteeism and job turnover. Managers must be alert to destructive conflicts, quickly acting to prevent or eliminate them, or at least minimise their resulting disadvantages. The effective manager 13.3 (overleaf) looks at ways to prevent destructive conflict.

Constructive conflict is conflict that results in positive benefits to the group.

Destructive conflict is conflict that works to the group's or organisation's disadvantage.

How to prevent destructive conflict

- Listen carefully to employees to prevent misunderstanding.
- Use open-ended questions.
- Paraphrase by reflecting on the message by saying it back in your own words.
- Acknowledge feelings.
- Monitor employees' work to assist them to understand and coordinate their actions.
- Encourage employees to approach you when they cannot solve difficulties with coworkers on their own.
- Clear the air with regular meetings that give employees a chance to discuss their grievances.
- Provide a suggestion box, check it frequently and personally reply to all signed suggestions.
- Offer as much information as possible about decisions to minimise confusion and resentment.
- Use employee surveys to identify potential conflicts that have not yet surfaced.

Conflict situations faced by managers

The very nature of the manager's position in an organisation guarantees that conflict will be a part of his or her work experience. The manager may encounter conflict in supervisor–employee relationships, in peer or intergroup relationships, and in relationships with senior management. The manager's ability to deal with such situations may in large part determine whether they have constructive or destructive impacts on the work situation. More specifically, an effective manager is able to recognise and deal with each of the following conflict situations.

- *Vertical conflict* occurs between hierarchical levels, and commonly involves supervisor — employee disagreements over resources, goals, deadlines or performance results.
- *Horizontal conflict* occurs between people or groups at the same hierarchical level, and commonly involves goal incompatibilities, resource scarcities or purely interpersonal factors.
- *Line–staff conflict* occurs between line and staff representatives, and commonly involves disagreements over who has authority and control over certain matters, such as personnel selection and termination practices.
- *Role conflict* occurs when the communication of task expectations proves inadequate or upsetting, and commonly involves uncertainties of expectations, overloads or underloads in expectations, and/or incompatibilities among expectations.[25]

Conflict becomes more likely in each of these situations when certain conditions exist. In general, managers should be aware that work situations with one or more of the following characteristics may be predisposed to conflict:

- work flow interdependence
- power and/or value asymmetry
- role ambiguity or domain ambiguity
- resource scarcity (actual or perceived).[26]

As discussed in chapters 8 and 9, the various parts of a complex organisation must be well integrated for it to function well. However, interdependencies among components can breed conflicts. When work flow interdependence is high — that is, when a person or group must rely on task contributions from one or more others to achieve its goals — conflicts often occur. You will notice this, for example, in a fast-food restaurant, when the people serving the food have to wait too long for it to be delivered from the cooks. Good managers understand that the performance expectations and other aspects of such links must be handled carefully to ensure smooth working relationships. Indeed, one of the central precepts of total quality management is that 'internal customers' — other people or groups inside the organisation — should receive the same dedicated attention and service that external customers receive.

Power or value asymmetries in work relationships exist when interdependent people or groups differ substantially from one another in status and influence, or in values. Conflict due to asymmetry is prone to occur, for example, when a low-power person needs the help of a high-power person who will not respond; when people who hold dramatically different values are forced to work together on a task; or when a high-status person is required to interact with — and perhaps depend on — someone of lower status. A common example of the latter case occurs when a manager is forced to deal with another manager through his or her secretary.

When individuals or groups operate with a lack of adequate task direction or clarity of goals, a stressful and conflict-prone situation exists. In chapters 7 and 11 we discussed how role ambiguities may cause problems for people at work. At the group or department level, similar effects in terms of domain ambiguities can occur. These ambiguities involve misunderstandings over such things as customer jurisdiction or scope of authority. Conflict is likely when individuals and/or groups are placed in situations in which it is difficult for them to understand just who is responsible for what. It may also occur where people resent the fact that their 'territory' is being trespassed.

A common managerial responsibility is the allocation of resources among different groups. Actual or perceived resource scarcity is a conflict-prone situation. When people sense the need to compete for scarce resources, working relationships are likely to suffer. This is especially true in organisations experiencing the financial difficulties associated with a period of decline. As cutbacks occur, various individuals or groups will try to position themselves to gain or retain maximum shares of the shrinking resource pool; they are also likely to try to resist or employ countermeasures to defend their resources from redistribution to others.

Most conflicts develop in stages, as shown in figure 13.3. These stages include antecedent conditions, perceived and felt conflict, manifest conflict, conflict resolution or suppression, and conflict aftermath.[27] The conditions that create conflict, as discussed, are examples of conflict antecedents; that is, they establish the conditions from which conflicts are likely to develop. In addition, managers should recognise that unresolved prior conflicts help set the stage for future conflicts of the same or related sort. Rather than try to deny the existence of conflict or settle on a temporary resolution, it is always best to deal with important conflicts so they are completely resolved.

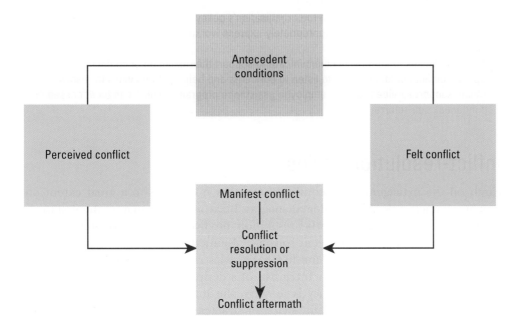

FIGURE 13.3 The stages of conflict

When the antecedent conditions actually become the basis for substantive or emotional differences between people and/or groups, such as those situations already described, the stage of perceived conflict exists. Of course, this perception may be held by only one of the conflicting parties. There is also a difference between perceived conflict and the stage of felt conflict. When people feel conflict, they experience it as tension that motivates them to take action to reduce feelings of discomfort. For conflict to be resolved, all parties should both perceive it and feel the need to do something about it.

When conflict is openly expressed in behaviour it is said to be manifest. A state of **manifest conflict** can be resolved by removing or correcting its antecedents. It can also be suppressed through controlling the behaviour (although no change in antecedent conditions occurs); for example, one or both parties may choose to ignore the conflict in their dealings with each other. This is a superficial and often temporary form of conflict resolution. Indeed, we have already noted that unresolved conflicts — and a suppressed conflict falls into this category — may continue to fester and cause future conflicts over similar issues.

Unresolved conflicts of any type can result in sustained emotional discomfort and stress, and escalate into dysfunctional relationships between individuals and work units. In contrast, truly resolved conflicts may establish conditions that reduce the potential for future conflicts and/or make it easier to deal with them. Thus, any manager should be sensitive to the influence of conflict aftermath on future conflict episodes.

Manifest conflict occurs when conflict is openly expressed in behaviour.

Conflict-management approaches

Conflict in organisations is inevitable. The process of managing conflict to achieve constructive rather than destructive results is clearly essential to organisational success. This process of conflict management can be pursued in a variety of ways. An important goal should always be to achieve or set the stage for true **conflict resolution** — that is, a situation in which the underlying reasons for a given conflict are eliminated.

Conflict resolution occurs when the reasons for a conflict are eliminated.

THE **EffectiveManager** 13.4

What can be done to better manage workplace conflict?

- Reinforce to managers their responsibility for managing conflict.
- Develop conflict management strategies.
- Ensure employees are familiar with the organisation's policy on interpersonal conflict.
- Facilitate discussion sessions to appropriately express workplace relationships and interpersonal tensions.
- Coach employees to effectively communicate to support the resolution of conflict.
- Appoint conflict contact officers to listen to concerns and help staff find ways to resolve them.
- Provide support services such as employee assistance programs, which can be accessed on a confidential, self-referral basis.[28]

Conflict-resolution styles

Research on the management of conflict shows that it depends to a great extent on the personality characteristics of individual managers. Blake and Mouton were the first to classify personality strategies or styles of conflict resolution into five basic types: forcing, withdrawing, soothing, compromising and problem solving.[29] Kenneth Thomas developed this line of analysis further by suggesting that the five basic styles could be compared in two aspects: assertiveness or self-confidence, which consists of a desire to serve one's own interests; and cooperativeness, where the tendency is to serve the interests of others.[30] Afzalur Rahim also points to five different personality styles, or strategies, in conflict resolution, which he analyses according to the orientation towards self or others. His five styles are: integrating, obliging, compromising, dominating and avoiding.[31]

Rahim draws attention to the fact that there is no one best style, because each has its advantages and disadvantages. The effectiveness of an application of a particular style depends on the situation. In everyday life people tend to show a preference for a certain conflict-resolution style; for example, a person with high affiliation needs will generally choose an obliging style and avoid a dominating style. It appears that in organisational life, the status of an organisational member could well influence the choice of conflict-resolution style.[32] for example, people may choose different strategies when dealing with a boss, an employee or a peer.

Most researchers share the view that an integrating style is best for managing conflicts in organisations, because this style is aimed at solving the problem, it respects the needs and interests of both sides, and is based on achieving a satisfactory outcome for each side.[33] However, choice of style needs to be contingent on the situation. A manager may choose a dominating style where the goals of the conflicting parties are incompatible, there has been a previous failure to reach agreement and a quick decision needs to be made.[34] In contrast, an integrating style would probably work best in a conflict caused by communication problems or in solving strategic problems linked to goals, policies and long-term planning in organisations. Research shows that managers believe that the frequent use of a compromising style hampers performance and the attainment of goals, but that they may endorse such a style in certain situations where mutual concessions are the only possible solution.[35] Research by Krum Krumov showed that the integrating style is used more often by women than men, and that its use increases gradually with age. In contrast, the compromising style is used equally by women and men, and its use tends to increase with age. However, the use of this style is more typical of employees than managers.[36]

Wayne Pace suggests that preferred ways of handling conflict occur because, when two people come together expecting to claim their share of scarce resources, they think somewhat habitually about themselves and the other person. Thus, conflict-resolution styles appear to be some combination of the amount of concern you have about accomplishing your own goals and the amount of concern you have about others accomplishing their goals. These concerns can be portrayed as two axes running from low concern to high concern. This paradigm results in a two-dimensional conceptualisation of personal conflict-resolution styles, as depicted in figure 13.4 and briefly described here. Unfortunately, when conflict occurs people have the tendency to do and say things that perpetuate the conflict.[37]

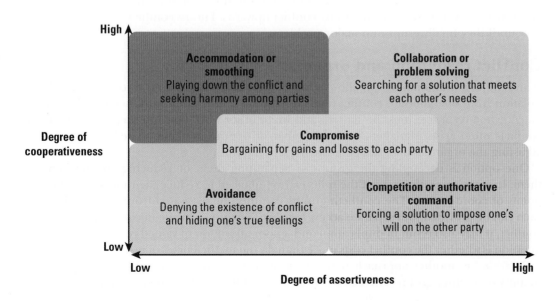

FIGURE 13.4 Personal conflict-resolution styles

Source: R Wayne Pace and Don F Faules, *Organizational communication*, 3rd ed. (Boston, MA: Allyn & Bacon, 1994), p. 250.

- Cell 1 — competitor or tough battler. People who employ this style pursue their own concerns somewhat ruthlessly and generally at the expense of other members of the group. The tough battler views losing as an indication of weakness, reduced status and a crumbling self-image. Winning is the only worthwhile goal and results in accomplishment and exhilaration.
- Cell 2 — collaborator or problem solver. People who employ this style seek to create a situation in which the goals of all parties involved can be accomplished. Problem solvers work at finding mutually acceptable solutions. Winning and losing are not part of their way of looking at conflict.
- Cell 3 — compromiser or manoeuvring conciliator. The person who employs this style assumes that everyone involved in a disagreement stands to lose and works to help find a workable position. A pattern of 'giving in' often develops.
- Cell 4 — accommodator or friendly helper. People who employ this style are somewhat nonassertive and quite cooperative, neglecting their own concerns in favour of those of others. The friendly helper feels that harmony should prevail and that anger and confrontation are bad. When a decision is reached, accommodators may go along with it and wish later that they had expressed some reservations.
- Cell 5 — avoider or impersonal complier. The person who employs this style tends to view conflict as unproductive and somewhat punishing. Thus, the avoider sidesteps an uncomfortable situation by refusing to be concerned. The result is usually an impersonal reaction to the decision and little commitment to future actions.[38]

Conflict resolution through hierarchical referral

Hierarchical referral uses the chain of command for conflict resolution; problems are referred up the hierarchy for more senior managers to reconcile.

Hierarchical referral makes use of the chain of command for conflict resolution; problems are simply referred up the hierarchy for more senior managers to reconcile. The managers involved will typically be those to whom the conflicting parties mutually report; they will be managers who ultimately have the formal authority to resolve such disputes by directive if necessary.

While hierarchical referral can be definitive in a given case, it also has limitations. If conflict is severe and recurring, the continual use of hierarchical referral may not result in true conflict resolution. For instance, managers may have the tendency to consider most conflicts a result of poor interpersonal relations. They may consequently seek outward signs of harmony as evidence of their conflict management skills, or they may act quickly to replace a person with a perceived 'personality' problem.[39] In so doing, they may actually fail to delve into the real causes of a conflict, and conflict resolution may be superficial. Employees may also learn that it is best not to refer any conflict upwards. Future conflicts may be kept from view until they finally erupt into major problems.

Conflict resolution and organisational design

Decoupling involves separating or reducing the contact between two conflicting groups.

Buffering is a conflict management approach that sets up inventories to reduce conflicts when the inputs of one group are the outputs of another group.

When the organisational design allows groups, units and departments to operate in relative isolation from one another, conflict tends to be muted. But when work needs to be coordinated, when resources must be shared, and when other work flow interdependencies exist, conflicts often arise. Managers have a number of options available to reduce conflicts by adjusting the organisational design at such friction points.[40]

One option is **decoupling** the groups — separating them or reducing contact between them. In some cases, the tasks of the units can be adjusted to reduce the number of required points of coordination. The conflicting units can then be separated from one another and each can be provided with separate access to valued resources. While decoupling may reduce conflict, it may also result in duplication and a poor allocation of valued resources. Often the question is whether the conflict costs more than do the inefficiencies of resource allocation.

Buffering is another approach that can be used when the inputs of one group are the outputs of another group. The classic buffering technique is to build an inventory between the two groups so any output slowdown or excess is absorbed by the inventory and does not directly pressure the target group. Although it reduces conflict, this technique is increasingly out of favour because it increases inventory costs. This consequence is quite contrary to the practice of 'just-in-time' delivery that is now valued in operations management.

Conflict management can be facilitated by assigning people to serve as formal linking pins between groups that are prone to conflict.[41] People in linking-pin roles, such as project liaison officers, are expected to understand the operations, members' needs and the norms of their host group. Linking pins are supposed to use this knowledge to help their group work better with other groups to accomplish mutual tasks. Although expensive, this technique is often used when different specialised groups, such as engineering and sales, must closely coordinate their efforts on complex and long-term projects.

> **Linking pins** are people who are assigned to manage conflict between groups that are prone to conflict.

A variation of the linking-pin concept is the liaison group.[42] The purpose of such a group, team or department is to coordinate the activities of certain units and to prevent destructive clashes between them. Members of the department may be given formal authority to resolve disputes on everything from technical matters to resource claims or work assignments. The International spotlight considers how the use of email can lead to conflict in the workplace.

> **Liaison groups** are groups that coordinate the activities of certain units to prevent destructive conflicts between them.

Email and conflict escalation

Email communication is almost unique in that it is asynchronous (the parties are not co-present, but, rather, each reads the other's email whenever desired and responds whenever desired), textual, and electronic. It is textual because it contains written words only, not the facial expressions inherent in face-to-face conversations or in videoconferencing, or the verbal nuances displayed during a telephone conversation. The result is not an actual conversation, but a series of intermittent, one-directional comments. If the parties happen to be online at the same time and choose to respond immediately, the communication can be nearly instantaneous; however, it is more likely that responses will occur after hours or even days. When colleagues in a workplace interact, they instantaneously look for clues about how the other reacts to their comments, and make constant adjustments and modifications. However, this cannot be done without information about their reactions. In email, there is mostly an absence of

International **SPOTLIGHT**

> co-presence, which allows each party to be in the same surroundings and see what the other is doing and looking at, visibility, which allows each party to see the other (albeit not necessarily their surroundings), audibility, which allows each party to hear timing of speech and intonation, co-temporality, where each party receives an utterance just as it is produced, simultaneity, where both parties can send and receive messages at once, and sequentiality, where turn-taking cannot get out of sequence.[43]

Consequently, insults could unintentionally occur, which the other party may view as more aggressive than intended. Furthermore, in audible conversations participants in the conversation can correct each other immediately when misunderstandings take place. In contrast, in email, without the nuances of face-to-face communication, it is much more difficult to steer conversations in specific directions, and mistakes and misunderstandings are likely to occur to a much greater extent. In lengthy messages, the reader of the email may, through selective attention, focus on specific parts of a message, which may cause misunderstandings and skew the interpretation of the intended message. This can lead to

(continued)

anger, and a desire to respond in a defensive manner. This is especially true of emails containing numerous messages. There are some counter-arguments that email can be highly personal, such as in email romances and online support groups; however, in these instances the objective is to build a relationship and provide support, not assert one's needs or wishes through differences of opinion.[44] The potential of email to escalate conflict is even greater when cross-cultural influences of participants in the communication are present, since personal cultural values and attitudes can create even greater 'noise' in the process. Therefore, where possible, other media should be used — such as face-to-face or audio-rich channels — to communicate messages that could potentially cause conflict.

Negotiation

Conflict between individuals, groups and organisations is a common phenomenon. When parties are involved in conflict, negotiation is frequently used to resolve differences. This section introduces you to negotiation as an important process in managing people and organisations.

Managers need to understand some of the key areas of negotiation in order to improve workplace effectiveness and performance. **Negotiation** is the process of making joint decisions when the parties involved have different preferences. In other words, negotiation can be considered a way of getting what managers want from others in the process of making decisions.

Negotiation is especially significant in today's work settings, where more people are being offered opportunities to be involved in decisions affecting them and their work. As more people get involved in any decision-making process, so more disagreements are likely to arise over such diverse matters as wage rates, task objectives, performance evaluations, job assignments, work schedules, work locations and special privileges. Given that organisations are becoming increasingly participative, a manager's familiarity with basic negotiation concepts and processes is increasingly important for dealing with such day-to-day affairs.

> **Negotiation** is the process of making joint decisions when the parties involved have different preferences.

Four types of negotiation situations

In the course of their work, managers may be faced with different types of negotiation situations. As shown in figure 13.5, there are four main types of situations with which managers should be familiar.

- *Two-party negotiation.* The manager negotiates directly with one other person; for example, a manager and an employee negotiating a salary increase during an annual performance appraisal.
- *Group negotiation.* The manager is part of a team or group whose members are negotiating to arrive at a common decision; for example, a committee that must reach agreement on recommending a new sexual harassment policy.
- *Intergroup negotiation.* The manager is part of a group that is negotiating with another group to arrive at a decision regarding a problem or situation affecting both; for example, negotiation between management groups from two organisations to form a joint venture or strategic alliance.
- *Constituency negotiation.* The manager is involved in negotiation with other people and each individual party represents a broad constituency. A common example is a team representing 'management' negotiating with a team representing 'labour' to arrive at an agreement.

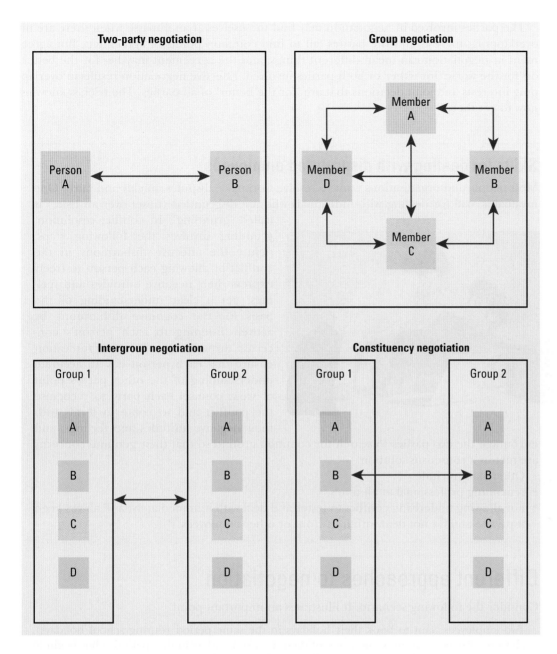

FIGURE 13.5 Four types of negotiation situation faced by managers

Two-party negotiation

Person A ⟷ Person B

Group negotiation

Member A
Member D
Member B
Member C

Intergroup negotiation

Group 1: A, B, C, D
Group 2: A, B, C, D

Constituency negotiation

Group 1: A, B, C, D
Group 2: A, B, C, D

Negotiation goals and outcomes

Two goals are at stake in any negotiation. **Substance goals** are concerned with outcomes relative to the 'content' issues at hand, such as the dollar amount of a wage agreement in a collective bargaining situation. **Relationship goals** are concerned with outcomes relating to how well people involved in the negotiation and any constituencies they may represent are able to work with one another once the process is concluded. An example is the ability of union members and management representatives to work together effectively after a contract dispute has been settled.

Unfortunately, many negotiations result in a sacrifice of relationships, as parties become preoccupied with substance goals and self-interest. In contrast, **effective negotiation** occurs when substance issues are resolved and working relationships are maintained or even improved.

Substance goals are concerned with outcomes tied to the 'content' issues at hand in a negotiation.

Relationship goals are concerned with how well people involved in a negotiation, and their constituencies, are able to work with one another once the process is concluded.

Effective negotiation occurs when issues of substance are resolved without any harm to the working relationships among the parties involved.

The parties involved in negotiation may find themselves at an impasse when there are no overlapping interests and the parties fail to find common points of agreement. But agreement in negotiation can mean different things, and the agreement may be 'for the better' or 'for the worse' for either or both parties involved. Effective negotiation results in overlapping interests and joint decisions that are 'for the better' of all parties. The trick is knowing how to get there.

OBinAction

Skills for dealing with disgruntled employees

Most people and organisations want to resolve workplace disputes quickly and fairly. One invaluable skill for dealing with individuals who are disgruntled (upset over an issue) is  called 'gruntling'. In conflict resolution, gruntling involves the following steps: defuse the affective disharmony in the conflict by allowing each person to freely express their negative attitudes and feelings; get a clear understanding of the basis for the cognitive disharmony by actively listening to each person's concerns; through effective communication ensure that each person has an accurate understanding of the other party's point of view; counsel each party to recognise the conflict and to come to terms with their negative attitudes and feelings; and encourage the two parties to search for common ground so that their genuine concerns are met in a consensus solution.

Other skills include:
* remaining professional at all times
* not allowing underlying conflict to fester and deal with it immediately; and always keep it private and do not deal with it in front of other employees.[45]

Different approaches to negotiation

Consider the following scenario. It illustrates an important point.

Two employees want to book their holidays in the same period (during school holidays). However, the boss can only allow one of them to take holidays in that period. They begin to negotiate over who should take the holiday in that period.

For our purposes, the 'holiday' represents a valued outcome for both employees. The approach taken to the negotiation can have a major influence on its outcomes. It is useful to discuss two alternative approaches: distributive negotiation and integrative negotiation.[46]

Distributive negotiation

Distributive negotiation is negotiation in which the focus is on 'positions' staked out or declared by the parties involved, who are each trying to claim certain portions of the available 'pie'.

In **distributive negotiation**, the focus is on 'positions' that conflicting parties stake out or declare. Each party is trying to 'claim' certain portions of the available 'pie'. Distributive negotiation is sometimes referred to as competitive or positional negotiation. Returning to the holiday scenario, if the two workers adopted distributive bargaining approaches, they would each ask the question: 'Who is going to get the holiday at the requested time?' This question, and the way in which it frames subsequent behaviour, will have a major impact on the negotiation process and outcomes.

A case of distributive negotiation usually unfolds in one of two directions, neither of which yields optimal results. 'Hard' distributive negotiation takes place when each party holds out to get its own way. This leads to competition, whereby each party seeks dominance over the other and tries to maximise self-interests. 'Soft' distributive negotiation takes place when one party is willing to make concessions to the other to get things over with. In this case, one party tries to find ways to meet the other's desires. A soft approach leads to accommodation (one party gives in to the other) or compromise (each party gives up something of value in order to reach agreement).

In the case of the two employees wanting the same holiday period, the hard approach may lead to a win–lose outcome, in which one employee will dominate (perhaps by putting forth a stronger and more convincing case to the boss) and therefore wins the round. Or it may lead to an impasse, in which case neither employee will get the holiday. A soft approach (or compromise) may result in the holiday period being split equally between the two employees, where one employee gets half of the period and the second takes the other half. But here, too, dissatisfaction may exist because each employee is still deprived of what they originally wanted — the entire holiday period at the preferred time.

Integrative negotiation

In integrative negotiation, sometimes called principled negotiation, the focus is on the 'merits' of the issues. Everyone involved tries to enlarge the available 'pie' rather than stake claims to certain portions of it. For this reason, integrative negotiation is also sometimes referred to as problem-solving or interest-based negotiation. In the case of the employees, the integrative approach to negotiation would be prompted by asking the question: 'How can the available leave best be used?' Notice that this is a very different question from the one described for distributive negotiation. It is much less confrontational and allows for a broader range of alternatives.

> Integrative negotiation is negotiation in which the focus is on the merits of the issues and the parties involved try to enlarge the available 'pie' rather than stake claims to certain portions of it.

The integrative approach to negotiation has much more of a 'win–win' orientation than does the distributive approach; it seeks ways of satisfying the needs and interests of all parties. At one extreme, this may involve selective avoidance, wherein both parties simply realise that there are more important things on which to focus their time and attention. In the holiday scenario, the two workers may mutually decide to forget about the holiday and to attend work. Compromise can also play a role in the integrative approach, but it must have an enduring basis. This is most likely to occur when the compromise involves each party giving up something of perceived lesser personal value to gain something of greater value. In the case of the workers, one may get the holiday this time in return for the other getting one during the next school holidays.

Finally, integrative negotiation may involve true cooperation. In this case, the negotiating parties engage in problem solving to arrive at a mutual agreement that truly maximises benefit to each. In the case of the holidays, this ideal approach could lead to both workers getting half the time off, and spending the other half working, but from home so they can still attend to their children. As you can see, this solution would be almost impossible to realise using the distributive approach because each worker would be preoccupied with getting the holiday. Only under the direction provided by the integrative approach — 'How can the available leave best be used?' — is such a mutually optimal solution possible. However, it is important to appreciate that the most effective negotiators will have a wide array of negotiation skills and will be able to use both approaches, mixing and matching them, depending on what they think works best for a specific issue or situation.

Managerial issues in negotiation

Given the distinctions between distributive and integrative negotiation, it is appropriate to identify some negotiation issues of special relevance to managers — specifically, the foundations for gaining integrative agreements, classic two-party negotiation and communication problems in negotiation.

Gaining integrative agreements

Underlying the concept of 'principled' negotiation is negotiation based on the 'merits' of the situation. The foundations for gaining truly integrative agreements cover three main areas: attitudes, behaviours and information.[47] To begin with, there are *three attitudinal foundations of integrative agreements.*

1. Each party must approach the negotiation with a willingness to trust the other party.
2. Each party must be willing to share information with the other party.
3. Each party must be willing to ask concrete questions of the other party.

As implied, the *information foundations of integrative agreements* are substantial; they involve each party becoming familiar with the **BATNA**, or 'best alternative to a negotiated agreement'. That is, both parties must know what they will do if an agreement cannot be reached. This requires that both negotiating parties identify and understand their personal interests in the situation. They must know what is really important to them in the case at hand, and they must come to understand the relative importance of the other party's interests. As difficult as it may seem, each party must achieve anunderstanding of what the other party values, even to the point of determining its BATNA.

Reaching this point of understanding is certainly not easy. In the complex social setting of a negotiation, things may happen that lead parties astray. An unpleasant comment uttered during a stressful situation, for example, may cause the other party to terminate direct communication for a time. Even when they return, the memory of this comment may overshadow any future overtures made by the offending party. In negotiation, all behaviour is important both for its actual impact and for the impression it leaves. Accordingly, the following behavioural foundations of integrative agreements must be carefully considered and included in any negotiator's repertoire of skills and capabilities:

- the ability to separate the people from the problem and to avoid letting emotional considerations affect the negotiation
- the ability to focus on interests rather than positions
- the ability to avoid making premature judgements
- the ability to judge possible agreements according to an objective set of criteria or standards.

Classic two-party negotiation

Figure 13.6 introduces the case of the new graduate.[48] In this case, a graduate is negotiating a job offer with a corporate recruiter. The example illustrates the basic elements of classic two-party negotiation in many contexts.

To begin with, look at the situation from the graduate's perspective. She has told the recruiter that she would like a salary of $50 000; this is her initial offer. But she also has in mind a minimum reservation point of $40 000 — the lowest salary that she will accept for this job.

BATNA is the 'best alternative to a negotiated agreement', or each party's position on what they must do if an agreement cannot be reached.

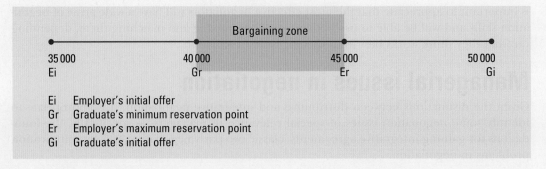

FIGURE 13.6 An example of the bargaining zone in classic two-party negotiation

Thus, she communicates a salary request of $50 000 but is willing to accept one as low as $40 000. The situation is somewhat reversed from the recruiter's perspective. The recruiter's initial offer to the graduate is $35 000 and the maximum reservation point is $45 000; this is the most the recruiter is prepared to pay.

The bargaining zone is defined as the range between one party's minimum reservation point and the other party's maximum reservation point. In figure 13.6, the bargaining zone is $40 000–$45 000; it is a positive bargaining zone because the reservation points of the two parties overlap. Whenever a positive bargaining zone exists, bargaining has room to unfold. Had the graduate's minimum reservation point been greater than the recruiter's maximum reservation point (for example, $47 000), there would have been no room for bargaining. Classic two-party bargaining always involves the delicate tasks of first discovering the respective reservation points (your own and the other's) and then working towards an agreement that lies somewhere within the resulting bargaining zone and that is acceptable to each party. The What would you do? discusses underlying conflict.

The **bargaining zone** is the zone between one party's minimum reservation point and the other party's maximum reservation point in a negotiating situation.

Underlying conflict

Due to Queensland government reforms, a particular department is affected by the merger of three local government organisations. The proposed vision of this merger is to deliver a stronger, more efficient and more modern local government system that has a greater ability to deliver services and infrastructure for all Queenslanders. As part of the merger, a new CEO has been appointed. Even in times of no significant change, the appointment of a new CEO may result in major changes to the organisation by way of a change in leadership style.

The new CEO has not only brought a very different style of leadership to the merged organisation, but has done so in a time of radical change. The merger could be described as a planned event, with the state government acting as an initial change agent, placing various levels of control over the merger in the form of policies and procedures. This has allowed for a change management strategy to be developed to direct the process of restructure in the new organisation.

This strategy has been implemented by a management team consisting of the CEO and senior management. This management team has been affected by organisational power and political issues. As a restructure of the new organisation is required, this has created opportunity for individuals to pursue greater positional power — sometimes through political means. As the process of positional restructure progresses, the use of political means to gain positional power is increasing. As with many mergers, organisational culture can be a major barrier. Each of the three original organisations has a different culture in some form. This directly relates to all the employees as it involves aspects of their sense of identity, values, behaviours and motivation.

Reflecting on this scenario, with such a major change affecting staff at all levels of the organisation, conflicts are bound to occur. Various types of disagreement have already been occurring and the management team needs to ensure that the conflict is effectively managed to limit the negative aspects of this conflict.

Questions

1. Discuss the types and sources of conflict that could occur in this case.
2. If you were appointed as a consultant, what recommendations would you make in relation to managing the potential conflict in this case?

It is too easy in negotiation to stake out your position based on the assumption that to gain your way, something must be 'subtracted' from the other party's way. This myth of the 'fixed pie' is a purely distributive approach to negotiation. The whole concept of integrative negotiation is based on the premise that the 'pie' can sometimes be expanded and/or used to the maximum advantage of all parties, not just one.

Parties to negotiations often begin by stating extreme demands, so the possibility of escalating commitment is high. That is, once 'demands' have been stated, people become committed to them and are reluctant to back down. As a result, they may be prone to non-rational escalation of conflict. Concerns for 'protecting your ego' and 'saving face' may enhance these tendencies. It takes self-discipline to spot this tendency in your own behaviour as well as that of others.

It is also common for negotiators to develop the belief that their positions are the only 'correct' ones. This is characterised by overconfidence and ignoring others' needs. In some cases, negotiators completely fail to see merits in the other party's position — merits that an outside observer would be sure to spot. Such overconfidence makes it harder to reach a positive common agreement. It may even set the stage for disappointment if the negotiation is turned over to a neutral third party for resolution. In **arbitration**, such as the salary arbitration now common in professional sports, this third party acts as the 'judge' and issues a binding decision after listening to the positions advanced by the parties involved in a dispute. Sometimes, a manager may be asked to serve as an arbitrator of disputes between employees, from matters as important as the distribution of task assignments to those as seemingly trivial as access to a photocopy machine. The Counterpoint considers conflict in a workplace.

Arbitration occurs when a neutral third party acts as judge and issues a binding decision affecting parties at a negotiation impasse.

COUNTER**POINT**

The virtue and vice of workplace conflict

Workplace conflict is seen generally as a hurdle to overcome. Often, it is considered as the consequence of ineffective coordination by the leader and a lack of joint task performance by the team. Furthermore, to solve conflict in a constructive manner takes time, which could result in time-off costs and missed business opportunities owing to the conflict taking valuable focus away from business progress. Extensive research exists arguing that conflict involving cognitive conflict and emotional conflict has a negative impact upon team member satisfaction. Conflict creates stress and could lead to psychosomatic complaints and feelings of burnout.[49] However, even though conflict can be destructive, it can also benefit group work. When conflict revolves around differences in opinions or decisions, neglected problems and opportunities can be identified. The latter is referred to as cognitive conflict or functional conflict.[50] For example, there could a disagreement between members of a group regarding how to achieve a specific team goal. A debate between members of the group is likely to take place, each defending her or his argument to reach the final decision. This debate will bring forward a variety of problems and opportunities to which group members are exposed and which may not have surfaced otherwise. In contrast, when members agree with other group members about concepts or actions without presenting or considering differing viewpoints, superior alternatives may be overlooked and subsequent performance may be less than optimal. This in turn could allow for better decision making and problem solving to take place. In addition, controversy associated with conflict allows group members to be exposed to a variety of positions, which in turn is likely to develop a deeper understanding of others' positions and arguments. Controversy may result in open-mindedness, interpersonal attraction, and incorporation of opposing views into one's own. Members tend to be closer after the stress of conflict and the associated release that comes with successful conflict resolution. One strategy to manage effectively and utilise controversy in a positive way is to ensure a climate of openness and cooperation in the group. Another way is to utilise members' skills and abilities. By achieving an open atmosphere in the group members can openly and honestly contribute to the group's decision-making process while being accepting of each other's points of view. A greater commitment to the final decision is another positive outcome. Conflict can also prevent stagnation, stimulate interest and foster creativity. Because conflict tends to open up a range of different ideas, perceptions and ways of processing and judging information, creativity and curiosity can result. In the process group members could re-evaluate their positions, which could ultimately lead to greater cohesion in the group and enhanced productivity. Group members who see the world differently have the opportunity to cooperate even when the parties have different viewpoints.[51]

Questions

1. Which argument about the effect of conflict do you most strongly support and why? Provide an example to argue your point.
2. What can organisations do in order to minimise and/or manage conflict effectively?

Summary

Communication and its role in organisations

Communication in an organisation is a process by which organisational members share meanings by exchanging information. We communicate to inform, instruct, motivate or seek information, to achieve coordinated action throughout the organisation, to develop information for the benefit of the organisation, to express our feelings and emotions, and to explain respective job responsibilities, roles and expectations. The interpersonal communication process involves an intricate matching of information that is encoded, sent, received and decoded, sometimes with and sometimes without feedback, but always affected by noise. Communication is effective when both sender and receiver interpret a message in the same way. It is efficient when messages are transferred at a low cost. Communication channels include formal, informal and quasiformal relationships among members of the organisation. The organisation is a network of information and communication channels. The electronic age has provided organisations with new opportunities to link managers effectively. Barriers to communication include special sources of noise common to most interpersonal exchanges: physical distractions, cultural differences, and the absence of feedback and status effects. Each of these sources of noise should be recognised and subjected to special managerial control. Managers can eliminate or reduce barriers through techniques such as wandering around, developing active listening skills, providing effective feedback to the sender of the communication, and articulating job roles and responsibilities.

Conflict and its effect on organisations

Conflict can be either emotional (based on personal feelings) or substantive (based on work goals). Both forms can be harmful in organisations if, as a result, individuals and/or groups are unable to work constructively with one another. Conflict situations in organisations occur in vertical and lateral working relations and in line–staff relations. Often, they result from work flow interdependencies and resource scarcities. Most typically, conflict develops through a series of stages, beginning with antecedent conditions and progressing into manifest conflict. The conflict may or may not be entirely 'resolved' in the sense that the underlying reasons for the emotional and/or substantive conflict are eliminated. Unresolved conflicts set the stage for future conflicts of a similar nature. When kept within tolerable limits, conflict can be a source of creativity and performance enhancement.

Even when managers have different viewpoints, ongoing questioning and discussion about their differences may unleash more creative approaches to a situation as they are further probed. On the other hand, such situations can become destructive when these limits are exceeded and the hostility between individuals or groups continues. In this case, managers must be made aware of such conflicts and take appropriate action to resolve them.

Managing conflict

Conflict management should always proceed with the goal of true conflict resolution. Indirect forms of conflict management include appeals to common goals, hierarchical referral and organisational redesign. Direct conflict management proceeds with different combinations of assertiveness and cooperativeness on the part of conflicting parties. Win–win outcomes are achieved through cooperation and problem solving most often associated with high assertiveness and high cooperation. Win–lose outcomes usually occur through direct competition or authoritative command. Lose–lose outcomes are typically found as a result of avoidance, smoothing and compromise approaches.

Negotiation and its role in organisations

Negotiation in organisations occurs whenever two or more people with different preferences must make joint decisions. Managers may find themselves involved in various types of negotiation situations, including two-party, group, intergroup and constituency negotiation. Both substance goals and relationship goals are at stake. Effective negotiation occurs when issues of substance are resolved and human relationships are maintained, or even improved, in the process. To achieve such results, ethical conduct must be carefully maintained, even as negotiating parties represent viewpoints and preferences that differ greatly from one another.

Managers' issues in negotiation

Different approaches to negotiation can have substantially different results. In distributive negotiation, the focus of each party is on staking out positions in the attempt to claim desired portions of a 'fixed pie'. In integrative negotiation, sometimes called principled negotiation, the focus is on determining the merits of the issues and finding ways to satisfy one another's needs. The distributive approach is often associated with individual styles of competition (the 'hard' approach) or accommodation (the 'soft' approach). The integrative approach ideally leads to some form of cooperation or problem solving to achieve a mutually desirable solution.

CHAPTER 13 study guide

Key terms

arbitration, *p. 518*
bargaining zone, *p. 517*
BATNA, *p. 516*
buffering, *p. 510*
channels, *p. 494*
conflict, *p. 500*
conflict resolution, *p. 508*
constructive conflict, *p. 505*
decoding, *p. 495*
decoupling, *p. 510*
destructive conflict, *p. 505*
distributive negotiation, *p. 514*
effective communication, *p. 495*
effective negotiation, *p. 513*

efficient communication, *p. 495*
emotional conflict, *p. 501*
encoding, *p. 494*
feedback, *p. 495*
formal communication
channels, *p. 496*
hierarchical referral, *p. 510*
informal communication
channels, *p. 496*
information source, *p. 494*
integrative negotiation, *p. 515*
intergroup conflict, *p. 503*
interorganisational conflict, *p. 503*
interpersonal conflict, *p. 503*

intrapersonal conflict, *p. 503*
liaison groups, *p. 511*
linking pins, *p. 511*
manifest conflict, *p. 508*
negotiation, *p. 512*
noise, *p. 495*
organisational communication, *p. 493*
quasiformal channels, *p. 496*
receiver, *p. 495*
relationship goals, *p. 513*
substance goals, *p. 513*
substantive conflict, *p. 501*
transmission, *p. 494*

Review questions

1. Describe the main sources of noise and disturbance in communication. Give examples.
2. Discuss the challenges to the workplace of the use of social media at work.
3. Under what circumstances would conflict be accepted and considered to be positive? Give examples.

4. What are some of the most common strategies used in resolving conflict? Briefly explain why conflict in the workplace can be positive.
5. Describe some of the most common managerial issues in negotiations.

Application questions

1. Imagine you are the CEO of a large manufacturing company that has five factories in Asia employing a total of 5000 people. What are some of the ways you would select to communicate your company's vision throughout the organisation?
2. If, as a manager, you felt it necessary to criticise the productivity of one of your employees, what would be some of the important factors you would consider before approaching that person?
3. The text states 'when conflict arises, most people's first reaction is to become angry or distressed, and to seek to eliminate the problem'. Provide an example in which you have been an *observer only* of a conflict situation. The example you describe could be from your workplace or a different environment, such as

a bank or an airport. Write down how the reaction of the parties involved in the conflict appeared to an onlooker — in this case, yourself. Then explain how you would have handled the situation if you had been one of the parties in conflict, remembering to take into consideration the emotional aspect that can escalate conflict. *Note:* If more than one student is involved, each should have the opportunity to take the role of each of the parties involved.
4. According to the text, 'managers are known to spend up to 20 per cent of their time dealing with conflict, including conflicts in which managers are themselves directly involved'. What implications does this have for business school educators and new managers?

5. Using an example, explain how destructive conflict can have a negative impact on performance. How would you remedy the conflict situation you have discussed?
6. Discuss the statement: 'Social media are changing contemporary workplaces on a number of fronts'. Provide some examples in arguing your case.
7. Design a half-day awareness workshop aimed at teaching administrative staff the meaning of conflict and the various approaches to conflict resolution.

Research questions

1. Access the website of a large company with which you are familiar. Search the site with a view to identifying how the company:
   (a) communicates its commitment to new and existing employees and its external customers, such as yourself
   (b) addresses issues of conflict that are most common in the organisation (for example, bargaining with trade unions with a view to establishing enterprise agreements)
   (c) uses social media (if any) and for what purposes.

2. Select a well-known case of conflict involving multiple parties (including, for example, managers, customers, government and the community).
   (a) Examine the reasons for the conflict.
   (b) Outline how and why the conflict escalated.
   (c) Describe the approach(es) used in attempting to resolve the conflict.
   (d) Critically examine the effectiveness of these approach(es).

Running project

Complete the following activities for your organisation.
1. Describe the formal communication channels likely to exist, based on the information on its organisational chart.
2. Find a job advertisement from your organisation (its website or its social media may be a likely source) and assess how well it communicates the job role. Apart from the job description, where else would you expect to obtain information about the expectations of the employer, both before and after joining the organisation?
3. What internal communication processes does your organisation use? Try to find examples of each and assess what criteria the organisation uses in choosing which communication channel to use. (For example, why does it advertise its products in newspapers, but use its website for job advertisements?)

4. What social media does your organisation use to communicate with various audiences? Discuss two examples.
5. Negotiation is especially significant in today's workplace, where more people are being offered opportunities to be involved in decisions. This can often lead to disagreements. If possible, arrange an interview with a manager or other person of authority in your organisation. Ask the manager what formal and informal processes the organisation has in place to deal with situations that may arise from intergroup conflict caused by any of the following issues: wage rates, task objectives, performance evaluations, job assignments, work schedules and locations, and special privileges.

Individual activity

Conflict management strategies

Instructions
Think of how you behave in conflict situations in which your wishes differ from those of others. In the space to the left, rate reach of the following statements on a scale of '1' 'not at all' to '5' 'very much'.

When I have a conflict at work, school or in my personal life, I do the following.
1. I give in to the wishes of the other party.
2. I try to realise a middle-of-the-road solution.
3. I push my own point of view.
4. I examine issues until I find a solution that really satisfies me and the other party.

5. I avoid a confrontation about our differences.
6. I concur with the other party.
7. I emphasise that we have to find a compromise solution.
8. I search for gains.
9. I stand for my own and the other's goals.
10. I avoid differences of opinion as much as possible.
11. I try to accommodate the other party.
12. I insist we both give in a little.
13. I fight for a good outcome for myself.
14. I examine ideas from both sides to find a mutually optimal solution.
15. I try to make differences that seem less severe.
16. I adapt to the other party's goals and interests.
17. I strive whenever possible towards a fifty-fifty compromise.
18. I do everything to win.
19. I work out a solution that serves my own as well as other's interests as much as possible.
20. I try to avoid a confrontation with the other person.

Scoring

Total your scores for items as follows.

Yielding tendency: 1 + 6 + 11 + 16 = _____.
Compromising tendency: 2 + 7 + 12 + 17 = _____.
Forcing tendency: 3 + 8 + 13 + 18 = _____.
Problem-solving tendency: 4 + 9 + 14 + 19 = _____.
Avoiding tendency: 5 + 10 + 15 + 20 = _____.

Interpretation

Each of the scores above approximates a conflict management style. Although each style is part of management, only collaboration or problem solving leads to true conflict resolution. You should consider any patterns that may be evident in your scores and think about how to best handle the conflict situations in which you become involved.

Source: This instrument is described in Carsten KW De Drew, Arne Evers, Bianca Beersma, Esther S Kluwer and Aukje Nauta, 'A theory-based measure of conflict management strategies in the workplace', *Journal of Organizational Behavior*, vol. 22 (2001), pp. 645–668. Used by permission.

Group activity

Conflict resolution

Preparation

You will be given the opportunity to role play handling a conflict you face or have faced. Select the conflict and write out the information for a class member who will play the role of the person with whom you are in conflict.

1. Define the situation and list pertinent information about the other party (that is, relationship to you, knowledge of the situation, age, background and so on).
2. State what you wish to accomplish during the conflict resolution.
3. Identify the other party's possible reaction to your confrontation (resistance to change).

Plan how you will overcome resistance to change using the problem-solving conflict management style. A good way to open the conflict resolution is to use an X (behaviour), Y (consequences), Z (feelings) statement: for example, 'When you smoke in my room (behaviour), I have trouble breathing and become nauseous (consequences), and feel uncomfortable and irritated (feeling)'. Write out an XYZ statement to open your selected conflict resolution. During the role play, open with your XYZ statement, then allow the person to respond as you seek true satisfaction of everyone's concerns by working through differences, and finding and solving problems so everyone gains as a result.

Objective

To develop your conflict resolution skills

Total time: 30–40 minutes

Procedure 1

Break into groups of three. If there are any people not in a triad, make one or two groups of two. Each member selects the number 1, 2 or 3. Number 1 will be the first to initiate a conflict role play, then 2, followed by 3.

Procedure 2

1. Initiator number 1 gives his or her information from the preparation to number 2 (the responder) to read. Once number 2 understands, role play (see step 2 below). Number 3 is the observer.
2. Role play the conflict resolution. Number 3, the observer, writes his or her observation. Focus on what was done and how to improve.
3. Integration. When the role play is over, the observer leads a discussion on the effectiveness of the conflict resolution. All three should discuss the effectiveness. Number 3 is not a lecturer. Do not go on until told to do so.

Procedure 3

Same as procedure 2, only number 2 is now the initiator, number 3 is the responder and number 1 is the observer.

Procedure 4

Same as procedure 2, only number 3 is the initiator, number 1 is the responder and number 2 is the observer.

Various cases involving the issues of social media and the workplace have surfaced recently. Following are three scenarios involving social media that created a lot of problems for the organisations involved.

KitchenAid
@KitchenAidUSA

Obamas gma even knew it was going 2 b bad! 'She died 3 days b4 he became president'. #nbcpolitics

The KichenAid scenario: A staff member of KitchenAid posted an insensitive tweet about President Obama's grandmother to the Kitchenaid Twitter account, instead of the personal account of the staff member.[52]

The staff member quickly deleted the tweet; however, the tweet was already viewed by many people. Cynthia Soledad, the head of the KitchenAid brand, quickly tried to remedy the situation by tweeting an explanation 15 minutes later. She apologised to President Obama and the public and advised that the person sending the tweet would not be doing any more tweets for the company.[53] Cynthia Soledad's honest explanation and personal apology limited the damage to the brand and was well received.

The DKNY scenario: A photographer, who realised that DKNY were using his photos in a window display without his permission, took to the digital community and asked them to share a post asking DKNY to donate $100 000 to a local YMCA in lieu of compensation. DKNY was quick to come forward with an apology and explained that the Bangkok store involved had mistakenly used the 'mock-up' photos and DKNY would donate $25 000 to the YMCA. The photographer accepted it was an honest mistake and thanked them for the donation. DKNY's quick and strong response successfully defused the situation before a social media crisis erupted.[54]

The Australian Olympic swimming team scenario: A photograph on the back page of *The Courier-Mail* during the 2012 Olympics created a stir. Seven members of the Australian Olympic swim team were photographed at the pool with their heads down, looking intensely at their mobile phones. This particular image accompanied a news story about the distraction posed by Twitter and questions to the Australian team officials from readers about whether the athletes should have been given unrestrained access to social media. Some Australian officials reflected on the issue when it was claimed that silver medallist Emily Seebohm was distracted by her use of Twitter. After she competed, the athlete was involved in a Twitter row with an aggressive fan who ridiculed her tears after she took second place in the race.[55]

Questions

1. Given the content on communication, especially the reference to social media in the chapter, analyse the main problems in the scenarios above.
2. In view of the scenarios above, what can organisations do to limit the negative impact of the use of social media?

End notes

1. Robert Walters, 'Understanding the role of social media to complement attraction strategies' (2013), www.robertwalters.com.au.
2. Reprezent, 'In search of employment: an insight into how young people look for work' (2014), www.wereprezent.co.uk.
3. JP Medved, 'Find new talent and nurture existing employees with the help of HR software', Capterra Talent Management blog (4 April 2014), http://blog.capterra.com/examples-companies-facebook-recruiting/Social media — a recruitment revolution?
4. T Dahle, 'An objective and comparative study of five methods of transmitting information from management to business and industrial employees', *Speech monographs*, vol. 21 (March 1954).

5. EG Wertheim, 'The importance of effective communication', Northeastern University College of Business Administration, http://cba.neu.edu.

6. Randstad, 'Shaping the world of work' (2013), www.randstad.com.au.

7. Wertheim, op. cit.

8. T Iggulden, 'A slap in the interface', *Australian Financial Review BOSS Magazine* (August 2001), p. 8.

9. C Donaldson, 'Social media the next frontier', *HR Leader* (1 April 2008), www.humanresourcesmagazine.com.au.

10. R DeMatteo, 'Social media: 6 functions HR can't do without' *Personnel Today* (19 April 2010), www.personneltoday.com/articles

11. J Griffin, 'SR7 getting to grips with social media risks', *HR Leader* (14 September 2010), p. 27.

12. J Field and J Chelliah, 'Employers need to get to grips with social-media risks', *Human Resource Management International Digest*, vol. 21, no. 7 (2013), pp. 25–6.

13. J Froud, 'How employers can embrace social media and protect their business', *The Guardian* (5 March 2013), www.theguardian.com.

14. J Walton, 'Board dynamics', *Australian Financial Review BOSS Magazine* (August 2001), pp. 60–1.

15. RE Walton, *Interpersonal peacemaking: confrontations and third-party consultation* (Reading, MA: Addison-Wesley, 1969).

16. KW Thomas and WH Schmidt, 'A survey of managerial interests with respect to conflict', *Academy of Management Journal*, vol. 19 (1976), pp. 315–18.

17. R Bolton, *People skills: how to assert yourself, listen to others, and resolve conflicts* (Sydney: Prentice Hall, 1986), ch. 12.

18. Walton, op. cit.

19. ibid.

20. RE Walton and JM Dutton, 'The management of interdepartmental conflict: a model and review', *Administrative Science Quarterly*, vol. 14 (1969), pp. 73–84.

21. 'Supporting a healthy organisation: Effective communication', *EAP Messenger*, vol. 12, no. 1 (2010).

22. Queensland University of Technology (QUT), 'Cultural diversity policy', www.qut.edu.au.

23. See A Jassawalla, C Truglia and J Garvey, 'Cross-cultural conflict and expatriate manager adjustment: an exploratory study', *Management Decision*, vol. 42, no. 7 (August 2004), pp. 837–49.

24. D Leonard and S Straus, 'Putting your company's whole brain to work', *Harvard Business Review*, vol. 75, no. 4 (July/August 1997), p. 111.

25. Developed from D Hellriegel, JW Slocum, Jr and RW Woodman, *Organizational behavior*, 3rd ed. (St. Paul: West, 1983), pp. 471–4.

26. Developed from G Johns, *Organizational behavior* (Glenview, IL: Scott, Foresman, 1983), pp. 415–17; RE Walton and JM Dutton, 'The management of interdepartmental conflict: a model and review', *Administrative Science Quarterly*, vol. 14 (1969), pp. 73–84.

27. These stages are consistent with the conflict models described by Alan C Filley, *Interpersonal conflict resolution* (Glenview, IL: Scott, Foresman, 1975); LR Pondy, 'Organizational conflict: concepts and models', *Administrative Science Quarterly*, vol. 12 (September 1967), pp. 269–320.

28. Adapted from R Gaskell, 'How effectively is your organisation managing conflict?', *hrconnection*, vol. 8 (2003), www.davidsontrahaire.com.au.

29. RR Blake and JS Mouton, *The managerial grid* (Houston, TX: Gulf, 1964).

30. KW Thomas, 'Organizational conflict' in S Kerr (ed.), *Organizational behavior* (Columbus, OH: Grid, 1979), pp. 151–81.

31. M Afzalur Rahim, 'A strategy for managing conflict in complex organizations', *Human Relations*, vol. 38, no. 1 (1985), pp. 83–5.

32. RE Jones and BH Melcher, 'Personality and preference for modes of conflict resolution', *Human Relations*, vol. 35, no. 8 (1982), pp. 649–58.

33. PR Lawrence and JW Lorsch, 'Differentiation and integration in complex organizations', *Administrative Science Quarterly*, vol. 12, no. 1 (1967), pp. 1–47.

34. SP Robbins, '"Conflict management" and "conflict resolution" are not synonymous terms', *California Management Review*, vol. 21, no. 2 (1978), pp. 67–75.

35. PR Lawrence and Jay W Lorsch, *Organization and environment* (Cambridge, MA: Harvard University Press, 1967).

36. K Krumov, S Ilieva, S Karabeliova and L Alexieva, 'Conflict resolution strategies in the transition to market economy', *Annals of the American Academy of Political and Social Science*, vol. 552, no. 10 (1997), p. 65.

37. W Pace, *Organizational communication* (Englewood Cliffs, NJ: Prentice Hall, 1983), p. 145.

38. ibid.

39. SP Robbins, *Organization theory: structure design and applications* (Englewood Cliffs, NJ: Prentice Hall, 1987).

40. See J Galbraith, *Designing complex organizations* (Reading, MA: Addison-Wesley, 1973).

41. R Likert and JB Likert, *New ways of managing conflict* (New York: McGraw-Hill, 1976).

42. D Nadler and M Tushman, *Strategic organizational design* (Glenview, IL: Scott, Foresman, 1988).

43. RA Friedman and SC Currall, *Conflict Escalation: Dispute Exacerbating Elements of E-Mail Communication* (2004), p. 6, http://ssrn.com.

44. J Walther, 'Computer-mediated communication: impersonal, interpersonal, and hyperpersonal interaction', *Communication Research*, vol. 23 (1996) pp. 3–43.

45. M Michalowicz, '5 steps to managing a disgruntled employee', (28 September 2011), www.americanexpress.com.

46. Following discussion based on R Fisher and W Ury, *Getting to yes: negotiating agreement without giving in* (New York: Penguin, 1983); RJ Lewicki and JA Litterer, *Negotiation* (Homewood, IL: Richard D. Irwin, 1985), pp. 315–19.

47. R Fisher and W Ury, *Getting to yes: negotiating agreement without giving in* (New York: Penguin, 1983), pp. 10–14.

48. This example is developed from MH Bazerman, *Judgment in managerial decision making*, 2nd ed. (New York: John Wiley & Sons, 1990), pp. 106–8.

49. CKW De Dreu, 'The virtue and vice of workplace conflict: food for (pessimistic) thought', *Journal of Organizational Behavior*, vol. 29 (2008), pp. 5–18.

50. SH Appelbaum, C Abdallah and BT Shapiro, 'The self-directed team: a conflict resolution analysis', *Team Performance Management*, vol. 5, no. 2 (1999), pp. 60–77.

51. B Eunson, *Communicating in the 21st Century*, 3rd ed. (Milton Qld: John Wiley & Sons, 2007).

52. Our Social Media Limited, 'KitchenAidUSA: handling a Twitter crisis' (4 October 2013), http://oursocialtimes.com.

53. J Rick, 'How KitchenAid spun a Twitter crisis into a PR coup' (4 October 2012), www.fastcompany.com.

54. L Mensching, 'A photo is worth 25 000 words — or in this case, dollars' (21 March 2013), http://bohlsengroup.com.

55. *News.com.au*, 'Social media serves up yet another modern dilemma for brilliant Games' (4 August 2012), www.news.com.au.

CHAPTER 14

ORGANISATIONAL CHANGE AND INNOVATION

LEARNING OBJECTIVES

After studying this chapter, you should be able to:

1. distinguish between radical and incremental planned change

2. discuss the forces favouring change and the targets of change in contemporary organisations

3. identify the change strategies used by managers

4. explain why people resist change and describe strategies to overcome resistance

5. discuss workplace stress in the context of change

6. explain why innovation is so important to organisations today and list the features you would expect to find in an innovative organisation.

LEADING CHANGE WHEN GOING PUBLIC

Bulletproof Networks became the first pure-play, publicly-listed cloud services company in Australia (ASX: BPF) in January 2014, the company's world-class support and management targets leading private and public cloud platforms, including VMware and Amazon Web Services (AWS). Bulletproof has driven industry innovation since being the first provider in Australia to launch a VMware public cloud service in 2006, leading to ZDNet's Emerging Innovation Award. This was followed with the first Managed AWS service in Australia in 2012, leading to Bulletproof being nominated as a finalist in the BRW Digital Innovation Awards in 2013.[1]

Prior to deciding to list, founder Anthony Woodward made a conscious decision to maintain who they are as a company through the process and decided to have a key focus on the continued development of the company culture. Woodward argues that one of the company's values is transparency — a factor coming into play whenever they deal with their people, customers and suppliers. Being open to the company team about what the listing would mean for them, why the company did it and what the company hoped would come from it, was a priority to Woodward.

Woodward believes company culture needs to be managed through the process of going public to ensure it keeps on growing and doesn't fade or change in a negative direction. He argues that going public means taking on a new set of important stakeholders in the form of generally unrelated public shareholders, with some shareholders even being employees. He believes even though Bulletproof's core value of transparency serves the requirement of continuous disclosure well, the method and manner of releasing information has to be controlled since it is important that all shareholders and the rest of the market receive

sensitive information simultaneously (via the ASX platform). As a leader he believes 'providing a great service to your clients, looking after your team, remaining viable, profitable and growing are all key components to achieving company success whether you are public or private'.[2]

According to Woodward the measures of success don't alter when a company goes public. The ongoing development of a culture that enables your people to reach their full potential and work in a great environment is another major measure of success.

Recruitment is a big factor in the ongoing success and change of Bulletproof. Recruiting staff who add value to the company culture and continue to develop it in a positive way is essential. He stresses the importance of ensuring diversity of staff to guard against a monoculture.[3]

Introduction

In today's turbulent socioeconomic environment, organisations need to constantly adapt to a changing environment. Furthermore, organisations need to be innovative in their management approaches, since we have entered an era in which increasingly greater premiums are attached to effective and positive approaches to innovation and change. Apart from demographic challenges, such as changing demographics, the Information Age is transforming all before it — like the Industrial Revolution did 200 years ago. The rules of the game have fundamentally changed: 'control' was important in the industrial era, but the Information Age demands innovation and flexibility as prerequisites for success. In order to survive and prosper and to ensure they remain economically competitive and responsive, organisations must be willing and able to make substantial changes to their practice.

For organisations, this means continual innovation. As our society becomes more technologically demanding, the need for change reaches all sectors of the economy, including industry, government, professional development programs and various institutional frameworks. This requires managers to reassess how they develop and implement change strategies and encourage innovation. Even in the public sector, organisations are facing great challenges. There is relentless pressure to change the missions and innovative practices of these organisations.[4]

This chapter will help you understand the importance of change and innovation. It examines the various types of and approaches to change. We shall also deal with the increasingly important topic of innovation in an organisational context.

What is organisational change?

'Change' is the watchword of the day for most organisations. In organisational behaviour, 'organisational change' refers to organisation-wide change rather than to small changes, such as adding a new person or making minor modifications to a process. Examples of organisation-wide change might include a change in mission, restructuring operations, the adoption of major new technologies, and mergers. Some experts refer to organisational transformation to designate a fundamental and radical reorientation in the way the organisation operates. Some of this change may be described as **radical change**.[5] This is change that results in a major make-over of the organisation and/or of its component systems. In today's business environments, radical changes are often initiated by a critical event, such as the arrival of a new chief executive officer (CEO), a new ownership brought about by a merger or takeover, or a dramatic failure in operating results. Radical change occurs infrequently in the life cycle of an organisation. However, when it does occur, this change is intense and all-encompassing. There may be times in an organisation's life when its survival depends on an ability to undergo successfully the rigours and demands of radical change. Radical change occurs when an industry's core assets and activities are both threatened with obsolescence, and knowledge and brand capital erode along with the customer and supplier relationships. It is most commonly caused by the introduction of new technologies or regulations, or by changing consumer preferences.

Another and more common form of organisational change is **incremental change**. This is change that occurs more frequently and less traumatically as part of an organisation's natural evolution. Typical changes of this type include new products, new technologies and new systems. Although the nature of the organisation remains relatively unaltered, incremental change builds on the existing ways of operating and seeks to enhance them or extend them in new directions. The ability to improve continually through incremental change is an important asset to organisations in today's demanding environments.

The success of both radical and incremental change in organisations depends in part on **change agents** who facilitate and support the change processes. A change agent is a person or group who takes responsibility for changing the existing pattern of behaviour of another person or social system. It makes sense, therefore, that part of every manager's job in today's dynamic times is to act as a change agent in the work setting. This means being alert to situations or people needing change, open to good ideas, and able to support the implementation of new ideas into actual practice.

Planned and unplanned change

Changes in organisations can be planned or unplanned. Planned change occurs when an organisation deliberately attempts to make internal changes to meet specified goals or to pursue a set of strategies. For example, organisations often change their structures to meet

Radical change is change that results in a major make-over of the organisation and/or its component systems.

Incremental change is change that occurs more frequently and less traumatically as part of an organisation's natural evolution.

Change agents are individuals or groups that take responsibility for changing the existing pattern of behaviour of a person or social system.

given objectives or to pursue cost-cutting strategies. Also, an organisation may engage in major updating of its operational systems, which would mean engaging in some form of technological change.

Unplanned change is usually prompted by some external driver, such as market forces, economic crises, economic opportunities or social changes. Typically, organisations engage in organisation-wide change to respond to these forces and thereby evolve to a different level in their life cycle; for example, going from a highly reactive to a more proactive and planned development. However, not all change in organisations happens as a result of an intended (or change agent's) direction. **Unplanned change** occurs spontaneously or randomly, and without a change agent's attention. The appropriate goal in managing unplanned change, once the change is recognised, is to act immediately to minimise any negative consequences, and to maximise any possible benefits.

In this chapter we are particularly interested in **planned change** — that is, change that comes about as a result of specific efforts on the part of a change agent. Planned change is a direct response to someone's perception of a **performance gap**. This is a discrepancy between the desired and actual state of affairs. Performance gaps may represent problems to be resolved or opportunities to be explored. It is useful to think of most planned changes as efforts initiated by managers to resolve performance gaps to the benefit of the organisation and its members.

However, planned change often assumes that the future is predictable and there is an end state to be reached. In other words, managers tend to regard change as a once-only, major alteration to the organisation. In reality, in the vast majority of cases change occurs in an incremental way, reflecting the assumption that what worked in the past will also work in the future. However, with contextual dynamism and complexity being the new rule, any linear extrapolation is at best misleading. The line representing the link between past and future is at best dotted, and sometimes even discontinuous, with twists and thresholds everywhere.[6]

As Bowman has discovered, 'organisations are constrained by routines, but, paradoxically, routines are the very stuff of organisations; without routines organisations could not function. The problems start when routines get in the way of strategic thinking and strategic change'[7], and when routine thinking gets in the way of lateral/innovative thinking. Processes that challenge the taken-for-granted assumptions that underpin routine thinking are then needed for the organisation to progress.

Leadership of change

Most change initiatives, especially radical change, require effective leadership, not just on the part of the chief executive and other senior managers, but from leaders at all levels in the organisation.

The more recent Australian studies show that change processes that have the support of the workforce require good leadership, an appropriate model of change, some room for negotiation and compromise, and well-planned communication. In particular, a study focusing on six case studies in the Australian public sector found great support for the proposition that a prominent CEO role was important in 'driving' change, and in enlisting support for it.[8]

So, what does the leadership of change involve? It encompasses many dimensions that need to be adapted to each situation. Initially, leadership involves preparing people for the change by challenging the status quo and communicating a vision of what the organisation can aspire to become. Next, it involves building the commitment of employees and change agents throughout the organisation, and enabling them to act by providing resources and training, delegating power, building change teams and putting appropriate systems and structures in place. Then, leaders act as effective role models, maintaining the momentum of change through symbolic and substantive actions that reward progress and recognise the reaching of milestones.[9]

Unplanned change is change that occurs at random or spontaneously and without a change agent's direction.

Planned change is change that happens as a result of specific efforts on the part of a change agent.

The **performance gap** is the discrepancy between an actual and a desired state of affairs.

Robert Miles, a successful change management consultant and writer, has summarised the leadership of change in the following terms. First and foremost, according to Miles, radical change is vision-led. That is, it involves the creation of goals that stretch the organisation beyond its current horizons and capacities. Secondly, it is based on a total-system perspective, wherein all major elements of the organisation are carried forward. And thirdly, it requires a sustained process of organisational learning so that people and processes develop synergistically.[10] Figure 14.1 provides a picture of the four essential ingredients of a successful change process.

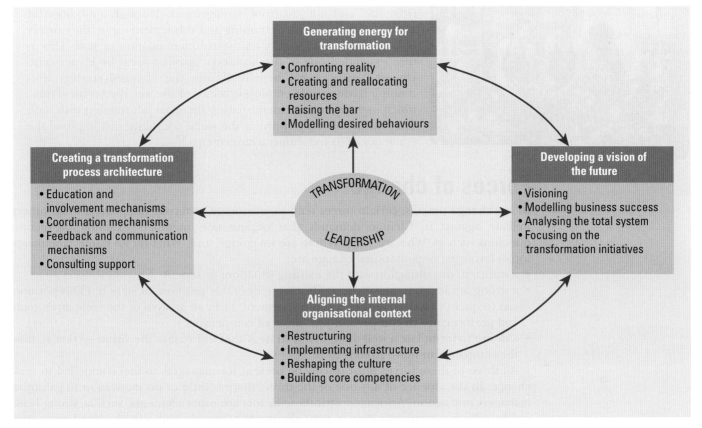

FIGURE 14.1 A framework for planned organisational change leadership

Source: Robert H Miles, *Corporate comeback: the story of renewal and transformation at National Semiconductor* (San Francisco: Jossey-Bass, 1997), p. 6.

As figure 14.1 suggests, the process hinges on 'generating energy for transformation'. A key to this is in revealing to employees the shortfalls in current organisational performance — in essence, providing a reality check. One way to do this is by benchmarking the organisation against customer expectations, industry leaders or competitors. Another method is to diagnose internal strengths and weaknesses; for example, by conducting a skills profile of employees to gauge their capacity to work cross-culturally. Based on such assessments, resources are released or reallocated to prepare the organisation and its staff for the next ingredient — 'developing a vision'. While 'generating energy' puts people into a frame of mind that supports change, the vision provides them with a sense of what the future organisation could be like and where they will be heading. A thorough organisational analysis is also needed as a basis for detailed planning of the change, which Miles describes as 'aligning the internal context'. The internal context consists of all the components that make an organisation what it is — its structure, culture, technology and so on. Any or all of these components can become targets for change. The final ingredient is 'creating a transformation process architecture'. Key words that express what this is about are education, involvement and communication.

Planting seeds of success

Leadership certainly doesn't happen only in the corporate world. Kyle Newport of United Nurseries not only plants seeds literally to grow his business, but he also plants seeds of success through his focused leadership approach to help his people grow. Newport took his business to the next level by encouraging staff to participate in a business efficiency program. The training shifted everybody's mindset, which Kyle found of great benefit in having ideas coming from staff and not just from management. Through application of continuous improvement training and subsequent input, the nursery re-laid garden beds purely on the recommendation of staff. This in turn expanded one of the business's growing areas by 15 per cent. United Nurseries has benefited from the changed strategy with training having made employees aware of the way the business runs, which includes management sharing financial information with staff. The business is now applying the same techniques to improve the efficiency of its freighting arrangements.[11]

Forces of change

In any change process, certain forces tend to encourage or favour the process while others militate against it. Change demands that organisation members examine big-picture questions such as 'Who are we?', 'Where are we going?' and 'What do we want?' The major forces favouring organisational change are:

- a sufficient dissatisfaction with the existing situation, or state A
- a strong attraction to moving towards a more desirable position, or state B. (This position can frequently be described in a vision statement, or in an analysis of the company's goals and performance in comparison with those of competitors.)
- a desire to formulate a well-thought-out strategy that will realise the vision — that is, how the company can move from A to B.[12]

All three of these forces must usually be present for managers to feel compelled to seek change. In the absence of any one of the three, there is little or no motivation to galvanise managers into action. Associated with these factors are other elements, such as strong leadership, effective communication, a tight alignment of people and organisational goals, and a clear definition of the compelling reasons to change.

Change may be triggered by internal or external forces. External forces include politics (for example, a change in government or government policy), laws (for example, anti-spam legislation), markets (for example, competition from foreign companies entering the home market) and technology (for example, the convergence of communications devices). Internal triggers include changes of ownership, products, services and processes and measures of effectiveness that can happen in an organisational setting. Today's organisations must be able to react quickly and correctly to external change, while managing internal change effectively. External change is usually obvious and has immediate impact. In contrast, the need for internal change is often less obvious.

Cultural change

As we saw in chapter 9, organisational culture is the pattern of an organisation's shared beliefs, values, expectations and assumptions. Culture is a strong influence on people's thoughts and behaviour, and affects all aspects of organisational life. It can significantly influence — positively and negatively — the outcomes of change so it cannot be ignored when considering a change initiative. Even the most rigid of organisational cultures can be subject to significant change under the right circumstances.

It is a massive task to achieve a major culture change, one in which new values are antagonistic to the old ones. Successful culture change, in which there is a change in the underlying values that drive behaviour, can take a long time, even years.[13] Pathways to effective culture change are listed in The effective manager 14.1.

Organisational growth will engender change, and new companies tend to see a rapid evolution of organisational culture as they undergo consistent change. Established companies tend to be more structured and slower to undertake change. A long-established company may not seek change until change is forced upon it as the result of a merger or acquisition, adverse media attention or undeniable changes in the environment. When a merger occurs, the question of which partner's organisational culture will become dominant inevitably arises. Both companies may be able to allow a new organisational culture to emerge. Cultural change may also occur internally in an unplanned fashion as the result of a labour dispute, a scandal or an accident.[15]

Technological change

The increased complexity of the business environment and of competition is due to a number of factors, but technology is a key driving force for change. Companies are generally receptive to technological change and are ready to accommodate further technological change. Companies use sophisticated networks and information systems that have unprecedented capacity for meeting customer and other business needs. Business transactions take place almost instantaneously via email and the internet. These changes have increased the pace of business. This pace is another force of change with which managers must contend.[16]

Technological change that occurred slowly over centuries (such as the invention of the wheel) accelerated to change measured in decades (for instance, the impact of the car), which has now transformed into continuous and pervasive change brought about by the computer chip and its successors.

Organisational targets for change

The forces for change are ever present in today's dynamic work settings.[17] They are found in the relationship between an organisation and its environment; mergers, strategic alliances and divestitures are examples of organisational attempts to redefine relationships with challenging environments. They are found in the life cycle of the organisation as it passes from birth through growth towards maturity; changes in culture and structures are examples of organisational attempts to adjust to these patterns of growth. They are found in the political nature of organisational life; changes in internal control structures (including benefits and reward systems) are examples of organisational attempts to deal with shifting political currents.

Driving change that is environmentally friendly

One major change organisations in modern and sophisticated economies have to manage effectively is environmental sustainability. The Good Guys retail electrical goods store at Capalaba, in South-East Queensland is a company that does not take sustainability lightly — particularly environmental sustainability. Owner and manager James Brockhurst, who won the Minister's Award for ClimateSmart Leadership in Queensland in 2010 and who is still a strong business sustainability leader today, says that the company wanted to make a positive difference, as well as himself personally. He thinks everyone is motivated by something, whether it is money, position or something else, but for him it is about leaving a legacy.

Under Brockhurst's leadership, the organisation has implemented numerous sustainability initiatives, and asked the question, 'How do we make the biggest difference in our community?' Many of the company's appliances use a lot of water and energy, so it developed a training program to assist staff in educating consumers on their purchases and informing them of what they can do for the environment. He also identified a staff 'eco-champion' to encourage momentum in the sustainability initiatives, and involved an external eco-champion to act as a coach and motivator on environmental issues. Under Brockhurst's leadership, the company developed the SERB guide (Sustainable Electrical

Retailers Induction Business). This ensured that their induction guide has all The Good Guys' usual cultural, functional ideals, but linked to sustainability actions.

The company has progressively employed incremental changes in creating a cultural change, and key stakeholders and the eco-champions are involved in permeating the sustainability message, with Brockhurst holding the occasional motivational session. The company shares its knowledge with its competitors and the community. The Good Guys has become a role model for other businesses in achieving sustainability outcomes. For the company, this means cost savings as well as substantial environmental benefits; for its staff, it means greater employee engagement and motivation; and for the community, it means an increased community spirit of being environmentally aware and friendly.[18]

Planned change based on any of these forces can be directed towards a wide variety of organisational components or targets. As shown in figure 14.2, these targets include organisational purpose, strategy, structure and people, as well as objectives, culture, tasks and technology.

Sometimes, these targets for change are addressed mistakenly by management through 'fad' solutions that are offered by consultants and adopted by managers without much thought for the real situation and/or people involved. The logic of truly planned change requires a managerial willingness and ability to address problems concretely and systematically, and to avoid tendencies towards an easy but questionable 'quick fix'.[19]

Further, the manager must recognise that the various targets of planned organisational change are highly intertwined. For example, a change in the basic tasks performed by an organisation (that is, a modification in what it is the organisation does) is almost inevitably accompanied by a change in technology (that is, a modification in the way in which tasks are accomplished). Changes in tasks and technology usually require alterations in the structure of the organisation, including changes in the patterns of authority and communication as well as in the roles of members. These technological and structural changes can, in turn, necessitate changes on the part of the organisation's members. For example, members may have to acquire additional knowledge and develop new skills to perform their modified roles and work with the new technology.[20]

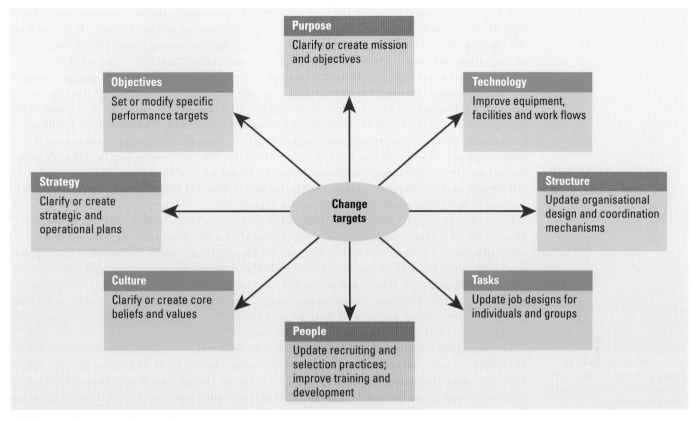

FIGURE 14.2 Organisational targets for planned change

Phases of planned change

Kurt Lewin, a famous psychologist, recommends that any change effort should be viewed as a process that includes the phases shown in figure 14.3.

FIGURE 14.3 Lewin's three phases of planned change

Managers using Lewin's ideas will be sensitive to the need to ensure that any change effort properly addresses each of these three phases of change:

1. unfreezing — getting people and things ready for change
2. changing — implementing the change
3. refreezing — making sure the change 'sticks' as part of new routines.[21]

Unfreezing is the managerial responsibility of preparing a situation for change. It involves disconfirming existing attitudes and behaviours to create a felt need for something new. Unfreezing is facilitated by environmental pressures, declining performance, the recognition of a problem, or awareness that someone else has found a better way, among other factors. Many changes are never tried or fail simply because situations are not properly unfrozen to begin with. As a concept, unfreezing is similar in meaning to 'generating energy for transformation', which was discussed in relation to figure 14.1. 'Force field analysis' is a useful

Unfreezing is the first stage of the planned change process in which a situation is prepared for change.

tool for identifying the forces for and against change during the unfreezing stage. Force field analysis is a management technique to diagnose and encourage change. It is based on the idea that in any situation there are both driving and restraining forces that influence any change that may occur. Driving forces push in a particular direction; they tend to initiate a change and keep it going. In terms of improving productivity in a work group, pressure from a supervisor, incentive earnings and competition may be examples of driving forces. Restraining forces restrain or decrease the driving forces. Apathy, hostility and poor maintenance of equipment may be examples of restraining forces against increased production. Changes occur when the driving and restraining forces are shifted out of equilibrium.[22] The basic steps are to identify the driving forces, identify the restraining forces, identify which forces can be changed, and weigh those forces based on the degree to which they can be influenced and the likely effects of that influence.[23] You will find an exercise on force field analysis in the study guide at the end of this chapter.

Large systems seem particularly susceptible to the so-called boiled frog phenomenon.[24] This refers to a classic physiological proposition that a live frog will immediately jump out when placed in a pan of hot water; but when placed in cold water that is then heated very slowly, the frog will stay in the water until it boils to death. Organisations can fall victim to similar circumstances. When managers fail to monitor their environments, recognise the important trends, or sense the need to change, their organisations may slowly suffer and lose their competitive edge. The best organisations, by contrast, have managers who are always on the alert for 'unfreezing' opportunities.

The **changing** stage involves a managerial responsibility to modify a situation — that is, to change people, tasks, structure and/or technology. Lewin feels that many change agents enter this stage prematurely or are too quick to change things. As a result, they often end up creating resistance to change in a situation that is not adequately unfrozen. Changing something is hard enough, let alone having to do it without the proper foundations. Successful change requires sustained energy and clear goals to maintain the process.

Successful change also depends on the degree of readiness to change, which suggests that two distinct forces act on people.[25] Firstly, there are the forces within the individual. Secondly, there are the forces within the system, which (as we have discussed) include the type of leadership, the culture, the climate of the organisation and the perceived consequences of success or failure within the organisation. The combination of these factors affects the individual's degree of felt security. That is, if the degree of felt security is either high or low, then the efforts to introduce change will most likely be rejected. If people feel secure in their current work situation, then what need is there for them to change? If an individual's degree of felt security is low, then anything you do to disturb that low state of security will be seen to be highly threatening. Thus, only in the middle ranges of felt security is the response to change most likely to be positive. Such positive response will be expressed through behaviours including listening, clarifying, negotiating and a willingness to explore alternatives.

Refreezing is the final stage of managerial responsibility in the planned change process. Designed to maintain the momentum of a change, refreezing positively reinforces desired outcomes and provides extra support when difficulties are encountered. Evaluation is a key element in this final step of the change process. It provides data on the costs and benefits of a change, and offers opportunities to make constructive modifications in the change over time. Improper refreezing results in changes that are abandoned or incompletely implemented.

The foundational work of Kurt Lewin has had a significant and long-lasting effect on the field of organisational change. However, there is now a growing recognition of the need for alternative strategies for change.

Change levers and change cycles

Managers may limit their capacity to manage change by focusing on a restricted set of organisational change levers. In other words, regardless of the nature of the problem that the change is meant to solve, they reach for the same levers every time. This means that the

---

Changing involves a managerial responsibility to modify a situation — that is, to change people, tasks, structure and/or technology.

Refreezing is the final stage of the planned change process in which changes are positively reinforced.

change process is viewed from only one perspective. It may be viewed as a technical problem, a political problem or a cultural problem that needs resolving. Noel Tichy argues that those who design, manage, and change organisations face the following three fundamental sets of problems, and effective change managers can recognise all three.

1. *Technical design problem.* The organisation faces a production or operational problem. Social and technical resources must be allocated to solve the problem and achieve a desired outcome.
2. *Political allocation problem.* The organisation faces an allocation of power and resources problem. It must determine how it will use its resources, as well as which parts of the organisation will benefit.
3. *Culture/ideological mix problem.* An organisation is held together by shared beliefs. The organisation must determine what values need to be held by what people.[26]

All of these problems tend to occur simultaneously in organisations. They constitute the fundamental levers that prompt managers to contemplate strategic change. They form the basic parts of what could be described as the engine of change, as shown in figure 14.4. When these areas are considered over time, you can identify cycles in their relative importance. Attempts to resolve each set of problems give rise to new situations and, hence, new problems which in turn require new solutions.[27]

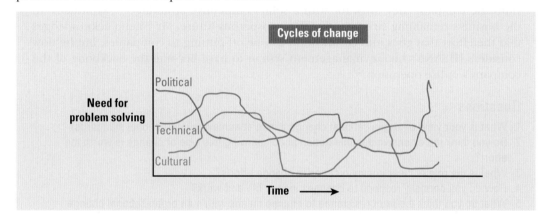

FIGURE 14.4 The engine of change

Source: Adapted from N Tichy, *Managing strategic change: technical, political and cultural dynamics* (New York: John Wiley & Sons, 1983). Reprinted by permission of John Wiley & Sons Inc.

Seeing the change process as an engine allows us to understand some of the practical aspects of change. Managers may experience all of the problems outlined by Tichy, but to a varying degree. At some stage of organisational development, technical problems may be the most pressing. At another stage, cultural problems may need the most urgent attention. As with the oil or water that feeds an engine, none of these issues can be ignored if the engine of change is to run. All components of the engine need attention to ensure high performance. Change agents and participants often fail to understand this. Too often during a change process, one group becomes frustrated because their problems are not seen to be the most pressing. Managers need to understand that each group's problems are intertwined and that they must be dealt with simultaneously. In doing so, managers will find themselves addressing strategic change. Resistance to change and change processes are discussed in detail in the next Counterpoint.[28]

Dealing with resistance through clear communication and anchoring

Established in Singapore in 1992 and specialising in mechanical motion products, HISAKA has transformed into a leading automation solutions provider in the Asia–Pacific region. When the company expanded into the medical devices sector in order

COUNTER**POINT**

(continued)

to capitalise on new growth opportunities and create new revenue streams, staff initially struggled to adapt to the new and additional procedures necessary to meet International Standards. CEO Jackie Cheng believes that applying International Standards and stringent quality management systems in order to conform to international criteria gives companies like HISAKA instant credibility and accountability. However, Mr Cheng acknowledges that the improved practices included the extensive documentation of processes. This meant staff had to begin completing forms to document quality checks and generate product failure data. These new procedures were met with resistance by employees who found it hard to adapt due to the number of international requirements that were very strict and unique to medical devices. Clear communication by management about the necessity and importance of standards anchored employees to the degree that management were able to get them on-board with the need for a more structured approach to quality assurance. Through management's clear communication, employees were able to recognise that information needed to be documented and shared if the company was to function effectively with standardised procedures to eliminate mistakes and inconsistencies. Through this process employees also came to realise that standards are prized by the industry and that certification provides the company they work for with a solid competitive advantage — conducive to the business remaining strong and with a prosperous future. Mr Cheng acknowledges that the effort that goes into certification can be off-putting to companies, but he now considers HISAKA's quality management system to have become the backbone of the company's entire operation.[29]

Questions

1. What is your view on organisational change aimed at achieving international standards?
2. Do you think the extensive documentation accompanying this type of change is worth the effort?
3. What is the role of clear communication in change efforts?
4. How do you normally respond to changes in your life and work?
5. What do you think the term resistance to change means within an organisational change context?

The idea that people will naturally resist change and that management must plan ways to overcome this is firmly entrenched in the management literature. Furthermore, resistance to change is recognised as a critical variable in influencing the success or failure of change efforts[30] and some authors even argue that the failure of some large-scale corporate change can be directly attributed to employee resistance to change.[31] Many practitioners also regard resistance to change as a highly influential and problematic factor in the workplace.[32] There is an expectation that resistance to change actually hinders the implementation of change processes.

However, there is another side to this argument. Resistance to change can be seen as enhancing the change process. So, a question can be asked. Is resistance the most useful framework to categorise employees' responses to change?

It has been argued that people do not resist change, per se. What they do resist is the impact of change on their personal status quo, such as potential loss of status, loss of pay and comfort.[33] However, this is not the same as resisting change in its totality. The pervading belief that employees resist change creates psychological and systemic barriers within the organisation that hinder the process and progress of change. The fact that employees are uncertain about certain aspects of the impact of change and require more information about the change in order to allay their fears does not mean they resist change. So, resistance to change can be seen as a response to the change management process, rather than to the change itself.[34] Employees may not be resisting the change itself, but rather the uncertainty that the change engenders, especially in the beginning stages of the process.

In their book *Built to change*, Worley and Lawler suggest that the best way to promote change is to identify the things that won't change — in other words, identify change anchors. For example, a company manufacturing expensive running shoes for the New Zealand and Australian market may recognise the need to change. When it communicates to its employees that anything could happen and all options are open, a great deal of anxiety can be created within the workforce. Conversely, the company could communicate to its employees that they may drop other lines of business and/or implement new marketing strategies, but that one thing won't change: 'we will never give up on the athletic shoe business'. In other words, they create an anchor that employees can hang onto by identifying that the core business of the company will remain the same.[35]

Planned change strategies

Managers and other change agents use various means for mobilising power, exerting influence over others and getting people to support planned change efforts. As described in figure 14.5, each of these strategies builds from different foundations of social power (as discussed in chapter 10) and each has somewhat different implications for the planned change process. Among the change strategies commonly used by managers to bring about planned organisational change are:

- *top-down approach to change* — using centralised power to force compliance with change directives
- *force-coercion* — using authority to force compliance with change directives
- *rational persuasion* — using logic and information to persuade people to accept change directives
- *shared power* — involving others in decisions identifying the need for change and desired change directions.[36]

FIGURE 14.5 Power bases, change strategies, management behaviours and predicted outcomes

Top-down approach to change

In pursuing the top-down (or directional) approach to change, executives and managers believe that one-way communication backed by the formal authority of their position is enough to implement change. This approach to change is akin to the military model in its style and assumes that members lower down in the hierarchy will understand what is intended and follow through exactly as requested.

In many situations, this approach is problematic and ineffective, especially when the situation facing the organisation is complex and difficult to interpret.[37] With complex problems requiring change, top managers do not have a monopoly on expertise, information[38] and inputs. In such situations, having the additional perspectives of the lower-level managers and employees is an advantage.

Given that members at the lower levels are generally on the firing line (that is, closest to the machinery, the consumer and the community), they are in an excellent position to observe problems and to provide varied and valuable inputs to any required changes. When a directive approach to change pervades the organisation, higher-level managers are unlikely to listen. Thus, the lower levels become increasingly frustrated and may even refuse to lend their cooperation. Further, the extent to which the change process requires member commitment for successful implementation suggests that the lower-level members may not comply automatically.[39] If members do not commit to the change process as intended, what is finally implemented may be a far cry from what top management had in mind.

Many eminent management scholars, such as Tom Lupton, have also voiced the idiosyncracies of authoritarian change. For instance, Lupton sees that change can be more successfully introduced from the bottom up than from the top down.[40] In general, individuals who are struggling to assert their autonomy tend to resist the efforts of people in authority to exercise control over them. By doing so, individuals do not necessarily reject the legitimacy of the authority, but rather seek to extend their own autonomy by working to control their interactions with the authority.

However, the 'bottom-up' (participative) approach to change is often not possible. In the case of public sector organisations, for example, the change process may be imposed on them by drastic changes in government policies and legislation. In this situation, change may be more directive and less participative.

Force-coercion and planned change

Force-coercion strategy tries to 'command' change through the formal authority of legitimacy, rewards and punishments.

A **force-coercion strategy** uses legitimacy, rewards and/or punishments as primary inducements to change. That is, the change agent acts unilaterally to try to 'command' change through the formal authority of their position, to induce change via an offer of special rewards, or to bring about change via threats of punishment. People respond to this strategy mainly out of fear of being punished if they do not comply with a change directive, or out of desire to gain a reward if they do. Compliance is usually temporary and will continue only so long as the change agent remains visible in their legitimate authority, or so long as the opportunity for rewards and punishments remains obvious. If, as a change agent, you were to use the force-coercion strategy for bringing about planned change, the following profile might apply:

> You believe that people who run things are basically motivated by self-interest and by what the situation offers in terms of potential personal gains or losses. Since you feel that people change only in response to such motives, you try to find out where their vested interests lie and then put the pressure on. If you have formal authority, you use it. If not, you resort to whatever possible rewards and punishments you have access to and do not hesitate to threaten others with these weapons. Once you find a weakness, you exploit it and are always wise to work 'politically' by building supporting alliances wherever possible.[41]

Rational persuasion and planned change

Rational persuasion strategy attempts to bring about change through persuasion based on empirical facts, special knowledge and rational argument.

Change agents using a **rational persuasion strategy** attempt to bring about change through the use of special knowledge, empirical support or rational arguments. This strategy assumes that rational people will be guided by reason and self-interest in deciding whether to support a change. Expert power is mobilised to convince others that the cost–benefit value of a proposed change is high; that is, that the change will leave them better off than before. When successful, this strategy results in a longer-lasting, more internalised change than does the force-coercion strategy. If you use a rational persuasion strategy, the following profile may apply:

> You believe that people are inherently rational and are guided by reason in their actions and decision making. Once a specific course of action is demonstrated to be in a person's

self-interest, you assume that reason and rationality will cause the person to adopt it. You approach change with the objective of communicating, through information and facts, the essential 'desirability' of change from the perspective of the person whose behaviour you seek to influence. If this logic is effectively communicated, you are sure that the person(s) will adopt the proposed change.

Shared power and planned change

In order to minimise the likelihood of resistance, some of the best approaches to change put strong emphasis on involving all parties affected by the change. For example, a leader might meet with all managers and employees to explain reasons for the change, and generally how it will be carried out. A plan may be developed and communicated. Staff forums may be organised to give members the opportunity to express their ideas about the proposed change. They are also given the opportunity to express their concerns and frustrations. This approach to change coincides with what is commonly known as a **shared power strategy** to change. This strategy actively and sincerely involves other people who will be affected by a change in planning and making key decisions in respect to it. Sometimes called a **normative-reeducative strategy**, this approach seeks to establish directions and social support for change through the empowerment of others. It builds essential foundations, such as personal values, group norms and shared goals, so support for a proposed change emerges naturally. Managers using this approach emphasise personal reference and share power by allowing others to participate in planning and implementing the change. Given this high level of involvement, the strategy is likely to result in a longer-lasting and internalised change. If you use a shared power strategy for bringing about planned change, the following profile may apply:

> You believe that people have complex motivations. You feel that people behave as they do as a result of sociocultural norms and commitments to these norms. You also recognise that changes in these orientations involve changes in attitudes, values, skills and significant relationships, not just changes in knowledge, information or intellectual rationales for action and practice. When seeking to change others, you are sensitive to the supporting or inhibiting effects of any group pressures and norms that may be operating. You try to find out their side of things and to identify their feelings and expectations.

On a final note, in a study examining the controversy between 'one best way' and contingent approaches to corporate change in 13 service sector organisations in Australia, Dunphy and Stace concluded that the 'one best way' models are inadequate because they do not capture the diversity of approaches actually used by these organisations. In particular, they concluded that the traditional organisational development model emphasising employee participation and shared power is unrepresentative of how change in many contemporary organisations is made. According to them, the model is also inadequate as a prescriptive model because different change strategies, some dramatically different from organisational development, resulted in successful financial performance.[42] The effective manager 14.2 lists guidelines for effective change.

A **shared power strategy** (or **normative-reeducative strategy**) attempts to bring about change by identifying or establishing values and assumptions so that support for the change emerges naturally.

Guidelines for effective change

Managers should keep in mind the following when planning change:
- consider using an expert consultant
- communicate the need for change
- gather as much information and feedback from employees as possible
- do not fall into the trap of change for change's sake
- study organisational change, including new forms and structures.[43]

THE **EffectiveManager** 14.2

Resistance to change

Typically, change initiatives are met by some resistance. This is because employees are often afraid of the unknown. Many of them may think things are already just fine and do not understand the need for change. Many may also be cynical about change. Some may even think that the proposed change goes against the values held by members in the organisation. That is why much organisational change is often discussed in conjunction with needed changes in the culture of the organisation, including changes in members' values and beliefs. In essence, resistance to change is often viewed by change agents as something that must be 'overcome' for change to be successful. This is not always the case. It is helpful to view resistance to change as feedback that can be used by the astute change agent to help accomplish his or her change objectives.[44] The essence of this notion is to recognise that when people resist change, they are defending something important that appears to be threatened by the change attempt. Formally defined, **resistance to change** is any attitude or behaviour that reflects a person's unwillingness to make or support a desired change.

Both passive and active resistance work against organisational change. Passive resistance can include the widespread cynicism often found among workers exposed to frequent management change initiatives, in cases in which insufficient attention is paid to implementation and the effects on organisational members. Passive resistance can also occur when organisational members feel that the psychological cost of adjusting to new systems and processes is greater than any recommended or perceived benefits. Active resistance occurs when the redistribution of power threatens vested self-interest. This form of resistance can be dangerous for an organisation and can undermine even well-thought-out change programs.[45]

> **Resistance to change** is any attitude or behaviour that reflects a person's unwillingness to make or support a desired change.

Why people resist change

There are several reasons for possible resistance to the introduction of a new management practice. People who directly report to a manager, for example, may resist the introduction and use of e-commerce (electronic commerce) in their workplace because:

- they are not familiar with online business and internet use and wonder whether they could become familiar with it successfully (*fear of the unknown*)
- they may wonder if the manager is introducing e-commerce just to 'get rid' of some of the workers eventually (*need for security*)
- they may feel they are doing their jobs well and do not need the new facility (*no felt need for change*)
- they may sense that the manager is forcing e-commerce on them without first discussing their feelings on the matter (*vested interests threatened*)
- they may have heard from workers in other departments that e-commerce is being introduced to get more work out of people with no increase in pay (*contrasting interpretations*)
- they are really busy at the present time and do not want to try something new until the work slackens a bit (*poor timing*)
- they may believe that they will be left on their own to learn how to operate the new systems (*lack of resources*).

These and other viewpoints often create resistance to even the best and most well-intended planned changes. To deal better with these forces, managers often find it useful to separate such responses into resistance to change directed towards the change itself, the change strategy, and the change agent as a person.

Sometimes, a manager may experience resistance to the change itself. A good manager understands that people may reject a change because they believe it is not worth their time, effort and/or attention. To minimise resistance in such cases, the change agent should make sure that the people affected by the change know specifically how it satisfies the following criteria.

1. *Benefit.* The change should have a clear relative advantage for the individuals being asked to change; that is, it should be perceived as 'a better way'.
2. *Compatibility.* The change should be as compatible as possible with the existing values and experiences of the people being asked to change.
3. *Complexity.* The change should be no more complex than necessary. It must be as easy as possible to understand and use.
4. *Triability.* The change should be something that people can try on a step-by-step basis and make adjustments as things progress.

Managers will always experience some resistance to their change strategy. Someone who attempts to bring about change via force-coercion, for example, may create resistance among individuals who resent management by 'command' or the threatened use of punishment. People may also resist an empirical–rational strategy in which the data are suspect or expertise is not clearly demonstrated, or a normative-reeducative strategy that appears manipulative and insincere.

Finally, managers may experience resistance to the change agent. In this case, resistance is directed at the person implementing the change and may reflect inadequacies in the personality and attributes of the manager as a change agent. Change agents who are isolated from other people in the change situation, who appear self-centred or who have a high emotional involvement in the changes are especially prone to such problems. Research also indicates that change agents who are different from other key people on such dimensions as age, education and socioeconomic factors are likely to experience greater resistance to change.[46]

How to deal with resistance to change

An informed change agent can do many things to deal constructively with resistance to change in any of its forms. In general, resistance will be managed best if it is recognised early in the change process. All things considered, the following general approaches for dealing with resistance to change have been identified:

- *education and communication* — using one-on-one discussions, presentations to groups, memos, reports or demonstrations to educate people about a change before it is implemented and to help them see the logic of the change
- *participation and involvement* — allowing others to help design and implement the changes; asking individuals to contribute ideas and advice; forming task forces or committees to work on the change
- *facilitation and support* — providing socioemotional support for the hardships of change; actively listening to problems and complaints; providing training in the new ways; helping to overcome performance pressures
- *negotiation and agreement* — offering incentives to actual or potential resistors; working out tradeoffs to provide special benefits in exchange for assurance that the change will not be blocked
- *manipulation and cooptation* — using covert attempts to influence others; selectively providing information and consciously structuring events so the desired change receives maximum support; buying off leaders of resistance to gain their support
- *explicit or implicit coercion* — using force to get people to accept change; threatening resistors with a variety of undesirable consequences if they do not go along as planned.[47]

Figure 14.6 (overleaf) summarises additional insights into how and when each method may be used by managers when dealing with resistance to change. When such resistance seems to be based on a lack of information or the presence of inaccurate information, education and communication are good managerial responses. Once persuaded that the change is for the best, people will often help implement the change. The downside is that the process of education and communication can be time consuming if too many people are involved. Participation and involvement is a good approach when the manager or change agent does not have all the information needed to design the required change. This is especially true if other people have a lot of power to resist. People who are allowed to participate in designing a change tend to be highly committed to its implementation. But, again, this process can be time consuming.

In cases in which people are resisting the change because there will be adjustment problems, facilitation and support are recommended responses. In such circumstances, people are most likely trying hard to implement a change, but they are frustrated by external constraints and difficulties. Here a manager must play the 'supportive' role and try to make it as easy as possible to continue with the planned change. Of course, the manager must be able to invest the time and energy needed to provide this support and to gain needed commitments from the organisation. Negotiation and agreement tends to be most useful when a person or group will clearly lose something as a result of the planned change. When the person or group has considerable power, resistance can be particularly costly to the change effort. Direct negotiation can sometimes prove a relatively easy way of avoiding or eliminating this form of resistance. This response requires a foundation of trust and may involve extra 'costs' in terms of any agreements that may be reached.

METHOD →	USE WHEN →	ADVANTAGES →	DISADVANTAGES
Education and communication	People lack information or have inaccurate information	Creates willingness to help with the change	Can be very time consuming
Participation and involvement	Other people have important information and/or power to resist	Adds information to change planning; builds commitment to the change	Can be very time consuming
Facilitation and support	Resistance traces to resource or adjustment problems	Satisfies directly specific resource or adjustment needs	Can be time consuming; can be expensive
Negotiation and agreement	A person or group will 'lose' something due to the change	Helps avoid major resistance	Can be expensive; can cause others to seek similar 'deals'
Manipulation and cooptation	Other methods do not work or are too expensive	Can be quick and inexpensive	Can create future problems if people sense manipulation
Explicit and implicit coercion	Speed is important and change agent has power	Quick; overpowers resistance	Risky if people get angry

FIGURE 14.6 Methods for dealing with resistance to change

There is no avoiding the fact that resistance to change can be — and is — managed at times through manipulation and cooptation. These responses may be used when other tactics just do not work or are too expensive. They may also make up a 'style' that a manager or change agent uses on most occasions. In some cases, manipulation and cooptation can provide a relatively quick and inexpensive solution to resistance problems. But a good manager understands that these approaches can also lead to future problems if people feel manipulated. A more extreme approach is explicit or implicit coercion. Coercion is often used when speed is of the essence or when the manager or change agent possesses considerable power. It is a fast response and can overpower resistance. It also runs the risk of offending people, however. People who experience coercion may feel angry at the manager or change agent, and be left without any true commitments to ensuring that the change is fully implemented. As Lewin might say, 'coercion may unfreeze and change things, but it does not do much to refreeze them'.

Regardless of the chosen strategy, managers must understand that resistance to change is something to be recognised and constructively addressed instead of feared. The presence of resistance typically suggests that something can be done to achieve a better 'fit' between the change, the situation and the people affected. A manager should deal with resistance to change by 'listening' to such feedback and acting accordingly.

Change and stress

More and more employers today are concerned about stress in the workplace. Organisational change can often be stressful, although it is certainly not the only cause of stress. When experienced for a prolonged period of time, stress can lead to employee illness and even death. Employers and managers need be concerned not only for humanitarian reasons, but also because of the costs to their companies. Change of any sort in organisations is often accompanied by increased stress for the people involved. Managers and change agents alike need to understand the meaning and causes of stress as well as ways of preventing and managing it.

What is stress?

Stress is a state of tension experienced by individuals facing extraordinary demands, constraints or opportunities.[48] Any look towards your managerial future would be incomplete without confronting stress as something you are sure to encounter along the way.[49] Consider this statement by a psychologist working with top-level managers with severe drinking problems: 'All executives deal with stress. They wouldn't be executives if they didn't. Some handle it well, others handle it poorly.' If you understand stress and how it operates in the work setting, you should be more likely to handle it well. This goes for both the stress you may experience personally and the stress experienced by persons you supervise.

Stress is a state of tension experienced by individuals facing extraordinary demands, constraints or opportunities.

Sources of stress

Simply put, **stressors** are the things that cause stress. One study of stress experienced by executives around the world reports that managers in mature industrialised countries worry about losing their jobs, about family and social pressures, lack of autonomy and poorly trained employees.[50] In contrast, managers in developing and recently industrialised countries worry about work overloads, interpersonal relations, competition for promotion and lack of autonomy. It is important for a manager to understand and be able to recognise these and other potential stressors, for they are the root causes of job-related stress. In turn, job-related stress influences work attitudes and behaviour. Figure 14.7 (overleaf) shows three categories of stressors that can act in this fashion: work, non-work and personal factors.

Stressors are things that cause stress (for example, work, non-work and personal factors).

Stress and our health

In responding to a stressor, employees could choose behaviours that may have a positive, negative or neutral effect on physical and emotional wellbeing. They could choose to behave in a neutral manner, such as practising early detection or avoidance; for example, they could decide to use social networks (such as talking with friends and family), exercising, or spiritual activities in an attempt to lower the negative response they may feel about stressors in their lives. Negative responses can include aggressive behaviours, or indulging in smoking, drinking or drugs.

In reacting to stress, our bodies do not know the difference between physical and psychological threats. If you feel stressed about a work project, a very busy work schedule, work overload or conflict with a coworker, your body react just as strongly as if you were facing a life-or-death situation. This is known as the 'flight' response. Even though small incidences of stress have little risk to an employee's health, prolonged stress leaves the body in a state of continuous activity, or stress overload. This gradually wears down the body's defence system, and the employee becomes progressively more susceptible to illness. The impact of chronic stress could be compared to trying to hold a heavy object in front of you. Initially, the object may not feel very heavy; however, the longer you hold it, the heavier it becomes. If a person were forced to hold the object for several days, that person may need medical attention. Stress operates in a similar way.

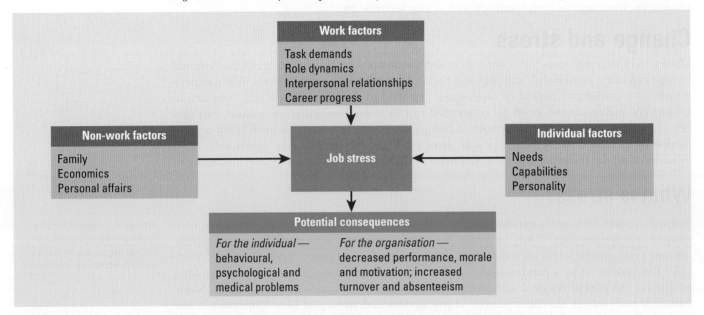

FIGURE 14.7 Potential consequences of work, non-work and personal stressors for individuals and organisations

One of the keys to stress management is taking regular breaks. If we put the object or the 'stress' down and rest from it for a while, we will be able to pick it up again and carry on with motivation and a new attitude.[51] Therefore, it is essential to find ways in which we can take a break from stress, whatever the cause may be.

There are numerous signs and symptoms of stress overload. Stress affects the mind, body and behaviour in many ways. Psychologist Connie Lillas uses a driving analogy to describe the three most common ways people respond when they are overwhelmed by stress.

1. **Foot on the gas.** This is an irritated or angry response to stress. The person is easily irritable, very emotional, and needs to be doing something.
2. **Foot on the brake.** This is a depressed or closure response. The person loses focus, has little energy, and little emotion.
3. **Foot on both.** This is a tense and frozen response, where the person can no longer complete their normal tasks. They look frozen, but under the surface are extremely agitated.[52]

Some symptoms of stress that employees may experience include:

- thought or reasoning symptoms, such as memory problems, inability to concentrate, poor judgement, negative attitude, anxious thoughts and constant worrying
- physical symptoms, such as aches and pains, diarrhoea or constipation, nausea, dizziness, chest pain, rapid heartbeat and frequent colds
- emotional symptoms, such as moodiness, irritability or short temper, agitation, inability to relax, feeling overwhelmed, a sense of loneliness and isolation, depression and general unhappiness
- behavioural symptoms, such as changes in eating habits, isolation from others, procrastination or neglect of responsibilities, the use of substances to relax (e.g. alcohol, cigarettes or drugs), and nervous habits (e.g. nail biting, pacing).

From an organisational behaviour perspective, it is essential that we try and recognise these symptoms in ourselves and colleagues.

One of the major challenges employees are currently dealing with is the increased use of technology in the workplace. Increasingly, employees are required to communicate via email and social media technologies with their employers and customers anywhere and anytime, even when they are not at work. The stress associated with these technologies will eventually lead to high absenteeism rates and higher healthcare costs. Cardiovascular disease, back and upper-extremity musculoskeletal disorders, depression, ulcers and burnout could be just a few of the negative consequences of an overuse of new technologies — especially with increased blurring between the working and home lives of employees. Stress associated with new technologies includes problems like information overload, fear of data loss, and a constant need to remain connected. Furthermore, pressure to keep up with new technologies (like web applications and changes to methods of personal communication) is constantly placing demands on both employees and managers.

The American Psychological Association encourages employees to turn off their mobile phones and limit the use of email when they get home from work. Allocating specific response times is one way of placing personal boundaries on the time spent engaging in email and phone communication. Discussion about finding solutions to stress-related problems stemming from communication technologies in the workplace is also essential.[53]

Preventing or coping with stress

Stress prevention is the best first-line strategy for dealing with stress. It involves taking action for yourself or others to keep stress from reaching destructive levels in the first place. In particular, stressors emerging from personal and non-work factors must be recognised so that action can be taken to prevent them from adversely affecting the work experience. Persons with type A orientations, for example, may exercise self-discipline; managers of type A employees may try to model a lower-key, more relaxed approach to work. At another level, family difficulties may be relieved by a change of work schedule; or the anxiety caused by family concerns may be reduced by knowing that your supervisor understands. Work stressors such as role ambiguities, conflicts and overloads can be prevented by good supervisor–employee communication, a willingness of employees to 'speak up' when role dynamics are creating difficulties, and sensitivity on the part of supervisors to behaviours or other symptoms indicating that employees are experiencing problems. The Ethical perspective considers long hours and stress at work.

Stress prevention involves taking action to prevent the emergence of stress that becomes destructive.

Utilising tools to keep stress in check

Australian software development company Atlassian has focused heavily on an enviable work culture that aims to retain employees by providing them with a stress-preventative workplace. Cofounder and chief executive Scott Farquhar says Atlassian's approach to looking after staff is by way of creating an enjoyable workplace with readily available tools aimed at reducing stress. One of these tools is the Mood App, which was designed to allow employees to express their level of happiness at work on a daily basis. By tapping on the screen, employees register an answer to daily questions provided by management. In addition to providing feedback, staff are also given access to the collective response across the organisation for each question. After its immediate implementation this useful stress-reduction tool revealed to management that leaders were not communicating with employees about performance as much as staff wanted them to. In response, Atlassian established some leadership development sessions to ensure management

ETHICAL
Perspective

(continued)

recognised what effective feedback looked like in order to provide it in the future. Through utilising such initiatives and being immediately responsive, Atlassian prides itself on being a self-correcting organisation. Management are able to quickly go to an employee to ask follow-up questions in order to address issues of stress or dissatisfaction as they arise. The Mood App allows the company to track and quickly correct stress felt by employees. This means tensions don't have a chance to build up for months, which means consistent maintenance of employee health and satisfaction.[54]

The consequences of stress from excessive working hours and other pressures have also been noted among senior executives around the world. The problem is so acute that the World Economic Forum held a discussion on the topic. The forum noted that chief executives increasingly suffer from stress, sleep deprivation, heart disease, failed personal relationships, loneliness and depression. In response, some commentators have argued that the high salaries and other benefits make executive jobs attractive, implying that the health risks are part of the package.[55] But should this be the end of the story? Are employers considering the long-term effect of long hours on worker productivity, or do they, in general, take a short-term view? How can organisations and their managerial employees (at all levels in the hierarchy) share the responsibility for individual health and welfare?[56]

Innovation in organisations

In order to survive and prosper, organisations need to build capabilities to make substantial changes to ensure they remain economically competitive and responsive to the environment. In most cases, this involves continual innovation. Innovation comes in many forms and degrees, but is typically defined as the creation of new and improved products and processes. There are various types of innovations: organisational innovation, market innovation, process innovation and so on. The simplest form of innovation is the variation of an existing idea or system (product, service or method of doing things) that may cause us to look at its function in a new way. The highest form of innovation is pure invention, which occurs when the product has no precedent. This must be considered to be a rare thing.

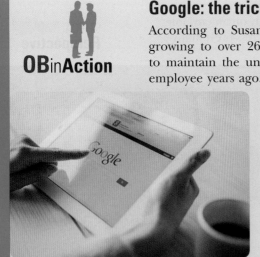

OBinAction

Google: the trick to grow exponentially and still stay innovative

According to Susan Wojcicki, Google's Senior Vice President of Advertising, despite growing to over 26 000 employees in more than 60 offices, Google has worked hard to maintain the unique spirit that characterised the company when she joined as an employee years ago. She cites some of the key processes and principles in ensuring the company doesn't get bogged down in the past as it keeps moving on a path to success. These include: (1) have a mission that matters; (2) think big, but start small; (3) strive for continual innovation, not instant perfection; (4) look for ideas everywhere; (5) share everything with your employees; (6) spark with imagination, fuel with data; (7) be a platform by utilising the power of open technologies (in Google's case they enable anyone, anywhere, to apply their unique skills, perspectives and passions to the creation of new products and features on top of Google's platforms); and (8) never fail to fail as long as you learn from your mistakes and correct them fast.[57]

The best organisations are able to 'innovate' on an ongoing basis; the best managers are able to help people use their 'innovative' talents to the fullest. Formally stated, **innovation** can be defined as the process of creating new ideas and putting them into practice.[58] It is the means by which creative ideas find their way into everyday practice in the form of new goods or services that satisfy customers, or as new systems or practices that help organisations better produce them. The former represents **product innovation** — innovation that results in the creation of a new or improved good or service. The latter represents **process innovation** — that is, innovation that results in a better way of doing things.

Today's managers bear increasing responsibility for ensuring that both product and process innovation take place. They must be concerned with two main aspects of innovation as expressed in this equation:

$$\text{Innovation} = \text{invention} + \text{application}$$

In the equation, *invention* is the act of discovery, while *application* is the act of use. Both are critical to the innovation process. New ideas for improved products and services emerge from invention, but they achieve their full value only through application. In too many organisations invention occurs, but application does not. One key aspect of application is marketing. Suggestions for promoting innovation are listed in The effective manager 14.3.

Promoting an innovation culture

To promote a culture of innovation throughout an organisation:
- define what a culture of innovation really is
- determine and communicate what it is that people have to change
- involve all levels of management in developing and implementing the cultural change plan
- train management and staff in the techniques of creative thinking
- develop a knowledge management system
- establish an evaluation and feedback system.

Source: Adapted from Australian Continuous Improvement Group, 'Leadership and innovation', www.acig.com.au

THE **EffectiveManager** 14.3

The innovation process

The various steps involved in a typical process of organisational innovation are shown in figure 14.8 (overleaf). These steps include:
- *idea creation* — gathering new product or process ideas that arise from spontaneous creativity, ingenuity and information processing
- *initial experimentation* — examining new ideas in concept to establish their potential values and applications
- *feasibility determination* — conducting formal studies to determine the feasibility of adopting the new product or process, including the costs and benefits
- *final application* — producing and marketing the new product or service, or fully implementing the new process.[59]

Central to this view of the innovation process is the idea that any new product or process idea must offer true benefits to the organisation and/or marketplace. Further, the process is not complete until the point of final application has been reached.

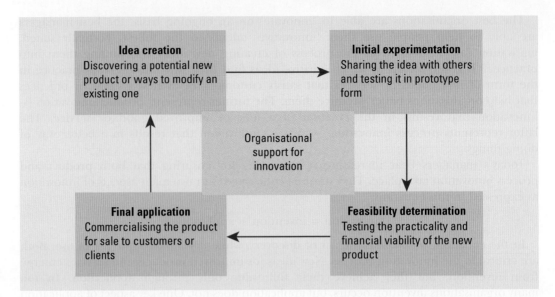

FIGURE 14.8 The innovation process: a case of new product development

International SPOTLIGHT

Stimulating social innovation through crowdfunding

Innovation doesn't only take place in business contexts — more and more innovation is driven in social contexts. Social innovation could be described as the generation and implementation of new ideas about how people should organise interpersonal activities, or social interactions, to meet one or more common goals. Social innovation might, for example, involve the creation of new kinds of social institutions, the formation of new ideas about government, or the development of new social movements. It could also involve the creation of new processes and procedures for structuring collaborative work, the introduction of new social practices in a group, or the development of new business practices.[60]

One innovative medium that facilitates raising funds for social causes is the innovation in fund sourcing, crowdfunding. Crowdfunding is a way of raising finance by asking a large number of people each for a small amount of money. Crowdfunding switches the traditional idea of asking a few people for large sums of money around to using the internet to talk to thousands — if not millions — of potential funders. Fund seekers will typically set up a profile of their project on a website and then use social media, alongside traditional networks of friends, family and work acquaintances, to raise money.

More and more social causes are turning to crowdfunding to initiate their social innovations; for example, 'Catalyst' (crowdfunding for a better world), www.csicatalyst .org, and 'Start Some Good' (raise funds for good), http://startsomegood.com. However, there are also platforms such as OpenIDEO, https://openideo.com, which has the aim to include a broader range of people in the design process through brainstorms, conception and evaluation. OpenIDEO partners with a non-profit to present the community with a social issue 'challenge'. Community members then contribute to the process by providing feedback each step of the way until a solution is created and supported by the community.

This creative approach to fundraising could be done from anywhere in the world and enables the spread of the creative idea or message to millions of people.

Established companies can avoid fall into the classic traps that stifle innovation by widening the search for new ideas, loosening overly tight controls and rigid structures, forging better connections between innovators and mainstream operators and cultivating communication and collaboration skills. But the quest for innovation is doomed unless managers who seek it take the time to learn from the past.

These are the wise words of management guru Rosabeth Moss Kanter. She also argues that the essence of effective innovation is to get the balance right between exploiting (getting the highest returns from current activities) and exploring (seeking the new), which requires organisational flexibility and significant attention to relationships.[61]

Governments and industry groups can promote innovation by several means. The India Semiconductor Association (ISA), for example, has an initiative to promote technology and innovation in the Indian semiconductor industry. The initiative includes a series of awards to encourage the commercialisation of innovations from university research, as well as recognising innovation generally. The awards also operate at the school level, helping create a pervasive culture of innovation.[62]

In a highly innovative organisation, staffing is handled with a clear commitment to innovation. The organisation's strategies, cultures and structures support every member or employee, allowing them to use their creative talents to the full. This is what tends to happen in highly innovative organisations in which managers tend to espouse a more flexible and open style of management, encouraging innovation and problem solving. In addition, managers in highly innovative organisations pay special attention to filling critical innovative roles, such as idea generators, information gatherers and project leaders.

Finally, an innovative organisation benefits from top-management support. Part of this responsibility involves setting a good personal example and maintaining a positive tone.

WhatWould YouDo?

Creating an innovation culture

Shutterstock, 25th on the most innovative companies list in 2014, is certainly not one of those companies that can be accused of becoming slower innovators after going public.[63] The company achieved a 40 per cent growth in revenue and has been consistently releasing new programs. Through Spectrum, users can search images by colour; through Skillfeed, various online video classes and imaging software are made accessible; and through Offset, higher-quality visuals are available. In addition to integrating with Dropbox, Shutterstock's images are freely available to Facebook advertisers who formerly littered the site's ad space with cheap but poor-quality photos.

Shutterstock's founder and CEO, John Oringer, explained to *Fast Company* that the Facebook advertising deal is a win–win: advertisers are happy as their ads have high quality photos for no cost; Facebook gets more advertisers and better looking ads; and Shutterstock sells more images. Oringer said that Facebook pays Shutterstock a fee per image, with the photograph contributor receiving approximately 30 per cent of that fee. That all of Shutterstock's images are ready to be used commercially also helps advertisers avoid the threat of litigation that they would be exposed to had they simply copied and pasted an image from the internet.[64]

The company has brought in the concept of collaborative experimentation, which can help companies to not only boost their products, but instil a progressive innovative mentality into the company culture. Shutterstock's Vice President of Product, Wyatt Jenkins, argues that through the continuous testing of ideas, a culture of experimentation can begin to manifest in the organisation. Jenkins says that the benefits

(continued)

of an experimental culture include the death of 'HiPPOs', which he describes as the 'Highest paid person's Opinion'. 'A/B testing is a sure way to get to the bottom of a decision without relying on anyone's gut instinct. At Shutterstock, if a senior executive has an idea in a meeting, the response is simply, "Let's test it".'

This process spills over into teams, which results in better engagement since their ideas are valued and will be tested. Even if the result is failure, many positive spin-offs are achieved such as improved self-esteem and employee growth, especially the growth of critical ideas. Jenkins is an advocate of keeping the testing teams small; for example, a business analyst, an engineer and a designer/front-end developer (in the case of Shutterstock). The idea is to get a mix of different business functions, but related to what is being tested. The concept of the '20 per cent time' phenomena of the tech world is relevant here. In essence, it allows employees to use some of their work time to work on any company-related product they want. They experiment with ideas that would not normally see the light of day. This kind of experimentation has led to Gmail, Adsense and many other Google initiatives.[65]

Questions

1. What are your views on experimenting in the workplace?
2. What impact can this have on your company or a company you know of?
3. What other strategies could be employed in stimulating innovation in the workplace?

Management responsibility for innovation leadership further extends to putting the right strategies, cultures, structures and staffing in place, and keeping them updated. At any level of responsibility, such support for innovation begins with the ability to spot organisational barriers to innovation such as a leader who is not open to new ideas, insufficient time and resources to allocate to innovation, and the inability to implement and commercialise new ideas.[66] But true management support for innovation goes further than mere recognition of potential barriers; it means being able to take the actions required to eliminate these barriers and to unlock the full innovation potential of the organisation. More specifically, it means decentralising authority and empowering people. It means redesigning work to create a sense of ownership for individuals and groups. It means making every effort to build a democratic workplace based on mutual trust. It means working with people to encourage experimentation and risk taking, and to eliminate the fear of failure. And, it means being willing to reward those who do experiment and take risks and who support change.[67]

Summary

Radical versus incremental planned change
Planned change is directed by managers and others acting as change agents. Radical change involves a significant transformation of the organisation and/or its objectives, systems and processes. It often occurs in response to a critical event, such as the presence of a new CEO, an emerging competitive threat, or a merger with another company. Incremental change is more gradual and involves an adjustment to the way things are currently done in one or a limited number of organisational departments. It is less disruptive and generally more frequent than radical change.

Forces favouring change and the targets of change
Within organisations, change is more likely to take place successfully when there is sufficient dissatisfaction with the way things are currently done, a strong attraction towards a more desirable state and a willingness to work towards a strategic approach to change. External

factors in favour of change include increasing complexity in the business environment. Complexity is increased through globalisation, technological change, competition, and the need to be more efficient, innovative and responsive to customer demands. Organisational targets for planned change include purpose, strategy, culture, structure, people, tasks and technology.

Change strategies

Planned change strategies are the means used by change agents to implement desired change. Force-coercion strategies of change use aspects of a manager's position power to try to 'command' that the change will take place as directed. Temporary compliance is a common response of people who are 'forced' to change in this manner. Rational persuasion strategies of change use logical arguments and appeal to knowledge and facts to convince people to support change. When successful, this method can lead to more commitment to change. Shared-power strategies of change seek to involve other people in planning and implementing change. Of the three strategies, shared power creates the longest-lasting and most internalised commitments to the change.

Resistance to change and what can be done about it

Resistance to change is to be expected. Dealing successfully with resistance begins with an awareness that it represents 'feedback' that can be used by a change agent to increase the effectiveness of a change effort. People sometimes resist because they do not find value or believe in the change. They sometimes resist because they find the change strategy offensive or inappropriate. Sometimes, they resist because they do not like or identify positively with the change agent as a person. Successful change agents are open to resistance and are capable of responding to it in ways that create a better 'fit' between the change, the situation and all the people involved.

Workplace stress

Stress is a state of tension experienced by individuals facing extraordinary demands, constraints or opportunities. Stress in the workplace is caused by work, non-work and personal factors (collectively known as stressors), including organisational change. Managers need to be able to minimise stress, cope with it themselves and help their employees cope with it.

Innovation in organisations

Innovation in organisations is the process of creating new ideas and putting those new ideas into practice. It is a process of 'invention + application' that turns creative ideas into products and/or processes of real benefit to people and organisations. Innovation is important to the private sector because it is so closely linked to competitiveness; that is, new or improved goods and services, or better ways of doing things ensure the financial viability of the enterprise. Innovation is also important in government business enterprises. Highly innovative organisations share certain features in common. They have supportive strategies, cultures, structures, staffing and top management. They tolerate mistakes and have a client-focused approach.

CHAPTER 14 study guide

Key terms

change agents, *p. 529*

changing, *p. 536*

force-coercion strategy, *p. 540*

incremental change, *p. 529*

innovation, *p. 549*

performance gap, *p. 530*

planned change, *p. 530*

process innovation, *p. 549*

product innovation, *p. 549*

radical change, *p. 529*

rational persuasion
strategy, *p. 540*

refreezing, *p. 536*

resistance to change, *p. 542*

shared power strategy (normative-
reeducative strategy), *p. 541*

stress, *p. 545*

stress prevention, *p. 547*

stressors, *p. 545*

unfreezing, *p. 535*

unplanned change, *p. 530*

Review questions

1. Explain the difference between planned and unplanned change. Give examples of situations in which these may occur.
2. Explain what managers can do to manage change and minimise resistance.
3. Explain the importance and benefits of innovation in organisations.
4. Discuss some of the things that managers can do to encourage and promote innovation in their organisations.
5. Discuss the notion that innovating too fast and too much is not always a good thing.

Application questions

1. Design a one-day training course targeting the mid-level managers of a medium-size organisation. There would be 20 participants coming from a diverse range of functions in the organisation, including production, design, administration, marketing, sales and product development. The aims of the program are to make participants aware of the meaning of 'cultural change', and also to gauge views on the current culture and potential required changes.
2. As a team leader in an organisation facing increasing competition from new entrants to your industry, you have been tasked with implementing changes within your unit. These changes are likely to disrupt current schedules, rosters and work processes significantly. Prepare a strategy for the unfreezing stage of the change process for your team, with a view to minimising resistance so that the changes can be implemented as smoothly as possible.
3. The best way to approach change is through the 'shared power' approach. Do you agree?
4. Discuss some of the work-related factors that can cause stress, then compare and contrast the following occupations in terms of the degree of stress they might generate: bus driver, call-centre operator, team leader and security guard. Choose one of these occupations and discuss the potential consequences of stress on the job holder and the organisation.
5. Many great ideas and inventions never achieve their full potential because of barriers within the organisational culture. Discuss.
6. You have developed a unique, simple-to-use and highly effective software package that will enable teachers to detect plagiarism from internet sources in student assignments. As you have just completed your university degree, you are determined to set up your own business and market this product to universities around Australia. You also realise that, to build up your business, you will need to create an organisation that encourages further innovation and product development. Based on the four features of an innovative organisation, describe the organisation that you would create to realise your dream of becoming a successful business entrepreneur.

Research questions

1. Resistance to change is a complex response by employees when confronted with the possibility of unwelcome changes to their working lives. It is based on employee beliefs about the change (for example, there will be job cuts); emotions (such as anxiety, anger); and behaviours (for example, absenteeism, reduced work quality, undermining the changes). Conduct a search on the topic of resistance, identifying a range of employee response types encompassing beliefs, emotions and behaviours. If possible, identify organisations and situations in which these various responses have occurred. What can you conclude about the way people respond to the possibility of unwelcome changes to their working lives? What can managers do to anticipate and minimise resistance to change?

2. What skills and competencies do good change agents have? Search the internet to identify people who are presented as successful agents of change. You should find some good examples among the senior managers of large organisations in the business, public or community sectors. What skills and competencies do these people demonstrate? How have they used these skills and competencies to bring about change in their organisations?

3. Choose three companies on the list of the world's 50 most innovative companies (type the term 'the world's 50 most innovative companies' into a search engine) that you feel you can learn from most regarding the principles they use in their innovation. Explain why.

Running project

Complete the following tasks for your chosen organisation.

1. Identify factors that are driving change at your organisation. Try also to identify factors that are likely to produce a need for change in the near future.
2. (a) Choose one current factor from part 1 and explain the organisation's response.
   (b) Choose one future factor from part 1 and suggest an appropriate response. Does the organisation need to act now?
3. Referring to your answer to question 2(b), identify what resistance to change might be encountered, why it might arise and how it might be overcome.
4. How important is innovation to your organisation? Explain.
5. Identify factors in your organisation that (a) promote and (b) discourage innovation.
6. What lessons can your organisation take away from some of the innovative companies featured in this chapter?

Individual activity

Innovative attitude scale

Introduction

Change and innovation are important to organisations. The following assessment surveys your readiness to accept and participate in innovation.

Instructions

Indicate the extent to which each of the following statements is true of either your actual behaviour or your intentions at work. That is, describe the way you are, or the way you intend to be, on the job. Use the following scale for your responses:

Almost always true = 5
Often true = 4
Not applicable = 3
Seldom true = 2
Almost never true = 1

1. I openly discuss with my boss how to get ahead.
2. I try new ideas and approaches to problems.
3. I take things or situations apart to find out how they work.
4. I welcome uncertainty and unusual circumstances related to my tasks.
5. I negotiate my salary openly with my supervisor.
6. I can be counted on to find a new use for existing methods or equipment.
7. Among my colleagues and coworkers, I will be the first or nearly the first to try out a new idea or method.

8. I take the opportunity to translate communications from other departments for my work group.
9. I demonstrate originality.
10. I will work on a problem that has caused others great difficulty.
11. I provide critical input towards a new solution.
12. I provide written evaluations of proposed ideas.
13. I develop contacts with experts outside my firm.
14. I use personal contacts to manoeuvre myself into choice work assignments.

15. I make time to pursue my own pet ideas or projects.
16. I set aside resources for the pursuit of a risky project.
17. I tolerate people who depart from organisational routine.
18. I speak out in staff meetings.
19. I work in teams to try to solve complex problems.
20. If my coworkers are asked, they will say I am a wit.[68]

For an interpretation of your responses, turn to page 558.

Group activity

Force field analysis

Objectives
1. To improve your analytical skills for addressing complex situations.
2. To show how force field analysis can aid understanding of change.

Total time: 30–60 minutes

Procedure
1. Choose a situation in which you have high personal stakes (for example, how to get a better grade in a particular course, or how to get a promotion).
2. Using the following force field analysis form, apply the technique to your situation.
   (a) Describe the situation as it now exists.
   (b) Describe the situation as you would like it to be.
   (c) Identify the 'driving forces' — the factors that are presently helping to move things in the desired direction.
   (d) Identify the 'restraining forces' — the factors that are presently holding things back from moving in the desired direction.
3. Try to be as specific as possible in these descriptions of your situation. You should attempt to be exhaustive in your listing of these forces. List them all!
4. Now go back and classify the strength of each force as weak, medium or strong. Do this for both the driving and restraining forces.
5. At this point you should rank the forces on their ability to influence or control the situation.
6. In groups of three to four, share your analyses. Discuss the usefulness of and drawbacks to using this method for (a) personal situations and (b) organisations.
7. Be prepared to share the results of your group's discussion with the rest of the class.

Force field analysis form

CURRENT SITUATION

_____

_____

_____

_____

PREFERRED SITUATION

_____

_____

_____

_____

DRIVING FORCES

_____

_____

_____

_____

RESTRAINING FORCES

_____

_____

_____

_____

Founded in 1932, the Danish company LEGO is one of the most famous brands in the world of children's toys and has grown significantly since its early beginnings in 1932. LEGO secured one of Denmark's first plastic injection moulding machines in 1946 and patented the plastic building brick in 1958. Following this, the organisation experienced many years of annual growth and success. In 1978, the 'Minifigure' was introduced and the next 15 years were marked by growth of 14 to 15 per cent per year, with the company doubling in size every five years in size.[69] As an iconic name in the toy business world, when customers thought about plastic building block toys, they were thinking of 'LEGOs'. Dissimilar to other very large companies, the firm was still run by the founding family.

However, things start falling apart and a growth in sales halted in 1994. Even though LEGO had always looked for new products, this sales slump prompted the company to triple its offerings, and in 2000 the company went on an innovation spree by adding on LEGO-branded electronics, amusement parks, interactive video games, jewellery, education centres, and alliances with the Harry Potter franchise and the Star Wars movies.[70]

LEGO's leadership team followed nearly every key innovation principle advocated by experts. They introduced what Professor Robertson from Wharton University of Pennsylvania calls a 'frenzy of innovation'.[71] The company sought relatively competition-free markets where LEGO could dominate; management sought out the participation of a diverse range of stakeholders both inside and outside the company and recruited a diverse and creative staff. The company set out to create new products that disrupted existing markets, and sought out and took customer feedback on-board. LEGO also tried a blue ocean strategy approach to innovation when it developed after-school learning centres to teach science, technology, mathematics and engineering. A blue ocean strategy entails the creation by a company of a new, uncontested market space that makes competitors irrelevant and creates new consumer value, often while decreasing costs.[72] Another example was opening a movie studio with Steven Spielberg that allowed builders to do stop-motion animation to create their own movies. The key focus of the company was innovation with the aim of transforming the company into the world's strongest brand among families by 2005.[73]

In short the company followed the seven truths of innovation.

1. Build an innovation culture.
2. Become customer driven.
3. Explore the full spectrum of innovation.
4. Foster open innovation.
5. Attempt a disruptive innovation.
6. Sail for a blue ocean.
7. Leverage diverse and creative people.

However, despite following the advice of experts and building an innovative culture that seemingly would have been the envy of any firm, the company almost went bankrupt.[74]

Some observers argued that LEGO over-diversified its product line with directing efforts into such areas as apparel and theme parks while others pointed to the exploding popularity of video games or pressure from low-cost producers in China.[75] These may have been contributing factors; however, other factors also had a negative impact, including its innovation capabilities and its supply chain.

LEGO lost focus by applying every innovation strategy, among multiple product lines and departments throughout the company.

All of those innovation strategies worked, but they worked too well. It was like strapping a jet engine onto a car: when they lit up the engines of innovation, the company became an unguided missile. If a company is going to accelerate innovation, it needs a different way to guide itself.[76]

LEGO's supply chain was at least ten years outdated and poor customer service and irregular availability of products were eroding the company's franchise in crucial markets.[77] LEGO was essentially out of cash by 2003 with a $300 million loss that year and a projected loss for the next year of up to $400 million. Professor Robertson from Wharton argues, 'Basically, LEGO had strapped on wings and was flying at 30 000 feet'. He further argues that the company had not asked or answered the questions needed to financially sustain such growth — questions such as, 'Where do you want to go?', 'Where are you now?' and 'How will you get there?' 'If you are going to accelerate innovation, you need to know which way you are going.'[78]

With a view to rebuild profitability, the company revamped its supply chain. Inefficiencies were eliminated, its innovation capacity was aligned with the market, and the company re-directed its strategy to compete in the new big-box world.

The company's chief of product innovation worked closely with supply chain leadership to devise a series of day-to-day solutions to the constraints puzzle. It was decided to cut the palette of roughly 100 colours in half. LEGO cut back on the thousands of different police officers, pirates, and other figures in production. The leadership team took a deliberate approach to analysing the true costs of each element and identify those whose costs were out of line with the rest of the stock. This helped LEGO to shrink its supplier roster by 80 per cent. Similarly, the operational team initiated a process where designers were assisted with more cost-effective choices. Basic rules were developed regarding the creation of new colours and shapes and ordering new materials. They created a cost matrix, clearly showing the price associated with each change after which designers were encouraged to use existing elements in new ways, rather than devise new elements requiring new moulds and colours. This enabled designers to link price trade-offs when designing new items.

This was a major change management challenge for CEO Jorgen Vig Knudstorp, who took the top job in 2004, since the company had grown to roughly 7300 employees, working mostly in two factories and three packaging centres — each in a different country — producing more than 10 000 variations of its products packaged in hundreds of configurations. The leadership team realised that speedy attention to the supply chain would not only assist them with dealing with the other challenges, but it could start a circle of improvements that would support subsequent changes in the rest of the company.

The leadership set up a war room where the operational team gathered every day to make detailed decisions about what toys to make, how tasks should be prioritised, and how to deal with obstacles. Team members scrutinised progress of key initiatives and opened bottlenecks as they occurred. A major focus was placed on solving problems instead of pointing fingers. Time was allocated to consensus building since an autocratic change management approach wouldn't work in a close-knit, family-owned company. A focus was placed on building the loyalty of its workforce, and leadership adopted a strategy of complete transparency. Workforce loyalty was developed through shared communication and consultation throughout, even when redundancy of some employees became a reality. The advantage of the consensus approach is that when the teams finally reached consensus, the decision stuck.[79]

Thanks to LEGO's rationalisation and streamlining, its product development, sourcing, manufacturing and distribution the company is profitable once more.

LEGO's experience shows that having a strategy (or two or three) to boost innovation is not enough to be successful. Before launching any innovation-boosting initiative, companies must identify where they want their innovation initiatives to take them. Ultimately, a clear vision for what a successful innovation will produce is essential as is ensuring the right personnel and resources to monitor and guide its execution. Following mantras of innovation isn't enough; neither is unrestrained innovation as shown by the LEGO experience.[80]

Questions

1. What were some of the reasons why LEGO found itself in trouble?
2. Discuss the types of changes LEGO implemented from a change and innovation perspective.
3. What lessons are to be learnt from this case study?

Interpretation of individual activity

To determine your score on the 'Innovative attitude scale', simply add the numbers associated with your responses to the 20 items. The higher your score, the more receptive to innovation you are. You can compare your score with that of others to see if you seem to be more or less receptive to innovation than a comparable group of business students.

Score	Percentile*
39	5
53	16
62	33
71	50
80	68
89	86
97	95

*Percentile indicates the percentage of the people who are expected to score below you.

End notes

1. Bulletproof: Mission critical cloud, 'About us', www.bulletproof.net.au/bulletproof.
2. A Woodward, 'How to keep (and improve) your company culture when you go public: Bulletproof Networks founder Anthony Woodward', *BRW* (22 August 2014), www.brw.com.au.
3. ibid.
4. RM Zeffane, 'Patterns of organizational commitment and perceived management styles: a comparison of public and private sector employees', *Tavistock Institute Journal of Human Relations*, vol. 47, no. 8 (1994), pp. 13–27.
5. For more on the concepts of frame-breaking and frame-bending change see D Nadler and M Tushman, *Strategic organizational design* (Glenview, IL: Scott, Foresman, 1988).
6. N Tichy, *Managing strategic change: technical, political and cultural dynamics* (New York: John Wiley & Sons, 1983).
7. C Bowman, 'Stuck in the old routines', *European Management Journal*, vol. 12, no. 1 (1994), p. 76.
8. J Stewart and P Kringas, 'Change management — strategy and values: six case studies from the Australian public sector', Centre for Research in Public Sector Management, University of Canberra, www.blis.canberra.edu.au
9. F Graetz, 'Strategic change leadership', *Management Decision*, vol. 38, no. 8 (2000), pp. 550–62.
10. R Miles, *Corporate comeback: the story of renewal and transformation at National Semiconductor* (San Francisco: Jossey-Bass, 1997).
11. R Greenwood, 'TAFE not just a school for apprentices' (26 May 2014), http://www.news.com.au; United Nurseries, 'About us', http://united-nurseries.com.au.
12. WE Deming, *Out of the crisis* (Cambridge, MA: MIT Center for Advanced Engineering Study, 1986).
13. See for example Sharon Parker, 'Tactical change' (2004), www2.agsm.edu.au.
14. P Gagliardi, 'The creation and change of organisational cultures: a conceptual framework', *Organisation Studies*, vol. 7, no. 2, (1986), pp. 117–34, cited in S Parker, 'Tactical change' (2004), www2.agsm.edu.au.
15. J Silvester, NR Anderson and F Patterson, 'Organizational culture change: an intergroup attributional analysis', *Journal of Occupational and Organizational Psychology*, vol. 72, no. 1 (March 1999), p. 1.
16. S Weston and J Harper, 'The challenge of change', *Ivey Business Quarterly*, vol. 63, no. 2 (Winter 1998), p. 78.
17. R Moss Kanter, BA Stein and TD Jick, 'Meeting the challenges of change', *World Executive's Digest* (May 1993), pp. 22–7.
18. R Wiesner, D Chadee and P Best, *A research report on developing a best practice framework for managing environmental sustainability in Australian small and medium size enterprises (SMEs)* (CPA Australia, January 2010).
19. See for example RH Kilmann, *Beyond the quick fix* (San Francisco: Jossey-Bass, 1984); Noel M Tichy and Mary Anne Devanna, The transformational leader (New York: John Wiley & Sons, 1986).
20. RA Cooke, 'Managing change in organizations' in Gerald Zaltman (ed.), *Management principles for nonprofit organizations* (New York: American Management Association, 1979). See also David A Nadler, 'The effective management of organizational change' in JW Lorsch (ed.), *Handbook of organizational behavior* (Englewood Cliffs, NJ: Prentice Hall, 1987), pp. 358–69.
21. K Lewin, 'Group decision and social change' in GE Swanson, TM Newcomb and EL Hartley (eds), *Readings in social psychology* (New York: Holt, Rinehart and Winston, 1952), p. 4.
22. Accel Team, 'Team building', www.accel-team.com.
23. Charles Sturt University, 'Managing change', NSW HSC online, http://hsc.csu.edu.au.
24. Tichy and Devanna, op. cit., p. 44.
25. R Zeffane, 'Dynamics of strategic change: critical issues in fostering positive organizational change', *Leadership and Organization Development Journal*, vol. 17, no. 7 (1996), pp. 36–43.
26. Tichy, op. cit.
27. See NM Tichy, *Managing strategic change: technical, political, and cultural dynamics* (New York: John Wiley & Sons, 1983).
28. ibid.
29. J Cheng, 'Singapore — How International Standards helped HISAKA grow' (18 February 2013), www.iso.org.
30. D Waddell and A Sohal, 'Resistance: a constructive tool for change management', *Management Decision*, vol. 36, no. 8 (1998), p. 543.
31. W Bovey and A Hede, 'Resistance to organisational change: the role of defense mechanisms', *Journal of Managerial Psychology*, vol. 16, no. 7 (2001), p. 534.
32. S Palo and S Panigrahi, 'Managing change during a transition period: the case of an Indian State', *Development and Learning in organizations*, vol. 18, no. 6 (2004), p. 7.
33. E Dent and S Goldberg, 'Challenging resistance to change', *Journal of Applied Behavioral Science*, vol. 35, no. 1 (1999), pp. 25–41.
34. C Carnall, *Managing change in organisations* (Harlow: Prentice Hall, 2003).
35. EE Lawler and CG Worley, *Built to change* (San Francisco: Jossey-Bass, 2006).
36. R Chin and KD Benne, 'General strategies for effecting changes in human systems', in WG Bennis, KD Benne, R Chin and KE Corey (eds), *The planning of change*, 3rd ed. (New York: Holt, Rinehart and Winston, 1969), pp. 22–45.
37. RM Zeffane, 'The downsizing paradox: problems in the quest for leaner organizations', *Journal of Industrial Affairs*, vol. 4, no. 1 (1995), pp. 45–8.
38. RM Zeffane and F Gul, 'The effects of task characteristics and sub-unit structure on information processing', *Information Processing and Management*, vol. 29, no. 1 (1993), pp. 21–37.

39. RM Zeffane, 'Patterns of organizational commitment and perceived management styles: a comparison of public and private sector employees', *Tavistock Institute Journal of Human Relations*, vol. 47, no. 8 (1994), pp. 13–27; M Emery and M Emery, 'Participative design: work and community life', in M Emery (ed.), *Participative design for participative democracy* (Canberra: Australian National University, Centre for Continuing Education, 1992).

40. T Lupton, 'Organisational change: "top-down" or "bottom-up" management?', *Personnel Review*, vol. 20, no. 3 (1991), pp. 4–10.

41. The change strategy examples in this part are developed from an exercise reported in J William Pfeiffer and John E Jones, *A handbook of structured experiences for human relations training*, vol. II (La Jolla, CA: University Associates, 1973).

42. D Dunphy and D Stace, 'The strategic management of corporate change', *Human Relations*, vol. 46, no. 8 (August 1993), pp. 905–20.

43. C McNamara, 'Basic context for organizational change', www.managementhelp.org.

44. D Klein, 'Some notes on the dynamics of resistance to change: the defender role' in Bennis et al. (eds), op. cit., pp. 117–24.

45. K N Dervitsiotis, 'The challenge of managing organizational change: exploring the relationship of re-engineering, developing learning organizations and total quality management', *Total Quality Management*, vol. 9, no. 1 (February 1998), p. 109.

46. See EM Rogers and F Floyd Shoemaker, *Communication of innovations*, 2nd ed. (New York: The Free Press, 1971).

47. JP Kotter and LA Schlesinger, 'Choosing strategies for change', *Harvard Business Review*, vol. 57 (March/April 1979), pp. 109–12.

48. AP Brief, RS Schuler and M Van Sell, *Managing job stress* (Boston: Little, Brown and Company, 1981).

49. Portions of this treatment of stress developed from JR Schermerhorn, Jr, *Management for productivity*, 3rd ed. (New York: John Wiley & Sons, 1989), pp. 647–52.

50. CL Cooper, 'Executive stress around the world', *University of Wales Review of Business and Economics* (Winter 1987), pp. 3–8.

51. J Carr, B Kelley, R Keaton and C Albrecht, 'Getting to grips with stress in the workplace: strategies for promoting a healthier, more productive environment', *Human Resource Management International Digest*, vol. 19, no. 4 (2011), p. 33.

52. J Segal and M Smith, 'Conflict resolution skills: building the skills that can turn conflicts into opportunities', *Helpguide* (November 2010), http://helpguide.org/mental/eq8_conflict_resolution.htm.

53. R Huebsch, 'How has the increased use of technology impacted workplace stress?', *eHow* (updated 29 June 2011), www.ehow.com.

54. F Smith, 'Atlassian: Is this the first self-correcting organisation?', *BRW*, (10 April 2013), www.brw.com.au.

55. N Way, 'The fast lane speeds up', *Business Review Weekly* (11 June 1999), pp. 84–7.

56. Savery and Luks, op. cit.

57. S Wojcicki, 'The eight pillars of innovation', *Think Newsletter* (July 2011), www.thinkwithgoogle.com.

58. See EB Roberts, 'Managing invention and innovation', *Research Technology Management* (January/February 1988), pp. 1–19.

59. JR Schermerhorn, Jr, *Management for productivity*, 4th ed. (New York: John Wiley & Sons, 1993), p. 661.

60. MD Mumford, 'Social innovation: ten cases from Benjamin Franklin', *Creativity Research Journal*, vol. 14, no. 2 (2002), pp. 253–66.

61. Kanter, op. cit.

62. Cyber India Online, 'ISA launches initiative to promote innovation', www.ciol.com.

63. M McCue, 'Shutterstock, The world's 50 most innovative companies', *Fast Company* (2014), www.fastcompany.com.

64. ibid.

65. ibid.; C Edmond, 'How experimentation can bolster company culture', *HR Magazine* (11 February 2014), www.hcamag.com.

66. SmallBizConnect, 'Introduction to innovation', http://toolkit.smallbiz.nsw.gov.au.

67. Based on VSL Tan, 'Change is the CEO's imperative', *New Straits Times* (22 May 1993), p. A1.

68. JE Ettlie and RD O'Keefe, 'Innovative attitudes, values and intentions in organizations', *Journal of Management Studies*, vol. 19 (1982), p. 176.

69. D Robertson, 'The seven deadly truths of innovation: how the accepted wisdom on innovation management almost bankrupted LEGO, in learning from failure in innovation — turning setbacks into advantages', https://mackinstitute.wharton.upenn.edu.

70. Wharton University of Pennsylvania, 'Innovation almost bankrupted LEGO — until it rebuilt with a better blueprint' (18 July 2012), http://knowledge.wharton.upenn.edu.

71. ibid.

72. W Chan Kim and R Mauborgne, 'Blue ocean strategy', *Harvard Business Review* (October 2004), http://hbr.org.

73. Robertson, op cit.

74. D Robertson, *Brick by brick: how LEGO rewrote the rules of innovation and conquered the global toy industry* (New York: Crown Business, 2013).

75. K Oliver, E Samakh and P Heckmann, 'Rebuilding LEGO, brick by brick — how a supply chain transformation helped put the beloved toymaker back together again', *Strategy and Business* (29 August 2007), issue 48, www.strategy-business.com.

76. Robertson, op. cit.

77. Oliver, Samakh and Heckmann, op. cit.

78. Wharton University of Pennsylvania, op. cit.

79. Oliver, Samakh and Heckmann, op. cit.

80. Robertson, op cit.

Part 5

CASE STUDIES

	CHAPTER/S CASE APPLIES TO													
	1	2	3	4	5	6	7	8	9	10	11	12	13	14
CASE STUDY 1 The Princess Polly story								■						■
CASE STUDY 2 Management style and employee–management relations		■			■	■		■	■	■	■	■	■	
CASE STUDY 3 Manukau Water: it's not only about pipes	■	■	■	■		■			■	■	■	■	■	
CASE STUDY 4 Woolworths: what it DOES take		■		■	■		■	■					■	

THE PRINCESS POLLY STORY

Innovation and culture — the formula for success

Princess Polly captures the hip, fresh, colourful vibrancy of life under the Australian sun. Founded in the summer of 2005, Princess Polly kicked off as a cute and quirky boutique in Surfers Paradise. A combination of good quality fabrics and unique femme styles soon created a cult-like following among local fashionistas.

Until Princess Polly arrived, these customers only had access to the bulk 'cookie cutter' fashion offered by larger, long-established retailers (i.e. those found in every mall across Australia). Princess Polly offered something new, exciting and distinctively different. The Princess Polly founders adopted the mantra 'Money doesn't buy style. What counts is that it's *gorgeous* and customers see value in it'. In essence, they found a formula to build a solid and loyal customer base.

Since their humble beginnings, Princess Polly has experienced an almost exponential growth in their sales. Whilst they initially concentrated on a bricks-and-mortar strategy, they soon extended the business to incorporate an online platform, which has proven to be very popular. Within just three years online sales have grown from zero to a $10 million turnover.

Their move to an online presence was driven primarily by the customers themselves. In early 2010, before Facebook gained mass-market popularity, customers were screaming out to shop online. Many girls from interstate had visited the Queensland store and the word was starting to spread virally across Australia.

Staying lean and flexible in times of rapid growth

Princess Polly's management decided to self-fund the online store, which immediately took off. However, during the initial rapid growth phase, management strived to remain lean and agile. The Australian fashion e-commerce market was only getting started and everything was changing quickly. According to co-founder Wez Bryett, Princess Polly remained flexible in the face of social media and mobile technology changes by focusing on keeping systems as manual as possible and avoiding investing in cumbersome IT systems. This allowed Princess Polly to test different systems, to adjust as necessary and then to develop the successful system.

Princess Polly's management are passionate about new possibilities for retail. Fast fashion and e-commerce have revolutionised the industry. They see the opportunity for Princess Polly to operate, not only as an online store, but as a 'new model' retailer. The aim is to achieve vertical retailing across online and in-store, with a strong in-house brand, digital presence, and a global outlook. Princess Polly currently has its sights set on borderless trade opportunities. Wez describes, 'We are developing a US and Asian marketing immersion strategy to expand beyond the shores of Australia, and leveraging social media will be an integral part of this strategy'.

Innovative social media engagement strategies

To be successful with a tech-savvy Gen Y customer base, companies must keep pace with the latest and greatest in social media. Companies that move fast and are constantly on the lookout for ways to differentiate their brands will succeed; those that neglect such innovation will be left behind.

In response to this market reality, Princess Polly has recently joined forces with Pirus Group, an innovative marketing consultancy, to implement a new social media platform called 'Stylechat'. This tool allows users to shop online with their Facebook friends and instantaneously share and chat about clothes right on the Polly site. The tool allows online users to participate in the social element of shopping that has predominantly been associated with in-store shopping, such as being able to get a second opinion and to avoid a fashion faux pas.

This is what the owners of Princess Polly are good at: identifying deficiencies in the online shopping experience and connecting with experts in the field to make the customer experience even more satisfying. Wez explains:

> Testing of Stylechat has shown that it substantially increases the customers' level of satisfaction, deepens our followers' sense of community and loyalty to the brand, increases time on site, boosts sales, and of course reduces returns.

This demonstrates how one innovation can have a simultaneous and positive impact on several aspects of the business at once.

The importance of company culture

During a growth phase, staff may struggle to handle constant change. To reduce this risk, the Princess Polly founders focused on creating a strong company culture. Co-founder Paul Lavender sees this strong culture as what gives staff the confidence to be able to stand strong in the face of change.

Ensuring staff intensely share the Princess Polly core values of 'authenticity, passion, sell what you love, and don't be afraid to be different' is of paramount importance. Encouraging such beliefs creates both high levels of cohesiveness and trust amongst employees as well as efficient norms. That is, employees naturally moderate their own behaviour *themselves* to fit in with the culture, reducing the need for managers to monitor their staff continually.

Creating a strong culture also begins with recruitment. In the hiring process, Princess Polly seeks out individuals who not only want to work in a fun and fast-moving fashion company, but also want to become part of the Polly family. Paul explains, 'We have mostly hired new staff with great attitudes and a willingness to learn and grow into positions'. Not only does the prospective employee have to be good for the position, but the position has to be good for the person. According to Paul:

> We look for individuals that are brand aware, live and breathe fashion, and are personable and quirky. You can train skills, but you can't train character, so finding those with characteristics that encapsulate the Princess Polly identity is very important to us.

Princess Polly is passionate about positively influencing young women's lives. They accomplish this by empowering employees and assisting them to road map their future involvement in the business, either with Princess Polly or on their own journeys. Management have strived to create an environment where the employees feel empowered and appreciated (as both individuals and as employees). They hold skills workshops to enhance abilities in sales, organise for life coach consultants to visit and offer yoga sessions to employees. This caring focus on the employees has led to the development of a loyal and dedicated workforce.

Princess Polly has also implemented a mentor system, where business or design students come on board as interns to gain valuable firsthand industry experience. Wez highlights:

> We have found this to be a very positive experience where value is created from both sides. Not only do the interns get real fashion experience, but they inject a youthful perspective that helps inform us about the direction of the industry, and what customers in that demographic really want.

The Princess Polly owners believe there is a formula for success; however, this formula must be flexible. 'You need to change the direction of your focus depending on the environment, but as long as the main constituents of the formula are maintained, you will do well' says Paul. These foundation elements are good quality products that are individual and distinctive; a strong culture; loyal and engaged employees; keeping in touch with the customers; and keeping pace with innovation. Oh, and of course, 'Spreading love, peace and happiness'.[1]

Questions

1. What innovative technique is Princess Polly implementing? What aspects of the business will it improve, and why?
2. Determine two important factors in the creation of a strong culture and discuss what makes these factors so important.
3. What method does Princess Polly use to boost morale? What effect does boosting morale have for the company?
4. What does Princess Polly do to reduce the need for managers to engage in behaviour modification of their employees?

End note

1. S Amundsen and ØL Martinsen, 'Self–other agreement in empowering leadership: Relationships with leader effectiveness and subordinates' job satisfaction and turnover intention', *The Leadership Quarterly* (2014); GR Bushe, 'Advances in appreciative inquiry as an organization development intervention', *Organization Development Journal*, vol. 13 (2014), pp. 14–22; CA O'Reilly, J Chatman and DF Caldwell, 'People and organizational culture: A profile comparison approach to assessing person–organization fit', *Academy of Management Journal*, vol. 34, no. 3 (1991), pp. 487–516.

MANAGEMENT STYLE AND EMPLOYEE– MANAGEMENT RELATIONS[1]

Background

Fiji Ships and Heavy Industries Limited (FSHIL), once known as Government Shipyard and Public Slipways (GSPS), was initially a wholly Fijian government–owned entity. Fiji, one of the most developed of the Pacific Island economies, is an island nation located in the heart of the Pacific Ocean, southwest of Honolulu, midway to the equator and New Zealand. GSPS was later corporatised as Shipbuilding (Fiji) Limited (SFL) to pave the way for its privatisation process. When SFL underwent receivership in 1999, the Fijian government made a successful $6.25 m bid to acquire the assets from the receivers. It was in 2002 (effective 1 January 2003) that the Board decided to change the company name to FSHIL to better reflect the extensive range of heavy engineering work carried out by the company. In the same year, an international search was done for the appointment of a CEO.

November 2002 saw the appointment of a CEO who came to FSHIL from Papua New Guinea. The new CEO had thirty years of experience in shipbuilding and ship repairs and had been a ships engineer in the ten years prior. His role became effective in 2003. In the period prior to the appointment of this full-time CEO, FSHIL had an acting CEO — one that had to work to gain the acceptance of his employees. The way the acting CEO carried himself and how he not only consulted the union/workers, but was also receptive to their suggestions and requests, encouraged the employees to accept the acting CEO. With the introduction of the new CEO, problems began to surface between management and the 'managed'.

The situation breakdown

The CEO was unhappy with what he witnessed after joining FSHIL, contending that he had been brought into a politically sensitive shipyard that was not doing well, had old machinery and an overly tarnished reputation. He asserted that the biggest and the most difficult of all challenges was Fiji's laidback culture towards commercial operations. He had positive plans to further upgrade the shipyard, but was held back by finances and investor confidence. The members of the FSHIL in-house union decided that they would prefer to be a part of the Transport Workers Union (TWU) and to resign from the in-house union.

Following is a breakdown of the events in 2003 following the introduction of the new CEO and the in-house union's decision to change unions.

August	25	The secretary of the in-house union writes to the general secretary of TWU to join with them.
September	1	TWU writes to the CEO seeking voluntary recognition. The CEO advises that he will respond after the Board meeting on 4 September 2003.
	4	The first termination under the new CEO is made at FSHIL. The technical services manager (with 30 years' shipbuilding experience) receives a termination letter (effective immediately) from the CEO, with payment for only the one-month's pay that was stipulated in the manager's contract and no reason given for the termination. The technical services manager requests a written explanation for the reason of his termination from the CEO, but receives no response — he had only served eighteen months of his three-year contract.

	5	During a union–management meeting, the CEO advises that FSHIL will recognise the union and requests a draft recognition agreement. The draft is submitted and the CEO agrees to respond to TWU by 12 September 2003.
	8	32 workers receive temporary standdown letters from the CEO.
	12	The union feels insulted that they were not consulted or advised of the decision to standdown employees, and TWU writes to the CEO to explain this. TWU also requests the response to the draft recognition agreement due from the CEO today. No response is received.
		Further, TWU writes a letter explaining that the standdown was unjust and unfair, especially given the fact that all employees affected were members of the union. TWU accuses the CEO of failing to act in accordance with the relevant sections of the Labour Advisory Board's approved *Industrial Relations Code of Practice* in relation to reducing the workforce. The union calls for instantaneous reinstatement of the affected employees and the conclusion of the voluntary recognition agreement, requesting a response by 15 September. No response is received.
	15	After no response from the CEO for his previous request, the terminated technical services manager writes to the permanent secretary of the Public Enterprises Ministry to disclose the rift between himself and the CEO, suspecting this is the reason for his termination.
	23	After no response from the CEO, TWU reports a trade dispute to the permanent secretary of the Ministry of Labour, Industrial Relations and Productivity for the thirty-two staff members temporarily stood down without pay, for an unspecified period and without prior notice or consultation with the union, claiming that this action was in direct response to its request for voluntary recognition.
October	21	The Ministry informs TWU, as well as the CEO, of the acceptance of the trade dispute report and appoints a principal labour officer from the Ministry as the conciliator.
	24	A voluntary memorandum of agreement is signed for all union members, excluding the CEO and other selected staff.
	28	The Ministry is notified of the signing of the memorandum of agreement.
November	5	The Ministry-appointed conciliator advises the union and the CEO of a meeting on 18 November 2003 to discuss the standdown of the thirty-two employees.
	17	Forty frustrated workers submit a petition to the Public Enterprises Ministry with copies to the Prime Minister's Office, Board Chairman and TWU to draw attention to the attitude of the CEO, the state of shipyard and to request for a change in leadership.
	18	The meeting between the CEO and the union takes place. It is agreed that the thirty-two employees will work on a rotational basis as the company secures jobs.

The result

The result of these events was lingering negative feelings, poor impressions and mistrust. The CEO was the focus for a lot of the complaints. TWU complained that there were better people for the role. The union alleged that the CEO also employed his wife in the office, even though he received a quarter–million dollar salary package. The CEO defended the employment of his wife, saying she had a temporary advisory role for which she was paid an allowance.

Likewise, employees formed strong views of the salary package enjoyed by the CEO in contrast to the fewer jobs and the rising costs they faced. They felt that this package ensured that the CEO would do well, even if the company suffered. Employees claimed that the CEO quoted preference prices for his friends compared to the prices quoted to other clients. They compared their current situation with the pre-privatisation period, arguing that they were better off in the pre-privatisation period as they had contracts, employment and local heads who understood their culture. The employees did not believe in the CEO's comments about clients no longer having faith in FSHIL, its tarnished image and the lack of shipbuilding contracts being secured. It was continually implied by the employees that a local CEO would be preferable to having a 'foreigner' as CEO.

The FSHIL Board received these complaints and allegations from the employees and TWU and confirmed that they would take appropriate action. However, these actions were not disclosed. The Board reiterated that the CEO was there for a contract period of three years and that they would refer to objective evidence, such as the financial reports, to investigate and substantiate employee and union claims. The eventual respect of the previous acting CEO compared with the situation with the current CEO provides a strong contrast.

Questions

1. Compare the leadership styles of the two different CEOs — the acting CEO and the new CEO.

2. In your opinion (and given the knowledge you have gained from the preceding chapters), how could the resulting situation between management and the employees/union be solved?

3. If you were invited as a consultant, what would your suggestion be to improve the relationship between the CEO and the employees?

End note

1. This case has been adapted from J Narayan, 'Public enterprise reforms in Fiji: how 'not' to privatize — the case of Government Shipyard and Public Slipways', ePublished Master of Arts thesis (London: Cooperjal Ltd, 2004).

MANUKAU WATER: IT'S NOT ONLY ABOUT PIPES[1]

Background

Established in 1965, Manukau City was one of four cities — North Shore, Waitakere and Auckland — and three districts — Papakura and Rodney, part of Franklin District — that made up the Auckland Region. Manukau City had been — and was expected to continue to be — a driving force behind the metropolitan area's growth. To attract new growth, Manukau City Council (MCC) sought to hold down local government spending and thereby rates, or property taxes. Efforts to limit the budget stemmed not only from a desire to attract and retain new businesses and residents, but because some of New Zealand's poorest neighbourhoods were located in Manukau.[2]

Until 2006, Manukau Water was among a variety of services that MCC operated under its direct control. Too often, however, important water and wastewater issues were buried under other City Council issues. The city's growth was also beginning to take its toll. New residents and businesses brought in additional tax revenue, but they also raised new demands for better services and more facilities. The city's budget strained under the demands, as well as under new, tougher nationwide pollution requirements for water and sewer services.

Getting corporatised

Pressed to control costs, MCC decided in 2005 to turn Manukau Water into a non-profit, Council-controlled organisation, or CCO. The structure offered the benefits of corporatisation without the political baggage of being profit-driven, which residents opposed. A board of directors would run the company, hiring management, ensuring the business fulfilled its statement of intent, and acting as the liaison between the Council and management. Executives were to answer to the board, not to the local politicians. The Council, however, was responsible for writing the statement of intent, and it had to either hold shares that represented 50 per cent or more of voting rights, or appoint half or more of the board members.

MCC's next order of business was to establish the board of directors. They in turn would hire the new chief executive officer; negotiate the acquisition of the Council-owned water pipes, sewers, and pump stations; and approve Manukau Water's first budget as a CCO for the new fiscal year, which would begin 1 July 2006. MCC appointed six men to the board, including John Hendricks as Manukau Water's chairman. Richard Jackson, the old utility's head, was made CEO. No other top managers from the old utility were retained. Instead, Hendricks, the board, and Jackson brought in four people from the outside to head up the main departments within Manukau Water: Michael Barton as chief financial officer; Malcom Saunders as the general manager for infrastructure; Janine Cardwell as the general manager for customer services; and Alyson Gaynor as the human resources manager. Except for the board and the management team, Manukau Water 'inherited' most of the former utility's staff and operations.

Encountering problems

The new executives found that politics permeated the new company. An excessive use of consultants led to a lack of accountability. Employees clocked in and clocked out regardless of whether work was completed. Staff members blamed others when something failed; and too often they failed to show initiative, leaving problems unaddressed unless instructed to fix them.

Saunders noted that decisions about the parts of infrastructure that needed rebuilding were often nonsensical and there was no asset planning team. Gaynor found that the recruiting and screening of new employees by an external agency was poor. In addition, pay was only nominally tied to performance; in practice, managers set performance indicators to ensure employees got the raise. Employees were reluctant to admit to knowledge gaps or interest in training, because to do so was to jeopardise raises. Customer service quality was also erratic.

On the political front, Hendricks found himself intervening to ensure MCC's councillors and employees understood the new governance structure and did not go directly to Manukau Water's management with requests and complaints, as they would have in the past. Barton had to contend with Manukau Water employees who thought if they did not use up their budgets for a given year, they would face cutbacks the following year. As a result, as a fiscal year drew to an end, employees made purchases whether they made sense or not, and because employees did not see beyond their own budgets, they were not aware of Manukau Water's overall financial state, much less how to improve it.

Painful solutions

The new team began tackling Manukau Water's troubles. Jackson reorganised personnel, cutting the number of project managers. Gaynor wrote up human resources policies, took over hiring, established training programs and renegotiated contracts so pay followed performance. Saunders consolidated two of the three major contracts and for the first time identified high-risk assets to ensure they were in good condition and to replace those that were not. Barton fired consultants, reviewed billing processes to improve cash flow, introduced fundamental business concepts to employees, and rode contractors hard for failing to achieve agreed-upon service levels.

The changes frustrated employees. An August 2006 survey, in which 93 per cent participated, had staff give the new CCO an employee satisfaction rating of 52.7 on a scale of 1 to 100. In the first year, 28 per cent of employees quit.

Some problems persisted into 2008. Customer service quality was still erratic; daily routines needed be standardised and published, so employees could follow them consistently; and non-performing personnel had to be dealt with more swiftly. A contractor hired to read meters had made too many errors and needed to be replaced, and some MCC-provided services were not meeting management's standards, creating tension. Occasionally, too, councillors would still appear in Barton's office.

Still, the CEO and management considered the transition a success. In its first year as a CCO, Manukau Water came in under budget, reporting a loss of $6.6 million against a budgeted deficit of $8.2 million. A year later, they narrowed the loss again, to $2 million versus the expected deficit of $5.4 million.[3] The executives were proud of the changes they had made and their financial results.

The board, too, was pleased. In Manukau Water's 2007–2008 annual report, Hendricks lauded the company's ability to narrow its losses and maintain Auckland's lowest water and sewer charges; the performance was proof of the new management's capabilities and the advantages of the new governance structure.[4] The executive team could now take a deep breath and look to the future.

Looking ahead

This brightening picture allowed Baron to consider investments and expanding services — possibly through acquisitions — to bring greater economies of scale. The executive management group was working on an asset management plan to maintain pipes and install new ones to keep up with growth. In its final form, the plan called for expenditures of $675 million over 20 years, starting in July 2009. The capital investment included $146.5 million in assets[5] that developers were expected to build as part of their projects and then vest with the City Council.

Beyond those investments, Manukau Water had a variety of other options by which to expand and improve services and cut costs. One option was to buy the water and sewer operations of Papakura District. If Manukau Water took it over, the company might be able to boost revenues, have a broader base of customers, and enjoy larger economies of scale, reducing operational and borrowing costs. Government officials across Auckland, however, were having discussions as to whether customers would be better served, and the region's resources more efficiently utilised, if the area's six water and sewer retailers and Watercare (the government-owned wholesaler) were consolidated into a single enterprise and possibly sold to, or operated by, a privately held company.

Consolidation would be a blow to Manukau Water's new executive team and to the politicians who had fought for it. In its 27-page submission to the Royal Commission, MCC voiced its opposition. The water and sewer systems had served Manukau residents and businesses well. With the restructuring of the business into a CCO, the Council continued to be able to set the lowest rates in the Auckland Region. Those rates would likely be forced higher if Manukau consumers had to help fund capital investments in the city of Auckland (which needed to separate its decades-old stormwater pipes from its sewer system — an expensive project).

Merging the six retailers and Watercare also would result in only minimal savings, they said, because the companies employed relatively few people compared with their customer base. At the same time, consolidation would eliminate the retailers' ability to negotiate with Watercare to limit wholesale price increases, leading to higher charges for consumers, the City Council predicted. No national regulator exists to monitor a consolidated company, and Watercare, Manukau officials said, was run by engineers who would be inclined to 'gold-plate' assets, rather than make capital investments that addressed problems without overburdening consumers. The result of the Royal Commission could mean that rather than acquiring companies, Jackson and Barton might find Manukau Water is the one with a new owner.

Questions

1. In the case, Manukau Water's employees were said to be frustrated with the changes being made to the company. What are some of the reasons why people are resistant to change and what approaches could have been used by management to help overcome this resistance?
2. What are the pros and cons of consolidation of the water companies in the Auckland Region?
3. Given those pros and cons, should Manukau Water (if consolidated) pursue a vertical or horizontal specialisation organisational structure? Why?

End notes

1. This case was written for the 2006–2009 period with the cooperation of Manukau Water's senior executive team solely for the purpose of stimulating class discussion. The case is not intended to be used as illustration of either effective or ineffective handling of a managerial situation. The authors would like to acknowledge the financial support of The University of Auckland Business Case Centre.
2. Manukau City Council, *New Zealand index of deprivation 2001* (produced by Land Information, 2002).
3. Manukau Water Limited, *Annual Report 2007–2008* (Manukau: East Tamaki, 2008).
4. ibid.
5. Manukau Water Limited, *Asset Management Plan 2010–2029* (Manukau: East Tamaki, December 2008).

WOOLWORTHS: WHAT IT DOES TAKE

Background

Woolworths is the largest supermarket and grocery store chain in Australia. In 2014, Woolworths (and its premium supermarket brand, Thomas Dux) has 924 supermarkets[1] in Australia and employs more than 111 000 staff members within its supermarkets, distribution centres and support offices.[2] Woolworths serves more than 10 million customers each week and has a 39.6 per cent market share in the grocery industry.[3] Whilst essentially operating as a duopoly with major competitor Coles (owned by Wesfarmers Limited) with a 33.5 per cent market share, Woolworths also competes with ALDI (owned by ALDI Stores Supermarkets Pty Ltd) with a 10.3 per cent market share, and IGA and SuperIGA (owned by Metcash Limited) with a 9.5 per cent market share. In 2013–14, Woolworths is expected to grow its revenue by 3.3 per cent to $34.5 billion, with the grocery industry worth an estimated $87.2 billion.[4]

The fierce competition in the grocery industry is not just limited to sales and market share. Woolworths, as well as its competitors, aim to be an employer of choice for the 298 825 people employed in the food and beverage industry.[5] Being an employer of choice centres on a firm's ability to recognise and reward staff well, invest in employees' learning and development, operate ethically and fairly at all times, have work–life balance, and have management who are passionate and engaging to work with.[6]

The issue

The employment of someone with disability is often a difficult and sensitive issue for many businesses. Disability can be generally defined as a condition that may restrict a person's mental, sensory, or mobility functions to undertake or perform a task in the same way as a person who does not have disability. According to the *Disability Discrimination Act 1992* (Cwlth), disability may be classified as *physical* (affecting a person's mobility or dexterity), *intellectual* (affecting a person's abilities to learn), *psychiatric* (affecting a person's thinking processes), *sensory* (affecting a person's ability to hear or see), or *neurological* (resulting in the loss of some bodily or mental functions).[7] In Australia, more than 4 million people, or around 20 per cent of the population, identify as having disability.[8]

The number of people in Australia on the disability support pension (DSP) has risen 280 per cent over the past 30 years.[9] People with disability in Australia have a 31 per cent participation rate in the labour force as compared with 83 per cent for people without disability.[10] Further, people with disability are only 50 per cent as likely to be employed compared with people without disability — a situation that has been described as a social and economic disaster.[11] Despite the introduction of the *Disability Discrimination Act 1992* making it unlawful for an employer to discriminate against a person on the grounds of disability, the employment rate of people with disability in Australia has declined since the mid-2000s, with Australia ranking 21st out of 29 OECD countries.[12]

Many people with disability are excluded from employment opportunities and are actively discriminated against by employers.[13] Sue O'Reilly, disability advocate, notes:

> There's a huge amount of discrimination against people with physical disabilities . . . People have extremely strong innate assumptions that if you have a disability, you are automatically mentally inferior.[14]

Employers may engage in explicit or implicit discrimination against people with disability due to concerns about occupational health and safety, workplace disruption, legal obligations, and the anticipated expensive modifications that may need to be made to the workplace. In reality, most workplaces can be modified to be made accessible for employees with disability for less than $500.[15]

Further, studies have found that employees with disability are more job loyal, experience lower levels of absenteeism, are more dependable, and overall perform better than their fellow employees.[16]

Diversity and Woolworths

Woolworths takes its commitment to having a diverse workplace very seriously. This commitment includes having a formal diversity policy, which aims to continue to recognise and celebrate Australia's multicultural diversity by reflecting this in their workforce, to incrementally grow the number of women performing senior roles within the organisation, to assist Indigenous Australians to access employment opportunities within the company, and to provide people with disability employment opportunities and career development.[17] Woolworths CEO, Grant O'Brien, reaffirmed his company's responsibility by acknowledging:

> Whether someone is looking for a long term career, a technical skill, a casual job or just the chance to have a go, we can provide them. At Woolworths we are committed to having a diverse workforce.[18]

With specific regards to disability employment diversity, Woolworths has had longstanding partnerships with disability employment service providers and disability support organisations, such as CRS Australia and the National Disability Recruitment Coordinator (NDRC).[19] Woolworths was one of the first employers in Australia to employ people with significant intellectual disability.[20] It is this commitment to having a sustainable, diverse workforce that enables them to be an attractive workplace for Australian workers.

The 'What it DOES take' program

In order to demonstrate its dedication to maintaining a diverse workplace and to better understand the importance of disability employment in its stores, Woolworths participated in a project called the 'What it DOES take' program from May 2011 to June 2012. This initiative was in collaboration with WorkFocus Australia and funded by the Department of Education, Employment and Workplace Relations (DEEWR) through its Innovation Fund for disability employment initiatives.[21]

The 'What it DOES take' program focused on the Woolworths stores in Melbourne's south-east area. It analysed job roles at the stores with the aim of identifying and removing barriers to the employment of people with disability. Further, the 'What it DOES take' program focused on recognising opportunities and workplace adjustments that could be made for people with a range of disability types. A project officer from WorkFocus Australia and a disability employment officer from Woolworths worked together for the duration of the program. Having a specialist from Woolworths involved in the process meant that there was an immediate understanding of how Woolworths worked, which further assisted relationship building between management, the disability service providers, and the NDRC.[22] Woolworths' disability employment officer identified potential available positions in advance so that employment service providers were aware of such opportunities.[23] Candidates were then put forward by employment consultants for pre-screening and practice interviews.

Moving forward, Woolworths pledged that the outcomes of program, including the lessons learned and implemented in those stores, will lead to the creation of 'how to' guides and job customisation tools for Woolworths that are to be replicated on a national level.[24] This, in turn, may have broader applications for other major employers.[25]

The outcome

By the end of the 2011–12 financial year there had been a 375 per cent increase in people with disability being employed in Melbourne's south-east area, compared with the disability employment levels in the previous financial year in the same area. The remainder of Melbourne saw a 225 per cent increase and the whole of Victoria had an overall increase of 270 per cent for disability employment. Forty-four placements were made after the initiative was finalised.[26]

Woolworths also produced the *How to guide*, which has information about the employment of people with disability, and has made this guide available to all store, area, regional, and HR managers across Australia. The guide is written specifically for store managers and takes into consideration their views on employment of people with disability, their experiences, and needs. It aims to promote awareness and generate understanding for store managers responsible for employees with disability. Further, the role of the disability employment officer within Woolworths has proven to be a very effective tool given that they can network with local stores and promote awareness of disability employment. Following the success of the 'What it DOES take' project, the disability employment officer continues to work with Woolworths on delivery of disability employment opportunities and providing information to store managers.[27]

Woolworths gained recognition for their involvement in the 'What it DOES take' program from the Australian Human Resources Institute's (AHRI) 2013 Diversity Awards program. The judging panel took into consideration such aspects as the program's innovation, culture, outcomes and impact, sustainability, leadership, metrics, industry recognition, and community.[28] The AHRI judges noted that:

> Woolworths developed a very scalable program that could easily translate to other large organisations. They have

embraced the challenge of disability employment and have demonstrated great success and positive impact to the organisation and those in the local community with a disability.[29]

While Woolworths and other large employers, like Australia Post and Westpac, have benefited from the assistance of the National Disability Recruitment Coordinator (NDRC) program, there are many criticisms and problems associated with the program. The main issue is that the NDRC program is not meeting its employment targets (only 154 of the target 1000 jobs — or 15.4 per cent — were fulfilled in 2010–11), even after those targets were revised downward year after year.[30]

Questions

1. Why is disability employment an important issue? Discuss this from the employer, employee, and the government perspective.
2. In what ways can large organisations, like Woolworths, make a significant impact on the employment of people with disability?
3. What recommendations can you offer small businesses who wish to have a diverse workplace and employ people with disability?

End notes

1. Woolworths Limited, '*Third quarter sales results — financial year 2014: 13 weeks to 6 April 2014*' (30 April 2014), www.woolworthslimited.com.au (viewed 3 June 2014).
2. Woolworths Limited, '*Woolworths supermarkets*', www.woolworthslimited.com.au (viewed 3 June 2014).
3. B Tonkin, 'Supermarkets and grocery stores in Australia: market research report', *IBISWorld* (March 2014), http://www.ibisworld.com.au/industry/home.aspx (viewed 3 June 2014).
4. C Kruper, 'Biggest winner of price wars: supermarkets', *The Sydney Morning Herald* (2 November 2012), www.smh.com.au (viewed 11 June 2014).
5. KPMG, 'State of the industry 2013 — essential information: facts and figures', Australian Food and Grocery Council (2013), www.afgc.org.au (viewed 11 June 2014).
6. LMA, 'Top 5 characteristics of employers of choice — employee view (2010)', *Leadership Management Australasia* (2011), www.leadershipmanagement.com.au (viewed 11 June 2014).
7. Disability Works Australia Ltd, '*What is a disability?*', www.dwa.org.au (viewed 3 June 2014).
8. PwC, '*Disability expectations: investing in a better life, a stronger Australia*', www.pwc.com.au (viewed 3 June 2014).
9. I Hopkins, 'New figures show disabled still not entering workforce', *HC Online* (8 April 2013), www.hcamag.com (viewed 11 June 2014).
10. PwC, '*Disability expectations: investing in a better life, a stronger Australia*', www.pwc.com.au (viewed 3 June 2014).
11. OECD, '*Sickness, disability and work: breaking the barriers — a synthesis of findings across OECD countries*', OECD Publishing (2010), ec.europa.eu/health/mental_health/eu_compass (viewed 3 June 2014).
12. Commonwealth of Australia, *Disability Discrimination Act 1992* (Cwlth); PwC, '*Disability expectations: investing in a better life, a stronger Australia*', www.pwc.com.au (viewed 3 June 2014); OECD, '*Sickness, disability and work: breaking the barriers — a synthesis of findings across OECD countries*', OECD Publishing (2010), ec.europa.eu/health/mental_health/eu_compass (viewed 3 June 2014).
13. E Ross, 'Wake up call: employers need to wise up on their disability strategies', *HR Monthly* (June 2011), pp. 23–26.
14. F Carruthers, 'A rallying call from the heart', *The Australian Financial Review* (25 January 2011), p. 44.
15. E Ross, 'Wake up call: employers need to wise up on their disability strategies', *HR Monthly* (June 2011), pp. 23–26.
16. ibid; M Fastenau, 'Able or disabled: does it affect competence, or your comfort level?', *HR Monthly* (September 1996), pp. 39–40; DJ Peterson, 'Paving the way for hiring the handicapped', *Personnel*, vol. 58, no. 2 (March–April 1981), pp. 43–52.
17. Woolworths Limited, '*Diversity policy*', www.woolworthslimited.com.au (viewed 3 June 2014).
18. ibid.
19. WorkFocus Australia, '*Media release: Woolworths supported to employ more people with disability*' (2011), www.workfocus.com (viewed 3 June 2014).
20. Australian Human Resources Institute (AHRI), '*Disability employment — Woolworths Limited*' (2013), diversityawards.ahri.com.au (viewed 3 June 2014).
21. ibid.
22. ibid.
23. WorkFocus Australia, '*Media release: Woolworths supported to employ more people with disability*' (2011), www.workfocus.com (viewed 3 June 2014).
24. Australian Network on Disability, '*Woolworths sets an inspirational example for disability employment*', www.and.org.au (viewed 12 June 2014).
25. WorkFocus Australia, '*Media release: Woolworths supported to employ more people with disability*' (2011), www.workfocus.com (viewed 3 June 2014).
26. Australian Human Resources Institute (AHRI), '*Disability employment — Woolworths Limited*' (2013), diversityawards.ahri.com.au (viewed 3 June 2014).
27. ibid.
28. Australians for Disability and Diversity Employment Incorporated, '*Awards*', www.adde.org.au/awards (viewed 5 June 2014).
29. ibid.
30. A Baker, 'Disability employment: noble cause, failed policy', *Ramp Up* (6 July 2012), www.abc.net.au/rampup (viewed 5 June 2014).

GLOSSARY

Ability is the capacity to perform the various tasks needed for a given job. *p. 47*

Absenteeism is the failure of people to attend work on a given day. *p. 62*

Absorptive capacity is the ability to learn. *p. 424*

Achievement-oriented leadership is leadership behaviour that emphasises setting challenging goals, stressing excellence in performance and showing confidence in the group members' abilities to achieve high standards of performance. *p. 410*

Active management by exception involves watching for deviations from rules and standards and taking corrective action. *p. 416*

Adaptive capacity refers to the ability to change. *p. 424*

An **adhocracy** is an organisational structure that emphasises shared, decentralised decision making, extreme horizontal specialisation, few levels of management, the virtual absence of formal controls, and few rules, policies and procedures. *p. 319*

The **adjourning stage** is the fifth stage of group development, in which members of the group disband when the job is done. *p. 229*

The **affective components** of an attitude are the specific feelings regarding the personal impact of the antecedents. *p. 59*

Aptitude is the capability to learn something. *p. 47*

Arbitration occurs when a neutral third party acts as judge and issues a binding decision affecting parties at a negotiation impasse. *p. 518*

Artificial intelligence, or AI, studies how computers can be made to think like the human brain. *p. 475*

An **attitude** is a predisposition to respond in a positive or negative way to someone or something in your environment. *p. 59*

Authentic leadership involves both owning one's personal experiences (values, thoughts, emotions and beliefs) and acting in accordance with one's true self (expressing what you really think and believe, and acting accordingly). *p. 429*

Authoritarianism is a personality trait that focuses on the rigidity of a person's beliefs. *p. 53*

Automation is a job design that allows machines to do work previously accomplished by human effort. *p. 167*

Autonomous work teams are teams given significant authority and responsibility over their work in contexts of highly related or interdependent jobs. *p. 268*

The **bargaining zone** is the zone between one party's minimum reservation point and the other party's maximum reservation point in a negotiating situation. *p. 517*

BATNA is the 'best alternative to a negotiated agreement', or each party's position on what they must do if an agreement cannot be reached. *p. 516*

The **behavioural components** of an attitude are the intentions to behave in a certain way based on a person's specific feelings or attitudes. *p. 59*

Behavioural decision theory refers to the idea that people act only in terms of what they perceive about a given situation. *p. 458*

Behaviourists study observable behaviours and consequences of behaviour, and reject subjective human psychological states as topics for study. *p. 125*

Beliefs represent ideas about someone or something and the conclusions people draw about them. *p. 59*

Brain drain refers to a characteristic of today's skilled workforce whose members are now more mobile and prepared to take their knowledge with them to their new workplaces as they pursue opportunities across the globe. *p. 17*

Brainstorming is a technique by which team members generate as many ideas as possible, without being inhibited by other team members. *p. 260*

Buffering is a conflict management approach that sets up inventories to reduce conflicts when the inputs of one group are the outputs of another group. *p. 510*

A **bureaucracy** is an ideal form of organisation whose characteristics include a division of labour, hierarchical control, promotion by merit with career opportunities for employees, and administration by rule. *p. 312*

Casual work is work where the number and schedule of work hours vary and there is little or no security of ongoing employment. *p. 26*

Centralisation is the degree to which the authority to make decisions is restricted to higher levels of management. *p. 301*

Certain environments are decision environments in which information is sufficient to predict the results of each alternative in advance of implementation. *p. 455*

Change agents are individuals or groups that take responsibility for changing the existing pattern of behaviour of a person or social system. *p. 529*

Changing involves a managerial responsibility to modify a situation — that is, to change people, tasks, structure and/or technology. *p. 536*

Channels are the media through which the message may be delivered. *p. 494*

Charisma is a dimension of leadership that provides vision and a sense of mission, and instils pride, respect and trust. *p. 416*

Charismatic leaders are those leaders who, by force of their personal abilities, are capable of having a profound and extraordinary effect on followers. *p. 414*

Classical conditioning is a form of learning through association that involves the manipulation of stimuli to influence behaviour. *p. 126*

Classical decision theory views the manager as acting in a world of complete certainty. *p. 458*

Coercive power is the extent to which a manager can deny desired rewards or administer punishment to control other people. *p. 367*

Cognitive abilities refer to our mental capacity to process information and solve problems. *p. 47*

Cognitive complexity is the underlying assumption that those high in cognitive complexity process information differently and perform certain tasks better than less cognitively complex people. *p. 424*

The **cognitive components** of an attitude are the beliefs, opinions, knowledge or information a person possesses. *p. 59*

Cognitive dissonance is a state of perceived inconsistency between a person's expressed attitudes and actual behaviour. *p. 60*

Cognitive evaluation theory explains the effects of extrinsic rewards on intrinsic motivation. When people are offered a large payment for engaging in an activity, they infer that the activity must be difficult, tedious, risky, or unpleasant in some way, so their enjoyment of the task is decreased. *p. 141*

Cognitive learning is learning achieved by thinking about the perceived relationship between events and individual goals and expectations. *p. 128*

Cohesiveness is the degree to which members are attracted to and motivated to remain a part of a team. *pp. 235, 263*

Common assumptions are the collection of truths that organisational members share as a result of

their joint experiences and that guide values and behaviours. *p. 335*

Compressed work week is any scheduling of work that allows a full-time job to be completed in fewer than the standard five days. *p. 190*

Conflict occurs when two or more people disagree over issues of organisational substance and/or experience some emotional antagonism with one another. *p. 500*

Conflict resolution occurs when the reasons for a conflict are eliminated. *p. 508*

Conglomerates are organisations that own several unrelated businesses. *p. 315*

Constructive conflict is conflict that results in positive benefits to the group. *p. 505*

Consultative decisions are decisions made by an individual after seeking input from or consulting with members of a group. *p. 464*

Content theories offer ways to profile or analyse individuals to identify the needs that motivate their behaviours. *p. 87*

Contextual variables link observations to a set of relevant facts, events, or points of view, such as organisational characteristics, work functions, external environment factors, and demographic variables. *p. 419*

A **contingency approach** is the attempt by organisational behaviour scholars to identify how situations can be understood and managed in ways that appropriately respond to their unique characteristics. *p. 5*

Contingent rewards are rewards that are given in exchange for mutually agreed goal accomplishments. *p. 416*

Continuous reinforcement is a reinforcement schedule that administers a reward each time a desired behaviour occurs. *p. 133*

Control is the set of mechanisms used to keep actions and outputs within predetermined limits. *p. 294*

Controlling is the process of monitoring performance, comparing results with objectives and taking corrective action as necessary. *p. 13*

Coordination is the set of mechanisms used in an organisation to link the actions of its subunits into a consistent pattern. *p. 297*

Corporate social responsibility (CSR) is the obligation of organisations to behave in ethical and moral ways. It generally refers to the notion that corporations have a responsibility to the society that sustains them. *p. 28, 292*

Countercultures are the patterns of values and philosophies that outwardly reject those of the larger organisation or social system. *p. 336*

Crafted decisions are decisions created to deal specifically with a situation at hand. *p. 455*

Creativity is the development of unique and novel responses to problems and opportunities. *p. 463*

Crisis leadership is leadership during a traumatic period or event. *p. 427*

A **cultural symbol** is any object, act or event that serves to transmit cultural meaning. *p. 340*

Decentralisation is the degree to which the authority to make decisions is given to lower levels in an organisation's hierarchy. *p. 301*

Decision making is the process of identifying a problem or opportunity and choosing among alternative courses of action. *p. 454*

Decoding is the interpretation of the symbols sent from the sender to the receiver. *p. 495*

Decoupling involves separating or reducing the contact between two conflicting groups. *p. 510*

Demographic characteristics are background variables (for example, age and gender) that help shape what a person becomes over time. *p. 46*

Departmentalisation by customer is the grouping of individuals and resources by client. *p. 305*

Departmentalisation by geography is the grouping of individuals and resources by geographical territory. *p. 305*

Destructive conflict is conflict that works to the group's or organisation's disadvantage. *p. 505*

The **differentiation perspective** views an organisation's culture as a compilation of diverse and inconsistent beliefs that are shared at group level. *p. 346*

Directive leadership is leadership behaviour that spells out the what and how of employees' tasks. *p. 410*

Disruptive behaviour is any behaviour that harms the group process. *p. 217*

Distributed leadership is the sharing of responsibility for fulfilling group task and maintenance needs. *p. 234*

Distributive negotiation is negotiation in which the focus is on 'positions' staked out or declared by the parties involved, who are each trying to claim certain portions of the available 'pie'. *p. 514*

Division of labour is the process of breaking the work to be done into specialised tasks that individuals or groups can perform. *p. 8*

Divisional departmentalisation is the grouping of individuals and resources by product, service and/or client. *p. 305*

Divisionalised design is an organisational structure that establishes a separate structure for each business or division. *p. 315*

Dogmatism is a personality trait that regards legitimate authority as absolute. *p. 53*

Effective communication is communication in which the intended meaning of the source and the perceived meaning of the receiver are one and the same. *p. 495*

Effective groups are groups that achieve high levels of both task performance and human resource maintenance. *p. 218*

An **effective manager** is a manager whose work unit achieves high levels of task accomplishment and maintains itself as a capable workforce over time. *p. 10*

Effective negotiation occurs when issues of substance are resolved without any harm to the working relationships among the parties involved. *p. 513*

Efficient communication is communication at minimum cost in terms of resources expended. *p. 495*

Emergent behaviours are tasks group members do in addition to, or in place of, what is formally asked of them by the organisation. *p. 230*

Emotion management is exercising emotional self-control and self-regulation influenced by the context in which individuals find themselves. *p. 48*

Emotional conflict is conflict that involves interpersonal difficulties that arise over feelings of anger, mistrust, dislike, fear, resentment and the like. *p. 501*

Emotional intelligence is a form of social intelligence that allows us to monitor and shape our emotions and those of others. *pp. 6, 48*

Employee involvement teams are teams of workers who meet regularly outside their normal work units for the purpose of collectively addressing important workplace issues. *p. 267*

Empowerment is the process by which managers delegate power to employees to motivate greater responsibility in balancing the achievement of both personal and organisational goals. *pp. 108, 380*

Encoding is the process of translating an idea or thought into meaningful symbols. *p. 494*

Environmental complexity is the magnitude of the problems and opportunities in the organisation's environment, as evidenced by the degree of richness, interdependence and uncertainty. *p. 290*

Equity theory presents the idea that motivation is affected when people feel that work outcomes are unfair or inequitable, due to social comparison in the workplace. *p. 98*

ERG theory categorises needs into existence, relatedness and growth needs. *p. 91*

Escalating commitment is the tendency to continue with a previously chosen course of action even when feedback suggests that it is failing. *p. 473*

Ethical behaviour is behaviour that is morally accepted as 'good' and 'right' as opposed to 'bad' and 'wrong' in a particular social context. *p. 28*

The **ethical climate** is the shared set of understandings in an organisation about what is correct behaviour and how ethical issues will be handled. *p. 351*

An **ethical dilemma** occurs when a person must make a decision that requires a choice among competing sets of principles. *pp. 29, 477*

Ethical leadership is leadership that abides by core values and standards acceptable to both the institution and society. *p. 429*

Existence needs are about the desire for physiological and material wellbeing. *p. 91*

Expectancy is the probability that the individual assigns to work effort being followed by a given level of achieved task performance. *p. 101*

Expectancy theory argues that work motivation is determined by individual beliefs about effort–performance relationships and the desirability of various work outcomes from different performance levels. *p. 102*

Expert power is the ability to control another's behaviour through the possession of knowledge, experience or judgement that the other person does not have but needs. *p. 370*

External adaptation is the process of reaching goals and dealing with outsiders. *p. 347*

Externals are persons with an external locus of control, who believe what happens to them is beyond their control. *p. 52*

Extinction is the withdrawal of the reinforcing consequences for a given behaviour. *p. 138*

Extrinsic rewards are positively valued work outcomes that the individual receives from some other person in the work setting. *pp. 104, 131*

Feedback is the process of telling someone else how you feel about something the person did or said, or about the situation in general. *p. 495*

Felt negative inequity exists when individuals feel they have received relatively less than others have in proportion to work inputs. *p. 99*

Felt positive inequity exists when individuals feel they have received relatively more than others have. *p. 99*

The **five key dimensions of personality** are extroversion–introversion; conscientiousness; agreeableness; emotional stability; and openness to experience. *p. 52*

Flexible working hours (flexitime) is any work schedule that gives employees daily choice in the timing of work and non-work activities. *p. 191*

Flexiyear or **annual hours** is a system whereby total agreed annual hours are allocated by workers as they see fit. *p. 194*

Flow is complete absorption in an activity, where the task is well matched to one's abilities. *p. 189*

Force-coercion strategy tries to 'command' change through the formal authority of legitimacy, rewards and punishments. *p. 540*

Formal communication channels are communication channels that follow the chain of command established by the organisation's hierarchy. *p. 496*

Formal groups are 'official' groups that are designated by formal authority to serve a specific purpose. *p. 211*

Formal leadership is the process of exercising influence from a position of formal authority in an organisation. *p. 403*

The **formal structure** is the intended configuration of positions, job duties and lines of authority among the component parts of an organisation. *p. 287*

Formalisation is the written documentation of work rules, policies and procedures. *p. 296*

The **forming stage** is the first stage of group development, in which the primary concern is the initial entry of members to the group. *p. 228*

The **founding story** is the tale of the lessons learned and efforts of the founder of the organisation. *p. 339*

The **fragmentation perspective** views organisational culture as lacking any form of pattern as a result of differing meanings between individuals and within individuals over time. *p. 346*

Friendship groups consist of people with natural affinities for one another who may do things together inside or outside the workplace. *p. 213*

Full-range leadership theory (FRLT) involves nine dimensions covering both transformational and transactional leadership, *especially emphasising contextual variables. p. 419*

Functional departmentalisation is the grouping of individuals and resources by skill, knowledge and action. *p. 304*

Garbage can decision model views problems, solutions, participants and choice situations as all mixed together in a dynamic field of organisational forces. *p. 459*

Global management skills and competencies include understanding of international business strategy, cross-cultural management, international marketing, international finance, managing e-business and the internet, risk management, managing sustainable organisations, re-engineering organisations, managing the virtual workplace, knowledge management, international economics and trade, and Asian languages. *p. 14*

Globalisation is the process of becoming more international in scope, influence or application. *p. 14*

Goal setting is the process of developing, negotiating and formalising an employee's targets and objectives. *p. 179*

Group decisions are decisions made by all members of the group, ideally with consensus being achieved. *p. 464*

Group dynamics are the forces operating in groups that affect group performance and member satisfaction. *p. 227*

Group inputs are the initial 'givens' in a group situation that set the stage for all group processes. *p. 220*

Group norms are the standards of behaviour that group members are expected to display. *p. 230*

Group outputs are the results of the transformation of group inputs through group processes. *p. 234*

Group roles are the sets of behaviours expected by the managers of the organisation and the group members for the holder of a particular position. *p. 230*

Groups are collections of two or more people who work with one another regularly to achieve one or more common goals. *pp. 211, 250*

Groupthink is the tendency of members in highly cohesive groups to lose their critical, evaluative capabilities. *p. 469*

Growth needs are about the desire for continued personal growth and development. *p. 91*

Heterogeneous groups are groups whose members have diverse backgrounds, interests, values, attitudes and so on. *p. 225*

Heuristics are simplifying strategies or 'rules of thumb' that people use when making decisions. *p. 462*

Hierarchical referral uses the chain of command for conflict resolution; problems are referred up the hierarchy for more senior managers to reconcile. *p. 510*

Higher-order needs are esteem and self-actualisation needs in Maslow's hierarchy. *p. 88*

Homogeneous groups are groups whose members have similar backgrounds, interests, values, attitudes and so on. *p. 225*

Horizontal loading involves increasing the breadth of a job by adding to the variety of tasks that the worker performs. *p. 169*

Horizontal specialisation is the division of labour through the formation of work units or groups within an organisation. *p. 302*

Human resource maintenance is the attraction and continuation of a viable workforce. *p. 10*

Human resources are the individuals and groups whose contributions enable the organisation to serve a particular purpose. *p. 8*

Hygiene (hygiene factors) are dissatisfiers that are associated with aspects of a person's work setting *p. 96*

Incremental change is change that occurs more frequently and less traumatically as part of an organisation's natural evolution. *p. 529*

Individual decisions are decisions made by one individual on behalf of the group. *p. 464*

Individualised consideration is a leadership dimension by which the leader provides personal attention, treats each employee individually, and coaches and advises employees. *p. 417*

Influence is a behavioural response to the exercise of power. *p. 365*

Informal communication channels are communication channels that do not adhere to the organisation's hierarchy. *p. 496*

Informal groups are groups that emerge unofficially and are not formally designated as parts of the organisation. *p. 213*

Informal leadership is the process of exercising influence through special skills or resources that meet the needs of other people. *p. 403*

Information power is the extent to which individuals have control over information needed by others. *p. 369*

An **information source** is a person or group of persons with a reason to communicate with some other person(s), the receiver(s). *p. 494*

The **initial integration stage** is the third stage of group development, at which the group begins to come together as a coordinated unit; it is sometimes called the norming stage. *p. 229*

Innovation is the process of creating new ideas and putting them into practice. *p. 549*

Innovation leadership is leadership that makes a difference in the nature and success of creative efforts. *p. 424*

Inspiration is the communication of high expectations, the use of symbols to focus efforts, and the expression of important purposes in simple ways. *p. 416*

Instinct is made up of inherited patterns of unreasoned and unchangeable responses to particular actions and behaviours. *p. 51*

Instrumentality is the probability that the individual assigns to a level of achieved task performance leading to various work outcomes. *p. 101*

The **integration perspective** views organisational culture as a system of shared meanings, unity and harmony. *p. 345*

Integrative negotiation is negotiation in which the focus is on the merits of the issues and the parties involved try to enlarge the available 'pie' rather than stake claims to certain portions of it. *p. 515*

Intellectual stimulation promotes intelligence, rationality and careful problem-solving. *p. 417*

Interest groups consist of people who share common interests, whether those interests are work or non-work related. *p. 214*

Intergroup conflict is conflict that occurs between groups in an organisation. *p. 503*

Intergroup dynamics are the dynamics that take place between groups, as opposed to within groups. *p. 236*

Intermittent reinforcement is a reinforcement schedule that rewards behaviour only periodically. *p. 133*

Internal integration is the creation of a collective identity and the means of matching methods of working and living together. *p. 348*

Internals are persons with an internal locus of control, who believe they control their own fate or destiny. *p. 52*

Interorganisational conflict is conflict that occurs between organisations. *p. 503*

Interpersonal conflict is conflict that occurs between two or more individuals. *p. 503*

Intrapersonal conflict is conflict that occurs within the individual as a result of actual or perceived pressures from incompatible goals or expectations. *pp. 143, 503*

Intrinsic motivation is a desire to work hard solely for the pleasant experience of task accomplishment. *p. 165*

Intrinsic rewards are positively valued work outcomes that the individual receives directly as a result of task performance. *p. 104*

Intuition is the ability to know or recognise quickly and readily the possibilities of a given situation. *p. 460*

The **job characteristics model** identifies five core characteristics (skill variety, task identity, task significance, autonomy and job feedback) as having special importance to job designs. *p. 172*

Job content refers to what people do in their work. *p. 95*

Job context refers to a person's work setting. *p. 96*

Job control refers to the extent to which a person is capable of controlling their tasks and the way they work. *p. 184*

Job demands are the physical, psychological, social or organisational aspects of the job that require sustained psychological or physical effort or skills, and are associated with physiological or psychological costs. *p. 184*

Job design is the planning and specification of job tasks and the work setting in which they are to be accomplished. *p. 166*

A **job diagnostic survey** is a questionnaire used to examine each of the dimensions of the job characteristics model. *p. 174*

Job enlargement involves increasing task variety by combining into one job tasks of similar skill levels that were previously assigned to separate workers. *p. 168*

Job enrichment is the practice of building motivating factors into job content. *p. 170*

Job involvement is the degree to which a person is willing to work hard and apply effort beyond normal job expectations. *p. 62*

Job resources/support are the aspects of the job that function to reduce job demands, enable achievement of work goals, and/or stimulate personal growth, learning and development. *p. 185*

Job rotation involves increasing task variety by periodically shifting workers among jobs involving different tasks at similar levels of skill. *p. 168*

Job satisfaction is the degree to which individuals feel positively or negatively about their jobs. *p. 60*

Job sharing is the assignment of one full-time job to two or more persons, who divide the work according to agreements made between themselves and the employer. *p. 192*

Job simplification is standardising work procedures and employing people in clearly defined and specialised tasks. *p. 167*

Jobs are one or more tasks that an individual performs in direct support of an organisation's production purpose. *p. 166*

Judgement is the use of the intellect in making decisions. *p. 462*

Key performance indicators are standards against which individual and organisational performance can be measured. *p. 182*

Knowledge management (KM) focuses on processes designed to improve an organisation's ability to capture, share and diffuse knowledge in a manner that will improve business performance. *p. 17*

A **knowledge-based economy** is an economy in which the production, distribution and use of knowledge is the main driver of growth, wealth creation and employment across all industries — not only those classified as high-tech or knowledge intensive. *p. 17*

Laissez faire leadership involves abdicating responsibilities and avoiding decisions. *p. 416*

The **law of contingent reinforcement** is the view that for a reward to have maximum reinforcing value, it must be delivered only if the desired behaviour is exhibited. *p. 132*

The **law of effect** refers to Thorndike's observation that behaviour that results in a pleasant outcome is likely to be repeated while behaviour that results in an unpleasant outcome is not likely to be repeated. *p. 131*

The **law of immediate reinforcement** states the more immediate the delivery of a reward after the occurrence of a desirable behaviour, the greater the reinforcing effect on behaviour. *p. 132*

Leaders provide inspiration, create opportunities, coach and motivate people to gain their support on fundamental long-term choices. *p. 403*

Leadership is a special case of interpersonal influence that gets an individual or group to do what the leader wants done. *p. 403*

Leading is the process of directing and coordinating the work efforts of other people to help them to accomplish important tasks. *p. 13*

Learning is a relatively permanent change in behaviour which occurs as a result of experience. *p. 125*

Least preferred coworker (LPC) scale is a measure of a person's leadership style based on a description of the person with whom respondents have been able to work least well. *p. 407*

Legitimate power is the extent to which a manager can use the internalised belief of an employee that the 'boss' has a 'right of command' to control other people. *p. 368*

Liaison groups are groups that coordinate the activities of certain units to prevent destructive conflicts between them. *p. 511*

Line personnel are work groups that conduct the major business of the organisation. *p. 302*

Linking pins are people who are assigned to manage conflict between groups that are prone to conflict. *p. 511*

Locus of control is the internal–external orientation — that is, the extent to which people feel able to affect their lives. *p. 52*

Lower-order needs are physiological, safety and social needs in Maslow's hierarchy. *p. 88*

Machiavellians are people who view and manipulate others purely for personal gain. *p. 53*

Maintenance activities are activities that support the emotional life of the group as an ongoing social system. *p. 235*

A **management philosophy** links key goal-related issues with key collaboration issues to come up with general ways by which the organisation will manage its affairs. *p. 343*

The **management process** involves planning, organising, leading and controlling the use of organisational resources. *p. 13*

A **manager** is responsible for work that is accomplished through the performance contributions of others. *p. 10*

Managerial wisdom is the ability to perceive variations in the environment and having an understanding of social actors and their relationships. *p. 424*

Managers are concerned with making things happen and keeping work on schedule, engaging in routine interactions to fulfil planned actions. *p. 403*

Manifest conflict occurs when conflict is openly expressed in behaviour. *p. 508*

Material resources are the technology, information, physical equipment and facilities, raw material and money that are necessary for an organisation to produce some product or service. *p. 8*

A **matrix structure** is a combination of functional and divisional patterns in which an individual is assigned to more than one type of unit. *p. 307*

Mechanistic design emphasises vertical specialisation, hierarchical levels, tight control and coordination through rules, policies and other impersonal methods. *p. 299*

Merit pay is a compensation system that bases an individual's salary or wage increase on a measure of the person's performance accomplishments during a specified time period. *p. 144*

A **motivating potential score** is a summary of a job's overall potential for motivating those in the workplace. *p. 174*

Motivation to work refers to the forces within an individual that account for the level, direction and persistence of effort expended at work. *pp. 45, 80*

The **motivator-hygiene theory** distinguishes between sources of work dissatisfaction (hygiene factors) and satisfaction (motivators); it is also known as the two-factor theory. *p. 94*

Motivators (motivator factors) are satisfiers that are associated with what people do in their work. *p. 95*

Multiskilling helps employees acquire an array of skills needed to perform the multiple tasks in

an organisational production or customer service process. *p. 178*

The **nature/nurture controversy** is the argument over whether personality is determined by heredity, or genetic endowment, or by one's environment. *p. 50*

The **need for achievement (nAch)** is the desire to do something better, solve problems or master complex tasks. *p. 92*

The **need for affiliation (nAff)** is the desire to establish and maintain friendly and warm relations with others. *p. 92*

The **need for power (nPower)** is the desire to control others, influence their behaviour and be responsible for others. *p. 92*

Negative reinforcement is the withdrawal of negative consequences, which tends to increase the likelihood of the behaviour being repeated in similar settings; it is also known as avoidance. *p. 136*

Negotiation is the process of making joint decisions when the parties involved have different preferences. *p. 512*

A **network organisation** is a de-layered organisation aligned around the complementary competencies of players in a value chain. *p. 320*

Noise is anything that interferes with the effectiveness of the communication attempt. *p. 495*

Non-contingent reward is a reward that is given arbitrarily; being unrelated to, or not requiring, a behavioural response. *p. 138*

Non-routine problems are unique and new problems that call for creative problem solving. *p. 455*

Norms are rules or standards about the behaviour that group members are expected to display. *p. 262*

Observable culture is behavioural patterns that a group displays and teaches to new members. *p. 334*

Open systems transform human and physical resources received from their environment into goods and services that are then returned to the environment. *p. 8*

Operant conditioning is the process of controlling behaviour by manipulating its consequences. *p. 127*

Organic design is an organisational structure that emphasises horizontal specialisation, an extensive use of personal coordination, and loose rules, policies and procedures. *p. 299*

Organisation charts are diagrams that depict the formal structures of organisations. *p. 288*

Organisational behaviour is the study of individuals and groups in organisations. *p. 5*

Organisational behaviour modification is the systematic reinforcement of desirable work behaviour and the non-reinforcement or punishment of unwanted work behaviour. *p. 131*

Organisational commitment is the degree to which a person strongly identifies with, and feels a part of, the organisation. *p. 62*

Organisational communication is the process by which entities exchange information and establish a common understanding. *p. 493*

Organisational culture is a system of shared beliefs and values that guides behaviour. *p. 333*

Organisational design is the process of choosing and implementing a structural configuration for an organisation. *p. 287*

Organisational governance is the pattern of authority, influence and acceptable managerial behaviour established at the top of the organisation. *p. 388*

Organisational learning is acquiring or developing new knowledge that modifies or changes behaviour and improves organisational performance. *p. 148*

Organisational politics is the management of influence to obtain ends not sanctioned by the organisation, or to obtain sanctioned ends through non-sanctioned means of influence. *p. 383*

Organisational strategy is the process of positioning the organisation in the competitive environment and implementing actions to compete successfully. *p. 291*

Organising is the process of dividing the work to be done and coordinating the results to achieve a desired purpose. *p. 13*

Output controls are controls that focus on desired targets and allow managers to use their own methods for reaching defined targets. *p. 295*

Output goals are the goals that define the organisation's type of business. *p. 292*

Participative leadership is a leadership style that focuses on consulting with employees, and seeking and accounting for their suggestions before making decisions. *p. 410*

Passive management by exception involves intervening with employees only if standards are not met. *p. 416*

Perception is the process through which people receive, organise and interpret information from their environment. *p. 67*

Performance is a summary measure of the quantity and quality of task contributions made by an individual or group to the work unit and organisation. *p. 64*

Performance equation Job performance = attributes × work effort × organisational support. *p. 6*

The **performance gap** is the discrepancy between an actual and a desired state of affairs. *p. 530*

Permanent formal work groups perform a specific function on an ongoing basis. *p. 212*

Personality is the overall profile or combination of traits that characterise the unique nature of a person. *p. 50*

Physical abilities refer to our natural and developed motor capacities for speed, strength, flexibility and so on, as well as our use of the five senses. *p. 47*

Piece rate is a fixed ratio schedule where workers are paid for each unit or item at a fixed rate. *p. 133*

Planned change is change that happens as a result of specific efforts on the part of a change agent. *p. 530*

Planning is the process of setting performance objectives and identifying the actions needed to accomplish them. *p. 13*

A **policy** is a guideline for action that outlines important objectives and indicates how an activity is to be performed. *p. 295*

Positive reinforcement is the administration of positive consequences which tend to increase the likelihood of repeating the behaviour in similar settings. *p. 132*

Power is the ability to get someone else to do something you want done, or the ability to make things happen or get things done in the way you want. *p. 365*

Primary beneficiaries are particular groups expected to benefit from the efforts of specific organisations. *p. 292*

A **procedure** (or **rule**) is a more specific, rigid guideline that describes in detail how a task is to be performed. *p. 295*

Process controls are controls that attempt to specify the manner in which tasks will be accomplished. *p. 295*

Process innovation is innovation that results in a better way of doing things. *p. 549*

Process power is the control over methods of production and analysis. *p. 369*

Process re-engineering is the fundamental rethinking and radical redesign of business processes to achieve improvements in performance. *p. 14*

Process theories seek to understand the thought processes that take place in the minds of people and that act to motivate their behaviour. *p. 87*

Product innovation is innovation that results in the creation of a new or improved good or service. *p. 549*

Productivity is a summary measure of the quantity and quality of work performance that also accounts for resource use. *p. 10*

Programmed decisions are decisions that implement specific solutions determined by past experience as appropriate for the problems at hand. *p. 455*

Punishment is the administration of negative consequences or the withdrawal of positive consequences, which tends to reduce the likelihood of repeating the behaviour in similar settings. *p. 136*

Quality circles are groups of workers who meet periodically to discuss and develop solutions for problems relating to quality, productivity or cost. *p. 267*

Quality of work life refers to the overall quality of human experience in the workplace. QWL activities represent special applications of the many organisational behaviour concepts and theories discussed throughout this book. *p. 11*

Quasiformal channels are planned communication connections between holders of the various positions within the organisation. *p. 496*

Radical change is change that results in a major make-over of the organisation and/or its component systems. *p. 529*

Rational persuasion strategy attempts to bring about change through persuasion based on empirical facts, special knowledge and rational argument. *p. 540*

The **receiver** is the individual or group of individuals that hear or read or see the message. *p. 495*

Referent power is the ability to control another's behaviour because the individual wants to identify with the power source. *p. 372*

Refreezing is the final stage of the planned change process in which changes are positively reinforced. *p. 536*

Relatedness needs are about the desire for satisfying interpersonal relationships. *p. 91*

Relationship goals are concerned with how well people involved in a negotiation, and their constituencies, are able to work with one another once the process is concluded. *p. 513*

Required behaviours are those contributions the organisation formally requests from group members as a basis for continued affiliation and support. *p. 230*

Resistance to change is any attitude or behaviour that reflects a person's unwillingness to make or support a desired change. *p. 542*

Resource dependencies occur when the organisation needs resources that others control. *p. 387*

Reverse-incentive effect is when people are offered a large incentive or reward for doing a task, they will judge that task to be more difficult, more boring, or more unpleasant than when a small (or no) reward is offered. *p. 141*

Reward power is the extent to which a manager can use extrinsic and intrinsic rewards to control other people. *p. 367*

Risk environments are decision environments that involve a lack of complete certainty but that include an awareness of probabilities associated with the possible outcomes of various courses of action. *p. 455*

Rites are standardised and recurring activities used at special times to influence the behaviours and understanding of organisational members. *p. 339*

Rituals are systems of rites. *p. 339*

A **role** is a set of expectations for the behaviour of a person holding a particular office or position. *p. 262*

Role ambiguity is the uncertainty about what other group members expect of a person. *p. 263*

Role conflict occurs when a person is unable to respond to the expectations of one or more group members. *p. 263*

Routine problems are problems that arise routinely and that can be addressed through standard responses. *p. 455*

A **saga** is an embellished heroic account of the story of the founding of an organisation. *p. 339*

Satisficing means choosing the first satisfactory alternative rather than the optimal decision. *p. 458*

Schemas are cognitive frameworks developed through experience. *p. 68*

Self-concept is the concept that individuals have of themselves as physical, social and spiritual or moral beings. *p. 106*

Self-determination theory is a theory of human motivation, development and wellness. The theory focuses on types, rather than just amount, of motivation, paying particular attention to autonomous (intrinsic) motivation, controlled (extrinsic) motivation, and amotivation (lack of motivation) as predictors of performance and wellbeing outcomes. *p. 141*

Self-efficacy refers to a person's belief that they can perform adequately in a situation. *p. 109*

Self-managing teams (SMTs) are small groups of people empowered to manage themselves and the work they do on a day-to-day basis. *p. 268*

Servant leadership involves deliberately choosing to serve others and prioritising other people's needs, aspirations and interests. *p. 430*

Shaping is the creation of a new behaviour by the positive reinforcement of successive approximations to the desired behaviour. *p. 132*

Shared leadership is a dynamic, interactive influence process among individuals in groups for which the objective is to lead one another to the achievement of group or organisational goals or both. *p. 420*

A **shared power strategy** (or **normative-reeducative strategy**) attempts to bring about change by identifying or establishing values and assumptions so that support for the change emerges naturally. *p. 541*

Shared values are the set of coherent values held by members of the organisation and that link them together. *p. 335*

A **simple design** is a configuration involving one or two ways of specialising individuals and units. *p. 312*

Situational constraints are organisational inadequacies which do not allow workers to perform adequately. *p. 45*

Situational control is the extent to which leaders can determine what their group is going to do and what the outcomes of their actions and decisions are going to be. *p. 407*

The **social information-processing approach** argues that individual needs, task perceptions and reactions are a result of socially constructed realities. *p. 178*

Social learning is learning achieved through the reciprocal interaction between people and their environments. *p. 128*

Social loafing is the tendency of people not to work as hard in groups as they would individually. *p. 217*

Socio-technical job design is the design of jobs to optimise the relationship between the technology system and the social system. *p. 178*

The **span of control** is the number of individuals reporting to a supervisor. *p. 302*

Spiritual leadership is inclusive of religious and ethically based values, attitudes, and behaviours. *p. 430*

Staff personnel are groups that assist the line units by performing specialised services for the organisation. *p. 303*

Standardisation is the degree to which the range of actions in a job or series of jobs is limited. *p. 296*

Status is the indication of a person's relative rank, worth or standing within a group. *p. 225*

Status incongruence occurs when a person's expressed status within a group is inconsistent with their standing in another context. *p. 225*

Stimulus is something that incites action. *p. 126*

The **storming stage** is the second stage of group development, which is marked by a period of high emotion and tension among group members. *p. 228*

Strategic alliances are announced cooperative agreements or joint ventures between two independent organisations. *p. 319*

Strategic leadership is identified by concern for the advancement of the organisation, including its evolving capabilities and goals. *p. 421*

Stress is a state of tension experienced by individuals facing extraordinary demands, constraints or opportunities. *p. 545*

Stress prevention involves taking action to prevent the emergence of stress that becomes destructive. *p. 547*

Stressors are things that cause stress (for example, work, non-work and personal factors). *p. 545*

Sub-goal optimisation occurs when a group achieves its goals at the expense of the goals of others. *p. 220*

Subcultures are unique patterns of values and philosophies within a group that are not inconsistent with the dominant culture of the larger organisation or social system. *p. 335*

Substance goals are concerned with outcomes tied to the 'content' issues at hand in a negotiation. *p. 513*

Substantive conflict is conflict that occurs in the form of a fundamental disagreement over ends or goals to be pursued and the means for their accomplishment. *p. 501*

Substitutes for leadership are organisation, individual or task-situational variables that substitute for leadership in causing performance/human resource maintenance. *p. 412*

Successive approximation is when someone acts in a way that gets closer and closer to the desired behaviour in order to receive a reward. *p. 132*

Supportive leadership is a leadership style that focuses on employee needs and wellbeing, and promotes a friendly work climate; it is similar to consideration. *p. 410*

Synergy is the creation of a whole that is greater than the sum of its parts. *pp. 8, 217*

Systems goals are goals concerned with conditions within the organisation that are expected to increase its survival potential. *p. 293*

Task activities are the various things members do that directly contribute to the performance of important group tasks. *p. 235*

Task forces are temporary teams created to fulfil a well-defined task within a fairly short period of time. *p. 268*

Task performance is the quality and quantity of work produced. *p. 10*

A **teaching organisation** aims to pass on learning experiences to others and, in doing so, allow the organisation to achieve and maintain success. *p. 151*

Team building is a sequence of planned action steps designed to gather and analyse data on the functioning of a group, and to implement changes to increase its operating effectiveness. *p. 253*

Team IQ is the ability of a group of individuals to tackle and manage complex and non-routine situations together. *p. 252*

Teams are small groups of people with complementary skills, who work together as a unit to achieve a common purpose for which they hold themselves collectively accountable. *p. 249*

Teamwork is when members of a team work together in a way that represents certain core values that promote the use of skills to accomplish certain goals. *p. 253*

The **technological imperative** is the idea that if an organisation does not adjust its internal structure to the requirements of the technology, it will not be successful. *p. 289*

Technology is the combination of resources, knowledge and techniques that creates a product or service output for an organisation. *p. 289*

Telework principles relate to work conducted remotely from the central organisation using information technology. *p. 193*

Temporary formal work groups are created for a specific purpose and typically disband once that purpose has been accomplished. *p. 212*

The **total integration stage** is the fourth stage of group development, which sees the emergence of a mature, organised and well-functioning group; it is also referred to as the performing stage. *p. 229*

Transactional leadership involves daily exchanges between leaders and followers, and is necessary for achieving routine performance on which leaders and followers agree. *p. 416*

Transformational leadership is a leadership style by which the followers' goals are broadened and elevated, and confidence is gained to go beyond expectations. *p. 416*

Transmission is the actual communication of a message from one person to another through a chosen channel. *p. 494*

Turnover is the decision by people to terminate their employment. *p. 62*

Uncertain environments are decision environments in which managers are unable to assign probabilities to the possible outcomes of various courses of action. *p. 456*

Unfreezing is the first stage of the planned change process in which a situation is prepared for change. *p. 535*

Unity of command is the situation in an organisation where each worker has a clear reporting relationship to only one supervisor. *p. 302*

Unplanned change is change that occurs at random or spontaneously and without a change agent's direction. *p. 530*

Valence represents the values that the individual attaches to various work outcomes. *p. 102*

Value congruence occurs when individuals express positive feelings on encountering others who exhibit values similar to their own. *p. 56*

Value-added managers are managers whose efforts clearly enable their work units to achieve high productivity and improve 'bottom-line' performance. *p. 11*

Values are global beliefs that guide actions and judgements across a variety of situations. *p. 56*

Vertical loading involves increasing job depth by adding responsibilities, like planning and controlling, previously held by supervisors. *p. 169*

Vertical specialisation is a hierarchical division of labour that distributes formal authority and establishes how critical decisions will be made. *p. 301*

Virtual organisations comprise individuals, groups and businesses that work together across time and space. *p. 320*

A **virtual team** is one whose members work interdependently towards the achievement of a common goal across space and time. *p. 270*

Voluntary reduced work time (V-Time or **time–income trade-offs)** is a scheme by which workers trade income for additional leisure time that is packaged to suit their needs. *p. 192*

Work flow interdependency is the way work flows in an organisation from one group to the next. *p. 236*

Work teams or **units** are task-oriented groups that include a manager and his or her direct reports. *p. 10*

Workforce diversity means a workforce consisting of a broad mix of workers from different racial and ethnic backgrounds, of different ages and genders, and of different domestic and national cultures. *p. 18*

The **zone of indifference** is the range of authoritative requests to which an employee is willing to respond without subjecting the directives to critical evaluation or judgement — that is, the requests to which the employee is indifferent. *p. 375*